When
Cultures
Collide

LEADING
ACROSS CULTURES

The Fourth Edition
of the Global Guide

Richard D. Lewis

NICHOLAS BREALEY
PUBLISHING

London • Boston

First published in 1996 by Nicholas Brealey International
This fourth edition published in 2018 by Nicholas Brealey International
An imprint of John Murray Press

An Hachette UK company

1

British Library Cataloguing-in-Publication Data
A catalogue record for this book is available from the British Library.

ISBN 978-1-473-68482-9
eBook ISBN (UK) 978-1-473-69780-5
eBook ISBN (US) 978-1-473-69781-2

Printed and bound by CPI Group (UK) Ltd, Croydon, CR0 4YY

John Murray Press policy is to use papers that are natural, renewable and recyclable products and made from wood grown in sustainable forests. The logging and manufacturing processes are expected to conform to the environmental regulations of the country of origin.

Nicholas Brealey Publishing
John Murray Press
Carmelite House
50 Victoria Embankment
London, EC4Y 0DZ, UK
Tel: 020 3122 6000

Nicholas Brealey Publishing
Hachette Book Group
Market Place Center, 53 State Street
Boston, MA 02109, USA
Tel: (617) 263 1834

www.nicholasbrealey.com
www.crossculture.com

To Jane, Caroline, Richard and David,
multicultural all …

Contents

PART ONE
Getting to Grips with Cultural Diversity

PART TWO

Managing and Leading in Different Cultures

PART THREE

Getting to Know Each Other

English-Speaking Countries

Western European Countries

Central and Eastern European Countries

Us and Them

I was once in charge of an English language summer course in North Wales for adult students from three countries—Italy, Japan, and Finland. Intensive instruction was relieved by entertainment in the evenings and by day excursions to places of scenic or historical interest. We had scheduled a trip up Mount Snowdon on a particular Wednesday, but on the Tuesday evening it rained heavily. Around 10 o'clock that night, during the after-dinner dancing, a dozen or so Finns approached me and suggested that we cancel the excursion, as it would be no fun climbing the muddy slopes of Snowdon in heavy rain. I, of course, agreed and announced the cancellation.

Immediately I was surrounded by protesting Italians disputing the decision. Why cancel the trip—they had been looking forward to it (escape from lessons), they had paid for it in their all-inclusive fee, a little rain would not hurt anyone and what was the matter with the Finns anyway—weren't they supposed to be tough people? A little embarrassed, I consulted the Japanese contingent. They were very, very nice. If the Italians wanted to go, they would go, too. If, on the other hand, we cancelled the trip they would be quite happy to stay in and take more lessons. The Italians jeered at the Finns, the Finns mumbled and scowled, and eventually, in order not to lose face, agreed they would go. The excursion was declared on. It rained torrentially all night and also while I took a quick breakfast. The bus was scheduled to leave at half past eight, and at twenty-five past, taking my umbrella in the downpour, I ran to the vehicle. Inside were 18 scowling Finns, 12 smiling Japanese, and no Italians. We left on time and had a terrible day. The rain never let up, we lunched in cloud at the summit, and returned covered in mud at 5 o'clock, in time to see the Italians taking tea and chocolate biscuits. They had sensibly stayed in bed. When the Finns asked them why, they said because it was raining . . .

Getting to Grips with Cultural Diversity

Cultural diversity is not something that is going to go away tomorrow, enabling us to plan our strategies on the assumption of mutual understanding. It is in itself a phenomenon with its own riches, the exploration of which could yield incalculable benefits for us, both in terms of wider and more profitable policies and activity. People of different cultures share basic concepts but view them from different angles and perspectives, leading them to behave in a manner which we may consider irrational or even in direct contradiction of what we hold sacred. We should nevertheless be optimistic about cultural diversity. The behavior of people of different cultures is not something willy-nilly. There exist clear trends, sequences and traditions. Reactions of Americans, Europeans, and Asians alike can be forecasted, usually justified and in the majority of cases managed. Even in countries where political and economic change has been rapid or sweeping (Russia, China, Hungary, Poland, Korea, Kazakhstan, etc.) deeply rooted attitudes and beliefs will resist a sudden transformation of values when pressured by reformists, governments or multinational conglomerates. Post-perestroika Russians exhibit individual and group behavioral traits strikingly similar to those recorded in Tsarist times—these had certainly persisted, in subdued form, in the Soviet era. By focusing on the cultural roots of national behavior, both in society and business, we can foresee and calculate with a surprising degree of accuracy how others will react to our plans for them, and we can make certain assumptions as to how they will approach us. A working knowledge of the basic traits of other cultures (as well as our own) will minimize unpleasant surprises (culture shock), give us insights in advance, and enable us to interact successfully with nationalities with whom we previously had difficulty. This book aims to facilitate the acquisition of such insights.

Cultural Differences in International Business

International business, especially where joint ventures or prolonged negotiations are involved, is fraught with difficulties. Apart from practical and technical problems (to which solutions are often readily found), national psychology and characteristics frequently interfere at the executive level, where decisions tend to be more complex than the practical accords reached between accountants, engineers and other technicians. Corporate cultures vary widely inside one country (compare Apple and IBM in the US, or Sony and Mitsubishi in Japan); national business styles are markedly more diverse. In a Japanese–U.S. joint venture, where the Americans are interested mainly in profit and the Japanese in market share, which direction is to be taken? When a capitalistic company from the west sets up business in a socialist country, the areas for conflict are even more obvious. But how similar will be the business ethics or cultural background of Sweden and Greece, both European?

National Characteristics

Determining **national** characteristics is treading a minefield of inaccurate assessment and surprising exception. There exist excitable Finns, wooden Italians, cautious Americans and charismatic Japanese. There is, however, such a thing as a national norm. For instance, Italians are in general more loquacious than Finns. Yet talkative Finns and silent Italians will overlap. The individuals who overlap are actually deviates in terms of that particular characteristic. In this book, with the object of making meaningful comparisons between different cultures, I have made certain generalizations regarding the national characteristics of one people or another. Such generalizations carry with them the risk of stereotyping as one talks about the typical Italian, German, American, etc. It is evident that Americans differ greatly from each other and that no two Italians are alike. However, my experience during 30 years of living abroad and rubbing shoulders with individuals of many nationalities has led me to the conviction that the inhabitants of any country possess certain core beliefs and assumptions of reality which will manifest themselves in their behavior. Culture, in the sense that it represents one's outlook and world view, is not, however, a strictly national phenomenon.

In some countries **regional** characteristics can prevail to the extent that they relegate the 'national type' to second position. Basques and Andalucians have little in common apart from a Spanish passport; Milanese businesspeople often feel more at home with French and Austrians than with Sicilians. In the U.S.—nation of many subcultures—differences in race and language have led to the creation of three major divisions: Black, Hispanic, and English-speaking whites. In certain cases **cities** have developed such a strong cultural identity that it transcends the traits of the region. Thus Londoners are not just southern English, Parisians not simply northern French, Berliners are more than just eastern Germans. The inhabitants of Marseille have created their own city culture, the citizens of Liverpool have an accent and lifestyle completely different from the northerners surrounding them. Hong Kong, even after integration, is likely to be a special enclave in southern China.

Cultural groups can cross or span frontiers of nations or regions; they may also align themselves in ways other than geographical. Muslims and Christians are cultural groups; so are engineers and accountants. Graduates of the universities of Oxford, Cambridge, Harvard and Yale would claim separate cultural identities. **Corporate** culture affects the lives of many of us to a greater or lesser degree. It is particularly strong in Japan. In other countries, such as Italy, Spain and China, **family** culture is considered more important. The smallest cultural unit is the personal one—the **individual**. Individualistic views are shown great respect in countries such as Britain, France, Australia and the USA. Perhaps the greatest cultural divide is not national, religious, corporate or professional, but that based on **gender**. It is quite possible that an Italian woman has a world outlook more similar to that of a German woman than to that of a male Italian.

What the Book Is About

In Part One we explore the vital question of how the mind is **conditioned**, culturally, at an early age. Once one realizes the almost irreversible nature of this childhood training, creating in each of us a set of values so different from those extolled in other parts of the world, the possibilities for complex or hampered interaction in later life become clear. This book attempts to show that there is no good or bad, logical or illogical, in cultural values, just as one cannot argue about taste. The British, American, Chinese each see themselves as rational and normal. Cross-cultural training makes one see others as normal too, when viewed from a different perspective. We also discuss the fascinating subject of the inter-relationship between **language and thought**.

Next we classify the world's cultures in three rough categories:

- **Linear-actives**—those who plan, schedule, organize, pursue action chains, do one thing at a time. Germans and Swiss are in this group.
- **Multi-actives**—those lively, loquacious peoples who do many things at once, planning their priorities not according to a time schedule, but according to the relative thrill or importance that each appointment brings with it. Italians, Latin Americans and Arabs are members of this group.
- **Reactives**—those cultures that prioritize courtesy and respect, listening quietly and calmly to their interlocutors and reacting carefully to the other side's proposals. Chinese, Japanese and Finns are in this group.

The chapter on categorization emphasizes the rising importance of companies finding and assessing the existing **cultural capital** within the organization. The hundreds or thousands of people they employ may possess cultural traits which would make them excellent ambassadors, mediators or leaders in certain foreign cultures. Correctly placed, they augment the fruits of recruitment. Such expatriates mingle easily with their colleagues in the country they are sent to. Usually they will stay five years or more and make a profitable contribution to their firm's activities. The costs of sending untrained or unsuitable staff to take up foreign assignments are well known. Repatriation used to be estimated between $150,000–200,000. Now it is nearer half a million. There is also the reputation cost. If firms such as Nestlé, Nokia, Ericsson, Hewlett-Packard, Kraft and HSBC can tackle this problem successfully, why did DaimlerChrysler fail to do so?

The LMR assessment system described in Part One, pages 1–80 has given such companies as Nokia, Beiersdorf, Ericsson, LSG-Lufthansa, Unilever and Rolls Royce an insight into the cultural assets among their staff. Other organizations such as the World Bank, OneWorld and the Nordic government ministries have benefited from the clarity of the terminology of the LMR classification and the testing system: linear-active, multi-active and reactive characteristics are readily identifiable by HR managers around the world. The LMR method steers clear of the diffuse and long-winded terminology of some assessment systems, which may line up a dozen or more aspects or dimensions to be analysed.

In Chapter 3 I do stress, however, that most individuals, though basically linear, multi-active or reactive as a type, will inevitably be to some extent hybrid. This is because, in any place or time, a person is subjected to a **contextual** influence involving his/her background of study, profession and own personality preferences. At all events an advisable route for a company to take in staff training is a.) assess, b.) fine tune the assessment, and c.) prepare.

We go on to demonstrate how each group **gathers information** in a different way—the linear-actives relying mostly on data, the multi-actives on face-to-face encounters and dialogues, the reactives on a combination of both styles. Further chapters in Part Two show how the values taught to us in early life give us an entrenched approach to the use of **space and time** and how we accord **status**, respond to different types of **leadership**, and organize our society and business to fit in with these attitudes.

Language is an important part of our functional activity and we indicate, often in diagrammatic form, the varying **communication patterns** used in meetings and during negotiations. **Listening habits** are also important to communication, and a discussion of these leads us on to aspects of sales, marketing and advertising.

The last chapter in Part One gives a comprehensive survey on manners in business and society around the world.

Part Two, now devoted entirely to business, anticipates the changing perspectives of management and strategy at the turn of the twenty-first century and shows that widely diverging horizons and credos can be managed—collapsed together—especially in the creation of **international teams**. The very language of management itself becomes a vital inspirational tool for the leaders of tomorrow. Empathy, tact, understanding, subtlety, positive reaction—these are the resources of the multicultural executive.

Part Two is vital reading for managers whose task it is to put into practice the insights into cultural issues outlined in Part One and apply them systematically in an international business context.

Chapters 7–10 analyze how cultures accord **status**, respond to different types of **leadership** and organize their societies to fit in with these attitudes. One entirely new section, "Success and Failure in the Twenty-First Century," has been added to Chapter 7, as has new material on leadership. These chapters indicate how successful **team-building** can be achieved by harmonizing the diverse horizons of team members.

Chapter 9, "Motivating People and Building Trust," is a totally new chapter, revealing in depth the cultural factors involved in motivating staff and creating trust, particularly in multicultural and—increasingly—virtual teams. There is no international magic formula for either motivating or building trust across cultures, but I can say that establishing and maintaining relationships are the key concept when interacting across (and within) linear-active, multi-active and reactive boundaries. I also introduce some general factors that influence motivation within LMR-category countries.

Part Two ends by describing how **meeting styles** vary around the world— nuances of settings, protocol and structure—and contrasts different routes of **negotiation** and **decision-making**.

Part Three constitutes a comprehensive reference source giving an in-depth analysis of the background and cultural characteristics of over 90 of the world's major countries and regions. Each chapter is devoted to a separate state or area, explains why the behavior of its inhabitants follows certain paths and agendas and gives practical advice on how to minimize friction with each group.

Features of This New Edition

The 2006 Edition added most countries in the EU, including those in the queue for membership. In addition to Romania, Bulgaria, Croatia, Serbia, Montenegro, Slovenia, Slovakia, Hungary, Poland, the Czech Republic and the Baltic States, this Fourth Edition now includes Malta, Cyprus, Albania, Armenia, Georgia, Ukraine, Belarus and Azerbaijan. Further East, the only major Asian country not in previous editions—Myanmar—has now been covered in some detail.

Most country chapters include the following sections: introduction to and background about the country, cultural values, concepts of space and time, communication patterns, listening habits, behavior at meetings and negotiations, and suggestions for empathizing with the locals. An entirely new section has been added to almost all of the countries and regions: "Motivation." These Motivation charts provide a quick look at the Key motivating factor for each country. In addition, the charts offer insight as to what to emphasize and what to avoid during your business interactions.

• • •

The twenty-first century will be crunch time for Western managers in terms of meeting fierce and unrelenting Asian competition (especially from China) and in attempting to gain a share of the mammoth markets that rapidly changing demographics will create in India, China, Pakistan, Indonesia, Bangladesh, Nigeria and Brazil (in 2050 their total population will be around 5 billion). The goal of this new, expanded edition of *When Cultures Collide* is to keep pace with these emerging and changing markets.

Acknowledgments

No new work on cross culture escapes the influence of Edward and Mildred Hall and Geert Hofstede, and I would like to acknowledge their pioneering of certain concepts which figure prominently in this book. I am equally indebted to the perceptive writings of Desmond Morris on body language, to Glen Fisher for his comprehensive analysis of the international negotiation scene, and to David Rearwin and John Paul Fieg for their authoritative views on Asian countries. Yale Richmond, Margaret Nydell, and Joy Hendry have written impeccably penetrating insights into the cultures of Russia, the Arab world, and Japan respectively, and I have leaned heavily on their experience in the relevant chapters of *When Cultures Collide*.

Deirdre Holding helped me with the chapter on Armenia and Alex Berozashvili kindly aided me in writing about Georgia.

Eminent culturalists such as Professor Arie Lewin of Duke University, Professor James Téboul of INSEAD, Professor Susan Schneider of the University of Geneva, and Professor Peter Shikhirev of the Graduate School of International Business, Moscow, have given me valuable advice. Marta Szabo White of Georgia State University, Ulla Ladau-Harjulin of the Swedish School of Economics, Helsinki, Jeff Russell of the Fuqua School of Business, and Michael Gearin-Tosh and Roger Ainsworth of St Catherine's College, Oxford University, have also been unstinting in their encouragement.

The impressive multiculturalism of individuals such as Dr. Saul Lanyado, Chairman of Rolls Royce Marine, Iouri Bairatchnyi and Gabriela Gold of the World Bank, Yolanda Hengne of the IFC, Jorma Ollila and Pekka Ala-Pietilä of Nokia, Richard d'Souza of Pfizer, Dr. Francesco Ingrassia of the Bank of Sicily, Steffen Seeger and Per Jacobsson of Bearing Point, Sir Eldon Griffiths of the World Affairs Council and Markku Vartiainen of Finn-Niche have been recent sources of further inspiration.

Finally I wish to acknowledge the expertise and helpful comments of my co-seminarists in workshops—Michael Gates for his knowledge of Europe and India, Marit Imeland Gjesma with regard to Islamic, Nordic and Japanese cultures, Dr Iouri Bairatchnyi for enlightenment on things Russian, and finally, last but not least, my trilingual daughter, Caroline Lewis, arguably the U.K.'s foremost consultant on Japanese matters.

PART 1

Getting to Grips with Cultural Diversity

1

Different Languages, Different Worlds

For a German and a Finn, the truth is the truth. In Japan and Britain it is all right if it doesn't rock the boat. In China there is no absolute truth. In Italy it is negotiable.

Comparisons of national cultures often begin by highlighting differences in social behavior. The Japanese do not like shaking hands, bow when greeting each other and do not blow their nose in public. Brazilians form unruly bus lines, prefer brown shoes to black and arrive two hours late at cocktail parties. Greeks stare you in the eye, nod their heads when they mean no and occasionally smash plates against walls in restaurants. The French wipe their plates clean with a piece of bread, throw pastry into their coffee and offer handshakes to strangers in bistros. Brits tip their soup bowls away from them, eat peas with their forks upside down and play golf in the rain.

Appearance and Reality

These various manners and mannerisms cause us great amusement. We smile at foreign eccentricity, congratulating ourselves on our normality. And yet we are aware that these idiosyncrasies are largely superficial. If we stay in France a while, we are sooner or later happy to dunk our croissants and make a mess; we discover the unhurried delight of turning up outrageously late in Brazil; we throw vodka glasses over our shoulders with abandon in St. Petersburg. Such adaptation of our behavior leaves no scars on our psyche. We join strangers in their social ways partly to conform and partly for fun. We can become French or Greek for an evening, we can sit on *tatami* with Japanese colleagues and eat legs of lamb with one hand among Arabs. But what goes on in our heads remains a private, well-protected constant. We may put on a show for others, but all the while we follow our own silent program.

Concepts and Notions

Part of the superficial public behavior cited here is cultural in origin, and yet we can adopt these manners without prejudice to our own core beliefs. Actions are not difficult to emulate, and even different varieties of speech can be imitated to some extent. Thought is a different matter. We cannot see it; we cannot hear it; it may be revealed to us with reluctance, simulation or cunning. Cross-cultural problems arise not so much on account of our unfamiliarity with a bow, a Gallic shrug or chopsticks. Neither do they crop up because of certain concepts, because many of these concepts are shared by other cultures. We can teach a Spaniard nothing about honor; the Japanese are masters of courtesy. Swedes, Brits and Germans are all convinced of their own honesty; honor, duty, love, justice, gratitude and revenge are basic tenets of the German, Chinese, Arab and Polynesian alike. A Tasmanian knows his or her duty as clearly as a Greenlander does. Given the size of the world, its long history and immeasurable variety, it is remarkable how many common concepts are rooted so firmly in a similar manner in very different societies. What we often overlook is the fact that everyone has different *notions* of these concepts that appeal to so many cultures. Romantic love is seen differently in France and Finland, and the English notion of revenge bears little similarity to the Sicilian.

We readily accept that cultural diversity is vast and formidable. If we take an extreme example, the barriers against communication or mutual comprehension between an Inuit hunter and a Nigerian herdsman might prove insurmountable. Given their different backgrounds, what could they talk about? They probably would be completely unaware of the structure or politics of each other's society; it is hardly likely that they could imagine the opposite extremity of climate; their religions, taboos, values, aspirations, disappointments and lifestyle would be in stark contrast. Available subjects of conversation (if they had some mode of communication) would be minimal, approaching zero.

The wildly differing notions of time, space, life after death, nature and reality held by isolated societies will have little impact on international business (although they may contribute usefully to our morals or philosophy). The Navahos with their nuclear concept of speech, the Zulus with their 39 colors of green, the Aborigines with their dreamtime, the Inuit with their 42 types of snow and the Lapps with their eight seasons provide us with striking insights and unique thought and speech processes that intrigue and fascinate those of us who have time to study them. We can observe, learn about and sometimes understand some of these groups' world views, but deceived we are not. We know, more or less, where we stand with these people. They live in their worlds and we live in ours.

Closer to Home

In our world, there are others who are more like us. They have modern civilizations, political parties, industrial complexes and stocks and shares. Their clothes resemble ours. We appear to have similar concepts and values. Yet for some reason, the French and Germans don't always get on. In Belgium half of society dislikes the other. The Chinese and Japanese are wary of each other, to say the least; neighborly Swedes and Norwegians snipe at each other, and the mutual exasperation that British and American cousins experience is only too well documented.

Truth. The concepts are shining and clear; our notions of them are different. The German notion is that truth, absolute honest truth, even if somewhat unpalatable, will allow participants to achieve a successful outcome to a business meeting. "*Die Wahrheit ist die Wahrheit,*" say the Germans. Not so, the Chinese would argue—there is no absolute truth. These two conflicting views may both be correct. Many Americans, Norwegians and Finns would agree with the Germans; most Asians and many Italians would agree with the Chinese.

In Germany, Sweden and Finland, where people are generally concerned about what the neighbors think, the drive toward conformity imposes checks and constraints on a person's ability to refashion veracity. The French, Italians and other Latins are not famous for their candor, which might interfere with the smooth social intercourse they are so fond of. In Japan, where no one must face exposure, be confronted or lose face, truth is a dangerous concept. In Asia, Africa and South America, strict adherence to the truth would destroy the harmony of the relationships between individuals, companies and entire segments of society. Only in Australia is a spade called a spade continent wide, and even there truth often occasions dismay and leads to fistfights.

Contracts and Ethics. As the globalization of business brings executives more frequently together, there is a growing realization that if we examine concepts and values, we can take almost nothing for granted. The word *contract* translates easily from language to language, but like *truth*, it has many interpretations. To a Swiss, Scandinavian, American or Brit, a contract is a formal document that has been signed and should be adhered to. Signatures give it a sense of finality. But a Japanese businessperson regards a contract as a starting document to be rewritten and modified as circumstances require. A South American sees it as an ideal that is unlikely to be achieved but that is signed to avoid argument.

Members of most cultures see themselves as ethical, but ethics can be turned upside down. The American calls the Japanese unethical if the latter breaks a contract. The Japanese says it is unethical for the American to apply the terms of the contract if things have changed. Italians have very flexible views on what is ethical and what is not, which sometimes causes Northern Europeans to question their honesty. When Italians bend the rules or "get around" some laws or regulations, they consider they are less ideal-bound than, say, the Swiss, and cut actually closer to reality. They do not consider themselves corrupt or immoral, nor do they admit to illegality. There are many gray areas where "shortcuts" are, in Italian eyes, the only intelligent course of action. In a country where excessive bureaucracy can hold up business for months, currying favor with an official is a matter of common sense.

Common Sense. The very term *common sense* has to be treated carefully, for it is not as common as it seems. British dictionaries define it as "judgment gained from experience rather than study"; the American lexicon describes it as "judgment that is sound but unsophisticated." Academics are uncomfortable with common sense, which tends to pre-empt their research by coming to the same conclusion months earlier. But we must not think that this rough-and-ready wisdom will unite our mix of nationalities. Common sense, although basic and unsophisticated, cannot be neutral. It is derived from experience, but experience is culture-bound. It is common sense in Germany and Sweden to form an orderly bus line. In Naples and Rio it is common sense to get on the bus before anyone else. It would seem common sense for the Japanese to have discarded the Chinese writing system, which does not suit their language and which takes ten years for Japanese children to learn, but they have not done so.

Gossip. Gossip has negative connotations in the Nordic countries and hardly a good name in the Anglo-Saxon world. Yet gossip proves far more important to us than we would at first admit. It is a vital source of information in business circles in many countries. In Spain, Italy, Brazil and Japan, gossip quickly updates and bypasses facts and statistics, provides political background to commercial decisions and facilitates invaluable debate between people who do not meet officially. The cafés of Madrid and Lisbon overflow with businesspeople, and the whole of Central and South America "networks" merrily until one or two in the morning.

The corridors of power in Brussels, where European business and political legislation are inevitably intertwined, reverberate with gossip. Countries that do not have access to this hothouse exchange of information will be severely disadvantaged.

Another positive aspect of gossip is that it appears to be good for us—that is to say, in line with our natural evolution. Professor Robin Dunbar of University College London points out that humans live in much larger groups than other primates and that language may have evolved as a form of social glue to hold us together. While some animals obviously communicate well in small groups, it is hardly likely that they can gossip about third parties. This ability enables us to form large social or working groups of up to approximately 150 members. This number holds true for ancient "clans," military fighting units (a company) and even modern firms. Once a commercial enterprise swells well beyond that magic number, it has to be organized into divisions or it becomes less manageable. Intense interest in what other people are doing, finding out from our "group" the latest news about third parties, enables us to network on a large scale and calculate our positions and reactions accordingly. So the Latins, Greeks, and Arabs have got it right after all!

Silence. Silence can be interpreted in different ways. A silent reaction to a business proposal would seem negative to American, German, French, Southern European and Arab executives. In countries as dissimilar as the United States, Peru and Kuwait, conversation is a two-way process, where one partner takes up when the other one leaves off. The intervening silence is two or three seconds in Britain and Germany, less than that in Greece and Kuwait and hardly noticeable in France, Italy and the U.S. However, East Asians and Finns find nothing wrong with silence as a response. "Those who know do not speak; those who speak do not know," says an old Chinese proverb. In these countries silence is not equated with failure to communicate, but is an integral part of social interaction. What is *not* said is regarded as important, and lulls in conversation are considered restful, friendly and appropriate. Silence means that you listen and learn; talking a lot merely expresses your cleverness, perhaps egoism and arrogance. Silence protects your individualism and privacy; it also shows respect for the individualism of others. In Finland and Japan it is considered impolite to force one's opinions on others—it is more appropriate to nod in agreement, smile quietly, avoid opinionated argument or discord.

Powerful Mental Blocks

As international trade and scientific and political exchange intensify, there is a growing effort on the part of academics, multinational organizations and even nations and governments to improve communication and dialogue. It is becoming increasingly apparent that in pursuit of this goal it is desirable not only to learn foreign languages on a much wider scale but to show a sympathetic understanding of other peoples' customs, societies and culture. Many binational and international bodies have been created to further this aim, and the personnel and training departments of many large companies have invested substantial sums of money in cross-cultural and internationalization programs and briefings for those staff members who will represent them abroad.

The question I would like to raise is whether or not cross-cultural training and a willingness to adapt will achieve anything at the end of the day, in view of the interlocking nature of our own language and thought. I am not necessarily suggesting that cross-cultural training might eventually be seen to be in vain—I believe the contrary to be true—but I would like to play devil's advocate for a little while and consider how powerful mental blocks may hinder our ability to change our attitudes or adopt new approaches. From infancy we are conditioned by various factors and influences—not least by the behavior and guidance of our parents, teachers and society. But they and we are subjected at every turn to that dominating and pervasive "conditioner"—our common language.

Many linguists adhere to anthropologist Benjamin Whorf's hypothesis, which states that the language we speak largely determines our way of thinking, as distinct from merely expressing it. In other words, Germans and Japanese behave in a certain manner because the way they think is governed by the language in which they think. A Spaniard and a Briton see the world in different ways because one is thinking in Spanish and the other in English. People in the British Isles act and live in a certain way because their thoughts are channeled along Anglo-Saxon grooves which are different from neo-Latin, Japanese or Chinese grooves.

The Briton, the German and the Inuit may share a common experience, but it appears to each as a kaleidoscopic flux of impressions that has to be organized by the mind. The mind does this largely by means of language. Thus the three individuals end up seeing three different things. What is fair play to the Briton may be something else to the German, who needs to translate the concept into different words, and it may mean nothing at all in a society where there are no organized games.

English and Zulu

If you think the notion of fair play is rather abstract, let us go to another instance where a very basic concept is seen in completely different ways by two people of diverse origins. My example involves an Englishman and a Zulu. While the cultural chasm is clear, it is the linguistic factor that dominates this instance.

As mentioned earlier, the Zulu language has 39 words for *green*. I was interested in how the Zulus could build up 39 one-word concepts for *green*, while English has only one, and discussed this at length with a former Zulu chief who had earned a doctorate in philology at Oxford. He began by explaining why Zulus needed 39 words for green. In the days before automotive transport and national highways, the Zulu people would often make long treks across their savannah grasslands. There were no signposts or maps and lengthy journeys had to be described by those who had traveled the route before. The language adapted itself to the requirements of its speakers. English copes with concepts such as contract deadlines and stock futures, but our tongue is seen as poverty stricken and inadequately descriptive by Africans and Native Americans, whose languages abound in finely wrought, beautifully logical descriptions of nature, causation, repetition, duration and result.

"Give me some examples of different green-words," I said to my Zulu friend. He picked up a leaf. "What color is this?" he asked.

"Green," I replied.

The sun was shining. He waited until a cloud intervened. "What color is the leaf now?" he asked.

"Green," I answered, already sensing my inadequacy.

"It isn't the same green, is it?"

"No, it isn't."

"We have a different word in Zulu." He dipped the leaf in water and held it out again. "Has the color changed?"

"Yes."

"In Zulu we have a word for *green shining wet*."

The sun came out again and I needed another word (leaf-green-wet-but-with-sunshine-on-it!).

My friend retreated 20 yards and showed me the leaf. "Has the color changed again?"

"Yes," I yelled.

"We have another word," he said with a smile.

He went on to indicate how different Zulu greens would deal with tree leaves, bush leaves, leaves vibrating in the wind, river greens, pool greens, tree trunk greens, crocodile greens… He got to 39 without even raising a sweat.

Language Straitjacket

It was evident that my Zulu friend and I saw the world through different eyes. And yet it was not a question of eyes. However international, multicultural or all-embracing I wished to be, there was no way I could perceive or feel about nature the way he did, *because I didn't have the language to do it with*. It was not just a matter of familiarizing myself with the cultural habits, preferences and taboos of his tribe or even adopting his religion and philosophies. I could only experience reality as fully as he did by learning his language and escaping (in terms of descriptive ability) from the straitjacket of my own.

Just as seeing with two eyes gives us stereoscopic vision and a sense of depth, thinking in two different languages gives us added dimensions of reality. The bilingual Swedish Finn is a case in point. A striking idea is that while French (a language very similar to English) would expand our world view by maybe an extra 10 percent, a "primitive" language totally different from our own, with its other logic and set of assumptions, might show us things we have never dreamed of!

Translation Inadequate

The Greeks, who were the first people to inquire in depth into logic and reason, assumed that language was a universal untampered-with element of reason. They believed it was a phenomenon shared by all mankind and, in the case of educated people, would provide a standard yardstick for comparison of ideas, experience and reality. They also assumed that ideas could be translated freely into any language. This is only true up to a point.

Those of us who have learned languages at school have noticed the difficulty our teachers have in translating such words as *panache, esprit de corps, Gemütlichkeit* and *Zeitgeist* into English. Interpreters at the United Nations are faced daily with similar problems, even with languages that are closely related. In one recorded case, the English speaker said "I assume," the French interpreter translated it as "I deduce," and this was rendered by the Russian as "I consider"—by which time the idea of assumption had been lost!

Different Worlds

If this can happen working with three close relatives of the Indo-European group, we see that two languages as different as English and Navaho literally operate in two different worlds. I think it is important for businesspeople to consider carefully the implication of the expression in *different worlds*. All observers are not led by the same physical evidence to the same picture of the universe, unless their linguistic backgrounds are similar, or can in some way be calibrated. English, French, German, Russian and other Indo-European languages can be roughly calibrated (although not always satisfactorily), but where does this leave us with Chinese, Indonesian, Finnish or Japanese? If the structure of a person's language influences the manner in which he or she understands reality and behaves with respect to it, then we could have four individuals who will see the universe through Sino-Tibetan, Polynesian, Altaic and Japanese eyes respectively and then comport themselves accordingly.

Thought = Internalized Language

There is a good deal of scientific support for the hypothesis that higher levels of thinking depend on language. Thought can be regarded as internalized language. Most of us conduct an interior monologue, often accompanied by visual imagery. The more educated and literate the individual, the more complex and sophisticated this monologue becomes, and there is no doubt that most of this goes on "in words," whether expressed aloud or not.

We can assume that German, Italian and Malaysian businesspeople do the same thing in their own language. When each speaks, we merely glimpse the tip of a huge iceberg of verbal activity that never breaks the surface of audibility. If you make this reasonable assumption, then you can presume that whatever is said to you will be a brief projection of the inner world of the other person's thoughts. What is said may be grammatically accurate or erroneous in the extreme, but it will be colored by the person's view of reality, which is itself influenced by the rigidity of his or her own language structure. This line of reasoning tends to become somewhat involved, but to clarify the point, let's take a few practical examples.

The German language is a tightly disciplined, no-nonsense entity with long, compound words often expressing complex concepts. We might therefore expect the internal monologue of a German person to be serious rather than casual, concentrating on weighty issues, and resulting in verbalized thoughts that will be anything but flippant.

Contrast this with the interior monologue of an American counterpart. The nature of American English is interwoven with the character and history of the youthful United States. American speech or thought is mobile and opportunistic; it shifts quickly for advantage or compromise and excels in casual and humorous shafts. Germans will take Americans seriously when they do not intend to be taken as such. A further complication is the deep slide that American English has taken into clichés and "tough talk." Such expressions as *gotta deal, gotta be jokin', no way, full of shit, over the top, you can't do this to me* and *give away the store* fail to indicate properly what the American is really thinking, but are verbal escape routes to simplified analyses or solutions not necessarily in their favor. Britons are guilty of other clichés indicative of near-stultifying vagueness of thought, well designed to convey very little or nothing at all to their foreign interlocutors. Such expressions, occasionally derived from sport, include *fair play, sticky wicket, a good innings, good show, bad news, not on* and *a bit thick.*

The French thought monologue is quite different. They have dissected their universe better than most of us, and they try to think about it clearly. They know where they are going and what it is that they want. Their clinical vocabulary is conducive to quick thinking, its lack of vagueness leads to a cutting directness, and their ruthless pursuit of logic will often irritate

Anglo-Saxons or Japanese, who tend to "feel their way" toward a solution. The Spanish speaker's monologue is earthy, emotional and generous. The wealth of Spanish vocabulary and the wide range of endearments and diminutives (shared with Italian and Portuguese) enable the Spaniard to communicate in a warm, human manner indicative of an expansive character and a lack of cunning. One should not, however, read this warmth as a sign that the Spaniard can easily be taken advantage of.

The Japanese have the most difficult task of all in making the transition from their internal monologues to actual verbal utterances. In their thoughts they agonize over striking a balance between gaining advantage and correctness of behavior. Their internalized speech has to be polite in the extreme in view of the fact that they are to address others. But the speech mechanisms involved in such politeness often lead to incredible vagueness of expression, so that whatever message they seek to convey may well get lost in a fog of impeccable behavior. On top of that, their formidable battery of honorific expressions—so useful in communication between Japanese—are rendered useless in the face of the impossibility of translation, so that their conversation with their foreign counterpart emerges as terribly platitudinous, even if grammatically correct.

Humor across Frontiers

It has been said that humor crosses national boundaries with difficulty, especially when heading east. If we analyze this assertion for a moment, several implications emerge. First, it is self-evident that the victim of a humorous attack is hardly likely to see the funny side of it. French anecdotes depicting the Belgians as a collection of slow-witted yokels fail to gain appreciation in Brussels. The Dutch resent similar treatment at the hands of the Belgians.

Secondly, failure to appreciate the funny side of an anecdote does not necessarily depend on one's being the victim. Serious-minded, factual Germans do not split their sides on hearing American jokes about Texas, which usually depend on gross exaggeration. The story about the Mexican driving just as fast as he could for 24 hours to get out of Texas but finding he had not managed it, thrills the American imagination but sounds far-fetched to the German, who might reply, "He should have used a German car." This reply would be considered very funny in Germany and fairly humorous in England and Scandinavia.

Apart from the Koreans, who seem to like everybody's jokes, few Asians are amused by American or (most) European jokes. The Confucian and Buddhist pre-occupation with truth, sincerity, kindliness and politeness automatically eliminates humor techniques such as sarcasm, satire, exaggeration and parody. They also find little merit in jokes about religion, sex and underprivileged minorities. Sick or black humor is definitely out.

So what is left, you might ask? Eastern humor, such as we understand it, is couched in subtlety, gentle, indirect reproach or reprimand, occasionally victimizing listeners in a sly but nonaggressive manner that yet leaves them room for response and stops short of depriving them of their dignity. Even the rougher, occasionally bawdy Koreans take great care to protect the listener's "wholeness" or standing. Chinese are noted for their aphorisms and proverbs, and they and Indians find great sources of humor in parables, which we in the West find only moderately funny, although they do combine wisdom, moralizing and a sense of perspective

Is there such a thing as a "national style" of humor? Before answering this question directly, one must accept the fact that there *is* such a thing as international humor—that is to say, some types of humor and some jokes gain international acceptance. In particular, this is true of slapstick, which is age-old in its use and laughed at by Europeans, Americans, Africans and Asians alike. It is very much in evidence, for instance, on Japanese television. There are also "international" jokes repeated across many borders, such as the one about who must jump first out of the airplane, elephant jokes, restaurant jokes and hilarious stories about golfers.

Even in the area of international jokes, however, the national "rinse" begins to show. Take, for example, the old joke about the journalists who organized a competition to write an article about elephants. The titles were as follows:

English	Hunting Elephants in British East Africa
French	The Love Life of Elephants
German	The Origin and Development of the Indian Elephant from 1200 to 1950 (600 pages)
American	How to Breed Bigger and Better Elephants
Russian	How We Sent an Elephant to the Moon
Swede	Elephants and the Welfare State
Spaniard	Techniques of Elephant Fighting
Indian	The Elephant as a Means of Transportation before Railroads
Finn	What Elephants Think about Finland

This joke, which probably originated at a conference of journalists, pokes fun at various national *faiblesses* (weaknesses): French lust, German seriousness, American bragging, British colonialism and so on. The punch line is the Finns' preoccupation with what others think about them. In Helsinki, however, the Finns developed an alternative punch line by adding a Norwegian title: "Norway and Norway's Mountains." Finns, Swedes and Danes find this alternative absolutely side-splitting. The Norwegians, who consider themselves a humorous people, do not find this ending funny at all. In fact, *they do not understand it*. Do you?

Humor in Business

As world trade becomes increasingly globalized, businesspeople meet their foreign partners more frequently and consequently feel that they know each other better. It is only natural that when they develop a closer relationship, they begin to converse in a more relaxed manner. A funny incident involving some personal discomfort or embarrassment is a good start; a sly attack on a "common enemy" may soon follow.

Humor during business meetings is not infrequent in most European countries, although it is less common among Latins than with Northern peoples, where it is a valuable tool for breaking the ice. Perhaps among the Spaniards, Portuguese and Italians, there is little ice to break. Their own racy, gossipy, confiding conversation style constitutes in itself a valid humorous element.

It is in the Anglo-Saxon countries that humor is used systematically. Relaxed in Canada and New Zealand, it can be barbed and provocative in Australia. In the United States, particularly, sarcasm, kidding and feigned indignation are regarded as factors that move the meeting along and help get more done in less time. Time is, after all, money. It is perhaps in Britain, though, that humor is most intertwined in business talks. The British hate heavy or drawn-out meetings and will resort to various forms of humor and distracting tactics to keep it all nice and lively.

However, two nationalities in particular avoid jokes and other forms of humor during the actual business sessions. Germans find it out of place during negotiations. Business is serious and should be treated as such, without irrelevant stories or distractions. If you do not concentrate on the issue, you are not showing respect to your interlocutor. Kidding is, in their eyes, not honest and creates confusion in business discussion. They want to know about price, quality and delivery dates, with some precision, please.

After the meetings are over, Germans are quite willing to relax and joke with their partners in bars, restaurants and at home. Humor and anecdotes are more than welcome in these circumstances. Relaxation, like business discussion and many other activities in Germany, is fairly strictly compartmentalized.

The Japanese also fail to see any benefit in introducing humor into business meetings. They will laugh if they are aware that you have told a joke (it is unlikely they will have understood it), but that is out of sheer politeness. They are normally nervous about understanding your straight talk in the first place, so that any clever nuances or tongue-in-cheek utterances will leave them floundering. They take anything you say quite literally. Americans using expressions like "You are killing me" or "Say that once again and I'll walk away from this deal" will cause great consternation among their Japanese partners. One U.S. executive, who said a certain clause would "blow the deal out of the water," was asked, "What water?"

While the introduction of humor in international business talks may bring considerable gain in terms of breaking the ice, speeding up the discussion, escaping from deadlock, putting your partners at ease and winning their confidence in you as a human being, the downside risks are often just as great. What is funny for the French may be anathema to an Arab; your very best story may be utterly incomprehensible to a Chinese; your most innocent anecdote may seriously offend a Turk. Cultural and religious differences may make it impossible for some people to laugh at the same thing. Who can say with certainty what is funny? If all values are relative and culture based, then these include humor, tolerance, even truth itself. And remember that laughter, more often than not, symbolizes embarrassment, nervousness or possibly scorn among Asians.

Making Allowances

International businesspeople cannot escape the "bottom line"—a good American expression—of the considerations just mentioned. The picture of the universe shifts from tongue to tongue, and the way of doing business shifts accordingly. There is no one metaphysical pool of human thought—or of behavior. Different languages provide different "segments of experience," and there is little we can do about it, except to learn more languages. But at least being aware of cultural differences, and being sensitive to those differences, will help us establish whatever degree of communication our different mentalities permit.

2

Cultural Conditioning

We think our minds are free, but, like captured American pilots in Vietnam and North Korea, we have been thoroughly brainwashed. Collective programming in our culture, begun in the cradle and reinforced in kindergarten, school and the workplace, convinces us that we are normal, others eccentric.

What Is Culture?

Geert Hofstede defined culture as "the collective programming of the mind that distinguishes the members of one category of people from another." The key expression in this definition is *collective programming*. Although not as sinister as *brainwashing*, with its connotations of political coercion, it nevertheless describes a process to which each one of us has been subjected since birth (some people would say even before birth, but that is a little deep for me). When parents returning from the hospital carry their baby over the threshold, they have often already made one of their first culturally based decisions—where the baby will sleep. A Japanese child is invariably put in the same room as the parents, near the mother, for at least the first couple of years. British and American children are often put in a separate room, right away or after a few weeks or months. The inferences for the child's dependence or interdependence and problem-solving abilities are obvious.

Parents and teachers obviously give children the best advice they can to prepare them for successful interactions in their own culture and society, where good and bad, right and wrong, normal and abnormal are clearly defined. It is perhaps unfortunate in one sense that each cultural group gives its children a different set of instructions, each equally valid in their own environment.

As we grow up, these learned national and/or regional concepts become our core beliefs, which we find almost impossible to discard. We regard others' beliefs and habits (Russian, Chinese, Hungarian…) as strange or eccentric, mainly because they are unlike our own. There is no doubt about it, the Japanese are not like Americans!

On the other hand, we have a sneaking feeling (and we frequently hear it expressed) that "deep down all people are alike." There is also truth in this, for there are such things as universal human characteristics. They are not as numerous as you might think, for our national collective programming distorts some of our basic instincts (Scots' thrift versus American free spending). Figure 2.1 shows how national collective programming is "grafted onto" inherited traits. The top section adds individual characteristics. Some people, by dint of personal originality, extra powers of perception, stubbornness or even genius, stand apart

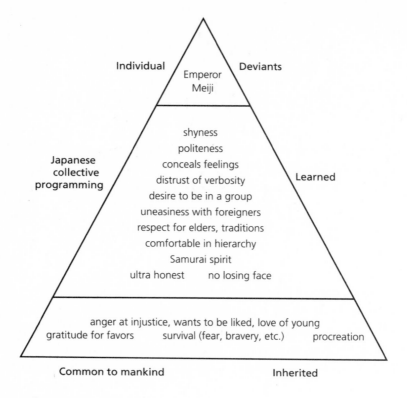

Figure 2.1 Human Mental Programming: Japan

from their colleagues and deviate sharply from the national track. Such people often become famous for their idiosyncrasies, and a few have actually changed the course of their nation's destiny (e.g., King Henry VIII, Kemal Atatürk, Emperor Meiji of Japan).

In general, however, our national or regional culture imposes itself on our behavior rather than the other way round, and we become a solid German, a good Swede, a real American or a true Brit, as the case may be. Interacting with our compatriots, we generally find that the closer we stick to the rules of our society, the more accepted we become.

Culture Shock

Our precious values and unshakeable core beliefs take a battering when we venture abroad. "Support the underdog!" cry Guy Fawkes–loving English. The Australians, famous historical underdogs themselves, echo this to the full. Germans and the Japanese, although temporary underdogs themselves after the Second World War, tend to support the *more powerful* of two adversaries, seeing the underdog as necessarily the less efficient. The Japanese government, through its Ministry of Trade and Industry, issues directives to the larger banks to lend money to those industries that are currently thriving and have the potential for further growth, while discouraging loans to enterprises that have become old-fashioned or have little

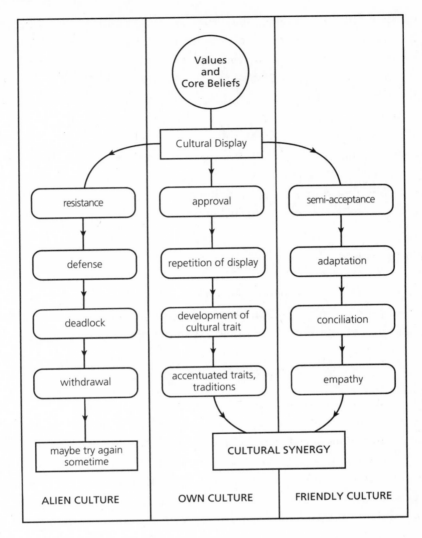

Figure 2.2 Paths for Core Beliefs

hope for success in the future. This attitude is in marked contrast to that so long prevalent in Britain, where ancient factories were kept alive and industrial underdogs such as textiles and coal mining were supported long after they were economically viable.

Figure 2.2 shows the different paths our core beliefs take according to the culture we try to impose them on. Others are not aware of our values simply by looking at us. They may draw certain conclusions from the manner in which we dress, but these days most businesspeople dress in a similar way. It is only when we *say* or *do* something that they can gain deeper insight into what makes us tick. This utterance or action may be described as a *cultural display* or *event*, since, by its execution, we reveal our cultural attitudes. The cultural display might be an Italian (probably from Rome) who turns up half an hour late for a scheduled meeting. In her own cultural environment this will make no waves, for most of the others will be late too. Were she to turn up 30 minutes late in an alien culture, say Germany, she would deliver a culture shock of no mean proportions. Germans do not like to be kept waiting for 3 minutes, let alone 30. Immediate resistance and protest by the German leads to Italian defense (traffic jam, ill daughter, etc.) and eventually a defense of the Italian way of life: "Why are you Germans so obsessed about time? You are like clocks!" Such confrontation often leads to deadlock and even withdrawal from a project.

In a friendly culture (say the French), the criticism will be couched in cynicism but will be less final or damning: "*Mon vieux, tu m'as volé une demie heure, tu sais!*" "You stole half an hour of my time, old chap!" The Italian, sensitive to Latin objections, next time comes only 20 minutes late. The Frenchman, no great believer in punctuality himself, eventually settles for 15 minutes. The Italian concurs. This is Latin understanding.

Who Is Normal, Anyway?

Most English people think they are normal and that all others (whom they call "foreigners") are abnormal—that is to say, they might be all right, but they really cannot act and think like the English, because, after all, they are foreign. You only have to look at them, you'll know what that means . . .

Chauvinism

Americans think America is the biggest and the best, the newest and the richest, and all others are a bit slow, old-fashioned, rather poor and somewhat on the small side. They can't call the British foreigners, so they call them *limeys*.

Spaniards think they are the bravest because they kill bulls, the French think they are intellectually superior to everybody else, the Japanese are quite sure they are superior to others, including the French. The Germans admit that they are not as big as the Americans, as agile as the Japanese, as eloquent as the French or as smooth as the British, but what really counts in life? Efficiency, punctuality, *Gründlichkeit* ("thoroughness"), method, consistency and organization, and who can match Germans on these counts?

There are few countries in the world where people do not believe, at the bottom of their hearts, that they are the best, or the most intelligent, or at least normal. Perhaps in Europe the Italians and the Finns are the most innocent in this regard, often being willing to criticize themselves before others, yet both still consider themselves normal.

Normal and Abnormal

If people from each culture consider themselves normal, then the corollary is that they consider everybody else abnormal. By this token Finns consider Italians overly emotional because they wave their arms while talking. The individualistic Spaniards consider the Swiss stuffy and excessively law-abiding. Lively Italians find Norwegians gloomy. French-influenced

Vietnamese find Japanese impassive. Most South Americans find Argentineans conceited. Germans think Australians are undisciplined. Japanese see straight-talking Americans as rude.

We can achieve a good understanding of our foreign counterparts only if we realize that our "cultural spectacles" are coloring our view of them. What is the route to better understanding? To begin with, we need to examine the special features of our own culture.

Our second task, once we realize that we, too, are a trifle strange, is to understand the subjective nature of our ethnic or national values. While Scots see stubbornness largely as a positive trait, flexible Italians may see it as mainly intransigence, the diplomatic English, possibly a lack of artfulness or dexterity. We also make assumptions on the basis of our subjective view and, even worse, assumptions about other people's assumptions. The Italian who assumes that French people feel intellectually superior also assumes that the French therefore think Italians are suitable mainly for manual labor when emigrating to France. Finns who judge Swedes as snobs also assume that Swedes stereotype Finns as rough and rustic. There may be a grain of truth in many of these judgments and assumptions of assumptions, but the danger involved in making them is only too obvious!

It Depends on Our Perception

Our perception of reality (what a word!) may be assisted if we can wear someone else's shoes for a moment—if we can see how he or she views some issue in a way very different from how we see it. Let's take, for example, the differing viewpoints of Finns and Spaniards on legality and illegality.

Both nationalities agree that trafficking in drugs is bad and that laws against drunken driving are socially beneficial and justified. When it comes to restrictive immigration laws, the Finns' subjective view is that the fragile, delicately balanced national economy must be protected, while semiconsciously their instinct is to protect the purity of their race. Spaniards, born in a country where no one dares trace his or her ancestry further back than 1500, have a reflexive distaste for prohibitive immigration policies that hinder the free movement of Spaniards seeking better wages abroad. Such policies or laws they see as negative, or simply bad.

As a second example, a Finn consistently making expensive telephone calls for which she need not pay will ultimately fall victim to her own inherent sense of independence, not least because she is building up a debt to her friend in Finnish Telecom. The Spaniard, on the other hand, would phone Easter Island nightly (if he could get away with it) with great relish and unashamed glee.

It is by considering such matters that we realize that all that is legal is not necessarily good, and everything illegal is not necessarily bad. Swedes, Swiss and Germans do not make this discovery very easily. Americans, Belgians, Hungarians, Koreans and Australians can accept it without losing too much sleep. Latins, Arabs, Polynesians, Africans and Russians see it clearly from the beginning. A Sicilian friend of mine has not paid for a telephone call since 1948. His father owns a vineyard.

Recently I tested mature Finnish executives on cross-cultural seminars with the following exercise:

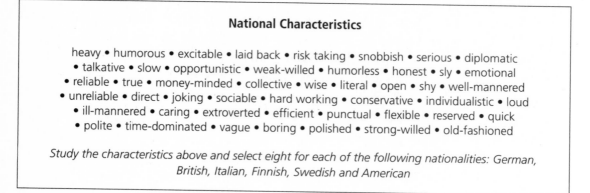

National Characteristics

heavy • humorous • excitable • laid back • risk taking • snobbish • serious • diplomatic • talkative • slow • opportunistic • weak-willed • humorless • honest • sly • emotional • reliable • true • money-minded • collective • wise • literal • open • shy • well-mannered • unreliable • direct • joking • sociable • hard working • conservative • individualistic • loud • ill-mannered • caring • extroverted • efficient • punctual • flexible • reserved • quick • polite • time-dominated • vague • boring • polished • strong-willed • old-fashioned

Study the characteristics above and select eight for each of the following nationalities: German, British, Italian, Finnish, Swedish and American

The Finns invariably select the following qualities to describe themselves:

honest, slow, reliable, true, shy, direct, reserved, punctual

Six of these characteristics are clearly positive; even *shy* and *slow* do not have negative connotations in Finnish ears.

Germans could be considered punctual, Swedes honest, Britons true and reliable, Americans direct, but the Finnish seminar participants had a natural tendency to paint a positive picture of themselves. Swedes, Germans and Britons, when tested in a similar manner, do the same, selecting positive adjectives to describe their own culture.

In another exercise, the same Finnish executives were asked to perform role plays in which Finnish, Russian, American and Polynesian characters were involved. The executives played the Finnish and Russian roles well but invariably exaggerated the traits of Americans and Polynesians, magnifying and distorting the brash and blustery nature of the former and the innocence and chatter of the latter. This illustrated the Finnish tendency to resort to stereotype categorizing when actual familiarity is lacking (Russian characteristics, on the other hand, are well known by Finns).

Stereotyping is dangerous, but generalizing is a fair guide at the national level. A particular Dane may resemble a certain Portuguese, but a Danish choir or soccer team is easily distinguishable from its Portuguese equivalent. Generalizing on national traits breaks down with individuals but stands firm with large numbers.

Our cultural spectacles, then, blur the vision of any nationals when they consider their foreign interlocutors. Figure 2.3 illustrates the barriers to communication Japanese reticence erects when faced with Latin exuberance, and Figure 2.4 shows the relative ease with which two Latin peoples can communicate with each other by virtue of wearing similar spectacles.

It is worth pointing out that the French and Italians do not like each other particularly, but they are both good communicators and there are no substantial barriers in the way of rapid and mutually intelligible discourse.

If a Japanese person or anyone else takes off his or her national spectacles, the world is initially blurred and out of focus. Many other pairs of spectacles will have to be tried on before 20/20 vision is achieved. This is the process of *developing intercultural sensitivity.*

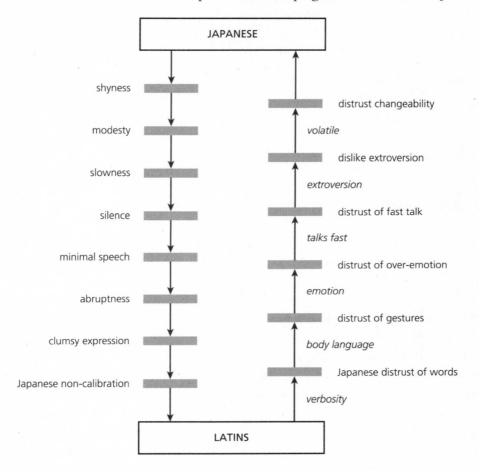

Figure 2.3 Barriers to Communication: Japanese and Latins

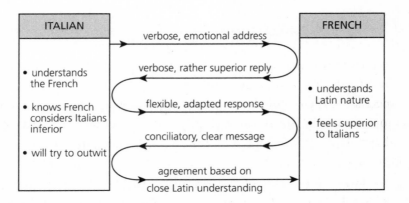

Figure 2.4 Interaction among Latins: French and Italians

3

Categorizing Cultures

The several hundred national and regional cultures of the world can be roughly classified into three groups: task-oriented, highly organized planners (linear-active); people-oriented, loquacious interrelators (multi-active); and introverted, respect-oriented listeners (reactive). Italians see Germans as stiff and time-dominated; Germans see Italians gesticulating in chaos; the Japanese observe and quietly learn from both.

Cultural Categories at Cross-Century

In the early years of the twenty-first century, we have many nation–states and different cultures, but enduring misunderstandings arise principally when there is a clash of *category* rather than *nationality*. For example, Germany and the Netherlands experience national friction, but they understand and cooperate with each other because they are both linear-active. Friction between Korea and Japan occasionally borders on hatred, but their common reactive nature leads to blossoming bilateral trade.

Let us examine for a moment the number and variety of cultures as they now stand and consider how classification and adaptation might guide us toward better understanding.

There are over 200 recognized countries or nation–states in the world, and the number of cultures is considerably greater because of strong regional variations. For instance, marked differences in values and behavior are observable in the north and south of such countries as Italy, France and Germany, while other states are formed of groups with clearly different historical backgrounds (the United Kingdom with her Celtic and Saxon components, Fiji with her Polynesians and Indians, Russia with numerous subcultures such as Tatar, Finnic, Chechen, etc.).

In a world of rapidly globalizing business, Internet electronic proximity and politico-economic associations, the ability to interact successfully with foreign partners in the spheres of commercial activity, diplomatic intercourse and scientific interchange is seen as increasingly essential and desirable. Cross-cultural training followed by international experience goes a long way toward facilitating better relationships and reducing misunderstandings. Ideally, the trainee acquires deepening insights into the target (partner's) culture and adopts a *cultural stance* towards the partner/colleague, designed (through *adaptation*) to fit in suitably with the attitudes of the other.

The question then arises as to how many adaptations or stances are required for effective international business relations. It is hardly likely that even the most informed and adaptable executive could envisage assuming 200 different personalities! Even handling the different national types on European Union (EU) committees and working groups has proved a daunting task for European delegates, not to mention the chairpersons.

Such chameleon-like behavior is out of the question and unattainable, but the question of adaptation remains nevertheless important. The reticent, factual Finn must grope toward a *modus operandi* with the loquacious, emotional Italian. Americans will turn over many more billions in trade if they learn to communicate effectively with the Japanese and Chinese.

Assuming a suitable cultural stance would be quickly simplified if there were fewer cultural types to familiarize oneself with, can we boil down 200 to 250 sets of behavior to 50 or 20 or 10 or half a dozen? Cross-culturalists have grappled with this problem over several decades. Some have looked at geographical divisions (north, south, east and west), but what is "Eastern" culture? And is it really unified? People can be classified according to their religion (Muslim, Christian, Hindu) or ethnic/racial origin (Caucasian, Asian, African, Polynesian, Indian, Eskimo, Arab), but such nomenclatures contain many inconsistencies—Christian Norwegians and Lebanese, Caucasian Scots and Georgians, Muslim Moroccans and Indonesians, and so on. Other classification attempts, such as professional, corporate or regional, have too many subcategories to be useful. Generational culture is important but ever changing. Political classification (Left, Right, Centrist) has many (changeable) hues, too.

Writers such as Geert Hofstede have sought dimensions to cover all cultures. His four dimensions included power distance, collectivism versus individualism, femininity versus masculinity and uncertainty avoidance. Later he added long-term versus short-term orientation. Edward T. Hall classified groups as monochronic or polychronic, high or low context and pastor future-oriented. Alfons Trompenaars' dimensions categorized universalist versus particularist, individualist versus collectivist, specific versus diffuse, achievement versus ascription and neutral versus emotional or affective. The German sociologist Ferdinand Tönnies dwelt on *Gemeinschaft* versus *Gesellschaft* cultures. Florence Kluckholn saw five dimensions/attitudes to problems: time, Nature, nature of man, form of activity and relation to one's cultural compatriots. Samuel Huntington drew fault lines between civilizations—West European, Islam, Hindu, Orthodox, Japanese, Sinic and African.

The need for a convincing categorization is obvious. It enables us to

- ✦ predict a culture's behavior,
- ✦ clarify why people did what they did,
- ✦ avoid giving offense,
- ✦ search for some kind of unity,
- ✦ standardize policies, and
- ✦ perceive neatness and *Ordnung*.

Linear-Active and Multi-Active Cultures

Sven Svensson is a Swedish businessman living in Lisbon. A few weeks ago he was invited by a Portuguese acquaintance, Antonio, to play tennis at 10:00 A.M. Sven turned up at the tennis court on time, in tennis gear and ready to play.

Antonio arrived half an hour late, in the company of a friend, Carlos, from whom he was buying some land. They had been discussing the purchase that morning and had prolonged the discussion, so Antonio had brought Carlos along in order to finalize the details during the journey. They continued the business while Antonio changed into his tennis clothes, with Sven listening to all they said. At 10:45 they got on the court, and Antonio continued the discussion with Carlos while hitting practice balls with Sven.

At this point another acquaintance of Antonio's, Pedro, arrived to confirm a sailing date with Antonio for the weekend. Antonio asked Sven to excuse him for a moment and walked off the court to talk to Pedro. After chatting with Pedro for five minutes, Antonio resumed his conversation with the waiting Carlos and eventually turned back to the waiting Sven to begin playing tennis at 11:00. When Sven remarked that the court had only been booked from 10:00 to 11:00, Antonio reassured him that he had phoned in advance to rebook it until noon. No problem.

It will probably come as no surprise to you to hear that Sven was very unhappy about the course of events. Why? He and Antonio live in two different worlds or, to put it more exactly, use two different time systems. Sven, as a good Swede, belongs to a culture which uses linear-active time—that is, he does one thing at a time in the sequence he has written down in his date book. His schedule that day said 8:00 A.M. get up, 9:00 breakfast, 9:15 change into tennis clothes, 9:30 drive to the tennis court, 10:00–11:00 play tennis, 11:00–11:30 beer and shower, 12:15 lunch, 2:00 P.M. go to the office, and so on.

Antonio, who had seemed to synchronize with him for tennis from 10:00 to 11:00, had disorganized Sven's day. Portuguese like Antonio follow a multi-active time system, that is, they do many things at once, often in an unplanned order.

Multi-active cultures are very flexible. If Pedro interrupted Carlos's conversation, which was already in the process of interrupting Sven's tennis, this was quite normal and acceptable in Portugal. It is not acceptable in Sweden, nor is it in Germany or Britain.

Linear-active people, like Swedes, Swiss, Dutch and Germans, do one thing at a time, concentrate hard on that thing and do it within a scheduled time period. These people think that in this way they are more efficient and get more done. Multi-active people *think they get more done their way.*

Let us look again at Sven and Antonio. If Sven had not been disorganized by Antonio, he would undoubtedly have played tennis, eaten at the right time and done some business. But Antonio had had breakfast, bought some land, played tennis and confirmed his sailing plans, all by lunchtime. He had even managed to rearrange the tennis booking. Sven could never live like this, but Antonio does, all the time.

Multi-active people are not very interested in schedules or punctuality. They pretend to observe them, especially if a linear-active partner insists. They consider reality to be more important than man-made appointments. Reality for Antonio that morning was that his talk with Carlos about land was unfinished. Multi-active people do not like to leave conversations unfinished. For them, completing a human transaction is the best way they can invest their time. So he took Carlos to the tennis court and finished buying the land while hitting balls. Pedro further delayed the tennis, but Antonio would not abandon the match with Sven. That was another human transaction he wished to complete. So they would play till 12:00 or 12:30 if necessary. But what about Sven's lunch at 12:15? Not important, says Antonio. It's only 12:15 because that's what Sven wrote in his date book.

A friend of mine, a BBC producer, often used to visit Europe to visit BBC agents. He never failed to get through his appointments in Denmark and Germany, but he always had trouble in Greece. The Greek agent was a popular man in Athens and had to see so many people each day that he invariably ran over-time. So my friend usually missed his appointment or waited three or four hours for the agent to turn up. Finally, after several trips, the producer adapted to the multi-active culture. He simply went to the Greek agent's secretary in late morning and asked for the agent's schedule for the day. As the Greek conducted most of his meetings in hotel rooms or bars, the BBC producer would wait in the hotel lobby and catch him rushing from one appointment to the next. The multi-active Greek, happy to see him, would not hesitate to spend half an hour with him and thus make himself late for his next appointment.

When people from a linear-active culture work together with people from a multi-active culture, irritation results on both sides. Unless one party adapts to the other—and they rarely do—constant crises will occur. "Why don't the Mexicans arrive on time?" ask the Germans. "Why don't they work to deadlines? Why don't they follow a plan?" The Mexicans, on the other hand, ask, "Why keep to the plan when circumstances have changed? Why keep to a deadline if we rush production and lose quality? Why try to sell this amount to that customer if we know they aren't ready to buy yet?"

Recently I visited a wonderful aviary in South Africa where exotic birds of all kinds were kept in a series of 100 large cages, to which the visiting public had direct access. There was plenty of room for the birds to fly around and it was quite exciting for us to be in the cage with them. You proceeded, at your leisure, from cage to cage, making sure all the doors were closed carefully.

Two small groups of tourists—one consisting of four Germans and the other of three French people—were visiting the aviary at the same time as we were. The Germans had made their calculations, obviously having decided to devote 100 minutes to the visit; consequently they spent one minute in each cage. One German read the captions, one took photographs, one videoed and one opened and closed doors. I followed happily in their wake. The three French people began their tour a few minutes later than the Germans but soon caught up with them as they galloped through the cages containing smaller birds. As the French were also taking pictures, they rather spoiled cage 10 for the Germans, as they made a lot of noise and generally got in the way. The Germans were relieved when the French rushed on ahead toward the more exciting cages.

The steady German progress continued through cages 11 to 15. Cage 16 contained the owls (most interesting). There we found our French friends again, who had occupied the cage for five minutes. They filmed the owls from every angle while the Germans waited their turn. When the French eventually rushed out, the Germans were five minutes behind schedule. Later on, the French stayed so long with the eagles in cage 62 that the Germans had to bypass them and come back to see the eagles later. They were furious at this forced departure from their linear progression, and eventually finished their visit half an hour late. By then the French had departed, having seen all they were interested in.

A study of attitudes toward time in a Swiss–Italian venture showed that, after some initial quarreling, each side learned something from the other. The Italians finally admitted that adherence at least in theory to schedules, production deadlines and budgets enabled them to clarify their goals and check on performances and efficiency. The Swiss, on the other hand, found that the more flexible Italian attitude allowed them to modify the timetable in reaction to unexpected developments in the market, to spot deficiencies in the planning that had not been evident earlier, and to make vital last-minute improvements with the extra time.

Germans, like the Swiss, are very high on the linear-active scale, since they attach great importance to analyzing a project, compartmentalizing it, tackling each problem one at a time in a linear fashion, concentrating on each segment and thereby achieving a near-perfect result. They are uneasy with people who do not work in this manner, such as Arabs and those from many Mediterranean cultures.

Americans are also very linear-active, but there are some differences in attitude. As Americans live very much in the present and race toward the near future, they sometimes push Germans into action before the latter want to act. Germans are very conscious of their history and their past and will often wish to explain a lot of background to American partners to put present actions in context. This often irritates Americans who want to "get on with it."

Figure 3.1 gives a suggested ranking on the linear/multi-active scale, showing some rather surprising regional variations. German and other European influences in Chile have caused Chileans to be less multi-active than, for instance, Brazilians or Argentineans. The differences in behavior between northern and southern Italians are well documented. Australians, with a large number of Southern European immigrants, are becoming less linear-active and more extroverted than most northern peoples.

Figure 3.2 lists the most common traits of linear-active, multi-active and reactive cultures.

Reactive Cultures

Japan belongs to the group of reactive, or listening, cultures, the members of which rarely initiate action or discussion, preferring to listen to and establish the other's position first, then react to it and formulate their own.

1. Germans, Swiss
2. Americans (WASPs)*
3. Scandinavians, Austrians
4. British, Canadians, New Zealanders
5. Australians, South Africans
6. Japanese
7. Dutch, Belgians
8. American subcultures (e.g., Jewish, Italian, Polish)
9. French, Belgians (Walloons)
10. Czechs, Slovenians, Croats, Hungarians
11. Northern Italians (Milan, Turin, Genoa)
12. Chileans
13. Russians, other Slavs
14. Portuguese
15. Polynesians
16. Spanish, Southern Italians, Mediterranean peoples
17. Indians, Pakistanis, etc.
18. Latin Americans, Arabs, Africans

*White Anglo-Saxon Protestants

Figure 3.1 Linear-Active/Multi-Active Scale

Linear-Active	Multi-Active	Reactive
✦ introvert	✦ extrovert	✦ introvert
✦ patient	✦ impatient	✦ patient
✦ quiet	✦ talkative	✦ silent
✦ minds own business	✦ inquisitive	✦ respectful
✦ likes privacy	✦ gregarious	✦ good listener
✦ plans ahead methodically	✦ plans grand outline only	✦ looks at general principles
✦ does one thing at a time	✦ does several things at once	✦ reacts
✦ works fixed hours	✦ works any hours	✦ flexible hours
✦ punctual	✦ not punctual	✦ punctual
✦ dominated by timetables and schedules	✦ timetable unpredictable	✦ reacts to partner's timetable

(continued)

Figure 3.2 Common Traits of Linear-Active, Multi-Active, and Reactive Categories

Linear-Active	Multi-Active	Reactive
✦ compartmentalizes projects	✦ lets one project influence another	✦ sees whole picture
✦ sticks to plans	✦ changes plans	✦ makes slight changes
✦ sticks to facts	✦ juggles facts	✦ statements are promises
✦ gets information from statistics, reference books, database, Internet	✦ gets first-hand (oral) information	✦ uses both first-hand and researched information
✦ job-oriented	✦ people-oriented	✦ people-oriented
✦ unemotional	✦ emotional	✦ quietly caring
✦ works within department	✦ gets around all departments	✦ considers all departments
✦ follows correct procedures	✦ pulls strings	✦ networks
✦ accepts favors reluctantly	✦ seeks favors	✦ protects face of other
✦ delegates to competent colleagues	✦ delegates to relations	✦ delegates to reliable people
✦ completes action chains	✦ completes human transactions	✦ reacts to partner
✦ likes fixed agendas	✦ interrelates everything	✦ thoughtful
✦ brief on telephone	✦ talks for hours	✦ summarizes well
✦ uses memoranda	✦ rarely writes memos	✦ plans slowly
✦ respects officialdom	✦ seeks out (top) key person	✦ ultra-honest
✦ dislikes losing face	✦ has ready excuses	✦ must not lose face
✦ confronts with logic	✦ confronts emotionally	✦ avoids confrontation
✦ limited body language	✦ unrestricted body language	✦ subtle body language
✦ rarely interrupts	✦ interrupts frequently	✦ doesn't interrupt
✦ separates social/ professional	✦ interweaves social/ professional	✦ connects social and professional

Reactive cultures are also found in China, Taiwan, Singapore, Korea, Turkey and Finland. Several other East Asian countries, although occasionally multi-active and excitable, have certain reactive characteristics. In Europe, only Finns are strongly reactive, but Britons, Turks and Swedes fall easily into "listening mode" on occasion.

Reactive cultures listen before they leap. Reactive cultures are the world's best listeners in as much as they concentrate on what the speaker is saying, do not let their minds wander (difficult for Latins) and rarely, if ever, interrupt a speaker while the discourse or presentation is on-going. When it is finished, they do not reply immediately. A decent period of silence after the speaker has stopped shows respect for the weight of the remarks, which must be considered unhurriedly and with due deference.

Even when representatives of a reactive culture begin their reply, they are unlikely to voice any strong opinion immediately. A more probable tactic is to ask further questions on what has been said in order to clarify the speaker's intent and aspirations. Japanese, particularly, go over each point many times in detail to make sure there are no misunderstandings. Finns, although blunt and direct in the end, shy away from confrontation as long as they can, trying to formulate an approach that suits the other party. The Chinese take their time to assemble a variety of strategies that will avoid discord with the initial proposal.

Reactives are introverted; they distrust a surfeit of words and consequently are adept at nonverbal communication. This is achieved by subtle body language, worlds apart from the excitable gestures of Latins and Africans. Linear-active people find reactive tactics hard to fathom because they do not slot into the linear system (question/reply, cause/effect). Multi-active people, used to extroverted behavior, find them inscrutable—giving little or no feedback. The Finns are the best example of this behavior, reacting even less than the Japanese, who at least pretend to be pleased.

In reactive cultures the preferred mode of communication is *monologue*—pause—reflection—monologue. If possible, one lets the other side deliver its monologue first. In linear-active and multi-active cultures, the communication mode is a *dialogue*. One interrupts the other's monologue with frequent comments, even questions, which signify polite interest in what is being said. As soon as one person stops speaking, the other takes up his or her turn immediately, since the Westerner has an extremely weak tolerance for silence.

People belonging to reactive cultures not only tolerate silences well but regard them as a very meaningful, almost refined, part of discourse. The opinions of the other party are not to be taken lightly or dismissed with a snappy or flippant retort. Clever, well-formulated arguments require—deserve—lengthy silent consideration. The American, having delivered a sales pitch in Helsinki, leans forward and asks, "Well, Pekka, what do you think?" If you ask Finns what they think, they begin to *think*. Finns, like Asians, think in silence. An American asked the same question might well pipe up and exclaim, "I'll tell you what I think!"—allowing no pause to punctuate the proceedings or interfere with Western momentum. Asian momentum takes much longer to achieve. One can compare reactions to shifting the gears of a car, where multi-active people go immediately into first gear, which enables them to put their foot down to accelerate (the discussion) and to pass quickly through second and third gears as the argument intensifies. Reactive cultures prefer to avoid crashing through the gearbox. Too many revs might cause damage to the engine (discussion). The big wheel turns slower at first and the foot is put down gently. But when momentum is finally achieved, it is likely to be maintained and, moreover, it tends to be in the right direction.

The reactive "reply-monologue" will accordingly be context centered and will presume a considerable amount of knowledge on the part of the listener (who, after all, probably spoke first). Because the listener is presumed to be knowledgeable, Japanese, Chinese and Finns will often be satisfied with expressing their thoughts in *half-utterances*, indicating that the listener can fill in the rest. It is a kind of compliment one pays one's interlocutor. At such times multi-active, dialogue-oriented people are more receptive than linear-oriented people, who thrive on clearly expressed linear argument.

Reactive cultures not only rely on utterances and semi-statements to further the conversation, but they indulge in other Eastern habits that confuse the Westerner. They are, for instance, "roundabout," using impersonal pronouns ("one is leaving") or the passive voice ("one of the machines seems to have been tampered with"), either to deflect blame or with the general aim of politeness.

As reactive cultures tend to use names less frequently than Westerners, the impersonal, vague nature of the discussion is further accentuated. Lack of eye contact, so typical of the East, does not help the situation. The Japanese, evading the Spaniard's earnest stare, makes the latter feel that they are being boring or saying something distasteful. Asian inscrutability (often appearing on a Finn's face as a sullen expression) adds to the feeling that the discussion is leading nowhere. Finns and Japanese, embarrassed by another's stare, seek eye contact only at the beginning of the discussion or when they wish their opponent to take their "turn" in the conversation.

Japanese delegations in opposition with each other are often quite happy to sit in a line on one side of the table and contemplate a neutral spot on the wall facing them as they converse sporadically or muse in joint silence. The occasional sidelong glance will be used to seek confirmation of a point made. Then it's back to studying the wall again.

Small talk does not come easily to reactive cultures. While Japanese and Chinese trot out well-tried formalisms to indicate courtesy, they tend to regard questions such as "Well, how goes it?" as direct questions and may take the opportunity to voice a complaint. On other occasions their overlong pauses or slow reactions cause Westerners to think they are slow witted or have nothing to say. Turks, in discussion with Germans in Berlin, complained that they never got the chance to present their views fully, while the Germans, for their part, thought the Turks had nothing to say. A high-ranking delegation from the Bank of Finland once told me that, for the same reason, their group found it hard to get a word in at international meetings. "How can we make an impact?" they asked. The Japanese suffer more than any other people in this type of gathering.

The Westerner should always bear in mind that the actual content of the response delivered by a person from a reactive culture represents only a small part of the significance surrounding the event. Context-centered utterances inevitably attach more importance not to what is said, but *how* it is said, *who* said it and what is *behind* what is said. Also, what is *not* said may be the main point of the reply.

Self-disparagement is another favorite tactic of reactive cultures. It eliminates the possibility of offending through self-esteem; it may draw the opponent into praising the Asian's conduct or decisions. The Westerner must beware of presuming that self-disparagement is connected with a weak position.

Finally, reactive cultures excel in subtle, nonverbal communication, which compensates for the absence of frequent interjections. Finns, Japanese and Chinese alike are noted for

		Strongly Reactive
1.	Japan	
2.	China	
3.	Taiwan	
4.	Singapore, Hong Kong*	
5.	Finland*	
6.	Korea	
7.	Turkey†	
8.	Vietnam, Cambodia, Laos†	
9.	Malaysia, Indonesia†	
10.	Pacific Islands (Fiji, Tonga, etc.)†	
11.	Sweden*	Occasionally Reactive
12.	Britain*	

*Linear-active tendencies when reacting
†Multi-active tendencies when reacting

Figure 3.3 Ranking of Countries on the Reactive Scale

their sighs, almost inaudible groans and agreeable grunts. A sudden intake of breath in Finland indicates agreement, not shock, as it would in the case of a Latin. The "oh," "ha" or "e" of the Japanese is a far surer indication of concurrence than the fixed smile they often assume.

Reactive people have large reserves of energy. They are economical in movement and effort and do not waste time reinventing the wheel. Although they always give the impression of having power in reserve, they are seldom aggressive and rarely aspire to leadership (in the case of Japan, this is somewhat surprising in view of her economic might). France, Britain, and the U.S., on the other hand, have not hesitated to seize world leadership in periods of economic or military dominance.

Figure 3.3 gives a suggested ranking of countries on the reactive scale, from strongly reactive to occasionally reactive.

Intercategory Comparisons

Common linear-active behavior will facilitate smooth relations between, for instance, Swedes and Flemish Belgians. A common multi-active mentality will help contacts between Italians and Argentineans or Brazilians. In the Vietnam War, the most popular foreign troops with the South Vietnamese were reactive Koreans. There are naturally underlying similarities between members belonging to the same cultural category.

When members of *different* cultural categories begin to interact, the differences far outnumber the commonalities (see Figure 3.4).

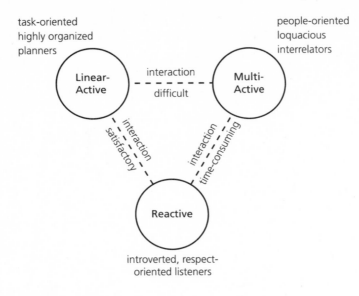

task-oriented
highly organized
planners

people-oriented
loquacious
interrelators

Figure 3.4 Levels of Difficulty in LMR Interactions

Figures 3.5 to 3.7 illustrate intercategory relationships. When you look carefully at these diagrams, you can see that commonalities exist between all types, but tend to be thin on the ground between linear-actives and multi-actives.

Reactives fit better with the other two, because they *react* rather than initiate. Consequently the trade-hungry Japanese settle comfortably in conservative, orderly Britain, but also have reasonably few problems adapting to excitable Latins on account of their similar views on people orientation, diplomatic communication and power distance.

The entirely disparate world views of linear-active and multi-active people pose a problem of great magnitude in the early years of a new century of international trade and aspiring globalization. Can the pedantic, linear German and the voluble, exuberant Brazilian really share a "globalized" view of, for instance, duty, commitments or personnel policies? How do the French reconcile their sense of intellectual superiority with cold Swedish logic or American bottom line successes? Will Anglo-Saxon hiring and firing procedures ever gain acceptability in people-orientated, multi-active Spain, Portugal or Argentina? When will product-oriented Americans, Britons and Germans come to the realization that products make their own way only in linear-active societies and that *relationships* pave the way for product penetration in multi-active cultures? One can well say, "Let's concentrate on selling to the 800 million linear-active customers in the world," but what about multi-active and reactive customers? The fact is, there are a lot of them: four billion multi-active and just under three billion reactive at the last count. Figure 3.8 shows approximate numbers in each category for the year 2020.

Figure 3.9 is a diagrammatic disposition of linear-active, multi-active and reactive variations among major cultures, based on decades-long observation and thousands of assessments

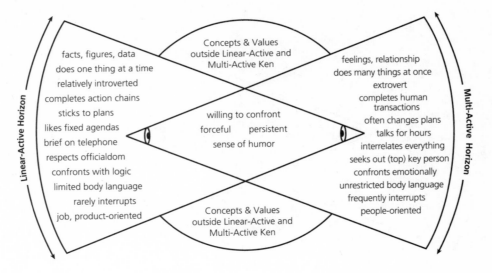

Figure 3.5 Linear-Active/Multi-Active Horizons

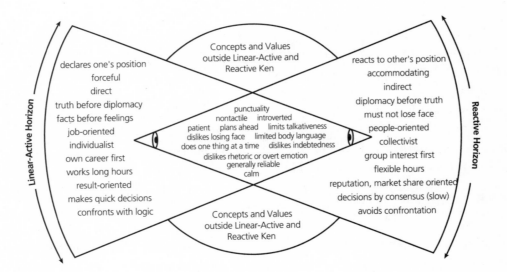

Figure 3.6 Linear-Active/Reactive Horizons

of cultural profiles with respondents of 68 nationalities. The diagram, which is repeated in color on the back cover, is not drawn to scale as far as the cultural distance between each nationality is concerned. What it does indicate is the relative positioning of each culture in terms of its linear-active, multi-active or reactive nature. Thus the juxtaposition of Russia and Italy on the left side indicates they are linear-active/multi-active to a similar degree. It does not impute other cultural resemblances (core beliefs, religion, taboos, etc.). Spaniards and Arabs, though strikingly different in ideological and theological convictions, are able

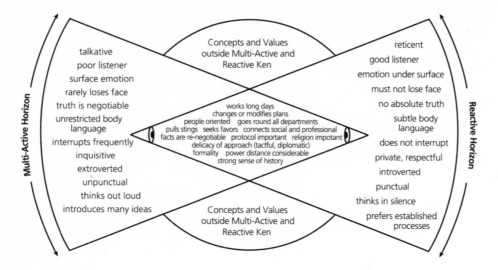

Figure 3.7 Multi-Active/Reactive Horizons

Linear-Active	800,000,000
Multi-Active	4,000,000,000
Reactive	3,000,000,000
Hybrid (Multi-Active and Reactive)	
Indonesia	215,000,000
Philippines	75,000,000
TOTAL	**8 billion (approximately)**

Figure 3.8 Cultural Category Statistics for 2020

to benefit from their similar multi-active nature in communicating in an intensely personal and often compassionate manner. A Norwegian, though, is not on the same wavelength with either. As mentioned earlier, a senior multi-active Indian was able to combine his characteristics of warmth and people orientation to achieve success in managing the entire South American division of his company.

I developed the LMR (linear/multi/reactive) method of testing so that individuals can determine their own cultural profiles. This classification or categorization of cultural groups is straightforward when compared with the somewhat diffuse instruments of the other cross-culturalists, and it has consequently proven comprehensible and user-friendly to students in hundreds of universities, schools of business and multinationals in industry, banking and commerce. It has also proven valuable to European government ministries that have the task of training personnel to interact on EU committees. As the assessment can be completed

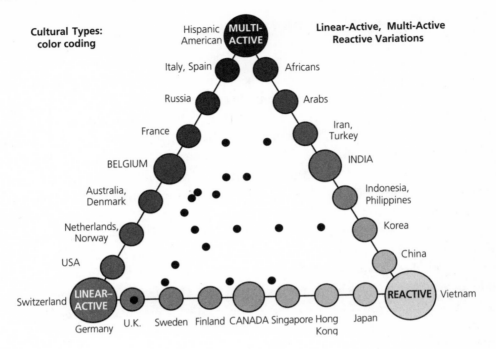

Figure 3.9 Cultural Types Model

in 60–90 minutes on the Internet, it has enabled multinationals with staff scattered over several dozen countries to collect and collate profiles electronically. This gives them an insight as to which cultural areas of the world might prove appropriate for certain managers and employees. A senior British manager, for example, was determined to take over his company's large Chinese market, but because he tested completely linear-active, the human resources department firmly steered him to a five-year stint in the Nordic division, where he excelled and made profits. In China he would have had to undergo a lengthy period of cultural adaptation.

In the majority of cases, the LMR Personal Cultural Profile assessment points the respondent toward a sympathetic relationship with a particular cultural group. A very linear person will find comfort in the orderliness and precision of Germans and Swiss. A multi-active, emotional person will not offend Italians or Latin Americans with his or her extroversion. A good listener, calm and nonconfrontational, will be appreciated and probably liked by the Japanese and Chinese.

Yet none of us is an island unto ourselves. Both personality and context will make us hybrid to some extent. Personal traits can occasionally contradict the national norm. A compassionate German may occasionally forsake his love of truth and directness in order to avoid giving offense. An introverted Finn may be subject to bursts of imagination. Some Americans may have a cautious streak.

Fine-Tuning Categorization

As well as the personal or psychological traits of an individual, the *context* within which he or she operates is an important factor in fine-tuning categorization. Situational context is infinite in its variations, but three ingredients stand out: *age, profession* and *field of study. Age* is, of course, a well-recognized "layer of culture"—attitudes about society, authority, law and freedom are often generational. Younger people test strongly linear-active or multi-active according to their culture, but both groups become more reactive as they get older.

A person's *profession* is also an influential factor. Linear-active people often wind up as engineers, accountants and technologists, and the exercise of their profession reinforces their linearity. Teachers, artists and sales and marketing staff lean toward multi-active options, where flexibility and feelings before facts fit their chosen type of work. Doctors and lawyers either need to be reactive by nature or develop reactive skills in order to listen carefully to their clients' plights. Human resource managers tend to be more hybrid, as they seek and promote diversity in a firm's human and cultural capital. Successful managers are also generally hybrid, with evenly balanced LMR scores. Skilled senior managers are usually more multi-active than the norm, especially in cultures where linearity is the norm.

Cultural profiles reveal many poor fits in people's chosen careers. Accountants testing strongly as multi-active are often unhappy in their jobs. Linear scientists sent out to "sell" their company's products have met with spectacular failures.

One's *field of study* also influences his or her cultural profile. Assessments carried out with respondents in Western MBA degree programs show a high score for linearity, especially those from reactive cultures. Japanese students in such programs go for linear options that seem appropriate in the earnestly efficient MBA environment. Tested at home in Japan, however, their reactive score would be much higher.

Multi-actives are less "obedient" to Western-style MBA doctrines, but they will still test higher on the linear scale than they would in their home countries. Students of mathematics find it hard to ignore the linear options, and students of literature find that multi-active choices reflect more adequately the richness and poetic side of human nature. Those studying medicine, law or history have everything to gain by developing their own ability to react to suffering, legal predicaments and the enigma of history itself. Someone studying politics and championing human rights would be obliged to consider most multi-active solutions.

Such contextual considerations play an important role in fine-tuning cultural profiles. Yet they have limitations. One or two thousand years of cultural conditioning lend great momentum to an individual's core beliefs and manner of expressing them. Ideally, cultural assessments like the Personal Cultural Profile should be carried out in one's home environment, where natural reactions emerge from the ambience of close social bonds and where instinct prevails.

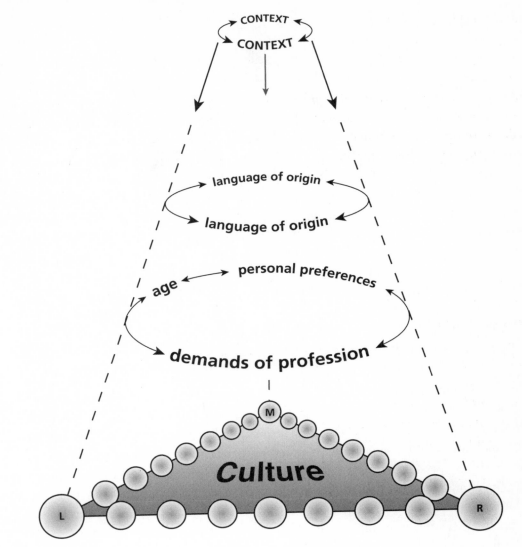

Figure 3.10 The Fourth Dimension

Moving along the LMR Planes

Let's begin our discussion near the end of the multi-active point, where we encounter populations whose characteristics, though differing significantly in terms of historical background, religion and basic mindset, resemble each other considerably in the shape of outstanding traits, needs and aspirations (refer to Figure 3.9, page 35, throughout this section). For example, Latin Americans, Arabs, and Africans are multi-active in the extreme. They are excitable, emotional, very human, mostly nonaffluent and often suffer from previous economic exploitation or cultural larceny. Turkey and Iran, with more Eastern culture intact, are furthest from the multi-active point.

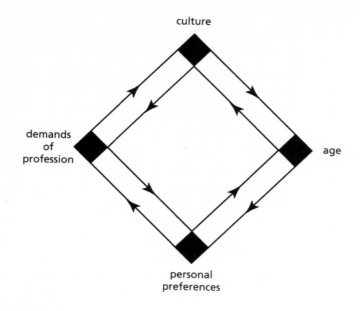

Figure 3.11 Mindset Tug-of-War

To switch our commentary to Northern European cultures, and proceeding along the linear-active/reactive axis, let's consider three decidedly linear countries that exhibit reactive tendencies (when compared with the Germans and Swiss): Britain, Sweden and Finland. British individuals often seek agreement among colleagues (a reactive trait) before taking decisive action. Swedes are even further along the reactive line, seeking unanimity if possible. The Finns, however, are the most reactive of Europeans in that their firm decision-making stance is strongly offset by their soft, diffident, Asian communication style (plenty of silence) and their uncanny ability to listen at great length without interrupting.

The linear-active/multi-active axis is fairly straightforward. The United States, Norway and the Netherlands plan their lives along agenda-like lines. Australia has multi-active flashes due to substantial immigration from Italy, Greece and former Yugoslavia. Danes, though linear, are often referred to as the "Nordic Latins." France is the most linear of the Latins, Italy and Spain the least. Russia, with its Slavic soul, classifies as a loquacious multi-active, but it slots in a little higher on the linear-active side on account of its many millions living in severely cold environments.

Belgium, India and Canada occupy median positions on their respective axes. These positions can be seen as positive and productive. Belgium runs a highly prosperous and democratic economy by maintaining a successful compromise between linear-active (Flemish) and multi-active (Walloon) administrations. Canada, because of massive immigration and intelligent government cultural care, is the most multicultural country in the world. Indians, though natural orators and communicators, have combined these natural skills and warmth with Eastern wisdom and courtesy. On top of that they have inherited a considerable number of British institutions, which enables them to relate to the West as well.

The early years of the twenty-first century find some degree of blending of cultural categories—in other words, movement along the linear-active/multi-active/reactive planes. Globalization, especially in business, has been one of the major forces behind this phenomenon. Nowhere is this trend more visible than along the linear-active/reactive plane. The successful Japanese, for instance, with their logical manufacturing processes and considerable financial acumen, are becoming more amenable to Western linear thinking. Hong Kong was created to make money, a very linear and countable commodity, while Lee Kuan Yew's brilliant economic management of Singapore—the result of combining his innate Confucianism with his degree from Cambridge—pushed that tiny island city–state to the very borders of linear-activity, in spite of its 72 percent Chinese majority population.

Other East Asian reactive nations tend to temper their inherent reactivity by occasionally wandering along the reactive/multi-active plane. The Chinese are less interested in Western linear thinking and logic ("there is no absolute truth") than in gut feelings and their periodic, highly emotional assertion of their inalienable rights and dominance based on a culture that is over 5,000 years old. They have no interest whatsoever in Western logic as applied to Tibet, Taiwan or human rights. Koreans, while extremely correct in their surface courtesy, actually suppress seething multi-active emotion, even tendencies toward violence, more than any other Asians. They frequently demonstrate explosive rage or unreliability vis-à-vis foreign partners or among themselves. Further along this plane, Indonesians and Filipinos, after many centuries of colonization, have developed into cultural hybrids, sometimes opposing, sometimes endorsing the policies and cultural styles of their former colonizers.

Individuals from certain nationalities sharing characteristics from two categories may find areas of cooperation or common conduct. Those close to the linear-active/reactive axis are likely to be strong, silent types who can work together calmly and tend to shun multi-active extroversion and loquacity. Those close to the multi-active/reactive axis will, in spite of visible differences, attach great importance to relationships and circumvent official channels by using personal contacts or networks. People close to the linear-active/multi-active axis, though opposites in many ways, are inevitably broad-minded on account of their range of traits and are likely to be forceful and persistent in their actions.

Individuals whose cultural profiles wander away from the axes and who occupy a central location inside the triangle may possess qualities that enable them to be efficient mediators or international team leaders.

Data-Oriented, Dialogue-Oriented and Listening Cultures

Interaction among different peoples involves not only methods of communication but also the process of gathering information. This brings us to the question of dialogue-oriented and data-oriented cultures. In data-oriented cultures, one does research to produce lots of information that is then acted on. Swedes, Germans, Americans, Swiss and Northern Euro-peans in general love to gather solid information and move steadily forward from this database. The communications and information revolution is a dream come true for data-oriented cultures. It provides them quickly and efficiently with what dialogue-oriented cultures already know.

Which are the dialogue-orientated cultures? Examples are the Italians and other Latins, Arabs and Indians. These people see events and business possibilities "in context" because they already possess an enormous amount of information through their own personal infor-mation network (refer to Chapter 9 for a complete explanation of "context"). Arabs and Por-tuguese will be well informed about the facts surrounding a deal since they will already have queried, discussed and gossiped in their circle of friends, business acquaintances and exten-sive family connections. The Japanese (basically listeners) may be even better informed, since the very nature of Japan's "web" society involves them in an incredibly intricate infor-mation network operational during schooldays, college, university, judo and karate clubs, student societies, developed intelligence systems and family and political connections.

People from dialogue-oriented cultures like the French and Spanish tend to get impatient when Americans or Swiss feed them with facts and figures that are accurate but, in their opinion, only a part of the big human picture. A French businessperson would consider that an American sales forecast in France is of little meaning unless there is time to develop the correct relationship with the customer on whom the success of the business depends. It is quite normal in dialogue-oriented cultures for managers to take customers and colleagues with them when they leave a job. They have developed their relationships.

There is a strong correlation between dialogue-oriented and multi-active people. Anto-nio (introduced earlier) does ten things at once and is therefore in continuous contact with humans. He obtains from these people an enormous amount of information—far more than Americans or Germans will gather by spending a large part of the day in a private office, door closed, looking at the computer screen.

Multi-active people are knee-deep in information. They know so much that the very brevity of an agenda makes it useless to them. At meetings they tend to ignore agendas or speak out of turn. How can you forecast a conversation? Discussion of one item could make another meaningless. How can you deal with feedback in advance? How can an agenda solve deadlock? Dialogue-oriented people wish to use their personal relations to solve the prob-lem from the human angle. Once this is mentally achieved, then appointments, schedules, agendas, even meetings become superfluous.

If these remarks seem to indicate that dialogue-oriented people, relying on only word of mouth, suffer from serious disadvantages and drawbacks, it should be emphasized that it is very difficult to change from one system to the other. It is hard to imagine a Neapolitan company organizing its business along American lines with five-year rolling forecasts, quar-terly reporting, six-month audits and twice-yearly performance appraisals. It is equally hard to imagine Germans introducing a new product in a strange country without first doing a market survey.

Most of the successful economies, with the striking exception of Japan, are in data-oriented cultures. Japan, although dialogue-oriented, also uses a large amount of printed information. Moreover, productivity also depends on other significant factors, particularly climate, so that information systems, while important, are not the whole story of efficiency and its logic. One might summarize by saying that a compromise between data-oriented and dialogue-oriented systems would probably lead to good results, but there are no *clear* examples of this having happened consistently in modern international business communities.

Figure 3.12 gives a suggested ranking for dialogue-oriented and data-oriented cultures. Figures 3.13, 3.14, and 3.15 illustrate the relatively few sources of information that data-oriented cultures draw on. The more developed the society, the more we tend to turn to printed sources and databases to obtain our facts. The information revolution has accentuated this trend and Germany, along with the United States, Britain and Scandinavia, is well to the fore. Yet printed information and databases are almost necessarily out of date (as anyone who has purchased mailing lists has found out to their cost). Last night's whispers in a Madrid bar or café are hot off the press—Pedro was in Oslo last week and talked to Olav till two in the morning. Few data-oriented people will dig for information and then spread it in this way, although Germans do not fare badly once they get out of their cloistered offices. Northerners' lack of gregariousness again proves a hindrance. By upbringing they are taught *not to pry*—inquisitiveness gains no points in their society—and gossip is even worse. What their database cannot tell them they try to find out through official channels: embassies, chambers of commerce, circulated information sheets, perhaps hints provided by friendly companies with experience in the country in question. In business, especially when negotiating, information is power. Sweden, Norway, Australia, New Zealand and several other data-oriented cultures will have to expand and intensify their intelligence-gathering networks in the future if they are to compete with information-hot France, Japan, Italy, Korea, Taiwan and Singapore. It may well be that the EU itself will develop into a *hothouse exchange* of business information to compete with the Japanese network.

Listening cultures, reactive in nature, combine deference to database and print information (Japan, Finland, Singapore and Taiwan are high tech) with a natural tendency to listen well and enter into sympathetic dialogue. Japanese and Chinese will entertain the prospect of very lengthy discourse in order to attain ultimate harmony. In this respect, they are as people oriented as the Latins. The Finns, inevitably more brief, nevertheless base their dialogue on careful consideration of the wishes of the other party. They rarely employ "steamrollering" tactics frequently observable in American, German and French debate. Monologues are unknown in Finland, unless practiced by the other party.

Listening cultures believe they have the right attitude toward information gathering. They do not precipitate improvident action, they allow ideas to mature and they are ultimately accommodating in their decisions. The success of Japan and the four Asian tigers—South Korea, Taiwan, Hong Kong and Singapore—as well as Finland's prosperity, all bear witness to the resilience of the listening cultures.

Dialogue

1. Latin Americans
2. Italians, Spanish, Portuguese, French, Mediterranean peoples
3. Arabs, Africans
4. Indians, Pakistanis
5. Chileans
6. Hungarians, Romanians
7. Slavs
8. American sub-cultures
9. Chinese, Japanese, Koreans
10. British, Australians, Benelux
11. Scandinavians
12. North Americans (U.S. and Canada), New Zealanders, South Africans
13. Germans, Swiss, Finns

Data

Figure 3.12 Dialogue-Oriented, Data-Oriented Cultures

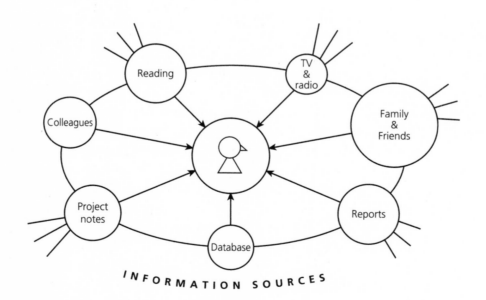

Figure 3.13 Information Sources: Data-Oriented Cultures

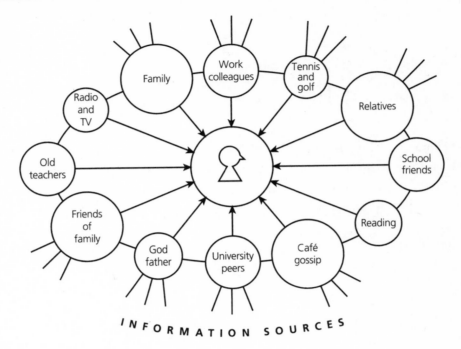

Figure 3.14 Information Sources: Dialogue-Oriented Cultures

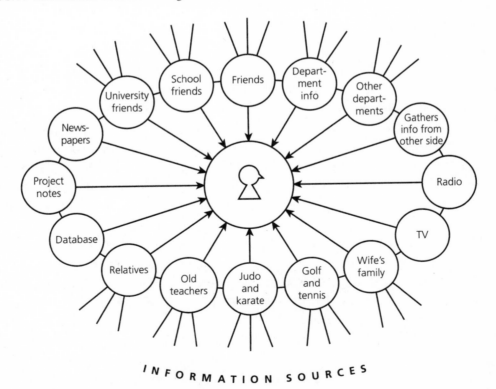

Figure 3.15 Information Sources: Listening Cultures (Japan)

4

The Use of Time

The world views held by different cultures vary widely, as do a multiplicity of concepts that constitute and represent a kaleidoscopic outlook on the nature of reality. Some of these concepts—fatalism, work ethic, reincarnation, Confucianism, *Weltschmerz* and so on—are readily identifiable within specific groups, societies or nations. Other concepts—central and vital to human experience—are essentially universal, but notions of their nature and essence are strikingly different, such as space and time.

Time, particularly, is seen in a different light by Eastern and Western cultures, and even within these groupings assumes quite dissimilar aspects from country to country. In the Western Hemisphere, the United States and Mexico employ time in such diametrically opposing manners that it causes intense friction between the two peoples. In Western Europe, the Swiss attitude to time bears little relation to that of neighboring Italy. Thais do not evaluate the passing of time in the same way that the Japanese do. In Britain the future stretches out in front of you. In Madagascar it flows into the back of your head from behind.

Linear Time

Let us begin with the American concept of time, for theirs is the most expensive, as anyone who has had to deal with American doctors, dentists or lawyers will tell you.

For an American, time is truly money. In a profit-oriented society, time is a precious, even scarce, commodity. It flows fast, like a mountain river in the spring, and if you want to benefit from its passing, you have to move fast with it. Americans are people of action; they cannot bear to be idle. The past is over, but the present you can seize, parcel and package and make it work for you in the immediate future. Figure 4.1 illustrates how Americans view time and Figure 4.2 shows how they use it.

In the U.S. you have to make money, otherwise you are nobody. If you have 40 years of earning capacity and you want to make $4 million, that means $100,000 per annum. If you can achieve this in 250 working days, that comes to $400 a day or $50 an hour. With this orientation Americans can say that their *time costs* $50 an hour. Americans also talk about *wasting, spending, budgeting* and *saving* time.

This seems logical enough, until one begins to apply the idea to other cultures. Has the Portuguese fisherman, who failed to hook a fish in two hours, wasted his time? Has the Sicilian priest, failing to make a convert on Thursday, lost ground? Have the German composer, the French poet, the Spanish painter, devoid of ideas last week, missed opportunities that can be qualified in monetary terms?

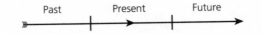

Figure 4.1 American Flow of Time

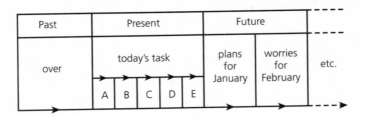

Figure 4.2 Carving Up American Time

The Americans are not the only ones who sanctify timekeeping, for it is practically a religion in Switzerland and Germany, too. These countries, along with Britain, the Anglo-Saxon world in general, the Netherlands, Austria and Scandinavia, have a linear vision of time and action. They suspect, like the Americans, that time is passing (being wasted) without decisions being made or actions being performed. These groups are also monochronic; that is, they prefer to do only one thing at a time, to concentrate on it and do it within a fixed schedule. They think that in this way they get more things done—and more efficiently. Furthermore, being imbued with the Protestant work ethic, they equate working time with success: the harder you work—the more hours, that is—the more successful you will be and the more money you will make. This idea makes perfect sense to American ears, would carry less weight in class-conscious Britain, and would be viewed as entirely unrealistic in Southern European countries, where authority, privilege and birthright negate the theory at every turn. In a society such as existed in the Soviet Union, one could postulate that those who achieved substantial remuneration by working little (or not at all) were the most successful of all.

Multi-Active Time

Southern Europeans are multi-active, rather than linear-active. The more things they can do at the same time, the happier and the more fulfilled they feel. They organize their time (and lives) in an entirely different way from Americans, Germans and the Swiss. Multi-active peoples are not very interested in schedules or punctuality. They pretend to observe them, especially if a linear-active partner or colleague insists on it, but they consider the present reality to be more important than appointments. In their ordering of things, priority is given to the relative thrill or significance of each meeting.

Spaniards, Italians and Arabs will ignore the passing of time if it means that conversations will be left unfinished. For them, completing a *human transaction* is the best way they can invest their time. For an Italian, time considerations will usually be subjected to human feelings. "Why are you so angry because I came at 9:30?" he asks his German colleague. "Because it says 9:00 in my diary," says the German. "Then why don't you write 9:30 and then we'll both be happy?" is a logical Italian response. The business we have to do and our close relations are so important that it is irrelevant at what time we meet. The *meeting* is what counts. Germans and Swiss cannot swallow this, as it offends their sense of order, of tidiness, of planning.

A Spaniard would take the side of the Italian. There is a reason for the Spaniard's lax adherence to punctuality. The German believes in a simple truth—scientific truth. The Spaniard, in contrast, is always conscious of the double truth—that of immediate reality as well as that of the poetic whole. The German thinks they see eye to eye, as in Figure 4.3, while the Spaniard, with the consciousness of double truth, sees it as in Figure 4.4.

As far as meetings are concerned, it is better not to turn up strictly on time for Spanish appointments. *In Spain, punctuality messes up schedules,* as illustrated in Figure 4.5.

Few Northern Europeans or North Americans can reconcile themselves to the multi-active use of time. Germans and Swiss, unless they reach an understanding of the underlying psychology, will be driven to distraction. Germans see compartmentalization of programs, schedules, procedures and production as the surest route to efficiency. The Swiss, even more time and regulation dominated, have made *precision* a national symbol. This applies to their watch industry, their optical instruments, their pharmaceutical products, their banking. Planes, buses and trains leave on the dot. Accordingly, everything can be exactly calculated and predicted.

In countries inhabited by linear-active people, time is clock- and calendar-related, seg-mented in an abstract manner for our convenience, measurement, and disposal. In multi-active

Figure 4.3 What Germans and Spaniards Think They See

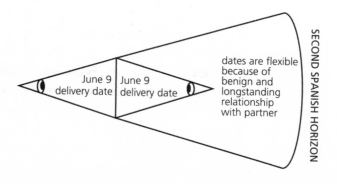

Figure 4.4 How the Spaniard Actually Sees

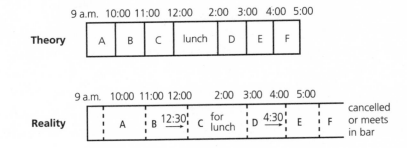

Figure 4.5 Spanish Schedules: In Theory, in Reality

cultures like the Arab and Latin spheres, time is event- or personality-related, a subjective commodity which can be manipulated, molded, stretched, or dispensed with, irrespective of what the clock says.

"I have to rush," says the American, "my time is up." The Spaniard or Arab, scornful of this submissive attitude to schedules, would only use this expression if death were imminent.

Cyclic Time

Both the linear-active northerner and the multi-active Latin think that they manage time in the best way possible. In some Eastern cultures, however, the adaptation of humans to time is seen as a viable alternative. In these cultures, time is viewed neither as linear nor event–relationship related, but as *cyclic*. Each day the sun rises and sets, the seasons follow one another, the heavenly bodies revolve around us, people grow old and die, but their children reconstitute the process. We know this cycle has gone on for 100,000 years and more. Cyclical time is not a scarce commodity. There seems always to be an unlimited supply of it just around the next bend. As they say in the East, when God made time, He made plenty of it.

It's not surprising, then, that business decisions are arrived at in a different way from in the West. Westerners often expect an Asian to make a quick decision or to treat a current deal on its present merits, irrespective of what has happened in the past. Asians cannot do this. The past formulates the contextual background to the present decision, about which in any case, as Asians, they must think long term—their hands are tied in many ways. Americans see time passing without decisions being made or actions performed as having been "wasted." Asians do not see time as racing away unutilized in a linear future, but coming around again in a circle, where the same opportunities, risks and dangers will represent themselves when people are so many days, weeks or months wiser. As proof of the veracity of the cyclical nature of time, how often do we (in the West) say, "If I had known then what I know now, I would never have done what I did?"

Figure 4.6 compares the speed of Western *action chains* with Asian reflection. The American, German and Swiss go home satisfied that all tasks have been completed. The French or Italian might leave some "mopping up" for the following day. John Paul Fieg, author of *A Common Core: Thais and Americans*, describing the Thai attitude toward time, saw it as a pool one could gradually walk around. This metaphor applies to most Asians, who, instead of tackling problems immediately in sequential fashion, circle around them for a few days or weeks before committing themselves. After a suitable period of reflection, tasks A, D and F may indeed seem worthy of pursuing (refer to Figure 4.6). Tasks B, C and E may be quietly dropped. Contemplation of the whole scene has indicated, however, that task G, perhaps not even envisaged at all earlier on, might be the most significant of all.

In a Buddhist culture (e.g., Thailand, Tibet), not only time but also life itself goes around in a circle. Whatever we plan, however we organize our particular world, generation follows generation; governments and rulers will succeed each other; crops will be harvested; monsoons, earthquakes and other catastrophes will recur; taxes will be paid; the sun and moon will rise and set; stocks and shares will rise and fall. Even the Americans will not change such events, certainly not by rushing things.

Chinese

The Chinese, like most Asians, "walk around the pool" in order to make well-considered decisions, but they also have a keen sense of the value of time. This can be noticed especially in their attitude toward taking up other people's time, for which they frequently apologize. At the end of a meeting in China, it is customary to thank the participants for contributing their valuable time. Punctuality on arrival is also considered important—more so than in many other Asian countries. Indeed, when meetings are scheduled between two people, it is not unusual for a Chinese to arrive 15 to 30 minutes early "in order to finish the business before the time appointed for its discussion," so not stealing any of the other person's time! It is also considered polite in China to announce, 10 or 15 minutes after a meeting has begun, that one will soon have to be going. Again, the worthy aim involved is to economize on their use of your time. The Chinese will not go, of course, until the transaction has been completed, but the point has been made.

This is indeed a double standard. The Chinese penchant for humility demands that the other person's time be seen as precious; on the other hand, the Chinese expect a liberal amount of time to be allocated for repeated consideration of the details of a transaction and to the careful nurturing of personal relationships surrounding the deal. They frequently complain that Americans, in China to do business, often have to catch their plane back to the U.S. "in the middle of the discussion." The American sees the facts as having been adequately discussed; the Chinese feel that they have not yet attained that degree of closeness—that satisfying sense of common trust and intent—that is for the Chinese the bedrock of the deal and of other transactions in the future.

Japanese

The Japanese have a keen sense of the *unfolding* or *unwrapping* of time—this is well described by Joy Hendry in her book *Wrapping Culture*. People familiar with Japan are well aware of

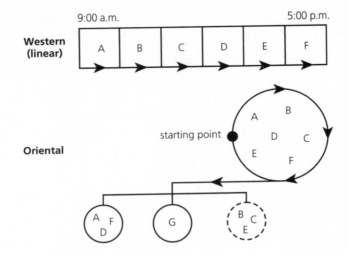

Figure 4.6 Western Action Chains/Asian Reflection

the contrast between the breakneck pace maintained by the Japanese factory worker on the one hand, and the unhurried contemplation to be observed in Japanese gardens or the agonizingly slow tempo of a Noh play on the other. What Hendry emphasizes, however, is the meticulous, resolute manner in which the Japanese *segment* time. This segmentation does not follow the American or German pattern, where tasks are assigned in a logical sequence aimed at maximum efficiency and speed in implementation. The Japanese are more concerned not with how long something takes to happen, but with how time is divided up in the interests of properness, courtesy and tradition.

For instance, in most Japanese social gatherings, there are various phases and layers—marked beginnings and endings—for retirement parties, weddings, parent–teacher association meetings and so on.

In Japan's conformist and carefully regulated society, people like to know at all times where they stand and where they are at: this applies both to social and business situations. The mandatory, two-minute exchange of business cards between executives meeting each other for the first time is one of the clearest examples of a time activity segment being used to mark the beginning of a relationship. Another example is the start and finish of all types of classes in Japan, where the lesson cannot begin without being preceded by a formal request on the part of the students for the teacher to start. Similarly, they must offer a ritualistic expression of appreciation at the end of the class.

Other events that require not only clearly defined beginnings and endings but also unambiguous phase-switching signals are the tea ceremony, New Year routines, annual cleaning of the house, cherry blossom viewing, spring "offensives" (strikes), midsummer festivities, gift-giving routines, company picnics, sake-drinking sessions, even the peripheral rituals surrounding judo, karate and kendo sessions. A Japanese person cannot enter any of the above activities in the casual, direct manner a Westerner might adopt. The American or Northern European has a natural tendency to make a quick approach to the heart of things.

The Japanese, in direct contrast, must experience an unfolding or unwrapping of the significant phases of the event. It has to do with Asian indirectness, but in Japan it also involves love of compartmentalization of procedure, of tradition, of the beauty of ritual.

To summarize, when dealing with the Japanese, you can assume that they will be generous in their allocation of time to you or your particular transaction. In return, you are advised to try to do the "right thing at the right time." In Japan, form and symbols are more important than content.

Back to the Future

In the linear-active, industrialized Western cultures time is seen as a road along which we proceed. Life is sometimes referred to as a "journey"; death is often referred to as the "end of the road." We imagine ourselves as having traveled along the part of the road that is behind us (the past) and we see the untrodden path of the future stretching out in front of us.

Linear-oriented people do not regard the future as entirely unknowable for they have already nudged it along certain channels by meticulous planning. American executives, with their quarterly forecasts, will tell you how much money they are going to make in the next three months. The Swiss stationmaster will assure you, without any hesitation, that the train from Zurich to Luzern will leave at 9:03 tomorrow morning and arrive at exactly 10:05. He is probably right, too. Watches, calendars and computers are devices that not only encourage punctuality but also get us into the habit of working toward targets and deadlines. In a sense, we are "making the future happen." We cannot know everything (it would be disastrous for horse racing and detective stories), but we eliminate future unknowns to the best of our ability. Our personal programming tells us that over the next year we are going to get up at certain times, work so many hours, take vacations for designated periods, play tennis on Saturday mornings and pay our taxes on fixed dates.

Cyclic time is not seen as a straight road leading from our feet to the horizon, but as a curved one which in one year's time will lead us through "scenery" and conditions very similar to what we experience at the present moment. Observers of cyclic time are less disciplined in their planning of the future, since they believe that it cannot be managed and that humans make life easier for themselves by "harmonizing" with the laws and cyclic events of nature. Yet in such cultures a general form of planning is still possible, for many things are fairly regular and well understood.

Cultures observing both linear and cyclic concepts of time see the past as something we have put behind us and the future as something that lies before us. In Madagascar, the opposite is the case (see Figure 4.7). The Malagasy imagine the future as flowing into the back of their heads, or passing them from behind, then becoming the past as it stretches out in front of them. The past is *in front of* their eyes because it is visible, known and influential. They can look at it, enjoy it, learn from it, even "play" with it. The Malagasy people spend an inordinate amount of time consulting their ancestors, exhuming their bones, even partying with them.

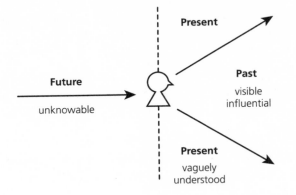

Figure 4.7 Malagasy Concept of Time

By contrast, the Malagasy consider the future unknowable. It is behind their head where they do not have eyes. Their plans for this unknown area will be far from meticulous, for what can they be based on? Buses in Madagascar leave, not according to a predetermined timetable, but when the bus is full. The situation triggers the event. Not only does this make economic sense, but it is also the time that most passengers have chosen to leave. Consequently, in Madagascar stocks are not replenished until shelves are empty, filling stations order gas only when they run dry, and hordes of would-be passengers at the airport find that, in spite of their tickets, in reality everybody is wait-listed. The actual assignation of seats takes place between the opening of the check-in desk and the (eventual) departure of the plane.

Validity of Time Concepts

The Malagasy, Thais, Japanese, Spaniards and many others will continue to use time in ways that will conflict with linear-oriented cultures in social and business spheres.

The objective view of time and its sequential effects is, however, favorable to historicity and to everything connected with industrialized organization. Just as we conceive of our objectified time as extending in the future in the same way that it extends in the past, we mirror our records of the past in our estimates, budgets, and schedules. We build up a commercial structure based on time pro rata values: time wages, rent, credit, interest, depreciation charges, and insurance premiums.

In general we are confident (in North America and Northern Europe) that we have approached the optimum management of time. Many cultures (including powerful economies of the future, such as China, Japan and Southeast Asia) will only allow the linear-oriented concept of time to dictate their behavior to a limited extent. Industrial organization demands a certain degree of synchronization of schedules and targets, but the underlying philosophies concerning the best and most efficient use of time—and the manner in which it should be spent— may remain radically different.

5

Bridging the Communication Gap

Whatever the culture, there's a tongue in our head. Some use it, some hold it, some bite it. For the French it is a rapier, thrusting in attack; the English, using it defensively, mumble a vague, confusing reply; for Italians and Spaniards it is an instrument of eloquence; Finns and East Asians throw you with constructive silence. Silence is a form of speech, so don't interrupt it!

Use of Language

One of the factors leading to poor communication is often overlooked: the nationals of each country use their language and speech in a different way. Language is a tool of communication, delivering a message—but it is much more than that: it has strengths and weaknesses which project national character and even philosophy.

How do the French use their language? Like a rapier. French is a quick, exact, logical language and the French fence with it, cutting, thrusting and parrying, using it for advantage, expecting counter thrusts, retorts, repartee and indeed the odd touché against them. French is a good tool for arguing and proving one's point. It is fair play for the French to manipulate their language, often at great speed, to bewilder and eventually corner their opponent, leaving the latter breathless and without reply.

The English use their language differently—to its best advantage, certainly, but they are not quick to attack with it. They will lean heavily on understatement and reservation; they will concede points to their opponent early on to take the steam out of the argument, but their tone implies that even so, right is on their side. They know how to be vague in order to maintain politeness or avoid confrontation, and they are adept at waffling when they wish to procrastinate or cloud an issue. (It is impossible to waffle in French, as each word has a precise meaning.) The English will use a quiet tone to score points, always attempting to remain low key. Scots and the Northern English may emphasize their accents in order to come across as genuine, sincere or warm-hearted, while the Southern English may use certain accents to indicate an influential background, a particular school or good breeding.

Spaniards and Italians regard their languages as instruments of eloquence and they will go up and down the scale at will, pulling out every stop if need be to achieve greater expressiveness. To convey their ideas fully they will ransack an extensive vocabulary, use their hands, arms and facial expressions and make maximum use of pitch and tone. They are not necessarily being dramatic or overemotional. They want you to know how they feel. They will appeal, directly and strongly, to your good sense, warm heart or generosity if they want something from you, and often you have to decide there and then whether to say yes or no.

Germans, like the French, rely to a large extent on logic, but tend to amass more evidence and labor their points more than either the British or the French. The French, having delivered their thrust, are quite prepared to be parried and then have their defense pierced by a superior counter thrust. Germans are not; they come in with heavier armor and have usually thought through the counter arguments. Often the best way to deal with a German is to find common ground and emphasize solidarity and reliability in cooperation. The splendid German language is heavy, cumbersome, logical, disciplined and has such momentum that it is invincible in any head-on collision with another language. But that momentum can be deflected by a sensitive negotiator and all parties can benefit.

Scandinavians are something else. In the long dark nights they have thought about matters well in advance and they list all the "pros and cons" before giving you their conclusion, which they will justify. They will not abandon their decision easily for they believe they have proven their case, but on the other hand they do not ask for too much. Swedes wield their language in a democratic manner with only a modicum of personal deference and with great egalitarian informality. They cut out the niceties and get down to brass tacks. Finns are friendlier and more reticent, but with the same modern equal-footing approach. The Finnish language is much more eloquent and flowery than Swedish, Danish or Norwegian, but the bottom line is still dryly factual, succinct and well thought out. You can use any kind of humor with a Finn, linguistic or otherwise. A Dane will go along with you for a while, especially if the joke is at the expense of the Swedes. Swedes will accept your humor if it doesn't affect their profit margin. But never tell jokes about Norway to Norwegians—they don't understand them.

American speech is quick, mobile and opportunistic, reflecting the speed and agility of the young country. The wisecrack is basic to their discourse. American humor excels in quips, barbed retorts and repartee, typical of the dog-eat-dog society of early America.

Exaggeration and hyperbole are at the bottom of most American expressions, contrasting sharply with the understated nature of the British. In the early days of pioneering, when immigrants speaking many varieties of halting English were thrown together in simple, often primitive surroundings, plainness and unsophisticated language were at a premium. The well-worn cliché was more understandable than originality or elegance of expression. The American language has never recovered from the exigencies of this period. The ordinary man's speech tends to be "tough talk," rather reminiscent of cowboy parlance or Chicago gangland speech of the 1920s. The nation's obsession with show business and the pervasive influence of Hollywood have accentuated and, to some extent, perpetuated this trend. To make a start is to get the show on the road, to take a risk in a business venture is to fly by the seat of your pants, lawyers are shysters, accountants are bean counters, and, if you have no choice, it's the only game in town.

The Japanese use language in a completely different way from everyone else. What is actually said has hardly any meaning or significance whatsoever. The Japanese use their language as a tool of communication, but the words and sentences themselves give little indication of what they are saying. What they want and how they feel are indicated by the *way* they address their conversation partner. Smiles, pauses, sighs, grunts, nods and eye movements convey everything. The Japanese leave their fellow Japanese knowing perfectly well what has been agreed to, no matter what was said. Foreigners leave a conversation or meeting with the Japanese with a completely different idea. Usually they think that everything has gone swimmingly, as the Japanese would never offend them by saying anything negative or unpleasant.

In British English, French and a good number of languages, people often aspire to elegantly polite discourse in order to show respect to their interlocutor. This process is carried on to a much greater degree in Japanese, where standards of politeness are much higher than in the United States and Europe. On all ceremonial occasions, and these may include formal business meetings, attendees use a whole sequence of expressions that bears little or no relation to the actual sentiments of the individuals present. The language is instead aimed at conveying the long-term relationships which are envisaged and the depth of expectation that each participant has.

When they translate Japanese conversations, other nationalities tend to look at the content rather than the mood. Consequently, all they hear is platitudes or, even more suspicious, flattery. When at each meeting hosted by the Japanese, they go through the ritual of thanking their visitors for giving up their valuable time and for suffering the prevailing weather conditions, Anglo-Saxons in particular begin to doubt the sincerity of their hosts. The Japanese, however, are simply being courteous and caring.

The whole question of people using different speech styles and wielding their language in the national manner inevitably leads to misunderstandings not only of expression but also of intent. The Japanese and English may distrust Italians because they wave their hands about, or Spaniards and Arabs because they sound emotional and loud or prone to exaggeration. The French may appear offensive because of their directness or frequent use of cynicism. No one may really know what the Japanese and Finns are thinking or what they actually said, if they said anything at all. Germans may take the English too literally and completely miss nuances of humor, understatement or irony. Northern peoples may simply consider that Latins speak too fast to be relied on. Languages are indeed spoken at different speeds. Hawaiian and some Polynesian languages barely get through 100 syllables per minute, while English has been measured at 200, German at 250, Japanese at 310 and French at 350 syllables per minute.

The Communication Gap

We have, therefore, a variety of cultures using speech not only according to the strictures imposed by grammar, vocabulary and syntax, but in a manner designed to achieve the maximum impact. These different speech styles, whether used in translation or not, do nothing to improve communication in the international forum.

Not many people are clever linguists, and all over the world thousands of misunderstandings are caused every day through simple mistakes. Here are some enjoyable—and not terribly damaging—examples.

Germany

- ✦ Next week I shall become a new car. (get)
- ✦ Thank you for your kidneys. (kindness)
- ✦ What is your death line? (deadline)

Japan

- ✦ I have split up my boyfriend.
- ✦ My father is a doctor, my mother is a typewriter.
- ✦ I work hardly 10 hours a day. (hard)

Portugal

- ✦ What will you do when you retire? I will breed with my horses.

Sweden

- ✦ Are you hopeful of any change? No, I am hopeless.

Finland

- ✦ He took two trucks every night. (drugs = pills)
- ✦ He took a fast watch. (quick look)
- ✦ How old is your son? Half past seven.

Communication Patterns during Meetings

We attempt to surmount the linguistic hurdle by learning the language of our partner well or by using an interpreter. The former method is preferable, as we can become more fully involved in the conversation and are better able to express ourselves in terms of intent, mood, nuance and emotion. When the issues are noncontroversial and the agenda is smooth, few obstacles arise. When a misunderstanding arises, however, we abandon neutrality and cultural sensitivity, and our language swings back into culture-bound mode.

The following figures give you an idea of how some countries' communication patterns look when they are mapped out. Italians believe in full explicitness and will wax eloquent (see Figure 5.1). Finns, by contrast, strive to phrase their statement of intent in as few words as possible, as in their culture this is the route to succinctness and clarity (see Figure 5.2).

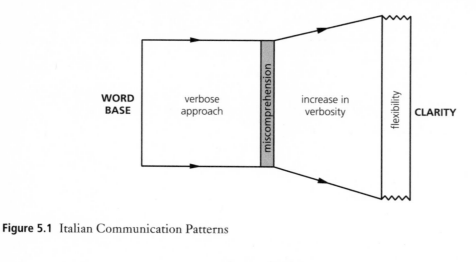

Figure 5.1 Italian Communication Patterns

Figure 5.2 Finnish Communication Patterns

Germans tend to push resolutely forward in a constant, believing-in-oneself style (Figure 5.3). The French use a variety of tactics, including imaginative appeal, but invariably adhere to strict principles of logic throughout their discourse (Figure 5.4).

The English, like Germans, go steadily forward, but often introduce humor or understatement to soften their style (Figure 5.5). South Americans and Swedes go in for long discussions although in entirely different manners (Figure 5.6).

Spaniards use lengthy discourse to get to know their interlocutor well and to develop friendship and loyalty as a basis on which they can build their transaction (Figure 5.7).

Americans regard negotiation as a give-and-take scenario, where both sides should put all their cards on the table at the beginning and waste no time beating around the bush. Their style is confrontational and often aggressive (Figure 5.8).

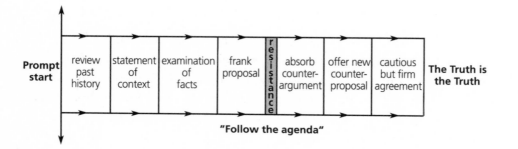

Figure 5.3 German Communication Patterns

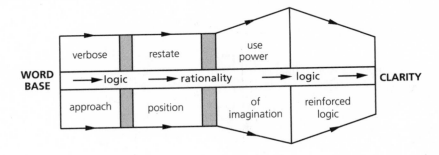

Figure 5.4 French Communication Patterns

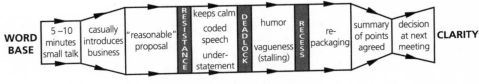

Figure 5.5 English Communication Patterns

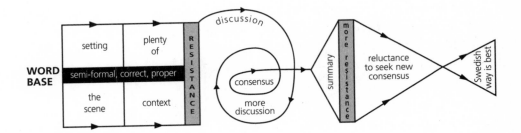

Figure 5.6 Swedish Communication Patterns

Listening Habits

Communication is a two-way process, involving not only the communicative skill of the speaker but, just as important, the listening habits of the interlocutor or audience. Just as different cultures don't use speech the same way, neither do they listen the same way. There are good listeners (Germans, Swedes, Finns) and there are bad ones (French, Spaniards). Others, such as the Americans, listen carefully or indifferently, depending on the nature of the conversation or address. Figures 5.9 through 5.17 give some indication of the main concerns of several nationalities when they are obliged to listen. Figure 5.18 summarizes the principal expectations of audiences belonging to different cultures.

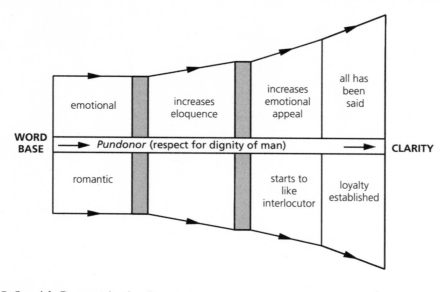

Figure 5.7 Spanish Communication Patterns

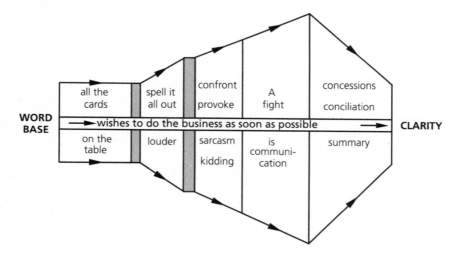

Figure 5.8 American Communication Patterns

The Language of Management

Different languages are used in different ways and with a variety of effects. Managers of all nationalities know how to speak to best effect to their compatriots, yet they are in fact only vaguely aware of their dependence on the built-in linguistic characteristics that make their job easier.

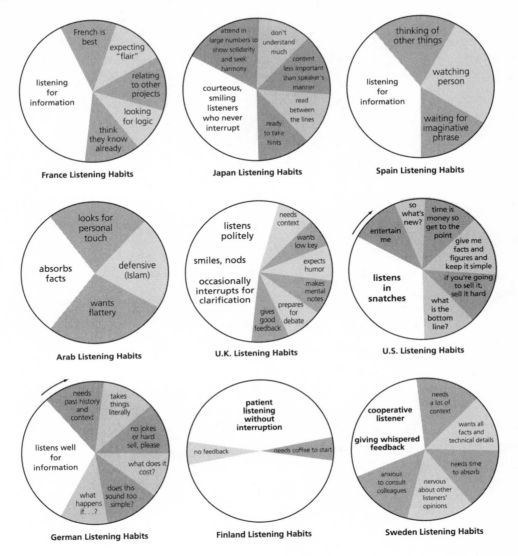

Figures 5.9 to 5.17 Listening Habits

German

Germans belong to a data-oriented, low-context culture (see Chapter 3 for an explanation of these concepts) and like receiving detailed information and instruction to guide them in the performance of tasks at which they wish to excel. In business situations German is not used in a humorous way, neither do its rigid case-endings and strict word order allow the speaker to think aloud very easily. With few homonyms (in contrast, for example, to Chinese) and a transparent word-building system, the language is especially conducive to the issuing of clear orders. The almost invariable use of the formal *Sie* (you) in business fits in well with the expectation of obedience and reinforces the hierarchical nature of the communication.

U.S.	U.K.	GERMANY
◆ humor	◆ humor	◆ solidity of company
◆ joking	◆ a story	◆ solidity of product
◆ modernity	◆ "nice" product	◆ technical information
◆ gimmicks	◆ reasonable price	◆ context
◆ slogans	◆ quality	◆ beginning—middle—end
◆ catch phrases	◆ traditional rather than modern	◆ lots of print
◆ hard sell		◆ no jokes
		◆ good price
		◆ quality
		◆ delivery date
attention span: 30 mins	attention span: 30–45 mins	attention span: 1+ hour

FRANCE	JAPAN	SWEDEN
◆ formality	◆ good price	◆ modernity
◆ innovative product	◆ USP	◆ quality
◆ "sexy" appeal	◆ synergy with corporate image	◆ design
◆ imagination	◆ harmony	◆ technical information
◆ logical presentation	◆ politeness	◆ delivery dates
◆ reference to France	◆ respect for their company	
◆ style, appearance	◆ good name of your company	
◆ personal touch	◆ quiet presentation	
◆ may interrupt	◆ well-dressed presenter	
	◆ formality	
	◆ diagrams	
attention span: 30 mins	attention span: 1 hour	attention span: 45 mins

(continued)

As far as motivating subordinates is concerned, German would seem to be less flexible than, for instance, bubbly American English. The constrictive effect of case-endings makes it difficult for German speakers to chop and change in the middle of a sentence. They embark on a course, plotted partly by gender, partly by morphology, in a straitjacket of Teutonic word order. Because the verb comes at the end of the sentence, the hearer is obliged to

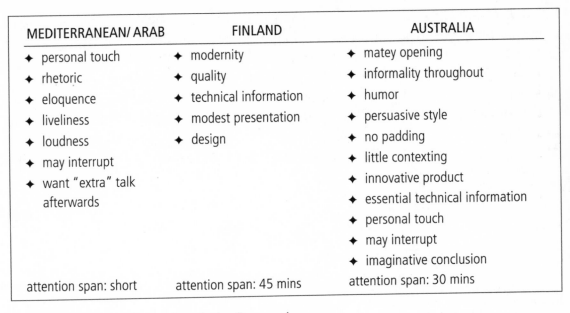

MEDITERRANEAN/ARAB	FINLAND	AUSTRALIA
✦ personal touch	✦ modernity	✦ matey opening
✦ rhetoric	✦ quality	✦ informality throughout
✦ eloquence	✦ technical information	✦ humor
✦ liveliness	✦ modest presentation	✦ persuasive style
✦ loudness	✦ design	✦ no padding
✦ may interrupt		✦ little contexting
✦ want "extra" talk afterwards		✦ innovative product
		✦ essential technical information
		✦ personal touch
		✦ may interrupt
		✦ imaginative conclusion
attention span: short	attention span: 45 mins	attention span: 30 mins

Figure 5.18 Audience Expectations during Presentations

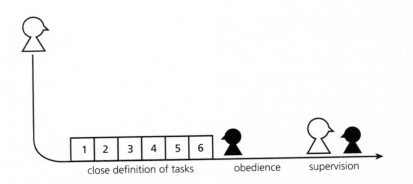

Figure 5.19 German Language of Management

listen carefully to extract the full meaning. The length and complexity of German sentences reflect the German tendency to distrust simple utterances. Information-hungry Germans are among the best listeners in the world, and their language fits the bill.

American English

The United States is a young, vigorous, ebullient nation and its language reflects the national energy and enthusiasm. Americans exaggerate in order to simplify—low-key Britons feel Americans go "over the top," but the dynamic cliché wears well in the U.S.

The frequent tendency to hyperbolize, exaggerate chances of success and overstate aims or targets allows American managers to "pump up" their subordinates—to drive them on to longer hours and speedier results. American salespeople are also used to the "hard sell" approach. Tough talk, quips, wisecracks, barbed repartee—all available in good supply in American English—help them on their way.

The ubiquitous use of *get* facilitates clear, direct orders. You get up early, you get going, you get there first, you get the client and you get the order, got it? The many neologisms in American English, used liberally by managers, permit them to appear up to date, aphoristic, humorous and democratic.

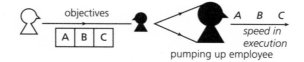

Figure 5.20 American English Language of Management

British English

In Britain the English language has quite different qualities and, as a management tool, is much more subtle. British staff members who are put off by American exaggeration and tough talk will fall for a more understated, laid-back version of English that reflects their own characteristics. Managers manipulate subordinates with friendly small talk, humor, reserved statements of objectives and a very casual approach to getting down to work. You don't arrive on the dot and work around the clock. The variety of types of humor available in the U.K. enables managers to be humorous, to praise, change direction, chide, insinuate and criticize (themselves as well as others) at will. Irony is a powerful weapon either way.

Both British and American English facilitate the coining of new words. American managers and staff often use business terminologies coined yesterday, which neither fully understands but which unite them in wonder at the spanking newness of the expression. Britons, in contrast, shy away from neologisms, often preferring woolly, old-fashioned phrases that frequently lead to sluggish thinking. "Muddling through" is the result—and the British are famous for it.

Foreigners follow British English with difficulty, for in fact they are listening to messages in a code. American and German criticism is blunt and direct; the British version is incidental and oblique. Managers, when praising, may seem to condemn. When persuading, they will strive to appear laid back. When closing a project they will take a casual stance, and when being tough they will feign great consideration, even kindness.

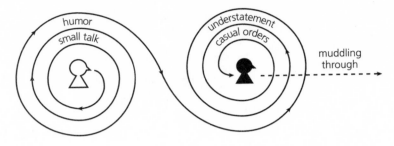

Figure 5.21 British English Language of Management

Japanese

There is a certain similarity in the language of management in Britain and Japan, although the basic and ever-present indirectness of the Japanese style makes the British, by comparison, seem like clinical thinkers! Nevertheless, the Japanese have an aversion to "rocking the boat." British managers' understated criticisms, their humorous shafts in attack and their apparent reasonableness of expression at all times are gambits to preserve harmony in their teams. In Japan the drive toward harmony is so strong that it takes priority over clarity, even over truth.

Japanese managers do not issue orders: they only hint at what has to be done. The language is custom designed for this. The structure, which normally stacks up a line of subordinate clauses before the main one, invariably lists the justifications for the directive before it reaches the listener.

"Complete September's final report by 5:30 P.M." comes out in Japanese as "It's October 10th today, isn't it? Our controller hasn't asked to see September's report yet. I wonder if he'll come around tomorrow. You never know with him..." The actual order is never given—there is no need, the staff are already scrambling to their books.

Japanese has built-in mechanisms that create a strong impact on the listener. The general mandatory politeness creates a climate where staff appear to be quietly consulted in the most courteous manner. This very courtesy encourages their support and compliance. In fact, though, they have no choice, as the hierarchy of communication is already settled by the status of the manager based on the quality and date of his university degree. The use of honorifics, moreover, reinforces the hierarchical situation. The different set of expressions (again mandatory) used in formulating the subordinates' responses to the manager's remarks closes the circle of suggestion, absorption, compliance.

Other features of the Japanese language that serve managers in instructing and motivating staff are the passive voice, used for extra politeness; the impersonal verb, which avoids casting direct blame; and the use of silence on certain issues, which clearly indicates the manager's opinion to the subordinate. Reported speech is not popular in Japan, for Japanese people subscribe to the myth that all one-to-one conversations are delivered in confidence and should not be repeated to others, and indeed the language does not possess a mechanism for reported speech.

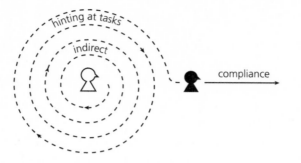

Figure 5.22 Japanese Language of Management

French

French managers inhabit quite a different linguistic world. They are clinically direct in their approach and see no advantage in ambiguity or ambivalence. The French language is crisp and incisive, a kind of verbal dance or gymnastics of the mouth, which presses home its points with an undisguised, logical urgency. It is rational, precise, ruthless in its clarity.

The French educational system, from childhood, places a premium on articulateness and eloquence of expression. Unlike Japanese, Finnish or British children, French children are rarely discouraged from being talkative. In the French culture loquacity is equated with intelligence, and silence does not have a particularly golden sheen. Lycée, university and *École normale supérieure* education reinforces the emphasis on good speaking, purity of grammar and mastery of the French idiom. The French language, unquestionably, is the chief weapon wielded by managers in directing, motivating and dominating their staff. Less articulate French staff members will show no resentment. Masterful use of language and logic implies, in their understanding, masterful management.

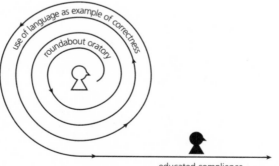

Figure 5.23 French Language of Management

Other Languages

In the Gulf States a good manager is a good Muslim. The language used will make frequent references to Allah and align itself with the precepts and style of the Koran. A didactic management style is the result. The inherent rhetorical qualities of the Arabic language (see Figure 5.24) lend themselves to reinforcing the speaker's sincerity. A raised voice is a sign not of anger, but of genuine feeling and exhortation.

University Professor Nigel Holden sees Russian, where social distance is encoded in highly subtle ways, as resembling Japanese as a flexible management language. Areas such as leadership or motivation of employees was not of importance to Soviet managers. They used threats and coercion to produce the results demanded by socialist "planning." How Russian will develop as a language of management in the future will depend on modes of address using names and titles and on the development of formal and informal mechanisms which do not remind subordinates of coercion and control.

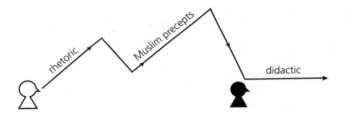

Figure 5.24 Arabic Language of Management

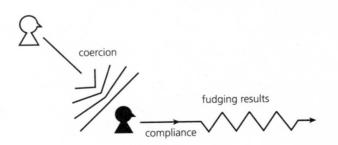

Figure 5.25 Russian Language of Management

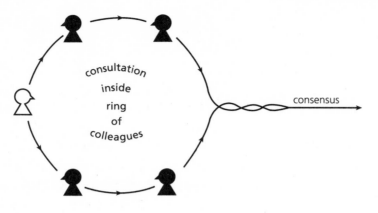

Figure 5.26 Swedish Language of Management

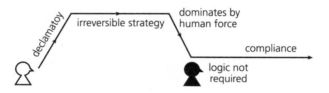

Figure 5.27 Spanish Language of Management

Swedish as a language of management leans heavily on the *Du* (informal) form of *you* and on dry, courteous expressions that clearly put managers at the same level as their colleagues. I recently heard a TV journalist in his mid-twenties address the prime minister as *Du*.

To take a very different example of the use of the informal second-person pronoun, the Spanish *tu* is directed toward staff at a much more vertical angle. However, the declaimed nature of their delivery, with typical Spanish fire and emphasis, makes their pronouncements and opinions virtually irreversible. Spanish, with its wealth of diminutive endings, its rich vocabulary and multiple options on most nouns, is extremely suitable for expressing emotion, endearments, nuances and intimacies. Spanish managers woo, persuade and cajole. They want you to know how they feel. The language exudes warmth, excitement, sensuousness, ardor, ecstasy and sympathy.

6

Manners (and Mannerisms)

"Manners maketh man." Cross-culturally speaking, they can unmaketh him as well. In a really free world we should be able to wipe our plates with bread like the French, hawk and spit like the Mongolians, belch like the Fijians, drink ourselves legless like the Finns, voice unpopular opinions like the Germans, turn up late like the Spaniards, snub people like the English and eat with our left hand in Saudi Arabia. In theory, there is no such thing as international etiquette, but certain mannerisms are acceptable only at home!

In our own culture we are provided with a code for behavior. There is right and wrong, proper and improper, respectable and disreputable. The code, taught by parents and teachers and confirmed by peers and contemporaries, covers not only basic values and beliefs but also correctness of comportment and attitudes in varying circumstances. The rules may or may not be enshrined in law, but in one's own society they may not be broken without censure or with impunity. Unless we are eccentric, we conform. At home we know how to behave at the dinner table, at cocktail parties, in restaurants, at meetings and at a variety of social occasions. We are also fully cognizant of the particular taboos our own culture imposes.

The well-brought-up citizen not only feels comfortable with the code, but in the main actually welcomes it. It is a familiar regulatory mechanism which stops people from making fools of themselves or being considered outsiders. All societies have outsiders, of course, but most of us prefer to be insiders. Generally speaking, it is less hassle. A problem arises, however, when we go abroad. As a representative of our country, we would like to show what good manners we have. Unfortunately, what are good manners in one country can be eccentricity or downright bad manners in another, as anyone who blows his or her nose in a beautiful white handkerchief in front of a Japanese will soon find out. International travelers face a dilemma: should they maintain their impeccable behavior from back home and risk inevitable *faux pas*, or should they imitate the people they visit and risk ridicule by not getting it quite right?

Unfortunately, there is no such thing as international etiquette. When someone begins to formulate an international code for correct behavior, they instinctively look to their own norms as being the logical, acceptable, inoffensive ones. So we are back where we started.

Sincerity Helps

Sincerity takes us a long way. Europeans, Asians and Americans meet regularly on business and at conferences and manage to avoid giving offense, by and large, by being their honest selves. Americans are genial and sincere, the French gallant and sincere, the British reasonable and sincere, Germans and Russians unsmiling but sincere, Finns clumsy but sincere, the Japanese smiling and sincere (although unfortunately Europeans and Americans think their smiles are insincere). The odd dinner or business meeting we carry off well in the euphoria generated by the host's generosity and the guest's appreciative attentiveness. At such initial gatherings *faux pas* are ignored, even considered charming.

The question of correct comportment in a foreign environment only becomes pressing when the exposure is lengthened. A protracted host–guest relationship or, even more, an ongoing business relationship, places greater strain on the tolerance and patience thresholds of both parties as time goes by. The American habit of sprawling in chairs at business conferences may seem friendly and disarming to the British but would place Germans in a constant state of unease. Mexican unpunctuality, forgiven once, becomes unacceptable if endemic. Latin loquacity, engaging at first for Finns and Swedes, soon drives them up the wall. There is a limit to the number of cups of green tea a European can accept in a day.

Once the honeymoon of first acquaintance is over, international travelers/ businesspeople seek a behavior pattern that will serve them adequately wherever they find themselves. Some things come easily—handshaking or bowing, ladies first or ladies last, chocolates or flowers for the hostess. Other features give a little more trouble—the use of chopsticks, the texture of local small talk, the concept of time in a particular country. The deeper we delve, the harder it gets. What are the important social norms, the core beliefs, the real sensitivities? Above all, what is strictly taboo?

They don't always tell you. Everyone knows that it is inadvisable to send the firm's best-known drinker to represent you in Saudi Arabia and that Arabs do not eat pork, but is everyone aware that it is bad manners to point one's foot at an Arab in conversation or ask about the health of any of his womenfolk? Did you know that sending yellow flowers to a woman signifies, in some European countries, that she has been unfaithful to her husband? Let us take a look at the areas where major etiquette *gaffes* may cause offense and minor ones some embarrassment—dining etiquette, cocktail parties, restaurant behavior, social norms and finally taboos.

Dining Etiquette

According to an old Malagasy proverb, "Men are like the lip of a cooking pot, which forms just one circle." By this one might understand that the basic human need for food serves as a uniting factor, at least temporarily. This is more than likely, though what people do around that cooking pot can differ to a startling degree. To begin with, eating is actually more important to some of us than to others. We often hear it said that Americans eat to live and that the French live to eat. This may be an oversimplification, but it is a fact that many Americans have a Coke and burger in the office and Scandinavians are in and out of the company cafeteria in 30 minutes flat. In contrast, the French, Spaniards, Portuguese and Greeks attach social importance to the midday meal, which may last from one to two hours.

Eating Hours

People also eat at very different times. Nordics, who begin work early, eat very little breakfast and are starving by noon. Spaniards rarely get the midday meal on the table before 2:00 P.M. and used to carry on for a couple of hours, although their membership in the European Union is causing the younger executives, at least, to get back to the office by 3:00 P.M. and cut out the siesta.

An even greater variety of eating times is apparent for the evening meal. Finns are starving again around 4:00 P.M., and they, along with the Japanese "salarymen" and the British working classes, precede the rest of us to the table around 5:30 P.M. The Americans prefer to eat dinner around 6:00 or 6:30 P.M., and most Northern and Central Europeans sit down around 7:30 P.M., while the Spaniards and Portuguese, still digesting lunch at that time, do not want to see food again until at least 9:00 or 10:00 P.M., often leaving it much later than that. A dinner invitation in Spain or Portugal for 8:00 or 8:30 P.M. means that the main course is likely to be served between 10:00 and 11:00 P.M. Chinese and other Asians start the evening meal between 7:00 and 9:00 P.M., although Indonesians have an aversion to dining early.

When invited to dinner at someone's home, most nationalities turn up at the appointed time. Lack of concern regarding punctuality, is, however, no disgrace in Spain, when an invitation for 9:00 P.M. means 9:30 in any case.

Seating arrangements, when around a table, are often casual and left to the last minute in many countries, although Asians invariably seat the most important guest facing the door. In Europe, the French and Germans are more careful about placing people, bearing in mind their various interests and status. It is the Swedes, however, who are the most formal. Swedish hospitality notwithstanding, dinner in Stockholm can be quite an ordeal.

Bon Appétit

In most countries the signal to start eating is given by the host or hostess. In France, for example, it is *bon appétit*, in Germany *guten Appetit*, in Italy *buon appetito*, and so on. Anglo-Saxons have no equivalent for this formula and often mutter "right" or say nothing. The Japanese formula is *itadakimasu* (I am receiving), although they will probably have preceded this by saying something nice about the appearance of the food. Because the Japanese attach as much importance to the aesthetic arrangement or layout of the food as to its actual taste, you should not attack a dish without complimenting your host on the artistry.

How Many Courses?

Anglo-Saxons are used to eating three courses: starters, the main dish accompanied by a starch and vegetables, and dessert. In other societies, the number of dishes may be far more numerous. The French, for instance, serve many side dishes separately, whereas the British tend to put as much as they can on one plate. In Asia one can lose count of the number of dishes. The Japanese, when seeking to impress, can serve a very large number of dishes one after the other, each containing a small, easily digestible amount. When once hosted by a Japanese college principal, I counted 19 consecutive courses, all paper-thin slices of fish or, occasionally, meat and arranged artfully to cover the whole plate. My mother, who was 92 at the time, was worried that the very multiplicity of cuts would be too much for her aging stomach, but the principal, who was 90 himself, assured her that she would be able to digest it all without any problem. This proved to be true, until they served up the twentieth dish (strawberries), which promptly sent them both off to the restroom to be sick.

Customs

According to the customs of the country, meals may be taken around a table sitting on chairs, on the floor or on the ground. In Japan it is common to sit on tatami matting; in Arabian countries, on carpets, linoleum or polished surfaces; in Tonga, Fiji and most of Polynesia on grass or firm soil. Chopsticks are used in several Asian countries, particularly Japan and China, and Caucasians are advised to acquire enough aptitude with them at least to get morsels into the mouth. Clumsiness is normally overlooked, although goodness knows what they really think of us. We get our own back when some of them use knives and forks. In Arab countries one usually eats with the hand—the right one—as the left one is reserved for unclean tasks. The choicest cuts of meat are handed to you by the host; it is bad manners to take a piece yourself or to decline the piece he offers you, no matter how big. Rice will be squeezed into balls by the host (by hand) and given to you directly. Don't touch any food with your left hand unless you have informed the host at the beginning of the meal that you are left-handed, in which case remember that your right hand is the dirty one.

Starters

Starters vary in different countries. Japanese *sashimi* (raw fish) is arguably among the most delicious (and expensive), raw or smoked fish also being popular in Scandinavian countries. French *hors d'oeuvre* often consist of crudités. Italians favor *antipasta* (often Parma ham), Americans shrimp cocktails and (recently) potato skins, Greeks *tsatsiki* and *taramasalata* and Turks yogurt. Spaniards like to have a *tapas* session before dinner. Americans whet their appetites with pre-dinner guacamole and cheese dips. In virtually all countries, however, soups are a great stand-by and often a particular soup is closely associated with the national cuisine. In Spain, it is *gazpacho*, in France *soupe à l'oignon* and *bouillabaisse*, in Austro-Hungary *goulasch,* in Russia *bortsch,* in China shark's fin or bird's nest, in Nordic countries pea, in Italy *minestrone,* in Germany oxtail and in the United States clam chowder. All of these soups, whether hot or cold, are normally ordered as starters. In Japan, *misoshiro* soup is eaten at or near the end of the meal, as is the *sopa alentejana* in the Portuguese province of Alentejo. In the latter case, the peasants used to fill up on soup, as main courses were often inadequate in this once poverty-stricken region.

Soups are normally eaten with metal soup spoons; in China spoons are ceramic and a special shape. In Japan and Korea, one lifts the soup bowl to the mouth and drinks the contents accompanied by legitimate slurping. In these countries rice is also slurped up from close quarters with chopsticks. It is a noisy process, but perfectly good manners. Most Europeans tip their soup dishes towards themselves when spooning out the last dregs—in England, it is considered good manners to tilt the soup plate away from oneself in the closing stages.

Main Courses

Main courses around the world are too numerous and varied to describe here. Strange though many foods may seem, most dishes are edible and even tasty once you have familiarized yourself with them. Sashimi, which puts a lot of Anglo-Saxons off at first tasting, is one of the world's great dishes, priceless for its subtlety and delicate flavor. One can hardly say the same of Korean *kimshi,* some Vietnamese fish and eel dishes and various offerings in the small villages along the Yangtse. Fijian *kava* tastes (and looks) like mud to the uninitiated, and I would not recommend the Pyongyang sake with a snake in the bottle even to people who owe me money. Finnish *kalakukko* and *mämmi* take a little negotiating but are good in the end, although *calamares en su tinta* (squid in its own ink) has few supporters outside the Hispanic world.

You should eat as much as you can, to avoid offending your hosts. Americans, and particularly English, are well placed to get their revenge if they want to by offering their own cooking to visitors on Anglo-Saxon shores. Even though you may not consider what you are eating a delicacy, your host is most likely offering the best, so you should try to follow the good manners of the host country. It is as well to know that an Australian country breakfast may consist of a huge beefsteak with two fried eggs on top and that in Madagascar you should not hand an egg directly to another person, but place it on the floor first. In Tonga and Hawaii you bury meat for a while before you eat it, in Japan you can eat whale meat and live lobsters (they watch you eat them) and in Finland I have enjoyed succulent steaks of bear, beaver, elk and reindeer. Portuguese mix pork and clams and cook cod in 53 different ways. Malagasy slaughter zebu cattle on sacrificial occasions and put a little blood on guests' heads to integrate them into the festivities.

Unusual table manners are not limited to Third-World or out-of-the-way countries. The English take the use of a knife and fork for granted, but Americans do not keep a knife in their hand while eating. First they cut the meat with their knife in the right hand and fork in the left. Then they put the knife down by the side of the plate, transfer the fork from left hand to right, slightly dip the left shoulder and start eating in what to the British looks like a lopsided manner. The British habit of eating vegetables (even peas) with the fork upside down is viewed as ridiculous by the Americans and Europeans. The French—great eaters—use bread as an extra utensil, pushing anything else around with it and eventually employing a chunk to wipe the plate clean and save the dish washers extra effort.

In Japan the main things to remember are to say how nice everything looks, keep eating a little of each dish at a time without finishing any off, and lifting up your glass when someone offers to fill it. You in turn should fill up their glasses, and any others you can reach. When you have drunk enough sake, turn your sake cup upside down. In China you should never take the last morsel from a serving plate and never at any time during the meal say you are hungry.

In the Finnish countryside they serve new potatoes with their skins on at the table and you are supposed to peel them before eating. In England we are told not to put our elbows on the dining table and to sit with our hands in our lap when we have finished. Mexicans are told to put both hands on the table during and after the meal; it is taboo to hide them under the table. In Fiji and some other countries it is polite (even mandatory) to belch or burp after completing your meal, to show appreciation. Don't do it in the wrong country, though. Swedish hostesses would faint. In China you know when the meal is ended, for the host stands up and thanks you for coming.

Cocktail Parties

There are no fixed rules for cocktail parties, which in themselves are often interesting exercises in cross-cultural behavior. What is the best time to arrive, the best time to leave? How long should the party last? Then there is the question of what to drink, how much to eat and what to talk about. Having a few friends at home for drinks in one's own country is a relatively simple affair. Larger parties with a multinational guest list require considerably more thought.

My wife and I spent five years on the Tokyo cocktail circuit—a very lively one—where attendances averaged well over 50 and involved a minimum of a dozen different nationalities, often more. They were usually held in the homes of business executives; embassies entertained on a somewhat larger scale on National Days and other occasions.

We counted among our circle of friends in Tokyo acquaintances from 20-odd countries as well as a liberal sprinkling of Japanese. Under such circumstances there is no such thing as a cocktail party of short duration. How does one schedule an event where the Japanese will turn up 10 minutes early, the Germans and the Swiss on time, the Americans and British a bit late, the French after them and the Brazilians arriving an hour after the party was due to end? One could put something like 6:30–8:30 P.M. on the invitation card, but nobody took any notice of it. Few parties ended before 11 P.M. or 12 A.M. unless one ran out of liquor.

Another basic problem was how many people to invite. Even among the British and American communities, with which we were chiefly involved, it was likely that there would be half a dozen cocktail parties held every night. Consequently, one counted on an acceptance rate of one in three and invited 150. If you were unlucky enough to hit a day when for some reason there were few parties, you might get landed with 100 guests or more—this happened to us on more than one occasion. The problem was further complicated by the fact that Japanese tend not to answer the RSVP—but they usually turn up. Furthermore, most Japanese executives do not bring their wives, although some do! One just had to play the averages.

Small Talk

Some nationalities thrive in the cocktail party atmosphere and others do not. Russians, for instance, like drinking sitting down, especially as they devote a considerable amount of time to it. Chinese, too—used to mammoth dinners seated at banquet tables—are less at ease shuffling around from group to group of noisy strangers. Americans, with their mobile nature and easy social manners, excel at small talk. Australians and Canadians, used to formulating strategies for meeting new arrivals, also have no difficulty, and conversation always comes easily to them. The British and the French—past masters at small talk—are also practiced cocktailers.

Yet the very thought of small talk poses substantial problems for some other nationalities. Germans simply do not believe in it, Finns and Japanese are frightened to death by it and Swedes usually dry up after about 10 minutes. Russians and Germans—more than willing to have long, soul-searching conversations with close friends—see no point in trotting out trivialities and platitudes for two hours to a complete stranger. Swedes—fluent in English and happy to talk about their job and technical matters—find little to say in addition and often admit they become boring after the first half-hour. Finns, unused to chatter, actually buy booklets on small talk (one recently published in Helsinki was a great success).

The Japanese—masters of polite trivia among themselves—are never quite sure what to talk about with foreigners. At Japanese business meetings, there is the obligatory 15-minute session of platitudes and harmonizing, after which one can get down to business. At cocktail parties they run up against a void.

Not so the South Americans. Although relatively deficient in foreign language skills, they maintain an incessant patter, which often saves the day for Japanese and Scandinavian partners. Mexicans, Peruvians and Argentineans never run out of steam. I once attended an all Latin American cocktail party in Caracas, which began at 7:00 P.M. and finished at 1:00 A.M. There were 300 people present, very little to eat, and nobody stopped talking except to draw breath for six hours flat; I do not remember a single word that was said.

Personal Space

At cocktail parties it is sometimes difficult to maintain the integrity of one's "space bubble," especially when there are a few Latins around. A common sight in Tokyo was a Brazilian or Colombian businessman towering over a diminutive Japanese, gripping his upper arm to show confidence, while the Japanese would backpedal, striving to keep his glass and himself on an even keel. In 20 minutes they would traverse the length of the room, the Japanese ending up with his back against a wall.

What to Drink

For a big party it is necessary to stock a large variety of drinks, although drinking habits are now far more standard than they used to be. This is largely due to the ascendancy of whiskey and gin and tonic as international beverages. The French, for instance, who formerly drank Scotch only after dinner, now regard it as an apéritif and import huge quantities of it. English frequently drink it with soda, Americans often on the rocks, Scots neat and Japanese with water (*mizuwari*). Gin and tonic sells well on hot evenings and is a favorite with ladies of most nationalities, as is Campari soda or Campari and orange. Germans like white wine, Spaniards and Portuguese red, Russians vodka, Scandinavians anything with a label on it.

When Americans ask for a martini they mean 99 percent dry gin with just a drop of vermouth in it, often with an olive or cocktail onion for good looks. With the olive it is called a martini, with an onion a Gibson. When Americans ask for whiskey, they mean bourbon; if they want whiskey they say Scotch. When you've worked this out, they ask for whiskey sour, so you don't know what to put in it. When you think you're well stocked they will request things like Manhattans, Screwdrivers and White Ladies and see if you know the difference between Tom and John Collins.

Embassies

Embassy cocktail parties can be long and boring affairs where most of the diplomats talk to each other for hours and leave businesspeople and other lesser mortals to fend for themselves. On these occasions it is advisable to arrive and leave early, as the food usually runs out after the first hour. Japanese embassies provide the best food, the Germans and Americans at least serve enough. Paradoxically the embassies most oriented towards businesspeople were the Soviet, Chinese and Eastern bloc countries, as their attachés were actually the people who developed commercial outlets for command economies.

Leaving

There is no foolproof way of calling an end to cocktail festivities. American businesspeople can get so involved in discussing deals over drinks that they sometimes forget they are at a party, never mind the time. Latins can talk forever. British, Germans, Dutch, Swiss and Japanese are relatively disciplined cocktail party leavers, but the same cannot be said for Danes, Scots, Slavs and Irish. In Asia it is the duty of a host to end a party; in Europe and the United States it usually depends on the guest. An old English gentleman I knew used to go to the front door at midnight, open it and stand quietly by it. After 10 minutes or so everybody would get the idea and leave. A Swedish party-giver told me recently that there was only one way to make Finns and Russians leave: announce there was plenty of food left, but nothing more to drink.

Restaurant Behavior

Restaurant entertaining plays an important part in the life of the international businessperson. It is not unusual for traveling executives to find themselves being hosted four or five times a week when on a foreign trip. They will be required to reciprocate when their partners or associates return the visit. The choice between entertaining at home or at a restaurant depends on varying circumstances. American, British, Canadian, Australian and New Zealand hosts are quick to open their homes to foreign visitors. Spaniards, Portuguese and other Latins are less inclined to do so, until firm personal relationships have been established. Dining out is still a rather good value for the money in Madrid, Lisbon, Athens and Istanbul, whereas the astronomical prices in Oslo, Stockholm and Helsinki make Nordics think twice about indulging in this once popular and time-honored practice. Restaurants tend to be packed in the evenings in cities renowned for their gastronomic excellence—Brussels, Paris, Lyon, San Francisco, New York, New Orleans, Vienna, Florence, Bologna and some other big Italian cities are good examples.

Nowhere is dining out more popular than in Japan, where restaurant bills are fully tax deductible and where companies or fiscal authorities rarely question the validity of entertaining expenses unless they exceed 4 percent of the firm's turnover. Japanese and other Asians, furthermore, consider that the relative smallness of their homes, in comparison to, say, those of their American or European counterparts, prohibits them from being able to entertain at home.

Ethnic Cuisines

When being entertained by a foreign colleague in a restaurant, one need not be so fully attuned to the table manners of the country, since often the establishment will be chosen on account of its ethnic cuisine, which could be from anywhere.

It is as well to remember that some national cuisines are best represented outside their country of origin. This is certainly true of Russian food, for which Russian restaurants in Paris, Helsinki and Stockholm set standards nearly impossible to reach at establishments within the former Soviet Union. The best Hungarian meals I have ever eaten have been in

Vienna, while nothing I ate during my month-long odyssey down the Yangtze even vaguely approached the excellence of Chinese dishes available in London or Hong Kong. London and England in general have unbelievably good Indian restaurants. Most astonishing of all, Tokyo arguably possesses the best French restaurants in the world! The variety of dishes available covers most of the regional specialties of France. The quality of Kobe beef and Japanese seafood ensures that no ingredients are lacking. Wine is flown in from France—wine lists can include 200–300 of the best vintages from Burgundy and Bordeaux—and it is not unusual for a good bottle to cost $3,000–$5,000. One shudders when envisaging what the total bill might be when half a dozen Japanese executives who know their wines (and they really do) have a good evening out.

Major League and Minor League

Somewhat removed from this fast-lane living are middle managers anxious to impress their foreign customers on a night out on the limited budget that their enterprise permits. It is often a good idea to ask the guests which ethnic type of meal they prefer. There are, surprisingly, a very small number of cuisines that can be said to be truly famous internationally: French, Italian, Chinese and Indian. Such restaurants can be found in good numbers in almost every city in the world. Most businesspeople automatically opt for one of these styles.

There is a growing "second-division league" of ethnic cuisines that are gradually establishing their reputation on an international basis; these include Greek, Mexican, Russian, Spanish, Korean, Indonesian, Thai and Japanese restaurants. One rarely talks about Anglo-Saxon cuisine (American, British, Australian, New Zealand, Canadian), unless one is addicted to pig meat for breakfast.

Varying Ambiences

Given such a variety of restaurants, dining out offers a multiplicity of experiences. In general one adapts to the ambience. Restaurants in Spain, South America, China, Hong Kong and Indonesia are usually convivial and noisy. In England, the United States and Japan the atmosphere is more conducive to quiet socializing or business discussion, while in Sweden and Finland guests are asked to leave if they are too boisterous or unduly inebriated. Moderate intoxication is readily permitted in restaurants in Germany, Austria, Denmark and Greece, while in Japan it is considered good form for the boss to drink more than his subordinates, then perhaps leave early.

In Russia and Bavaria it is not uncommon for strangers to join you at your table, particularly if the restaurant is rather large or has certain beer hall characteristics. In Munich people occasionally bring their dogs and ask if they may sit them under the table.

When taking Japanese out to a restaurant, you should exercise care that they are not allowed to choose freely from the menu, because the senior Japanese in the group will usually choose the least expensive entrée listed and his colleagues will have to follow suit. In

Japan it is good manners, when given the choice of dish, to show that you are not being extravagant with your host's money. This is certainly very meritorious behavior on the part of the Japanese, but it may not be what you want. Most likely, for business reasons, you will wish them to have a costly meal and wind up in your debt. The correct course of action is not to let them choose, but to recommend strongly the most expensive dish on the menu. "The châteaubriand is what I am having, Mr. Suzuki; it's the best dish in this restaurant and I insist you accompany me." He (and his subordinates) will be delighted to concur. It is not a cheap way of doing business, but it will almost certainly get you orders. And Mr. Suzuki will have no hesitation in treating you with equal generosity in Japan.

Paying the Bill and Tipping

When it comes to paying the bill, it is customary to pay on one's home ground. Junior managers often agree to pay their own way if they meet frequently. Under no circumstances should one propose this arrangement with Asians. In most Asian countries, especially in Japan and China, the question of who pays the bill is quite clear before the evening commences. It is permissible for you to invite them out in their own country, though normally only after they have entertained you at least once. Guests are given the seat facing the door, and from this position you should never try to pay. When you have seen the amount on the bill in many Japanese restaurants, it is unlikely you will be eager to pay in any case.

Tipping can be such a minefield of errors and embarrassment that it is better to ask host nationals what the accepted custom is. Suffice it to say that tips are awaited more anxiously by some waiters than others. The safest situation is when service is included in the bill, although it is not unusual for Latin waiters to expect an additional sum in recognition of smart attention. In most Asian countries the standard of service is excellent, whether you tip or not. In Japan and China tipping is not expected. In France waiters are capable of throwing the tip on the floor if they consider it insufficient.

Home in Safety

Once the bill is paid, the waiter rewarded and the appropriate belching (if required) executed, then you are free to leave. In Asia the host generally will include your transportation home as part of the evening's obligations. This is not so common in the West, but care should be taken to ensure safe delivery of your guest in such cities as Naples, St. Petersburg, Rio, Los Angeles and New York, not to mention spots such as Bogotá and Antananarivo, where not even locals venture out on the street after dark.

Manners in Society

In addition to the accepted practices for wining and dining, most cultures have an intricate set of rules governing general social behavior.

Fortunately, manners are not what they used to be. In England they reached their peak of stringency in the days of Queen Victoria, when gentlemen wore hats just so they could take them off when meeting ladies on the street and inexperienced diners almost starved to death at table for fear of exhibiting inadequate etiquette. Alice Thomas Ellis recently reviewed a terrifying Victorian volume, *Manners and Tone of Good Society, or Solecisms to Be Avoided* (circa 1899), which devoted 22 pages to the etiquette of leaving cards and went on to detail suitable instructions for morning calls, introductions, titles, periods of mourning and five o'clock teas.

At the beginning of the twentieth century, similar behavior was being advocated in Paris, Budapest, Vienna and St. Petersburg, and other fashionable metropoles. Good manners, invented by the upper classes theoretically in the interests of smooth social intercourse, in fact developed into a repressive code which put people in their place. Happily, Americans resent being sorted out in this way and shortly afterwards invented bad manners, which saved us all a lot of trouble. In this they were capably supported by the Canadians, with their disarmingly casual social graces, and particularly by the Australians, who, as we all know, don't give a XXXX about etiquette and generally behave as they please.

If some of England's colonies scrapped the tenets of correct behavior held by the mother country, others imitated them well into the twentieth century. This was particularly true of India, where formality of posture and flowery speech habits even today retain Victorian overtones. Also New Zealanders and many South Africans appear very polite to present-day English people, who, since the Second World War, have largely adopted easy-going American social attitudes.

The Anglo-Saxons, along with the Scandinavians, are probably the most informal societies in the early twenty-first century. The Japanese lead the world in standards of politeness, while Asians in general display consistent courtesy to foreigners and to each other. In Europe, social ease fluctuates from Spanish warmth and Italian flexibility to Swiss pedantry and German righteousness; the French are probably the most formal of the Europeans.

The problem with observing the manners of others is not so much the degree of formality or informality to adopt (this can be quickly regulated) but to know what the manners are in certain regions. In Japan, for instance, the correct thing to do for a bereaved neighbor is to send the family money in a sealed envelope. This custom makes some Westerners uncomfortable, but nevertheless has considerable merit. If the family is rich, they send the money back; if they are poor, they keep it for funeral expenses. What more practical way to help them in their misfortune? To complicate the situation, bereaved Japanese often send you and your wife gifts in appreciation of your gesture.

Gift Giving

Gift giving, particularly in Japan and China, is in itself a difficult area to negotiate. In brief, Westerners cannot avoid indulging in this practice in the long run without running the risk of being considered churlish or stingy. Gift giving will almost invariably be initiated by the Asian; when reciprocating, don't try to "outgift" a Japanese or a Chinese. It is a game you are not going to win anyway; extravagance on your part will only result in escalating expense on theirs. More important is the thought behind the gift. Something ethnic and tasteful from your own country is the safest (prints, ceramics, a specialty from your own region, illustrated books and so on). In general, do not open gifts in front of Asians and Arabs when an exchange of presents is taking place. The danger of someone losing face is too great.

When in Rome, Do as the Romans Do

In Rome, imitating people's behavior entails little hardship, as foreign visitors are more often than not quite willing to indulge in the wining, dining and other aspects of *la dolce vita* available in the Italian capital. In some countries and environments, however, you will have to use your own judgment as to how far you are expected to "go native."

Taking one's shoes off in Japanese homes comes easily, but what degree of politeness should one exhibit? For instance, the Japanese apologize regularly for personal defects, minor transgressions and even for wrongs they have not done and can be embarrassingly self-deprecating in front of Westerners. How much should Americans or Europeans run themselves down or accept Japanese apologies? Paradoxically, Japanese wives, in flower arranging or *origami* classes, speak disparagingly about their husbands, as this is regarded as a sign of modesty and good manners. Should the British wife follow suit? In Japan, Korea and some other countries men walk in front of women and precede them up and down stairs. British, French and Nordic males find this hard to do, though Australians manage it.

In Russia it is polite to make a short speech with every toast, but it is better not to smash your vodka glass to the floor unless it is evident that your host expects you to. It's the same with plates in Greece—check it out. In Thailand, a pale face is a sign of beauty in a woman (don't ask if she is unwell); in Asia one generally wraps up presents in red paper; white, on the other hand, is an unlucky color associated with death. In Russia, people don't answer other people's telephones—they just let them ring. And so it goes on—one just lives and learns how other people behave.

Strange or Far Out

Some traditions are so unusual that it is not advisable to imitate them. Cattle stealing is a proof of manhood in some African areas and it may be the only route to secure a worth-while wife. In other, drought-stricken regions it is customary to take soap with you on long journeys, in case opportunities arise for running water. Polynesians bite the head of a newly deceased relative to make sure he has really passed away; it is better to stand respectfully at one side, if you are present.

Chinese decide how to construct buildings and arrange furniture according to their *feng shui* beliefs, which may mean little to you. Few customs, however, are stranger or more impressive than the Malagasy *famadihana*, which means "the turning of the bones." In Madagascar when a relative has been dead and buried for a decent period of time, he or she is exhumed on some suitable anniversary or auspicious occasion, the bones are wrapped in a shroud and lovingly paraded at a family ceremony where a hundred or more people may be present. The bones are examined, fondled, shown to others and even talked to. In Madagascar the dead are considered more important and more influential than the living and the occasion often sees their reinstallation in a costly family tomb which offers considerably more comforts and amenities than the average Malagasy home.

Taboos

Taboos exist in every country, and we do well to observe them as they are often deep rooted in the history and beliefs of the region. Madagascar again leads the field with a bewildering list of forbidden practices:

- ✦ A woman may not wash her brother's clothes.
- ✦ Pregnant women may not eat brains or sit in doorways.
- ✦ Children may not say their father's name or refer to any part of his body.

Closer to Europe, Russians also have an impressive list:

- ✦ Coats should not be worn indoors.
- ✦ It is bad form to stand with your hands in your pockets.
- ✦ You should not sit with your legs apart.
- ✦ No whistling in the street.
- ✦ No lunches on park lawns.
- ✦ No public displays of affection.
- ✦ It is poor form to ask people where the toilet is, and never from the opposite sex.

On the other hand, it is perfectly acceptable to wander round hotel corridors at all hours of the evening or night wearing only pajamas.

In Malaysia it is taboo to point with your index finger, although you may point with your thumb. In Indonesia the head is regarded as a sacred, inviolable part of the body and should not be touched by another, so you must suppress the desire to pat young children on the head. It is also taboo in Indonesia for your head to be higher than that of a senior person. This point of deference is easily engineered while sitting (a low chair or a crouch) but harder to achieve when meeting someone on the street. It is common to see Indonesians bobbing up and down on bent knees as they pass senior citizens or people of authority.

In Korea well-brought-up young people do not smoke or drink in front of elders. In Taiwan it is unthinkable to write messages in red ink. In England, Scandinavia, Japan and China it is bad form to blow your own trumpet, although others seem to see nothing wrong with it.

In Arab countries it is taboo to drink alcohol, eat pork or to ask about the health of a man's womenfolk. Do not openly admire his possessions either, as he may feel obliged to give them to you.

PART TWO

Managing and Leading in Different Cultures

7

Status, Leadership and Organization

In Part One, we examined the cultural roots of behavior and assessed the effects of cultural diversity on people's lives and destinies. Part Two deals principally with the world of business and tackles head-on the issues and problems of international exchanges. The twenty-first century promises to be crunch time for powerful governments, trading blocs and manufacturing powerhouses. The hegemony enjoyed by Western Europe, the United States and Japan is no longer guaranteed. With six to seven billion consumers, the stakes are terrifyingly high. They include not only access to gigantic markets and astronomical profits, but also prospects of failure, recession, even survival.

Success or Failure in the Twenty-First Century

Western and Japanese managers face enormous challenges. They have to come to grips with the problems posed by the rapid expansion of globalized trade and they have to abandon previous habits of arrogance and complacency. They have many economic weapons with which to defend themselves, but they are seriously outnumbered. It is imperative that Western and Japanese managers learn how to *lead, manage, motivate* and *inspire* their growing number of foreign staff and customers. This is attainable: the top level has gone global (at the time of writing a Frenchman runs Nissan), but this has to happen at many organizational levels. Contact among middle managers and international teams can lead to success or failure for many organizations. Is there such a thing as a global leadership style? Does it work in practice? What are its elements? How does one get there? Get there one must, as there is no alternative if Western managers wish to compete and survive.

Asian competition in the twenty-first century will be fierce and unrelenting. The Asians have endured centuries of playing second fiddle to the West; now they intend to reverse the situation. In many instances they have already done so. In industries such as textiles, garments, shoes, toys and plastics the West has no chance to compete, nor will it have in the future. In high-tech industries, especially consumer hardware, the West is already threatened by Malaysia, Thailand, Korea and Taiwan; China is replacing these as the implacable competitor. How can the West fight all this?

The United States can be expected to widen its technological lead over competitors for another couple of decades, but not indefinitely. Finland, who in 2003 surpassed the U.S. in global competitiveness, may follow a similar path. Germany, Britain, France and Sweden, all high tech, will have to innovate constantly to stay ahead of Japan and China.

The West's most effective weapons have to be *dynamic leadership, perspicacity, psychological skills, willingness to innovate* and clever use of their *democratic institutions.* A lot is achieved in the West in its clubs, societies, committees, charities, associations, sport and leisure activity groups, alumni fraternities and so on. The influence of such institutions, with their inherent social vibrancy, should not be underestimated and, furthermore, are hard for Eastern cultures to put a finger on.

There remains also the question of control of worldwide organizations such as the WTO, WHO, WWF, OECD, the World Bank, G8, the EU, NAFTA and NATO as well as substantial funding of the UN, UNESCO, UNICEF and so forth. Western control will eventually weaken, China has entered the WTO and countries with burgeoning populations play greater roles, but there is still a bit of *breathing space* for Western and Japanese managers and executives to confront cross-cultural issues, begin to understand others' cultural habitats and learn how to stand in the shoes of foreign colleagues. If they do so, they at least stand a chance of influencing and leading the staff of Western companies in the East, such as those of IBM, Microsoft, Nokia, Unilever, Hewlett-Packard, Motorola and Volkswagen.

It is already late in the day for many organizations to begin this learning curve. Huge multinationals have avoided or postponed cultural training for decades. A few have excelled in their approach, such as Nokia, Ericsson, HSBC, Motorola, ABB, Coca Cola and Unilever.

Which national cultures are reluctant to learn about others? The problem lies with the Big Five, that is to say the globe's biggest economies: the United States, Japan, Germany, Britain and France. These countries (and the companies originating in them) have been particularly insensitive in their handling of intercultural issues. The very size of their own economies endows them with a certain sense of complacency, but the problem runs deeper than that. Britain, France and Spain assumed that they could continue indefinitely the ways of Empire— with one language, one policy, one supreme authority, one educational system, one code of ethics, one jurisdiction, one way of doing business. One can see how convenient it was!

The United States and Japan fail consistently to understand others because of *isolation* or *insularity,* both geographical and mental. They wallow in powerful, all-encompassing "cultural black holes," core beliefs of such gravity that they cannot be questioned (Lewis 2003). These cultural black holes prohibit intelligent or perceptive analysis of others' cultures and agendas. If you swallow, hook, line and sinker, the concept of the American Dream, no other agenda is really worthwhile contemplating. If you devote your life to avoiding loss of face and affirm unswerving obedience to the Emperor, you can hardly be a free agent in assessing others' values and ways of advancing (this means no disrespect to the Emperor of Japan, who happens to be far more enlightened and perceptive than most of the world's executives).

With Germans, the problem is different again. On intercultural issues they are in advance of the other members of the Big Five, but they are so honest, frank and, consequently, tactless that they lack the delicacy to fully understand those who do not meet strict German (ethical and organizational) standards. But at least they try.

Smaller countries have no such impasses. They learned long ago that to play the game with the Big Boys, you had to play by their rules. The rules they learned differed from country to country, but they adapted to them, case by case, which meant that they *aspired to multiculturalism*. Consequently, Dutch, Belgians, Finns, Swedes, Danes and Swiss, and to a lesser extent Greeks, Hungarians, Czechs, the Baltic states and Norwegians, have studied and achieved a certain degree of empathy with the cultures of more powerful countries. Poles, Turks and Slovenians are beginning to go down the same track. In the Americas, Canada is an outstanding example of a successful and consciously multicultural society.

When it comes to competing for world markets in terms of understanding the aspirations of others, one can make significant comparisons as to how different national cultures are dealing with the issue.

1. Small Northern European countries—the Netherlands, Belgium, Switzerland and the Nordics—have intercultural skills and are performing well internationally (Nokia, Ericsson, Scania, Volvo, Carlsberg, Heineken, Shell, Unilever, Tetra-pak, Nestlé). Their impact on world trade is limited by their size.
2. Multicultural Canada has great future potential.
3. The Big Five—the United States, Japan, Germany, Britain and France—have a long way to go in learning about how to manage successfully across cultures.
4. The Latin countries, including France, Italy and Spain, are hampered by their inadequate level of English-language proficiency.

If we compare the performance of Asians in this respect, we see they are no laggards. They have not only learned English, but they have developed sensitivity toward the aspirations of Western consumers. In this they have been greatly aided by the existence and activity of millions of overseas Chinese and overseas Indians. Singapore and Hong Kong have had their own built-in advantages. Thais and Koreans have familiarized themselves with American cultural habits. Malaysians know the British well. The Philippines is the second largest English-speaking country in the world.

Japan's successful penetration of Western markets took place *in spite of* poor intercultural skills. Rising labor costs and Chinese high-tech competition pose an imminent threat to the Japanese economy. Like the Americans, the Japanese are on the right side of a technological gap, which gives them a few years' breathing space. Like the Americans, they will have to learn how to continue to project their success across borders by developing more intercultural sensitivity. The mammoth markets of the future—China, India, Indonesia, Pakistan, Nigeria and Brazil—have wildly different mindsets!

Leaders

Leaders can be born, elected, or trained and groomed; they can seize power or have leadership thrust upon them. Leadership can be autocratic or democratic, collective or individual, merit-based or ascribed, desired or imposed.

It is not surprising that business leaders (managers) often wield their power in conformity with the national setup. For instance, a confirmed democracy like Sweden produces low-key democratic managers; Arab managers are good Muslims; Chinese managers usually have government or party affiliations.

Leaders cannot readily be transferred from culture to culture. Japanese prime ministers would be largely ineffective in the United States; American politicians would fare badly in most Arab countries; mullahs would not be tolerated in Norway.

Cross-national transfers are becoming increasingly common with the globalization of business, so it becomes even more imperative that the composition of international teams, and particularly the choice of their leaders, be carefully considered. Autocratic French managers have to tread warily in consensus-minded Japan and Sweden. Courteous Asian leaders have to adopt a more vigorous style in argumentative Holland and theatrical Spain if they wish to hold the stage. German managers sent to Australia are somewhat alarmed at the irreverence of their staff and their apparent lack of respect for authority.

Changing Notions of Leadership

In the twenty-first century, with multinationals and conglomerates expanding their global reach, corporate governance and international teams will learn a lot about leading multicultural enterprises and workforces. The new impetus provided by fresh managers from Asia, Russia, Poland, Hungary, East European states, Latin America and Africa will change notions of leadership as will the increasing number of women in management positions.

At cross-century, two of the world's most respected leaders—Nelson Mandela and Kofi Annan—were African. The ultimate numerical superiority of non-white leaders, already significant in the political world, will permeate business. Based on Singapore's commercial success and development within a given time frame, Lee Kuan Yew stakes a reasonable claim to have been the most successful "manager" of the last three decades of the twentieth century. His tenets were largely those enshrined in Asian precepts. This does not mean that Confucian rules are equally applicable everywhere. Lee concocted his own individual version of leadership style, not unaffected by his Cambridge education. The diagrams in Figures 7.1, 7.2 and 7.3 show some special and widely varying leadership styles.

Cultural Roots of Organization and Leadership

The development of concepts of leadership is a historical phenomenon, closely connected with the organizational structure of society. Each society breeds the type of leader it wants, and expects him or her to keep to the path their age-old cultural habits have chosen.

The behavior of the members of any cultural group is dependent, almost entirely, on the history of the people in that society. It is often said that we fail to learn the lessons of history—and indeed we have seen mistakes repeated over hundreds of years by successive generations—but in the very long run (and we may be talking in millennia) a people will adhere collectively to the set of norms, reactions and activities which their experience and development have shown to be most beneficial for them. Their history may have consisted of good and bad years (or centuries), migrations, invasions, conquests, religious disputes or crusades, tempests, floods, droughts, subzero temperatures, disease and pestilence. They may have experienced brutality, oppression or near-genocide. Yet, if they survive, their culture, to some extent, has proven successful.

Besides being a creation of historical influence and climatic environment, the mentality of a culture—the inner workings and genius of the mindset—are also dictated by the nature and characteristics of the language of the group. The restricted liberties of thought that any particular tongue allows will have a pervasive influence on considerations of vision, charisma, emotion, poetic feeling, discipline and hierarchy.

Historical experience, geographic and geolinguistic position, physiology and appearance, language, instinct for survival—all combine to produce a core of beliefs and values that will sustain and satisfy the aspirations and needs of a given society. Based on these influences and beliefs, societal cultural conditioning of the members of the group is consolidated and continued, for as many generations as the revered values continue to assure survival and success. Infants and youth are trained by their parents, teachers, peers and elders. The characteristics of the group gradually emerge and diverge from those of other groups. Basic needs for food, shelter and escaping from predators are dealt with first. Social, economic and military challenges will ensue. Traumatic historical developments may also have an impact. For example, Japan's samurai traditions, discredited in 1945–46, gave way to growing enthusiasm for success in industry and commerce.

At all events, in victory or defeat, in prosperity or recession, a society needs to organize, adapt and reorganize according to external pressures and its own objectives. Cultural groups organize themselves in strikingly different ways and think about such matters as authority, power, cooperation, aims, results and satisfaction in a variety of manners. The term *organization* automatically implies leadership, people in authority who write the rules for the system. There are many historical examples of leadership having been vested in the person of one man or woman—Alexander the Great, Tamerlane, Louis XIV, Napoleon, Queen Elizabeth I, Joan of Arc are clear examples. Others, equally renowned and powerful but less despotic (Washington, Bismarck, Churchill), ruled and acted with the acquiescence of their fellow statesmen. Parliamentary rule,

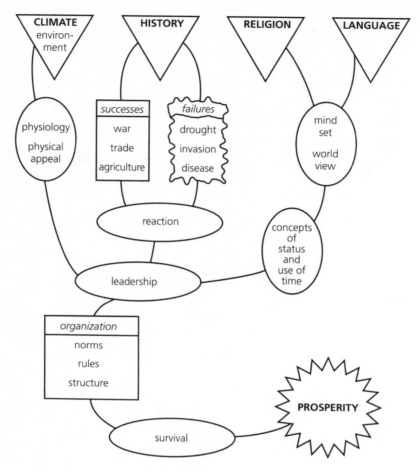

Figure 7.1 Factors Leading to the Organization of Society

introduced by the British in the early part of the seventeenth century, initiated a new type of collective leadership at government level, although this had existed at regional, local and tribal levels for many centuries. Minoan collective rule—one of the earliest examples we know about—inspired a similar type of leadership both in the Greek city–states and later in Rome. In another hemisphere, Mayan and North American Indians held similar traditions.

In the business world, a series of individuals have also demonstrated outstanding abilities and success in leadership—Ford, Rockefeller, Agnelli, Berlusconi, Barnevik, Gyllenhammer, Iacocca, Geneen, Matsushita and Morita are some of them. It is now common for leadership and authority also to be vested in boards of directors or management committees.

The way in which a cultural group goes about structuring its commercial and industrial enterprises or other types of organizations usually reflects to a considerable degree the manner in which it itself is organized. The two basic questions to be answered are these: (a) How is authority organized? and (b) What is authority based on? Western and Eastern answers to these questions vary enormously, but in the West alone there are striking differences in attitude.

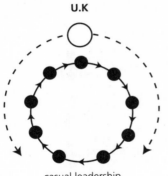

U.K

casual leadership

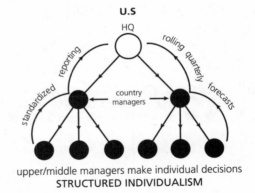

U.S

upper/middle managers make individual decisions
STRUCTURED INDIVIDUALISM

FRANCE

autocratic

SWEDEN

primus inter pares

GERMANY

hierarchy, consensus

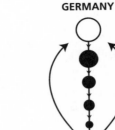

ASIA

consensus rule

LATIN/ARAB

nepotism

INDONESIA

military
Chinese

using know-how

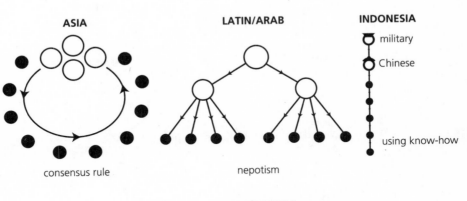

NETHERLANDS

meritocratic

Figure 7.2 Leadership Styles

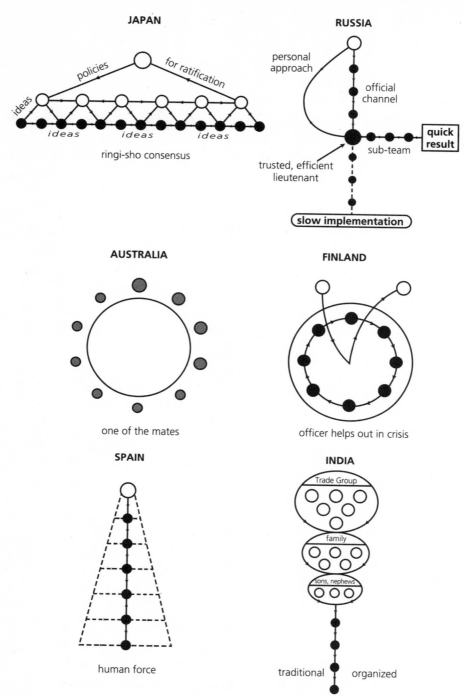

JAPAN

policies   for ratification

ideas

ideas   ideas   ideas

ringi-sho consensus

RUSSIA

personal
approach

official
channel

trusted, efficient
lieutenant

sub-team

**quick
result**

(slow implementation)

AUSTRALIA

one of the mates

FINLAND

officer helps out in crisis

SPAIN

human force

INDIA

Trade Group

family

sons, nephews

traditional   organized

There is, for instance, precious little similarity in the organizational patterns of French and Swedish companies, while Germans and Australians have almost diametrically opposing views as to the basis of authority. Organizations are usually created by leaders, whether the leadership is despotic, individual or collective. Leadership functions in two modes—*networking* and *task orientation*. In networking mode, the concerns, in order of appearance, are the status of the leader(s), the chain of command, the management style, the motivation of the employees, and the language of management used to achieve this. In task-orientation mode, the leadership must tackle issues, formulate strategies, create some form of work ethic and decide on efficiency, task distribution and use of time.

Managers in linear-active cultures will generally demonstrate a task orientation. They look for technical competence, place facts before sentiment, logic before emotion; they will be deal oriented, focusing their own attention and that of their staff on immediate achievements and results. They are orderly, stick to agendas and inspire staff with their careful planning.

Multi-active managers are much more extroverted, rely on their eloquence and ability to persuade and use human force as an inspirational factor. They often complete human transactions emotionally, assigning the time this may take—developing the contact to the limit. Such managers are usually more oriented to networking.

Leaders in reactive cultures are equally people oriented but dominate with knowledge, patience and quiet control. They display modesty and courtesy, despite their accepted seniority. They excel in creating a harmonious atmosphere for teamwork. Subtle body language obviates the need for an abundance of words. They know their companies well (having spent years going around the various departments); this gives them balance, the ability to react to a web of pressures. They are also paternalistic.

Because of the diverse values and core beliefs of different societies, concepts of leadership and organization are inevitably culture-bound. Authority might be based on achievement, wealth, education, charisma or birthright (ascription). Corporations may be structured in a vertical, horizontal or matrix fashion and may be molded according to religious, philosophical or governmental considerations and requirements. No two cultures view the essence of authority, hierarchy or optimum structure in an identical light.

Different Concepts of Status, Leadership and Organization

Germany

Germans believe in a world governed by *Ordnung*, where everything and everyone has a place in a grand design calculated to produce maximum efficiency. It is difficult for the impulsive Spaniard, the improvising Portuguese or the soulful Russian to conceive of German Ordnung in all its tidiness and symmetry. It is essentially a German concept which goes further in its theoretical perfection than even the pragmatic and orderly intent of Americans, British, Dutch and Scandinavians.

Just as they believe in simple, scientific truth, Germans believe that true *Ordnung* is achievable, provided that sufficient rules, regulations and procedures are firmly in place. In the business world, established, well-tried procedures have emerged from the long experience of Germany's older companies and conglomerates, guided by the maturity of tested senior executives. In Germany, more than anywhere else, there is no substitute for *experience.* Senior employees pass on their knowledge to people immediately below them. There is a clear chain of command in each department and information and instructions are passed down from the top. The status of managers is based partly on achievement, but this is seen as interwoven with the length of service and ascribed wisdom of the individual, as well as formal qualifications and depth of education.

German management is, however, not exclusively autocratic. While the vertical structure in each department is clear, considerable value is placed on consensus. German striving for perfection of systems carries with it the implication that the manager who vigorously applies and monitors these processes is showing faith in a framework which has proved successful for all. Although few junior employees would question the rules, there is adequate protection in German law for dissenting staff. Most Germans feel comfortable in a rather tight framework which would irritate Americans and British. Germans welcome close instruction: they know where they stand and what they are expected to do. They enjoy being told twice, or three or four times.

German managers, issuing orders, can motivate by showing solidarity with their staff in following procedures. They work long hours, obey the rules themselves and, although they generally expect immediate obedience, they insist on fair play.

In task orientation, Germany's use of time resembles the American: meetings begin on the dot, appointments are strictly observed, late arrivals must be phoned in prior to the appointed arrival time. A strong work ethic is taken for granted, and although staff working hours are not overlong and holidays are frequent, the German obsession with completing action chains means that projects are usually completed within the assigned period. Each department is responsible for its own tasks and there is far less horizontal communication between equals across the divisions of a German company than there is in U.S. and British firms. Secrecy is respected in Germany both in business and private. Few German companies publish their figures for public consumption or even for the benefit of their own employees.

Latins and some Anglo-Saxons frequently experience some difficulty in working or dealing with Germans on account of the relatively rigid framework of procedures within which many German companies operate.

Cooperating successfully with Germans means respecting their primary values. First, status must be established according to **their** standards. Efficiency and results will win the day in due course, but a foreign national must have adequate formal qualifications to make an initial impression. Punctuality and orderliness are basic; get there first and avoid sloppiness or untidiness in appearance, behavior and thought. Procedures should always be written down, for Germans read them, and so should you. Any instructions you issue should be firm and unambiguous. If you want something written in black ink, not blue, then you should make this clear. Germans want content, detail and clarity—they hate misunderstandings.

Strive for consensus at all times. Consensus is obtained by clarification and justification, not by persuasion or truly open discussion. Consensus creates solidarity, which makes everyone feel comfortable. Each participant in the discussion makes a contribution, but does not query a superior too energetically and certainly does not question his or her judgment.

Hierarchical constraints necessitate your knowing the exact pecking order in the ladder of command, including *your* own rung. German directness enables you to point out when something is being done in an incorrect manner or when mistakes are being made, as long as the criticism is clearly constructive or designed to help. If you are too subtle in your criticism, it may not register at all.

Subordinates with difficulties should be supervised, helped, advised, instructed, monitored. If no help is asked for or required, tasks should not be interrupted. Quiet single-mindedness is admired in Germany, so don't try to do six things at once, and don't leave anything unfinished. If you are working hard, *show* it; a casual approach will be misunderstood.

Finally, communication is vertical, not horizontal. Don't go *across* the company to chat with people at your level in other departments. Most of your business ideas should be communicated to either your immediate superior or immediate subordinate. You do *not* have the ear of the chairman, however benignly he may smile at you—unless you are vice chairman.

France

French management style is more autocratic than the German, although this is not always evident at first glance. In France the boss often seems to have a roving style, using *tu* to subordinates and often patting them on the back. Such behavior is, however, quite deceptive.

The French chief executive's status is attributed according to family, age, education and professional qualifications, with the emphasis on oratorical ability and mastery of the French language. Preferably the executive was "finished" at the *École normale supérieure,* an elitist establishment way ahead in prestige of any French university. French managers have less specialization than U.S. or British managers, but they generally have wider horizons and an impressive grasp of the many issues facing their company. They can handle production, organizational procedures, meetings, marketing, personnel matters and accounting systems as the occasion requires.

French history has spawned great leaders who have often enjoyed (frequently with little justification) the confidence of the nation. Napoleon and Pétain are remembered for their heroics rather than for their disasters; Louis XIV, Joan of Arc, Charles de Gaulle, and André Malraux were charismatic figures who excited the French penchant for *panache* and smashed the mediocrity and mundanity that surrounded them. Ultimate success in French culture is less important than the collective soaring of the national pulse—the thrill of the chase or crusade. French failures are always glorious ones (check with Napoleon Bonaparte).

While mistakes by German executives are not easily forgiven and American managers are summarily fired if they lose money, there is a high tolerance in French companies for management blunders. As management is highly personalized, it falls on the manager to make many decisions on a daily basis, and it is expected that a good proportion of them will be incorrect. The humanistic leanings of French and other Latin-based cultures encourage the view that human error must be anticipated and allowed for. Managers assume responsibility for their decisions, but it is unlikely that they will be expected to resign if these backfire. If they are of the right age and experience and possess impeccable professional qualifications, replacing them would not only be futile, it would point a dagger at the heart of the system. For the French, attainment of immediate objectives is secondary to the ascribed reputation of the organization and its sociopolitical goals. The highly organic nature of a French enterprise implies interdependence, mutual tolerance and teamwork among its members as well as demonstrated faith in the (carefully) appointed leader. French managers, who relish the art of commanding, are encouraged to excel in their work by the high expectations on the part of their subordinates.

Such expectation produces a paternalistic attitude among French managers (not unlike that demonstrated by Japanese, Malaysian and other Asian executives), and they will concern themselves with the personal and private problems of their staff.

In addition to their commercial role in the company, French managers see themselves as valued leaders in society, indeed, as contributing to the well-being of the state itself. Among the largest economies of the world, only Japan exercises more governmental control over business than the French. Modern French companies such as Aérospatiale, Dassault, Elf Aquitaine, Michelin, Renault and Peugeot are seen as symbols of French grandeur and are "looked after" by the state. A similar situation exists in Japan and to some extent Sweden.

The prestige and exalted position enjoyed by the French manager is not without its drawbacks, both for the enterprise and for the national economy. By concentrating authority around the chief executive, opinions of experienced middle managers and technical staff (often close to customers and markets) do not always carry the weight that they would in Anglo-Saxon or Scandinavian companies. It is true that French managers debate issues at length with their staff, often examining all aspects in great detail. The decision, however, is usually made alone and not always on the basis of the evidence. If the chief executive's views are known in advance, it is not easy to reverse them. Furthermore, senior managers are less interested in the bottom line than in the perpetuation of their power and influence in the company and in society. Again, their contacts and relationships at the highest levels may transcend the implications of any particular transaction.

Britain

The feudal and imperial origins of status and leadership in England are still evident in some aspects of British management. A century has passed since Britain occupied a preeminent position in industry and commerce, but there still lingers in the national consciousness the proud recollection of once having ruled 15 million square miles of territory on 5 continents.

The class system persists in the U.K., and status is still derived, in some degree, from pedigree, title and family name. There is little doubt that the system is on its way to becoming a meritocracy—the emergence of a very large middle class and the efforts of the Left and Centrist politicians will eventually align British egalitarianism with that of Northern Europe.

British managers could be described as diplomatic, tactful, laid back, casual, reasonable, helpful, willing to compromise and seeking to be fair. They also consider themselves to be inventive and, on occasion, lateral thinkers. They see themselves as conducting business with grace, style, humor, wit, eloquence and self-possession. They have the English fondness for debate and regard meetings as occasions to seek agreement rather than to issue instructions.

Under the veneer of casual refinement and sophistication in British management style there exists a hard streak of pragmatism and mercenary intent. When the occasion warrants it, British managers can be as resilient and ruthless as their tough American cousins, but less explicitly and with disarming poise. Subordinates appreciate their willingness to debate with them and the tendency to compromise, but they also anticipate a certain amount of deviousness and dissimulation. Codes of behavior within a British company equip staff to absorb and cope with a rather obscure management style.

Other problems arise when British senior executives deal with European, American and Eastern businesspeople. In spite of their penchant for friendliness, hospitality and desire to be fair, British managers' adherence to tradition endows them with an insular obstinacy resulting in a failure to comprehend differing values in others.

Although British delegates at international meetings frequently distinguish themselves by their poise, charm and eloquence, they often leave the scene having learned little or nothing from their more successful trading partners. As such conferences are usually held in English, they easily win the war of words; this unfortunately increases their linguistic arrogance.

I once gave a series of cross-cultural seminars to executives of an English car company that had been taken over by a German auto industry giant. The Germans attending the seminars, although occasionally struggling with terminology, listened eagerly to the remarks about British psychology and cultural habits. The British participants, with one or two notable exceptions, paid only casual attention to the description of German characteristics, took hardly any notes, were unduly flippant about Germany's role in Europe and thought the population and the gross domestic product (GDP) of the two countries were roughly equal. Only one of the British spoke German and that at a very modest level.

As far as task orientation is concerned, British managers perform better. They are not sticklers for punctuality, but time wasting is not endemic in British companies, and staff take pride in completing tasks thoroughly, although in their own time frame. British managers like to leave work at 5:00 or 6:00 P.M., as do their subordinates, but work is often taken home.

As for strategies, managers generally achieve a balance between short- and long-term planning. Interim failures are not unduly frowned on and there are few pressures to make a quick buck. Teamwork is encouraged and often achieved, although it is understood that individual competition may be fierce. It is not unusual for managers to have "direct lines" to staff members, especially those whom they favor or consider intelligent and progressive. Chains of command are observed less than in German and French companies. The organization subscribes in general to the Protestant work ethic, but this must be observed against a background of smooth, unhurried functions and traditional self-confidence.

The contrast with the immediacy and driving force of American management is quite striking when one considers the commonality of language and heritage as well as the Anglo-Celtic roots of U.S. business.

United States

The Puritan work ethic and the right to dissent dominated the mentality of the early American settlers. It was an Anglo-Saxon-Celtic, Northern European culture, but the very nature and hugeness of the land, along with the advent of independence, soon led to the "frontier spirit."

The vast lands of America were an entrepreneur's dream. Unlimited expanses of wilderness were seen as unlimited wealth which could be exploited, if one moved quickly enough. Only Siberia has offered a similar challenge in modern times.

The nature of the challenge soon produced American values: speed was of the essence; you acted individually and in your own interest; the wilderness forced you to be self-reliant, tough, risk taking; you did not easily cede what you had claimed and owned; you needed to be aggressive against foreign neighbors; anyone with talent and initiative could get ahead; if you suffered a setback, it was not ultimate failure, there was always more land or opportunity; bonds broken with the past meant that future orientation was all important; you were optimistic about change, for the past had brought little reward; throwing off the yoke of the King of England led to a distrust of supreme authority.

American managers symbolize the vitality and audacity of the land of free enterprise. In most cases they retain the frontier spirit that has characterized the U.S. mindset since the end of the eighteenth century: they are assertive, aggressive, goal and action oriented, confident, vigorous, optimistic and ready for change. They are achievers who are used to hard work, instant mobility and decision making. They are capable of teamwork and corporate spirit, but they value individual freedom above the welfare of the company, and their first interest is furthering their own career.

In view of their rebellious beginnings, Americans are reluctant to accord social status to anyone for reasons other than visible achievement. In a land with no traditions of (indeed aversion to) aristocracy, money was seen as the yardstick of progress, and very few Americans distance themselves from the pursuit of wealth. Intellectuality and refinement as qualities of leadership are prized less in the United States than in Europe. Leadership means getting things done, improving one's standard of living by making money for oneself, finding short-cuts to prosperity and making a profit for one's firm and its shareholders.

With status accorded almost exclusively on grounds of achievement and wealth, age and seniority assume less importance. American managers are often young, female or both. Chief executives are given responsibility and authority and then expected to act; they seldom fail to do so. How long they retain power depends on the results they achieve.

Motivation of American managers and their staff does not have the labyrinthine connotations that it does in European and Asian companies, for it is usually monetary. Bonuses, performance payments, profit-sharing schemes and stock options are common. New staff, however, are often motivated by the very challenge of getting ahead. Problem solving, the thrill of competition and the chance to demonstrate resolute action satisfy the aspirations of many young Americans. Unlike Europeans and Asians, however, they need constant feedback, encouragement and praise from the senior executive.

In terms of organization, the rampant individualism in American society is rigidly controlled in business life through strict procedures. American executives are allowed to make individual decisions, especially when traveling abroad, but usually within the framework of corporate restrictions. Young Americans' need for continual appraisal means that they are constantly supervised. In German companies staff are regularly monitored, but German seniors do not "hover." In the United States senior executives pop in and out of offices, sharing information and inspiration with their subordinates: "Say, Jack, I've just had a terrific idea." Memos, directives, suggestions in writing are ubiquitous. Shareholder pressure makes quarterly reporting and rolling forecasts imperative. The focus is on the bottom line.

American managers can be quickly hired and just as rapidly fired (often without compensation). Being sacked often carries less stigma than elsewhere: "It just didn't work out, we have to let you go." For the talented, other jobs and companies beckon. There is precious little sentimentality in American business. The deal comes before personal feeling. If the figures are right, you can deal with the Devil. If there is no profit, a transaction with a friend is hardly worthwhile. Business is based on punctuality, solid figures, proven techniques, pragmatic reasoning and technical competence. Time is money, and Americans show impatience during meetings if Europeans get bogged down in details or when Asians demur in showing their hand.

Europeans, by contrast, are often miffed by American informality and what they consider to be an overly simplistic approach toward exclusively material goals. Eastern cultures are wary of the litigious nature of American business (two-thirds of the lawyers on earth are American), a formidable deterrent for members of those societies who settle disputes out of court and believe in long-term harmony with their business partners.

Sweden

The Swedish concept of leadership and management differs considerably from other European models and is dealt with in some detail in Chapter 43. Like Swedish society itself, enterprises are essentially "democratic," although a large percentage of Swedish capital is in private hands. Managers of thousands of middle-sized and even large firms have attained managerial success through subtle self-effacement, but the big multinationals have also thrown up some famous executives who might well claim to be among the most far-seeing business leaders in the world: Carstedt, Gyllenhammar, Wennergren, Barnevik, Carlzon, Wallenberg, and Svedberg.

Modern Swedish egalitarianism has age-old cultural roots. Although some historical Swedish monarchs such as Gustav av Vasa and Charles the Great were dominating, compelling figures, the Swedish royals, like those of Denmark and Norway, have espoused democratic principles for many centuries, no doubt mindful of the old Viking *lagom* tradition, when warriors passed round the drinking horn (or huge bowl) in a circle and each man had to decide what amount to drink. Not too little to arouse scorn; not too much to deprive others of the liquid.

Latins

The business cultures of Italy, Spain and Portugal are described in later chapters. In Latin Europe, as well as in South America, the management pattern generally follows that of France, where authority is centered around the chief executive. In middle-sized companies, the CEO is very often the owner of the enterprise and even in very large firms a family name or connections may dominate the structure. More than in France, sons, nephews, cousins and close family friends will figure prominently in key positions. Ubiquitous nepotism means that business partners are often confronted with younger people who seem to have considerable influence on decision making. Delegations may often consist of the company owner, flanked by his brother, son, cousin or even grandson. Women are generally, although not always, excluded from negotiating sessions.

Status is based on age, reputation and often wealth. The management style is autocratic, particularly in Portugal, Spain and South America, where family money is often on the line. There is a growing meritocracy in Brazil, Chile and in the big Northern Italian industrial firms, but Latin employees in general indicate willing and trusting subservience to their "establishments."

Task orientation is dictated from above; strategies and success depend largely on social and ministerial connections and mutually beneficial cooperation between dominant families. Knowing the right people oils the wheels of commerce in Latin countries, just as it does in Arab and Asian cultures. It helps anywhere, but assumes greater importance in those societies that prioritize nurturing human relationships over pragmatic, rapid implementation of transactions based on mere notions of opportunity, technical feasibility and profit.

Netherlands

Leadership in the Netherlands is based on merit, competence and achievement. Managers are vigorous and decisive, but consensus is mandatory, as there are many key players in the decision-making process. Long "Dutch debates" lead to action, taken at the top, but with constant reference to the "ranks." Ideas from low levels are allowed to filter freely upward in the hierarchy.

Indonesia

In colonial times, leadership came from the Dutch. Under Sukarno and Suharto leadership was exercised principally by the military and was therefore autocratic. The indifferent nature of many Indonesians to the business process has, however, resulted in a lot of business management being entrusted to a resident Chinese professional class, which has the commercial know-how and international connections. Overseas Chinese shareholding in many Indonesian companies encourages this situation.

Japan

Japanese top executives have great power in conformity with Confucian hierarchy, but actually have little involvement in the everyday affairs of the company. On appropriate occasions they initiate policies that are conveyed to middle managers and rank and file. Ideas often originate on the factory floor or with other lower-level sources. Signatures are collected among workers and middle managers as suggestions, ideas and inventions make their way up the company hierarchy. Many people are involved. Top executives take the final step in ratifying items that have won sufficient approval.

Russia

The leadership concept is undergoing profound changes in Russia following the demise of the Soviet Communist state. Efforts made by managers to promote business through official channels only are likely to founder on the rocks of bureaucracy and Russian apathy. Using key people and personal alliances, the "system" is often bypassed and a result achieved.

Finland

Finnish leaders, like many British leaders, exercise control from a position just outside and above the ring of middle managers, who are allowed to make day-to-day decisions. Finnish top executives have the reputation of being decisive at crunch time and do not hesitate to stand shoulder to shoulder with staff and help out in crises.

Australia

Australian managers, like Swedes, must sit in the ring with the "mates." From this position, once it is accepted that they will not pull rank, they actually exert much more influence than their Swedish counterparts, as the semi-Americanized nature of Australian business requires quick thinking and rapid decision making.

Spain

Spanish leaders, like French, are autocratic and charismatic. Unlike the French, they work less from logic than from intuition, and pride themselves on their personal influence on all their staff members. Possessed often of great human force, they are able to persuade and inspire at all levels. Nepotism is also common in many companies. Declamatory in style, Spanish managers often see their decisions as irreversible.

India

Nepotism is also rife in traditional Indian companies. Family members hold key positions and work in close unison. Policy is also dictated by the trade group, e.g. fruit merchants, jewelers, etc. These groups work in concert, often develop close personal relations (through intermarriage, etc.) and come to each other's support in difficult times.

Japan and The East

Cultural values dominate the structure, organization and behavior of Eastern enterprises more than in the West, because deeply rooted religious and philosophical beliefs impose near-irresistible codes of conduct.

In the Chinese sphere of influence—People's Republic of China, Hong Kong, Taiwan, Singapore—as well as in Japan and Korea, Confucian principles hold sway. (Thailand is Buddhist; Indonesia and Malaysia, strongly Muslim.) Although national differences account for variations in the concepts of status, leadership and organization, there is a clearly discernible "Eastern model" that is compatible with general Asian values. The Confucian model, whether applied to corporations, departments of civil service or government, strongly resembles family structure.

Confucianism, which took final shape in China in the twelfth century, designated family as the prototype of all social organization. We are members of a group, not individuals. Stability of society is based on unequal relationships between people, as in a family. The hierarchies are father–son, older brother–younger brother, male–female, ruler–subject, senior friend–junior friend. In the past, loyalty to the ruler, filial piety to one's father and right living would lead to a harmonious social order based on strict ethical rules and headed up in a unified state, governed by men of education and superior ethical wisdom. Virtuous behavior, protection of the weak, moderation, calmness and thrift were also prescribed.

Confucianism entered Japan with the first great wave of Chinese influence between the sixth and ninth centuries A.D. For some time it was overshadowed by Buddhism, but the emergence of the centralized Tokugawa system in the seventeenth century made it more relevant than it had been before. Both Japan and Korea had become thoroughly Confucian by the early nineteenth century in spite of their feudal political systems. In the twentieth century the Japanese wholeheartedly accepted modern science, universalistic principles of ethics, as well as democratic ideals, but they are still permeated, as are the Koreans, with Confucian ethical values. While focusing on progress and growth, strong Confucian traits still lurk beneath the surface, such as the belief in the moral basis of government, the emphasis on interpersonal relationships and loyalties, the faith in education and hard work. Few Japanese and Koreans consider themselves Confucianists today, but in a sense almost all of them are.

Confucianism in Leadership. What do these cultural influences mean in terms of status and leadership today? Japanese and Korean business leaders today flaunt qualifications, university and professorial connections more than family name or wealth. Many of the traditional Japanese companies are classic models of Confucian theory, where paternalistic attitudes to employees and their dependants, top-down obligations, bottom-up loyalty, obedience and blind faith are observed to a greater degree than in China itself. Prosperity makes it easier to put Confucianism into practice: in this regard Japan has enjoyed certain advantages over other countries. The sacred nature of the group and the benevolence attributed to its leaders, however, permeate Asian concepts of organization from Rangoon to Tokyo.

Japanese top executives today, although they have great power in conformity with Confucian hierarchy, actually have little involvement in the everyday affairs of the company. On appropriate occasions they initiate policies which are conveyed to middle managers and the rank and file. Ideas often originate on the factory floor or with other lower-level sources. Signatures are collected among workers and middle managers as suggestions, ideas and inventions make their way up the company hierarchy. Top executives take the final step in ratifying items that have won sufficient approval.

Buddhist and Islamic Variations. In Buddhist Thailand and Islamic Malaysia and Indonesia, slight variations in the concept of leadership do little to challenge the idea of benign authority. Thais see a strict hierarchy with the King at its apex, but there is social mobility in Thailand, where several monarchs had humble origins. The patronage system requires complete obedience, but flexibility is assured by the Thai principle that leaders must be sensitive to the problems of their subordinates and that blame must always be passed upward. Bosses treat their inferiors in an informal manner and give them time off when domestic pressures weigh heavily. Subordinates like the hierarchy. Buddhism decrees that the man at the top earned his place by meritorious performance in a previous life.

In Malaysia and Indonesia status is *inherited,* not earned, but leaders are expected to be paternal, religious, sincere and above all gentle. The Malay seeks a definite role in the hierarchy, and neither Malaysians nor Indonesians strive for self-betterment. Promotion must be initiated from above; better conformity and obedience than struggling for change. Age and seniority will bring progress.

Life in a Group. Although Confucianism, Buddhism and Islam differ greatly in many respects, their adherents see eye-to-eye in terms of the family nature of the group, the noncompetitive according of status, the smooth dispersal of power, the automatic chain of command and the collective nature of decision making. There are variations on this theme, such as the preponderance of influence among certain families in Korea, governmental intervention in China, the tight rein on the media in Singapore and fierce competition and individualism among the entrepreneurs of Hong Kong. Typical Asians, however, acknowledge that they live in a high-context culture within a vital circle of associations from which withdrawal would be unthinkable. Their behavior, both social and professional, is contextualized at all times, whether in the fulfillment of obligations and duties to the group (families, community, company, school friends) or taking refuge in its support and solidarity. They do not see this as a trade-off of autonomy for security, but rather as a fundamental, correct way of living and interacting in a highly developed social context.

In a hierarchical, family-type company, managers guide subordinates and work longer hours as a shining example. As far as task orientation is concerned, immediate objectives are not as clearly expressed as they would be in, for example, an American company. Long-term considerations take priority and the slow development of personal relationships, both internally and with customers, often blur real aims and intent. Asian staff seem to understand perfectly the long-term objectives without having to have them spelled out explicitly. In Japan, particularly, staff seem to benefit from a form of corporate telepathy—a consequence of the homogeneous nature of the people.

What Is Work?

The work ethic is taken for granted in Japan, Korea and China, but this is not the case throughout Asia. Malaysians and Indonesians see work as only one of many activities that contribute to the progress and welfare of the group. Time spent (during working hours) at lunch, on the beach or playing sports may be beneficial in deepening relationships between colleagues or clients. Time may be needed to draw on the advice of a valued mentor or to see to some pressing family matter that was distracting an employee from properly perform-ing their duties. Gossip in the office is a form of networking and interaction. Work and play are mixed both in and out of the office in Thailand, where either activity must be fun or it is not worth pursuing. Thais, like Russians, tend to work in fits and starts, depending partly on the proximity of authority and partly on their mood. Koreans, all hustle and bustle when compared to the methodic Japanese, like to be seen to be busy all day long and of all Asians most resemble the Americans in their competitive vigor.

Asian management attaches tremendous importance to form, symbolism and gesture. The showing of respect, in speech and actions, to those higher in the hierarchy is mandatory. There must be no loss of face, either for oneself or one's opponent, and as far as business partners are concerned, red carpet treatment, including lavish entertaining and gift giv-ing, is imperative. Ultimate victory in business deals is the objective, but one must have the patience to achieve this in the right time frame and in the correct manner. This attitude is more deeply rooted among the Chinese and Japanese than in Korea, where wheeling and dealing is frequently indulged in.

Looking Ahead

Is the Asian "family model" efficient? The economic success of Japan and the rates of growth in China, Korea, Malaysia and Taiwan, among others, would indicate that it is. Whatever the reality may be, it will not be easy for Westerners to convert to Asiatic systems. Individualism, democratic ideals, material goals, compulsive consumerism, penchant for speed, environmental concerns and a growing obsession with the quality of life (a strange concept in Asia) are powerful, irreversible factors to be reckoned with in North America and Northern Europe. The globalization process and the increasing determination of the multinational and transnational giants to standardize procedures will result in some convergence between East and West in terms of goals, concepts and organizational structure, but divergence in values and world view will sustain organizational diversity well into the twenty-first century.

8

Team Building and Horizons

Team Building

What kinds of new challenges do twenty-first century international teams face? Previously, executives who worked surrounded by their own nationals were secure in a cocoon of established norms and rules that led to decisions based on (their) common sense and best precedents. The head office—perhaps their base—had a comforting permanence about it. Now team members are rapidly assembled in a variety of locations and must learn to make quick decisions in an organizational setting that may feel unfamiliar or uncomfortable. Change, often chaos, is in the air, and the twenty-first century executive must manage it. This century will be characterized by ferocious competition, often emanating from Asia or, indeed, from other emerging areas. Western and Japanese companies will have to face and adapt to this challenge and acquire some of the strategies that are needed for this new type of flexible, savvy team. Versatility will be the name of the game, moving and improving faster than competitors, and this very versatility also has to be managed. What is for sure is that no single business model will win the day or ensure survival. Quick thinking, shifting strategies, taking risks, using intuition, collecting information, scrapping plans and starting afresh, innovating constantly—these are some of the ingredients needed—and none of them is particularly easy for companies and organizations used to sealing success through traditional procedures or established reputation.

Innovation and Change

While the agility of an international team will be a prerequisite for its survival, not all team members will be equally disposed toward change and innovation. Arabs, especially Saudi Arabians, are more interested in the status quo. The Russians fear change; historically it has always been bad news for them. Conservatives everywhere, by definition, object to change. Germans in general are very attached to tried, established and successful processes. Thais believe there is no real change—we just came around in a circle. In Western Europe, Swiss, Norwegians, Portuguese and Sicilians are less amenable to change than, for instance, Czechs, Swedes, Spaniards and Milanese.

Americans are the drivers of change and innovative technology, closely followed by Finns, Canadians, Australians and, in theory, the British. In Britain you can change anything except the Church of England, the Monarchy, Wimbledon, Ascot, cricket, rugby, warm beer and five o'clock tea.

Because of the wide-ranging internationalism and economic strength of the Big Five—the United States, Britain, France, Japan and Germany—most international teams have at least a fair number of linear-active members. Linear-actives in principle favor change and innovation. Multi-actives and Asian reactives subscribe to change, too, but see it in a different light. Linear-actives emphasize practicality and necessity. Multi-actives find change exciting. Reactives stress prudence.

Replies to questionnaires on change and innovation during seminars I conducted in 2012 elicited the comments in the following table.

The international team, functioning comfortably or not, is likely to be the central operating mode for a global enterprise. Companies must also address the question of how to balance centralized strategy at the head office with local expertise regarding markets and customers. Directives from the head office will be counterbalanced by information and strategies flowing back from global outposts. The inflow is likely to turn the tide against the outflow as effective globalized units begin to bite. International teams will have to buzz around fast; their fingers must be on many pulses.

In this context, the cultural diversity of the team (including a mix of linear-active, multi-active and reactive members) emerges as the most likely successful formula. The international team is small, agile, hopefully versatile and multifaceted. These qualities will offer varied solutions for a plethora of suddenly arising problems and dilemmas. Italian charisma, American drive, overseas Chinese experience and wisdom, French logic, Nordic common sense, Japanese intuition and German thoroughness will combine to address a complex situation. A well-known experiment in Atlanta in the 1990s concluded that international teams were better than national ones at solving complex problems, while national teams did well on routine tasks. International business in the twenty-first century will rarely just be routine. Globalization and huge organizations such as NAFTA and the EU will cause business to increase in complexity, not to mention the huge change in context that will soon take place when China flexes its huge commercial and manufacturing muscles. Later, India will have tremendous impact, especially as the world's largest market (along with China) to sell to.

Before we go further with international teams and team building, we need to go back to the basics of world view—what I prefer to call *horizons*.

Linear-Active	Multi-Active	Reactive
Change is constantly necessary	Change is imaginative and exciting	Change should be gradual
We must innovate to survive	Innovation should be aesthetic	Imitation and improvement are safer than innovation
Decisions should be future-oriented	Decisions should be bold and original	Decisions should be based on best past precedents

(continued)

(continued from previous page)

Linear-Active	Multi-Active	Reactive
Change stimulates growth and improvement	Change stimulates people	If it ain't broke, don't fix it
Plan in detail, then change	Change charismatically, then plan details	Plan change slowly, in harmony with others
Change is top-down	Change after key lateral clearances	Change if all agree
Change should be profit-oriented	Change involves the social reputation of the company	Change should be employment-oriented
Innovation comes from individuals	Innovation is discovered in lengthy discussion	There is little new under the sun
Make innovation a goal	Innovate elegantly	Introduce innovations only when necessary
Democratic brainstorming is an excellent way to foster creativity	Brainstorming is great, but it must be restrained in the presence of superiors	It is better to think in silence than aloud
Customers should be asked about their changing priorities	Customers should be advised what their changing priorities are	One should try to anticipate what customers' changing priorities are and try to prepare for them
Show support for others' new ideas but voice any reservations about them immediately	Imply you agree to others' suggestions for innovations but modify or drop them later	Approve of others' new ideas even if you fully disagree
One learns best by querying the wisdom of past actions and debating the future	One learns best by discussing actions/decisions from every possible angle	One learns best by just listening to more experienced mentors
Concentrate on worst-case scenarios	Concentrate on best-case scenarios	Don't have scenarios—discuss all options until the best one becomes evident
Innovation comes largely from eccentrics and deviants from the company or national norm	Innovation comes from brilliance born of first-class education and training	Innovation is born of the aggregate of collective thought and effort
Any change is better than no change	Change usually benefits top dogs	Change is often dangerous

Life within Horizons

Our genes, our parental and educational training, our societal rules, our very language, enable us to see only so far—as far as our horizon. We can broaden our horizon to some degree by living in other countries; learning foreign languages; and reading books on philosophy, psychology, other cultures and a variety of other subjects. Unless we make such efforts, our horizon remains a South African horizon, a Colombian horizon, an Egyptian horizon or one of many other world views. In other words, each cultural group enjoys a certain segment of experience, which is no more than a fraction of the total possible available experience. Benjamin Whorf believed that such segments of experience were limited by the vocabulary and concepts inherent in one's language. By learning more languages, especially those with excitingly different concepts, we can widen our vision and gain deeper insight into the nature of reality. Many graduates in Romance studies feel enriched by being able to see the world through Spanish eyes or using French rationality. Scholars of Chinese or Japanese often develop two personalities when immersing themselves in one of these two languages.

We can widen our horizons not only by learning foreign tongues but also by cultivating empathy with the views of others; standing in their shoes in their geographical, historical and philosophical location; seeing ourselves from that perspective. But for the moment, let's assume that we live within our own limited horizons. Figures 8.1 and 8.2 show how Americans and the French look at the world from different standpoints, see some things in a similar light (science, profit, consumerism) while other concepts are visible only to one nationality. A third area, containing a variety of beliefs and philosophies, lies outside the ken of either Americans or the French.

Figure 8.3 shows how two nationalities speaking different languages miss out on several linguistically based concepts. Figure 8.4 illustrates how two countries' cultures (the U.K. and the U.S.) united by the same language have developed different horizons, where concepts such as subtlety and understatement are invisible to many Americans, and tough talk, clichés or a certain variety of hype are meaningless to most English. In the case of Brits and Yanks, however, the overlapping areas of common experience still dominate thinking. This is far from being the case with the Australians and Japanese, or even neighbors like Poles and Germans.

The Education Factor

We live in an era of improved education and training, but educational systems vary considerably from country to country, both as to content and objectives. The French all-around senior manager, carefully groomed in wide-ranging skills in the *hautes écoles,* views the vocationally trained manager from a German *Volkswirtschaftshochschule* as a highly competent technician. Practical Japanese engineers wonder why their French and Arab counterparts evince no inclination to change tires or fix malfunctioning TV sets. The German *Diplom-Kaufmann*

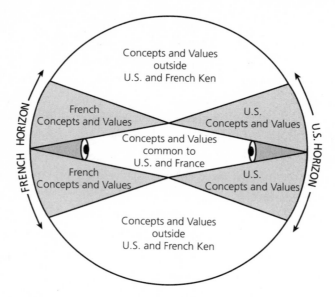

Figure 8.1 French and U.S. Horizons: General Concepts

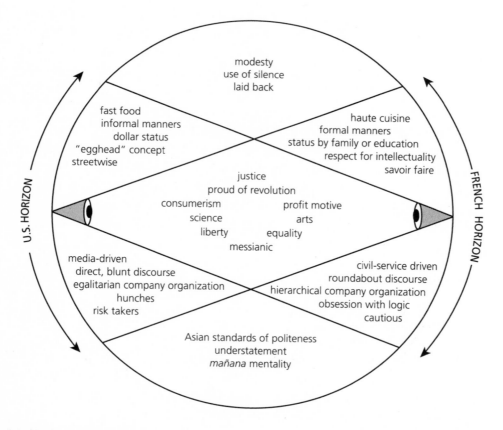

Figure 8.2 Horizons: French and U.S.

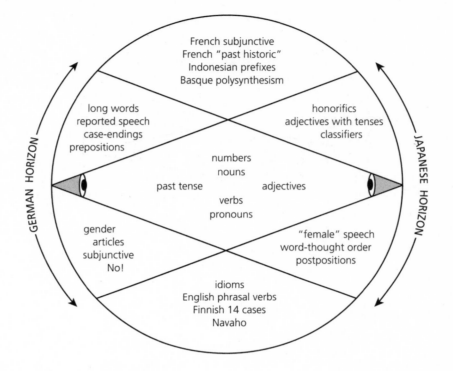

Figure 8.3 Horizons: Japanese and German

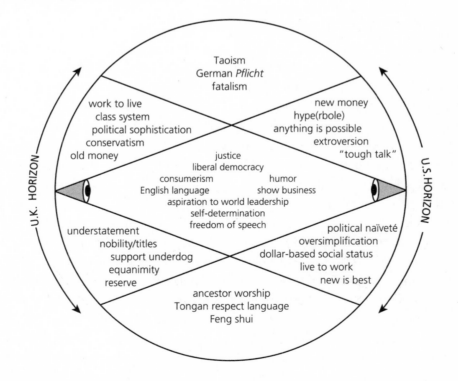

Figure 8.4 Horizons: British and American

may wonder why his British opposite number seems to have no official qualifications in commerce. Action-oriented American managers, many of whom climbed from the bottom rung of the corporate ladder to the very top through sheer ability, energy and aggressive ambition, may set no store by diplomas of any kind. These vastly different culturally based concepts certainly play a role in how members of the international team view each other's qualifications and the degree of respect that they have for each other.

Even if all the members of a team have had a "good" university education, there is no guarantee that this will facilitate international understanding. While universities have revolutionized their teaching of science, mathematics, engineering and medicine over the past two or three decades, there has been little change in the social sciences; only those graduates in foreign languages, literature, philosophy or history are in some ways equipped to interact in a more meaningful way with foreign nationals, and few of these graduates end up in international business.

Language and Culture

How can we set about achieving a relatively harmonious and integrated international team? To begin with, we must face the fact that to understand what makes foreign colleagues tick, there is no substitute for learning their language, reading books produced by the culture and familiarizing ourselves with the country's history, particularly if we plan to live and work within the country's borders. This means a sizeable investment, not so much in financial terms as in time. Assuming you come from an English-speaking country, in order for you to achieve modest fluency in a European language, 250 to 500 hours of direct teaching will be required, preferably over a three-month period. This should include an intensive course of two to three weeks of full-time (minimum forty hours) immersion. Japanese, Chinese, Arabic and Russian (to name four other major languages) will require almost double the time. By contrast, you can do a reasonable study of the country's basic history, geography, politics and economy along with the main cultural traits within two or three weeks, and simultaneously with the language training. Add to this a knowledge of the country's business behavior, and you should be ready for whatever will be thrown at you in the new country.

Companies that discount the importance of such training do so at their peril. A malfunctioning joint venture with a foreign partner can result in a catastrophic financial loss. One large, traditional British company (turnover of several billion pounds per year) branched out into three European countries five years ago without giving sufficient attention to language and culture learning. The initial investment was around £10 million. Probably language and cultural training as outlined above for 20 key executives would have cost in the region of £200,000. In 1994, in one European branch alone, the British company incurred losses of £100 million. Yet the subsidiary in question was showing a profit at the time of its acquisition!

What had happened? The British parent, vastly successful in the U.K., had moved quickly to grow the size and scope of the branch operation, applying strategies and policies that had proven successful for many years in the U.K. Most of the new products and the general monolithic approach found little favor in the local culture. The problems were magnified by the local managers, who offered polite, guarded criticism and advice. The British, although reasonable, bulldozed onward in the firm belief that their company name, impressive home record and lengthy experience would carry the day. The locals, in retaliation for the snub they perceived from the clueless British executives, clammed up. The much-heralded synergy was lost.

Horizons, Common Ground and Divergence

Now that we've discussed national horizons and how they overlap with the world views of other nationalities, we're ready to put the two together. There are areas of agreement between any two nationalities. Latins are generally considered difficult partners for the British, yet Britons can find common ground with the French, Spaniards and Italians, although that ground differs in each case. As an example, let's say you are from the United Kingdom and a member of an international team that includes French, Spanish and Italian members. What is your common ground with each of the three nationalities? Where are the areas of divergence?

Just as it is valuable to focus on common ground, divergences of approach merit no less attention. The descriptions of countries and regions in Part Three will go a long way toward helping you identify both the common ground you share and the divergent characteristics.

One's first step toward adaptation must at the very least be to avoid irritants. An Italian, however well-disposed toward a Brit, finds little subtlety of humor in being reminded that the best-known Italian product is spaghetti. The English may weary of incessant French ramblings at meetings, but they risk hostility if they attempt to quash it as irrelevant. Spaniards, touchy about personal style, do not take kindly to British references to their lack of concern for punctuality or their overt body language. Japanese and most Asians should be treated with as much respect and deference as Anglo-Saxons can muster: a good performance will in any case only slightly mitigate their opinion of us as somewhat unsophisticated types. Latins

U.K./France	U.K./Spain	U.K./Italy
sense of superiority	love of theater, plots	flexible
messianic	support underdog	reasonable
long term	vague, "muddle through"	exports to survive
conservative	humorous	diplomatic, tactful
interest in arts and science	distrustful of the French	love of art
ex-imperialistic	dignified	sociable, good at small talk
linguistic arrogance	individualists	use of first names
	poor linguists	compromisers
	out of European mainstream	

and Germans alike take liberties in judging Brits as slow-moving, old-fashioned amateurs with no linguistic skills, while Americans are often categorized as dollar-mad salespeople lacking a sense of tasteful dress, tact, finesse and any values other than material.

Common sense, self-awareness and a modicum of unhurried thought are all useful resources for avoiding behavior that might prove irritable to our partners. If we accept that certain traits are not going to disappear (American drive, German seriousness, French sense of superiority, Japanese opacity, Spanish tardiness, Italian deviousness, Norwegian obstinacy, Swiss secrecy, Russian sentiment, Arab passion), we may come to the realization that these very differing traits can make a positive contribution to our team effort. For example, American enthusiasm harnessed by thorough German planning and supervision can be very effective. Spaniards are slow starters, but they can be good finishers, often displaying stamina and verve in the hours leading up to midnight. Italians are generally good at making deals, when others may be entrenched or even deadlocked. They are valuable, too, in working with other Latins.

Managers in experienced multinationals like IBM, Unilever and ABB are skilled at choosing the right person for each environment. Unilever recently needed a manager to supervise their marketing operations in South America. A Brazilian or an Argentinean might have been resented in some of the smaller countries and certainly in each other's. They chose an Indian executive and provided him with quality language and cross-cultural training. Not only did his nationality place him above interregional rivalry, but his keen perception and his Indian characteristics of people orientation, subtle negotiating skills and warmth made him someone Latin Americans could easily relate to.

National Strengths, Insights and Blind Spots

There is another important factor to be considered in choosing international teams, apart from the desirability of wider horizons gained through diverse views. That is the question of competence. Though an individual's ability depends in the last analysis on his or her personal talents, education and experience, members of international teams often display strengths that derive to some extent from the rock-solid characteristics of their national culture. The following table indicates some natural strengths of certain cultural groups.

INTERNATIONAL TEAMS—STRENGTHS	
French	Logical, visionary, imaginative ideas, intelligent leadership, used to develop a conceptual and all-embracing approach to a project
Italians	Visionary, human relations, provide social glue for team, good at settling disputes, especially between other Latins; flexibility, reasonableness, never neglects peripheral business, works all hours

Germans	Technical details, forward planning, general competence, keep to schedules, spot difficulties, try to avoid future problems
Americans	Action-oriented, get things going, simplify, focus on return on investment, think big, take risks, willing to invest, entrepreneurial, to the point, good at planning sales and marketing, monitor budget, energetic and enthusiastic
Brits	Calm and phlegmatic, like to arbitrate, inventive, reasonable, avoid offense, diplomatic, think long-term, good at administration, like chairperson's role, fair
Spaniards	Human force, warmth, vision, focus on ideals, good at persuading, often settle disputes through mediation, loyal team members when feeling appreciated, work long hours
Belgians	Compromisers, practical, make things work, avoid dogmatic approach, use gradualist approach to problems
Dutch	Always busy, work quickly, sense business opportunities, spot weaknesses, good organizers, hate wasting time, international in outlook, democratic, persist in finding solutions, hate to lose business
Swedes	Logical and practical; strong on processes, rules and laws; compromisers in deadlock, maintain politeness in rough situations, strong on technical planning, always consult others
Finns	Calm, unflappable, inventive, reliable, good with facts and figures, good at planning and implementation, listen well and modify stance, use scientific truth, cut through hypocrisy and wasting time, summarize well

Besides unique and specific insight strengths, team members may also have cultural insights and blind spots—or weaknesses—that can lead to creative breakthrough in the first instance or misunderstanding or ignorance of colleagues' motives in the second. Some examples of both follow.

Nationality	Insights	Blind Spots
Finns	✦ common sense ✦ accuracy	✦ small talk ✦ why Latins say one thing and do another
Germans	✦ order ✦ processes ✦ details	✦ subtle humor
Americans	✦ drive ✦ bottom-line focus ✦ optimism	✦ insensitivity to non-American values

(continued)

(continued from previous page)

Nationality	Insights	Blind Spots
Japanese	✦ courtesy ✦ patience	✦ individual decision making ✦ Western humor
French	✦ logic ✦ rhetoric	✦ seek to win the argument rather than discover the truth
Italians	✦ communicative skills	✦ agendas ✦ punctuality
Spaniards	✦ idealism ✦ imagination ✦ human warmth	✦ shaky planning ✦ impatience with details
Brits	✦ diplomacy ✦ reasonableness	✦ foreign languages ✦ "up-to-dateness"
Swedes	✦ collective skills ✦ planning	✦ slow decision makers ✦ complacency
Chinese	✦ negotiating skills ✦ patience ✦ courtesy	✦ lack of international exposure ✦ sense of urgency ✦ Western humor
Overseas Chinese	✦ experienced ✦ risk takers ✦ bottom-line focus ✦ organized	✦ almost none
Indians	✦ skilled negotiators ✦ communicative ✦ warmth	✦ strict planning
Koreans	✦ energetic ✦ hard-working ✦ good planners	✦ distorted world view due to excessive nationalism
Latin Americans	✦ imaginative ✦ risk takers	✦ *mañana* ✦ cooperation ✦ accuracy
Arabs	✦ sincerity ✦ morality	✦ unity ✦ teamwork

(continued)

Nationality	Insights	Blind Spots
Africans	✦ warmth ✦ colorful ✦ humor	✦ organizational skills
Russians	✦ warmth ✦ directness	✦ sustained effort ✦ trust
Malaysians	✦ moral ✦ educated ✦ culturally sensitive	✦ ambition ✦ drive
Thais	✦ easy-going ✦ cooperative	✦ ambition ✦ dislike responsibility
Vietnamese	✦ educated ✦ hard-working ✦ persistent	✦ modern management techniques
Filipinos	✦ democratic ✦ friendly ✦ neat	✦ punctuality ✦ accountability
Eastern Europeans	✦ culturally aware	✦ structure of business in a democracy

Advantages of Diverse Teams

Versatility in Problem Solving

- ✦ Generate more alternatives
- ✦ Respond better to cultural preferences in local markets
- ✦ Better local forecasting
- ✦ Better critical analysis

Creativity

- ✦ Broader perspectives, less emphasis on conformity
- ✦ Better product design

Diversity in General

- ✦ Not only "black" and "white" but also "both-and"
- ✦ Not only "one-way" assumptions

- ✦ Asians, Africans and women have different cognitive styles
- ✦ Bilinguals have higher level of divergent thinking
- ✦ More charisma, stimulation and real dialogue
- ✦ Better tolerance with ambiguity and chaos
- ✦ Diverse talent compensates for inability to attract top local talent
- ✦ Sound moral basis
- ✦ Demographic trends indicate that in the second half of the twenty-first century, most of the workforce will be non-Western, non-white, non-male

Team-Building Exercises

There is a wide variety of team-building exercises, and multinational corporations have tried all of them. At business schools, budding MBAs work together on hundreds of case studies. Promising managers and key staff from different countries are assembled to go camping, climb mountains, raft down rivers and cross deserts together. A basic principle of most team-building exercises is that all members shall face some kind of difficulty together and help each other out according to individual ability and with the resources that are at hand. The environmental constraints of a tent, raft, yacht or classroom necessitate working closely together and avoiding needless friction.

When the teams are international, interesting things occur. Individuals strive to put their personal skills at the service of the team—sometimes practical, sometimes inspirational, sometimes intuitive. Leaders emerge: different people take charge of provisioning, planning, directions and destination planning, financing, logistics, social affairs, even cooking. A language of communication evolves, as do problem-solving routines. Even in an immersion language course, this spirit of cooperation emerges. Latins recognize long literary or scientific words in English easily, but have difficulty with pronunciation; Dutch and Scandinavians pronounce beautifully, but are short on Latin-based vocabulary. Swedes help Finns with unfamiliar prepositions. Germans struggle with English word order. Everyone learns from everyone else.

Back to cultural cooperation: working with someone from another nation and culture at close quarters for a protracted period of time enables you not only to observe unfamiliar patterns of behavior but to perceive some of the reasoning behind them. You also have the opportunity to explain your own actions and thinking (perhaps eccentric for others) as you go along. The talkative Italian, possibly irritating at first, may prove to be the social adhesive holding the group together. The disconcertingly withdrawn, opaque Japanese, sitting quietly in the corner, may later remind the group of things they have forgotten. The hustling American gets everyone to the restaurant on time, the superior Frenchman gets you the right wine, the fussy German has a minibus and umbrellas waiting for you in the rain.

9

Motivating People
and Building Trust

Motivation is closely linked to leadership and management—the ability of leaders to get people to do what they want done while at the same time making them feel that it is a good idea, or even their own idea. It is a skill daily exercised by managers dealing with their own nationals, with differing degrees of success. In theory, motivating people who generally head toward the same goals and objectives and who entertain the same hopes, ideas and aspirations, in a familiar, national context, should be achievable through reasonably sensitive management. Companies post "corporate values" and "mission statements" to this end. Talented managers occasionally secure complete allegiance from their staff by individual brilliance or charisma. But no one would disagree that motivating staff, particularly at different levels, can prove difficult.

Gaining the allegiance of people who do *not* share the same values, customs, habits, aspirations, preferences, rules and laws will, naturally, be even more difficult. Yet the mergers and acquisitions, the joint ventures and the globalization of business in the twenty-first century are ushering in an era of kaleidoscopic international contact between corporate staff, managers and workers on a hitherto unimaginable scale. The necessity of directing and managing other nationals will oblige head offices to familiarize themselves with motivation factors around the globe.

There is no international formula for motivation. It is essentially a national phenomenon; it can vary enormously between close neighbors, for instance, Americans and Canadians, French and Germans and Swedes and Finns.

The international manager who is unaware of or chooses to ignore the manner in which certain cultures are motivated does so at his or her peril. Failure to motivate foreign staff or management will result in discontent, resistance, frustration, possible alienation and deadlock. Multicultural managers will do best by standing in the shoes of their colleagues and partners and trying to understand how they were motivated in the past. Then they should consider current and future national and cultural aspirations in the twenty-first century.

Up to the advent of parliamentary democracy, coercion was a major factor in getting people to do things. Absolute rulers, slavery, feudalism, totalitarianism, conscription and industrial exploitation held sway over the centuries. Yet group motivation and inspiration were not entirely absent. The enlightened era of the Greek city–states devalued coercion.

Kings and queens often commanded blind allegiance from their subjects down through the centuries, from Boadicea and Henry V to Peter the Great and Queen Victoria. Japanese samurai, in their allegiance to their lord, were faithful unto death and demonstrated that quality regularly, as indeed did the cavalry and foot soldiers of Napoleon Bonaparte. Great leaders captivated willing disciples through sheer charisma—Alexander the Great, Caesar, Tamerlane, Hernan Cortés, Simón Bolívar, Kemal Atatürk, Mahatma Gandhi, Winston Churchill, Chou-en-Lai and Nelson Mandela are a few who come to mind.

In the modern era, business leaders have occasionally shown the charismatic and visionary leadership that attracts loyal followers; examples are Henry Ford, Akio Morita, Konosuke Matsushita and Richard Branson. Religion has also played a major role in mass-motivation throughout the historical era.

Twenty-First Century Aspirations

If you consider the main cultural categories I introduced in Chapter 3—linear-active, multi-active and reactive—you can discern differences in the motivational patterns of cultural groups in each category, both in terms of traditional features and developing aspirations as a new century of opportunity gets under way.

Linear-active people were traditionally motivated by achievement rather than words (*do* what you have said you are going to do). In the twentieth century, climbing as high as possible in one's chosen career was important, as was money or other forms of remuneration. The general alignment of Protestant values and linear-active behavior meant that work equated with success which equated with prosperity. These, taken together, were usually sufficient motivation.

In this century the concept of globalization itself constitutes a motivational factor. For many linear-actives, *globalization* means globalization of business that leans strongly toward the imposition of Western management styles on joint ventures, mergers and acquired companies. Linear individuals are motivated by access to high-level technology, generous funding for research, increased opportunities for individual flair and entrepreneurialism through the Internet and direct business-to-business contacts free of stifling bureaucratic controls. They also like the idea of lower taxes, less government and/or more honesty in politics.

Multi-active people were traditionally motivated by words more than deeds—by emotion, compassion, expression of human understanding. Their idea of globalization in the twentieth century was a more "civilized" one, where there was a compromise between materialistic goals and the recognition of softer human values. In this century globalization should usher in an era of market opportunities that are available also to those who are poor and underprivileged. Multi-actives gain inspiration from people or circumstances that are conducive to boosting their self-confidence. Nurture and security are important for this cultural category.

Reactive people were traditionally motivated by the reassuring comfort of collective goals and action, common loyalty to respectable organizations, discovery of enduring trust and unswerving diligence in preserving integrity and face for family, friends and colleagues.

Reactives have a third view of globalization, that in which the huge Asian markets of the future (India, China, Indonesia) will benefit from strategic East–West alliances, especially in high-tech fields. Motivational factors in Asia, particularly, are increased leisure time and opportunities for foreign travel and international contact (things denied to Japanese, Chinese and other East Asians in the nineteenth and twentieth centuries). Young people, especially, hunger for more education and training and long to taste Western lifestyles and participate in trend-setting in fashion, food, films and so on. These twenty-first century motivations, however, are not going to replace traditional motivators to any great degree in the twenty-first century.

Product versus Relationship

One of the outstanding shortcomings of linear-active businesspeople (particularly Americans, Germans, Scandinavians and British) is their failure to understand the relative importance of two salient factors involved in business deals. The linear-active assumes almost automatically that an excellent product sells itself, that it paves the way for a successful relationship. Similarly, a sound idea or policy, backed by incontestable facts and figures, must inevitably be accepted. Neither supposition is true. While other linear-actives may agree, other cultures have different priorities. In Italy, Japan or Saudi Arabia, the personal relationship paves the way for the product (or blocks its purchase). Arabs, Asians and Latins buy from people they like, not necessarily from those who offer the best product at the best price.

Similarly, a business project or agenda will follow a smooth course if its viability has been discussed at length during a process of warm socializing and personal contact.

Motivation, of customers or one's own staff, has to take place in the context of personal relationships. Once Latins and Asians know you and trust you, they will be motivated to buy from you, tell you if something is amiss, protect you from losing face, look after your interests, help you in need, and make allowances for your different cultural view. If they work for you, they will do so loyally, do quality work, contribute overtime hours without extra pay and wait for you to suggest promotion or better remuneration without pushing for it. Such are the positive human qualities of (motivated) Latins and Asians.

On the other hand, if they are not properly motivated by their trust in you, there is a risk that they will be disloyal, hide things from you, invent excuses, lack incentive and originality, and spread boredom or unrest among other employees.

For decades to come, in spite of the convergence and micro-level adaptation of major cultures facilitated by electronic proximity and global trading, the motivation of employees, partners and collaborators will remain largely a nation-specific phenomenon. To this end, I have added—new in this edition—motivation charts to almost all of the countries and regions in Part Three.

Building Trust

One of the most convincing ways of motivating someone is to install strategies which lead to early trust, particularly among multi-active and reactive employees, managers, customers and prospective partners. When considering building trust in an international group, national traits must, of course, be kept in mind. To ensure a smooth-running team based on mutual trust, it is perhaps best to start with a set of basic trust-building strategies, the kinds that are outlined in numerous management manuals:

- ✦ Set clear, transparent aims and goals
- ✦ Prepare clear instructions
- ✦ Communicate them effectively
- ✦ Insist on an information-sharing policy
- ✦ Provide practical, user-friendly tools
- ✦ Set up time-efficient processes
- ✦ Recognize contributions
- ✦ Back up the "team"
- ✦ Act on the team's recommendations
- ✦ Work toward transparency

Few Westerners would argue with these principles—they appear to be transnational. They cease to be straightforward, however, when they form part of a matrix with intercultural factors. For instance, in some cultures managers and executives are much less willing to share information (especially vertically) than others. Effective communication is not the same in France as it is in Australia. The Japanese way of giving orders would not be seen as "clear instructions" by Americans and Germans. Transparency is much more common in linear-active cultures than among multi-active and reactive cultures. None of these factors constitute insurmountable barriers, but if they are not taken into account they can seriously impede understanding and trust in a multicultural team.

High-Trust and Low-Trust Societies

Let us examine the concept of trust *inside* a cultural group. Professor Francis Fukuyama divides societies into high-trust and low-trust categories. My own findings, which are close to his, are illustrated in the figures in the remainder of this chapter.

Members of high-trust societies normally have a ready trust for their compatriots. They are usually linear-active and assume that their fellow nationals "follow the rules"; in other words, trust a person until he or she proves untrustworthy. Members of low-trust cultural groups are initially suspicious of fellow nationals—they are often multi-actives or reactives who have a more flexible adherence to rules, regulations and laws. I asked a German

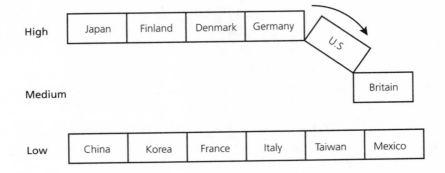

Figure 9.1 High- and Low-Trust Countries

executive how he would react to stumbling across a fellow German in a Tokyo bar. "We would have a friendly chat, of course," was his reply. When I asked an Italian friend for his reaction to spotting a fellow Italian, he quickly replied, "What is this Italian doing here?"

Several surveys have been carried out regarding trust in fellow nationals. Usually the Danes, Finns and fellow Nordics score highest, with the Germans and Japanese close behind. Britons are in the medium category. Americans, who once fit in the high-trust category, have a declining trust level due to perceived corruption in state and national government and in their financial institutions, particularly in corporate governance.

Low-trust cultural groups are exemplified by such countries as China, Mexico, France and the Latin and Arab countries. People in these groups trust completely only those they know best: family and one or two close, lifetime friends (see Figure 9.2).

Fukuyama makes much of the vast difference in how people's lives are structured between high- and low-trust societies. In countries such as China and Korea (low trust) where both the family and the state wield great influence, there is an "empty middle"—a kind of vacuum of social activity or extraneous influence (see Figure 9.3). The demands of both state and family take up much of the individual's time. He or she is not sure what to do with whatever spare time is left. In high or medium-trust societies such as Sweden, Germany, Britain, Canada and the United States, there is a superabundance of extra time because the demands on people's time outside of work are not nearly as great. A plethora of leisure, educational and volunteer organizations offer the individual rich social and personal opportunities, as represented in Figure 9.4. Such individuals enjoy experiences that serve as excellent training for international teamwork.

Whatever the preparation for participation in international interaction, the nature of the team member's trust will be strongly affected by the cultural category he or she belongs to. Figure 9.5 illustrates this trust variance.

Word–deed correlation is essential among linear-actives. If you always do what you have said you are going to do, on a consistent basis, you build trust by cementing your integrity. This has to be. Truth is recognized as scientific, based on facts and figures, almost tangible. No window-dressing, please. As official institutions in linear-active cultures are normally

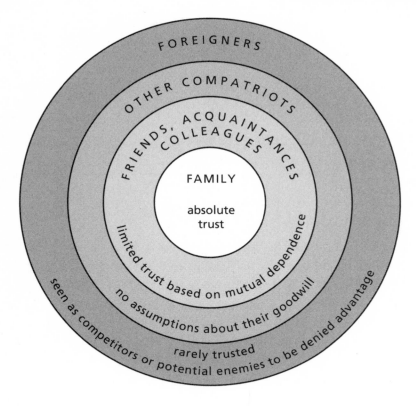

Figure 9.2 Low Trust

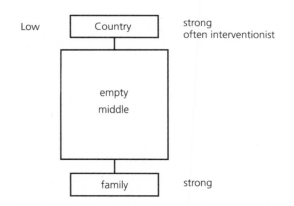

Figure 9.3 Structure of High- and Low-Trust Societies

efficient and relatively speedy, individuals place their trust in those institutions (banks, schools, the post office, etc.). Trust is fairly impersonal. In general, people do what they are paid to do.

This linear-active type of trust is a scarce commodity among multi-actives (Italians, Hispanics, Greeks, Turks, Slavs, among others). Their truth is more flexible (creative), their wheels of bureaucracy turn more slowly, their faith in institutions is less firm. They prefer

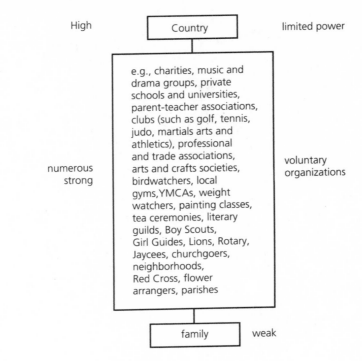

High   Country   limited power

e.g., charities, music and
drama groups, private
schools and universities,
parent-teacher associations,
clubs (such as golf, tennis,
judo, martials arts and
athletics), professional
numerous   and trade associations,   voluntary
strong   arts and crafts societies,   organizations
birdwatchers, local
gyms, YMCAs, weight
watchers, painting classes,
tea ceremonies, literary
guilds, Boy Scouts,
Girl Guides, Lions, Rotary,
Jaycees, churchgoers,
neighborhoods,
Red Cross, flower
arrangers, parishes

family   weak

Figure 9.4 Structure of High- and Low-Trust Societies (2)

to place their trust (strong indeed) in in-group intimates—family, former teachers, close friends. They trust people who show them compassion, accept closeness, protect their vulnerabilities and disobey regulations in keeping that trust if it is necessary. Such trust is even firmer than the linear-active's trust in official bodies and laws.

In highly reactive cultures such as Japan, China and Korea, trust is gained through respectful behavior, protecting the other's face, reciprocating favors and exhibiting predictable courtesies. Westerners can score points and earn trust through mirroring this behavior. Compassion and closeness are not required; flattery and reference to shared experience or common friends are. The Japanese particularly place great trust in their schoolmates and former schoolmates who graduated from their university. Trust is also given to former teachers and tutors.

Trust in Virtual Teams

International teams meeting once a month or six, seven times a year usually develop an easy familiarity with each other and look forward to their get-togethers at different venues. The social aspects of the meetings contribute greatly to the bonding of the team. Face-to-face meetings are especially important for multi-active and reactive members, for whom personal relationships and genial socializing have great significance. While Germans, Finns

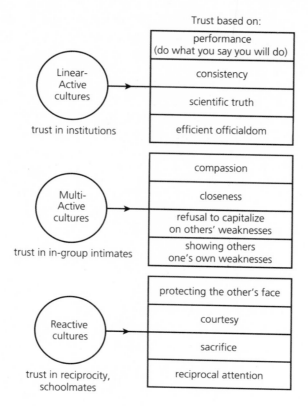

Trust based on:

Linear-Active cultures
- performance (do what you say you will do)
- consistency
- scientific truth
- efficient officialdom

trust in institutions

Multi-Active cultures
- compassion
- closeness
- refusal to capitalize on others' weaknesses
- showing others one's own weaknesses

trust in in-group intimates

Reactive cultures
- protecting the other's face
- courtesy
- sacrifice
- reciprocal attention

trust in reciprocity, schoolmates

Figure 9.5 Trust Variance in Different Cultural Categories

and Swedes shine in the "nitty-gritty" let's-get-down-to-work areas, Latins contribute most effectively in a committee atmosphere enhanced by close social contact. For reactive Asians, too, the feeling of togetherness is reassuring and brings out their best qualities.

In a virtual team that meets rarely, or not at all, face-to-face interaction is not there for reassurance, and mistrust can slip into the cracks between the less-precise long-distance communication.

Distance, as they say, breeds distance, and this is particularly true for reactive and multi-active nationalities. Nordics function fairly well at a distance in a cool, common-sense way. Americans generally accept that electronic proximity is with us to stay and are experts at impersonalizing communication. For Hispanics, Italians, Portuguese, Chinese and Japanese, the lack of face-to-face interaction is a far more serious matter. Asian customers, in general, want to be visited, visited, visited. They want—and take—time to evaluate and absorb what and whom they see. Tactile Hispanics need the warming handshake, embrace or arm around the shoulder. The French want to display their oratorical skills (difficult by e-mail). Italians wish to convince you through persuasive tones and expressive use of eyes, hands, arms and shoulders.

One can ask the question, why use virtual teams at all? Surely big business can afford the plane fares and hotel bills. It is of course more a question of time and availability. Perhaps even more important is that a thoughtfully selected virtual team can call upon the very best brains in an organization or corporation without anyone needing to travel.

In any case, trust in a virtual team will be harder to create. Integrity and competence are less visible, and proficiency can be hard to verify at a distance. There is also the matter of first impressions. First impressions are complete and swift when accompanied by personal presence. First impressions nearly always endure; it would be a pity if an early misunderstanding occurred through a slip in a written or electronic message. At any rate, all of the general guidelines for working and communicating across cultures that have been presented so far in this book—and the specific suggestions in the country-specific section (Part Three)—become all the more critical to your success with a virtual team.

High- and low-context communication assumes great significance when people from different categories interact and therefore contributes to trust building—or the lack of such. Edward T. Hall is the originator of the concept of context in communication; his concise definition in *Understanding Cultural Differences* is quoted here in full:

> A high-context communication or message is one in which *most* of the information is already in the person, while very little is in the coded, explicit, transmitted part of the message. A low-context communication is just the opposite; that is, the mass of the information is vested in the explicit code.
>
> Twins who have grown up together can and do communicate more economically than two lawyers in a courtroom during a trial, a mathematician programming a computer, two politicians drafting legislation, two administrators writing a regulation (1990, 6).

In face-to-face meetings, low-context Germans and Nordics will require explicitness about how they are to proceed. High-context French, Indians and Japanese will leave a lot unsaid, paying their colleagues the compliment of assuming they know the situation. High-context people speak more, but they say less. Low-context people speak less, but every word counts. These different communication styles can be augmented in a variety of ways with body language, tone of voice and subtle timing when people are face-to-face. A virtual team, working at a distance, runs the risk of context confusion and with it, loss of trust. The low-context individuals on the team assume their high-context teammates are hiding information from them or are being purposefully vague. These same low-context Germans and Americans frequently exasperate the high-context French and Italians with their painstaking emphasis on instructions, explanation and clarification. Tell a Frenchman something twice and he is likely to reply, "*Je ne suis pas stupide.*"

There are no easy answers as to how to establish trust in a totally virtual team. Steady asynchronous messaging with fairly swift responses and regular contact will help. Low-context, linear-active team members normally focus on tasks; they get moving first and then build up trust. They must remember that high-context, multi-active teammates will first deal with the question of trust (i.e., relationship building) before getting down to the tasks. At the very least, backgrounds and pedigrees must be exchanged before a task can be started. For Latins and Asians, protocol is important, even electronically. It is said that Japanese bow on the phone. I don't see anything wrong in that.

10

Meetings of the Minds

Meetings can be interesting, boring, long, short, or unnecessary. Decisions, which are best made on the golf course, over dinner, in the sauna or in the corridor, rarely materialize at meetings called to make them. Protracted meetings are successful only if transportation, seating, room temperature, lunch, coffee breaks, dinner, theater outings, nightcaps and cable television facilities are properly organized.

There are more meetings than there used to be. Businesspeople can now go to a meeting in another continent and often leave for home the same day. Videoconferencing and Skype are already reducing business travel, but these, too, are types of meeting.

Beginnings

For the moment, however, consider how people conduct meetings, face-to-face, in different countries. Meetings are not begun in the same way as we move from culture to culture. Some are opened punctually, briskly and in a "businesslike" fashion. Others start with chitchat, and some meetings have difficulty getting going at all. Figure 10.1 gives some examples of different kinds of starts in a selection of countries.

Germans, Scandinavians and Americans like to get on with it. They see no point in delay. Americans are well known for their business breakfasts (a barbaric custom in Spanish eyes). In England, France, Italy and Spain it would be considered rude to broach serious issues immediately; it's much more civilized to ease into the subject after exchanging pleasantries for 10 minutes—or half an hour. The English, particularly, are almost shame-faced at indicating when one should start: "Well, Charlie, I suppose we ought to have a look at this bunch of paperwork." In Japan, where platitudes are mandatory, there is almost a fixed period that has to elapse before the senior person present says: "*Jitsu wa ne...*" ("The fact of the matter is..."), at which point everybody gets down to work.

Structuring a Meeting

Just as ways of beginning a meeting vary, so do methods of structuring them. Linear-active people are fond of strict agendas, for agendas have linear shape. Other, more imaginative minds (usually Latins) tend to wander, wishing to revisit or embellish, at will, points already

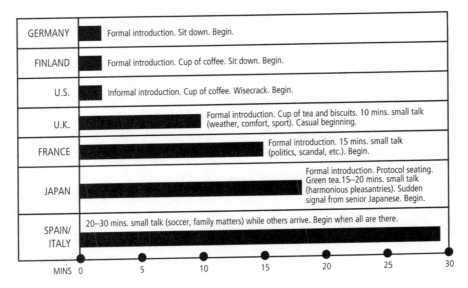

GERMANY	Formal introduction. Sit down. Begin.
FINLAND	Formal introduction. Cup of coffee. Sit down. Begin.
U.S.	Informal introduction. Cup of coffee. Wisecrack. Begin.
U.K.	Formal introduction. Cup of tea and biscuits. 10 mins. small talk (weather, comfort, sport). Casual beginning.
FRANCE	Formal introduction. 15 mins. small talk (politics, scandal, etc.). Begin.
JAPAN	Formal introduction. Protocol seating. Green tea.15–20 mins. small talk (harmonious pleasantries). Sudden signal from senior Japanese. Begin.
SPAIN/ITALY	20–30 mins. small talk (soccer, family matters) while others arrive. Begin when all are there.

MINS 0   5   10   15   20   25   30

Figure 10.1 Beginning a Meeting

discussed. Their agenda, if one can call it that, might be described as roundabout, or circuitous, which for Germans and Americans means no real agenda at all. Asians, especially Japanese, have another approach again, one that concentrates on harmonizing general principles prior to examining any details. At meetings where two or more cultural groups are involved, or at any meeting of an international team, the chairperson has the task of establishing a procedural and communicative style that will be acceptable to, even welcomed by, all the participants.

The purpose of a meeting depends on where one is coming from. Britons and Americans see a meeting as an opportunity to make decisions and get things done. The French see it as a forum where a briefing can be delivered to cover all aspects of a problem. They hunger for elegant processes. Germans, more concerned with precision and exactness, expect to gain compliance. Italians use meetings to evaluate support for their plans. The Japanese regard the first few sessions as occasions for establishing status and trust and finding out what possible sources of discord need to be eliminated from the outset. All of these objectives may be seen as worthy by everyone, but the priorities will vary. A skillful chairperson must be sensitive to these expectations and be quick to define a mutually shared aim.

My recent experience with a *oneworld* international team (British, American, Australian, Irish, Spanish, Chilean, Finnish and Chinese airlines alliance) indicated that skillful team leaders—in this case a Canadian, followed by a Finn—are able to blend procedural styles to mutual satisfaction among their colleagues. Contrasting requirements were addressed openly; certain wishes were analyzed and accommodated. The team leaders recognized that the linear-active, multi-active and reactive procedural styles each possessed unique strengths that could be combined to produce a successful *oneworld* style. Tolerance and a sense of humor on the part of the team leaders were also significant contributory factors.

Figures 10.2, 10.3 and 10.4 reflect the different preferences of the linear-active, multi-active and reactive team members.

Linear-active members need relatively little preamble or small talk before getting down to business. They like to introduce bullet points that can serve as an agenda. Tasks or issues are segmented, discussed and dealt with one after the other. Solutions reached are summarized in the minutes.

Multi-active members are not happy with the bullet-point approach, which they see as premature conclusions reached by their linear colleagues. They prefer to take points in random order (or in order of importance) and discuss them for hours before listing bullet points as *conclusions*. When they see topics listed at the beginning, they feel they have been manipulated.

Reactive people do not have the linear obsession with agendas, neither are they wooed by multi-active arguments. In Japanese eyes, for instance, things are not black and white, possible or impossible, right or wrong. They see arguments and ideas as points converging and ultimately merging. An emotional coming together is considered more important than an intellectual approach.

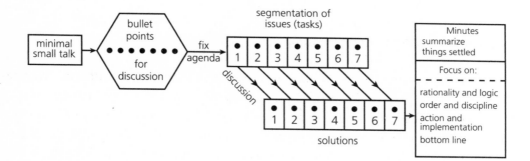

Figure 10.2 Structuring a Meeting—Linear-Active

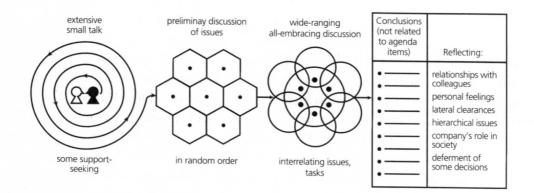

Figure 10.3 Structuring a Meeting—Multi-Active

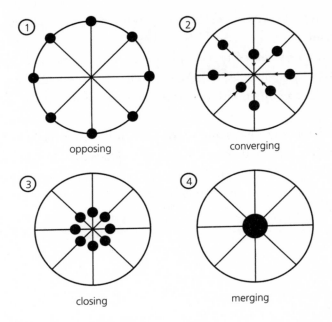

opposing

converging

closing

merging

Figure 10.4 Structuring a Meeting—Reactive

Meeting Behavior and Comportment

There are no universal rules for holding meetings. In addition to the different viewpoints regarding the structure of the proceedings, the nonverbal dimension and the physical comportment of participants is of utmost importance and varies to a great degree.

While verbal discussion might occupy 80–90 percent of the time devoted to a negotiation, psychologists tell us that the "message" conveyed by our actual words may be 20 percent or even less. Where, then, is the message?

The *venue* of the meeting itself may have positive or negative implications. Are we *home* or *away*? Are we seated comfortably? French negotiators, for example, are said to arrange lower seats for their opponents! *Hierarchy of seating* is also important. *Dress*, formal and informal, correct and inappropriate, can also give negotiators false impressions of the seriousness or casualness of the other side. The deliberate use of *silence* can be an invaluable advantage in negotiations, especially against Americans, who cannot stand more than a few seconds of silence. In Finland and Japan, for instance, silence is not uncomfortable but is an integral part of social interaction. In both countries what is *not* said is regarded as important. *Listening habits* can also play an important part in the negotiating process. Finns and Japanese again excel in their ability to listen closely for long periods of time.

Protocol is important in France, Germany, Japan and some other countries, whereas it is minimized in the Netherlands, Australia, Canada, the Nordic countries and in the United States.

Linear-actives enhance their rational, factual approach with a calm demeanor, little show of emotion or sentiment, and restricted body language. Reactives behave likewise; impassivity is a frequent description of their composure. Multi-actives, on the other hand—the French, Hispanics, Italians, Greeks, Southern Slavs, Arabs and Africans in particular—are often uninhibited in expressing their views with vigorous gesticulation and dramatic change of facial expression.

This striking variance in physical behavior, which results in linear-actives and reactives perceiving multi-active people as excitable, overly emotional and possibly unreliable and neurotic, can have such a profound effect on the process and outcome of meetings that it deserves some commentary and analysis here before we go on to the subject of negotiating and decision making.

Body Language

Body language, including facial expressions and loudness of voice or manner, gestures, degree of eye contact and so on, may play an enormous role in the success—or failure—of a meeting. Members of a Spanish delegation may argue fiercely with each other while opponents are present, causing the Japanese to think they are fighting. Asians are bemused when the same "quarreling Spaniards" pat each other like lifelong friends a few moments later. Smiles, while signifying good progress when on the faces of Britons, Scandinavians and Germans, might mean embarrassment or anger when adopted by Chinese and often appear insincere in the features of beaming Americans. Finns and Japanese often look doleful when perfectly happy, whereas gloom on an Arab face indicates true despondency. The frequent bowing of the Japanese is seen as ingratiating by Americans, while the hearty nose-blowing of Westerners in public is abhorred by the Japanese, who invariably leave the room to do this.

Anthropologists assume that speech developed to make body language more explicit, and that as the former became more sophisticated, gestures became less necessary. It is not that simple. In spite of the incredible sophistication, subtlety and flexibility of speech, it seems that some human groups still rely basically on body language to convey what they really mean, especially where intense feelings are concerned. Such people are the Italians, Greeks, South Americans and most other Latins, as well as many Africans and people from the Middle East. Others, such as Japanese, Chinese, Finns and Scandinavians, have virtually eliminated overt body language from their communication.

The Space Bubble

People from reactive and linear-active cultures are generally uncomfortable when their "space bubble" is invaded by excitable multi-actives. They regard the space within 1.2 meters of their body as inviolable territory for strangers, with a smaller bubble of 0.5 meters for close friends and relatives.

When a multi-active Mexican positions himself 0.5 meters away from an Englishman, he is ready to talk business. The Englishman sees him in English personal space and backs off to a more comfortable distance. In doing so, he relegates the Mexican to the South American "public zone" (1.2 meters) and the latter thinks the Englishman finds his physical presence distasteful or does not want to talk business. For a Mexican to talk business over a yawning chasm of 1.2 meters is like an English person shouting out confidential figures to someone at the other end of the room.

Different Types of Body Language

Finns and Japanese do not seem to have any body language. I say *do not seem* because in fact both cultural groups do use body language that is well understood by fellow nationals in each country. In both societies the control and disciplined management of emotions leads to the creation of a restrained type of body language that is so subtle that it goes unnoticed by the foreign eye. Because Finns and Japanese are accustomed to looking for minimal signs, the blatantly demonstrative body language of multi-active Italians, Arabs and South Americans is very disconcerting for them (cultural shock). It is as if someone used to listening to the subtle melodies of Chopin or Mozart were suddenly thrown into a modern disco. The danger is, of course, that overreaction sets in—a judgmental reaction to the multi-active's expressive body language. Japanese consider Americans and Germans as charging bulls; Finns see the French as too clever, Italians as overemotional and even Danes as a bit slick.

Because the body language of multi-actives can cause such shock to those not used to it, let's discuss it before going on.

Head. Eyes are among the more expressive parts of the body. In multi-active cultures, speakers will maintain close eye contact while they deliver their message. This is particularly noticeable in Spain, Greece and Arab countries. Such close eye contact (some linear-actives and reactives would call it staring) implies dominance and reinforces one's position and message. In Japan this is considered improper and rude. Japanese avoid eye contact 90 percent of the time, looking at a speaker's neck while listening and at their own feet or knees when they speak themselves.

In societies where hierarchy is important, it is easy to detect the "pecking order" by observing people's eye behavior. Lower-ranking staff often look at superiors, who ignore them unless they are in direct conversation with them. When anyone cracks a joke or says something controversial, all the subordinates' eyes will switch immediately to the chief personage to assess his or her reaction. This is less evident in northern countries where head and eye switching would be much more restrained.

French and Hispanic people indulge in the nose twitch, snort or sniff to express alertness, disapproval or disdain respectively. The Portuguese tug their earlobes to indicate tasty food, though this gesture has sexual connotations in Italy. In Spain the same action means someone is not paying for his drinks, and in Malta it signifies an informer. It is best to recognize these signs, but not embark on the risky venture of attempting to imitate them.

It is said that the mouth is one of the busiest parts of the human body, except in Finland where it is hardly used (except for eating and drinking). This is, of course, not strictly true, but most societies convey a variety of expressive moods by the way they cast their lips. Charles De Gaulle, Saddam Hussein and Marilyn Monroe made their mouths work overtime to reinforce their message or appeal. The tight-lipped Finn shrinks away from such communicative indulgences as the mouth shrug (French), the pout (Italian), the broad and trust-inviting smile (American) or even the fixed polite smile of the Asian. Kissing one's fingertips to indicate praise (Latin) or blowing at one's finger-tip (Saudi Arabian) to request silence are gestures alien to the Nordic and Asian cultures.

The Rest of the Body. Multi-active cultural groups, far more than others, also use all the rest of their bodies to express themselves. For example, they have very mobile shoulders, normally kept still in northern societies. The Gallic shoulder shrug is well known from our observations of Maurice Chevalier, Jean Gabin and Yves Montand. Latins keep their shoulders back and down when tranquil and observant but push them up and forward when alarmed, anxious or hostile.

Arms, which are used little by Nordics during conversation, are an indispensable element in one's communicative weaponry in Italy, Spain and South America. Frequent gesticulating with the arms is one of the features Northern Europeans find hardest to tolerate or imitate, being associated with insincerity, overdramatization and therefore unreliability. As far as touching is concerned, however, the arm is the most neutral of body zones; even the English will take guests by the elbow to guide them through doorways or indulge in the occasional arm pat to deserving subordinates or approaching friends.

The hands are among the most expressive parts of the body. Immanuel Kant called them "the visible parts of the brain." Italians watching Finnish hands may be forgiven for thinking that Finns have sluggish brains. It is undeniable that Northern peoples use their hands less expressively than Latins or Arabs, who recognize them as a brilliant piece of biological engineering. There are so many signals given by the use of the hands that we cannot even begin to name them all here. There are entire books written on hand gestures. I offer only a couple of examples here: "thumbs up," used in many cultures but so ubiquitous among Brazilians that they drive you mad with it; the hands clasped behind one's back to emphasize a superior standing (e.g., Prince Philip and various other royalty as well as company presidents); and the akimbo posture (hands on hips), which denotes rejection or defiance, especially in Mediterranean cultures.

As we move even further down the body, less evident but equally significant factors come into play. Even Northern Europeans participate in "leg language like everybody else. As no speech is required, it inflicts no strain on them." In general the "legs together" position signifies basically defensiveness against a background of formality, politeness or subordination. Most people sit with their legs together when applying for a job; it indicates correctness of attitude. This position is quite common for Anglo-Saxons at first meetings, but they usually change to "legs crossed" as discussions become more informal. The formal Germans and Japanese can go through several meetings maintaining the legs-together position. There are at least half a dozen different ways of crossing your legs; the most formal is the crossing of ankles only, the average is crossing the knees, and the most relaxed and informal is the "ankle-on-knee" cross so common in North America.

When it comes to walking, the English and Nordics walk in a fairly neutral manner, avoiding the Latin bounce, the American swagger and the German march. It is more of a brisk plod, especially brisk in winter, when the Spanish dawdle would lead to possible frostbite.

It is said that the feet are the most honest part of the body: we are so self-conscious about our speech or eye and hand movements that we actually forget what our feet are doing most of the time. The honest Nordics, therefore, send out as many signals with their feet as the Latins do. Foot messages include tapping on the floor (boredom), flapping up and down (want to escape), heel lifting (desperate to escape) and multi-kicking from a knees-crossed position (desire to kick the other speaker). Nordic reticence sometimes reduces the kicking action to wiggling of the toes up and down inside shoes, but the desire is the same. Foot stamping in anger is common in Italy and other Latin countries, but virtually unused north of Paris.

Body Language in Sales

Some forms of sales training actually include a close study of body language, especially in those societies where it is demonstrative. Italian salespeople, for instance, are told to pay great attention to the way their clients sit during a meeting. If they are leaning forward on the edge of their chairs, they are interested in the discussion or proposal. If they sit back in their chairs, they are either bored or confident that things will turn their way if they are patient. Buttoned jackets and arms or legs tightly crossed betray defensiveness and withdrawal. A savvy Italian salesperson will not try to close a sale in such a situation. Neither should a proposal be made to someone who is tapping with feet or fingers—they should be asked to speak. Italian salespeople are also taught to sit as close as they can to their customers when attempting to close the deal. Latin people will tend to buy more from a person sitting close to them than from someone at a distance.

Negotiating

Negotiations are the heart of many, perhaps most, meetings. Western business schools, management gurus, trade consultants and industrial psychologists focused, for most of the twentieth century, on the goal of reducing the process of negotiation to a fine art, if not a science.

One could be forgiven for assuming that relatively unchanging, universally accepted principles of negotiation would by now have been established—that an international consensus would have been reached on how negotiators should conduct themselves in meetings, how the phases of negotiation should proceed and how hierarchies of goals and objectives should be dealt with. One might assume that negotiators—with their common concepts (learned from manuals) of ploys, bargaining strategies, fallback positions, closing techniques and mix of factual, intuitive and psychological approaches—are interchangeable players in a serious game where internationally recognized rules of principles and tactics lead to a civilized agreement on the division of the spoils. This "game plan" and its outcome are not unusual in domestic negotiation between nationals of one culture.

But the moment people of different cultures are involved, the approach of each side will be defined or influenced by cultural characteristics. In fact, one could say nationals of different cultures negotiate in completely different ways. In Part Three I set out in some detail the negotiation styles of the major countries. The following pages give an overview of the cross-cultural factors that are likely to have a bearing on the negotiation process, but first, a few examples of cultural differences.

Germans will ask you all the difficult questions from the start. You must convince them of your efficiency, quality of goods and promptness of service. These are features Germans consider among their own strong cards and they expect the same from you, at the lowest possible price. They will give you little business at first but will give you much more later when they have tested you—and if you prove trustworthy and your product of good quality. The French tend to move much faster, but they may also withdraw their business more quickly. Spaniards often seem not to appreciate the preparations you have made to facilitate a deal. They do not study all the details of your proposal or play, but they do study *you*. They will only do business with you if they like you and think you are honorable.

The Japanese are similar in this respect. They must like you and trust you, otherwise there is no deal. Like the Germans, they will ask many questions about price, delivery and quality, but the Japanese will ask them all ten times. You have to be patient. The Japanese are not interested in profits immediately, only in the market share and reputation of the company.

Finns and Swedes expect modernity, efficiency and new ideas. They like to think of themselves as being up to date and sophisticated. They will expect your company to have the latest office computers and streamlined factories. The American business approach is to get down quickly to a discussion of investment, budgets and profits. They hurry you along and make you sign the five-year plan.

Businesspeople from small nations with a long tradition of trading, such as the Netherlands and Portugal, are usually friendly and adaptable, but prove to be excellent negotiators. Brazilians never believe your first price to be the real one and expect you to come down later, so you must take this into your calculations.

The Problems

Two problems arise almost immediately: professionalism of the negotiating team and cross-cultural bias.

As far as professionalism is concerned, what is often forgotten is that negotiating teams rarely consist of professional or trained negotiators. While this does not apply so much to government negotiation, it is often readily observable with companies. A small company, when establishing contact with a foreign partner, is often represented by its managing director and an assistant. A medium-sized firm will probably involve its export director, finance director and necessary technical support. Even large companies rely on the performance of the managing director supported by, perhaps, highly specialized technical and finance staff who have no experience whatsoever in negotiating. Engineers, accountants and managers used to directing their own nationals are usually completely lacking in foreign experience. When confronted with a different mindset, they are not equipped to figure out the logic, intent and ethical stance of the other side and may waste time talking past each other. This leads us to cross-cultural bias.

When we find ourselves seated opposite well-dressed individuals politely listening to our remarks, their pens poised over notepads similar to ours, their briefcases and calculators bearing the familiar brand names, we often assume that they see what we see, hear what we say and understand our intent and motives. In all likelihood they start with the same innocent assumptions, for they, too, have not yet penetrated our cosmopolitan veneer. But the two sets of minds are working in different ways, in different languages regulated by different norms and certainly envisaging different objectives. It is here with objectives that we begin our discussion.

Objectives in Negotiation

Even before the meeting begins, the divergence of outlooks is exerting decisive influence on the negotiation to come. If we take three cultural groups as an example—American, Japanese and Latin-American—the hierarchy of negotiating objectives are likely to be as in Figure 10.5.

Americans are deal-oriented; they see it as a present opportunity that must be seized. American prosperity was built on opportunities quickly taken, and immediate profit is seen as the paramount reality. Today, shareholders' expectation of dividends creates rolling forecasts that put pressure on U.S. executives to make the deal now in order to meet their quarterly figures. For the Japanese, the current project or proposal is a trivial item in comparison with the momentous decision they have to make about whether or not to enter into a lasting business relationship with the foreigners. Can they harmonize the objectives and action style of the other company with the well-established operational principles of their own *kaisha* (company)? Is this the right direction for their company to be heading in? Can they see the way forward to a steadily increasing market share? The Latin Americans, particularly if they are from a country such as Mexico or Argentina (where memories of U.S. exploitation and interference are a contextual background to discussion), are anxious to establish notions of

United States	Japan	Latin America
1. Current deal	1. Harmonious relationships and "direction taking"	1. National honor
2. Short-term profit and rapid growth	2. Securing market share	2. Personal prestige of chief negotiator
3. Consistent profit	3. Long-term profit	3. Long-term relationship
4. Relationships with partner	4. Current deal	4. Current deal

Figure 10.5 Negotiating Objectives

equality of standing and respect for their team's national characteristics before getting down to the business of making money. Like the Japanese, they seek a long-term relationship, although they will inject into this a greater personal input than their group-thinking Eastern counterparts.

This master programming supplied by our culture not only prioritizes our concerns in different ways, but makes it difficult for us to "see" the priorities or intention pattern of others. Stereotyping is one of the flaws in our master program, often leading us to false assumptions. Here are three examples:

- ✦ French refusal to compromise indicates obstinacy.
  (Reality: The French see no reason to compromise if their logic stands undefeated.)
- ✦ Japanese negotiators cannot make decisions.
  (Reality: The decision was already made before the meeting, by consensus. The Japanese see meetings as an occasion for presenting decisions, not changing them.)
- ✦ Mexican senior negotiators are too "personal" in conducting negotiations. (Reality: Their personal position reflects their level of authority within the power structure back home.)

The Social Setting

The French, Spaniards, most Latin Americans and the Japanese regard a negotiation as a social ceremony to which important considerations of venue, participants, hospitality and protocol, timescale, courtesy of discussion and the ultimate significance of the session are attached. Americans, Australians, Britons and Scandinavians have a much more pragmatic view and are less concerned about the social aspects of business meetings. The Germans and Swiss are somewhere in between.

U.S. executives generally want to get the session over with as quickly as possible, with entertaining and protocol kept to a minimum. Mutual profit is the object of the exercise, and Americans send technically competent people to drive the deal through. They persuade with facts and figures and expect some give-and-take, horse-trading when necessary. They will be argumentative to the point of rudeness in a deadlock and regard confrontation and in-fighting as conducive to progress. No social egos are on the line: if they win, they win; if they lose, what the hell, too bad.

Senior Mexican negotiators cannot afford to lose to Americans, least of all to technicians. Their social position is on the line. They do not enter into a negotiation to swap marbles with engineers and accountants. Their Spanish heritage causes them to view the meeting as a social occasion where everybody is to show great respect for the dignity of the others; discuss grand outlines as opposed to petty details; speak at length in an unhurried, eloquent manner; and show sincerity of intent while maintaining a modicum of discretion to retain some privacy of view.

The Japanese view the session as an occasion to ratify ceremonially decisions that have previously been reached by consensus. They are uncomfortable with both Mexican rhetoric and American argumentativeness, although they are closer to the Latins in their acceptance of protocol, lavish entertainment and preservation of dignity. As befits a social occasion, the Japanese will be led by a senior executive who sets standards of courtesy and deference. He may have no technical competence, but he represents the weighty consensus that backs his authority.

The French view the setting of the negotiation as a social occasion and a forum for their own cleverness. Their sense of history primes them for the traditional French role of international mediator. Their leader will be their best speaker, usually highly educated and self-assured. It will require a skillful American, Briton or Japanese to best him or her in debate. The leader will be unimpressed by American aggressive ploys. French Cartesian logic will reduce the "muddling-through" English and "belly-talking" Japanese to temporary incoherence. This is not a session for give and take, but for presenting well-formulated solutions. Lavish French hospitality will compensate for sitting through lengthy speeches.

Scandinavians, while relatively at home with Americans and Anglo-Saxons and familiar enough with German bluntness and protocol, have little feel for the social nuances displayed by Latins and the Japanese. In their straightforward egalitarian cultures, business meetings are conducted without regard to social status. Who the other negotiators are, their class, their connections, who they are related to—all these things are irrelevant to Finns and Swedes. Although more polite than Americans, Scandinavians have difficulty in settling down to a role in meetings where social competence dominates technical know-how.

Values and Self-Image

We see, therefore, how diverse cultures view the negotiating process in a different light, with dissimilar expectations about its conduct and outcome. Once the talks begin, the values, phobias and rituals of the particular cultural groups soon make themselves evident. The Americans rely on statistical data and personal drive to compress as much action and decision making as possible into the hours available. The Dutch, Finns and Swiss, although somewhat less headlong, will be similarly concerned with the time/efficiency equation. The Germans will place emphasis on thoroughness, punctuality and meeting deadlines. For this they require full information and context and, unlike Latins, will leave nothing "up in the air."

The French give pride of place to logic and rational argument. The aesthetics of the discussion are also important to them, and this will be reflected in their dress sense, choice of venue, imaginative debating style and preoccupation with proper form. The Japanese have their own aesthetic norms, also requiring proper form, which in their case is bound up with a complex set of obligations (vertical, horizontal and circular!). In discussion they value the creation of harmony and quiet "groupthink" above all else. The British also give priority to quiet, reasonable, diplomatic discussion. Their preoccupation with "fair play" often comes to the fore and they like to see this as a yardstick for decision making. Latins, as we have learned, place emphasis on personal relationships, honorable confidences and the development of trust between the parties. This is a slow process and they require an unhurried tempo to enable them to get to know their counterparts. This is well understood by the Japanese, but conflicts with the American desire for quick progress.

Self-image is part and parcel of value perception, and negotiators see themselves in a light that may never reach their foreign counterpart, although their playing of that role may irritate other nationalities. The English often assume a condescending and arbitrary role, a carryover from the days when they settled disputes among the subjects of Her Majesty's Empire. They may still see themselves as judges of situations that can be controlled with calm firmness and funny stories. The French have an equally strong sense of history and consider themselves the principal propagators of Western European culture. This encourages them to take a central role in most discussions, and they tend to "hold the floor" longer than their counterparts would wish.

Because Latin Americans see themselves as exploited by the United States, they often display heightened defensive sensitivity, which may frequently delay progress. They consider themselves culturally superior to North Americans and resent the latter's position of power and dominance.

The Japanese, on the other hand, are comfortable with American power. As victors in the Second World War, the U.S. earned the number one spot. Inequality is basic in both Japanese and Chinese philosophies, and the former are quite satisfied with the number two spot—for the time being. The Japanese see themselves as farsighted negotiators and courteous conversationalists. They have no aspirations to dominate discussion any more than they have to become world or even Asian leaders. They are privately convinced, however, of their uniqueness, of which one facet is intellectual superiority. Unlike the French, they base this belief not on intellectual verbal prowess, but on the power of strong intuition.

Compromise

It is not uncommon for negotiations to enter a difficult stage where the teams get bogged down or even find themselves in a deadlock. When such situations occur between nationals of one culture, there is usually a well-tried mechanism—changing negotiators or venue, adjourning the session, or "repackaging" the deal—that constitutes an escape route whereby momentum can be regained without loss of face for either side. Arab teams will take a recess for prayer and come back with a more conciliatory stance; Japanese delegations will bring in senior executives to "see what the problem is"; Swedish opponents will go out drinking together; Finns will retire to the sauna.

Mutually agreeable mechanisms are not always available in international negotiations, however. The mechanism for breaking a deadlock that is used by Anglo-Saxons and Scandinavians is usually that of compromise. Other cultures, however, do not see compromise in the same favorable light and remain unconvinced of its merit. In French eyes, *give-and-take* is Anglo-speak for *wheel-and-deal*, which they see as an inelegant, crude tactic for chiseling away at the legitimate edifice of reason they have so painstakingly constructed. Yes, let's all be reasonable, they say, but what is irrational in what we have already said?

For the Japanese, compromise during a negotiation is a departure from the company-backed consensus, and woe betide the Japanese negotiators who concede points without authority. Adjournment is sometimes the only way out. Many a senior Tokyo-based executive has been awakened in the middle of the night by trans-Pacific telephone calls asking for directives. Delays are, of course, inevitable.

Among the Latins, attitudes toward compromise vary. The Italians, although they respect logic almost as much as the French, know that our world is indeed irrational and pride themselves on their flexibility. The Spaniards and South Americans see compromise as a threat to their *pundonor* (dignity), and several nations, including Argentina, Mexico and Panama, display obstinacy in conceding anything to "insensitive, arrogant Americans."

Compromise may be defined as finding a middle course and, to this end, both the Japanese and Chinese make good use of "go-betweens." This is less acceptable to Westerners, who prefer more direct contact (even confrontation) to seek clarity. Confrontation is anathema to Asians and most Latins and disliked by Brits and Swedes. Only Germans, Finns, Americans and Australians might rank directness, bluntness and honesty above subtle diplomacy in business discussions. Arabs also like to use go-betweens. The repeated offer of King Hussein of Jordan to mediate in the dispute between Saddam Hussein and George Bush (Senior) unfortunately fell on deaf ears, even though, as a thoroughly Westernized Arab (with British and American wives to boot) he was the ideal middleman for that particular cross-cultural situation.

The problem remains that intelligent, meaningful compromise is only possible when one is able to see how the other side prioritizes its goals and views the related concepts of dignity, conciliation and reasonableness. These are culturally relative concepts and therefore emotion-bound and prickly. However, an understanding of such concepts and an effort to accommodate them form the unfailing means of unblocking the impasse. Such moves are less difficult to make than one might believe. They do, however, require knowledge and understanding of the traditions, cultural characteristics and ways of thinking of the other side. What, for example, is logical and illogical?

Logic

French debating logic is Cartesian in its essence, which means that all presuppositions and traditional opinions must be cast aside from the outset, as they are possibly untrustworthy. Discussion must be based on one or two indubitable truths upon which one can build, through mechanical and deductive processes, one's hypotheses. Descartes decreed that all problems should be divided into as many parts as possible and the review should be so complete that nothing could be omitted or forgotten. Given these instructions and doctrine, it is hardly surprising that French negotiators appear complacently confident and long-winded. They have a hypothesis to build and are not in a hurry.

Opponents may indeed doubt some of the French "indubitable truths" and ask who is qualified to establish the initial premises. Descartes has an answer to this: rational intellect is not rare; it can be found in anyone who has been given help in clear thinking (French education) and is free from prejudice. What is more, conclusions reached through Cartesian logic "compel assent by their own natural clarity." There, in essence, is the basis for French self-assurance and an unwillingness to compromise.

The fellow French would certainly meet thrust with counter-thrust, attempting to defeat the other side's logic. Many cultures feel little inclined to do this. The Japanese—easy meat to corner with logic—have no stomach for the French style of arguing or public demonstrations of cleverness.

Anglo-Saxons, particularly Americans, show a preference for Hegelian precepts. According to Hegel, people who first present diametrically opposed points of view ultimately agree to accept a new and broader view that does justice to the substance of each. The thesis and antithesis come together to form a synthesis (now we're back to compromise). The essence of this doctrine is activity and movement, on which Americans thrive. An American negotiator is always happy to be the catalyst, ever willing to make the first move to initiate action.

Chinese logic is different again, founded as it is on Confucian philosophy. The Chinese consider the French search for truth less important than the search for virtue. To do what is right is better than to do what is logical. They also may show disdain for Western insistence that something is black or white, that opposite courses of action must be right or wrong. Chinese consider both courses may be right if they are both virtuous. Confucianism decrees moderation in all things (including opinion and argument); therefore, behavior toward others must be virtuous. Politeness must be observed and others must be protected from loss of face. Taoist teaching encourages the Chinese to show generosity of spirit in their utterances. The strong are supposed to protect the weak, so the Chinese negotiator will expect you not to take advantage of your superior knowledge or financial strength!

Language

Unless they are using interpreters, negotiators need a common language. English is now the language of diplomacy as well as international trade, but beware. English can be a communication link, or it can be a barrier. When Americans use in discussion terms like *democratic, fair, reasonable, level playing field, evidence, common sense, equitable* or *makes business sense*, they often fail to realize that the Japanese interpret these words and expressions in a different light and that most Latins will instinctively distrust each and every one of them. *Democracy* has a different meaning in every country. American evidence is statistical; in many other cultures it is emotional. In Russia the expression *makes business sense* has virtually no meaning. Language is a poor communication tool unless each word or phrase is seen in its original cultural context. This is naturally true of other languages as well. Words such as *Weltschmerz* (German), *sisu* (Finnish) and *saudades* (Portuguese) mean little to people from other cultures even when translated, and no Westerner could possibly appreciate the web of duties and obligations implied by the Japanese words *giri* and *on*.

Decision Making

Negotiations lead to decisions. How these are made, how long they take to be made and how final they are once made are all factors that will depend on the cultural groups involved.

Americans love making decisions because they usually lead to action and Americans are primarily action oriented. The French love talking about decisions, which may or may not be made in the future. If their reasoned arguments do not produce what in their eyes is a logical solution, then they will delay decisions for days or weeks if necessary.

The Japanese hate making decisions and prefer to let decisions be made for them by gradually building up a weighty consensus. In their case, a decision may take months. This exasperates Americans and many Northern Europeans, but the Japanese insist that big decisions take time. They see American negotiators as technicians making a series of small decisions to expedite one (perhaps relatively unimportant) deal. Once the Japanese have made their decisions, however, they expect their American partner to move like lightning toward implementation. This leads to further exasperation.

What Westerners fail to understand is that the Japanese, during the long, painstaking process of building a consensus for a decision, are simultaneously making preparations for the implementation of the project or deal. The famous *ringi-sho* system of Japanese decision making is one of the most democratic procedures of an otherwise autocratic structure. In many Western countries action is usually initiated at the top. In Japan, younger or lower-ranking people often propose ideas that are developed by middle management and ultimately shown to the president. There is a long, slow process during which many meetings are held to digest the new idea and at length a draft will be made to be passed around for all to see. Each person is invited to attach his or her seal of approval so that unanimity of agreement is already assumed before the president confirms it. He will not do this lightly since he, not middle management, will have to resign if there is a catastrophe. To ask a Japanese negotiator during a meeting to take "another direction" is quite unacceptable. No hunches or sudden turnabouts here. Drastic swings of intent would force the Japanese team to go right back to the drawing board.

Mediterranean and Latin American teams look to their leader to make decisions and do not question his or her personal authority. The leader's decision making, however, will not be as impromptu or arbitrary as it seems. Latins, like the Japanese, tend to bring a cemented-in position to the negotiating table, which is that of the power structure back home. This contrasts strongly with the Anglo-Saxon and Scandinavian willingness to modify stances continuously during the talk if new openings are perceived.

French negotiators seldom reach a decision on the first day. Many a British negotiator has asked (in vain) French colleagues at 4:00 P.M., "Well, can we summarize what we have agreed so far?" The French dislike such interim summaries, since every item on the agenda may be affected by later discussion. Only at the end can everything fit into the "Grand Design." Short-term decisions are seen as of little consequence.

Once a decision has been made, the question then arises as to how final or binding it is. Anglo-Saxons and Germans see a decision, once it has been entered into the minutes of a meeting, as an oral contract that will shortly be formalized in a written, legal document. Ethically, one sticks to one's decisions. Agenda items that have been agreed on are not to be resurrected or discussed again.

Neither Japanese nor Southern Europeans see anything wrong, ethically, in going back to items previously agreed on. "Chop and change" (anathema to Anglo-Saxons) holds no terrors for many cultures.

The French show lack of respect for adherence to agenda points or early mini-decisions. This is due not so much to their concern about changing circumstances as to the possibility (even likelihood) that, as the discussions progress, Latin imagination will spawn clever new ideas, uncover new avenues of approach, improve and embellish accords that later may seem naïve or rudimentary. For them a negotiation is often a brainstorming exercise. Brainwaves must be accommodated! Italians, Spanish, Portuguese and South Americans all share this attitude.

Contracts

Different ethical approaches or standards reveal themselves in the way diverse cultures view written contracts. Americans, British, Germans, Swiss and Finns are among those who regard a written agreement as something that, if not holy, is certainly final.

For the Japanese, on the other hand, the contract they were uncomfortable in signing anyway is merely a statement of intent. They will adhere to it as best they can but will not feel bound by it if market conditions suddenly change, if anything in it contradicts common sense, or if they feel cheated or legally trapped by it. New tax laws, currency devaluations or drastic political changes can make previous accords meaningless. If the small print turns out to be rather nasty, they will ignore or contravene it without qualms of conscience. Many problems arise between Japanese and U.S. firms on account of this attitude. The Americans love detailed written agreements that protect them against all contingencies with legal redress. They have 300,000 lawyers to back them up. The Japanese, who have only 10,000 registered lawyers, regard contingencies to be *force majeure* and consider that contracts should be sensibly reworked and modified at another meeting or negotiation.

The French tend to be precise in the drawing up of contracts, but other Latins require more flexibility in adhering to them. An Italian or Argentinean sees the contract as either an ideal scheme in the best of worlds, which sets out the prices, delivery dates, standards of quality and expected gain, or as a fine project that has been discussed. But the way they see it, we do not live in the best of worlds, and the outcome we can realistically expect will fall somewhat short of the actual terms agreed. Delivery of payment may be late, there may be heated exchanges of letters or faxes, but things will not be so bad that further deals with the partner are completely out of the question. A customer who pays six months late is better than one who does not pay at all. A foreign market, however volatile, may still be a better alternative to a stagnating or dead-end domestic one.

If Anglo-Saxons and Scandinavians have a problem with the ethics of breaking or modifying a contract, they have an even greater one with those of propriety. Which culture or authority can deliver the verdict on acceptable standards of behavior or appropriate conduct of business?

Italian flexibility in business often leads Anglo-Saxons to think they are dishonest. They frequently bend rules, break or get around some laws and put a very flexible interpretation on certain agreements, controls and regulations. There are many gray areas where shortcuts are, in Italian eyes, a matter of common sense. In a country where excessive bureaucracy can hold "business" up for months, smoothing the palm of an official or even being related to a minister is not a sin. It is done in most countries, but in Italy they talk about it.

When does lavish entertaining or regular gift giving constitute elegant bribery or agreeable corruption? French, Portuguese and Arab hosts will alternate the negotiation sessions with feasting far superior to that offered by the Scandinavian cafeteria or British pub lunch. The expense-account-culture Japanese would consider themselves inhospitable if they had not taken their visiting negotiators on the restaurant nightclub circuit and showered them with expensive gifts.

Few Anglo-Saxons or Scandinavians would openly condone making a covert payment to an opposing negotiator, but in practice this is not an uncommon occurrence when competition is fierce. I once heard an American define an honest Brazilian negotiator as one who, when bought, stays bought. More recently the leader of the negotiating team of a large Swedish concern tacitly admitted having greased the palm of a certain South American gentleman without securing the contract. When the Swede quietly referred to the payment made, the beneficiary explained, "Ah, but that was to get you a place in the last round!"

Judgments on such procedures are inevitably cultural. Recipients of under-the-table payments may see them as no more unethical than using one's influence with a minister (who happens to be one's uncle), accepting a trip around the world (via Tahiti or Hawaii) to attend a "conference" or wielding brute force (financial or political) to extract a favorable deal from a weaker opponent. All such maneuvers can be viewed (depending on one's mindset) as normal strategies in the hard world of business. One just has to build these factors into the deal or relationship.

Solutions

Cross-cultural factors will continue to influence international negotiation and there is no general panacea of strategies which ensure quick understanding. The only possible solutions lie in a close analysis of the likely problems. These will vary in the case of each negotiation; therefore, the combination of strategies required to facilitate the discussions will be specific on each occasion. Before the first meeting is entered into, the following questions should be answered:

1. What is the intended purpose of the meeting? (Preliminary, fact-finding, actual negotiation, social?)
2. Which is the best venue?
3. Who will attend? (Level, number, technicians?)
4. How long will it last? (Hours, days, weeks?)
5. Are the physical arrangements suitable? (Room size, seating, temperature, equipment, transportation, accommodation for visitors?)
6. What entertainment arrangements are appropriate? (Meals, excursions, theater?)
7. How much protocol does the other side expect? (Formality, dress, agendas?)
8. Which debating style are they likely to adopt? (Deductive, inductive, freewheeling, aggressive, courteous?)
9. Who on their side is the decision maker? (One person, several, or only consensus?)
10. How much flexibility can be expected during negotiation? (Give-and-take, moderation, fixed positions?)
11. How sensitive is the other side? (National, personal?)
12. How much posturing and body language can be expected? (Facial expressions, impassivity, gestures, emotion?)
13. What are the likely priorities of the other side? (Profit, long-term relationship, victory, harmony?)
14. How wide is the cultural gap between the two sides? (Logic, religion, political, emotional?)
15. How acceptable are their ethics to us? (Observance of contracts, time frame?)
16. Will there be a language problem? (Common language, interpreters?)
17. What mechanisms exist for breaking deadlocks or smoothing over difficulties?
18. To what extent may such factors as humor, sarcasm, wit, wisecracking and impatience be allowed to spice the proceedings?

Good answers to the questions in the preceding checklist will help to clear the decks for a meeting that will have a reasonable chance of a smooth passage. It is to be hoped that the other side has made an attempt to clarify the same issues. The French often hold a preliminary meeting to do just this—to establish the framework and background for discussion. This is very sensible, although some regard the French as being nitpicking in this respect.

PART THREE

Getting to Know Each Other

We are normal, they are abnormal. Why do they have to be so devious, unpunctual, unsmiling, unreliable, undisciplined, cunning, lazy, corrupt, two-faced, aloof, distant, inscrutable? Why can't they be more like us? But appearance is not reality. Let's see why they are so difficult, obstinate and so on.

11

United States of America

The United States of America has the world's largest economy—four times greater than anyone else's (with the exception of China). America is first in volume of trade, first in industry, first in food output and first in aid to others. They spend, too, being the top consumers of energy, oil, oil seeds, grain, rubber, copper, lead, zinc, aluminum, tin, coffee and cocoa. They have the busiest airport in the world (Atlanta) and fly more passengers than anyone else. They have the world's longest road network and longest rail network. They own more cars, telephones, refrigerators, television sets, dishwashers, microwave ovens and cellular phones than any other people. They are the second to China in tourist spending but gross the biggest tourist receipts (twice as much as popular China). The U.S. leads the rest of the world as water users and polluters. They also have the highest rates of prison populations.

Concepts

Time

The pace of American life is different from that of other countries. In the eighteenth and nineteenth centuries vast tracts of open, unclaimed land to the west beckoned with some urgency to poorer settlers and new arrivals. For decades it was first come, first served—you staked your claim, cleared the land, tilled, planted and defended it. They were days of land grab and gold rush. There was no time to lose as immigrants poured in; out west there were no ruling classes or aristocrats, royal claims or decrees, no constraining ideologies or regulations—only practicality; if it worked, you did it, before anyone else did.

One might have assumed that with the majority of goals attained and the visible advent of the affluent society, this frenzied tempo of life would have slackened. It has not. Modern Americans continue at the headlong pace of their nineteenth-century forebears. Work equates with success, time is money. They have to get there first. The chief difference is that in the nineteenth century, everybody knew where "there" was. Today's Americans, unrelentingly driven by the traditional national habit of pressing forward, conquering the environment, effecting change and reaching their destination, are no longer sure what that destination is.

The rest of the world looks on in awe, for none of us are in the same grip of this achievement fever. It can be argued that the Germans and Japanese share the same work tempo as Americans, but the Germans, with their long vacations, social welfare and impressive culture, value quality of life much more. The Japanese, with no more leisure than the Americans, nevertheless achieve what they do at a much more relaxed pace and have created a calm, relatively crime-free society where moral and spiritual values take priority over materialistic goals. This, however, is changing. The four "Asian tigers"—Singapore, Hong Kong, Korea and Taiwan, breakneck export powerhouses all—most closely resemble the U.S. in unrelenting effort, although their Eastern philosophies incline them to view success as collectivist as opposed to the American view that the individual must triumph. In the U.S. you start at the very bottom, give it all you've got, pull yourself up by your own boot straps, guts it out and get to the very top. It's rags to riches, in a land where everybody is equal—in theory. It's a daunting task, but fortunately Americans are unfailing optimists and future-oriented.

Americans are not afraid of challenge or competition, although the strain is beginning to tell. Up to the 1970s the economic and political development of the U.S. had unquestionably been a success story. Other nations had had their ups and downs, peaks and valleys, successes and reverses. Only in America had progress been invariably forward, up and one way. Then came Vietnam, mounting trade balance deficits and the slowing of the economy. Even so, no one in his or her right mind writes off the Americans. Their industrial, commercial, financial and military assets are of a muscular nature not yet approached by their rivals for twenty-first-century dominance. A greater problem for the American people is not so much the maintenance of their material strengths as the attainment of inner harmony.

How should wise Asians, or Europeans with their variety of ideals, handle this time-keeping, media-driven, dollar-minded phenomenon? Hitch one's star to their wagon and make a fast buck? Or tough it out with them?

Cultural Factors in Communication

Behavior at Meetings and Negotiations

American businesspeople have the reputation of being the toughest in the world, but they are, in many respects, the easiest to deal with. That is because their business philosophy is uncomplicated. Their aim is to make as much money as they can as quickly as they can, using hard work, speed, opportunism and power (also of money itself) as the means toward this end. Their business decisions are usually not affected by sentiment, and the dollar, if not God, is considered at least almighty. This single-minded pursuit of profit results in their often being described as ruthless.

Northern Europeans are well placed to deal with Americans successfully. Their reputation as straightforward managers is well received by the open, frank Americans, who often get seriously irritated by what they see as the "devious" manners of Latins and Asians. At meetings, Americans show the following tendencies:

✦ They are individualistic; they like to go it alone without checking with the head office. Anything goes unless it has been restricted.

+ They introduce informality immediately: take their jackets off, use first names, discuss personal details, for example, family.

+ They give the impression of being naïve by not speaking anything but English and by showing immediate trust through ultra-friendliness.

+ They use humor whenever they can, even though their partner fails to understand it or regards it as out of place.

+ They "put their cards on the table" right from the start, then proceed on an offer and counteroffer basis. They often have difficulty when the other side doesn't reveal what they want.

+ They take risks but make a definite (financial) plan which must be adhered to.

+ They try to extract an oral agreement at the first meeting. "Have we got a deal?" They want to shake hands on it. The other party often feels the matter is far too complex to agree on the spot.

+ They want *yes* in principle and will work out details later. But they can be very tough in the details and check on everything in spite of apparent trust. Germans, French and others prefer to settle details first.

+ They are opportunistic, quick to take chances. The history of the U.S. presented many golden opportunities to those who grabbed fastest.

+ They often lack patience and will say irritating or provoking things ("Look at our generous offer") to get things moving.

+ They are persistent. There is always a solution. They will explore all options when deadlocked.

+ They put everything in words, but when they use words like *fair, democratic, honest, good deal, value* and *assume*, they think the other party interprets the words the same as they do. This is because U.S. subcultures (e.g., Czechs, Germans, Poles) do understand.

+ They are blunt; they will disagree and say so. This causes embarrassment to Japanese, Arabs, Italians and other Latins.

+ They assume all negotiators are technically competent and expect to win on their own technical knowledge. They forget the other side may see the status of the chief negotiator as most important. How can a Mexican company president lose to an American engineer?

+ They regard negotiating as problem solving through give-and-take based on respective strengths. They do not appreciate that the other side may have only one position.

+ Americans feel they are the best. But successful negotiating must enter the cultural world of the other party. Many Americans assume that American norms are the only correct ones.

+ This leads to lack of interest in or knowledge of the foreign culture. Americans often know little of such matters as saving face, correct dress, use of business cards, social niceties and formalities important to Arabs, Greeks, Spaniards, and others.

+ In the U.S. the dollar is almighty and will win most arguments. Americans don't always realize that Mexicans, Arabs, Japanese and others will rarely, if ever, sacrifice status, protocol or national honor for financial gain.

How to Empathize with Americans

Calm, pragmatic northerners such as the British, Dutch, Nordics, Canadians and other English speakers can live with most of these characteristics. They, too, are used to informality, first names, humor, persistence, bluntness, technical competence, give-and-take bargaining and general consistency in sticking to what has been agreed. They also wish to conclude the deal without unnecessary time wasting or labyrinthine procedures. Yet care must be exercised; Americans are fast talking, and if the language is English, there may be certain traps. With Americans one always has to read the "fine print," for their apparent openness and trust in the other party are usually underpinned by tight legal control in their contracts, and they will not hesitate to sue you later if you do not comply with every clause you have put your name to. American law is also quite different from many other legal systems.

You should always attempt to appear straightforward, honest, but quite tough in your dealings with Americans, who will respect resilience, open disagreement and alertness and strong cards. You don't have to "beat about the bush" as you would have to with the Japanese or Italians. "Yes, but what happens if . . . ?" is a good question to ask Americans.

If you appear tough often enough, Americans will argue, provoke and certainly push brute strength, but it is all part of their game. They, too, want the deal. They will use far more words than you are comfortable with, but your relative quietness will cause them discomfiture and will eventually gain you points. You will only irritate Latins with reticence, but Americans will respect it. The answer to the oft-repeated "Have we got a deal?" should be "Maybe." Don't be rushed. They, too, are taking risks, but more likely than not, they can afford to lose more than you can. They are looking at this particular deal more than the long-term relationship. They have quarterly forecasts to satisfy. They want profit now, as opposed to the Japanese, who want your market. Realization of such American aims helps you in dealing with them. Their friendliness means nothing, although it is pleasant while it lasts. They will forget your name the day after the deal is made.

You have a lot of cards up your sleeve. You know a lot more about Americans and their country than they know about you and yours. Many Americans think Finland is in Canada and confuse Lapps with Inuits. You can enter their cultural world without difficulty—you have seen hundreds of American films, read many U.S. books and journals. You speak their language and therefore have insight into their thought processes. They will find many Europeans disarming, but also deep. British people deal with Americans by occasionally using Americanisms in their speech, then retreating into British vagueness or semi-incoherence when they wish to confuse. Americans are tough, cunning, but also naïve. You should blow hot and cold with them, appearing half the time to be on the American wavelength and the other half of the time your own person. Americans find this disconcerting; they want to follow the script, or *scenario* as they often call it.

This is never more apparent than when the Americans are buying—they want to hear your sales pitch. Soft sell is not necessary in the U.S. Any American walking into a car showroom expects the salesperson to attack him from the start. He wishes to be told every good point about the car, the true and the peripheral, the fine discount and the personal concession; he then wants to hit back hard with his own demands. Finally, after much tough talk the buyer and seller arrive at the "deal" neither of them trusts but both want and fully accept. You can improve on this dialogue by showing all your toughness but slipping in a quiet injection of "niceness," even humility.

A certain amount of modesty scores points with Americans. If you are too modest with Latins, you run the risk of their believing you ("they have a lot to be modest about"), but the Americans, as native English speakers, will hear the linguistic nuances and respect your reserve. They, for their part, are incapable of being modest in speech, as American English is irrevocably tough, clever and tending toward the exaggerated and sensational. The chart below compares British modesty with blunt American tough talk.

Finally, when dealing with Americans, it is advisable to have on your team someone who knows their country well. This applies when dealing with any nationality, but at least many Europeans have spent years in the U.S. and such experts are readily available. Northern Europeans, with their language abilities and wide knowledge of the Anglo-Saxon world, are today quite close culturally to the British. Their mistake is in often assuming that Americans are similar because they speak the same tongue. But Americans live in a different hemisphere and a different world. They do things their way and people who have lived in the U.S. know the shortcuts in doing business with them.

Americans	British
Jack'll blow his top.	Our chairman might tend to disagree.
You're talking bullshit.	I'm not quite with you on that one.
You gotta be kidding.	Hmm, that's an interesting idea. (disagreement)
I tell you, I can walk away from this deal.	We'll have to do our homework.
You're going to get hurt.	I'm not sure this is advantageous for you.
Bean counters drive me mad.	Accountants can be frustrating.
It's the only game in town.	There is no other choice.
We had sticker-shocked the consumers right off their feet.	We had overpriced the product.
Go for broke.	Stake everything on one venture.
He'll do his best to make it fly.	He'll do all he can to ensure success.
If they ever come back from the grave . . .	If they are ever a force in business again . . .
When you scramble, you scramble like a son-of-a-bitch.	Speed of action is advisable.

MOTIVATION	
KEY	*Remuneration, new challenges*
Cross-century mood	✦ Rapidly increasing distaste for "too much government." ✦ Rapidly increasing distrust of the media and media hype. ✦ Growing disgust with lawyers and greedy executives and dissatisfaction with the litigious nature of American society. ✦ Slowly developing awareness of the complex interlocking nature of international interests and the dangers of isolationism.

Motivating Factors

✦ Money.
✦ Career challenge.
✦ Use of humor.
✦ Put your cards on the table and look at theirs.
✦ Launch quickly into a who-does-what mode.
✦ Remember that nothing is impossible in the U.S.
✦ Be persistent in chasing results.
✦ Link work and effort to return on investment.
✦ Americans are not willing to go into great detail unless they are sure there is a deal. Settle this early.
✦ Settle for the grand outline first, but make sure the fine print is acceptable subsequently.
✦ Americans like simplification of issues and get irritated with what they see as unnecessary complications.
✦ You will often have to explain to them possible intricacies in your culture.
✦ Otherwise they will judge everything by American standards.
✦ Remember that time is money.
✦ They are not averse to taking risks; you often have to match this.
✦ They often think aloud at business meetings; you should do the same. It shows you have nothing to hide and you may cook up some joint solutions.
✦ They dislike protocol. Anyone can say what he or she thinks at a meeting irrespective of the status of the participants.
✦ They often use clichés. Sometimes you need to probe for the meaning.
✦ Accept sarcasm, irony and kidding from their side.
✦ Show toughness, but eventual willingness to make concessions.
✦ Show great confidence in your own product and sell it hard.
✦ Remember that they have a great work ethic and hate people taking time off or going on vacation when there is an important project underway.

(continued)

MOTIVATION *(continued)*
◆ Be innovative. Change and improvement are an obsession with them.
◆ They are more interested in their future than your past.
Avoid
◆ Playing your cards too close to your chest, or they will quickly conclude that you are devious.
◆ Long silences; they are not used to them.
◆ Pulling rank.
◆ Challenging the American Dream.

12

Canada

In 1565 a ship carrying French explorers sank in Hudson Bay. The survivors, once ashore, encountered local Indians, whom they addressed in friendly terms and asked how they were. "*Apaizak obeto*," replied the Indians. They were speaking Basque ("The priests are better off ").

This startling incident not only pays tribute to the peripatetic initiatives of the Basque people, but is indicative of the early multiculturalism of the huge land mass that the Huron-Iroquois called *Kanata*.

The groundwork for multicultural Canada was laid more than 30,000 years ago when a diverse range of aboriginals crossed the land bridge between Siberia and Alaska and settled around Hudson Bay and the western and eastern coasts. They were originally inland hunters, but as they moved east across the north they adapted to coastal conditions and began to hunt seal and walrus. Eventually more than 700 groups of Inuit were scattered across the north, each one with its distinct customs and language.

English and French explorers plied the waters of North America in the sixteenth century as they sought a northwest passage to lead them to the rich markets of the Orient. Although explorers such as Cabot, Cartier and Champlain never found a route to China, they found something just as valuable—rich fishing grounds and teeming populations of beaver, fox and bear, all valued for their furs. Permanent French and English settlements began in the early 1600s and increased throughout the century. The settlers were obliged to interact with the First Nations people to build a unique Canadian heritage. During the nineteenth and early twentieth centuries, many Eastern and Northern Europeans emigrated to Canada in search of land and freedom. During this same period, large numbers of Chinese and South Asians also came to work as laborers in the mines, on the railroad or in service industries.

Today Canada is arguably the most multicultural country in the world. In 2000, over 12 million Canadians, or 40 percent of the population, were reported as having an ethnic origin other than British or French. Among the larger groups are German, Italian, Ukrainian, Dutch, Polish, Chinese, Vietnamese, Korean, Jewish, Caribbean, Portuguese, Finnish and Scandinavian.

Over 60 languages are spoken by more than 70 ethnocultural groups across the country. The Canadian government is very active in protecting this heritage, and multicultural and antiracist education programs exist at all levels. Ethnic newspapers flourish across Canada— in Toronto alone there are more than 100. Multicultural radio and television broadcasting thrives. Toronto has a full-time ethnic television station, with a large number of programs in Italian, Ukrainian, German, Greek, Portuguese and Chinese. Canada's Broadcasting Act (1991) and the Canadian Multiculturalism Act (1988) acknowledge that multiculturalism is woven into the very fabric of Canadian life. Canadians of all cultural origins have the opportunity to contribute to the common goals of equality, national unity, social harmony and economic prosperity.

The story of Canadian multiculturalism is not without its discordant note, however. Inevitably, North America became a focal point for the historical bitter rivalry between England and France. Quebec City was conquered by the British in 1759 and the Treaty of Paris assigned all French territory east of the Mississippi River to Britain, except for the islands of St. Pierre and Miquelon, off the island of Newfoundland.

Now under British rule, the French-speaking inhabitants of Canada had a single aim: to retain their traditions, language and culture. This endeavor continues today.

When Britain lost her American colony, large numbers of English-speaking colonists sought refuge in Canada. Canada first existed as Upper and Lower Canada, then in 1848 as the Province of Canada with a measure of autonomy, but part of the British Empire. The country subsequently expanded westwards to the Pacific Coast.

Canada played a substantial role in the Second World War and is the only nation to have taken part in all of the UN's major peacekeeping operations. It is the tenth biggest economy in the world; only half a dozen countries enjoy a higher standard of living as far as quality of life is concerned. Canada is normally among the top three on the Human Development Index.

Culture

Values

honest	fair, gentle, laid back
friendly, easy-going	generous, parochial
practical, savers	pioneers, independent

humorous   low key, uncomplicated
tolerant, but critical of U.S.   love family, mother nature
prudish, often traditional   internationally impartial

Canadians and Americans

Canadians are often defined in comparison and contrast to the Americans, with whom they share a 5,000-mile (8,000-kilometer) border and for whom they have conceived a love–hate relationship. Although no other neighbors in the world enjoy such a warm rapport, Canadians love to spell out U.S.–Canadian differences in the following manner:

Americans	Canadians
self-centered	world awareness
pushy	low key
boastful	modest
exaggerate	understate
jump to conclusions	methodical approach
individual is paramount	the society counts too
nationalistic	moderate, even apathetic
don't respect cultural differences	multicultural
distrustful	trusting
superiority complex	occasional inferiority complex
reckless	moderate caution
restless	internal comfort
rushing	measured pace
expansionist	conservative, consolidating

Concepts

Leadership and Status

In English-speaking Canada, leading statespeople are generally low key. Not many non-Canadians can remember the name of any Canadian premier except perhaps Pierre Trudeau. Leaders in Quebec have more Gallic flair.

Canadian managers behave in a subdued manner in comparison with their American counterparts and are expected by their staff to be truthful, trusting and egalitarian. Though results oriented, their route to success is governed by common sense rather than aggressive methods.

Canadian leaders have big homes and fine cars, but ostentatious behavior is definitely frowned on. They rarely talk about their possessions or money.

Space and Time

Canada is the world's second largest country. Its total area of 3,850,000 square miles (9,970,000 square kilometers) tops that of China, the U.S. and Brazil and contains one-third of all the world's fresh water. With fewer than six people per square mile (three per square kilometer), it has the lowest population density of any developed country except Australia. Most Canadians, however, live within 50 miles (80 kilometers) of the U.S. border and the vast expanses of the north (772,000 square miles/2 million square kilometers and 20 million lakes) are virtually uninhabited. The personal distance of comfort is 4 feet (1.2 meters).

Canadians are generally punctual, though the vast expanses of land in the prairies and in the north make people more relaxed about scheduling and other things. They are not obsessed by the time-is-money concept. The Inuits have their own sense of time.

Cultural Factors in Communication

Communication Pattern

Canadian English sounds pleasing to most ears, being measured, well articulated and lacking the extreme nasal tones of some U.S. accents. French Canadians possess more Gallic fervor, but in fact are much more anglicized (linguistically) than they would care to admit and are less roundabout and loquacious than the European French.

Listening Habits

Canadians are polite listeners and rarely interrupt a sensible speech or presentation. It is, however, a basic tenet of Canadian education that even young people may challenge the precepts of others. Canadians excel in courteous give-and-take debate. Instruction in schools is less teacher-led than student-directed.

Behavior at Meetings and Negotiations

Meetings are essentially democratic and everyone is allowed to air their own views. Decisions are not rushed and a certain amount of caution is advised, but Canadians of all origins dislike wasting time. Agreement is sought rather than dictated and negotiations must lead to a clear action plan. Pragmatism is the order of the day. Rhetoric and overly tough talk are not generally appreciated. Humor is always welcome.

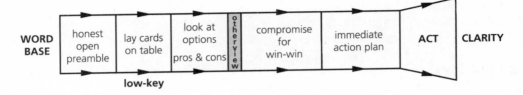

Figure 12.1 Canadian Communication Pattern

Figure 12.2 Canadian Listening Habits

Manners and Taboos

Canada is a very open society, exercising maximum social tolerance. There are consequently few taboos apart from boasting and other forms of ostentation. Canadians possess easy social graces—they are the world's best cocktail partiers! They invite people readily for supper in their homes, where old-fashioned hospitality shows no bounds. Clothing on most occasions is comfortable and tasteful rather than snazzy.

How to Empathize with Canadians

One has to mirror to some extent the typical Canadian values of tolerance, calm, reason-ableness and low-key utterances and behavior. Although they are not very nationalistic, they like you to appreciate the uniqueness of their identity and to distinguish them clearly from Americans. They are easy to deal with, as they are genuinely interested in other countries and are keen on being internationally popular (which they are).

With French Canadians, empathy is quickly gained by speaking French, if you can. They have sustained their isolation from Ontario and the rest of the country by clinging to the bonds of family, language and religion.

MOTIVATION	
KEY	*Be laid back on political issues*
Cross-century mood	✦ Hanging on (somewhat tenaciously) to national unity; this is mood not guaranteed forever with such a huge spread of thinly populated territory. ✦ Inclination to settle the Inuit question. ✦ Willingness to cooperate ever more closely (economically) with the U.S., as long as national integrity is guaranteed. ✦ A growing feeling that Canadian morals and standards will set the pace for human progress in coming decades.

Motivating Factors

✦ Distinguish them clearly from the Americans. Appreciate the uniqueness of their culture.
✦ Exercise cultural sensitivity. Canada is arguably the world's most multicultural country.
✦ Show tolerance at all times.
✦ Be low key and reliable.
✦ Lead from the front.
✦ Discussion style should be calm and reasonable.
✦ Stress impartiality in most matters.
✦ Dress well, but comfortably. Tastes are more conservative than in the U.S.
✦ Boasting and ostentatiousness are taboo.
✦ Too many status symbols irritate.
✦ Home entertaining is popular and rather folksy.
✦ They respond well to humor.
✦ Amusing after-dinner speeches are popular.
✦ Meetings are essentially democratic, where everyone airs his or her views.
✦ They like quick action, but do not tackle business at the American tempo. An unhurried decision followed by rapid implementation is the name of the game.
✦ When instructing Canadians, expect pleasant interruptions and a lot of give-and-take.
✦ They like the soft sell.
✦ Compromise is usually part of the process.
✦ Try to get the agreement of everyone in the room (if possible) before finalizing decisions or initiating action.
✦ Know your Canadian geography. Canadians have world awareness.
✦ Impute the best motives. Most Canadians are trustworthy and will appreciate your confidence.
✦ Exercise generosity. Canadians themselves are generous people.

(continued)

MOTIVATION *(continued)*

◆ Canadians dislike unnecessary complication. Simplify issues but avoid oversimplification.

◆ Bear in mind that Canadians are rather prudish and traditional, so tailor your behavior accordingly.

◆ Quality of life is important. According to the UN's Human Development Index, Canada is often assessed in first place.

◆ Remember that Canadians respect underdogs; they are the only nation to have taken part in all of the UN's peace-keeping operations and are big aid donors.

◆ When dealing with French Canadians, you may liven up considerably.

Avoid

◆ Being too individualistic or expecting them to be.

◆ Being overly opinionated or intense.

◆ Getting overly excited about anything, particularly politics.

◆ Underestimating Canada's economic impact, fine humanitarian record and moral authority.

13

Britain

For decades the British film industry, enriched by the talents of such actors as Alec Guinness, Peter O'Toole, John Gielgud, Ralph Richardson, Alastair Sim, George Cole and Charles Laughton, has put the typical Englishman on the screen for the world to see. The BBC, in such admirable programs as *Upstairs, Downstairs* and *Yes, Minister,* has reinforced the image.

The Englishman dresses in tweeds or a three-piece pin-striped suit and a Burberry raincoat on rainy days. He wears a bowler hat, carries a tightly furled, black umbrella with a cane handle and has a pink newspaper tucked under his left armpit. He goes to church on Sunday mornings and eats roast beef with Yorkshire pudding for Sunday lunch. He is a man of principle, insists on fair play for underdogs, does things in a proper manner and shows more affection for horses, cats and dogs than for children, foxes and grouse. He probably went to Eton and Oxford (Cambridge?) and frequents Ascot, Wimbledon, Twickenham, Lord's and Wentworth. He believes in the Monarchy, the Empire and the Conservative Party. When not in his Club (no ladies allowed), he sits in the local pub with gardeners and game wardens, with whom he sips warm beer called *real ale*. Often he has tea with the vicar, with whom he discusses the Church of England, farming, poaching, the village fête and his years with the Guards.

Englishmen are fond of cricket, croquet, rugby, sheepdog trials, detective stories and queuing (getting in lines). When lines are slow, you do not complain, as English people must never make a scene, not even if they have a double-barreled name. The same applies to poor service in restaurants, railway stations and that place where you get your passport.

The antidote to such frustrating situations is the stiff upper lip. When standing in line or sitting in a train one does not enter into conversation with others— that is the reason for carrying a newspaper everywhere. When a train was derailed in a tunnel in the London Underground a few years ago, an elderly City gentleman walked half a mile down the line to the next station, where he proclaimed: "It's horrible down there in the dark. People are talking to each other!"

This powerful stereotype of the British character has been etched on other nations' minds by several generations of British films. Huge populations abroad, including the Japanese, Indians, Southeast Asians and Africans, still subscribe to it and send their children to Britain to be educated along the same lines.

The majority of British people bear little resemblance to the stereotype. Not only is the image one of an upper-class personage of a former era, but it does not take into account regional differences, which in the U.K. are extremely marked. If you draw a latitudinal line through the city of Oxford, it is questionable if you will find anyone north of it who behaves in the manner of the stereotype. In the first place, nearly 10 million Britons are Celts (Scots, Welsh, Irish, Cornish and Manx). These people are essentially romantic, poetic and emotional. They, like millions of midland and Northern English people in the "wilds" beyond Oxford, are extremely critical of the archetypal Englishman existing in foreign minds. There is a type of English person who roughly corresponds to the projected image, but he is southern, upper class and almost extinct! Even in the south, we are talking about a tiny, although often highly visible (and audible) fraction of society. Foreigners, often laughing at the eccentric English stereotype, are unaware that 50-odd million Britons laugh at him too. Northern, midland and Celtic Britons feel much more affinity with some Europeans (Norwegians, Danes, Swedes, Finns, Dutch, Belgians, Germans, Swiss) than they do with the braying figure in tweeds. Britons are supposed to be poor at learning languages—this is a myth (it applies only to the Southern English). Scots, Welsh, Irish and most people north of Watford learn foreign languages well and often with a good accent.

What are real English people like? The "world image" bears some resemblance to the reality, but not much. The class system is still in evidence in Britain—an unfortunate anachronism which North America and most of Europe have dispensed with—but in fact most British people could be called middle class. They do not have a strong political party to represent them, although both Conservatives and Labour eagerly pretend to do so. The absence of a moderate centrist party contributes, sadly, to the continuing polarization of British society.

Polarized or not, how do British people behave? Whatever the status, a pattern can be observed. Yes, we are a nation of queuers, and probably the only time British people complain vociferously is when someone jumps ahead in the queue. But the stiff upper lip can move—British people today hold nothing sacred. While royalty is respected, the Royal Family is often ridiculed, both in the press and on TV. If the British can laugh at themselves, so can the monarchs—what could be more democratic than that?

Humor is a saving factor in British life—some say it is a product of a fickle climate—and many English people feel that as long as there is humor, there can never be utter despair. It is no accident that the BBC—the most humorous television service in the world—is highly popular in most countries fortunate enough to be able to receive it.

It is true that British people love detective stories. Agatha Christie is the world's most translated novelist and the British easily lead the world in library book loans. Sherlock Holmes is one of the most famous and popular Englishmen of all time. The fact is, the British have a strong conspiratorial streak—they love plotting. The most beloved characters in the extensive British theatrical literature are villains. Guy Fawkes, who was hung after failing to blow up Parliament, became an instant hero and the nation still celebrates his anniversary every November 5th. The biggest heroes of British naval history were Francis Drake and John Hawkins—both pirates. Apparently polished and sophisticated in diplomacy, the British are masters of intelligence gathering and political blackmail.

And yet British people regard themselves as honest, reasonable, caring and considerate. Their originality often borders on the eccentric, but it is true that throughout history they have been lateral thinkers with great powers of invention. Often academic and woolly, they can excel in science and technology. Portrayed as a nation of amateurs who "muddle through" crises, they have shown their visceral strength in the worst adversity.

Their insularity is incurable. Each evening on television British weather forecasters routinely end their message with the prognosis of the next day's temperature: "The high will be 22 degrees Celsius—that is 72 degrees Fahrenheit." That after five decades of metric systems!

Don't ask the British to change their double-decker buses or red mailboxes, or to drive on the right. Even when they venture abroad, they take their cocoon of insularity with them. It used to be five o'clock tea in long dresses in the heat of the African jungle; now it's fish and chips and bacon and eggs eagerly provided by Spanish hoteliers on the Costa del Sol.

Fixed habits, fixed ideas, slow to change, unprofessional. How do these characteristics apply to the British way of doing business? How should these eccentrics be handled? (For illustrations of the British communication pattern and listening habits, see Figures 5.5 and 5.13.)

How to Empathize with the British

The British feel at home with other English-speaking nationalities, with whom they have little difficulty in establishing an easy-going but effective relationship. They also feel comfortable with Nordics, the Dutch and (when they get to know them) the Japanese. They think that they strike the golden mean between excessive formality (French, German tendencies) and premature familiarity (American, Australian traits).

Britons, of course, belong to different classes, and you should always bear this in mind. When dealing with the wealthier, more class-conscious Southern English, stress your civilized, educated side; when dealing with the more hard-headed northern English, Scots or Welsh, you should lay more emphasis on sincerity and straight, uncomplicated dealing.

At business meetings, the British are rather formal at first, using first names only after two or three encounters. After that they become very informal (jackets off, sleeves rolled up) and first names will be used and maintained from then on. British people like to show themselves as family oriented (though less than the Latins) and it is normal for you to discuss children, vacations and reminiscences during and between meetings. Humor is important in business sessions in the U.K., and it is advisable for you to arrive well stocked with jokes and anecdotes. People who are good at this should use their talent to the full.

British people expect you to match story with story and an atmosphere conducive to doing business will result. A word of warning: British executives can use humor (especially irony or sarcasm) as a weapon in ridiculing an opponent or showing disagreement or even contempt. Sarcasm is rarely used against Nordics, however, since their modesty and restraint hardly ever deserve it. The British can use humor cruelly against some Latins and overly demonstrative people.

One can learn a lot about the British by observing how they use humor against themselves or their own colleagues. The following uses are common:

+ self-deprecation
+ to break up tension in a situation which is developing intransigence
+ to speed up discussion when excessive formality is slowing it down
+ to direct criticism toward a superior without getting fired
+ to introduce a new, possibly wild idea to unimaginative colleagues (the "trial balloon")
+ to introduce the unexpected in over-rigid negotiation
+ to laugh at overly elaborate or "mysterious" management priorities and perspective in solemn corporate planning

In short, humor is regarded as one of the most effective weapons in the British manager's arsenal, and some people can gain the confidence of the British by showing that they can be a match for them in this area. (A Swiss, Austrian, Turk or German has difficulty in doing this.)

British executives try to show during meetings that they are guided by reasonableness, compromise and common sense. You may find, however, that the British, even in the absence of disagreement, will rarely make a final decision at the first meeting. They do not like to be hurried. With them you should suggest, "Could we have a final decision at our next meeting?"

The British rarely disagree openly with proposals from the other side. They agree whenever possible, but qualify their agreement ("Hmm, that's a very interesting idea."). Other nationals are more open in this respect. You must watch for hidden signs of disagreement, for example,

+ "Well, we quite like that, however . . . ,"
+ vagueness in reply,
+ understatement indicating, in fact, opposition ("That might be a bit tricky"),
+ humor.

Some nationalities understand the use of understatement and humor well, but can be irritated by British vagueness. They use it to stall, confuse opponents, or delay the business. Ask them for a decision and they are likely to reply, "Let me tell you a story." You listen to the story with interest, for it will probably be a good one. When it ends you will say "Fine, but what about a decision?" "I already told you," the Briton will say. You would do well to show you understand the relevance of the story, or tell one back.

Using charm, vagueness, humor, understatement and apparent reasonableness, British negotiators can be smiling but quite tough for lengthy periods. They always have a fallback position which they disguise for as long as possible. You should attempt to discover this position by being equally reasonable, smiling, modest and tenacious. In the end you may find it is similar to your own fallback plan in most circumstances. The area for bargaining may be somewhat greater with the British (remember that they have hundreds of years of experience with India, the Middle East and the Far East).

Representatives of a British company will make normal use of their firm's reputation, size and wealth in their negotiating hand, and you can do likewise in dealing with them. What they do not reveal so readily is the strength of their behind-the-scenes connections. The "old school tie," or the "old-boys' network," is very much a reality in British executive life and should not be underestimated. It is particularly active in the City, the ministries and in legal circles, and nationals from a small country should always bear in mind that they may be dealing with greater influences than are apparent on the surface.

Finally, there is the question of British insularity. Brits generally have a feeling that "foreigners" intend to outsmart them.

MOTIVATION		
KEY	*At meetings, don't rock the boat*	
Cross-century mood	+ A liking for consultative managing style is growing.	
	+ Becoming more aware of the need for cross-cultural instruction.	
	+ Hard-nosed U.S. concepts on the wane.	
	+ Access to the latest technology increasingly desired.	
		(continued)

MOTIVATION *(continued)*

Motivating Factors

- ✦ Your strongest weapon is dry humor, supported by a cool, laid-back approach.
- ✦ Business and making money is a serious matter, but you should always try to look casual about it.
- ✦ Brits accept career challenge.
- ✦ Be competitive, but don't tread openly on others' toes. There are unwritten rules about fair play.
- ✦ Statements and actions should be low key. Everything should seem to be under control: Let's keep it jolly nice, chaps.
- ✦ Open debate is okay, as long as you make it clear that people's opinions are separate from their integrity.
- ✦ When you wish to criticize, disagree or even praise, do it obliquely (using understatement and coded speech).
- ✦ On-the-dot punctuality may sometimes be seen as overdone. You may arrive a few minutes late at a meeting as long as you are well-prepared. Most meetings begin with a few minutes of small talk.
- ✦ Managers usually want to be considered one of the team but maintain a slight (power) distance.
- ✦ English like orders to be given in the form of suggestions and hints ("Perhaps we might try this . . ."). They hate regimentation and see it as unwelcome in a twenty-first-century context.
- ✦ In discussion Brits accept occasional ambiguities and are prepared to read between the lines.
- ✦ It is good policy to use self-disparagement with English people and laugh at yourself.
- ✦ It is good form to be entrepreneurial. You should also admire another's success.
- ✦ Put things in writing, generally after some oral discussion. The English like confirmation of agreements, minutes of meetings, thank-you notes and friendly or informative memos. They keep thick files. Don't forget Christmas cards, either.
- ✦ Tell English colleagues about yourself and your family, but don't reveal many private details.
- ✦ Common sense, as in the Nordic countries, is a major factor with the English.
- ✦ Appeals to tradition and attractive precedents are usually successful.
- ✦ Remember that Brits are basically more interested in long-term relationships than in quick deals. They are very interested in profits, but often show great patience in waiting for them.
- ✦ Be prepared to accept some idiosyncratic or even eccentric behavior. This is often seen as a sign of originality leading to inventiveness. Teachers, professors, engineers, scientists and computer programmers are often dressed far from smartly.
- ✦ Remember that there are many types of Brits. Most of the above applies to the Southern English. People north of Birmingham, as well as Celtic Brits, tend to be more focused and hardheaded, show more openness and warmth, have less respect for class distinctions, resemble Nordics in many ways and often get on well with Americans. You should take these factors into account and modify your own stance accordingly.

(continued)

MOTIVATION (*continued*)

Avoid

+ Being sentimental, emotional and openly critical in public.
+ Boasting about your connections or indulging in name-dropping.
+ Talking too much; on the other hand, don't lapse into silence too often.
+ Taking sides in class questions.
+ Pushing logic too much; the English pride themselves on their intuition.
+ Putting forward too many strong opinions; it may jeopardize future compromise.
+ Looking too serious or always taking things literally. The English like leg-pulling.
+ Pressing them if they become (suddenly) vague; they are probably stalling, so take another tack.

14

Ireland

Talk of "two Irelands" usually refers to the political division between North and South, but another distinction becoming increasingly evident lies in the contrasting image of postcard or mythical Ireland on the one hand, and the enterprising, modernizing EU state on the other. Mythical Ireland suggests the "little people" and the Emerald Isle, folk music and scenic hills imbued with fifty shades of green. The real Ireland is very different. The youngest country in Europe, it has been vigorously bolstered by EU subsidies, transforming itself from a predominantly agricultural society to a near-urban manufacturing one (one-third of the republic's inhabitants live in Dublin). The darling of EU economies with a high growth rate, particularly among high-tech companies, Ireland has reached (or exceeded) the British standard of living, although it still sends about 20 percent of its exports to the U.K.

The British Isles

Given the proximity of Ireland and the U.K. and their relative isolation from mainland Europe, it is not unreasonable to suppose that a close political union might have been realized. Both islands were occupied by the Celts before 300 B.C. and later shared ravaging attacks by numerous Viking raiders in the eighth and ninth centuries. Their historical heritages did not remain parallel, however, since the Romans conquered Great Britain in 55 B.C. but never ruled Ireland, having found England rainy enough. Wales and Scotland, like Ireland, remained largely Celtic, but the decisive political development that caused England to diverge from its neighbors was the Norman French invasion of 1066. The more sophisticated Anglo-Norman combination conquered Dublin in 1169 and English power was consolidated later, under Henry VIII and Elizabeth I. Henry's split with Rome left England largely Protestant, while Ireland remained Catholic. The hail of death and destruction left in Ireland by Oliver Cromwell during the English Civil War put an end to acceptable relations between the two countries.

Culture

Values

As a predominantly Celtic nation, Ireland differs culturally from Anglo-Saxon-Norman England. Celts embody both linear-active and multi-active tendencies and are clearly dialogue-oriented. The most notable Irish values (some of which are shared by the Welsh and Scots) are as follows:

rural simplicity	poetic tendencies
vision and imagination	love of literature, music, theater
romance and idealism	warmth, charm
irony, sense of humor	mistrust of the British
informality	social anchors of land, church, family

Religion

Many simply think of Northern Ireland as Protestant and Ireland as Roman Catholic. It is not so simple. The Protestant/Catholic split in Ulster is 58 to 42 percent. While the South is predominantly Catholic (95 percent), there are over 100,000 Protestants, several of whom have been and are very influential. The republic's first president, Douglas Hyde, was a Protestant, as were three outstanding writers, Oscar Wilde, Samuel Beckett and W. B. Yeats. Protestant citadels like Trinity College and the *Irish Times* championed nonsectarian liberalism.

Although Catholicism has long been the backbone of Irish Celtic identity, it has lost much of its influence in the modern republic, largely due to its attitude toward women. Former president Mary Robinson referred to it as the "patriarchal, male-dominated Catholic Church."

Concepts

Leadership and Status

Leadership was once invested in the kings of Ireland, and in the eighteenth and nineteenth centuries was greatly influenced by the Catholic Church. Priests were instrumental in guiding the flocks. In the twentieth century politicians came more to the fore. Writers were influential. In the first decade of the twenty-first century, Irish leaders, both in business and politics, are progressive-minded and favor meritocratic and open-minded procedures.

Space and Time

The distance of comfort in Ireland is slightly less than in Britain. Friendly backslapping and various degrees of tactile behavior are common. The Irish are relaxed about time, especially in the countryside. Modern urban Irish are as punctual as the British.

Cultural Factors in Communication

Communication Pattern

Irish people speak in a more animated manner than the English and have been described as "audacious in speech." This audacity often borders on hyperbole and not infrequent embroidery of the truth. This results in what the Irish call *blarney* and must be taken into account when conversing with them. Warmly informal at all times, the Irish are great improvisers during discussions and resemble the Italians in their skill at showing apparent agreement and compliance. They are definitely more poetic and philosophical in speech than the British.

Listening Habits

When listening, the Irish are courteous and attentive and rarely show open dissent. They often have a strong desire to interrupt (as they are bursting with ideas) but rarely do so. Their feedback is ample enough, but occasionally is rather ambiguous or even devious.

Behavior at Meetings and Negotiations

Meetings with Irish people are invariably warm and friendly, but they can sometimes also be confusing. They are not great agenda followers and digress enthusiastically when confronted with an interesting idea. Ideas are infinitely more important than plain facts. The Irish have a strong affinity for the abstract, the innovative, the theoretical. In this they are like the French, although less strong on logic. This characteristic causes a certain tendency toward procrastination, while they look at new ways of approaching problems and tasks. It also leads to creativity: they are unconventional and independent spirits who resist structure and routine. Latins find this easier to accept than Germans, English, Swedes and Finns do.

How to Empathize with the Irish

Be warm, friendly and hospitable, as they are. Show vision and use your imagination. Tell a lot of stories. Think in terms of beauty and aesthetics. Emphasize simplicity. Don't call them English or praise the English too much. Don't be sarcastic, but accept their gentle irony. Don't show any snobbery or keep them at a distance. Don't be too factual, and don't try to pull wool over what you see as rustic Celtic eyes.

MOTIVATION	
KEY	*Show warmth, friendliness and humor*
Cross-century mood	✦ The Irish are enjoying the fruits of their late-twentieth-century boom. ✦ English hesitancy about full EU involvement encourages the Irish to participate more fully. ✦ They are anxious to throw off their previous backwardness.

Motivating Factors

✦ Be original when you can.
✦ Show sympathy for past Irish problems.
✦ Be folksy.
✦ Be poetic, if you can.
✦ Be humorous whenever you can.
✦ Emphasize tolerance.
✦ Accept occasional procrastination on their part.
✦ Align yourself with their affinity for the abstract and the theoretical.
✦ Recognize their innovation and creativity.
✦ Respect their history, Catholicism and sense of nationhood.

Avoid

✦ Making things too complex.
✦ Confusing them with Scots.
✦ Trying to delude them and talking down to them.

15

Australia, New Zealand and South Africa

A survey of the world's cultures would be incomplete (dare I say top-heavy?) if it did not include some consideration of the cultural forces at work and the fascinating geographical, historical and racial influences observable among the English-speaking countries of the southern hemisphere.

There are a large number of islands and communities in the South Pacific where English is dominant, a lingua franca, or it coexists with melodious Polynesian tongues. Space constrains us to focus on only three of these peoples— Australians, inhabitants of the largest island in the world; New Zealanders, tyrannized by their remoteness; and vibrant South Africans, durable, multicultural, energetically building a new nation in the southern Atlantic.

What cultural traits do these peoples have in common? Is there such a thing as "down under" solidarity or mentality? Do these English-speaking peoples relate comfortably to each other, taking advantage of similarities in linguistic and literary heritage? Do they respect, envy or dislike each other?

Australia

There is no better clue to the 230-year development of Australian society and culture than the Australian language itself. Australia is the largest English-speaking country in the southern hemisphere. Australian—the sixth largest variety of English (after American, British, Filipino, Indian and Canadian)—is a fascinating, young, vibrant, irreverent, humorous, inventive language.

Newcomers to Australia, who now arrive by jet, not convict ship, get a distinct impression of southern hemisphere Cockney when they first hear the local pronunciation. The similarity is in fact far from accidental. In the decades leading up to the discovery of Australia, the Industrial Revolution caused tens of thousands of destitute farm workers from Kent, East Anglia and Essex to come tumbling into the East End of London in search of work. They linked together with the dockland people—street traders, hawkers and artisans who had been driven out of the City and West End by the upper and middle classes. This hybrid East End population, crowded together in eighteenth-century slums and cross-fertilizing their rural and urban traditions, developed a racy, witty, vulgar type of street English that became known as *Cockney*.

It was not unnatural that these needy, lowly but fast-living city dwellers provided a size-able number of candidates for the vessels bound for the penal colonies in Australia. They were joined aboard by town-bred petty criminals from the overcrowded cities of Yorkshire and Lancashire, and especially Liverpool, which had a large, out-of-work Irish population.

Let's Talk Strine! (Australian)

It is an interesting linguistic phenomenon that the Australian language, like American Black English 200 years earlier, had its first origins at sea. The officers and crew of the slave ships on the long voyage to America had to communicate with their charges in Pidgin, a mixture of basic English and several African languages, which gave an unalterable direction to Black English. On the much longer voyage to Australia, the melting pot of Cockney, Irish and Northern English dialects led to an onboard fusion of accents, grammar and syntax which formed the basis of penal colony speech as the convicts stepped ashore in New South Wales and Queensland.

In this hurly-burly of dialects, Cockney emerged as the clear winner (there were more Cockneys), and the resultant speech variant was larded with dozens of old English dialect forms (*cobber, dust-up, tucker*), with Irish lilt, euphemism and volubility, and with a definite slant toward convict slang (*swag, flog, nick, pinch*). Swear words and vulgar expressions were abundant, as might be expected under the circumstances, but picturesque Cockney rhyming slang also found its way into the mixture and remains one of the fascinating features of Australian English (*trouble 'n strife* = wife, *Bugs bunny* = money, *eau de cologne* = phone).

As the language developed, "outback" speech was quickly added to the already rich mixture. The language of the outback (or the bush) had two main elements—Aborigine and frontier inventions. The influence of the former was limited, although picturesque in the extreme. From the Aborigines came such words as *boomerang, kangaroo, wombat, koala, jumbuck, dingo* and *budgerigar*. Frontier words and expressions were more numerous and showed the hardy humor of the explorers: *digger* = Australian, *amber* = beer, *banana bender* = Queens-lander, *roo* = kangaroo, *heart starter* = first drink of the day, *neck oil* = beer, *grizzle* = complain, and *across the ditch* = New Zealand are some examples.

The modern Aussie is a townie through and through. Australia is the least densely populated country on earth; it is also among the most highly urbanized. It was in the cities where the Cockneys and the Irish ("both in love with talk") thrived, and it was here that the Australian language gained momentum and vitality.

Twenty-first-century Australian is still undergoing change, and because Australia is a relatively classless society, so is the language. There are hardly any regional variations, no class pressures on one's way of speaking, and people switch from broad to cultivated Australian at will. But although Australian speech is in the main uniform, boring it is not. The language of Crocodile Dundee is human, humorous, inventive, original and bursting with vitality. Few languages can come up with similes and metaphors to match "uglier than a robber's dog," "blind Freddie could have seen it" or "he has kangaroos in his top paddock" (he's crazy).

Most Australians refer to each other as *mate*, even at the first meeting. Women are called *love*. *Fair go* is also central to the Australian outlook, based on common sense, equality and a healthy disregard for authority and ideology. This is why Australians always sympathize with the "battler" and underdog—they don't like the exercise of power and privilege over the weak. The two deadly sins are scabbing and dobbing—informing against one's mates.

Cultural Factors in Communication

Communication Pattern

There is no manual for correct behavior in Australia, as the country lacks a clearly defined social and conversational map. Most Australians see this as a strength, a license to be either erudite or rude in any situation. This keeps conversation lively, no one knowing what twist or turn it is likely to take. Will it end up in a torrent of abuse, warm bonhomie and sensitive human exchange, or none of these?

While not entirely true, egalitarianism is a cherished myth and the foreigner must always be very careful not to threaten this notion when talking to an Australian from any background. This egalitarianism is based on the idea of a classless society in which everyone is treated equally—regardless of wealth, education or background.

Although the basic fabric of Australian society is complex (yet appears deceptively simple), there are certain subjects that are in general safe or dangerous. All sports are generally safe topics, and most Australians respond well to a sporting analogy. They love criticizing themselves, but take very poorly to being criticized. This makes it very difficult for you as the newcomer because you will often find yourself in the middle of torrid condemnation of Australia or Australians, but should you agree too enthusiastically or even mildly, you run the risk of being dubbed a *whinger* (complainer). This could lead to your own country being very negatively compared to Australia. If you persist, you could be told in a variety of ways to "go back where you came from."

But Australians also do not like or trust people who constantly or too enthusiastically praise them. They suspect that they are being set up to be either humiliated or deceived. Too much praise raises expectation and puts the high achiever under insufferable pressure—and Australians hate being pressured.

This tortured form of modesty is greatly respected by most Australians and if it is not observed by the successful, they will rapidly fall victim to the "tall poppy syndrome." Equally, never take yourself or your national symbols too seriously, or a similar fate will befall you. It is a source of great pride to Australians that the prime minister is frequently booed at public appearances and that quite a few Australians do not know the words of the national anthem. Perhaps the greatest strength of the Australian personality, although it is under threat, is their monumental cynicism. Australians are totally cynical of people in power or with too much wealth; they respect the little person, the "battler," rather than the winner.

If you keep this in mind and don't oversell yourself or undersell your Australian hosts, success, friendship and good times will be yours Down Under.

Australians in Their Hemisphere

The world's biggest island is also the smallest continent. Geographical location and climatic conditions play a large part in shaping national character. Australia is the flattest and driest of the continents—when traveling around it's hard not to be impressed by the awesome, mind-numbing, parched flatness.

The love of outdoor activities, the ubiquitous beach culture and the fashion for a suntan has led to a national health problem of major proportions—skin cancer. The heat produces a tendency toward apathy and procrastination in many areas, expressed in a general laissez-faire attitude: "no worries" or "She'll be all right in the end." The darker side of Australian life is not to be discounted—they consume more alcohol and painkillers per capita than any other English-speaking country. Their racial policy had been largely unsuccessful, and the Aborigines were in dire straits as a result. Yet Australians remain very positive human beings. Few can match their friendliness and even fewer their spontaneous generosity.

Australia has been a successful multicultural society since the late 1970s. 49 percent of the population (ABS 2016) was born overseas or has at least one parent born overseas. Australia has a higher proportion of overseas-born (26 percent) than Canada (22 percent). It has made great strides in recognizing and encouraging multiculturalism, with some states enacting a Multicultural Act. The SBS radio station broadcasts in over seventy languages. There are 201 ethnic TV stations, 185 press titles and 152 radio stations catering for 300 different languages and 100 religions!

The disadvantages of Australia's geographical remoteness have now been mitigated by the exponential increase in the capabilities of telecommunications. This technology will continue to improve, making geographically remote (and therefore inexpensive) locations such as Perth, Darwin and Adelaide far more attractive propositions for the Asia–Pacific headquarters of multinationals than crowded Tokyo, Hong Kong, Manila or Singapore. Several hundred large companies currently run their regional businesses out of Australia.

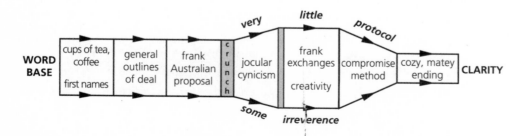

Figure 15.1 Australian Communication Pattern

With the entry of Britain into the EU in 1973, Australia lost its automatic access to traditional markets and was forced to face the reality of its location on the edge of Asia. Asian immigrants, with no sentimental attachments to British institutions, have accentuated this realization. Australian schoolchildren now learn Japanese, not French, as their first foreign language. The fact that Japanese people are not particularly fond of lamb or mutton may put at risk the future of the smallest continent's 60 million sheep!

However, with Britain's possible impending exit from the EU in 2019, the dynamics of the trading relationship may change yet again.

MOTIVATION	
KEY	*Accept "mateship"*
Cross-century mood	◆ A (hopeful) tendency to look to integration with nearby Asian countries as a solution to Australia's economic difficulties. ◆ Encouraged by a "Pacific Rim" mentality. ◆ Some ambivalence about Anglo-Celtic-American ties and how this clashes with Asian and Mediterranean immigrant views. ◆ Monarchy or republic? ◆ Tendency to want to settle the Aboriginal question.

Motivating Factors

◆ Show you are willing to be "one of the mates."
◆ While remaining law-abiding, show a healthy disrespect for many laws and too much government interference.
◆ Cut through red tape at every opportunity.
◆ Always lead from the front and never ask anyone to do anything you would not do yourself.
◆ Roll up your sleeves and help people to move tables.
◆ Develop deep friendships whenever this is appropriate.
◆ Moderate swearing is not taboo.
◆ Sarcasm and irony are popular, but when exercising them, let kindness shine through.
◆ Praise Australia—there is no reason why you shouldn't!
◆ They are free spenders, so be careful not to appear stingy.
◆ The "tall poppy syndrome" is a reality. Ride too high and the Australians will soon cut you down.
◆ Australians like cheerfulness and affability. Respond accordingly.
◆ Be prepared to chat amiably with relative strangers.
◆ Get a feel for how Australian males treat women. It is a rather special relationship.
◆ Give parties regularly if this is appropriate. Australians often mix business with social activities.

(continued)

MOTIVATION *(continued)*

+ You can make good progress with Australians if you let your hair down while drinking and socializing.
+ Although Australians often appear irreverent, take their irony with a pinch of salt. Many rough-and-ready Australians have hearts of gold.
+ Do them favors. They are quick to repay.
+ Jokes and anecdotes are very popular. A sense of humor is essential for getting the best out of Australians.
+ Always bear in mind that human rights are high on their list of priorities.

Avoid

+ Giving brusque orders or any other form of arrogance.
+ Criticizing anyone for not dressing smartly or for failing to observe etiquette; Australians love informality.
+ Intruding into their leisure time. At 4:00 or 5:00 P.M. they are usually thinking about the pub or the beach.
+ Using flowery or obscure speech.
+ Boasting about your past achievements.
+ Referring to their convict past; let them bring up the subject.

New Zealand

The original settlers who in the 1840s founded the colony of New Zealand were all English speaking—predominantly a middle-class and working population drawn principally from rural areas of England and Scotland. They were literate and, at least during the early settling-in period in the mid-nineteenth century, much of their educational thinking and all of their reading matter came from Britain. As New Zealand's "foreign" immigrants have always been small minorities, the English spoken in New Zealand has never been distorted (or invigorated) by waves of non-English speakers similar to those who posed a challenge to the English of the United States. It therefore has retained much old rural vocabulary from British dialects and remains resolutely Southern English, apart from some give-away front vowels (*pin* for *pen* and *fush* for *fish*).

The islands of New Zealand are similar in size to the British Isles and not entirely dissimilar in climate. New Zealanders tend to identify more strongly with their insular forebears and regard both Australians and Americans as a different, continental breed. The New Zealanders' stereotype of Australians is that they are loud-mouthed, brash and arrogant, they often interrupt others and they talk in tandem, all of which are frowned on in New Zealand.

New Zealanders are more conservative, placid and reserved than Australians. They are more British, not only in their calmness of manner, but in their racial composition. They see Australians as cosmopolitan and somewhat excitable.

New Zealanders see themselves as certainly being more laid back, cultured and much more likely to treat women sensitively than their Australian neighbors. Australians often regard New Zealanders as Victorian, outdated, poor country cousins—but New Zealand produces efficient, innovative managers who often do well in Australia, being more adventurous than their Ozzie counterparts. Deregulation has gone much further in New Zealand than in Australia, where business is often seen as a closed shop. Australians are more price-oriented than New Zealanders, who are more inclined to value quality.

New Zealanders emigrate in rather large numbers to Australia on account of the scarcity of work in their own country. The things they like about Australia (often referred to as "The West Island") are the wide-open outback and winter warmth, the cosmopolitan cities and shopping opportunities, the classless society and friendly, helpful attitude of the people.

Australians show a lot of down-under solidarity with New Zealanders, especially in moments of adversity, but on occasions when this bond is broken, the latter feel that they are not the ones who break it.

Many New Zealanders visit Europe and the "Old Country" once or twice in their lives, but they are increasingly oriented toward the Pacific and spend most of their vacations in Australia or the Pacific Islands. They have good relations with Pacific Islanders (Tonga, Fiji, Cook Island) and believe that their Maori policy has been fairly successful. Many Maoris do not share this opinion, feeling they were ruthlessly exploited in the past and that present atonement falls far short of what is morally required. The Maori attitude toward white New Zealanders is this: "They are guests in our country." An interesting cultural sideline is that the whites tend to behave like Maoris when living it up, for instance on certain sporting occasions and when singing and dancing. Most whites possess a fair knowledge of the Maori language (without being able to speak it) and sing Maori songs, as well as doing the *haka* with great gusto at ceremonies. This rather engaging symbiotic relationship is noticeably absent in the case of Australians and Aborigines.

NEW ZEALAND–AUSTRALIAN DIFFERENCES

New Zealand	Australia
conservative	liberal
cautious	adventurous
modest	confident
soft sell	medium-hard sell
reserved in speech	chatty
often rural attitude	urban

(continued)

(continued from previous page)

NEW ZEALAND–AUSTRALIAN DIFFERENCES

New Zealand	*Australia*
slow-medium tempo	quick
prioritize dependability	prioritize energy
British-oriented	cosmopolitan
educated speech	often broad
laid back	exploratory
usually calm	often excitable
often old-fashioned	up-to-date
polite	frank
careful with money	gamblers, generous
respect authority	irreverent
tight-lipped	bold speakers
properness in relations	warmth
insular, traditional	insular but continental
worriers	"no worries"

MOTIVATION	
KEY	*Show dependability and stamina*
Cross-century mood	◆ The tariffs of the EU and geographical isolation have led to crisis with regard to the future of New Zealand trade. ◆ They adhere strongly to the Anglo-Saxon cultural world, but look toward Asia as a future market for their products. ◆ Their best bet may be to make an "economic bloc" with Australia, but they are not ready for this step yet. *Motivating Factors* ◆ Distinguish them clearly from Australians. ◆ Recognize the Maori minority—it will eventually become the majority (faster growth rate). ◆ Show great interest in rugby and sports in general—all New Zealanders love sports. Rugby unites whites and Maoris. ◆ Accept that many New Zealanders have rural attitudes and may come across as steady plodders.

(continued)

MOTIVATION *(continued)*

- ✦ Share their laid-back tempo.
- ✦ Urban New Zealanders are often sharp businesspeople; have lively exchanges with them.
- ✦ Show personal steadiness and stamina; they respect these qualities.
- ✦ Laugh at the Australians with them (in a kind way).
- ✦ Appreciate New Zealand quality (produce and ideas)—"small is good."
- ✦ Be enthusiastic about their wonderful scenery.
- ✦ Share their concerns over the future of New Zealand trade and search for solutions with them.
- ✦ Show you are as dependable as they are.
- ✦ Restrict your ambitions to a New Zealand framework and context, as they must.
- ✦ Keep things direct and simple.

Avoid

- ✦ Too much flattery—the males react against it.
- ✦ Australian-style brashness—New Zealanders hate it.
- ✦ Any form of hard sell.
- ✦ Making statements you cannot back up.
- ✦ Overly ambitious schemes.
- ✦ Criticizing apparent national dullness ("New Zealand was closed when I was there").

South Africa

Post-apartheid South Africa is emerging into the world limelight as one of the most multi-cultural nations on earth. It is not a melting pot of immigrants like the United States or Australia, but a society where several communities and races— British, Afrikaans, Malay, Indian, Zulu, Xhosa and other black tribes—remain as separate and integral forces forging a new union that has aspirations to provide leadership to a depressed and seemingly disintegrating continent.

South Africa possesses the multicultural strengths of a Switzerland, a Singapore, and much more. The rich combination of British, French and Dutch experience, the artistry and ardent aspirations of the black South Africans and the diligence and tenacity of the Indians and Malays are ingredients for a dynamic, inspired and unique future. Yet the colorful variety of the country's cultures itself poses a number of problems.

White South Africans

The history of warfare between the British and Afrikaan settlers has left a residue of resentment between the two communities. Each group has inherited characteristics from their

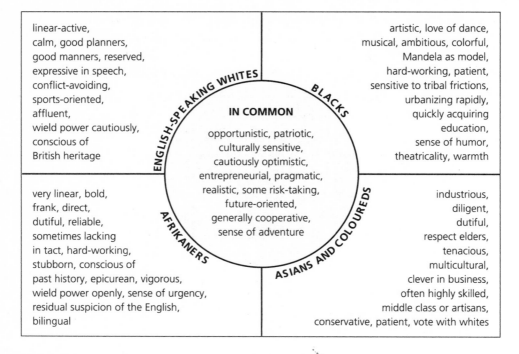

Figure 15.2 South African Values: English-Speaking Whites, Blacks, Afrikaners, Asians and Coloureds

forebears. English-speaking South Africans are somewhat reserved in nature, proud of their cultural heritage and set great store by good manners; elegant, expressive speech and avoidance of unnecessary conflict. In this respect they differ strongly from the Afrikaners, who, like their Dutch ancestors, are blunt (often tactless) and have the American tendency to "tell it like it is."

Although the British and Afrikaners differ sharply in their styles of communication, a white South African lifestyle is discernible. Pragmatism is paramount, but South Africans deeply resent the implication that they are insensitive to the plight of less fortunate human beings. A visitor to South Africa cannot avoid being aware of the eager hospitality and thoughtful kindness of the whites living there. Despite the years of racial suppression and injustice, there is in fact far less color consciousness in the country than in many other parts of the world. South Africans have been brought up in a multicolored society—it is a natural state.

White South Africans are entrepreneurial and decisive in business. At meetings they come well prepared and usually have a few cards up their sleeves. They are familiar with many African cultures and customs and accept that bribery and accommodation are part of life on their continent if one is to achieve anything. They are, however, flexible in such matters and do not apply the same judgments when dealing with the West. In a discussion they will often sit back to listen and learn, but they are not averse to assuming dominance and taking control of a meeting when they perceive an opportunity. In spite of the latitudinal distance, they focus much more on Europe than toward East or West. Africa, the continent they hope to lead, has close connections with Britain and France.

One hears many pessimistic predictions about the deterioration of South African society, similar to the manner that has been observed in other African states. South African whites recognize that their country can survive only if the black South Africans play an integral role in the development of the new South Africa.

Black South Africans really hold the key to the nation's future. They have many qualities that will help, not least of which are patience, tolerance and a delightful sense of humor. While they are not as well educated as the whites, they are very well educated in comparison with the rest of Africa, and their incomes are higher than other Africans, except Botswana. Furthermore, among the 50 percent who are already urbanized, there is a substantial and rapidly growing middle class. Their access to government posts and the international contact this will bring will quickly add to their experience and sophistication. Nelson Mandela himself was a shining example of a black South African politician. South Africa's gross domestic product (GDP) is already four times that of the combined GDP of the ten other countries of southern Africa.

Black South Africans

Because black South Africans are playing—and will continue to play—such a vital role in the development of the nation, I will emphasize this group above the whites, Indians, and Coloureds.

Black South Africans see themselves as human elements in a close pattern of kinship, to which they make sincere contributions and are consequently protected and secure. The tribe is everything. Without a tribal affiliation, the African is incomplete. This has little to do with the political nation–state boundaries drawn up in the 1880s by colonizing Europeans. About 1,000 tribes were collapsed into 50 political units, stripping millions of people of an accurate sense of self-identity. Only tribalism has rescued many Africans from this sense of loss (e.g., I may be Kenyan, but really I am Kikuyu, or South African perhaps, but Zulu for sure).

Though different in many aspects, black South Africans are as explicit and expressive as Latin peoples. More use is made of the eyes and facial expressions than would be the norm for even Southern Europeans. The African love of dance and rhythm is also visible in their body language. They often sway in rhythm with their verbal utterances, almost enacting a dance in moments of excitement. South African body language, like much of their music, is both stimulating and soothing, depending on the mood. You would do well to study the most favored signals.

Concepts

Leadership and Status

Traditionally, many societies were based on clans and lineages, with most authority being held by genealogically senior men. Clans might consist of a single kinship unit, but they would be linked with neighboring bands by ties of intermarriage and consciousness of common cultural identity. This type of leadership still exists, but economic change, when South Africa became part of the total worldwide system of economic production and exchange, has weakened clan and tribal influence. The traditional equality of living standards has been affected, especially in the cities, by the growth of new elites and the appearance of a poor and typically exploited urban proletariat.

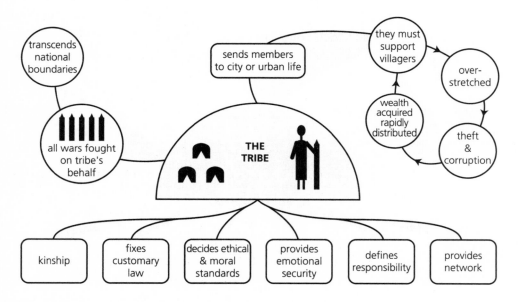

Figure 15.3 Black South African Leadership Style

Space and Time

In spite of a burgeoning population, South Africa as a whole has a relatively low population density of 90 persons per square mile (45 persons per square kilometer). The sense of space is exhilarating, and rural communities cling passionately to the wide open spaces of their land and their herds. Cities by contrast are overcrowded and cramp traditional African lifestyle.

   With regard to personal space, black South Africans are a very tactile people in terms of hugging. This occasionally causes Europeans some embarrassment (especially when

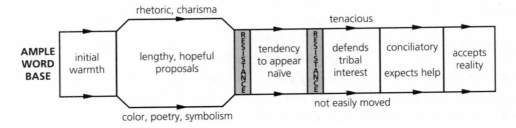

Figure 15.4 Black South African Communication Pattern

speaking to relative strangers), but this is a positive characteristic, emanating warmth, closeness and trust.

Black South Africans are not renowned for punctuality or any sense of urgency. Hot climates inhibit rushing around to keep appointments, and you will have to adjust to African time. Blacks themselves wait patiently for delayed transportation and meetings with important persons.

Cultural Factors in Communication

Communication Pattern

Black South African languages include Xhosa, Zulu, Swazi, Sotho, Tsonga, Venda and Ndebele. Communication at the outset is warm and friendly and in many cases is couched in poetic and symbolic terms. Color, charisma and rhetoric come naturally to Africans, enhanced, of course, by improved education. When conducting a business meeting, warmth is tempered by tenacity in defending tribal interest.

Listening Habits

Africans are courteous listeners, though some repetition is advisable. They do not like being rushed verbally—their own elders have innate patience. Although suspicious of "ex-colonialists," blacks are quickly gratified by reasonable establishment of trust between parties.

Behavior at Meetings and Negotiations

Meetings with black South Africans tend to be folksy and chatty and do not strictly adhere to agendas. Points are discussed in order of importance and are not abandoned until some measure of mutual satisfaction has been achieved. Older men usually decide when this point has been reached. Meetings can be noisy but are not necessarily aggressive. All-African meetings are more quarrelsome, with tribal rivalries rearing their heads. You will be expected to lead

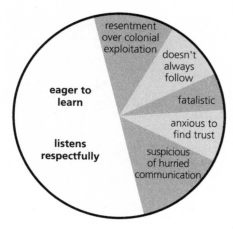

Figure 15.5 Black South African Listening Habits

meetings at which you present or at least make significant contributions. Show great respect and deference to senior Africans and protect everyone's "face" as much as possible. Don't be surprised—or annoyed—if subsequent meetings are repetitious; Africans normally do not mind going over old ground.

When you are negotiating, keep in mind the following characteristics:

+ Bargaining and haggling are part of the negotiation process.
+ Tribal or clan interests usually serve as a background to other commercial considerations.
+ Style is slow, plodding and repetitive.
+ Conviviality and affability are usually maintained (but not always).
+ Theatrical demands and explosive outbursts are not uncommon.
+ These are usually followed by conciliatory periods.
+ Older men are usually calm and finally make most of the decisions.
+ In the modern economy, blacks continue to show traditional wisdom, but inexperience with new economic factors is often a handicap.

Manners and Taboos

Dozens of tribal traditions entail many different customs, beliefs, rituals and taboos. Belief in a supreme being and other supernatural elements affect behavior continent-wide. Islamic core beliefs and taboos are in conformity with those of other Muslim communities. Various Christian sects exert their own influences. Black Africans are well known for their music, rhythm, drums and dance. Their art is incredibly rich and is clearly connected to religious and philosophical beliefs as well as to an amazing variety of rituals and ceremonial practices. The Western appreciation of traditional jazz music gives white people a certain feel for

African cultural sensitivity, poetry and drive. Music is one of the fruitful meeting grounds for black and white people and gives clues as to how common desires and feelings could, in better eras to come, be developed, coordinated and enjoyed.

How to Empathize with Black South Africans

Black South Africans in general need warmth, kindness, sympathy and practical help. They are also proud, so that aid and advice must be offered discreetly. You should recognize African strengths, which are numerous in many artistic, aesthetic and humanitarian fields. These should be seen as compensating for shortcomings (e.g., organizational and economic experience), which derive from situations often created by whites. From any point of view, blacks have an uphill struggle in the next few decades. Give them plentiful recognition where it is due, pay in full for good labor and services, and sacrifice short-term profit for long-term policies to develop trade, exchange and viable commercial prospects. Look at African efforts positively and keep an open mind as to their eventual potential.

South Africans from the Indian Subcontinent

The Indian community in South Africa is one million strong and is located mainly in Natal. Their cultural characteristics closely resemble those of Indians elsewhere (see Chapter 54 on India). Like the Chinese, overseas Indians tend to be more industrious and successful than those in the homeland. In South Africa, they are largely middle class and enjoy considerable prosperity. Their basic Indian culture is affected to some degree by rubbing shoulders with white and black South Africans, and to some extent they have acquired some traits from both sides, especially a South African worldview encompassing the aspirations of the country. Like minorities everywhere, the Indians of South Africa are somewhat nervous about the viability of their future, but they have proven their tenacity over many years.

South African Cape Coloureds

The 4.5 million population of Cape Coloureds (mixed white, black, Malay and Bushman) live mostly in the western and northern Capes. Although they exhibit certain characteristics deriving from their racial mix, in general they have developed a fairly standard culture and are either middle class or highly skilled workers and artisans. They have a strong work ethic and are more interested in commerce and earning a reasonable livelihood than in politics.

Like the Indians, they have a certain sense of precariousness in an overwhelmingly black country, but they are survivors, and they play a very useful and deserving role in the nation's economy. Education and the acquisition of skills are important for them.

MOTIVATION	
KEY	*Long-term commitment to the future of the country*
Cross-century mood	✦ Nelson Mandela achieved an impressive transition and this is the best hope in a society that cannot be easily managed. ✦ Currently things have proceeded peacefully, though there are enormous hills to climb economically, especially with regard to housing. ✦ If emigration of skilled people is diminished, the country could play an important part in leading the continent.

Motivating Factors

✦ Recognize and adapt to the main cultures—white, black, Indian and Cape Coloured, but search for commonalities among the groups.
✦ All South Africans would like to see their country prosper—decide how you can be of help.
✦ Introduce business which is meaningful and viable in the new South African context.
✦ Accept that return on investment will not be as rapid as "in the old days."
✦ Commit yourself to the future of the country—it is, after all, highly prosperous by African standards.
✦ Praise Mandela for his wise leadership and lasting charisma.
✦ Be even-handed with all cultural and racial groups.
✦ Acknowledge the multicultural sensitivity of many South Africans and the benefits thereof.
✦ Show an interest in sports, especially cricket and rugby (but also soccer); all groups participate to some extent.
✦ All South Africans are extremely hospitable; reflect their warmth.

Avoid

✦ The parlance and attitudes of the apartheid era.
✦ Dwelling on the country's problems without offering solutions.
✦ Short-term policies destined only to make a quick buck.
✦ Old-fashioned alliances with all-white interest groups.
✦ Open criticism of past policies—it is better to put them behind you.

16

Germany

The basic characteristics of German business culture are a monochronic attitude toward the use of time; for example, a desire to complete one action chain before embarking on another; a strong belief that Germans are honest, straightforward negotiators; and a tendency to be blunt and disagree openly rather than going for politeness or diplomacy. (For an explanation of monochronic and polychronic time, see Chapter 4.) German companies are traditional, slow-moving entities, encumbered by manuals, systems and hierarchical paths regarded by many Europeans and Americans as overly rigid and outmoded. Hierarchy is mandatory, often resulting in exaggerated deference for one's immediate superior and CEO.

The German boss is an extremely private person, normally sitting isolated in a large office behind a closed door. American and Scandinavian senior executives prefer an open door policy and like to wander round the corridors and chat with colleagues. This horizontal communication contrasts with the German vertical system, where instructions are passed down to immediate inferiors only and kept rigidly within one's own department. In many countries there exists inter-departmental rivalry, but when dealing with the Germans you should remember that they can be especially touchy in this area. Always try to find the right person for each message. Tread on a German executive's toes and he or she will remember it for a long time.

Germans have great respect for possessions and property. Solid buildings, furniture, cars and good clothing are important for them and they will try to impress you with all these things. You should acknowledge the grandeur of German possessions and not be afraid to display your own solidity, facilities, and so on. Germans wish to believe you are as solid as they are. When advertising your company's products to Germans, you should put as much as possible in print. Germans are unimpressed by flashy television advertising, clever slogans or artistic illustrations. Their newspapers are full of heavy, factual ads giving the maximum amount of information in the space available. Brochures aimed at the German market should be lengthy, factual and serious, and should make claims which can later be fully justified. No matter how long or boring your brochure is, the Germans will read it. They will also expect your product to conform exactly to the description you have given.

Culture

Values

fair	*Ordnung*
honest	frank, direct (truth before tact)
conformist	logical
time-dominated	private
tendency to complicate	serious
organized; good planners	law-abiding
strong sense of duty	faithful
requiring context	intense
soul-searching	serious

Concepts

Space and Time

Germans need less personal space and independence at work than Scandinavians or Americans, but they enthusiastically protect their rights to what space they have. It should not be reduced, interfered with or invaded by others. Working life and private life are usually kept strictly separate. Privacy is important and when a door is closed (as they often are), you should knock before entering.

Germans like to get close before greeting. They avoid shouting hellos across a crowded room or waving dramatically in airport arrival halls. Making a public scene of this sort would be seen as an emotional loss of control or discipline. In formal situations a polite distance is maintained, but physical contact is not always avoided in public spaces. When you bump into a German in a shop, a corridor or a train platform, apologies are restrained rather than effusive.

Germans are less than orderly in their attitude toward queues. Sometimes they are willing to wait their turn according to who came first. Sometimes they are organized by a numbered ticketing system. At other times Germans may push past each other to get to the front of a crowd or even the front of a line. There is no strong tradition of queuing in Germany.

Germans are the most punctual of all peoples. Foreigners arriving late for appointments will be reminded of their lateness, which will be seen as a sign of unreliability by Germans. "Arriving late" may mean a delay of only two or three minutes. Schedules, action plans and deliveries are strictly observed.

Germans value their leisure time greatly and will not welcome your attempts to cut into it with work. Meetings on Friday afternoons, when many offices close early, are not popular.

Cultural Factors in Communication

Communication Pattern

The German communication style is frank, open, direct and often loud. Truth comes before diplomacy. Many foreigners are surprised by German directness and honesty. Arguments are logical, weighty and thought out well. Their speech style is serious, often unsmiling and frequently repetitive. Germans do not seek humor in a work context, even when a joke may lighten the atmosphere. They do not look for a light working climate. There are few taboo subjects in Germany, and for many Germans, none at all. (See Figure 5.3 for an illustration of the German communication pattern.)

Listening Habits

Germans listen well because they are disciplined and always willing to learn more. They have a long attention span when absorbing information and especially like repetition and plenty of background information. Germans rarely expect or want to be entertained in a work context. They are serious-minded and when they hear your carefree comments, they may interpret them as important statements and ask for more information, examples or details. Simple messages sound incomplete to German ears. (See Figure 5.15 for an illustration of German listening habits.)

Behavior at Meetings and Negotiations

Germans have their own particular style of conducting meetings and negotiations, and you may find that procedures with big German companies are much more formalized than in your country. It is generally advisable to adopt a more formal approach with Germans at meetings and to note the following German characteristics, to which you must react appropriately:

- Germans will arrive at the meeting well dressed and with a disciplined appearance. You must match this.
- They will observe a hierarchical seating and order of speaking.
- They will arrive well informed as to the business to be discussed, and they will expect you to be also.
- They will present logical, often weighty arguments to support their case.
- They have often thought over your possible counterarguments and have their second line of attack ready.
- They do not concede their case or arguments easily, but tend to look for common ground. This is often your best approach for making progress. Head-on collision with a sizeable German company seldom leads to results.
- They believe they are more efficient than others and do not change positions easily.

- ✦ They compartmentalize their arguments, each member speaking about his or her specialty. They expect your side to do the same.
- ✦ They do not interfere with a colleague's remarks and generally show good teamwork throughout. They do, however, argue with each other in private between sessions. As they are not poker-faced (like the Japanese) or simulating (like the French), it is often possible to detect a difference of opinion among them by their facial expressions or body language.
- ✦ Like the Japanese, they like to go over details time and time again. They wish to avoid misunderstandings later. You must be patient.
- ✦ They are willing to make decisions within meetings (unlike the Japanese and French), but they are always cautious.
- ✦ They generally stick to what they have agreed to orally.
- ✦ If you are selling to them, they will question you aggressively on German strong points: quality of goods, delivery dates and competitive pricing. Be ready.
- ✦ They expect, in the end, to get the very best (lowest) price. They may only give you a little "trial" business even at that. Take it—it will lead to much more business later if they are satisfied.
- ✦ They will look earnestly for deficiencies in your products or services and will criticize you openly (even energetically) if you fail to match up to all your claims. Be prepared to apologize if you have failed in some respect. They like receiving apologies; it makes them feel better. Also, you will have to compensate them for your deficiencies.
- ✦ They can be very sensitive to criticism themselves; therefore you must go to great lengths to avoid embarrassing them, even unwittingly.
- ✦ Use surnames only and show respect for their titles. There are many *Doktors* in Germany.
- ✦ Do not introduce humor or jokes during business meetings. For them, business is serious.
- ✦ They will write up their notes carefully and come back well prepared the next day. It is advisable for you to do the same.
- ✦ They are generally convinced that they are the most honest, reliable and sincere people in the world, also in their business negotiations. Show them that in this respect you are their equal.

Germans are indeed very sincere people and assume that others are too. They are often disappointed, as other people who prefer a casual or flippant approach to life do not always give serious answers to serious questions. Germans tend to search long and deep for the true meaning of life and like to spend their time profitably, whether it is to enrich their coffers or their soul.

In their seriousness, they try hard to be dutiful, not being troublesome citizens. In a crowded country pressures to conform in public are very strong and Germans do not wish to be seen as mavericks or unorthodox. They have no desire (like many British, French and American people) to be eccentric. Germans try not to make mistakes and generally succeed. If you make a mistake they will tell you about it. They are not being rude—it is their unstoppable drive toward order and conformity. Germans like to be fair and often lean over backward to show how fair they are.

Germans often appear intense and humorless to Anglo-Saxons, who long for periodic levity in conversation. Germans do not have the British and American addiction to funny stories and wisecracks. They long for deep friendships and have heartfelt discussions of life's problems and enigmas. Anglo-Saxons do not always see the way toward making quick friendships with them, but when they succeed in entering into the somewhat complicated structure of a German friendship, they find rich rewards. A German is generally a loyal and true friend of incredible durability. Outwardly often glum and cautious, they are inwardly desperate for affection and popularity. They want to be cherished just as the rest of us do. When they find that English, American or French individuals—on the surface easy-going and witty—can also be as steadfast as a German, they are delighted and receptive. A German friendship is indeed a very worthwhile investment.

Manners and Taboos

Germans are great conformists and generally do the expected rather than the unexpected. Open criticism of opponents and colleagues is acceptable. The right to privacy, both at home and in one's office, is paramount. Eccentricity, ostentation, unpunctuality and disobedience are frowned upon.

How to Empathize with Germans

Be frank, truthful and as honest as possible. Respect their bluntness and accept criticism when it is directed toward you. Keep in regular touch; Germans are good correspondents. German businesspeople do not give or expect to receive expensive gifts. Gift giving often follows successful business, or occurs with loyal clients at certain times of the year.

Remember the importance of local identity. Being a Bavarian may be more important to your host than being a German, for example. Look for common ground in your and their views. Learn some German and use it. Show that you place trust in them. Avoid irony, sarcasm and quick wit. The people of Germany do have a sense of humor, but, as I've said, they do not use it at work. What amuses a German will not get all other cultures laughing either.

GERMANS AS SEEN BY OTHERS

Appearance	Reality
Germans are time-dominated, punctuality is an obsession.	Time is central to German culture. It is one of the principal ways of organizing life.
Germans are slow at making decisions, as they discuss things too long.	Germans' decision-making process requires extensive background research and often lateral clearances.
Germans give you very lengthy explanations, going right back to the beginning of every matter.	Germans, when explaining something, like to lay a proper foundation. For them events in the present are a result of the past.
Delays in delivery are common in Germany, contradicting their love of promptness.	Germans plan well into the future, not being preoccupied with immediate results or deliveries.
Germans are not good at providing quarterly financial reports according to the American system.	Germans prefer annual reports. Three months is too short a time frame to be meaningful.
Americans and Australians find the pace of German business life too slow.	Germans like to complete action chains and wish to be thorough rather than speedy.
You always have to knock on the door before entering a German's office.	Yes, it is good manners.
Germans are too private. They do not interact well with foreigners and are not mobile. They don't lend things easily.	Germany is not a melting-pot society, where people have developed strategies for interacting with strangers. Privacy is important in order to complete their work. They don't borrow things easily.
Germans are too formal, using only surnames with office colleagues.	Formality and use of surnames are signs of respect.
They are stiff, distant and do not smile much.	In Germany, smiling is for friends. They are reserved when being introduced to people; smiles are not always sincere!
Germans don't like people standing too close to them or touching them.	In Germany, the "distance of comfort" is approximately 4 feet (1.2 meters). It is a nontactile culture.
There is too much secrecy in German organizations. Information does not flow freely.	Knowledge is power. Power flows from the top down.
Germans admire military and economic power more than other kinds.	Not true. They admire intellectual power most. Many heads of German firms have doctorates.

(continued)

GERMANS AS SEEN BY OTHERS *(continued)*

Appearance	Reality
Germans display power and influence through material possessions rather immodestly.	Germans like to display symbols of power and success but handle them with reserve.
Germans are noisy people.	True only of German tourists abroad.
Germans have too many rules and regulations and do not take human needs into consideration sufficiently.	Germans believe good procedures and processes solve most problems and give order paramount importance.
Germans are too law-abiding, conform too much and are always worried about what others will think.	The German sense of order requires conformity. Signs and directions are there to be obeyed.
Decentralization and compartmentalization represent serious handicaps in German business.	These are structural features in German society. Germany was unified late and dislikes too much central power.
Germans, in conversation and when developing ideas, make things too complex.	Life is complicated. Germans think Americans and others oversimplify.
German possessions, especially furniture, buildings, cars and TV sets, are heavy and lack grace.	Germans like all their goods solid—like their characters!
Germans have a mania for keeping things in spotless order.	Germans do not believe in waste. If you keep things in good order they will last longer.
Germans criticize you if you do anything wrong or make too much noise. It is none of their business what I do!	In Germany, proper observation of the rules is everybody's business.
Germans are class-conscious, especially in top levels of business.	This is true to some extent, but top-level Germans are very well mannered.
The Germans persist in using Sie when most Anglo-Saxons would start using first names.	Germans are not casual about friendships. They do not wish to become immediately familiar with strangers.
Germans take work too seriously. They are boring.	Germans think business is a serious matter. Being serious is being honest, not boring.
Germans are stubborn and lack flexibility. They don't compromise enough.	Germans stick to what they believe in. If you want to change their minds, you must show them they are wrong.
Germans are often too frank at business meetings and lack delicacy. They upset people.	Frankness is honesty. "Diplomacy" can often mean deviousness or not saying what you think.

(continued)

GERMANS AS SEEN BY OTHERS (continued)

Appearance	Reality
Germans make poor conversation partners at cocktail parties. They can't make "small talk."	Germans do not see the point in "small talk." They say what there is to say. They do not wish to open their private lives to strangers at parties.
German head offices often fail to react to local conditions abroad and persist in doing things the "German way."	There is some truth in this, but German expatriate managers are often successful in convincing HQ of the need for flexibility.
Germans are not adaptable. They are unable to effect changes quickly within their organizations to meet changing circumstances.	Germans do not like making "lightning" decisions. They believe an organization will be successful if procedures are first perfected and then kept in place.
Germans spend an inordinate amount of time every day shaking hands with colleagues.	Shaking hands shows respect for one's colleagues and is the normal way for a German to say "hello."
German managers rarely compliment their workers on the job.	Germans expect a job to be well done. Why constantly compliment people who are simply doing their duty?
German advertising is heavy, boring and not visual enough.	Germans like lots of information, therefore they wish an advertisement to describe the product in detail. They are not impressed by clever slogans, catchphrases or hype.

MOTIVATION	
KEY	*Indicating trust, demonstrating solidity*
Cross-century mood	✦ They are very interested in financing development in Eastern Europe and establishing partnerships there. ✦ As the strongest nation, they intend to lead the EU. ✦ They value their good relationship with the United States. ✦ They have been successful in keeping their post-war democracy intact and want to continue doing so.

(continued)

MOTIVATION *(continued)*

Motivating Factors

◆ Germans are generally punctual, organized and efficient. You must match these qualities.

◆ Whatever you promise a German, you must deliver.

◆ When Germans criticize your actions, it is to help you avoid making mistakes. Accept their criticism as being constructive.

◆ You may also point out their errors frankly, but make sure you are right.

◆ Put as much in writing as you can. You can be as wordy as you like, they will read it.

◆ Once you have established your status (qualifications, competence, dress, reputation) then live up to it.

◆ Give serious answers to serious questions. Germans are uneasy when confronted with flippancy or (in their eyes) inappropriate humor.

◆ Be well prepared on the issues. They usually are.

◆ Display trust and expect it from them.

◆ They like consensus. Consult all people concerned before embarking on a course of action.

◆ Say what you mean—irony, sarcasm, subtle undertones usually fall on deaf ears.

◆ When Germans say they have a "problem," it usually means that there is an issue they wish to discuss. Most often a solution can be reached. Be positive.

◆ German companies are often successful because they have established reliable processes and procedures during their history. Respect these.

◆ In general it is a good policy to obey rules and laws without questioning them very much. They are not as flexible as Italians or as open-minded as Americans.

◆ Subordinates should be helped, advised and monitored, but once you have explained a task fully, then leave them alone to get on with it.

◆ Respect privacy at all times, both with regard to the person and the company's activities. Information does not flow freely in Germany.

◆ Remember to shake hands a lot and use proper greetings on meeting and departing.

◆ German friendships are deep. Work hard at them and maintain the relationship.

Avoid

◆ Displaying too much eccentricity.

◆ Meet them head on if you see their position is diametrically opposed to yours.

◆ Interrupting unfinished tasks or giving Germans too many tasks simultaneously. They are not multi-active Latins.

◆ Falling into the trap of oversimplifying. Germans often see Americans and some others as naïve.

◆ Overdoing small talk. Germans like facts, figures, reliable information.

◆ The hard sell.

◆ Wisecracks, gimmicks, slogans.

17

Austria

If we look at the map of Austria in outline we are tempted to imagine a rump with half a leg sticking out to the left. The metaphor, in fact, is not so inaccurate, since the country could be described as a *rump* state—what is left when others have taken their shares. The breakup of the vast Austro–Hungarian Empire hit Austrians hard. The Second World War, with the subsequent four-power occupation lasting until 1955, administered the coup de grâce to what was left of their self-assurance. The Austrians, heirs to a glorious imperial past, feel that there is a role for them, but do not quite know where to look for it.

Their search for identity is not an easy one. The dismemberment of the empire caused the loss of many lands and many citizens. Those who are left do not show great cohesion. Austria is compact neither in shape nor in mind. In the West the inhabitants of Vorarlberg would like to be Swiss, but the Swiss would not have them. Salzburg is compelling, but the east is dominated by Vienna—inhabited by large numbers of Czechs, Hungarians, Slovaks, Slovenians and Jews, not to mention recent immigrants from Eastern Europe.

Yet some statistics suggest a prosperous, healthy-minded Austria. Its 29th ranking in world economies is creditable, considering its small population and few resources. Its 19th place in GDP per capita is nothing less than astonishing. It is nineteenth in car ownership, nineteenth in tourist receipts and seventh in health spending. Its only "gold medal" in global achievement, however, hints at its "anonymous excellence": it is undisputed first in paper recycling!

Culture

Values

hospitable	traditional, old-fashioned
nostalgic	sentimental, romantic love
nature, clean	Catholic, pessimistic
respect education	self-deprecatory humor
hypersensitive to criticism	lack self-assurance
chivalrous, charming	class conscious, stylish

Concepts

Leadership and Status

In Austria there is a historical respect for aristocrats, not unrelated to the nostalgia felt about the old empire. The country (and especially Vienna) can still be categorized as class conscious. Austria is a democratic republic; business and industry, organized labor and the farming community work closely with the ministries in regulating the economy and political direction.

At business level, leadership is autocratic and authoritarian. Staff listen respectfully to what the boss has to say, without interrupting. Top managers maintain a sizeable power distance and delegate day-to-day tasks to middle managers, who work harder than they do. Middle managers enjoy authority over the rank and file, but object to the boss' policies at some risk. Workers tend to show exaggerated respect to seniors and are uncomfortable with a system where their voices are rarely heard and where major societal decisions are made behind closed doors. The general lack of self-confidence (observable at all levels of Austrian society) discourages workers from standing up for their rights.

Family connections and private networks are influential, and advancement in business and government is less transparent than it seems. The younger generation feels they are inadequately represented. Many Austrians list "knowing the right people" as the most important factor in advancing one's career; hard work and loyalty to the company come lower down.

Space and Time

In the west of Austria, love of nature and neat, well-nurtured spaces is dominant. Tyrolese keep at a respectful Germanic distance from each other (over a yard/meter) and kissing and hugging in public are rarely seen. Handshaking is mandatory.

The Viennese are much more tactile. Slavic, Jewish and Latin influence is observable in considerable physical closeness and displays of affection.

In the west of Austria people are punctual and hate wasting time. Vienna is different again. The "coffee house" culture of the capital encourages leisurely gatherings where gossip and networking thrive and clock watching takes a back seat.

Cultural Factors in Communication

Communication Pattern

Austrians are efficient communicators, using charm and small talk, and on the surface are open and friendly. They are also manipulative, but in an unconscious, natural way, not cold and calculating. They are eager talkers in monologue and are raconteurs who love telling stories and embellishing as they go along. In business discussions their weakness is that they often lapse into a rambling, convoluted style, feeling that they have to fill in all the background and context. Nordic and American directness is disconcerting to Viennese, who find it "uncivilized."

Listening Habits

Austrian politeness and agreeableness make them attentive listeners on the surface. They are, however, always anxious to speak themselves and, given the opportunity, they often take up where they left off. It is common for them to resume with "Yes, but..."

Behavior at Meetings and Negotiations

Austrians arrive at meetings well dressed in good-quality, smart clothes of a conservative nature. Their manner is formal and titles (*Frau Architekt*) are used. They maintain formality, as Germans do, but are less factual than Germans and often introduce personal details, talking about themselves and their emotions, not always with great tact. They attempt to maintain a veneer of self-assurance, but one senses insecurity underneath as they search for an appropriate role to play vis-à-vis their interlocutors. They are agreeable to most proposals, but may back out of today's statements tomorrow. They have a tendency to promise more than they can deliver and fall short of German or Nordic reliability in this respect. They avoid confrontation whenever possible and compromise rather than make a solid decision. Their agreeableness can quickly disappear if they are "cornered" or deadlocked.

It is advisable to check regularly on the performance of the Viennese with respect to what they have promised. "Did you remember..." is a useful start! Unlike Germans, the Viennese think short term rather than long; the dismemberment of the country probably has something to do with this. When reminded of their obligations, however, they do their best to comply.

Manners and Taboos

Austrians vary in lifestyle—the west is agricultural and tourist-oriented and maintains rural and folkloric traditions.

The Viennese, in spite of their underlying insecurity and tendency to be neurotic or melodramatic, are highly cultured people who enjoy a good lifestyle. They are invariably attracted to panache, fame and genius. Their standard of living is good, compared to most Europeans. They have always professed admiration for French grace and style—in their everyday language they use many French loan words.

The suicide rate is high—some victims are children who have failed their exams. Viennese tend to be over-strict with their children, who encounter frequent repression when young and resent it in their teens and later.

Taboo subjects of discussion in Austria are the Second World War, Adolf Hitler, the annexation, and criticism of Austrians. As for the rest, Austrians are exciting and knowledgeable interlocutors for whom conversation is a real art. They are extremely hospitable to visitors from abroad.

How to Empathize with Austrians

Be well dressed and presentable, generous and hospitable. Do not be overly familiar early on, maintain distance and respect and evince sophistication and erudition. Praise Austrian scenic beauty—it is stunning. Do not oversimplify issues with the Viennese, and remember in Vienna you may be dealing with people of Jewish, Hungarian, Czech, Slovak or Romanian origins. Avoid any form of deviousness in Western Austria.

MOTIVATION	
KEY	*Exhibit good manners and sophistication*
Cross-century mood	◆ Austrians are still searching for a positive identity after the collapse of the Austro–Hungarian Empire and the postwar four-power occupation. ◆ They are determined to hang on to their considerable prosperity. ◆ Their entry into the EU shows optimism tinged with caution.

Motivating Factors

◆ Refer to their high standard of living (currently 19th in GDP per capita).
◆ Dwell on Austrian strengths—scenery, skiing, music, folklore, neat infrastructure.
◆ Go along with their tendency to charm.
◆ Observe the class differences.
◆ Observe power distances.
◆ Respect education.
◆ Be well mannered and chivalrous.
◆ Accept that gossip and "coffee house" networking are part of the culture.
◆ Converse at a leisurely pace.
◆ Distinguish between Viennese and West Austrians.

Avoid

◆ Being too direct.
◆ Confusing them with Germans.
◆ Rushing matters.

18

Switzerland

In terms of cultural collisions, Switzerland is a prime candidate for polarization among its inhabitants, since its citizens speak four languages belonging to four diverse cultural groups, which, during the course of history, have not displayed any particular affection for each other. It is a brave prime minister who attempts to weld Germans, Italians, French and Romansh speakers into a harmonious whole. Perhaps that is why the Swiss settled instead for a council of seven prime ministers and an annually rotating presidency—a suitably weak and humble structure, since all issues of national importance are settled by direct-vote referenda.

Switzerland is the most mountainous country in Europe, with the result that most of its people live in deep and often isolated valleys. They are suspicious of those who live in other valleys and take refuge in steely, defensive parochialism. The country is divided into 26 cantons (and three half-cantons) where most decisions affecting local people are made—including tax systems, welfare schemes, infrastructure, laws, holidays and education.

With such a political system engineered to prevent strong leadership; with even the cantons having to listen to the demands of thousands of communes; with a female population denied the vote until 1971; with over a million foreigners on Swiss soil, 150,000 of whom cross the border daily (and go home again); with 46 percent of the people Catholic and 40 percent registered as Protestant; with stability only achieved in the twentieth century— one wonders how this improbable state came about, survived and even prospered. Yet the hodgepodge works. Divided by culture, the Swiss are united by force of will.

Switzerland as a country began with a three-cantonal alliance in 1291 between the men of Uri, Schwyz and Unterwalden. The French and Italians joined much later. Formerly a warlike people who took on and defeated French, German and Austrian armies before being eventually crushed at the battle of Marignano in 1515, the Swiss retreated to their mountain strongholds and never left them again. Security and armed neutrality became an obsession, taking precedence over internal squabbles and divisions. As the different cultural groups looked at each other, they realized that disunity and polarization would herald an early disintegration. In some manner they were able to adapt their inherited traits to produce a mainstream Swiss culture that has more than held its own amid the political and economic turbulence of the last 100 years.

In view of the restricted area available for agriculture, Switzerland has developed an industrial and urban nation. It is particularly strong in metalworking, watches and other precision instruments, textiles, chemical and pharmaceutical products, tourism and international banking. It trades almost entirely with the three countries whose languages the Swiss speak—Germany, France and Italy— although 14 percent of its exports go to the United

States and 6 percent to the United Kingdom. Unlike its continental neighbors, Switzerland has so far declined to become a member of the EU or NATO (no doubt preferring fierce neutrality). Its prosperity dates particularly from the end of the Second World War.

Some may argue that there is no such thing as a Swiss—one writer described them as a collection of sedated Germans, over-fussy French and starched Italians, all square like their national flag. An analysis of their behavior, however, reveals a unique and highly independent European.

Culture

Values

As the Swiss have various obsessions—security, punctuality, hygiene, rules and regulations, control, money, saving, perfectionism, propriety and others—we need a long list of adjectives to do justice to their qualities!

polite	clean
tidy, punctual	cautious, worrying
over-serious, dull	hardworking, proper
law-abiding, God-fearing	honest
frugal, saving	environmentally sensitive
family-oriented, disciplined	pragmatic, perfectionist
obsessed by security, neutral	keen on training and preparation
suspicious of all foreigners	anxious to control

Moreover, the Swiss take their values seriously, backing them up with visible and effective measures. Their neutrality, for instance, bristles with arms; Switzerland possesses more weapons per square mile than any other country in Europe. The Alps (their fighting redoubt and base) constitute a veritable fortress with hundreds of bunkers, invisible hangars, nuclear hideout shelters and underground hospitals. The strategy is simple and focused: the Swiss will fight to the last outpost and will blow up bridges, roads, railways, tunnels and even small mountains to cover advancing enemies with rubble! Every Swiss male between 20 and 50 is a member of the armed forces and keeps his weapons at home.

Concepts

Leadership and Status

As in the U.S., there is a deep-rooted distrust of government in Switzerland, and the system of rule resembles the American in its intricate and delicate array of checks and balances. The president has some powers but only one year to exercise them, and is closely bound by the Federal Council of Seven and the frequent referenda.

On account of the quarterly referenda, the common man or woman enjoys a higher status than in most countries. Wealth of course enhances power, but there are few poor Swiss to bully. Material possessions are more common status symbols than other forms of advancement, but as the Swiss say, "One does not talk about money, one just has it."

Space and Time

Only a small part of Swiss land is arable and only a small percentage of the people farm for a living. Space is therefore extremely valuable and cherished. Allied to a strong territorial instinct, this makes personal, communal and cantonal space important issues in Switzerland.

Only the Germans rival the Swiss in their respect for, and submission to, timetables and schedules. Time is not seen as money, in the American sense, but as an important tool in organizing daily life and society. The Swiss do not rush you, but they do not waste time either. Their accurate sense of timing enables them to predict and forecast events better than most nationalities. In Switzerland things usually happen when they are expected to and spontaneity is not a strong point.

Cultural Factors in Communication

Communication Pattern

The Swiss are extremely polite conversationalists, in both social and business situations. Their desire for privacy and propriety leads them to carry on discourse in a pragmatic and detached manner. They shun inquisitiveness and rarely pry. They are not exciting speakers; even the French Swiss lack the charisma and rhetoric of their cousins in France. Swiss Italians (in the Ticino) are more open but, living in a prosperous area, they display a smugness less noticeable among Italians over the border.

Swiss Germans, particularly, are cautious speakers, taking care not to offend and adhering to modesty and reserve in most pronouncements and predictions. They speak *Switzerdütsch*—not a very harmonic tongue—although they will speak real German (or English) if you address them that way.

Listening Habits

The Swiss are good listeners, not having any great urge to expound ideas at length themselves. They forget little of what you tell them, often taking notes while you speak, and they almost never interrupt. They are conservative in their opinions and it is unlikely that they will be greatly swayed by your advice or persuasion.

Behavior at Meetings and Negotiations

The Swiss have a knack of extracting the best deal from opponents without ever appearing demanding or aggressive. They often achieve this on the basis of self-confidence in the quality and value of the goods and services that they provide. The Swiss do not come cheap, whether it is watches, precision instruments, pharmaceuticals or ski slopes, but one is often tempted to pay the price.

The Swiss are good at making you feel that you get what you pay for. If you try to bargain with them too hard, they stiffen as if you have made a shady proposal. They are straightforward negotiators who honestly try hard to see matters from an opponent's point of view. You cannot call them inconsiderate—they are quick to make helpful suggestions when it does not hit their wallets. For the most part, they are reliable and efficient and can be counted on to deliver. They are strong on confidentiality.

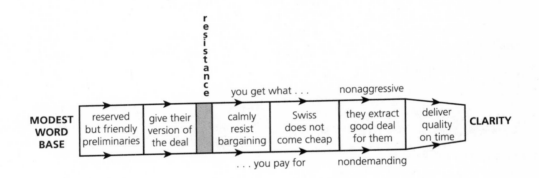

Figure 18.1 Swiss Communication Pattern

Manners and Taboos

The Swiss are rather heavy drinkers (ninth in the world) and inveterate smokers (13th). They also are third in drug offenses, although this figure may be artificially high due to the efficiency of the national police administration. The Swiss have a large number of manners, customs and festivals that vary from canton to canton, and you cannot be expected to know a great deal about these. They tend to bury themselves in these activities on public holidays and foreigners often feel left out. Taboos include boasting, undue curiosity, invasion of privacy and unpunctuality.

How to Empathize with the Swiss

You do not have to be exciting to make the Swiss like you; they are looking for solidity and reliability in the people they deal with. You should show that you are in good control of your emotions, private life and financial arrangements.

Meetings are always by appointment and it is advisable to be there five minutes early. You should be clean and well dressed and always display politeness, even if you are bored out of your mind.

Small gifts are appreciated when you come from abroad, though the Swiss do not make undue fuss. Propriety is much more important than affection, though when the Swiss begin to like you, they go out of their way to be friendly.

MOTIVATION	
KEY	*Correctness and propriety*
Cross-century mood	✦ The Swiss demonstrate no urgency to "join Europe." ✦ Steady in their pursuit of (armed) neutrality. ✦ See themselves as already having attained multicultural balance, while others strive to do so.

Motivating Factors

✦ Show you are dependable.
✦ Be conformist.
✦ Praise the unique Swiss system of government.
✦ Acknowledge the high quality of Swiss products.
✦ Demonstrate frugality.
✦ Address their worries and problems.
✦ Maintain administrative neatness.
✦ Indicate your financial solidity.

Avoid

✦ Showing you are bored.
✦ Breaking any laws, rules or regulations.
✦ Flippancy or too much humor.
✦ Ostentation.
✦ Eccentric behavior.

19

The Netherlands

Hemmed in against the North Sea by Germany and Belgium, the Dutch have made the best of the most crowded piece of land in the EU, creating on it the world's largest port and expanding seaward rather than landward. With the 18th biggest economy in the world, the Netherlands is a small nation with a big clout.

Culturally, the Dutch face north and west (and a bit east) but not south. Their Latin traits are few, but there are striking commonalities with the British, Germans, Swedes and Norwegians, as if at different times they followed different models. Perhaps this partly explains the paradoxical nature of Dutch society. With the Norwegians they share the exceptional characteristic of the national moral dilemma—how can a modern state embrace permissiveness, tolerance, sweeping innovation and pragmatic pursuit of wealth without losing the embedded historical values that served its straitlaced, frugal society so well in the past?

The pervasive egalitarianism in both the Netherlands and Sweden has led to the creation of Europe's two most comprehensive (and expensive) welfare states, with the subsequent corollary of high taxation. In both cases the expense of this luxury has been increased by a generous immigration policy: 10 percent of Swedes today were not born in Sweden and 15 percent of those in the Netherlands are not of Dutch descent.

In the business world, both the Netherlands and Sweden have many famous multinational conglomerates (Shell, Unilever, Philips, Volvo, Electrolux, Scania, Alfa-Laval, etc.) relative to the size of their economies. This is quite different to the situation in, for instance, Denmark, Norway, Finland and Belgium, where few companies are known worldwide (Nokia and Carlsberg are perhaps the only ones).

The proximity of Germany makes it only natural that the Dutch share many traits with their dynamic neighbor. Dynamism, industriousness and work ethic are among the most important of these characteristics. If the Germans are known to be efficient and punctual, the Dutch would claim to be their equals in these respects. Profit orientation is strong and money must be made (but not spent too quickly!). The Dutch and Germans are equally frugal, though their governments (especially the Dutch) are less tightfisted. Only the more conservative, older type of Dutch company resembles the German, but common management traits are frankness, a certain formality with regard to titles and the significance of education as an essential component of leadership. Education is conducted in Holland along German lines, with vocational schools, apprenticeships and on-the-job training major features. Both countries excel in the production of engineers and technicians. The Dutch and Germans rival each other in being rights conscious, but compensate by also being very conscious of their duties; rationality is another common factor.

Their forthright Germanic traits notwithstanding, it is perhaps with the British that the Dutch identify most strongly. When conversing with the English they have a confiding air of kinship easily straddling the narrow stretch of water between them. The inhabitants of the Frisian Islands speak a language somewhere between Dutch and English. The sea-going traditions of both countries give them a sense of sharing early internationalism, exciting eras of exploration and entrepreneurialism, and huge, rambling empires where durability, administrative skills and religious tolerance were notable features. The Dutch and the English cling to their royals and basic conservatism, but soften this with democratic parliamentary government, love of debate and a quiet, roll-up-your-sleeves self-determinism. Love of home, gardens and flowers are similar in both countries. In business, Dutch and English people resemble each other in dress, exploratory discussion, profit orientation and pragmatism. A surfeit of protocol is frowned on, food is not central to either culture and internal competitiveness, while keen, must remain covert.

Culture

Values

Dutch economic and geographic **paradoxes** are comprehensively matched by those of their values:

conservative	innovative
tolerant	dogmatic
international	parochial
materialist	moralist
puritanical	permissive
opinionated	consensual
rights conscious	dutiful
consultative	competitive
royalist	egalitarian
informal	proper
entrepreneurial	cautious
frugal	profligate (government)
self-determined	cooperative
frank, open	jealous of privacy

Concepts

Leadership and Status

The hierarchical pyramid in Dutch firms is decidedly flat: managers sit with other executives and decisions are made after lengthy consultation and consensus. As in Japan, one diligently avoids the "tyranny of the majority" and unanimity of decision is sought on most occasions. Individuals may stick to their opinions and cannot be steamrollered, but a great deal of pressure may be brought to bear on persistent lone dissenters.

Space and Time

The most important aspect of Dutch present-day culture is lack of space. Never tell a Dutch person that this must be an awful way to live. They will tell you to mind your own business as they take some more land from the waters of the Ijsselmeer (former Zuider Zee) and, slowly but surely, start building higher and higher apartment blocks everywhere. Indoor stairs and elevators are steep, and elevators are small, even in the largest office buildings. Working, walking and entertainment areas tend to be small and crowded. Living accommodations are cramped by American standards, and sleeping areas are even smaller. People are forced to think in terms of practicality and efficiency in the use and adaptation of space. They also have an obsession with "coziness," making good use of flowers in homes and gardens and even put Persian carpets on tables and walls to create an inviting atmosphere.

As far as personal space is concerned, formal contacts and strangers are kept outside of a 43 inch (1.1 meter) radius "space bubble." Physical contact is not welcomed and body language is limited.

Dutch people place a high value on punctuality. Arriving late or not honoring appointments may cause them to end a business relationship. Time is never to be wasted; agendas and schedules pack as much business as possible into meetings. In the Netherlands, trade union leaders tend to have a constructive attitude toward employers' problems and rarely strike, since that would be a horrendous waste of time!

Cultural Factors in Communication

Communication Pattern

The pragmatic Dutch, though mainly concerned with facts and figures, are also great talkers and rarely make final decisions without a long "Dutch" debate, sometimes approaching the danger zone of overanalysis. Foreign counterparts are also subjected to this and are routinely tested for bluffing, as Dutch people, with their long international experience in business, hate to think of themselves as being in any way gullible.

Listening Habits

The Dutch are cautious, skeptical listeners who prefer "cut-and-thrust" dialogue to any form of lecturing. Dutch audiences are both easy and difficult: easy in the sense that they are hungry for information and good ideas, difficult because they are very experienced and not open to much persuasion by others. Like the French, they tend to "know it all," but will in fact accept and seize viable plans and projects which are presented vigorously and backed up with convincing evidence.

Behavior at Meetings and Negotiations

Meetings are based on factual information; shows of emotion or ebullience are generally frowned on. Mutual help and dependence are general goals; confrontation is rare and not desirable.

Dutch meetings start on time in a rather formal atmosphere, which relaxes gradually as people get to know each other better. Surnames and sometimes titles are used at first. After four or five meetings the oldest or most senior Dutch person present may offer the use of first names. Even when discussions have entered a more relaxed stage, overt friendliness may

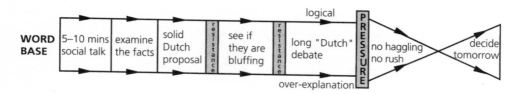

Figure 19.1 Dutch Communication Pattern

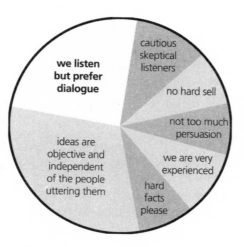

Figure 19.2 Dutch Listening Habits

be regarded as an imposition. This and personal questions about family, health, and so forth, are normally avoided during business conversations.

The Dutch shake hands with everyone at all meetings, both on arrival and departure. Introductions are short and to the point, and small talk is minimal. One feature of Dutch life is the "business luncheon," which can last up to three hours. Decisions may be made during such a lunch.

In general, the Dutch have a fairly high tolerance for bureaucracy: discussions are structured, correct and detailed.

Dutch meetings can be rather formal, though the Dutch adapt well to the informality of cultures elsewhere in Northern Europe. Small talk at the start of the meeting is limited. "Extra people" may be present at negotiations in order to allow on-the-spot delegation. Negotiation is analytical and fact-based; it moves quickly, although some issues may be debated in depth. The Dutch are practical and seek compromise. Often their first offer is what they believe to be a reasonable final outcome. Quality, reliability and cooperative relations are valued more than getting a low price.

The Dutch enjoy conflict and debate. Anyone may offer an opinion; negating his or her idea does not mean negating the person. Reason is always highly valued. With reason on your side, you can drive a hard bargain. Concessions are made with some reluctance; pressure is always firmly rejected.

Manners and Taboos

Dutch people usually entertain you in restaurants and cafés, only occasionally in their homes. If you are invited to a home, you are expected to bring flowers. Food is generally wholesome but unexciting. Don't help yourself to the hors d'oeuvres and don't drink until a toast has been proposed. Coffee, which is served at the end of the meal, not with dessert, is a signal for you to depart. A second serving of coffee is a clear signal to depart. Small talk includes soccer (very popular) and the international situation, both political and business, but avoid any discussion of religious views.

Handshakes are short, with a firm grip and an optional slight nod of the head. You should shake hands with the senior person first and then with everyone else in the room, including children.

It is common to exchange greetings with people you meet in elevators. It is not unknown for taxi drivers to invite you to sit next to them. They, like most Dutch people, are invariably fluent in English. Dutch people are obsessed with their rights, so you should never even hint at superiority over others—and that includes waiters, taxi drivers, shop assistants and hotel staff.

Things to avoid are any show of extravagance, ostentation or pretentiousness. You are expected to be competitive in business, but "cold calling" and influence-peddling are frowned upon.

How to Empathize with the Dutch

+ Know Dutch history, involvement in former colonies and achievements.
+ Congratulate them on their impressive linguistic abilities, but speak a few words of Dutch now and then.
+ Show that you are punctual, honest, dependable, rational and egalitarian.
+ Back up all you say with facts.
+ Focus on mutual profit.
+ Be willing to brainstorm and endure long debates.
+ Expect and practice verbal agility.
+ Drive a hard bargain, but keep your promises.
+ Be informative, informed and well prepared.
+ Engage in moderate small talk before getting down to business.

MOTIVATION	
KEY	*Respect individual rights*
Cross-century mood	+ The Dutch are among the most committed and enthusiastic members of the EU. + They see the twenty-first century as "going their way" in terms of increasing human rights, deepening tolerance of ideas and caring and nurturing environments. + There is general satisfaction with their economic performance, political goals and humanitarian standards. + National soul-searching continues as to how to combine maximum tolerance in society with adherence to straitlaced traditional values.

Motivating Factors

+ The Netherlands is a small country in area, but it has powerful international and economic clout. Show that you are fully aware of (and admire) their incredible achievements.
+ Congratulate them on their internationalism.
+ Be humorous. Dutch humor is earthy rather than witty.
+ Show some frugality; the Dutch dislike extravagance.
+ Indulge in give-and-take; this gets them going.

(continued)

MOTIVATION *(continued)*

+ In the Netherlands, personalities are separated from opinions. You may therefore object to what your Dutch hosts propose without incurring dislike. Similarly, they will feel free to criticize your views openly without offending you.
+ Be frank and open about most things; don't try to pull the wool over their eyes.
+ Attune yourself to their limited protocol. This means not being dressed too formally unless requested. They are not so concerned with graciousness, preferring to deal with people who are businesslike and straightforward.
+ Let them offer the use of first names and other informalities, especially when they are on their home ground.
+ Remember that Dutch cleanliness is legendary.
+ Demonstrating professional competence is a must. The Dutch are impressed by bottom-line achievements.

Avoid

+ Wasting their time; the Dutch are industrious and you should try to match their diligence and work rate.
+ Jokes or strong opinions about religion.
+ Too much ebullience or charisma; the Dutch are basically conservative.
+ Pushy tactics; the Dutch are skeptical.

20

Belgium

It is often said that Belgium is not a country, but a compromise. Belgium was created in 1830 when the Catholic provinces of the Low Countries that had achieved independence from Spain in the seventeenth century broke away from the Calvinist north. Basically Belgium is two nations—a Flemish-speaking one in the north and a French-speaking one in the south. The two groups do not like each other, particularly since the balance of power is currently passing from the formerly mine-rich French speakers (Walloons) to the nouveaux riches and numerically superior Flemish, who are developing the hinterland of Antwerp, Europe's second largest port. To complicate matters further, the city of Brussels is a predominantly French-speaking enclave in Flanders, and a German-speaking minority lives along the German border. In Brussels rival linguistic groups occasionally take down street signs in the offending language in the middle of the night.

Political compromise has been reached by the appointment of three prime ministers—Walloon, Flemish and Belgian. Parochial squabbles are numerous, but bad tempers rarely escalate into violence. With 66 ministers in the government and political divisions along linguistic lines, you can easily envisage the Belgian capital as a bureaucratic nightmare. As if this were not enough, Brussels has also been appointed the effective capital of Europe; 25 percent of its residents are well-paid bureaucrats from other countries.

Most Belgians are friendly, hard-working people characterized by an absence of dogma and strong opinions and an earnest desire to earn good money with the minimum of fuss. The Belgians worked hard to realize a Franco-German dream—the union of Europe—and their Europeanization may have contributed to their relative facelessness compared to other nationalities.

Yet Belgium, in spite of her smallness, has the 26th biggest economy in the world, ahead of such countries as Austria, Denmark and South Africa, not to mention Asian tigers such as Hong Kong and Singapore. Belgium's output almost equals that of exporting powerhouse Taiwan, which has twice her population. In GDP per capita, Belgium also ranks 24th in the world.

An industrial Mighty Mouse, Belgium is hard to evaluate in terms of its cultural influence on Europe and the rest of the world. The impact of its biculturalism is diminished by the fact that the intense rivalry tends to neutralize the effect of both sides. There is no such thing as a single Belgian national cultural profile.

Culture

Values

conservative	royalist
European-oriented	nonchauvinist
intellectual humility	common sense
avoidance of dogmatism	flexibility
compromise	avoidance of confrontation

Contrasting Flemish and Walloon values can be described as follows:

Flemish	Walloon
egalitarian	authoritarian
consensual decision making	autocratic decisions
approachable bosses	large power distance
delegation of responsibility	little delegation of power
relaxed relationships	vertical structure
few status symbols	status symbols important
dislike speaking French	French speakers
upwardly mobile	conscious of rank

Concepts

Leadership and Status

Flemish	Walloon
Bosses are relaxed and low-key. Responsibility is delegated downward to a considerable degree.	Leadership is exercised in a manner close to that of the French, where all final decisions rest with the boss.
Titles, perks and other status symbols are less important than salary. Authority is normally based on competence.	Rank is important and is demonstrated by car, office space, carpets, job title, furniture and parking space.
Punctuality is considered normal. Time should not be wasted	Walloons consider themselves more punctual than the French.

Cultural Factors in Communication

Flemish	Walloon

Communication Pattern

Flemish	Walloon
Communication is informal, and the boss mixes with staff and often acts on their ideas as well as his or her own. Facts are seen as more important than theories.	Communication goes through official channels as there is a definite hierarchy in place. Walloons are more imaginative but avoid rhetoric in favor of a toned-down style.

Listening Habits

Flemings listen to each other "in a circle." They are attentive, as the end result is likely to be an amalgamation of all ideas put forward. Everyone should know the strategy.	Meetings are for briefings, so subordinates tend to listen to superiors rather than the other way around. Staff don't always know what the strategy is.

Flemish	*Walloon*

Behavior at Meetings and Negotiations

You will normally be dealing with a group. The Flemish are nonassertive and welcome compromise. If you are really looking for solutions, there is a good chance of an agreement. They have a pragmatic bent and a calm style. Like most people from small countries, they are adaptable. The bottom line tends to dominate strategy. All members of the group are expected to show competence— nobody has a free ride.	Walloons are less grandiose and obstinate than the French, largely because they do not have an unswerving belief that they know better than others. You will not be dealing with a group but largely with the manager or delegation leader. His views must be analyzed, and he will also be accountable. He is expected to have charisma but should also show humility at the right times.

Manners and Taboos

The most important taboo is speaking French. Others are arrogance, over-assertiveness and pulling rank. They resent having been the lower classes in the past and are still rather annoyed at Brussels being a French-speaking enclave in the middle of Flanders.	Walloons resent being viewed as rather slow-witted French people and dislike the French tendency to make jokes at their expense. They are, however, slower than the French in speech and appear to other Latins to be rather plodding and deliberate.

How to Empathize with Belgians

Make it clear that you know that Flemings are not Dutch and that Walloons are not French. The main difference between the two groups is the question of consensual decision making versus hierarchical style, so you should adjust your approach accordingly.

Belgians of both persuasions will be looking for certain qualities in you: pragmatism, profit-mindedness, flexibility, willingness to compromise and the ability to respect the integrity and creativeness of a small country. Belgians are very European and assume that you share some of their enthusiasm for Europe (if you are in the EU).

MOTIVATION
KEY   *The ability to compromise*
Cross-century mood   ✦ Belgians worked hard to help realize the union of Europe and are more committed to this than most EU nations.   ✦ There is some doubt about the future of national unity (among Flemish and Walloons), but this is currently on a back burner.   ✦ In the meantime, Brussels is the capital of Europe.

Motivating Factors

✦ Show a certain amount of conservatism with both Flemings and Walloons.

✦ Show you know how to achieve solutions through compromise.

✦ Adopt a gradualist approach to problems in general.

✦ Demonstrate intellectual humility.

✦ In most situations resolve things through common sense.

✦ Show flexibility if deadlock threatens.

✦ Be enthusiastic about Europe (Belgians need it).

✦ Acknowledge Belgium's economic achievements in spite of her small size.

Avoid

✦ Too much dogma.

✦ Criticizing the monarchy.

✦ Direct confrontation.

✦ Discussion of politics (it is complicated).

✦ Any sign of temper.

✦ Being over-opinionated.

✦ Discussion of religious or language issues.

21

France

In both politics and business, the French like to be independent (at times maverick) and can appear frustrating to Americans, Japanese and Europeans alike.

French people live in a world of their own, the center of which is France. They are immersed in their own history and tend to believe that France has set the norms for such things as democracy, justice, government and legal systems, military strategy, philosophy, science, agriculture, viniculture, haute cuisine and *savoir vivre* in general. Other nations vary from these norms and, according to the French, have a lot to learn before they get things right.

The French know virtually nothing about many other countries, as their educational system teaches little of the history or geography of small nations or those that belonged to empires other than their own. Their general attitude toward foreigners is pleasant enough, neither positive nor negative. They will do business with you if you have a good product, or if you buy, but their initial posture will be somewhat condescending. If you don't speak French, you appear to be an Anglophile. That is not a good start in their eyes.

You are not seen as an equal. You may be better or worse, but you are different. The French, like the Japanese, believe they are unique and do not really expect you will ever be able to conform completely to their standards. What approach should you adopt when dealing with the French? Should you gallicize yourself to some degree, becoming more talkative, imaginative and intense? Or should you maintain stolid, honest manners at the risk of seeming wooden or failing to communicate?

Cultural Factors in Communication

Behavior at Meetings and Negotiations

In order to get the best of your dealings with the French, you have to study their psychology and tactics when they enter commercial transactions. They approach negotiation in a very French manner, which includes the following characteristics:

+ They arrive at a meeting formally dressed, regarding it as a formal occasion.
+ Surnames and formal introductions are used, and seating will be hierarchical.
+ Politeness and formal style will be maintained throughout negotiations managed by the French.

+ Logic will dominate their arguments and lead them to extensive analysis of all matters under discussion. They will pounce on anything illogical said by the opposition.
+ Meetings will be long and wordy.
+ They do not present their demands at the beginning, but lead up to them with a carefully constructed rationale.
+ They reveal their hand only late in the negotiations.
+ The French try to determine the other side's aims and demands at the beginning.
+ The French are suspicious of early friendliness in the discussion and dislike first names, removal of jackets, and disclosure of personal or family details.
+ They pride themselves on quickness of mind but dislike being rushed into decisions. For them, negotiation is not a quick procedure.
+ They rarely make important decisions inside a meeting.
+ They will prolong discussion, as they regard it as an intellectual exercise during which they are familiarizing themselves with the other party and perhaps discovering their weaknesses.
+ Their objectives are long-term; they try to establish firm personal relationships.
+ They will not make concessions in negotiations unless their logic has been defeated, which often makes them look stubborn to some.
+ During deadlock they remain intransigent but without rudeness, simply restating their position.
+ They try to be precise at all times. The French language facilitates this.
+ They believe they are intellectually superior to any other nationality.
+ They often depart from the agenda and talk at length on a number of issues in random order.
+ British and Americans often complain that the French talk for hours but make no decisions. (The French clarify their own thoughts through extensive discussion before arriving at any decisions or taking action.)
+ They arrive at the negotiation well informed in advance, but seeing things through French "spectacles" often blinds them to international implications. Sometimes they are hampered by their lack of language skills.

How to Empathize with the French

When dealing with the French, you should behave much more formally than usual, using only surnames and showing almost exaggerated politeness to French senior executives.

Stick to logic at all times, avoiding American-style hunches or British-style "feel for situations." If you contradict anything you said, even months earlier, a French person will pounce on the contradiction.

You should be willing to appear "more human" than usual, as the French are, after all, Latins in spite of their logic and exactness. They like a good discussion and observe few time limits for this. If you don't talk enough, they will label you as monosyllabic afterward.

If you want to gain points, you can score by criticizing the English—a favorite French pastime. You need not be unfair to anyone, just show that you are not entirely in the Anglo-Saxon camp. The French do not mind if you have a go at their other neighbors—the Italians and the Spaniards—either. Do not criticize Napoleon—he has a kind of lasting identity with the French soul. You can say what you want about Charles De Gaulle, François Mitterrand or any current French prime minister. They probably won't know who your president or prime minister is, so they can't crucify him or her.

The French are often criticized by people of other nationalities, and it is not difficult to see why. Essentially argumentative and opinionated, they frequently find themselves out on a limb at international meetings, isolated in their intransigence when all the others have settled for compromise. This naturally leaves them open to charges of arrogance. And yet one must have some sympathy for them; they are clear-sighted, perceptive thinkers who feel that they have a better historical perspective than most of us. They would rather be right than popular. Are they usually right? Like all others, they are fallible in their judgment and subject to bias, but they have great experience in politics, warfare, domestic and overseas organization and administration, and the humanities. Like the Germans, they cannot be accused of taking things lightly. Their long and significant involvement in European and world affairs gives the French the conviction that their voice should be heard loud and clear in international forums. Their political, military and economic strengths may no longer predominate as they once did, but the French perceive no diminishment in their moral and didactic authority. Like the Americans, British and Russians, they have a strong messianic streak. They would not be human if they did not resent the rise of the British after the fall of Napoleon, the decline of the French language as a world tongue, the incursions of the Japanese on the European economic scene, and, most of all, the pernicious Americanization of large parts of the world, including once-French-dominated Europe and even French culture itself.

Though often seen as selfish defenders of their own territory, it is not inconceivable that with their old-fashioned doggedness and resistance to precipitated globalization, they might one day emerge as the champions of the age-old values and philosophies that Europeans subconsciously cherish. The maverick of Europe may well turn out to be its moral bedrock. At all events, the French merit a closer examination of their apparent obstinacies and negative features.

THE FRENCH AS OTHERS SEE THEM

Appearance	Reality
The French are obstinate and always hold a different opinion from everybody else.	They stick to what they believe is right unless they are proven wrong.
They think they are cleverer than anyone else.	True. Their historical achievements leave them convinced that their mission is to civilize Europe.
They don't like to speak foreign languages, especially English.	French was once the internationally accepted language of diplomacy and was spoken widely on four continents. The French feel sadness at its decline vis-à-vis English. England was their traditional enemy, and American English seems anti-intellectual to them.
They know little about and are not interested in other countries.	Their educational system tends to concentrate on French history, but they know a lot about Asia and Africa as well as ancient cultures.
They are overly emotional.	Like all Latins, they raise their voice and gesticulate when excited, but they rarely abandon rationality.
They cannot mind their own business; they are inquisitive and ask personal questions.	French is such an exact language that it is difficult not to be direct when using it. They are interested in you personally, but they also have an innate politeness often unseen by foreigners.
They talk too much at meetings.	A logical argument takes longer to build up than an intuitive one. Cartesian theory requires building blocks. The French also like to consider everything before making decisions.
They can't keep to an agenda.	As they interrelate all the points, they feel they must go back and forth to balance their decisions.
They are finicky.	They generally have a clear idea of what they want and take pains to get things right.
They make grandiose plans.	True, they think big, but having established *les grandes lignes,* they are later analytical about details.
They make poor team members.	They are very individualistic and self-confident. This, and a good education, encourages them to go it alone. This is counteracted within France itself by a high degree of centralization.

(continued)

THE FRENCH AS OTHERS SEE THEM *(continued)*

Appearance	Reality
They can't relax.	Relaxing does not come easily to people who are quick and imaginative, and culture rich.
They are too quick to attack others.	The French feel compunction to redress what they perceive as injustice, stupidity or laxity. They do not hesitate to intervene.
They prefer ideas to facts and won't make decisions in a normal, straightforward manner.	Statistics can prove anything. Facts are not always what they seem. What is wrong with exploring ideas?
They are cynical.	If you have the British on one side, the Germans on the other and the Americans on your TV screen, you have to be.
The French are selfish, care little for others.	Not true. As André Malraux said, when the French fight for mankind, they are wonderful.
They are messianic.	True. Malraux's brief when being appointed minister of culture was the expansion and *rayonnement* of French culture. It's good for us.

MOTIVATION	
KEY	*Sharing visions, praising France*
Cross-century mood	✦ EU-oriented, but wish to preserve considerable independence. ✦ Anxious to retain place on world stage. ✦ Supporting the French language as a lingua franca as energetically as possible. ✦ Resisting American inroads into French (and European) economy. ✦ Defending French (and European) culture. ✦ Demonstrate a willingness to further French interests. ✦ In a working relationship, the French are not initially generous, but they will respond quickly to generosity from your side. ✦ Be willing to discuss topics and projects at great length—they wish to see things from every angle.

(continued)

MOTIVATION *(continued)*

- ◆ Go for an all-embracing solution rather than a segmented one.
- ◆ Be as imaginative and lively as you can.
- ◆ Use humor—they like it—but not always at their expense.
- ◆ They admire self-deprecation, not being very good at it themselves.
- ◆ Let them roam back and forth on the agenda; when they do this, they are thinking aloud.
- ◆ Show you are thinking long-term rather than short. They are much more relationship-oriented than deal-oriented.
- ◆ Deals and profits must fit into their vision of proper society. French companies are often organic and have sociopolitical undertones.

Avoid

- ◆ Expressing strong opinions until you know their position.
- ◆ Prolonged silences; they do not like them.
- ◆ American-style, bottom-line focus, quick deals, or opportunistic wheeling and dealing.
- ◆ Sarcasm and irony.

22

Italy

The Italians are charming, intelligent people to whom Europe owes a great cultural debt. They are excellent communicators and combine ultra-keen perception with ever-present flexibility. Their continuous exuberance and loquacious persuasiveness often produce an adverse reaction with reserved Britons, factual Germans and taciturn Scandinavians. Yet such northerners (including Americans) have everything to gain by adapting to Italians' outgoing nature, meeting them halfway in their taste for dialogue. There is plenty of business to be done with the Italians, who export vigorously in order to survive.

Concepts

Space and Time

There is a variance in the concept of space. Italians are used to being crowded and working in close proximity to each other. This creates an atmosphere of teamwork approximating that of the Japanese. A Briton, Finn or German needs more space or "elbow room" to work effectively, and this shows itself in such matters as office layout and use of space both in factories and in administrative areas. Be prepared to "rub shoulders" with Italians.

The "distance of comfort" is greater for northerners than for Italians. The English like to keep a minimum of 4 feet (1.2 meters) between themselves and their interlocutor. Italians are quite comfortable at 31 inches (80 centimeters). If you retreat from such a position, they will think you are avoiding them or that you find their physical presence distasteful. Make them feel more welcome by "standing your ground."

Italians may touch your arm or shoulder or perhaps hug you if they are feeling friendly. After some months' acquaintance, they may kiss you on both cheeks when greeting you or departing. They are showing affection and you must find some way of reciprocating. At least smile occasionally; your face will not break (in a southern climate). (Americans at least have no problem with smiling.)

Italians have a different concept of time from that of northerners and Americans. They do not arrive for appointments on time. Punctuality in Milan means they are 20 minutes late, in Rome 30 minutes and in the south, 45 minutes. You will not be able to change this, except in a fixed-hours factory or office environment. You must therefore adapt. Be prepared to wait 15 to 45 minutes before your Italian counterpart appears or lets you into his or her office. Take a good book or magazine. Alternatively, you can deliberately show up half an hour late, but in fact few northerners are able to do this.

Cultural Factors in Communication

Communication Pattern

Remember that the communication style is eloquent, wordy, demonstrative and apparently emotional. This is normal for them but may be overly dramatic for you. Do not be led into the belief that waving arms and talking with the hands denotes instability or unreliability. They think you, by contrast, are rather wooden and distant. Make them feel comfortable by showing more facial expression and body language. (See Figure 5.1 for an illustration of the Italian communication pattern.)

Behavior at Meetings and Negotiations

At meetings, Italians do not follow agendas as strictly as do northerners. They will jump ahead to later points or will loop back and discuss points you think have already been settled. They will talk loudly, excitedly and at length. Often several people will speak at once, and you may find two, three or more micromeetings going on simultaneously. They do not like silences of more than five seconds. If you are not running the meeting, there is nothing you can do except sit back and enjoy. If you are chairing the meeting, you have to create some kind of order, but you can only do this by establishing firm rules in advance. One German I know used yellow, red and green cards to discipline people at South American meetings. This humorous but firm approach achieved the desired result.

Italian wordiness versus northern succinctness is a constant pain in internal company communication, as both sides wish to achieve clarity, one through many words and the other through short messages and memos. A compromise must be reached. Northerners must teach themselves to be more explicit and explanatory, but also encourage their Italian colleagues to be more concise and economical with words and ideas and, whenever practical, to put them in writing. The inventions of the fax and e-mail have been valuable tools for Scandinavians and other concise peoples.

Italian negotiators are friendly, talkative, and ultimately flexible. They are less direct than northerners and often seem to proceed in a round about manner. Italians will discuss things from a personal or somewhat emotional angle, while northerners try to concentrate on the benefit for their company and stick to the facts of the particular deal. Northerners should approach negotiation with Italians with adequate time for the exercise and a large store of patience. They must be prepared to discuss at length and maintain calm. An Italian may get overheated on some point, but changes a moment later into the friendliest of negotiators. Italians may quarrel among themselves at the table, but are solid colleagues minutes later. Their starting price may be high, but they are prepared for a lot of negotiating down. The American, Scandinavian or Briton selling to them must show a first price which allows some room for a reduction later. They will expect it. They must come away from the deal showing they have won or gained something. Each member of their team must be granted something. Northerners will be at their best if they regard the negotiation as a kind of interesting game which must be played with many Italian rules, but which leads to a serious and beneficial result (for both).

North versus South

The unification of Italy was late in European terms, and the different regions still retain their particular characters. Northern Italians have a tendency to look down on "southerners" (any-one south of Rome). People living in the industrial areas around Milan, Turin, Genoa and the Veneto show little enthusiasm for the lifestyles of Sicilians, Neapolitans and Calabrians, whom they see as lazy, overly emotional, often untrustworthy; as living in a previous century; and as a sizeable economic burden on their industrious selves. Having heard this description, non-Italians, when visiting the south, are usually pleasantly surprised to meet people who are friendly, hospitable and generous, trustworthy and loyal, perceptive and essentially human.

Differences are, however, striking:

North	South
experience	value for money
factual	imaginative
modern	traditional
meritocratic	patronage system
industrial	agricultural
prosperous	poor
law-abiding	authorities coexisting with the Mafia
affinity with Austrians, Germans	affinity with Mediterraneans, Africans
often secular	church-guided
small families	extended families
family closeness	family dominance
upwardly mobile	mentor-guided
respect officialdom	key connections
scientific truth	contextual, situational truth
identification with company	identification with in-group
generalist	particularist

How to Empathize with Italians

Italians like to share details of families, vacations, hopes, aspirations, disappointments, preferences. Show photographs of children; reveal some of your political or religious opinions—this is normal in Italy, you need not be an island unto yourself. Discuss beliefs and values. Do not be afraid to appear talkative. No matter how hard you try, the Italian will always consider you reserved (and talk ten times as much as you).

One characteristic of Italians is that they are not very chauvinistic and do not automatically believe that Italy and Italians must be best. This national modesty is rarely seen outside Finland and Italy. Capitalize on this trait by discussing Italy in a frank manner.

Italians, unlike Spaniards, Germans and French, are not particularly sensitive or touchy. They accept criticism and are very flexible. You may speak much more freely with them than with most Europeans, but do not exaggerate directness or bluntness. They are flexible, but also delicate.

Italians are much more polite, on the surface, than northerners, so you will often appear overly frank, blunt and even rude, although you do not intend this. Try to adopt a certain Italian smoothness or delicacy and use flattery more than you normally would. They like it. Open doors for women and stand up and sit down at the right times. You probably do this anyway, but notice how the Italians do it with charm and style. When leaving a room an Italian often says, "*Con permesso.*" Try a few tricks like that. If you still feel a bit awkward, console yourself by remembering that to a Japanese an Italian looks clumsy, emotional and often rude.

You will often find it difficult to rid yourself of the impression that the Italians are an unruly, disorganized bunch. They do not seem to plan methodically like you do. Do not forget they are the eighth industrial nation in the world and have outperformed even the Germans and Americans in such areas as domestic appliances and some categories of cars. On top of that they have an enormous hidden, or "black," economy, the extent of which is unknown. Therefore they must be doing something right. Your task should be to discover where they act in a superior manner to you and whether you can learn to do the same. Their efficiency is not as "obvious" as yours, but it may have something to do with their gregariousness, flexibility, working hours, people orientation, teamwork, quickness and opportunism. Try to get into their shoes.

Italian flexibility in business often leads you to think they are dishonest. They frequently bend rules, break or "get around" some laws and put a very flexible interpretation on certain agreements, controls and regulations. Remember that this is the way they do business and you may well be able to benefit from this "flexibility." They will regard your rather rigid, law-abiding approach as somewhat old-fashioned, short-sighted or even blind. In this respect they probably are closer to reality than you are and less ideal bound. They do not consider their approach to be in any way corrupt, immoral or misleading. They will happily take you into their "conspiracy." They will share the "benefits" with you, if you accept. If you stick to the letter of the law, they will go on without you. We are not talking about clear illegalities. There are many gray areas where shortcuts are, in Italian eyes, a matter of common sense.

Italians are less private persons than linear-active people and they will occasionally borrow your property (or time) with some freedom. Eventually they will repay or return your property (calculator, car, report, etc.) so do not be unduly stuffy about it. Remember you can borrow from them whenever you like.

Italians often "borrow" your money in the sense that they pay late. This is another area where change of habit is very difficult to bring about. The best you can do is try to arrange satisfactory payment schedules in advance and/or take the probability of delayed payments strongly into consideration. Remember that the Italians will allow you similar latitude (if they can afford it).

MOTIVATION
KEY   *Share personal details; praise families*

Cross-century mood	✦ Very much in the EU (a founding member). ✦ Continued pursuit of intelligent industrialization and successful marketing of products. ✦ Some tendencies to consider separation of northern and southern halves of the country. ✦ Gradual subjection of Mafia and similar organizations.

Motivating Factors

✦ Be human at all times.

✦ Confide in them as much as you dare. This includes revealing family details, hopes, aspirations, disappointments and problems, particulars of past life, education, vacations and so on.

✦ They will reveal much of their private life to you. Listen sympathetically.

✦ Once a certain closeness has been established, maintain it through words and actions.

✦ Inquire always about their family's health and especially that of older relatives.

✦ Be prepared, in principle, to grant any personal favor they may ask you.

✦ They must feel that you are part of their in-group and they part of yours. This involves showing greater loyalty to them than to "outsiders" (including officials and authorities).

✦ Italians do not always obey the letter of the law. When approaching such issues, you should be as flexible as possible.

✦ Strive to be communicative. There is no advantage in leaving things unsaid with Italians. They rarely see the point of discreet silence, vagueness or ambiguity.

✦ Similarly, understatement will score no points. You should make your point very clear, though with delicacy.

✦ They are not insulted easily. You can criticize and joke with them. They are not touchy about nationalism.

✦ They misunderstand coded speech, for example, "Hmm, interesting idea" (stupid), "We must have a meeting about that" (forget it) or "We shall certainly consider it" (we won't do it).

✦ Better to tell them straight, with humor in your voice. They will laugh with you.

(continued)

MOTIVATION *(continued)*

- ◆ Be willing to share Italian conspiracies.
- ◆ There is not a strong correlation in Italy between word and deed. Accept quickly a change of heart or mind on their part. Often they agree to things euphorically, then renege in the cold light of day.
- ◆ Respect Italy's strong economy. They must be doing something right.
- ◆ Show more warmth for Italy than for France as a contributor to European civilization.
- ◆ In order to persuade them to do something, ask for help (on a personal basis).
- ◆ Contact them often.

Avoid

- ◆ Brusqueness and lack of delicacy.
- ◆ Insensitive remarks.
- ◆ Lack of appreciation of Italian thoughtfulness.
- ◆ Discussion of Mussolini or fascism.
- ◆ Reference to Italy's proclivity for changing governments.
- ◆ Reference to crime, corruption, the Mafia.

23

Spain

There is only one England or France, but there are several Spains. Castilians are in the majority and continue to dominate, but you would do well to check on a Spaniard's origins when beginning to do business with him or her. Galicians are practical and melancholy, sharing some common ground with British, Dutch and Nordics. Aragonese stubbornness finds an echo in Finnish *sisu*. Basques have a talent for industry and commerce and, along with Finns, Hungarians and Estonians, stand apart from Indo-European ancestry. Northern Europeans and Americans share the cult of efficiency with Catalans, who face France rather than Spain. On the other hand, they have little in common with two other regions—Asturias, where the people are extremely haughty, and Andalusia, where everyone is an orator and timetables are for cats and dogs.

At the time of writing, Spain's regions are still somewhat restive. The Catalans have already achieved a large degree of autonomy and self-rule. Catalan is firmly established as a literary tongue and is in daily use. Galician and Andalusian regionalism is relatively passive. In the Basque country, also, unrest is occasionally visible. The Islamic attack on a Madrid train in 2004 overshadowed Basque activities of a similar nature, but the aspirations of certain elements in the Basque provinces of Guipúzcoa, Vizcaya and Alava remain an obstacle to Spanish unity in the twenty-first century.

Culture

Values

So much for the regions—let us now take a close look at Castile and the values of its people.

guardians of the Roman heritage	proud
verbose	impractical crusaders, mystics eloquent individualists
inventive	not compliant with authority
romantic	scorn for laws and regulations
love to talk	personal dignity
fatalistic	energetic, adventuresome

Cultural Factors in Communication

Communication Pattern

We may insist that facts are stubborn things, but the Spaniard asserts things are not what they seem. There is a double truth, that of the immediate detail and that of the poetic whole. The second is more important for the Castilian, since it supplies a faith or vision to live by. One must realize the futility of material ambition.

Consideration of these Spanish concepts and credos makes it fairly clear that the Spaniard and some northerners (for instance, Nordics) have quite different perceptions of reality. Dialogue between them is never going to be easy. A grandiloquent, circumlocutory orator and supreme romanticist addresses a passive listener and taciturn pragmatist. There will probably be a language barrier. Yet dialogue there must be, in the world of business.

There are some bridges between Spanish and northern cultures. Castile is a barren land with extremes of cold and heat. The severity of climate and landscape has accustomed Castilians to austerity—a phenomenon not unknown to northerners—and hard times in many countries have encouraged frugality. Although Spain is a land of rich and poor, the egalitarian Britons, Scandinavians and Americans can detect in the Spaniards' protection of the underdog Spain's version of true democracy. (See Figure 5.7 for an illustration of Spanish communication pattern and Figure 5.11 for listening habits.)

Behavior at Meetings and Negotiations

Spaniards are generally friendly and affable, extremely hospitable when hosting. Enthusiastic small talk and socializing precede and procrastinate getting down to business. When they do formulate strategies, their proposals are often only "outlines" and vague to begin with. They maintain a genial stance throughout, but they are nobody's fools.

People wishing to do business with Spaniards must first accept that they will never act like northerners and that their scale of values is quite remote from the modern age.

Like other people, they buy and sell and are friendly, but they look at you in an old-fashioned way and they are more interested in you than in your goods. I once acted as interpreter for three German salesmen presenting their new product to the board of a Madrid company. The Germans had a slick presentation lasting 30 minutes, with slides, graphs, diagrams and video. The six Spanish managers facing them hardly watched the presentation at all. They were watching the salesmen. Were these the type of people they wanted to do business with? Did they like them? Were they really human? All Germans give perfect presentations, so why watch it? After the session was over the breathless Germans waited for the response. The Spaniards took them for lunch, which lasted until 4:00 P.M. After that everybody took a siesta. The deal was done three days later.

Manners and Taboos

Spain used to be well known for eating and drinking until the early hours of the morning and taking a siesta the following afternoon. Entry into the EU has obliged businesspeople to align their waking and working hours with the rest of Europe, so the siesta tradition is dying fast. Spaniards still eat late, however, very often in restaurants, and lunch is the bigger meal (starting as late as 2:00 or 3:00 P.M., if the office does not demand one's presence). An evening meal to follow may be just *tapas* if the lunch was enormous. Many Spaniards have two jobs. Work situations are more flexible than in Northern Europe or the United States. Contrary to popular belief, Spaniards are not huge wine drinkers, being ranked tenth in wine consumption, drinking only half the amount downed by their Portuguese and French neighbors. Spaniards smoke more than most Western Europeans. Taboos include failure to protect "face," lack of chivalry and bad treatment of the weak, poor or handicapped.

How to Empathize with Spaniards

You must work hard at making a Spaniard like you. If you succeed in this, the business will follow automatically. You must show you have a heart and that you do not take everything seriously. Northerners have big hearts, but some are often experts at hiding them. You need to talk to Spaniards with a twinkle in your eye. Their "distance of comfort" is much closer than that of most Europeans and they like both physical and eye contact. They are more robust than French, Italian or Portuguese people—they are the roughest of the Latins. *Macho* is a Spanish word, and the essential masculinity of the northern businessman stands him in good stead in a Spaniard's company. Northern businesswomen will also be comfortable with male Spaniards, as their relative aggressiveness will score points.

Spaniards are very human. When conversing with them it is best to shed some of your cool tendencies, forget the dictates of time, admit that some roguery actually exists in your country, confess to a few private sins or misdemeanors, ask them some rather personal questions, stay up drinking with them until 3:00 in the morning and in general let your hair down.

When relaxing in the company of Spaniards, keep one consideration in the forefront of your mind: they are touchy and sensitive. You may laugh at the French and Germans as much as you like, you can even criticize certain Spanish customs such as siestas or the bull fight, but do not under any circumstances say anything that might be interpreted to impinge on their personal dignity or honor. For many Spaniards *pundonor* (point of honor) is the most important word in the language. They may be poor, but they are noble. They may have been in jail, but they are honest. They may be unpunctual, but they are true. They may owe you money, but they are sure to pay you when they can. They may have failed, but they cannot be humiliated. Like the Japanese and Chinese, they cannot be made to lose face.

This deference to a Spaniard's dignity, the careful nurturing of their personal, human prowess, the respect shown for their station, personality and soul, is the key to their cooperation, alliance and affection. They will reciprocate in full—if you command a Castilian's loyalty, he will be your best friend. He will buy your company's product and send you Christmas cards for 25 years. He will lie and occasionally die for you. He is an honorable man.

MOTIVATION	
KEY	*Protect Spanish honor and integrity*
Cross-century mood	✦ Increasing tendency to "join Europe" after many decades of pursuing a separate way of life. ✦ Continued inability to solve regional problems, especially the Catalan. ✦ Increasing commitment to industrialization. ✦ Continued and increasing closeness of commercial ties with South America.

Motivating Factors

✦ Human relations count far more than logic or efficiency. Put business on a person-to-person basis.
✦ Be as familiar as you dare, but keep the dignity of man (*la dignidad del hombre*) in the forefront of your mind.

(continued)

MOTIVATION *(continued)*

✦ Always impute the best motives. Remember that, unlike Italians, they are touchy about personal honor and nationalism.

✦ Accept physical closeness, tactile behavior, back-slapping, etc.

✦ Hearty (sometimes rough) humor scores points. They are not subtle or delicate in such matters.

✦ Let them speak at length. They like to get things off their chest. Do not oppose or interrupt during this phase. The sympathetic listener will be granted favors later. You can even reverse their opinions, if you have gained their loyalty.

✦ Win their loyalty by listening well, trying to facilitate their task and fulfilling commitments diligently. Your diligence will impress them and put them in your debt.

✦ Spaniards "feel" situations rather than analyzing them logically. Therefore you may make emotional appeals. "My grandfather did business with your grandfather" is a very valid argument with Spaniards.

✦ Socialize as energetically (and as late) as possible. Relationship-building in Spain is nearly always associated with eating and drinking.

✦ Show some knowledge of Spanish history and literature/arts.

✦ Allude to Spain's glorious past. It is one of Europe's oldest countries; it dominated European politics and Catholicism for centuries, and it had a huge empire.

✦ Remember there are several Spains (Castile, Andalucia, Galicia, Catalonia, the Basques). Make sure you know where people's allegiances lie.

✦ Influence them through personal appeal, not rules, regulations or deadlines.

✦ They do not like being rushed, restricted, hindered or hedged in. Give them space as well as time.

✦ They have low legal consciousness.

✦ They need a vision or faith to live by. You must show them your idealism overlying your pragmatism.

✦ They are rather fatalistic and perceive "double truth"—the immediate reality and the enduring philosophical situation. There is nothing new under the sun. Try to share this attitude with them.

Avoid

✦ Confusing *mañana* behavior with laziness. If late deliveries (or payment) are causing you problems, indicate that you are under pressure from above and ask them to help you personally.

✦ Allowing any Spaniard to lose face in your presence.

✦ Paying too much personal attention to Spanish ladies. The men are unreasonably jealous!

✦ Referring to Spanish lack of punctuality, slowness, political or regional instability, violence or general inefficiencies or weaknesses. It is counterproductive.

24

Portugal

If the Portuguese people were not very different from the Spaniards, Portugal would not exist. Looking at a map of the Iberian Peninsula, we have the impression that the roughly pentagonal mass—so clearly separated from the rest of Europe by the Pyrenees and so narrowly cut off from Africa by the Straits of Gibraltar—seems geologically formed for unity: the intermediary between two seas and two continents.

Subconsciously most Spaniards think of the Iberian Peninsula as theirs, and subconsciously most Portuguese see the Spaniards as potential invaders. There is a parallel situation in the way English, Welsh and Scots feel about each other, although in their case the political union is a fact.

The Portuguese matter was settled with Spain in 1297, when Portugal won its independence under King Afonso Henriques. For 60 years (1580–1640) the Spaniards reestablished dominion, but since then the divorce has been made final. Geographically, in fact, the division makes sense, just as the separation of Norway and Sweden does. Each party wants its own side of the mountain, and the lifestyle has adapted to the environment. Norway and Portugal were forest-clad and coastal, inclining their populations toward seafaring and fishing occupations; in the case of Portugal the fishermen, sailors, foresters and fruit growers were too unlike the migratory shepherds on the Castilian plateau to share any lasting future with them. Spain has often been seen as a collection of separate provinces. With the advent of Portuguese independence, it counted one less.

Portugal is an Atlantic country; Spain is principally Mediterranean. The Portuguese, with their backs to Spain, face the ocean and the Western Hemisphere. Cut off from Europe by Spanish land, they had easy sea routes to the British Isles, the African coast, Madeira, the Canary Islands, the Azores and ultimately the Americas.

If you have stood by Vasco de Gama's statue on the seashore of his home town of Sines and looked out over the beckoning blue ocean on a fine sunny day, you are left in little doubt as to why the Portuguese sailed forth and sought lands beyond the horizon. The ocean is exhilarating and those people who are substantially exposed to it—the Vikings, Britons, French, Spaniards, Polynesians, Dutch and Portuguese—have proceeded literally to the ends of the earth and carved out their own destinies in times when such exploits were still feasible.

The Atlantic provided West-facing Portugal with an unhindered link with England, its natural ally against Spain and (later) Napoleon's France. It opened up a country that would otherwise have been claustrophobic, with no contact with fellow Europeans except through the Spanish filter.

Most importantly, the Atlantic gave newly independent Portugal the attractive opportunity for overseas exploration at the very time when large parts of the world were ripe for colonization. Science, although still in its infancy, was providing an invaluable aid to ocean-going vessels. England, France, Spain and Holland were all gearing up to expand by means of ambitious colonization. The 500-mile strip of Atlantic seacoast destined the Portuguese to join these maritime powers and enabled this tiny country to acquire an enormous empire, rivaling in size and resources those of France, Spain and Britain.

Cultural Factors in Communication

Behavior at Meetings and Negotiations

In business, although the organization of firms is based on vertical hierarchy with authority concentrated in the person at the top, Portuguese managers avoid direct conflicts with staff members whenever possible by adopting a benign manner of address and considering the personal problems of subordinates.

This same friendly attitude is observed in their relationships with clients. The Portuguese begin the relationship with the open assumption that trust exists between the two parties. Their manner is so cheerful and communicative that they have no difficulty in establishing this ambience, even in the initial stages of discussion. In Portugal clients are seen as friends; otherwise it is unlikely they will remain clients.

In countries where bureaucracy is heavy—and Portugal has this unfortunate characteristic—there is a tendency for business conduct to rely largely on good personal relations and mutual confidence of individuals; otherwise there will be no shortcuts. In Portugal, as in Italy, the ability to generate close relations and to secure good introductions, to create long-term goodwill, is not only an essential prerequisite to doing business; it is the criterion of efficiency itself! Portuguese executives, who have this gift, make excellent ice-breakers at international gatherings where some of the delegates exhibit initial stiffness.

The Portuguese possess great oratorical skills, but they also like things in writing. This is not only a product of Portuguese bureaucracy (they borrowed heavily from the Napoleonic model); they also think that well-expressed documents help to avoid uncertainty and ambiguity. There the contrast with Spaniards is startling. Portuguese generally write their language carefully and well; this characteristic serves them admirably in the bureaucratic procedures often required in large multinational companies.

The Portuguese are among the best negotiators in the world. When they negotiated the terms of their entry into the Common Market at the same time as the Spaniards, they obtained considerably better conditions than their fellow Iberians.

Their imperial past and inclination to distance themselves from the Spaniards have made them far more international in outlook than most people give them credit for. Their language abilities are excellent—among the Latins they are easily the best speakers of English, and enrollments in English, French and German courses are staggering. The famous Cambridge School of Languages in Lisbon regularly enrolls more than 10,000 students per annum.

- ✦ The Portuguese negotiate individually or in small teams whose members know each other well, and may be related.
- ✦ The negotiating team will achieve the best agreement for the company, but individual preferences, family and social position will be a background to the decisions.
- ✦ The results of a negotiation are regarded as a credit or debit to personal prowess.
- ✦ Their multi-active nature leads Portuguese to link the negotiation to other transactions or business in which they are currently involved. They do not compartmentalize the negotiation.
- ✦ Surnames and titles are used, but Portuguese negotiators are friendly, even charming, from the outset.
- ✦ They believe they are smarter than the other side, but they try to give the opposite impression.
- ✦ They know what they want from the outset but have an open mind as to
- ✦ how they will achieve it and will state what they really want as late as they can in the negotiation.
- ✦ Suspicious by nature, the Portuguese nevertheless disguise this trait.
- ✦ They are quick, perceptive and opportunistic, but exercise maximum flexibility.
- ✦ They often say they understand, when in fact they *plan* to understand.
- ✦ Although they begin with a high price to leave room for maneuvering later, they are quick to modify their bid if they sense tension.
- ✦ They argue in a roundabout manner as opposed to French logical buildup or American upfront demands.
- ✦ They often change course dramatically during a negotiation and make a platform out of something they didn't come to the table with, or they will throw an extremely imaginative (wild) proposal on the table to confuse the opponent or gain time.
- ✦ They rarely turn down any business offered during negotiation, scooping up whatever peripheral or accessorial transactions are available.
- ✦ Generous by nature, they entertain lavishly in between meetings, often choosing the entertainment themselves.
- ✦ The Portuguese expect to pay and be paid promptly.
- ✦ National honor is not a major factor; they are not touchy about race, religion or ethnicity.
- ✦ Their communicative style is personal, eloquent and emotional, but more restrained than Italian or Spanish (Atlantic influence).
- ✦ They come to the negotiation well informed about all aspects of the transaction.
- ✦ Having built on centuries of trading with India, Africa and the Far East, the Portuguese are experienced on a global scale. Experience has also taught them to be flexible, devious, realistic and "good losers."

◆ A lack of technology and resources often puts Portuguese negotiators in a disadvantageous position for which they must compensate with clever negotiation, resulting in a sophisticated approach.

Manners and Taboos

The Portuguese are more formal than the Spaniards, who nowadays use the familiar *tu* (you) form all over the place. *You* in Portugal can be *O Senhor* (*A Senhora*), *tu* or *Você,* and these forms can be combined with either first or second names or with titles such as *Professor* or *Engenheiro*. The permutations are many. When in doubt, it is advisable to err on the side of formality. Do not hesitate to address as *Doutor* anyone who appears well qualified or more intelligent than you are.

MOTIVATION	
KEY	*Showing compassion*
Cross-century mood	◆ Enthusiastic adherence to the EU after receiving generous grants for new infrastructure. ◆ Euphoric after the very successful Lisbon EXPO 1999. ◆ Rapid development of the Algarve as a successful tourist area.

Motivating Factors

- ◆ Distinguish them clearly from their Spanish neighbors.
- ◆ Establish closeness and show compassion at all times.
- ◆ Acknowledge their considerable language skills.
- ◆ Give ready advice when it is asked for.
- ◆ Be prepared to listen at length; they can be long-winded.
- ◆ Listen for subtlety—they occasionally want you to read between the lines.
- ◆ Show good planning and early trust.
- ◆ They like written documentation more than other Latins.
- ◆ Recognize their international attitude.

Avoid

- ◆ Appearing rough or brusque.
- ◆ Confrontation at all times.
- ◆ Talking down to them.
- ◆ Ignoring their problems.

25

Greece

Greek consciousness is keenly aware that the Greek city–state period laid the basis for Western European civilization and the liberal democracies. Greece is also a vociferous member of the EU. The collapse of its profitable market in former Yugoslavia (because of the war), the finicky quarrel with neighboring Macedonia, the unstable position in Russia and the enduring failure to resolve the Cyprus problem have been continuing sources of anxiety for successive Greek governments. Impatient with the Cyprus matter and annoyed at the country's threats to use its veto when it pleases, EU colleagues have not offered Greece their unbridled support.

Culture

Values

reason	rational debate
freedom	close family ties
thrift	talent for business
love of the sea	charisma

Concepts

Leadership and Status

The Greek view of leadership is somewhat similar to the French conception—that is, rooted in rational argument and skill in oratory. Mastery of the language is seen as essential for commanding the respect of subordinates. Family name is very important.

Status is gained in different ways. There is great respect for education, qualifications and intellectual prowess on the one hand, wealth and family connections on the other. There are several powerful family dynasties.

Space and Time

Greece is a tactile culture. Its distance of comfort is similar to the Italian, and hugging and kissing are common. The Mediterranean pace of life is slow. Greeks are usually late for appointments, but they always have a good excuse and warm apologies. They tend to lose all sense of time when engaged in animated discussion.

Cultural Factors in Communication

Communication Pattern

Greeks are verbose, theatrical and intense. Language is declaimed in a manner similar to Spanish; eye contact during address is the strongest in Europe. Emotion is used as a weapon in discourse. Greeks believe in their own powers of oratory; they use rational arguments like the French but spice them up with emotive content.

Listening Habits

Greeks are good listeners; they desire to be well informed about business. As they are very imaginative, they tend, however, to interrelate the subject under discussion with other matters.

Behavior at Meetings and Negotiations

Greeks often display great charm, but they are serious negotiators. The senior person will dominate the discussion, as is the rule in Mediterranean countries. They are shrewd, have great experience and do not give much away. They can talk late into the night and seem to get better as they go along. Their gestures are very similar to the Latin cultures, but a slight upward nod of the head means "no" and tilting the head to either side means "yes." Occasionally, Greeks smile when they are very angry.

Manners and Taboos

The multi-active nature of the Greeks means that they are often late for appointments. When they give interviews, they let them run on endlessly, even if someone else is waiting. Elderly people have a lot of authority and are not kept waiting.

Greeks are excellent hosts and their hospitality can be embarrassing. Flowers or a cake are suitable gifts for hostesses.

Do not mention Cyprus or say anything too laudatory about the Turks. Greeks are also sensitive about other aspects of their foreign policy, for example, their relations with Macedonia, Albania, Bulgaria and Serbia. Greek businesspeople are much more pragmatic than their politicians and in fact trade with Macedonia and put business before ideals in general. Like the Italians, they are willing to show you "shortcuts" to circumvent bureaucratic delays.

How to Empathize with Greeks

Learn the basic facts of Greek history and give them all credit for the "glory that was Greece." Personalize business as much as possible and get to know about their private lives, especially with regard to their families.

They will expect your approach, even when discussing business, to be warm and generous. Greeks like to think that the client is a friend. You should indicate trust as early in the proceedings as you can, although you must be watchful. They like eating and drinking, often quite late, and expect you to socialize.

MOTIVATION	
KEY	*Acknowledge former Greek glories*
Cross-century mood	✦ Their political stance is currently problematic—they are Western and an EU member, but their Orthodox religion aligns them with Russia, Serbia and Bulgaria. ✦ The Cyprus problem is still unresolved. ✦ Relations with the U.S. are somewhat ambivalent.

Motivating Factors

✦ Use a bit of Greek.
✦ Establish personal closeness with new business associates as soon as you can, but don't let their charm deceive you.
✦ Combine friendliness with shrewdness and firmness—they are tough negotiators.
✦ Show flexibility where rules and regulations are concerned.
✦ Accept some physical closeness.
✦ Be prepared for long-windedness.
✦ Allow them to digress when following an agenda.
✦ Socialize with them regularly, often late in the evening.
✦ Discussion may be occasionally grandiose, but they expect pragmatic conclusions.
✦ Maintain strong eye contact.

Avoid

✦ Discussing the decline of the importance of Greece since the city–state era.
✦ Talking about regional politics.
✦ Appearing too naïve.

26

Cyprus

The name "Cyprus" derives either from the Greek word for cypress tree (*kyparissos*) or possibly the Sumerian word for copper (*zubar*). The island has large deposits of copper ore. Cyprus is the third largest island in the Mediterranean, after Sicily and Sardinia.

Prehistoric hunter-gatherers were active on the island from around 10,500 BCE, as attested to by the presence of ancient water wells (the oldest in the world) at that time. Mycenaean Greek traders started visiting Cyprus around 1400 BCE and Phoenicians established colonies on the south coast from around 800 BCE. The strategic location of the island led to its being occupied successively by several major powers, including Assyrians, Egyptians and Persians. It was seized by Alexander the Great in 33 BCE. In the second millennium it fell under the rule of the Byzantine Empire, Arab caliphates, the French Lusignac dynasty and the Venetians, followed by over 300 years under the Ottoman Empire from 1571 to 1878.

The Cyprus Convention of 1878 placed the country under the administration of Britain, which formally annexed it in 1914. At that time Turkish Cypriots comprised around 20 percent of the population; the rest were fully Hellenized. However, the creation of a Turkish state in the north, and effective partition, became a policy of Turkish Cypriot leaders. In the 1950s they advocated the annexation of Cyprus to Turkey as an "extension of Anatolia." The Greek national policy was union with Greece (*enosis*).

Great Britain granted Cyprus independence in 1960. In 1963 intercommunal violence terminated in a coup d'état by Greek Cypriot nationalists in 1974. This precipitated the Turkish invasion of Cyprus on July 20 1974 and the proclamation of a separate Turkish state in the north established by unilateral declaration in 1983. The move was widely condemned by the international community. At the time of writing the Republic of Cyprus has *de jure* sovereignty over the entire island, except the sovereign base areas of Akrotiri and Dhekelia in the east, which remain under British control in accordance with the London and Zurich Agreements. However, the *de facto* division comprises the Greek Republic in the south and west (approximately 60 percent of the territory) and the Turkish Republic of Northern Cyprus (approximately 30 percent of the area). 4 percent is covered by the UN buffer zone.

The republic of Cyprus joined the EU on May 1 2004 and joined the Eurozone in 2008. The Turkish occupation is regarded as illegal occupation of EU territory since Cyprus became a member of the European Union.

Culture

The inherent duality of Cypriot culture is imposed upon the island's inhabitants by the political and linguistic division of the two communities. Greek and Turkish Cypriots exhibit some resemblances in terms of multi-active behavior, widespread religiosity, attention to tourism and not dissimilar cuisines. The pillars of Greek culture—reason, intellectuality and theatricality—differ wildly, however, from those of Turkey—male fierceness, Asian–European orientation and a moderated Islamic society.

Full descriptions of the cultural profiles of Greece and Turkey are given in Chapters 25 and 49 of this book. Readers are therefore directed to these chapters to familiarize themselves with the respective cultural factors that together combine to give an account of the comportment of Cypriots according to their particular community.

The question arises, do Greek and Turkish Cypriots differ in behavior from mainland Greeks and Turks? There is no easy answer to this, since Cypriots have been subjected to numerous foreign sources of influence over the centuries. The likelihood is, however, that they do not differ in any startling manner, since the protracted struggle between the two communities tends to reinforce the values and core beliefs of each side.

One cannot discount entirely, however, the impact of the British and their presence on the territory from 1878 to the present day (bases in the east). Cyprus is a high-income economy, a member of the Commonwealth, and still drives on the left. Eighty percent of Cypriots are fluent in English, and the discerning visitor can detect hints of some linear-active behavior, elements of reserve and a keen sense of fair play. Besides the English, a large number of Russians reside in Cyprus, and a significant number of Romanians, Bulgarians and other Eastern Europeans work in the service industries. There is little doubt that modern Cypriots are significantly more internationally oriented in outlook than their mainland counterparts.

The ultimate status of Cyprus and her relations with Greece and Turkey, the European Union, Britain, the Commonwealth and the rest of the world remains to be settled.

27

Malta

The Republic of Malta is one of the world's smallest archipelagos (five islands), lying in the middle of the Mediterranean Sea 93 km south of Sicily and 333 km north of Libya. The main islands—Malta, Gozo and Comino—cover just over 300 sq km, with a population of approximately 450,000. As such, Malta is the most densely populated country in the world after Singapore. The capital, Valletta, is the smallest capital in the EU. The country's thin soil restricts agriculture to a minimum—Malta is 95 percent urbanized. There is little wild life. The name Malta probably derives from the Greek word *meli*, meaning "honey." Resources are limestone, a strategic geographical location, a favorable climate and a productive labor force.

It is estimated that the Maltese islands were first settled around 5200 BCE by Stone Age hunters or farmers arriving from Sicily. Prehistoric Neolithic temples built around 3500 BCE are claimed to be the oldest standing structures in Europe. Phoenician traders colonized the islands after 1000 BCE, and the strategic position of Malta subsequently attracted the attention and rule of a succession of powers including Carthaginians, Greeks, Romans, Byzantines, Arabs, Normans, Sicilians, Spanish, Knights of St John, French and British. Milestones in Maltese history include the Great Siege of Malta in 1564 when the Knights of St John, with the help of Maltese infantry, withstood and repelled the hugely superior forces of the Ottoman fleet. After the siege the fortifications of the inner harbor of the capital (now named Valletta after the Grand Master of the Knights, Jean Parisot de la Valette) were greatly strengthened.

Napoleon captured Malta in 1798, but French financial and religious policies so angered the Maltese that they sought British support, and Malta eventually became a part of the British Empire in 1814.

Perhaps the most significant demonstration of the heroism of the Maltese people took place during the Second World War, when constant bombardment of Malta failed to subdue the island. In 1942 King George VI awarded the George Cross to the entire embattled colony— an unprecedented tribute.

Malta achieved independence in 1964, was declared a republic in 1974, joined the EU in 2004 and the Eurozone in 2008.

Malta's armed forces are tiny. She declares herself "a neutral state." The crime rate, though now increasing alarmingly, was traditionally low. Maltese society comprises a large number of associations and clubs, ensuring a healthy and sociably vibrant community.

Malta is one of the most multilingual countries in the European Union. One hundred percent of the people speak Maltese, 88 percent English, 66 percent Italian and 17 percent French. Maltese is a Semitic language descended from the now defunct Sicilian–Arabic dialect of South Italy.

Culture

Values

Roman Catholicism	bravery
importance of family	heroism
international orientation	hospitality

tenacity in adversity	fidelity
sense of humor	modesty
fair play	common sense
industriousness	simplicity

Religion

The predominant religion in Malta is Roman Catholicism, established as a state religion by the Constitution. St Paul was shipwrecked in Malta on his way from Jerusalem to Rome in AD 60 and spent three months on the island. There are 3,000 Muslims in the country, most of them foreigners.

Concepts

Leadership and Status

Nothing suggesting caste distinctions has existed in Maltese society since the expulsion of the ruling aristocratic knights. Neither do Maltese recognize any entrenched ethnic divisions. Relative stratification is evident, however, along the lines of higher education and economic status. Malta is a democratic republic whose parliamentary system is closely modeled on the Westminster system. Maltese demonstrated the second-highest voter turnout in the world in elections leading up to the turn of the century. The constitution gives both genders equal rights in employment. Males and females are free to circulate in public without sanction. Political and business leaders are expected to consider the well-being of subordinates. A social security system is supported by employee contributions and provides means-tested aid for people in financial difficulty. Flamboyant leadership is not popular in Malta.

Space and Time

The density of the population means that Maltese are used to crowded conditions. The distance of comfort is less than a meter, similar to the Italians. Maltese are, however, somewhat less tactile than Italians of Spaniards. Embracing is common amongst family members and close friends. In business circles overfamiliarity can be rebuffed if demonstrated too early.

Maltese are punctual in moderation, being rather laid back in their general behavior.

Cultural Factors in Communication

Communication Pattern

As multi-actives, Maltese are quite voluble in speech, though initial exchanges can seem rather tentative and shy, not unlike the British manner of engagement. Friendliness is, however, a premium requirement and a reasonable style of argument is adhered to. Maltese can talk at length and, like French and Italian speakers, can fall into digressive behavior when unsure of the subject. Use of humility, at the right intervals, is a strong card in their communicative style.

Listening Habits

On account of having been lectured to by many rulers, Maltese are respectful, but experienced listeners. They are receptive to hints, nuance and changes of tone and pride themselves on reading between the lines. They rarely raise strong objections to others' assertions, though they will ultimately defend their positions with polite tenacity. They rarely interrupt, and then only with the utmost courtesy. Sincerity is shown through strong eye contact.

Behavior at Meetings and Negotiations

Maltese have had wide experience of negotiating with multi-actives such as Italians and Arabs and reflect some of the facets of their manner and behavior. The equivalent paragraph in the chapter on Italy in this volume is a good guide on how to deal with full-blooded, multi-active comportment. There are, however, some differences which originate from the Maltese experience with the British. Though wordy, lively and digressive, Maltese like to demonstrate intermittent reserve and to show that they wish to be helpful to the other side. They fall short of using English "coded speech," but they avoid outright criticism, irony or cynicism.

When deadlock is threatened, they try to personalize discussion, hinting that as reasonable people they will "find a way." This is reminiscent of occasional Russian behavior, who like to conspire with a counterpart "to beat the system." In this area Maltese, like the British, will introduce humor. Another Maltese tactic, when negotiating, is to acknowledge the stronger position of an opponent and indirectly request a concession on a basis of friendliness. The Maltese have little appetite for excessive formality in business dealings. They consider "keeping the peace" is one of their strong points.

Manners and Taboos

Over 98 percent of the population are Roman Catholics and the year is filled with religious events and other celebrations indirectly connected with religion. Numerous pilgrimages also take place. Children are taken to church regularly and are usually sent to single-gender schools. With the young, sex is a taboo subject and puberty is rarely discussed. Open courtship is not encouraged before the age of 18. Scanty dress is taboo, as is immodest dress inside churches. Face-saving behavior is important in Maltese society.

Invitations into homes for tea or dinner are considered special favors. It is uncommon for single persons to leave the parental residence at any age. Divorce is still not legal in Malta.

How to Empathize with Maltese

Maltese are inherently modest; you should reflect their modesty but admire their vitality and share their enthusiasm. Learn about Maltese history and enthuse over their victory over the Turks during the 1565 Grand Siege. It is one of the most heroic events in world history. Show interest in the Maltese language—it is quite unique. Read between the lines when they are being indirect. Always be just and fair in their eyes.

MOTIVATION	
KEY	*Recognition of their courage and achievements*
Cross-century mood	✦ Enjoying their accession to the EU. ✦ Developing special tourism.

Motivating Factors

✦ Always be open and friendly.
✦ Understand that business and social life are intertwined.
✦ Give importance to their opinions.
✦ Be diplomatic rather than frank.

Avoid

✦ Brusque behavior.
✦ Considering them "small fry".
✦ Talking down to them.
✦ Confrontations.
✦ Rushing them.
✦ Any sign of temper.
✦ Appearing only results-oriented.
✦ Discussion of politics.

28

Poland

Poland should not be underestimated. Bigger than Italy and the U.K., its land area equals that of the Netherlands, Belgium, Denmark, Austria, Switzerland and the Czech Republic combined. In terms of population, there are as many Poles as Spaniards—only Germany, France, Italy and Britain in the EU have more citizens. Its GDP is not small either (25th in the world); its economy is as big as the combined output of Hungary, the Czech Republic, Bulgaria, Slovakia and Croatia.

If Poland continues to develop into a pivotal nation of considerable political, cultural and economic influence in Central Europe, it will not be for the first time. At the beginning of the seventeenth century, it was the largest state on the continent. Indeed, the celebrated Polish–Lithuanian Commonwealth, founded in 1386, had encompassed Lithuania, Latvia, Ukraine, Belarus and large parts of Russia and stretched from the Baltic to the Black Sea.

Medieval Poland saw itself as having a historic mission, that of the defender of Catholicism and the Christian West against the barbarous hordes spilling over the Russian Steppes and attempting to subjugate Europe. As early as 1240, Poland had faced a massive Mongol–Tartar invasion from the east that threatened to overrun the entire continent. In later years Polish armies were called upon to break the Turkish siege of Vienna. In modern times, one could say that Lech Walesa's Solidarity movement broke the communist siege of Central Europe and produced a domino effect in Hungary, the former Czechoslovakia, Slovenia, Croatia and elsewhere.

Poles, destined to a historical buffer role between expansionist Russian and German empires, have shown themselves to be ne plus ultra fighters down through the centuries. Their deep sense of vulnerability has engendered an unquenchable thirst for survival. Their stoicism in adversity, their shining courage and their enthusiasm for battle reached new heights during the Second World War. Polish pilots in the squadron fighting with the British Royal Air Force frequently lost planes through chasing enemy aircraft so far out over the North Sea that they ran out of fuel and were unable to return to their base. Such spirit, bordering on fanaticism, is the key to this vital, proud, sensitive, brave people, the most vigorous and westernized of the Slavs, now turning their face to the West more consistently than at any other time in their turbulent, tragic history.

Culture

Values

Poles, romantic idealists that they are, believe that they are imbued with so many virtues that it is quite impossible to make a short list.

the arts	generosity	bravery
education	hospitality	stoicism in adversity
rustic simplicity	sensitivity to criticism	self-sacrifice
family-oriented	flexibility	tolerance
pride, obstinacy	humility	

Religion

Slavs are divided by religion: Serbia, Bulgaria, Belarus, Eastern Ukraine and Russia are by tradition Orthodox; Bosnia, largely Muslim; Croatia, Slovenia, the Czech Republic, Western Ukraine and Poland, Roman Catholic. Among Catholic Slavs, however, it is in Poland that the faith assumes disproportionate importance. At the center of the problem of convergence of cultures, victimized repeatedly by invasion, mass deportations and even genocide, Poles have developed strong feelings of defensive nationalism and determination to survive no matter how devastating an oppression they face. In this defiance, they have consistently benefited from the power of Roman Catholic belief and have unhesitatingly used their religion as a source of identity to protect themselves against non-Roman Catholic enemies.

The fierce adherence of Poles to Roman Catholicism does not mean that they all go to church. They are less enthusiastic churchgoers than, for instance, Americans. But the refusal to separate church and state strengthened both the ecclesiastical and secular sides of Polish nationalism. Neither are Poles intolerant of other religions. There are Jewish, Orthodox, Lutheran, Calvinist and Muslim minorities. Religious tolerance has (like in the Netherlands) been part of the tradition of intellectual freedom down through the centuries.

Concepts

Leadership and Status

In Polish history, royals and nobles have figured largely as leaders and organizers. Gentry comprised a high percentage of feudal society and established a chivalrous, romanticist lifestyle. Honor and revenge are living concepts in the Polish mind, as are grace, nobleness of bearing, personal integrity, fearlessness and gallantry toward women, who still get their hands kissed in Poland.

In more recent years, Nazi suppression and 45 years of communism diminished the influence of the leading Polish families. Lech Walesa eventually emerged as a working-class leader of deeply nationalistic convictions. Meritocracy now dominates advancement in Polish society, although nationally the Polish Pope wielded enormous influence. Status is accorded unreservedly to great intellectuals and artists, both past and present, Chopin and Marie Curie being outstanding examples.

Space and Time

The Polish sense of space is typically Slavic, inasmuch as they stand and sit closer to each other than Anglo-Saxons and Nordics in conversation and often touch each other to give reassurance. Parents kiss their children well into their teens, often also as fully grown adults. Men kiss women on the hands and frequently kiss male acquaintances on both cheeks. As far as possession of space is concerned, territory has always been a major issue in Poland, in view of the acquisitive tendencies of her big neighbors.

Poles are relaxed about time, but not necessarily lacking punctuality. One should not steal others' time, but Polish society is not time-dominated in the German sense. Poles tend to turn up a little late, but they have an ambivalent attitude to the sequence of events, seeing ultimate reality as not being closely connected with present activity. They are definitely past-oriented—the length and significance of their history and heritage provide an indispensable background and launching pad for current action. There is a certain fatalism about their conduct, although they also possess drive and objectivity.

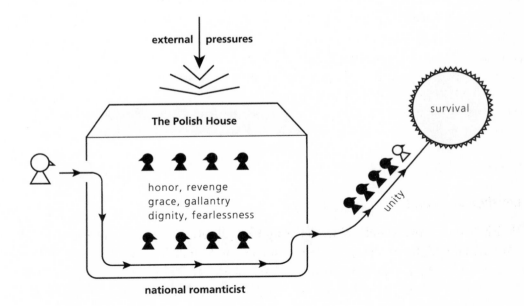

Figure 28.1 Polish Leadership Style

Cultural Factors in Communication

Communication Pattern

The Polish communication style is enigmatic, ranging from a matter-of-fact pragmatic style to a wordy, sentimental, romantic approach to any given subject. When in the latter mode, they are fond of metaphor and their speech is rich in implied meaning, allusions, images and ambiguity. Irony and even satire are used to great effect.

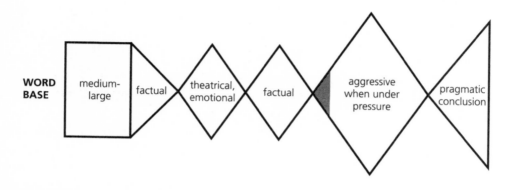

Figure 28.2 Polish Communication Pattern

Listening Habits

Poles are courteous and rarely interrupt, but they listen to official announcements with calm skepticism and distrust. They are quick to detect minor slights.

Behavior at Meetings and Negotiations

As with their speech style, in behavior Poles fluctuate between pragmatism and sentiment. Generally they seem to want a little of both. They are friendly and flexible when well treated, but react strongly if they suspect injustice. Not afraid to confront, they can be quite fiery when under pressure. A particular national characteristic is that they consider aggressive behavior on their part to be justified when they are severely criticized or insulted.

If they are handled with a combination of frankness and delicacy, they quickly try to establish close personal relationships. They have a basic shyness and nonassertive nature born of centuries of not questioning teachers or those in positions of influence and power.

Modern businesses are quickly growing in confidence, but you can still sense a disarming simplicity in Polish behavior toward others. Although personal, Polish negotiations are not particularly informal. A discreet distance is maintained between conversation partners. Often the third person (*he* or *she*) is used for direct address. Ideas are often introduced in a roundabout manner and you have to read between the lines.

Manners and Taboos

Toasting is common and consumption of hard liquor (vodka, cognac) is widespread. First names are reserved for close friends only. Body language is generally restricted, but the shrugging of shoulders and slapping of one's forehead (to indicate stupidity) is fairly frequent. An odd number of flowers (unwrapped) is a suitable present for a hostess.

How to Empathize with Poles

Treat such concepts as honor, chivalry and old-fashioned gallantry as meaningful qualities in a Polish context. Show interest in their old culture and considerable artistic achievements. Admire their religious tolerance and general tendency to accommodate the views of others. Show that you perceive their nationalism as a necessary survival mechanism.

Appreciate Polish food and learn some expressions in their language. Do not try to address Poles in Russian.

MOTIVATION	
KEY	*Love and help Poland*
Cross-century mood	✦ Adherence to the EU and NATO seen as trump cards for the nation's continued independence and survival. ✦ Young Poles, casting off the lethargy of Soviet-influenced times, are eager to exercise their initiative and energy to build a strong economy.

Motivating Factors

- ✦ Poles will do just about anything for a visitor who clearly demonstrates a love of Poland.
- ✦ Stay cool about your liking for Russians or Czechs. Poles are more enthusiastic about Hungarians than about other Slavs.
- ✦ Be courteous at all times and accord deferential treatment to women.
- ✦ Get a feeling for Polish romantic nationalism. Support it.
- ✦ Assume people are noble in spirit. Impute best motives.
- ✦ Be humorous and drink with them when you can.
- ✦ Compliment them on their lavish hospitality.
- ✦ Enter into eager debate with them, concentrating on positive issues.
- ✦ Appreciate Polish high standards of education and artistry.

(continued)

MOTIVATION *(continued)*

◆ Acknowledge the identification of Polish nationalism with Catholicism, and praise the deceased Polish Pope.

◆ In business Poles are impressed by hard facts, but they are also interested in your feelings about them.

◆ They are looking for trust, having been abused often in the past.

Avoid

◆ Being too direct, especially if there is a negative element involved.

◆ Criticism of anything inherently Polish.

◆ Being too serious about issues. Poles are considered "unserious" by other Slavs.

◆ Any form of bad manners (rudeness, lack of caring).

◆ Appearing only results-oriented.

◆ Impinging on anyone's rights.

◆ Risky comments that might be seen as offensive (they are very sensitive to slights).

29

Hungary

At the end of the ninth century, the Hungarians went through the Carpathian mountain passes to settle the Central Danube basin. There they established an empire that lasted 1,000 years, ruling what is now Hungary, Croatia, Slovakia, Transylvania, Western Ukraine and parts of Serbia and Austria. During this period they were devastated by the Mongols in the thirteenth century and endured 150 years of Ottoman rule in the sixteenth and seventeenth centuries. Although fighters by nature, they have not been successful in the conduct of their wars; in fact, they have never won one.

In a national sense, Hungary is somewhat claustrophobic. It is a severely truncated state, compared with the lands that it once ruled. These territories, taken away after military defeats, are still inhabited by Hungarians: two million Hungarians live in Romania alone, while another million inhabit Slovakia and Serbia.

Culture

Values

obsession to achieve

romanticism

sense of humor

vanity

individualism

national self-confidence

bon vivant

gallantry, chivalry

sensitivity

competitiveness

street wisdom

Concepts

Leadership and Status

Under their old aristocracy Hungarians were often led the wrong way. A conspicuous absence of military victories and political triumphs has made Hungarians adopt a cynical attitude toward any kind of leadership. The Soviet rule did nothing to change this attitude.

A nation of individualists, Hungarians have gained and encourage status in intellectual, artistic and scientific achievements. Teachers, poets, artists, theater and film directors, musicians, composers and so forth are well respected, though hardly properly remunerated.

Space and Time

In personal terms, Hungarians sit and stand close to each other. Physical contact is frequent, handshaking mandatory. Conditions are crowded in Budapest and extended families living under one roof are common. Buses and trains tend to be packed.

Hungarians are reasonably punctual in arriving for appointments but lose all sense of time when they get involved in animated conversation. In this respect they act in a very Latin manner, subjecting their behavior and activity not to the clock but to the psychological dictates of the encounter. The art of conversation cannot be scheduled—subsequent appointments are severely staggered or simply fall away.

Cultural Factors in Communication

Communication Pattern

Discussion with Hungarians can be deceptive in the extreme. They possess ample reserves of charm and charisma and give the impression that they are easy-going. Small talk invariably precedes commencement of business. They truly regard conversation as an art form—they are great storytellers and are not without humor.

Anglo-Saxons and Nordics may soon begin to lose their way in such an environment. As an argument develops, Hungarians begin to abandon rationality for emotion, logic for rhetoric. Fluency equates with intelligence, and Hungarians are great with words, often hiding what they are really saying. Exaggeration and flamboyance creep in, mixed with stylishly delivered flattery. Their natural easy-going approach can quickly switch to criticism, however. They are accomplished complainers. Pessimism and melancholy, suddenly introduced, can also be distracting.

Conversations are generally male-dominated. Turn taking is problematic; the tendency is for everyone to talk at once. Choose your moment of entry carefully.

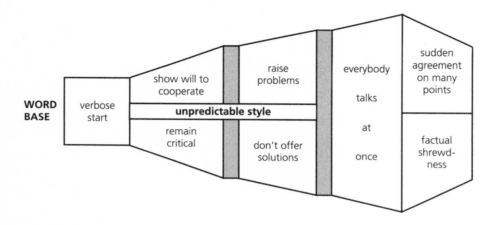

Figure 29.1 Hungarian Communication Pattern

Listening Habits

Hungarians have rather complex listening habits and require various ingredients to keep their attention. (see Fig 29.2)

Behavior at Meetings and Negotiations

When holding meetings with representatives of more powerful nations, Hungarians have an initial preoccupation with national honor. They must be treated delicately and not talked down to. They are quite touchy about this, but quickly relax once status has been established. Meetings are, however, generally far from relaxing in terms of negotiating style and duration.

Meetings are rarely quiet and orderly, and agendas are not respected. Hungarians are often moody and raise problems without offering solutions; they seem to expect the other party to come up with something. Bargaining is normal, prolonged and popular. In Northern eyes, they overanalyze constantly. Often pessimistic, they will lace pessimism with optimistic forecasts of deals to be done. They avoid saying no but often fail to answers questions directly. You really have to read between the lines.

Business must be carried on face-to-face, as only in this manner can trust be established. Hungarians are often unable to deliver their promises, but are skilled improvisers, although verbal energy often lapses into physical lassitude. At all times, you must watch your back. Grandiose in their intentions, they are weak on responsibility and even weaker on implementation.

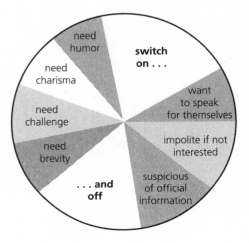

Figure 29.2 Hungarian Listening Habits

Manners and Taboos

The Hungarian is a bon vivant, a drinker of wine rather than beer, a lover of cholesterol-rich food and frequenter of traditional coffeehouses, where timeless conversation and bittersweet Turkish coffee remind you of the Ottoman occupation. Conversation in Hungary is very personal, with much handshaking, strong eye contact and frequent confidences. Women, although sometimes prominent in business, are idealized in the old-fashioned manner. Hand kissing is common and men walk to the left of women (to protect them with their sword). Women precede men into theaters, cinemas and private homes, but follow them into rougher environments such as bars, restaurants and cafés! Hungarians often use the third person (*he* or *she*) and have four forms for *you* to choose from, depending on the degree of politeness.

How to Empathize with Hungarians

Above all, be familiar with Hungarian history and their contributions to the wider world, particularly with reference to science and music. Listen to their complaints and problems, but do not offer any of your own.

Hungarians are impressed by plush offices, cars, clothes and so on, and they like to exhibit their wealth. Good clothes are essential and you should strive for immaculate presentation. This, a knowledge of Hungarian and a quick and flexible brain are assets in dealing with Hungarians. Most Hungarians in positions of power are very well educated, and they respect strong academic records and intelligent conversation about their own magnificent history. Always refer to Hungary as Central Europe rather than Eastern Europe.

Avoid talking about ethnic minorities (Jews, Gypsies, Romanians, etc.) unless you are well informed. A sense of humor is essential.

MOTIVATION	
KEY	Mix friendliness with shrewdness
Cross-century mood	◆ They are eager to demonstrate that they can recover from the communist era faster than anyone else. ◆ They seek investment. ◆ They are proud of having been early candidates for the EU.

Motivating Factors

- ◆ Demonstrate liveliness, energy and, if possible, sharp wit.
- ◆ Be prepared to eat, drink and socialize on a regular basis with colleagues.
- ◆ Enter into the spirit of the "coffeehouse" culture—gossip a bit.
- ◆ Show your status symbols; Hungarians will want to see them.
- ◆ Show your respect for their education and highly developed culture.
- ◆ Remember the glories of the Austro–Hungarian Empire.
- ◆ Enthuse about Budapest's beauty.

Avoid

- ◆ Praising Romanians or Slovakians too much.
- ◆ Dwelling too much on the communist times (they had their own version).

30

The Czech Republic

Czechs were once the 10th industrial power in the world. Democracy flourished under Tomas Garrique Masaryk and the country seemed to have the rosiest future of the Slavic lands. This fine progress was rudely interrupted by the German intrusion into Sudetenland in 1938 and by the Russian occupation from 1945 to 1989. During the presence of Soviet troops, the Czechs offered only passive resistance until Alexander Dubcek, who attempted to develop "socialism with a human face." This audacity produced the Prague Spring of 1968, which was quickly crushed by Russian tanks.

After the departure of the Soviets, Czechoslovakia wrestled with its internal problem—the growing schism between Czechs and Slovaks. The separation, as might have been foreseen, was civilized and bloodless (in stark contrast to the bloodletting in the former Yugoslavia). Czechs and Slovaks put their house in order in a manner not unlike that of the Portuguese in their 1974 revolution. The election of a playwright and poet—Vaclav Havel—to the Czech presidency crowned this serene political development.

The Czechs have had gnawing problems adjusting to a market economy. Nearly 50 years of being directed by the Soviets had left a legacy of lassitude and avoidance of responsibility that is also observable in other former communist states. Soul-searching in the Czech Republic is as pervasive as it is in more fortunate countries such as Norway and the Netherlands. The search for Czech identity goes on. Given the many skills and the high level of education of the Czech people, there is a high probability that it will be a creditable and inspiring one. Their cultural classification is linear-active, data-oriented (see Chapter 3 for an explanation of these terms).

Culture

Values

individualism, creativity	sense of humor
work ethic	flexibility
love of learning	pragmatism, egalitarianism
tolerance, tidiness, thrift	rationality
love of music and theater	discipline, steadiness, loyalty
morality	lack of self-confidence
lasting friendships	passive resistance

Concepts

Leadership and Status

Czechs resent power imposed from the outside and never accepted inequality imposed by foreign rulers. The high rate of literacy and general excellence of education over the centuries have enabled the Czechs to acquire and enjoy knowledge and to seek egalitarianism and democratic institutions. Liberty is seen as something that may be assured by laws, procedures and regulations. Orderliness in society has long been a characteristic of Czech society, though this has often led to excessive officialdom and periods of stifling bureaucracy. The Soviet influence in the communist period was met by passive resistance rather than by open confrontation.

Space and Time

Czechs are not particularly tactile people and kissing, embracing and hugging in public are very rare. Handshaking, however, is mandatory on greeting and taking leave. The "distance of comfort" is well over 40 inches (a meter).

Lines for buses are disciplined and orderly. Czechs arrive on time for appointments and often early for dinner. They are early risers. In the communist time, factories were in full swing by 7:00 A.M. or earlier and the working day often finished at 1:00 or 2:00 P.M.

Cultural Factors in Communication

Communication Pattern

The Czechs are soft speakers who communicate in a thoughtful manner and in measured tones. Rushing headlong into discussion is not their style, and rapid conclusions are rare. They often impress their interlocutors as being phlegmatic and lukewarm rather than just laid back. Their humor is dry and black.

Listening Habits

The Czechs are dutiful listeners, always polite and courteous. They rarely interrupt and give little feedback. As they think in a linear fashion, they are uncomfortable with roundabout or digressive discussions and have a low tolerance for ambiguity. Their response, if they are unhappy, can be ironic and contain veiled sarcasm.

Behavior at Meetings and Negotiations

Czech negotiations are contemplative, practical and rational. They do not like confrontation and pride themselves on their flexibility and adaptability. They have a gradualistic approach to problem solving, not unlike the Dutch and Belgian styles. Decisions can be deferred until tomorrow, but not indefinitely. Czechs are serious, even moralistic, but show flashes of creativity and unpredictability. They like to think of themselves as entrepreneurs, and there are now a very large number of registered, small companies. They believe that sound procedures are good for business and seek common ground with partners, just as Germans do. Their love of structure, regulations and incremental planning makes them poor at handling chaos.

Manners and Taboos

Czechs still adhere to old-fashioned concepts of formality and chivalry. Although they show less gallantry toward women than the Poles, they dress up conscientiously when going to the theater or opera and shake hands with all and sundry in a respectful (almost Germanic) manner. They do not forget to use academic titles when addressing people and respect education and good manners in others. Slouching or disrespectful body language is frowned on and generally they dislike ostentatious behavior or grandiose comportment. In short, they are (and wish to be) very civilized. They do not invite business associates immediately into their homes, but prove loyal and hospitable friends when acquaintanceship has matured.

How to Empathize with Czechs

Czechs are motivated by people behaving in what they consider to be a civilized manner.

They like their creativity to be challenged, and money is a secondary consideration. Brusque confrontation is taboo and they like an approach that leads to calm discussion and the discovery of solutions that suit all concerned.

All kinds of sports and home comforts are good topics of conversation. They have little inclination to talk about war, politics or religion.

MOTIVATION	
KEY	*Be steady, calm and loyal*
Cross-century mood	✦ Consolidating their new structure after the "Velvet Revolution." ✦ Trying to regain their high prewar ranking among industrial nations. This is difficult due to being smaller and on account of Asian competition. ✦ Hoping to prosper as a good and dutiful member of the EU.

Motivating Factors

✦ Show inventiveness, and look for solutions with them.
✦ Discuss things calmly, and be rational but flexible.
✦ Maintain a certain amount of formality; use academic titles with new acquaintances.
✦ Be chivalrous. Shaking hands is important.
✦ Demonstrate tolerance.
✦ Share their love of music and theater.

(continued)

MOTIVATION *(continued)*

- ✦ Enjoy their (original) humor.
- ✦ Steadiness, morality and loyalty are important.

Avoid

- ✦ Disrespectful body language or slouching.
- ✦ Being ostentatious.
- ✦ Praising Slovaks too much.

31

Slovakia

Slovaks are often defined in terms of their similarities or dissimilarities vis-à-vis their westerly "brothers," the Czechs. In fact, brothers they were during the Great Moravian Empire, which split up in A.D. 906 —the Czechs winding up in the Frankish (German) Empire and the Slovaks being absorbed by the Hungarians, recent arrivals on the Danube from the steppes of Asia. Czechs and Slovaks from then on lived in separate worlds for a whole millennium. Although they were reunited by the Allies in 1918, the brothers had developed different characters. Czechs, under mainly Austrian rule, had prospered. Slovaks, repressed culturally and economically by tough Hungarian regimes, had developed a victim mentality. In the new Czechoslovak state, the Czechs patronized them. The Slovaks, less sophisticated than the Czechs, became more nationalistic. The eventual "divorce" between the Czechs and the Slovaks in 1993 was mainly of their seeking. The "Velvet Revolution," as it was called, was bloodless, just as the Portuguese Revolution of 1974 had been. These events bore a striking contrast to the Spanish Civil War, not to mention the carnage that resulted from the more recent breakup of Yugoslavia (another Western creation). The Slovaks have emerged from the split with a more fragile economy than their Czech brothers, but after 1,100 years, they have finally satisfied their aspiration for self-rule. "When we divided, at least Slovakia had a name," remarked one of their politicians with dry humor. The Czech president, Vaclav Havel, offered a prize to anyone who could think of a more exciting name than the "Czech Republic."

Centuries of oppression, even slavery, have left Slovaks with a sense of having been victimized by historical circumstances. At the crossroads of many battles and invasions, they found it hard to consolidate their national identity. They are currently one of the youngest nation states in Europe, though they are fully aware that the Czechoslovak lands were possibly the earliest settled on the continent: 4000 B.C.

Culture

Values

extended families	closeness to nature
respect for education	attachment to folklore, folk art
love of music and sport	epicureanism
defense of their Slovak nation and culture	attachment to popular traditions
rather religious (marriage, baptism, funerals)	sense of historical victimization
lack of self-confidence	

Religion

The Slovak people are predominantly Catholic (60 percent) with Protestant and Jewish minorities. Their cultural classification is multi-active, dialogue-oriented (see Chapter 3 for an explanation of these terms).

Concepts

Leadership and Status

Slovakia is in transition from communist rule to a market economy. Former Communist officials have lost leadership positions in general, though a certain number of them have transformed their former political influence into executive power, and an autocratic style is still favored over a consensual one. Few people are anxious to embrace responsibility. Those who are willing to do so may wield their power fairly openly.

Status varies considerably according to age. In the Soviet-influenced years, it depended on one's political orientation and position within the Communist Party. People retaining their network of contacts from these years still command a certain status. Wealth certainly gives status, as does connection with certain families. With younger people, education and achievement provide upward mobility, though Slovakia cannot yet be described as a thoroughly meritocratic society.

Space and Time

The Slovak population density is fairly high, about 200 per square mile (109 per square kilometer), and Slovakians are used to rubbing shoulders with each other. They love to spend their time in rural areas—in former times most of them were peasants—and love nature and gardening. The distance of comfort is closer than that of Czechs or Germans, about 40 inches (one meter).

Slovaks, like Czechs, are more punctual than most Slavs. "Stealing" another's time is regarded as bad manners. The tempo of life is somewhat slower than that of Czech lands. They like to give issues the time they feel they need.

Cultural Factors in Communication

Communication Pattern

The Slovak language is a kind of lingua franca for Slavic peoples, inasmuch as it can be understood by Czechs, Poles, Bulgarians and ex-Yugoslavs more easily than any other. This gives Slovaks considerable confidence when conversing with Slavs, and they are regarded as quite loquacious and expressive in this context. When talking to Western Europeans (in English or German), a certain caution creeps into their speech pattern, partly for linguistic reasons, but also because of oppression suffered in the past. They have a tendency to distrust official information—a consequence of the Soviet-style years. There is a certain tendency toward vagueness, and they can often be ambiguous. This is because they are nonconfrontational and dislike saying anything that might offend the listener.

Listening Habits

Because Slovaks are normally polite and courteous and wish to learn, they listen well. They rarely interrupt a foreigner, though they occasionally do so with other Slovaks. They often ask for information to be repeated, as they wish to avoid misunderstandings. They admire daring, interesting conversationalists and get bored if they are not sufficiently entertained.

Behavior at Meetings and Negotiations

Meetings are held in a rather formal manner, with full use of titles until people get to know each other well. Hierarchy is generally respected, including seating arrangements, entering and leaving, and turns at speaking.

The purpose of meetings is to get to know the positions of others and to begin negotiations after some socializing and preliminary "sounding out." There is no rush to enter into commitments. Care is taken not to give offense and politeness in this respect may lead to ambiguity, as mentioned earlier, and may be seen as hypocrisy. Slovaks often say what you want to hear, but they are not being intentionally deceitful. They are merely observing certain Central European courtesies in diplomatic communication. They are cautious in their dealings; their social spontaneity is not matched by spontaneity in business proposals.

Business discussions follow a normally orderly course, but Slovaks have less rigid agendas than Germans and even Czechs. They often wish to digress on subjects which are of interest or importance to them, but they are more disciplined in their digressions than French, Italians or Hungarians.

Their style is generally sober, with occasional flashes of feelings. A formerly oppressed people, they expect Western partners to be generous and offer concessions when their own resources are inadequate. They are tenacious in negotiating, but not openly forceful; instead, they bluff to a certain extent to get what they can.

How to Empathize with Slovaks

First and foremost, show an interest in and respect for the new Republic of Slovakia. The Slovaks want to be distinguished from the Czechs and seen for what they are—a people who have lived a distinct European existence since their arrival in the fifth and sixth centuries. As a proud nation, they expect unqualified recognition as a fully fledged European state already in the EU. It is wise not to praise the Hungarians too much, the Czechs just a little. They appreciate a warm, personal approach. You should show sympathy for their troubled history and look positively on their new nationhood.

CZECHS AND SLOVAKS— SOME COMPARISONS

Czech	Slovak
linear-active	multi-active
calm, passive	charismatic
soft speakers	vigorous speakers
Germanic tendencies	Slavic tendencies
few likes and dislikes	somewhat opinionated
restrained nationalism	nationalistic
open to criticism	sensitive to criticism
reserved socially	party a lot
steady pace	slower pace
urban	parochial
sexes nearly equal	male-dominated

(continued)

(continued from previous page)

CZECHS AND SLOVAKS— SOME COMPARISONS

Czech	Slovak
nuclear family	extended family
stick to rules	relaxed about rules
low-key leaders	autocratic leaders
clear instructions	somewhat vague instructions
thrifty	spend and borrow
Protestant traditions	Catholic traditions
complain little	complain and grumble
non-tactile	non-tactile
procedures-oriented	some experimentation
not very religious	religious in the countryside
status by education	status by family, wealth and network contacts

MOTIVATION

KEY	Recognition of the Slovak nation
Cross-century mood	◆ Their primary concern is the building of their nation state after separation from the Czech Republic. ◆ They need a lot of investment from the West, and they know this. ◆ They are happy to have joined the EU and strive to meet the economic criteria.

Motivating Factors

◆ Slovaks consider themselves cultured, and you need to match their level of sophistication.

◆ They expect you to be well educated.

◆ They are motivated by solid achievement but are also susceptible to charm.

◆ They like to have their confidence bolstered. Encourage them.

◆ They want to see you relaxed about rules and regulations.

◆ Show interest in nature and enjoy their attractive countryside.

(continued)

MOTIVATION *(continued)*

Avoid

+ Patronizing the "young" nation.
+ Calling them Eastern Europeans.
+ Calling them a former communist regime.
+ Dwelling on their severe pollution problems.

32

Slovenia

Slovenia is a small Alpine country, slightly smaller than the state of New Jersey, with about two million inhabitants. The capital is Ljubljana. Slovenia was one of the six republics that made up the former Yugoslavia. Much of the land is mountainous; the small coastal strip has a Mediterranean climate.

The ancestors of the Slovenes, blond, blue-eyed and rather tall, settled in the area about A.D 600. They have managed to survive as a distinctive national group remarkably well, in spite of not having their own country since A.D. 788, when they fell to the Franks, then the Dukes of Bavaria (A.D. 843), then the Hapsburgs. Finally in 1918 Slovenia was included in the Versailles-designed country later named Yugoslavia. During the Second World War, Slovenia was divided among Germany, Italy and Hungary, then returned after the war to the reconstituted Yugoslavia under communist rule. When the time was ripe, Slovenia was the first to declare independence from Yugoslavia. It had several advantages in doing so: the language (Slovenian) is very distinctly its own (more than 95 percent of the population is ethnic Slovenian); in order to get to them, any large army coming from Belgrade would have to go through Croatia first; and most important, they would be perfectly able to make it on their own—they would in fact be better off.

Slovenia has emerged from communist rule with a fair degree of success—it was accepted into the EU in 2004—even though it has lost the majority of its markets within former Yugoslavia and has had to reorient most of its trade. The republic has not suffered from the hyper-inflation of other territories of ex-Yugoslavia.

Slovenes are Roman Catholic. As for the cultural category, they are linear active and data-oriented (see Chapter 3 for an explanation of these terms).

Culture

Values

thrifty	punctual
industrious	factual
clean	truthful
polite	direct, frank
hospitable	proud of their achievements
nationalistic	love of music
love of nature and mountain climbing	Catholic

Concepts

Leadership and Status

Often in their history Slovenes have been denied the right to rule themselves. After the Second World War leadership was invested in Belgrade and practiced according to rank in the Communist Party. Since 1992 Slovene leaders have arisen among non-Communist coalition politicians, characterized more by pragmatism than idealism or rhetoric: in business and academia, qualifications set standards; orderliness in society is seen as important; and there is little of the flamboyance displayed by Serbian and even Croatian leaders. Gradually Western European-style democracy is taking hold.

Like Germans and Czechs, Slovenes accord status according to level of education. Slovenes have succeeded better than most ex-communist peoples in casting off former party officials. This took time, but the regime is certainly becoming increasingly meritocratic as time passes. Although few women have reached top executive levels, the equality of the sexes is well-established in comparison with the other former Yugoslav cultures.

Space and Time

Slovenes are not a tactile people, requiring 47 inches (1.2 meters) as their distance of comfort. They love the outdoors and their mountains and make full use of these in hiking, rambling and climbing.

Their punctuality is almost Germanic, though they tolerate flexibility in timekeeping outside the business sphere. Buses and trains leave on time, and transportation is generally reliable.

Cultural Factors in Communication

Communication Pattern

Slovenes are not particularly talkative people (other former Yugoslavs often found them dull or boring). They resemble Western Austrians in their factual communicative style, Czechs in their thoughtful manner and measured tones. They rarely rush headlong into discussion and are reluctant to draw rapid conclusions. Many interlocutors find Slovenes phlegmatic and luke-warm. Slovene body language is the most restrained of the Balkans, and handshakes are firm.

Listening Habits

Slovenes are good listeners; they remain attentive and rarely interrupt. In Yugoslav days they often felt tricked by Serbs and even Croats and consequently are on their guard against loquacious or devious speakers. Like Germans, they listen for information and sift through facts carefully. They dislike emotion or loudness and have a low tolerance for ambiguity or vagueness. They give little feedback.

Behavior at Meetings and Negotiations

Meetings in Slovenia are orderly affairs. Slovenes are procedure-oriented and generally pre-fer to follow agendas, though some digression is often permitted. They are in general very businesslike. Like nationals of many small countries, they are persistent and leave no stone unturned to secure a deal. Also, as in most small states, everyone seems to know each other and networking is one of their strengths. Meetings start and finish on time and socializing is a frequent option afterwards. Slovenes will inquire politely about the well-being and comfort of visitors, even though they are not great on small talk. They like documentation and write careful minutes concerning what was discussed and agreed on. Red tape is not unknown, but it is less of a problem than it is in most Balkan countries.

Slovene negotiating characteristics are factuality, rationality, structure, procedures and persistence. Procedures and structures, then, are an important part of discussion. Bargaining is low-key—Slovenes prefer to keep within agreed parameters regarding price, delivery and so on. They like predictability and react negatively to new ideas suddenly thrust upon them. When they conclude a deal, they can be relied upon to meet their commitments.

Manners and Taboos

Slovenes are well-mannered people who shun ostentation, flamboyance and unruly behavior. They are very conscious of other Slavs' exaggerations and like to distance themselves from their eastern neighbors. Do not call them "Yugoslavs" and do not place them in the Balkans. They prefer to be considered as Central Europeans.

How to Empathize with Slovenes

Travel around Slovenia and share their enthusiasm for the country. Socialize whenever you can, and be generous at all times. Slovenes have a reputation for thrift but respond well to receiving gifts and favors. Bear in mind Slovenes respect correctness and civility. In their eyes, charisma is permitted, but unnecessary; they prefer solidity.

MOTIVATION	
KEY	*Recognizing the young nation*
Cross-century mood	✦ Consolidating their position in the EU. ✦ Distinguishing themselves from other ex-Yugoslavs. ✦ Facing West.

Motivating Factors

- ✦ Discuss solutions more than problems.
- ✦ Be logical at all times.
- ✦ Give plenty of context and explain motives.
- ✦ Consider worst-case scenarios as well as rosy ones.
- ✦ Evince calmness and sincerity.
- ✦ Recognize Slovenians' independence and uniqueness.
- ✦ Indicate trustworthiness and loyalty.
- ✦ Use academic titles.
- ✦ Talk about quality rather than quantity.

Avoid

- ✦ Political discussion.
- ✦ Praising Serbs, Croats or Bosnians.
- ✦ Ostentatious behavior.
- ✦ Calling them Slovaks.

33

Croatia

Croatia is the most maritime of the six republics that formed the former state of Yugoslavia. It has an extremely beautiful coastline and hundreds of picturesque islands, both inhabited and uninhabited, in its Adriatic waters.

The country is divided into two main areas (Mediterranean and Central European) by the Dinaric Alps, which run parallel to the coast. The population is correspondingly mixed with people of Hungarian and Germanic descent to the north and of Italian provenance in the south.

Even in these international times, Croatia is one of the most international countries around. The main reason for this is geography, but history and politics have also played a part. Croats arrived in the seventh century and settled in their present territory, which has unfortunately always been a thoroughfare and a bone of contention. Everybody wanted that piece of coast, warm and well provided with natural ports, so many peoples invaded Croatia. To give credit to Croatia, it never crossed its borders to invade anybody else's territory.

In 803 Croatia became part of the Roman Empire, only to be followed by other occupations: the Ottoman Empire, the Austrian Hapsburgs, the Austro–Hungarian Empire. Finally, in 1918, like Slovenia, Croatia became part of the new country later named Yugoslavia (1929). Germany occupied Yugoslavia during the Second World War; after the war, communists took power and Josip Broz Tito became the country's leader. Despite ethnic differences, Tito held Yugoslavia together until his death in 1980. A 1991 referendum voted overwhelmingly in favor of Croatia becoming an independent republic.

The Croatian economy is recovering gradually from the ravages inflicted by the civil war, which began following independence from Yugoslavia in 1991 and severely damaged much of Croatia's infrastructure, factories, farmland and tourist centers. The international community made substantial loans to help the country regain its economic footing. A bright spot for Croatia's future economic development is the prospect of increased tourism; the Croatian coast is arguably the most spectacular in Europe and other attractive locations are becoming internationally famous.

Culture

Values

antipathy toward Serbs	sense of belonging to Europe
Catholic attitudes	pride in cultural heritage
strong family attachments	pessimism
social envy	respect for education
passion for the Adriatic	

Although it is not actually a value, the Croatians' lasting hatred of the Serbs must be mentioned. It is an animosity that dates back to the tribal period. Centuries of subjugation politically emasculated the Croats' elite, who offered intellectual opposition rather than fighting for power. They fear and despise the more numerous Serbs, whom they regard as "Oriental barbarians."

Concepts

Leadership and Status

Croatia was used by the Hapsburgs as a defensive outpost against the Ottoman Empire. Croatian loyalty was to the Hapsburg emperor and to the Catholic Church. Leadership until independence emanated chiefly from imperial or church officials. During 45 years of communism, leadership was invested in Communist Party officials, often Serbian. Tito, however, was a Croat. In present-day Croatia (now converted to a market economy), some former communist luminaries still linger in the halls of power. The many opportunities offered by tourism, however, are leading to the creation of an entrepreneurial class of managers who embrace Western principles. Meritocracy is on the rise, though respect for status and hierarchical rank remain. Croatians respect money, power and influence. They strive to get qualified first, then use their education to achieve material ends. Trappings of status such as fine clothes, homes and cars are eagerly sought. Once money is available, there is a tendency toward consumption.

Space and Time

Croatians are tactile and demonstrative. The comfortable conversational distance is much closer than in Northern Europe. Like Hungarians, they are used to being crammed together in small spaces, and they are mostly very close to their families, in the literal as well as in every other sense. Occasionally one still encounters the Austro-Hungarian hand-kissing behavior, but this has largely been superseded by post-communist surliness.

Croatians are not particularly punctual, but they will make a special effort if they consider a meeting very important. Senior people make younger ones wait longer.

Cultural Factors in Communication

Communication Pattern

Croats possess strong opinions, especially in the political sphere, but also concerning social and business matters. They are somewhat restrained in expressing them, however, and are less open than the Serbs, who often demonstrate their views forcibly or even in a fiery manner. A high level of education often enables Croats to pursue their argument in a sophisticated manner. Their linguistic skills are considerable; they choose their words carefully for best effect.

Listening Habits

Croats are not the world's best listeners, inasmuch as they are suspicious of any arguments coming from an Eastern direction and lapse into cynicism easily. They are, however, swayed by sophisticated and rational discourse, especially from a Western source. They may interrupt interlocutors but generally do so in a courteous manner. Their quick minds cause them to evaluate speakers and formulate their reply while listening. Dalmatian Croats have a similar listening pattern to that of Italians. Further north they are influenced more by cold facts. Mainly they want logical arguments spiced with a little verve, but they are suspicious of rhetoric or too much charisma.

Behavior at Meetings and Negotiations

Croatians are very eager to join the rest of Europe, where they feel they belong. They expect to gain admittance to the EU some time in the second decade of this century. They learn foreign languages, travel as much as they can, and many of them have spent some time abroad.

When getting down to doing business with Croats, expect some delay. There will be lots of refreshments and digressions. It is best to prepare a strategy for keeping close to the agenda. Subdiscussions among those present may develop, and sometimes everybody will talk at the same time. Because they have a tendency to disagree with each other, negotiations may be slow, unless the power structure in the group is such that everybody simply has to follow the leader.

Croats generally do not use humor during a business meeting, but they will everywhere else. Their sense of humor is of a cynical, disenchanted nature, which they share in common with all Eastern Europeans. That, along with a certain lack of confidence, visible or not, is the result of never having been free to do what they wanted; someone was always there to stop them. Try to subtly encourage them toward positive thinking, indispensable in business.

Meetings are usually held in a formal manner with use of titles. The general respect for hierarchy can be noted in the seating arrangements. No commitments are entered into early on; trust must be established first. Croatians often say things that will please the other side. Although you should usually take such statements with a pinch of salt, remember that deceit is not in fact intended. Eastern Europeans tend to observe certain courtesies in communication.

Negotiations tend to include the following characteristics:

+ People from Zagreb are somewhat more linear in their discourse than Dalmatians.
+ When it comes to business, the style is generally sober, with occasional flashes of sentiment.
+ In view of their previous oppression by others, Croats expect to be treated generously and think Western partners will offer concessions when their own resources are inadequate.
+ Reluctance to accept responsibility is frequent, a carryover from communist control.
+ Negotiations are tenacious enough but rarely openly forceful. In the end Croats "get what they can," although meetings occasionally end in ambiguity.
+ Croats normally make an effort to keep commitments, though they sometimes fail to do so when they bite off more than they can chew.

Manners and Taboos

There is nothing Slavic, Latin, Hungarian, Germanic or Middle Eastern that seems totally strange to Croats. Having been invaded and occupied many times, they have learned to eat many different foods and have a feel for diverse mentalities. Eye contact is important; it is advisable to remove sunglasses while conversing with someone.

As a visitor to Croatia, you will be entertained lavishly, and forget about getting enough sleep. Croatian hospitality is sincere and generous. They will also be eager to show you as much of their beloved country as possible. Folklore and folk arts festivals are common, and Croats are happy to share these events and parties with strangers and visitors. As for eating and drinking, there is a lot of it. Socializing with friends in wine cellars and taverns is a way of life.

How to Empathize with Croats

In business and investment, make Croats understand that you are not trying to take over; there is some fear in certain circles that foreign investors are trying to "buy up Croatia." Express appreciation for their cultural and artistic patrimony, and the beauty of their country. Show them that you understand—and respect them—as being truly European. Personal contact is important. If mutual trust is established, you may make some good friends, your business is likely to benefit and you may be in for an enjoyable time.

MOTIVATION	
KEY	*Help them into Europe*
Cross-century mood	◆ Consolidating of the new state. ◆ Establishing separation from all things Serbian. ◆ Developing their best industry—tourism.

Motivating Factors

- ◆ Croats are proud of their country and expect recognition.
- ◆ They consider themselves cultured and expect you to match their level of sophistication.
- ◆ If you speak "Serbo-Croat," make sure you use the Croat version.
- ◆ Croats like entrepreneurial ideas.
- ◆ Indicate that you can be relaxed about certain laws and regulations.
- ◆ They sometimes lack self-confidence; try to encourage them without being obvious.
- ◆ Socialize if they indicate that they want to.
- ◆ Emphasize their "Westernness."

Avoid

- ◆ Praising Serbs.
- ◆ Querying their war record.
- ◆ Heavy arguments.

34

Serbia and Montenegro

Serbia and Montenegro (henceforth referred to in this chapter as *Serbia*) is the Yugoslav "rump state" that remains from the secession of Slovenia, Croatia, Bosnia and Macedonia. Montenegro, Kosovo and southern Serbia have rugged, mountainous, forested landscapes. Northern Serbia is mainly low-lying, drained by the Danube River system. Serbia includes the provinces of Vojvodina and Kosovo, formerly autonomous under the Yugoslav federation; the capital is Belgrade.

The area was settled by Serbs in the seventh century A.D., and they adopted Orthodox Christianity under Byzantine rule. Serbia became the leading Balkan power until, in 1389, it was defeated by the Ottoman Turks. The eighteenth-century decline of the Ottoman Empire encouraged Serbian nationalism. In 1829 Serbia gained autonomy under Russian protection, and in 1878, Turkey finally granted Serbia complete independence. In 1903 King Alexander Obrenovic was assassinated, and Peter I became king. The expansion of Serbian territory during the Balkan Wars antagonized Austria, and the assassination of Austrian Archduke Franz Ferdinand led to the outbreak of the First World War. In 1918 Serbia became the leading force in the kingdom of the Serbs, Croats and Slovenes, renamed Yugoslavia in 1929. During the Second World War, Yugoslavia was occupied and divided by the German army. In 1946 Serbia became an autonomous republic within Tito's neocommunist Yugoslavia. In 1987 President Slobodan Milosevic restated nationalist claims for a Greater Serbia, including Vojvodina, Kosovo and Serb-populated areas in Croatia, Bosnia-Herzegovina and Macedonia.

Between 1989 and 1995 a complex civil war accounted for thousands of deaths and the eventual involvement of the Western powers and peacekeeping operations. In 2001 Milosevic was finally forced out of office and extradited to the Netherlands, where he faced serious charges of crimes against humanity in the International Court in the Hague and died in 2006.

The Serbian economy was badly hurt by secessions, war and political uncertainty. When, in 1991 and 1992, Croatia, Bosnia and Herzegovina, and Macedonia became independent from Yugoslavia, Serbia and Montenegro were left as the principal republics within the country. This left the new state without its traditional trading partners and economic partnerships.

Tourism, once a very profitable industry in the days of the Yugoslav Federated Republic, was severely reduced, owing to most of former Yugoslavia's coastal territory now being included in the state of Croatia. Serbia had access to the sea only in Montenegro, and when that state became independent in 2006, Serbia became a landlocked country. Tourist attractions were then limited to the many inland mosques and monasteries as well as picturesque mountain villages and museums in Belgrade.

"Greater Serbia" remains a dream for Serbs—one which was rudely shattered in the 1990s. Paradoxically, they are traditionally both pro-American (they fought on the side of the Allies in both world wars) and pro-Russian (being Slavs and Orthodox). Relations with the Americans have deteriorated due to Serb behavior during the recent civil war, and Russia, with political and economic problems of her own, has been less of a paternal (or maternal) figure.

Ninety percent of Serbians are Orthodox Christians; 10 percent are Muslim. The cultural classification is multi-active, dialogue-oriented (see Chapter 3 for an explanation of these terms). The official language is Serbo-Croat.

Culture

In your interaction with the Serbs, do not ever lose sight of the fact that they hate the Croats implacably; they look down on other Balkan peoples and the Turks. They feel betrayed by the West and historically victimized by Austro-Hungarians, Ottomans, Croats and others.

Values

loquacity	flamboyance
generosity	hospitality
impulsiveness	charm
tendency to deceive	machismo
boastful manners	volatility
unpredictability	nationalism
stubbornness	romanticism
low legal consciousness	unpunctuality

Concepts

Leadership and Status

The Serbian aristocracy and nobility was more or less eradicated by the Ottomans and Turks during their 500-year dominance over the Serbs. Leadership concepts between the world wars was dominated by nationalistic issues, and the Second World War left Josip Broz Tito in sole charge. A Croat, he nevertheless represented all Yugoslavs and maintained authority in the fragmented nation successfully until his death in 1980. Leadership then became dictated by the needs and demands of each region. Serbian leaders were dictatorial—Slobodan Milosevic being the prime example. In Serbia, the person in power can get away with a lot.

Since Milosevic's removal, different figures have assumed authority, and although in theory the democratic process is functioning, power brokers are the reality. In business, Serbian managers reflect the national autocratic style of leadership. There is little consensual governance or participative management. Whoever has the power makes virtually all decisions, with ex-communist leaders still wielding power behind the scenes. People are admired for their intelligence, dexterity and ability to come out on top.

Status is achieved through success in politics, especially when this serves Serb nationalism. Wealth also confers status.

Space and Time

Serbs are tactile and personal; they prefer to stand and sit close to interlocutors. What used to be a big country has now been reduced to a rump state. Many Serbs feel a sort of national claustrophobia; they have lost a lot of territory, are surrounded by hostile neighbors and have lost their only outlet to the sea.

Serbs are unpunctual, showing up late for most appointments.

Cultural Factors in Communication

Communication Pattern

Serbs can be charismatic to an extraordinary degree, and they present themselves well to foreigners. They are, for example, renowned for efficient lobbying, especially in the United Kingdom and the United States.

Social and business discussions are preceded by extensive small talk; politics is a favorite subject. Serbs are an outspoken people, unafraid to voice their strong opinions on politics or business. In order to support their arguments, they may exaggerate some facts and invent others. It is advisable to take what they say with a pinch of salt. Boasting is common (Serbs do not see anything wrong with it). However, they accompany their boasts with charming anecdotes. They are good at speedy repartee but often make contradictory statements. If you pounce on these, Serbs invariably have a good excuse at hand. If they do not, find one for them, as they must not lose face.

They are practiced complainers and are quick to exploit what they see as weaknesses in others. Firmness and strict adherence to facts and figures is the only advisable approach for dealing with them. Serbs can be extremely generous on occasion, but you should ask yourself why. Their loquacity is notorious, their oratorical skills undeniable.

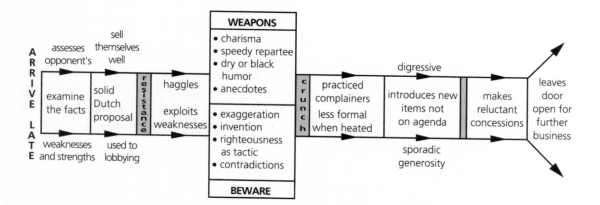

Figure 34.1 Serbian and Montenegrin Communication Pattern

Serb body language is explicit, demonstrative and often fiery. Eye contact is among the strongest in Europe. Gestures with hands and shoulders are also typical, accompanied by mobile facial expressions.

Listening Habits

Because Serbs feel they have frequently been betrayed and tricked in the past, they listen on the defensive. While listening, they are very attentive as they "size you up" and formulate their response or strategy.

Behavior at Meetings and Negotiations

Serbs usually turn up late for meetings and wish to carry on small talk for some time (30–60 minutes) before getting down to business. During this preamble they are getting to know you and assessing your strengths and weaknesses. Their initial proposals will be reasonable, optimistic and hint at expansiveness and generosity. On meeting resistance, they exhibit less cordiality and will continue to press their proposals until they see an impasse. When finally blocked, they will seek your side's opinions and listen carefully to them. Haggling is part of the process, and they will also throw in new ideas that are not part of the original agenda. Although they may present these ideas as being spontaneous, they have probably been planned in advance.

Serbs are mainly proud, but they are not averse to asking for sympathy and help (especially from Westerners) if their resources appear inadequate for them to carry out their side of the bargain. Considerable formality is exercised at the outset of meetings, but the tone becomes more informal when the Serbs get heated or upset. They frequently feign righteous indignation. They are often manipulative and may reply to questions with questions of their own. You need to be patient with them and resist many of their ploys. If you show them that they cannot pull the wool over your eyes, they eventually descend into reality and, in the process, become friendly, even generous. Serbian humor is dry and usually black.

Manners and Taboos

Serbia is rich in folklore and rural traditions; here the country and people are seen at their best. Although traditionally a male-dominated society, Serbs still occasionally observe old-fashioned gallantry toward the "gentler sex." As in Hungary and Poland (though less frequently), women's hands may be kissed and niceties of seating and other special attentions are often seen.

Drinking is common (slivovitz in particular) and often to excess. Men often drink hard liquor with black Turkish coffee first thing in the morning. It is not easy for many Westerners to join them in this habit, especially when the liquor and coffee are accompanied by large sweet cakes. Serbs are traditionally interested in music, history and politics. Taboos include criticizing their political record, especially such subjects as alleged atrocities and "ethnic cleansing."

How to Empathize with Serbs

Foreign males gain points by behaving in a macho and rather boisterous manner. Sympathize with them when you can; hold your tongue when you cannot. Socializing, eating and drinking are useful (and uncontroversial) pastimes with them. Participate, and drink their drinks (if you can!). Speak out for what you believe in, loud and clear, with strong eye contact. Serbs like firmness, as long as it is not too strongly directed against them. Scenery, folklore and the arts are uncontroversial subjects. Praise their soccer skills, and by all means do not mention any friendships you may have with Croats, Slovenes or Turks. Flatter them regularly; they usually do not see through it. Be broad-minded.

MOTIVATION	
KEY	*Stop raking up the controversial features of their recent history*
Cross-century mood	✦ Settling the "guilt" question. ✦ Obtaining international respect and recognition.

Motivating Factors

- ✦ Compare Serbs favorably with Croatians and Slovenes.
- ✦ Appeal to their national pride and rally them around their flag and aspirations.
- ✦ Admire their vitality.
- ✦ Give them credit for their outspoken style and frankness.
- ✦ Share their enthusiasms.
- ✦ Go along with their ideas, though with some caution.
- ✦ Show them how to make money.
- ✦ Take an interest in their culture, folk arts, etc.
- ✦ Be generous.
- ✦ Accept that coffeehouse networking and gossip are part of their culture.

Avoid

- ✦ Attacking their contradictory statements.
- ✦ Discussing their Civil War too much.
- ✦ Calling them Russianized.
- ✦ Discussing the parlous state of their economy.

35

Ukraine

The earliest records of human settlement in the territory of Ukraine date back to at least 4500 BCE. The land was subsequently occupied by numerous peoples, including Ancient Greeks, Ancient Rome and the Byzantine Empire.

Ukraine's modern history begins in the ninth century when the East Slavs founded the state of Kievan Rus. This became the largest and most powerful nation in Europe, but disintegrated in the twelfth century. By the ninetheenth century, Ukraine was partly part of the Russian Empire and partly under Austro–Hungarian control. Following World War One and the Russian Civil War, Ukraine emerged in 1922 as one of the founding republics of the Soviet Union. Ukraine became independent with the dissolution of the USSR. Nikita Khruschev, himself a Ukrainian, transferred Crimea from Russia to Ukraine in 1954. In 2014, after political pressure by Vladimir Putin, Crimea was annexed by the Russian Federation.

Most articles featuring Ukraine in the media these days centre round its possible accession to the European Union. Were it to join it would be the fifth-largest in population and the largest in area. Indeed Ukraine is the epicenter of the confrontation between the Western democratic world and authoritarian, totalitarian states. After centuries of subjugation by outside powers, Ukraine's "national idea" is resistance to authority. A pluralistic society is one of her strengths, but the country is more often than not fragmented by competing regional and economic interests. Among the country's advantages are a highly-educated population, fertile farmland and a vibrant civil society.

Ukrainians and Russians

Racially, the Ukrainian people are closely linked to the Russians and their East Slavic language is similar to Russian and Belorussian. It is only natural that Ukrainian values are often similar to those of their two neighbors. They did, however, not become a republic of the Soviet Union until 1924 and split from Russia on the demise of the Soviet Union in 1990. Consequently there are cultural and experiential differences as well as similarities between Ukrainians and Russians. These differences are more pronounced in West Ukraine. East Ukrainians differ only slightly in character from Russians. The dividing line between East and West Ukraine is the River Dnepr. West Ukraine shares a 500 km border with Poland; some Russians see West Ukrainians as sharing some Polish characteristics, such as obstinacy, self-sacrifice, romantic nationalism, stoicism, touchiness and sensitivity to criticism.

West Ukrainians consider they are more sophisticated and urban than Russians and tend to look down on them to some degree. They also think they are more mature politically. Their geographical proximity to Poland, Romania, Moldova and Bulgaria also makes them feel more European than Russians. They like the idea of being a Western-style democracy. They are more nationalistic than either Russians or East Ukrainians.

Russians see the strength of many West Ukrainian values—good education, developed social manners, punctuality, reasonable efficiency, sustained energy, tolerance of others, artistic skills and charming singers and musicians. They do however see some negative values such as touchiness, a certain lack of warmth and generosity, some absence of compassion, stubbornness and anti-Russian attitudes.

The closeness or drifting apart of Russian and Ukrainian values will depend greatly on political developments over the next few decades.

Culture

Ukrainians see themselves as brave, energetic, entrepreneurial, opportunistic people. They have a strong streak of independence and often show tenacity. They consider that the Russian state originated in Ukraine with its capital in Kiev. They have strong historical consciousness.

Values

patriotic	intellectual
emotional	well-educated
obstinate	wordy
collectivist	sentimental
tenacious	thrifty
sometimes cocksure	touchy
grandparents important in child-rearing	
women prominent in politics and business	

Religion

The dominant religion in Ukraine is Eastern Orthodox Christianity. There are about 1,000,000 Roman Catholics in the country and an equal number of Protestants (nearly 3 percent of the population). Muslims number just over 200,000, Jews about 120,000.

Concepts

Leadership and Status

The Ukrainian concept of leadership is derived from many widely differing styles in history. The word "Ukraine" means borderland and many races, both nomadic and settlers, have had their turn in dominating this region. In antiquity, Scythians ruled (700-200 BCE). The golden age of Kiev (Kievan Rus) was 800-1100 AD when Vladimir the Great turned Ukraine towards Byzantine Christianity. The rule of the Polish-Lithuanian Commonwealth pushed the country towards Catholicism, though the peasants remained East Orthodox. Later, the Cossacks (fiercely Orthodox) pushed Ukraine towards Russia. Huge civilian losses in the World War Two and the Great Famine of 1946-47 (caused by the Soviets) led to the Declaration of Independence in 1991. The Ukrainian leadership style reflects all these influences in its autocracy, political manipulation, tendency towards corruption and its preferences for males. West and East Ukrainian managers are polarised according to their political leanings.

Elderly people are generally more respected than younger. Well-educated people with doctors' degrees and so on have considerable status, as have well-known artists, musicians and literary figures. "Patriotic" politicians enjoyed popularity after separation from the

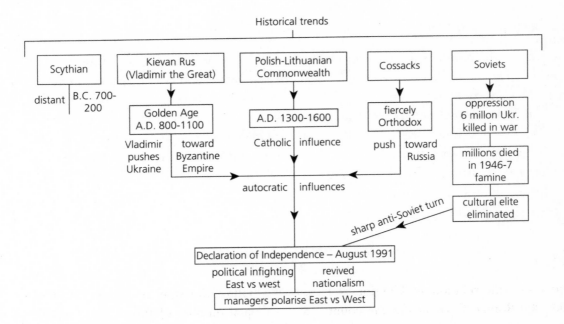

Figure 35.1 Ukrainian Leadership Style

Soviet Union, but have lost a lot of ground recently after several years of bickering, conniving and obdurate behavior.

Women are playing even greater roles in business and politics. The status of Ukrainian women is similar to that of women in Russia.

Space and Time

The Ukrainians, like the Russians, are tactile to a considerable degree, though less in the west than in the east. In terms of living space, Ukraine was one of the most densely populated areas in the Soviet Union, with around 80 people per square kilometer and much denser in the highly industrialised Donetsk basin and Dnepr lowland regions, which also account for 82 percent of the urban population.

West Ukrainian punctuality is similar to that of Polish—that is to say hardly on-the-dot time-keeping but making sure to be there when something important is at stake. In Eastern Ukraine, manners in this respect are similar to Russian, where respect is shown for appointments in general, but occasional apathy may occur. Older people are usually not kept waiting.

Cultural Factors in Communication

Communication Pattern

The Ukrainian communication pattern resembles the Russian in that it is rambling, wordy, emotional and somewhat unpredictable. Western Europeans and Americans may find unusual reactions to their own advances. Ukrainian pronouncements, including business decisions, are currently colored by political opinions—there is a serious cultural divide between East and West Ukraine. Foreign interlocutors should bear this in mind. All Ukrainians, after an initial display of warmth and hospitality, pursue a tough negotiating style typified by caution, tenacity, obstinacy and a win–lose mentality.

Listening Habits

Ukrainians are patient listeners, eagerly seeking benefits, but react strongly to differences of political opinion. The current politico-cultural divide between East and West Ukraine means that speakers must allow for their Russian-orientation or their EU-orientation. In both cases Ukrainian nationalism must be respected. Less political tendencies are listeners' expectations of emotional speech, animation, some humor and kindliness toward older people. Suspicion is usually a factor.

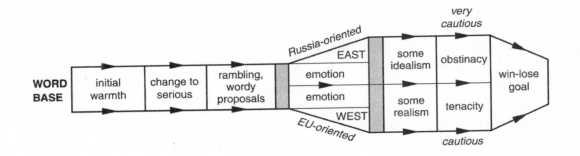

Figure 35.2 Ukrainian Communication Pattern

Figure 35.3 Ukrainian Listening Habits

Behavior at Meetings and Negotiations

Ukrainians are by nature loquacious and meetings are characterised by animated conversation, energy and directness of purpose. They show great respect for the views and attitudes of interlocutors and like to incorporate these into their own agendas when they can. They feel that they have a lot to learn from the West. In the Soviet times their own views were often tailored to calibrate with Russian agendas.

Western Ukrainians tend to behave in a more individualistic manner than their Eastern counterparts. In this way they resemble the Poles, expressing opinions in a forceful manner, but showing ready flexibility when they think they are respected. They try to establish personal relationships and later cling to them.

Eastern Ukrainians act more like Russians—more collectivist in voicing opinions and slower in reacting to opponents' differences of views. Like Russians they have no objection to drawing out issues (like chess players).

In both West and East Ukraine, approach to negotiation is conceptual and all-embracing as opposed to American or German step-by-step settlement. West Ukrainians are to some extent more direct and anxious to get on with things, but Ukrainians in general like to speak with one voice and quick, individual decisions are rare. Consensus is valued and proposals are examined from many perspectives. Negotiation consequently is a fairly slow process and often complex in U.S. or West European eyes. Like Poles, Ukrainians tend to switch styles during negotiation, sometimes linear and factual, sometimes theatrical and idealistic. In the end one would describe them as cautious and tenacious, but their wordy and sometimes emotional style can cloud issues.

Manners and Taboos

Ukrainian customs are heavily influenced by Christianity, which is the dominant religion in the country. Gender roles also tend to be more traditional, and grandparents play a greater role in raising children than in the West.

The tradition of the Easter egg, known as *pysanky*, has long roots in Ukraine.

The traditional Ukrainian diet includes chicken, pork, beef, fish and mushrooms. Ukrainians also tend to eat a lot of potatoes, grains, fresh and pickled vegetables. Popular traditional dishes include *varenyky* (boiled dumplings with mushrooms, potatoes, sauerkraut, cottage cheese or cherries), *borscht* (soup made of beets, cabbage and mushrooms or meat) and *holubsty* (stuffed cabbage rolls filled with rice, carrots and meat). Ukrainian specialties also include Chicken Kiev and Kiev Cake.

How to Empathize with Ukranians

Ukrainians are warm, generous, big-hearted people, who love eating, drinking, singing and dancing. They also are keen on all kinds of art—literature, poetry, architecture, folklore activities, painting and all visual arts. If you are epicurean by nature, you will enjoy the company of Ukrainians. It is appropriate for foreigners to evince enthusiasm for Ukrainian traditions, aims and aspirations. These of course vary from East to West, but all Ukrainians feel special and though East Ukrainians have no antipathy towards Russians, they do have a separate national consciousness that gives them pride. Outsiders have everything to gain by enthusing over Ukrainian tradition without taking up strong political views over the future of the country.

MOTIVATION

KEY	*Recognizing the importance of Kievan Rus in the origins of the Russian nation*
Cross-century mood	✦ Polarised perspectives in West and East dominate Ukrainian cross-century thinking. ✦ Though membership of the European Union is hardly imminent, the prospect has not been completely discarded.

Motivating Factors

- ✦ Stress their "Europeanness."
- ✦ Praise their educational standards.
- ✦ Praise their artistry and aesthetic achievements.
- ✦ Respect older people.
- ✦ Be well-mannered at all times.
- ✦ Tolerate their sense of nationalism.
- ✦ Show camaraderie.
- ✦ Be humorous and drink with them when you can.
- ✦ Distinguish between East and West Ukrainians.
- ✦ Do not take sides too irrevocably.

Avoid

- ✦ Criticism of things Ukrainian.
- ✦ Impinging on anyone's rights.
- ✦ Being wishy-washy.
- ✦ Talking down to them.
- ✦ Assuming they are identical to Russians.
- ✦ Being too casual.
- ✦ Being too pushy.

36

Belarus

Belarus is a landlocked country in Eastern Europe, bordered by Russia to the northeast, Ukraine to the south, Poland to the West and Lithuania and Latvia to the northwest. The capital is Minsk, with other major cities including Brest, Grodno, Gomel, Mogilev and Vitebsk. The country covers 207,000 sq km, of which 40 percent is forested. Agriculture and manufacturing make up its two most important economic sectors.

Before the twentieth century, Belarus belonged to several countries—the principality of Polotsk, the Grand Duchy of Lithuania, the Russian Empire and the Polish-Lithuanian Commonwealth. Following the Russian Revolution, Belarus became one of the founding republics of the Soviet Union and was known as the Belorussian Soviet Socialist Republic. In 1939, the land, which had been part of the Second Polish Republic, was united with the Belorussian SSR (Soviet Socialist Republic) as a result of the Soviet invasions of Poland. Belarus lost close to a third of its population and more than half of its economic resources during World War Two, but the impact of the war occasioned its founder membership of the United Nations, along with the Soviet Union and the Ukrainian SSR.

Sovereignty was declared in Belarus on July 27 1990, and independence one year later after the collapse of the Soviet Union. The country's president, elected in 1994, was Alexander Lukashenko, who implemented Soviet-era policies such as state ownership of the economy. In 2000, Belarus and Russia signed a treaty for greater cooperation.

The population of nearly 10 million live mostly in the urban areas around Minsk and the regional capitals, and are more than 80 percent native Belarusians. There are also sizeable numbers of Russians, Poles and Ukrainians, and the country has two official languages—Belarusian and Russian.

The origin of the name Belarus is not certain. It derives from the term "White Russia" (White Rus), and could refer to its snow-covered mountains or to the white clothing worn by the Slavs. During the time of the Russian Empire it was named Belorussia and was viewed as a part of the Russian nation, with its language as a dialect of Russian. It took its current name in 1991.

The region now known as Belarus was first settled by Slavic tribes in the sixth century. Bands of Scandinavian warriors and traders, called Varangians, came into contact with the tribes and, following a brief exile, were invited to return. The state of Kievan Rus was formed around A.D. 862.

Belarus has strained relations with the U.S., which supports various anti-Lukashenko NGOs. Belarus in turn made it harder for U.S.-based organizations to operate within the country. Nevertheless, there is cooperation on intellectual property protection, prevention of human trafficking and technology crime, and disaster relief.

Belarus belongs to the Eurasian Economic Community, the Collective Security Treaty Organization, the Non-Aligned Movement and the Organization for Security and Cooperation in Europe (OSCE).

The economy of Belarus remains, by and large, "Soviet-style" and state-controlled. Over 50 percent of the workforce of more than 4 million is employed by state-controlled companies, with 48 percent working for private Belarusian companies. Employment is high in agriculture, manufacturing sales, trading goods and education. Textile and wood-processing industries are both of historical importance. Russia is Belarus's largest trading partner, accounting for nearly half of total trade. It also has trade agreements with several EU member states.

The two official languages of Belarus are Russian and Belarusian. Russian is the main language, spoken by 72 percent of the population; Belarusian, the second official language, is used by under 12 percent.

Minority languages include Polish, Ukrainian and Eastern Yiddish.

Culture

Although Belarus has been conquered many times, it has never been a conqueror. Over the centuries, Belarusians have changed their faith, and accepted foreign cultures and languages to fit in with other races. However, in spite of everything, Belarus did not lose its national identity. They exhibit tolerance and the ability to understand the mentality of other cultures.

Racially, the Belarusians are closely linked with the Russians, and their language is similar to Russian, as are their values. As they did not become a republic of the Soviet Union until 1922 and split from Russia on the demise of the Soviet Union in 1990, there are cultural and experiential differences as well as similarities. They also share some Polish characteristics, such as obstinacy, self-sacrifice, romantic nationalism, stoicism, touchiness and sensitivity to criticism. They think of themselves as more sophisticated than Russians and also more politically mature. Their borders with EU countries make them feel more European, and several European countries have encouraged this sentiment.

Belarusians are Eastern Slavs but consider themselves European Slavs, being at the heart of Europe. They regard themselves as sophisticated vis-à-vis Russians.

Values

tolerant	willing to sacrifice
patient	intellectual
hard-working	well-educated
peace-loving	tenacious

Religion

Belarus has no official religion, but Belarusian Orthodox is the dominant religion in Belarus, followed by different denominations of Protestantism. Roman Catholics (about 10 percent) consist of a mixture of Belarusians and the country's Polish and Lithuanian minorities.

Concepts

Leadership and Status

Belarusians appreciate their high level of education. Well-educated people with doctors' degrees and so on have considerable status, as have well-known artists, musicians and literary figures. Family, stability, prosperity and good friends are valued. Elderly people are generally more respected than younger ones.

In a dictatorship, most managerial decisions have a political background or motive. The stultifying influence of Soviet bureaucracy and inefficiency has not been completely eradicated from the Belarusian business scene. Leadership, even when non-political, is of the old-fashioned autocratic kind, power distance is steadfastly maintained, consensus is rarely sought enthusiastically and female leaders are few.

Women are playing important roles in business and politics. Women in the large villages in rural areas still pursue traditional values of motherhood and home-making.

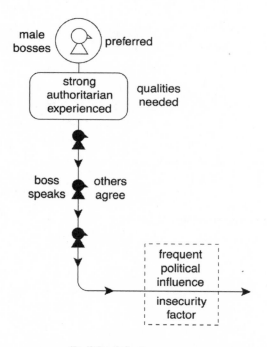

Political Autocracy

Figure 36.1 Belarusian Leadership Style

Space and Time

The country is not very densely populated (50 per sq km). The Belarusians are fairly tactile people, especially with children, though less than Latins. They can talk at close range. Men keep a respectful distance from women in public.

Belarusians, unlike Russians, are punctual, accustomed to a clear time-frame, although important officials may keep you waiting longer than you like. There is a general lack of sense of urgency for getting things done. People move cautiously.

Cultural Factors in Communication

Communication Pattern

In a period of history that included the break-up of the Soviet Union, Belarus's exit from it, and subsequent internal political dissension and dictatorship, Belarusians are cautious interlocutors who wish to seek solid personal relationships before "baring their soul." Conversations and negotiations are consequently preceded by long preambles, perhaps also socializing, before getting down to brass tacks. They watch the behavior of the head of delegation. They also like to follow the etiquette of the host and any previously agreed scenario. Even then, proposals may be well guarded, with high context inferences along the way. In later stages of discussion, agendas may be thrown to the wind and many people may talk over each other. Belarusians frequently prefer the "real deal" to be concluded in a private setting, but are always ready to celebrate the successful completion of a transaction informally.

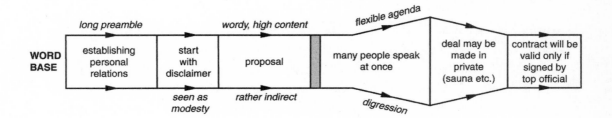

Figure 36.2 Belarusian Communication Pattern

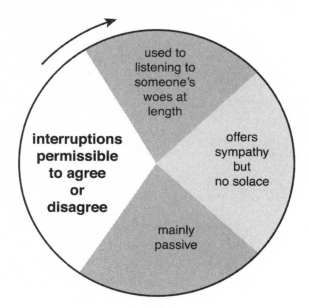

Figure 36.3 Belarusian Listening Habits

Listening Habits

Listening is mainly passive, but opinions may be voiced once a certain amount of trust has entered into the relationship. Life is somewhat bleak for many Belarusians, who listen sympathetically to others' problems but are not quick to offer remedies or solutions.

Behavior at Meetings and Negotiations

Belarusians are fairly voluble and express their opinions quite confidently, feeling somewhat "Western" when they do this. They maintain liveliness for long periods and are rather direct in letting yon know how they feel. There is a higher degree of individualism among western Belarusians. Those in the east part of the country tend to favor collectivist verdicts. They seek consensus and can talk at great length, which may disconcert nationalities such as Americans, Finns and Norwegians.

When negotiating they avoid going out on a limb and seek refuge in a collective approach. There is little urgency in their negotiating style. Emotion is occasionally permitted but they are reluctant to abandon factuality for long. Interlocutors must be patient in their dealings with them.

COMPARISON OF AUDIENCE EXPECTATIONS AT PRESENTATIONS		
Russia	Ukraine	Belarus
Official view is a lie	Do you lean East or West?	Hearing woes
Personal view is true	Make your own case	Keeping quiet
Changes are always bad	Emotional speech	Share emotions of speaker
Suspicious of foreigners	Considerable body language	Voicing own opinions may be
Expects rhetoric	Respect Ukraine's independence	a nuisance
Expects sentiment	What can you offer us?	Open debate unlikely
Expects complexity	Sincerity, please	Show us profit NOW
Needs recognition	Spice it with humor	"a bird in the hand"
People-oriented	We like anecdotes and examples	distrust of officialdom
Conspiratorial	Don't pull wool over our eyes	we have heard this before …
No war talk	We are not Russians and have a	love praise for their nation,
Dislikes greed	long separate history	national products and services
Let's beat the system	Remember we live next to Russia	

Manners and Taboos

"*Sardechna zaprashayem!*" is the traditional expression used when welcoming guests, who are usually presented with bread and salt. Shaking hands is the common form of greeting. Hospitality is part of the Belarusian tradition; people are welcoming and friendly; and gifts are given to friends and business associates.

The traditional two-piece dress is still worn today on special occasions. Clothes were made from flax or wool to cope with the cold climate, and decorated with intricate patterns influenced by those of neighboring cultures. Each region has its own particular designs. The Belarusian national flag, adopted in 1995, uses an ornate pattern which appeared on early clothing.

Literature

Literature in Belarus dates back to the eleventh–thirteenth centuries and religious writings. The Bible translated into Belarusian by Francysk Skaryna, published some time in the early 1500s, was the first book to be printed in Eastern Europe. Skaryna developed the Belarusian language and was one of the first to print in the Cyrillic alphabet.

Modern literature can be dated to the late 1800s, with the writer Yanka Kupala. Other writers of the time include Vladimir Zylka, Kazimir Svayak, Yakub Kolas, Zmitrok Biadula and Maksim Haretski, who wrote for a Belarusian-language paper, *Nasha Niva*.

Once Belarus had been subsumed into the Soviet Union, the Soviet government took control of the Republic's cultural affairs. Literature was only able to develop unhindered in Polish-held territory until Soviet occupation in 1939. Many writers went into exile after the Nazi occupation of Belarus, and did not return until the 1960s, when there was a revival of literature with novels by Vasil Bykau and Uladzimir Karatkievich.

How to Empathize with Belarusians

Relations are established over a dinner table and with alcohol. When you chat with them, remember that they believe rumors and gossip more than official attitudes or statements. They usually need help in drawing up business plans. They are not always clear about such terms as democracy, pluralism, accountability, turnover and profit. Guide them gently in business discussions when they seem out of their depth.

You should demonstrate friendliness and open-heartedness to secure their trust. If you want to do business with them, show willingness to build up long-term relations and be ready to make concessions. They often invite business partners to their home. Take simple gifts and be friendly.

MOTIVATION	
KEY	*Recognizing where they differ from Russians*
Cross-century mood	✦ Consolidation of their separate identiry vis-à-vis Russia and the Ukraine. ✦ Looking for a durable style of government. ✦ Trying to be as "European" as possible.

Motivating Factors

✦ Acknowledge their "Europeanness".
✦ Praise their country and its history and culture.
✦ Praise their educational standards.
✦ Praise their artistry and aesthetic achievements.
✦ Be well-mannered at all times, especially with older people.
✦ Accept their sense of nationalism.
✦ Respect the fact that they hold moral values above those of material wealth.

(continued)

MOTIVATION *(continued)*

◆ Be friendly and offer help.

◆ Be humorous and drink with them when you can.

◆ Do not take sides too irrevocably—if you share their opinion, show it. If not, just listen.

Avoid

◆ Criticism of things Belarusian.

◆ Talking politics and criticizing the existing system.

◆ Impinging on anyone's rights.

◆ Patronizing them.

◆ Assuming that they are identical to Russians.

37

Bulgaria

Bulgaria is a mountainous country in southeastern Europe, bordered by Romania to the north, Turkey and Greece to the south and Serbia and Macedonia to the west. The Black Sea is Bulgaria's eastern boundary. The name Bulgaria originates from the *Bulgars*, a tribe of Turkic warrior nomads from Central Asia, who entered Europe around A.D. 650.

The group known as the proto-Bulgarians, together with the Slavs, formed a Slav-Bulgarian state in A.D. 681. In the ninth and tenth centuries, the proto-Bulgarians and Slavs consolidated into a unified Slav people who, since that time, have retained the name Bulgarians. This national unity, present in embryonic form during the long Ottoman domination, flowered in the independence struggles of the nineteenth century, and the *Bulgarians* today share a unity unassailed by either ethnographic or linguistic differences.

Now, during the first decade of the twenty-first century, Bulgaria is a backward Balkan nation in comparison with Hungary, Croatia and Slovenia; nevertheless, it has enjoyed several years of political and economic stability. It joined the European Free Trade Association (EFTA) in 1993 and the EU in 2007. The majority of religious Bulgarians are Eastern Orthodox, with small numbers of Catholics, Protestants and Muslims, the latter including those Muslim Bulgarians who were forced to adopt Islam in the sixteenth and seventeenth centuries, but who have nevertheless retained Bulgarian language and customs. The Turks are Bulgaria's largest minority. Gypsies and Macedonians are two other sizeable minorities. There are a few thousand Russians, Armenians and Greeks (mostly in the towns), and Romanians and Tatars (mostly in the villages).

The cultural classification is multi-active (with some reactive tendencies) and dialogue-oriented (see Chapter 3 for an explanation of these terms).

Culture

Values

Bulgarians differ considerably from other Slavs in their values and communication style, probably because of their origins. In general they are cooler and more pragmatic than many Slavs, particularly when compared with Serbs. Quiet and soberness are valued; you will see little of the hotheaded discussion or noisy public disputes that are only too common in Belgrade.

They do, however, share with other Slavs a widespread feeling of pessimism about national helplessness. This is decreasing as the young post-communist generation begins to take the reins. In general, Bulgarian values tend to be rural, with homespun virtues, as one might expect from people living in a predominantly agricultural society.

disciplined	sober
pragmatic	cautious
persistent and stubborn	good organizers
industrious	determined
steady, with stamina	suspicious but tolerant of foreigners
animosity toward Turks	inventive
highly literate	thorough

Concepts

Leadership Style and Status

Bulgarian social barriers are few because of the lack of hereditary nobles. Although a wide range of people can aspire to leadership, no outstanding political or business leaders have emerged during the last decade; national pessimism and self-doubt hinder their development. In business, the future Bulgarian manager is likely to be less autocratic than Serbian or Greek top executives.

Bulgarian employees are docile in comparison with Serbs, Croats or Romanians.

Space and Time

Bulgaria is not an overcrowded country, but when engaged in interesting conversation, they sit closer to their interlocutor than would a Northern European. In public there is little pushing or shoving and lines are orderly.

Bulgarians are more punctual than most Slavs, though bureaucrats usually keep people waiting. On the surface, Bulgarians show little sense of urgency. Other Balkan peoples consider them slow-moving. Patience is certainly a virtue in Bulgaria, and it will be required of you—if you wish to achieve your ends, that is.

Cultural Factors in Communication

Communication Pattern

In comparison with the South Slavs, Bulgarians are reticent and reserved in the early stages of acquaintance. In this they resemble the Czechs and Slovenians. Before giving full expression to their feelings or opinions, Bulgarians engage in a series of preliminary encounters, during which they sound out and size up (albeit in a friendly manner) their conversation partners. During this period they are decidedly less flowery or rhetorical in their speech than the Serbs, Romanians or Hungarians. At this stage, it is very difficult to extract opinions or eventual attitudes from them. When this exploratory period has passed, Bulgarians open up to display a modicum of quiet charm and make their requests in a circuitous manner, avoiding confrontation whenever they can.

The Bulgarian language, being Slavic, is rich in vocabulary, similes, metaphors, symbolism and allegory. The better linguists among them enrich their English with the same tools. They enjoy conversation—an art for them—but are less prone to exaggeration than South Slavs or other Mediterranean people.

Bulgarians, like the Greeks, are famous for their unusual manner of saying *yes* and *no*. Nodding the head up and down signifies a negative. Shaking it from side to side means yes. The Bulgarians are well aware that this is the reverse of others' body language and sometimes nod in the Western European or American manner, which might be confusing.

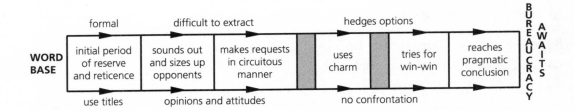

Figure 37.1 Bulgarian Communication Pattern

Listening Habits

Bulgarians are excellent listeners. They interrupt their compatriots rarely, foreigners hardly ever. Their attentiveness denotes their proclivity toward sizing up the speaker. In general, they respect Western opinions, though they do not always place the right connotation on what is said. A few minutes after absorbing a presentation or new idea, they will give a modicum of feedback, but they will not reveal the full extent of their reactions.

Behavior at Meetings and Negotiations

Meetings with Bulgarians are generally satisfactory affairs; a win–win goal combined with a solid, conservative approach will give you the feeling of steady progress and trust. Business in Bulgaria is rarely rushed. Goals are generally set in a slow, deliberate manner, and you need to allow plenty of time for Bulgarians to reach them. Endemic bureaucracy will do nothing to speed the process up. Keep in mind, though, that Bulgarians have an inner urge to succeed; patience can work wonders.

Initially, at meetings, Bulgarians exercise considerable reserve and hedge their options as long as you allow them to. Their requests will be made in an indirect and circuitous manner. Their reactions to your requests will also be circuitous. This does not imply negativity, but Byzantine habits that have little to do with straightforwardness.

Nationals from Norway, the Netherlands and the United States can get irritated with what they see as "deviousness," playing their cards close to their chest. It is unlikely that Bulgarians, however sincere, will depart from this practice. They do respond well to Westerners who give early evidence of trustworthiness. Their indirectness causes them to employ a roundabout approach to many issues, especially determining price or the bottom line. Calculation of profit does not come easily to them, particularly the Western meaning of profit. Most successful businesses in Bulgaria depend on a network of connections and the exchange of favors. Go-betweens are often necessary, especially when gifts or "facilitation" fees come into question.

Manners and Taboos

Bulgarians, like other Balkan people, are extremely hospitable and will share with guests what little they have. In their own country, they will always insist on paying the bills in restaurants and will often pick up other expenses they can ill afford. Compensate them the best you can—and be sure to reciprocate their hospitality when they visit you on your own turf. Eating, drinking and socializing are important features of Bulgarian life, both with each other and with foreign guests. Bulgaria is a big exporter of wines, many of which are of an excellent quality. When they want you to share *rakiya* (their fruit brandy) with them, do it. Herbal teas are another Bulgarian specialty. Coffee (Bulgarian, not Turkish) is black and strong. When visiting a Bulgarian home, take flowers for the hostess. Children, too, should be spoiled. Canned delicatessen items from the West are also greatly appreciated.

Bulgarians are famous for their folklore, especially song and dance. Music and opera are very important for most Bulgarians.

How to Empathize with Bulgarians

Bulgarians are naturally likeable people with whom it is easy to empathize, given their desire to please. They seek recognition of their sterling values and steadfastness and are prepared to show great loyalty to those who become their friends. You may find it necessary to initiate conversation with them, as their modesty and shyness make them hold back. They often need encouragement in their undertakings and are immensely grateful for genuine help. They love their country and it is wise to enthuse about things Bulgarian: the wonderful scenery, the good food and wine, the richness of their folklore and music. It is worthwhile learning how to read and pronounce Cyrillic, the basis of which was invented by the brothers (and saints) Cyril and Methodius in the ninth century. This attractive script is used today in Bulgaria, Russia, Serbia, Montenegro, Macedonia, Bosnia, Belarus and Ukraine.

MOTIVATION	
KEY	*Praise their potential. Be open and friendly*
Cross-century mood	✦ They are anxious to demonstrate that they have broken away from the Soviet Union. ✦ They are proud of being perceived as an island of stability in the Balkans. ✦ They are eager to be seen as part of Europe.

Motivating Factors

✦ Praise their potential. Be open and friendly.

✦ Demonstrate your appreciation of Bulgaria's resilience during half a millennium of Turkish domination, preserving its language and religion.

✦ Show your appreciation of the fact that the Cyrillic alphabet was created by Bulgarians and then spread to Russia and other parts of the world.

✦ Remember that the Bulgarians did not allow the Bulgarian Jews to be deported to Germany during the Second World War, even though Bulgaria was an ally of Germany at the time. They are very proud of "preserving their Jews."

✦ Recognize that Bulgarians are well-educated and well-informed.

✦ Listen to their complaints about problems and difficulties, but don't offer advice or solutions. Demonstrate your confidence that they can sort things out on their own.

(continued)

MOTIVATION *(continued)*

Avoid

+ Comparing them to Serbs and Romanians.
+ Being too enthusiastic about Turkey.
+ Talking about communist times, unless you wish to praise their survival skills and the lessons they have learned.

38

Romania

Romania is the twelfth largest country in Europe in area (including Russia and Ukraine). The earliest known inhabitants of Romania were the Dacians, a people coming from Thrace. Historical and archaeological evidence as well as the linguistic survival of Romanian (a Romance language) seem to confirm that the present territory of Romania had a fully developed population, with a high degree of economic, cultural and even political development, long before the Roman armies crossed the Danube in A.D. 106 into what became known as the province of Dacia. Roman influence was profound, creating a civilization that managed to maintain its identity after the collapse of the empire. During her turbulent history, Romania was ruled, after the Romans, by Ottoman Turks, as well as Hungarian and Hohenzollern monarchs. The Hohenzollern monarchy survived until 1947, when the Soviet Union, whose forces were maintaining the first Russian occupation (1944–1958) in the country's independent history, demanded a complete communist takeover.

In 1989 Romania emerged from a bleak period of corrupt communist dictatorship when Nicolae Ceausescu, who had ruled for 24 years, was deposed and executed. The revolution had been led by the National Salvation Front, and their leader, Ion Iliescu, became interim president. Since that time the now renamed Party of Social Democracy has remained the largest single party.

Romania joined the European Union in 2007. Communism's concentration on heavy industry devastated Romania's economy, which is still struggling. Its starting position was worse than some other countries: Ceausescu's rule was more centralized and indulged in more foolhardy projects than elsewhere.

Tourism has become of special significance to Romania. Tourist attractions range from winter sports in the mountains to summer seaside activities in the resort belt fringing the Black Sea and also the Danube Delta.

Eighty-five percent of Romanians are Romanian Orthodox, 5 percent are Roman Catholic and 4 percent are Greek Orthodox. Romania's cultural classification is multi-active, dialogue-oriented (see Chapter 3 for an explanation of these terms). Three languages are spoken on a daily basis in Romania: Romanian, Magyar (Hungarian) and Romany (Gypsy).

Culture

Values

Romanian values are largely forged in the crucible of an invasion-prone territory—the Ottoman Turks, Czarist (and later Soviet) Russia and the Austro–Hungarian Empire. Opportunism and maverick behavior have enabled Romania to survive as a state, its territory expanding and contracting periodically, depending on the success of its alliances. Such historical conditions and exigencies have led to anomalous positions on foreign policy. The enduring concept of *Romania Mare* (Greater Romania) may be less notorious than Milosevic's concept of *Great Serbia*, but it exists in Romanian minds nevertheless. Such a kaleidoscopic, complex historical background has led to Romanian values such as:

obsession to survive	pride in being a Balkan anomaly
opportunism	social corruption
apostasy	nepotism
volatility	self-importance
unpredictability	sense of the ridiculous
tendency to blame others	black humor
evasive techniques of action	

Concepts

Leadership and Status

Romania is situated in the part of Europe that was inhabited by peasant masses, ruled for centuries by sovereign lords, clan leaders and autocrats. In the post Ceausescu period, modern leadership styles were hampered in their development, since the government was still run by former communist leaders, who functioned under other labels. Business leaders are also affected by the continuing influence of the political apparatus. Romanian managers are gradually developing a style of their own that resembles that of Italian managers: autocratic but paternalistic and using emotion as a manipulative tool.

Space and Time

Romanians, though not on the Mediterranean, have the Mediterranean sense of space; that is to say, they like rubbing shoulders with people and are comfortable in groups or crowded conditions. They stand closer than Slavs, who require occasional moments of solitude.

Romanians are not punctual in general, especially with each other. Meetings usually start 30–45 minutes late. If you are invited to a Romanian home, it is best not to arrive early or on time, as the hosts will not be ready.

Cultural Factors in Communication

Communication Pattern

Romanians are oratorical by nature (neighbors say "long-winded") and are proud of their sophistication in discourse. They rarely answer questions with yes or no, so it is not advisable to ask direct questions requiring affirmative or negative answers. It is better to hint at what you want and then be prepared to read between the lines of their reply. Their answers are in any case long and complex and may to some extent reflect what you want to hear. Their delicacy is Italian in nature, as is their capacity for flexible truth when questioned aggressively. Their style of address is personal, and they seek your own opinion or support rather than that of your organization.

Listening Habits

Romanians are attentive but suspicious listeners, who may interrupt you if anything you say seems contradictory. They are used to lengthy presentations and arguments, so if you are too brief you will not make much impact.

Behavior at Meetings and Negotiations

Several decades of communism and repressive centralized rule have bequeathed Romania with a poor commercial infrastructure riddled with bureaucracy and corruption. The Westerner, consequently, must be wary of the possibility of being cheated—a common occurrence in a region with a hybrid Balkan and Turkish historical background.

Romanians are skilled diplomats and negotiators, and hard bargaining faces any foreigners who wish to do business with them. You will have to be careful to distinguish between apparent prospects and factual reality. Deals are rarely a straight transaction between two parties. Others are likely to be involved on a commission basis, exacting bribes or demanding "facilitation" payments. When you sense this is happening, bring in a Romanian go-between. Such "transaction costs" are generally laid at your door as the foreigner, unless you maintain vigilance.

Figure 38.1 Romanian Listening Habits

It is important to establish parameters at the outset of any business discussion, fixing procedures, limits and ultimate positions. Romanians will not be deterred from attempting to gain advantage, but once they have understood your position, they can behave in a constructive, creative and charming manner.

At meetings, extensive small talk is a necessary preamble. Be wary of painting yourself into a corner at this stage. When the Romanians get down to business, their statements must be taken with a pinch of salt. If you disagree with them, show this obliquely, as they hate being snubbed in any way. Never tell them what to do—it would upset their superiority complex. In general Romanians are risk takers (Turkish influence), and they will work hard to close a deal once everyone is on the same track. They are actually more open with foreigners than with each other, often showing reticence in front of their compatriots (a legacy of decades of spying, informing and eavesdropping). With foreigners they show their desire to please, but watch out for their frequent defense: "But that won't work in Romania." When things get bogged down, Romanians often come out with spontaneous (and apparently new) ideas. Although they are skilled negotiators, they often show little knowledge of Western exigencies, particularly with regard to speed, urgency or integrity.

Follow-through is not a Romanian strong point. When a deal is concluded, everything should be put in writing, witnessed by decision makers and the competent experts. After that, it is advisable to get further approval (in writing) from a very senior person in the organization. Romanians are often comfortable with ambiguity, whereas the Westerner wants final clarity. The communist legacy has left them with a poor sense of accountability, responsibility and best routes to the bottom line.

There may be attempts to alter conditions or clauses after the agreement has been signed. Such steps must be resisted unequivocally.

Manners and Taboos

Given its incredible ethnic diversity, Romania has an impressive storehouse of manners, customs, traditions, folklore and folk art. Romanians have the reputation of being excessively or embarrassingly hospitable. One Romanian writer describes this as "aggressive hospitality." You have to be, for example, very careful not to "under-indulge" at a meal in a Romanian home or to refuse anything being offered. The only defense against Romanian hospitality is to reciprocate their generosity. Items from your own country are often most appropriate. Well-illustrated books, prints, quality pens, attractive stationery, ties, scarves and packaged foods (delicatessen) are appreciated. Some Romanians like good whiskey or cognac.

Taboos include impolite or brusque behavior; blunt, direct remarks showing disagreement; and inquisitiveness as to personal details.

How to Empathize with Romanians

Romanians get on well with people who are happy to converse at length, especially about poetry, philosophy, history and the arts. Qualities they admire are erudition, delicacy of expression, intuition and compassion. Exchanges can be on a close personal basis, especially when you have attained a certain familiarity. Though more circumspect than Italians, Romanians resemble them in their desire for spiritual closeness, confidences and exploration of human feelings. The development of such relationships will make subsequent business dealings much easier to carry out, and, moreover, will lessen the likelihood of your being cheated.

Always keep the Romanians' animosity toward Hungarians in mind, but Romanians suffer from a national persecution complex as a result of centuries of mistreatment by foreign conquerors. Suspicion is a national habit.

Finally, remember that at heart they are epicureans and want to have a good time with you.

MOTIVATION	
KEY	*Respect the Romanian "difference"*
Cross-century mood	✦ Eagerness to play a role in the EU. ✦ Fight against corruption. ✦ Modernization. *Motivating Factors* ✦ Acknowledge Romania's special historical and linguistic position. ✦ Speak a few words of Romanian.

(continued)

MOTIVATION *(continued)*

Motivating Factors

◆ Admire the beauty of their language, scenery, churches and monasteries.

◆ Show you are willing to help them in their difficulties.

◆ Read between the lines to divine their wishes and aspirations.

◆ Elicit information indirectly.

◆ Indulge in small talk and politics, but do not "intervene."

◆ Accept their lavish hospitality and reciprocate soon.

◆ Understand that business and social life are intertwined.

Avoid

◆ Praising Hungarians and their qualities.

◆ Aggressive questioning.

◆ Brusque behavior.

◆ Causing anybody to lose face (they are very sensitive).

◆ Any reference to the country's backwardness, inefficiency and corruption.

39

Georgia

Georgia, with a population of just over 4 million (slightly lower than New Zealand), covers an area of 70,000 km, slightly smaller than the Czech Republic. The capital city is Tbilisi, home to 1.5 million inhabitants.

Georgia has its beginnings from several thousand years BCE. A cradle of wine, with archaeological evidence of wine-making from 6000 BCE, she was also an important contributor to Greek mythology.

The name "Georgia" originates from the Greek "geo," meaning "earth." Etymologically, it means a land where earthworks reside—most of the ancient Georgians were involved in agriculture. Another theory is, both the Western and the Russian exonyms are likely derived from the Persian designation of the Georgians, *gurğan*, from an Old Persian *varkâna* "land of the wolves" (also reflected in Old Armenian *Virk* and a source of the Greco–Roman *Iberia*). Throughout history, Georgia has had her ups and downs. Due to her strategic location between

Europe and Asia, she has suffered many invasions and defeats. She has, however, managed to preserve her own culture, traditions, even unique alphabet. She was one of the first countries in the world to officially convert to Christianity (in A.D. 337). The oldest archaeological findings of *Homo erectus* were discovered in Dmanisi, Georgia, and date from 1.8 million years ago.

Modern Georgian history started in 1918, when Georgia declared independence from Russia. This lasted only three years, but after the dissolution of the USSR, Georgia again declared herself an independent republic in 1991. Since then she has experienced many difficulties and conflicts, particularly with the breakaway republics of Abkhazia and South Ossetia. Nevertheless, there has been a slow but steady transition to a free-market economy. According to the World Bank report *Doing Business in 2018*, Georgia is the ninth-best country in the world in which to do business. Georgia has aspirations to join the EU, and a famous Georgian saying is "I am Georgian, therefore I am European."

The official language is Georgian. According to the Columbia Encyclopedia Georgian is a language related to the Iberico-Caucacian family of language. According to David Crystal's *Cambridge Encyclopedia of Lauguages*, there are about 40 languages which are recognized as belonging to a single Caucasian family. They are classified into three types—and the names Kartvelian as the third type, which contains Mingrelian, Svan and Laz.

Culture

Georgians see themselves as a strong, patriotic, warrior people, who fundamentally believe in freedom. They also think their country, culture and religion are unique. God's help is considered important.

Values

religion	family
own language	respect for elders
love of motherland	helping others
survival instinct	patriotism
epicureanism	extroversion
hard work	hospitality
education	irony

Religion

Religion is important in Georgia. 85.4 percent of Georgians are Christian Orthodox, 10.7 percent Muslims, 2.9 percent Armenian Apostolic Church, and 0.5 percent Catholics. Religious tolerance is observed.

Concepts

Leadership and Status

Traditionally, Georgian leaders have always been strong, eloquent orators, exhibiting decisiveness and dedication to their goals. The best-known is Joseph Stalin ("Man of Steel"). Most historical leaders were male, but gender equality is increasing rapidly.

Status is rather widely distributed in Georgia, as it can include rich people, but also renowned writers, painters, musicians, dancers and important civic figures, e.g. mayors. Women are well respected and make most decisions in families. A common Georgian saying is "Man is the head of the family and the woman is the neck." In the twelfth century, the most successful Georgian queen—Tamar—was addressed as King Tamar!

Space and Time

Georgian culture is basically collectivist, and a comfortable distance for conversation is 50–70 cm. Out of doors, they love nature, mountains and vistas.

Punctuality is not required at dinner or parties; no one takes offence at lateness. Official appointments in business allow people to arrive 5–15 minutes late.

Cultural Factors in Communication

Communication pattern

Georgians are communicative people, who usually are very direct about how they feel on many topics. They do not change opinions easily, but when something is agreed, they follow through with it. They are very verbal, emotional, often oratorical. Business communication is more formal than private conversations, where interruptions are frequent. Business people currently try to "Westernize" their dialogue.

Body language is an intrinsic part of Georgian communication, involving facial expression, use of shoulders, hands and even index fingers. They certainly let you know how they think about things.

Georgians are well known for their irony—one of their proverbs is "If your house is on fire, at least warm your hands."

Listening Habits

Georgians listen well, though they may interrupt occasionally. This is through curiosity and wish to be involved. Generally good, supportive audiences.

Behavior at Meetings and Negotiations

Since most Georgians are emotionally driven, agendas take second place to eloquent monologues and often to less than necessary divergence of topic. Spontaneity frequently results in more than one person speaking at once. In larger firms hierarchies are clearer: more discipline and respect are evident.

Georgians like to be straightforward, direct negotiators, making it clear what their goals are. Many negotiations can be seen as power comparisons, identifying networks, connections and external supports. The stronger party proceeds to lead the discussions, demonstrating superiority, but making token concessions at will.

Contracts and commitments, especially of a personal and oral nature, are closely adhered to on the basis of reputation. Written contracts may be renegotiated if conditions change, though this is somewhat unusual.

Manners and Taboos

Georgians are fairly tactile when greeting close acquaintances, kissing cheeks in the case of men or women. Handshaking is normal for business people. Eye contact, as in Greece, is intense. Hospitality is generous and profuse. Religious tolerance towards Muslim, Jews and others is widespread. However, religion is strongly anchored in Georgian culture and subjects related to sex and different expressions of sexuality are delicate issues approaching taboo.

How to Empathize with Georgians

Show great interest in, and appreciation of, the uniqueness of Georgian culture. Openness and genuine frankness in discussing personal or business matters wins medals in Georgia. Perceived deviousness is unpopular. Discussing challenges with which Georgians can identify themselves is a good way to get closer to them. Eating, drinking and generally socializing keenly is expected and appreciated.

MOTIVATION	
KEY	*Warm, frank, discussion*
Cross-century mood	✦ Aspiration to join EU. ✦ Wish to modernize. ✦ Concern with breakaway republics.
	(continued)

MOTIVATION *(continued)*

Motivating Factors

+ They respect courage, wit and knowledge.
+ Share emotions with them.
+ Talk about their history.
+ Reveal your own weaknesses.
+ Enquire about their family.
+ Shelter their dignity.
+ Win their loyalty by listening well.
+ Sympathize with their political difficulties.

Avoid

+ Discussion of sex-related issues.
+ Analyzing too much their politics.
+ Refusing hospitality.
+ Being too silent or withdrawn.
+ Pessimism.

40

Albania

Albania is one of the smallest countries in Europe, being slightly smaller than Belgium. The Albanian word for Albania is *Shqiperia*, deriving from the Albanian verb *shqipoi*, "to speak." It may also derive from the word for "eagle," *shqipe*, as this bird is the symbol of Albania. Albanians can be divided into two cultural groups: the Ghegs, the northern Albanians, and the Tosks, the southern Albanians. The population is just over 3,200,000, but Albanians in Europe total over 6 million, with 2 million in Kosovo and large numbers in Macedonia and Montenegro. Other smaller Albanian-speaking communities are to be found in Greece, Italy, Central Europe, the U.S., Canada and Australia.

Albanians are descended from ancient tribes called Illyrians. Romans and Bulgars ruled from 200 BCE to the fifth century A.D., followed by Slavs. Serbs conquered the country in the fourteenth century, but Turkish invasions began in the late 1300s. Skanderbeg, the revered national hero, resisted the Turks in the fifteenth century, but Albania was under Ottoman rule from 1500 until 1911. At an Ambassadors' Conference in 1912 an independent Albanian state was created. The country relapsed into poverty during and after the First World War. In 1928 King Zog came to power and ruled harshly until 1939, when Italy occupied Albania. The Germans invaded in 1943, but Albania was liberated in 1944.

The communist rule of President Enver Hoxha ruined Albania's economy and isolated her politically. (The country's only ally was Communist China!) After his death and the election of Sali Berisha, Albania became closely involved with the war between Serbia and Kosovo. More than a million ethnic Albanians fled from Kosovo to Albania during this period. When peace resumed, Albania joined NATO in 2009. Poverty and corruption continue to plague the country.

Albanian is an Indo-European language deriving from Illyrian. It is a synthetic tongue with masculine and feminine nouns, and five verbal inflections: nominative, genitive, dative, accusative and ablative. Verbal communication with different dialectal groups is difficult. In 1972 a Standard Albanian version was created at an orthography congress in Tirana.

Culture

No description of Albanian values and customs is complete without stressing the importance of *Kanun* (customary or traditional law), which historically has governed social behavior and almost every facet of life, especially in the north of the country. Widely respected today, *Kanun* lays down the "law" on matters of church, family, marriage, property, livestock, work, honor, damages, crimes and judicial law. It takes priority over all other laws, ecclesiastical or secular. With this code, the highland tribes were able to preserve their identity, autonomy and way of life under the Ottoman Empire for five centuries. Vengeance, for instance, is accepted as the prime instrument for exacting justice. Subsequent blood feuding is still a problem of social life in northern Albania.

Values

hospitality	nationalism
generosity	courage
obsession with survival	personal honor
family	hard-working
keeping promises (*besa*)	civically active
distrust of outsiders (northern)	neat in appearance

Religion

Organized religion plays only a marginal part in public life. In 1967, all religious communities were dissolved by the communist government. Since 1990 religious freedom has been restored. Roughly 57 percent of Albanians are Muslim, 10 percent Roman Catholic, 7 percent Orthodox Christian.

Concepts

Leadership and Status

Under the communist regime there were three social castes: communist families and clans, workers, and once prosperous farming families. Since the fall of the communist regime, status is determined exclusively by wealth. Albania is a patriarchal society based on male predominance. Women are granted subordinate roles.

Cultural Factors in Communication

Communication Pattern

Among acquaintances, Albanians are traditionally friendly in terms of address and use first names at once. With strangers the accepted style is more formal at first, but people try to introduce some form of familiarity as soon as they can, not through lack of respect but to offer friendship. The Albanian preference for conviviality is tempered, however, by a residual mistrust of foreigners. This is much more pronounced among northern Albanians than those in the south. The origin of mistrust is the memory of hardships and deceit imposed on the Albanian people during long periods of foreign oppression.

Listening Habits

The element of mistrust is also evident in Albanian listening habits. While they welcome friendliness in address and straight dealing, historical experience has taught them that they have often been deceived. By nature, they listen patiently and courteously, occasionally questioning certain statements in a polite manner. Eye contact is generally weak so as not to offend, but intensifies when vital points arise.

Behavior at Meetings and Negotiations

Adjusting to Western meetings, where free speech, entrepreneurism and competition are common features, has been different for those Albanians used to the communist style of discussion. Younger Albanians are gradually warming to the increased give-and-take of Western discussions. Anxious to be successful in business (and in earning power), they are more and more exploratory in their encounters. Professional men wear business suits and ties and pride themselves on their appearance.

A preoccupation with personal honor is usually just under the surface. One should treat Albanians with courtesy and avoid talking down to them in any way.

Manners and Taboos

Greetings are handshakes and kissing cheeks for women. Albanians normally smile when passing strangers on the street. Traditional costumes are worn for special events. Urban Albanians wear Western business suits etc. When a woman loses husband or children, she will wear a black scarf until the end of her life. Women's scarves are forbidden in schools or government buildings.

Visiting is important and involves food and *raki* (brandy). Coffee is Turkish-style. Breakfast is early (6 or 7am); lunch is the main meal of the day. Families often eat together, especially on Sundays. The Albanian diet is influenced by Greek, Turkish and Italian cuisines.

Weddings in Albania are impressive festivities and, in some cases, last several days. Birth rate is high.

Folk music, both traditional and current, plays an important part in Albanian culture. Featured are instruments such as the double flute, bagpipes, the lute and tambourine. Folk dances are performed by all ages during national and family celebrations.

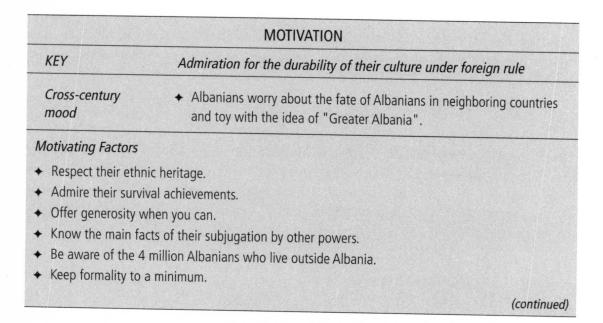

MOTIVATION		
KEY	*Admiration for the durability of their culture under foreign rule*	
Cross-century mood	◆ Albanians worry about the fate of Albanians in neighboring countries and toy with the idea of "Greater Albania".	

Motivating Factors

◆ Respect their ethnic heritage.
◆ Admire their survival achievements.
◆ Offer generosity when you can.
◆ Know the main facts of their subjugation by other powers.
◆ Be aware of the 4 million Albanians who live outside Albania.
◆ Keep formality to a minimum.

(continued)

MOTIVATION *(continued)*
Avoid
✦ Any form of stinginess.
✦ Dwelling on the Enver Hoxha period.
✦ Any brusqueness.
✦ Hurrying them.
✦ Risky humor.

41

Armenia

Armenia, a small country in the Caucasus region, is the same size as Albania (30,000 km) and has a similar population (3 million).

The capital city is Yerevan, which has just over 1 million inhabitants. More Armenians live outside of Armenia than inside it. The powerful diaspora numbers over 8 million.

Early records of habitation in Armenia featured the kingdom of Ararat (near Mount Ararat of biblical fame). Ruins of the fortress of Erebuni are still visible in Yerevan. During the centuries leading up to the birth of Christ, Armenia, like other areas in the Caucasus region, was overrun by invaders such as the Assyrians and Romans. From 95 to 55 BCE Armenia acquired territory stretching from the Caspian to the Mediterranean, but was later divided by the Romans and the Parthians. Armenia converted to Christianity in A.D. 301. At the beginning of the eleventh century the Seljuk Turks occupied large parts of the country, which was subsequently divided by Ottomans and Persians. In 1828 Russia annexed Yerevan. In the late nineteenth century Ottoman rulers ordered massacres, resulting in the deaths of 1.5 million Armenians. These culminated in the notorious Armenian genocide between 1915 and 1918.

In 1920 the invasion of the Red Army established Armenia as a Soviet Socialist republic. Armenian independence was finally declared in 1991.

Armenian life has continued to be unsettled on account of rival claims to the disputed territory of Nagorno-Karabakh by both Armenia and Azerbaijan. This became a full-scale war between the two countries. A ceasefire in 1994 was followed by further outbreaks of violence and killing in 2014 and 2016. No permanent settlement has been reached at the time of writing.

Life is not easy for present-day Armenians, many of whom live below the poverty line. Small and medium-size enterprises are numerous; many receive help from remittances from Armenians abroad. The country is a parliamentary republic led by a prime minister. While there is a reasonable modicum of liberty in religion, fragile rights to property and corruption are endemic in government and business. It is unlikely that the economy will attain satisfactory growth until the unresolved dispute with Azerbaijan reaches a settlement.

The Armenian language forms a separate branch of Indo-European, though it is heavily influenced by Persian. In classical times it was spoken over a far larger area than it is now, reaching across eastern Turkey as far south as Edessa (present-day Urfa). Today it is spoken by nearly 3 million people in its homeland as well as in well-established Armenian communities in the United States, Canada, France and Austria, to name a few. The Armenian alphabet, consisting of 39 characters, was invented early in the fifth century.

Culture

Values

Christianity	willingness to help
family	respect for elders
diligence	hospitality
national pride	love of music and dancing
dignity	passion for learning
sensitivity	anti-Turkish
entrepreneurship	love of freedom

Religion

The vast majority of Armenians belong to the Armenian Apostolic Church. This is not an Orthodox Church, but an autocephalous (self-governing) body; its head, the Catholicos, is the equivalent of the Roman Catholic Pope. Their Church is important to Armenians, since it and their language are what have held them together over centuries of oppression, conquest and dispersal. In fact, by these things are they defined as Armenians. Their Christian history makes them very aware of being on the borders of Christendom with the Muslim world.

Concepts

Leadership and Status

Most Armenians give the impression of being self-confident and speak of their past history with pride. They see themselves as strong-willed with a deep-rooted survival instinct. They have frequently had to adapt to historical disadvantage, but invariably stand firm.

Status is accorded to various heroes in past centuries including literary figures dating back to the fifth century A.D. Today people in authority are deferred to. Patronage is not uncommon.

Space and Time

Armenians sit or stand fairly close to each other when speaking, though they are less tactile than Italians or Spaniards. They are not particularly punctual—people's disposition is considered more important than time.

Cultural Factors in Communication

Communication Pattern

The Armenian communication pattern is extrovert by any standards, being very expressive both in tone of voice and accompanying body language. The latter is similar to Italian or Greek, where eyes, hands and shoulders reinforce feelings and opinions. Eye contact is intense, as in Greece, and Armenians are not averse to using the index finger to make a point or accusation. However, the general manner of address, though lively, shows concern for sociability and courtesy.

Overfamiliarity is not permitted in the early stages of business discussion, but Armenians are happy to adopt a friendly tone in due course and tend to use first names plus patronymics if they think it is permissible. Though enthusiastic, they have pragmatic goals, as they never depart too far from rationality.

Listening Habits

Their listening habits are respectful, as befits representatives of a small nation. They are keen on acquiring information which they can use for advantage. As they are ultra-sensitive, foreign counterparts must be careful to avoid offence, either by direct criticism or talking down to them. It is considered impolite to ask, "Do you understand?" as this implies stupidity. It is better to say, "I hope this is clear." Armenians like honest discussion, but subjects such as politics, history and integrity must be treated delicately. Courteous interruptions are permitted. Amongst themselves Armenians often resort to heated conversations and arguments.

Behavior at Meetings and Negotiations

Business dress is conservative—dark suits and ties. Business cards with one side printed in Armenian are useful. The establishment of personal relationships is central to doing good business. Punctuality and agendas at meetings are not particularly strict, and proceedings are occasionally interrupted by phone calls or visitors. Armenians are expert bargainers during negotiations, so it may be necessary to make certain concessions. Face should be protected for all. Direct refusal or saying simply "no" is not permitted. Foreigners are expected to be fair, though Armenians also respect firmness. One may therefore negotiate resolutely at all times. Hesitation creates a negative impression.

Manners and Taboos

Armenians are by nature gregarious and offer unlimited hospitality to foreigners. Young and middle-aged people will stand when elders enter a room. Teenagers will not smoke in front of elders. There are few taboos about drinking beer; vodka or Armenian cognac are popular with young and old. Guests are invited to meals and drinking sessions frequently. It is advisable to bring the hostess flowers, only in odd numbers. Armenians do not eat strictly at set times, but do so when they are hungry. Restaurants and cafés serve meals all day long. At work, men and women are on an equal footing, although it is still customary for a married woman to stay at home and look after the children while they are young. In the past few years, women drivers have become more numerous.

How to Empathize with Armenians

+ Be familiar with their unique and ancient history.
+ Respect their achievements.
+ Sympathize with their political aspirations.
+ Acknowledge the Armenian difference.
+ Offer help to the poor and disadvantaged.
+ Socialize vigorously.

MOTIVATION	
KEY	*Respect their long history*
Cross-century mood	+ Determination to consolidate their place in history. + Anxious about the territorial conflict with Azerbaijan.
	(continued)

MOTIVATION *(continued)*

Motivating Factors

+ Admire their courage.
+ Tacitly recognize their territorial claims.
+ Be aware of their huge and influential overseas diaspora (8 million).

Avoid

+ Talking about Turkey or Azerbaijan.
+ Do not dwell on the "genocide" question.
+ Pulling wool over their eyes.
+ Generally being lukewarm.
+ Directness which might offend.

42

Finland

The Finnish character remains mysterious to outsiders. Here we have an outstanding example of a hero nation, one with a virtually unblemished record in its internal and international dealings. After a long and what must have been an arduous migration, the Finns settled the Baltic shores some 2,000 to 3,000 years ago. A first testimony to their fortitude is that they have proven to be the only people capable of creating a successful society on territory lying in its entirety above 60° north latitude. (Iceland has done this on a smaller scale, though most Icelanders were forced to go northward, as their bloodstained history indicates.) For hundreds of years the Finns were subjected to foreign domination, yet neither once-mighty Sweden nor monolithic Russia was able to eliminate Finnish customs, language or culture, and historical references from both great powers constantly mention Finnish bravery, reliability and diligence.

When the opportunity came to gain their independence, the Finns took it, swiftly and efficiently, achieving their goal on 6 December 1917. Bloodshed was kept at a minimum, reprisals were few. As quickly as they could, the Finns set about establishing a modern state based on equality and freedom. Nationalist fervor was high, but arrogant chauvinism has been noticeably absent in Finnish history. Their treatment of the Swedish-speaking minority (now about 5 percent) was scrupulously fair. Swedish is retained along with Finnish as a national language and Finn-Swedes (who feel Finnish, not Swedish) have their own political party, newspapers and equal rights.

For 20 years (1919–1939) Finland's progress was steady, at times spectacular. Many athletic triumphs followed (particularly at the 1936 Olympics), women were given the vote and genuine democracy blossomed.

The Second World War was a cruel shock and a severe setback to the young nation, but even defeat was a victory: Finland maintained its independence. The subsequent fate of 10 East European countries has served to emphasize Finland's good fortune, earned by her determination to fight to the end for what she believed in.

After the war, the saga continued. The war-battered country immediately set about the task of paying off war reparations to the Soviet Union, which were settled in full by the appointed date. The 1950s and 1960s were difficult economically, with Finland starting off as the poor relation in the Nordic family. National diligence eventually triumphed. An environmentally clean, crime-free society without poverty entered the ranks of the world's 20 most prosperous countries in the early 1980s. And without ruining the environment.

Culture

Values

Finns sweep their nation's achievements under the carpet in periodic fits of pessimism and self-debasement. Foreigners are cleverer than we are, they say. We are rustic, gullible and easily deceived. We cannot learn languages (a myth) and we are rude and clumsy. It is hard for the British and French to imagine a nation that has triumphed over so much adversity can fall prey to an inferiority complex! There are a string of such contradictions. Here are some of them:

warm-hearted	desire for solitude
hardworking and intelligent	worry about emerging from a recession
love freedom	curtail their own liberty
admire coolness and calm judgment	drink far too much
want to communicate	wallow in introversion
tolerant	secretly despise overly emotional people
independent	hesitant to speak up in international arenas
democratic	often let the "tyranny of the majority" rule
fiercely individualistic	afraid of "what the neighbors might say"

Western in outlook	cannot lose face (like the Asians)
resourceful	often portray themselves as hapless
capable of acting alone	frequently take refuge in group collusion
desire to be liked	make no attempt to charm
love their country	seldom speak well of it

The Finns, probably on account of exceptional historical and geographical circumstance, have a higher degree of national self-consciousness than most peoples. It is a characteristic they share with the Japanese, Chinese and the French, although the Finns are less chauvinistic.

They are acutely aware of the special nature of their own culture, but they are also interested in cultural relativism, that is to say, the ways in which they differ from others. They discuss this subject at length and tend to develop complexes that do not always correspond to reality. The question of the Finnish difference once had its primary involvement in the arts, literature and assertion of political independence. Today Finland raises its head in the development and conduct of international business.

Concepts

Leadership and Status

In the business area, the Finnish low profile obviously causes problems for foreign managers who have to decide which role or profile of leadership they should adopt among Finnish colleagues. Should the French, with their great powers of imagination, attempt to fire and inspire the Finns with their exuberance and enthusiasm, or will they always be regarded as theatrical and overly emotional, with a lot of wild ideas? Should Germans, with their firm concepts of orderliness and *Gründlichkeit*, try to install solid systems and a greater sense of respect, or will they just be regarded as Teutonic, heavy, inflexible, or even old-fashioned or outdated? Modern Finnish managers, though usually decisive, are good team workers.

To sum up, Finnish leadership practices are sound. Finnish managers, like Finnish army officers, usually lead from the front and they generally strike the right balance between authoritarianism and consultative style.

Although the ice breaks slowly, foreign managers in Finland will find that the informal business climate gives them freedom of action. They will not be encumbered by too many manuals, systems or hierarchical paths. Finns leave work early, but they start early and can have achieved a fine day's work by the time most Britons are heading for lunch. Finnish employees are honest, reliable, punctual and generally loyal, and their *sisu* qualities are well documented. Bureaucracy is kept at a minimum.

Space and Time

In Finland, the concepts of space and time are clear-cut and unambiguous. A Finn needs ample mental and physical space—47 inches (1.2 meters) and "Do not follow me around." As for the use of time, you do not waste any and you arrive for meetings and appointments on the dot.

Cultural Factors in Communication

Communication Pattern

Finns display obvious weaknesses in communication—they speak little and often avoid showdowns with other peoples because of shyness or feeling that they lack savoir faire. Clashes between Finnish industry and the Finnish media in the 1970s and 1980s caused many business circles to avoid contact with the press and television. This reluctance to communicate has also extended to the foreign media. Finnish managers, with their reputation as straightforward players, would often be most favorably received by the foreign press.

In the future, Finnish industry cannot afford to neglect any viable out-of-country markets, which also means *getting on talking terms,* which is difficult for the taciturn Finns. In Finland silence is not equated with failure to communicate but as an integral part of social interaction. In the Anglo-Saxon world and in Latin and Middle Eastern countries, speech is a vital tool for getting to know people and establishing a quick relationship.

Their view of language appropriateness isolates Finland and Japan in international discourse. In both countries you hear the same whispers: "Foreigners talk so fast—we are slow by comparison—we can't learn languages—our pronunciation is terrible—it's because our own language is so difficult—foreigners are more experienced than we are—they are cleverer and often deceive us—they don't mean what they say—we can't rely on them—we are the truest people." Having lived many years in both countries, I have great respect for and sympathy with the admirable reserve and obvious sincerity of Finns and Japanese. But the fact is that Pekka Virtanen and Ichiro Tanaka have to enter the verbal fray, and both are in the process of doing so.

Behavior in the Business Environment

The image of the Finnish businessperson is still embedded in the general *Suomi-kuva* (Finnish image), which is perpetuated by the Finns themselves and accepted hook, line and sinker by foreigners who have little knowledge of Finland. In the Suomi-kuva the true Finn is fair-haired and blue-eyed (in both senses) and is slow, honest, reliable and easily deceived by other peoples. The Finn is a strong, silent type with a rural background, fiercely independent, a true friend, a good soldier, a bad enemy. Finns are uneasy with foreigners, but give them strong coffee and take them to the sauna. They are Lutheran, work hard when the money is right and always pay their debts.

The image of the Finnish manager cannot be completely separated from this myth (with its basis in truth). Finnish executives did not want to learn foreign languages, but disciplined themselves to do so. They prefer to keep quiet, but now and again they speak—and what they say they really mean (it might even be final). They pay their debts, but get their 90 days' credit. They make contracts with the Middle East and southern peoples, but they watch their backs and take precautions. They deal with the West, but with Eastern Europe too—and this includes the Russians, whom they understand like no other Europeans do. They know Finland cannot compete with the larger countries, but they sniff out niche industries, where Finnish original thinking can score points. Finnish managers insist on up-to-date technology, state-of-the-art factories and offices, and thorough training for all personnel. Profits are speedily reinvested in fine offices, training centers, sports facilities and anything else that will increase productivity.

Cold climates inevitably engender cool, sturdy, resilient peoples with an inordinate capacity for self-reliance and an instinct for survival. The Arctic survivor must have stamina, guts, self-sufficiency and powers of invention. In managerial terms, these qualities translate into persistence, courage, individuality and original thinking. Unlike their Scandinavian neighbors, the Finns originate from the east, though they are not Slavic. The uniqueness of their language and their outpost mentality encourage an independent outlook and lateral thinking, which extends to brilliance of industrial design and penetrative insight into various branches of technology.

Their lack of a strong national business culture enables them to consider membership of trade "clubs" readily, and Finland's successful experience within EFTA was followed by a successful entry into the EU. As a bridge between East and West, Finland has blossomed into a key EU member, particularly when East European nations such as Hungary and Poland gained entry.

Finnish business history is short, but it is replete with a succession of self-made men and rugged individuals who created the companies that are household names in the country today. Most Finnish managers make decisions without constant reference to headquarters, and this agility and mobile management is seen as a David-like advantage when dealing with foreign corporations of Goliathan proportions. Finns respect, even cherish, the rights of the underdog, so woe betide the Finnish (or any) boss who tries to bully or unduly coerce subordinates! This informality of corporate climate facilitates interchange of ideas and development of mutual respect within Finnish companies. The parallel distaste for foreign-imposed bureaucracy has led to Finnish business being seen as a meritocracy, and certainly the high level of education of Finnish executives gives them an edge over many foreign counterparts. The dynamism of Nokia exemplifies this Finnish excellence.

How to Empathize with Finns

Your best starting point is to get it crystal clear in your mind that a Finn is a formidable person. The slow, reticent and apparently backward behavior often referred to by many is no more than a deceptive veneer covering a very modern individual. The more you have to do with Finns, the more you will realize that they are, in effect, perfectionists. They defer politely to your cleverness or smoothness but, in fact, they usually upstage you.

The upstaging is done discreetly, but effectively. Your modest Finnish partners, so complimentary of your own attributes, turn out to be highly qualified technocrats with very solid assets. The Finns possess a squat, flat-footed solidity which always makes you feel you know where you are with them. They also look for solidity in others. Refer to your own culture's achievements, but always in a modest tone. Low profile works wonders with Finns. Never boast. When you have said your piece, do not expect any feedback. They are thinking about what you have said; they do not think and talk at the same time. Enjoy the silence—not many people give you this luxury. Consider silence as a positive sign; try to relax.

When working with Finns you should try to set clear goals and define objectives. Finnish businesspeople wish to have both their responsibility and authority well defined. They do not want one without the other. Also appeal to the inner resources of Finnish individuals to achieve the task under their own steam and to be fully accountable for it. Finns like to demonstrate their stamina in a lone task. They do not like being closely supervised; they prefer to come to you with the end result.

You should listen well to Finns, for when they eventually have something to say, it is often worth listening to. You have to watch for subtle body language, as they have no other. You can be humorous on any occasion, you can talk about the cultural values of others, but do not praise the Swedes too much. Finnish newspapers are among the best and most objective in the world, so they are probably better informed on most matters than you are. Show lively interest in Finnish culture—it is rewarding in any case. Make it clear that you know that Finland and Finnish products are high tech.

If you are managing Finns, remember that they are high on self-respect and inner harmony, as opposed to craving the support of teamwork. They like the idea of profit centers and accountability, but do not try to oversell to them. They will sometimes be slow in making up their minds but once they are made up, you are unlikely to succeed in changing them.

Finally, remember that they have a very dry humor (this quality, too, brings its delights). The great Finnish composer Jean Sibelius, who occasionally used to go on three- or four-day drinking sprees with other intellectuals, was once phoned by his long-suffering wife asking him for a forecast of when he might come back home. "My dear, I am a composer. I am involved in the business of composing music, not delivering forecasts," was the reply.

MOTIVATION	
KEY	*Low-key approach. Show you rely on them.*
Cross-century mood	✦ Determined to maintain their technological lead in telecommunications and other areas. ✦ Motivated by having the very best and latest equipment. ✦ Want training, training, training. ✦ Motivated strongly by EU entry and weighing NATO membership.

Motivating Factors

✦ Be frank, open, direct. Get to the point.
✦ Be modest and low-key. Do not talk too fast, raise your voice or gush.
✦ Use first names, dress casually and be relaxed about protocol and hierarchy. Eat lunch quickly.
✦ Use understatement and humor.
✦ Pay attention to and show respect for Finnish women; never underestimate them.
✦ Give Finns physical and mental space. Let them get on with the job and do not hover or follow them around.
✦ Show you rely on them.
✦ Be punctual, finish action chains—Finns hate slovenliness and loose ends.
✦ Appear just, keep your word and don't let them down, ever.
✦ Pay debts quickly.
✦ Listen carefully to what they say—it's not much, but they really mean it.
✦ Share your planning with them early on and constantly ask for their ideas. If you don't, they will proceed alone to an entrenched position from which it will be difficult to dislodge them.
✦ Be faithful and solid. Remember that in Finnish eyes a statement is often regarded as a promise.
✦ Enjoy shared silences. In Finland silence is cozy, restful—even fun.

Avoid

✦ Talking about Finlandization, and make it clear that you know they were never Russianized.
✦ Giving them the hard sell.
✦ Gossiping or prying.
✦ Staring. But you should shake hands very firmly.

43

Sweden

In the world at large, and especially in the English-speaking world, the Swedes seem to be universally popular. Their clean-cut profile as honest, caring, well-informed, efficient plodders who produce quality goods delivered on time sits well with their frequently well-groomed appearance, good sense of dress and (forgive the stereotyping) blond hair and blue eyes. Their English, grammatically proficient, is clean and crisp, like that of Scots who went to Oxford. They have impeccable manners and say all the right things—for the first 15 minutes. It is somewhat surprising, therefore, to discover that they are unpopular inside the Nordic area. The fact that none of the Swedes' neighbors—Denmark, Norway, Finland—have any undue reputation for aggressiveness makes their antipathy all the more unexpected. What is wrong with the Swedes?

This is a question which the Swedes themselves have been trying to answer over the last few decades. Statistically speaking, there is very little wrong with Sweden. Superb medical care has produced the oldest population in the world (over 18 percent of the population is older than 65) and only the Japanese have higher life expectancy. Infant mortality is the third lowest in the world, Sweden's population density is comfortably placed at about 35 per square mile (20 per square kilometer). Although only the 54th largest country in the world, Sweden is ranked 23rd in GDP and a meritorious 16th in GDP per capita.

This affluence is reflected in the Swedish standard of living. Sweden would seem to have few material problems. Sweden is also well to the fore in adult literacy, years of schooling and purchasing power. Foreign debt is low, foreign aid very high.

Sweden is, then, obviously a country that functions well, so why the friction between the Swedes and their neighbors? In the first place, they *are* neighbors: neighborly love is not a human characteristic. Norway, Denmark and Finland are less impressed than others by the splendor of the Swedish welfare state, as they have similar creations of their own (and there is a growing doubt in all four countries that the system will really work in the very long run). Nordic cynicism vis-à-vis Sweden seems to derive, rather, from historical factors:

- ✦ Denmark was for a long period a major player in the area.
- ✦ Swedes often laid siege to Copenhagen.
- ✦ Swedes ruled Finland for 600 years.
- ✦ Sweden and Norway shared an uncomfortable union until 1905.
- ✦ Norway, Denmark and Finland were battered in the Second World War; Sweden was not.

Swedish industry enjoyed a period of prosperity in the years 1945–1960, when Norway and Denmark got off to a much slower postwar start, and Finland was badly handicapped by having to pay huge war reparations to the Russians (1945–1952). The big Swedish multinationals—Volvo, Saab, Electrolux, SKF, Axel Johnson and so on—boomed during these years, when Swedish steel was reputedly the best in the world. Others' prosperity often gives rise to neighbors' envy, especially when accompanied by a certain complacency. In the Nordic zone, Sweden was seen as big, export-minded, financially strong, well-fed and irritatingly smug.

Cultural Values

In a survey I conducted among 100 Swedish businesspeople, the compilation of their values yielded the following list:

conscientiousness	honesty
loyalty	tolerance
equality	love of peace
love of nature	cleanliness
kindness	modesty

It is not without significance that the respondents chose 10 positive values and no negative ones. Laine-Sveiby, a cross-culturalist, comments that Swedes fail to see themselves as others see them; in this respect they differ from the more worldly Danes and also from the Finns, who are extremely interested in cultural relativism and constantly worry about what others think of them. Swedes, on the other hand, worry very much about what other Swedes think!

Behavior in the Business Environment

Swedish management is decentralized and democratic; the hierarchical structure of the typical Swedish company has a decidedly horizontal look about it. Power distance is small and the manager is generally accessible to staff and available for discussion. There will be fewer echelons in a Swedish firm than there would be, for instance, in France or Germany. There is actually a Swedish law (MBL) that stipulates that all important decisions must be discussed with all staff members before being implemented! The rationale is that better informed employees are more motivated and consequently perform better.

This collectivist form of decision making bears an interesting comparison with the Japanese system. In both countries it is seen as important that all colleagues have ample opportunity to discuss projects thoroughly, since the right to debate and express one's opinion is paid for by strict adherence to the company policy once it has been settled. In Sweden, as in Japan, decisions may be considerably delayed, but, once made, are unanimous; everyone in the company will subsequently be pulling the same way. This contrasts sharply with, for instance, the situation in many U.S. companies, where individual convictions often lead to internal discord and infighting.

A major difference, however, between the Swedish and Japanese models is that power distance between managers and employees is in reality much greater in Japan. In both systems, prolonged discussion and evaluation leads to good communication of information and generates a feeling of confidence and trust among employees.

The Swedish model is not without its critics. Robert Moran mentions the following as Swedish weaknesses in the implementation of business:

+ avoidance of conflict and taking sides
+ fear of confrontation
+ reliance on the team for initiatives
+ avoidance of competition with others in the company

While employee participation in decision making is clearly desirable in modern firms, the speed at which business is conducted today (enhanced by information technology) often requires quick and clear decisions. Probably decision making is faster in the U.S. than anywhere else; it is slowest in Japan and some other Asian countries. Most European countries lie somewhere in between these two extremes. Sweden is dangerously near Japan. I use the word *dangerously* in the sense that while it is an accepted Asian concept that big decisions take months, it is by no means the case in Europe and the U.S. French, British and Finnish managers have experienced frustration when working with or in Swedish companies, with the constant consultation going on at all levels, the endless meetings, habitual deferment of decisions, obsession with people-orientation, ultra-cautiousness, woolly personnel policies and unclear guidelines from managers.

Swedish managers are skilled at handling human resources, using charisma, a gentle but persuasive communication style and clever psychological approaches. They are good because they have to be! Their lot is not a simple one. As in Japan, it is not easy to get rid of an incompetent, even lazy or less than fully honest employee in Sweden. As it is also unseemly to get rich, managers lack both a carrot and a stick. They cannot fire and they cannot motivate very much with money (bonuses and use of a company car drive up taxes). Consequently, they take great pains to get the best out of those they command.

Unfortunately, managers don't command their supervisees very much either. They don't issue orders—these are better described as guidelines and are often not more than suggestions. They don't implement even these directives, but delegate authority downward to have them carried out. If the employee is incompetent or idle, there is a lot of mopping up to do. To be fair, one must point out that most Swedish staff members are extremely conscientious, cooperative and loyal.

The problem arises (as it often does in Japan) when the task assigned is too big for the capabilities of the individual.

A Swedish professor remarked that in order to exercise power in Sweden one has to create an image of not being powerful. Swedish managers walk a tightrope between undue personal intervention and woolly, ineffective control. They try to establish their effectiveness through careful planning and procedures. It is said that detailed planning helps Swedish managers to sleep better!

The Feminine Society

Geert Hofstede, in his well-known study of business cultures, concludes that of all those covered in the survey, Sweden is the most feminine. In masculine cultures the dominant values are success, money, rewards, objects and possessions. In feminine ones interpersonal aspects, quality of life, physical environment, rendering service and nurturance are considered more important—in short, the creation of a caring society. In the case of today's Sweden, people (including Swedes) are beginning to ask themselves if it is too caring. The welfare system— arguably the best in the world—is very expensive to maintain. Taxes are so high they hurt, and the country is aging fast. Every year there are fewer breadwinners for more dependents. In a noncompetitive world, Swedes might go on selling quality products at high prices to support their living standards, but competition in the twenty-first century is and will continue to be ferocious. Asians and Americans do not take six-week holidays plus all kinds of long weekends and rush out of the office at four in the summer. The Swedish manager is constantly confronted by requests to take leave for pregnancies, sick children, sabbaticals, right to study, home guard (similar to the National Guard in the U.S.), trade union work, and so forth.

Capital and industry had been left largely in private hands in Sweden, but the taxation system sees to it that nobody gets rich legally. Those who threaten to do so (Ingmar Bergman, Björn Borg), are forced to go and live abroad to avoid paying a tax that might reach more than 100 percent of income. Monte Carlo has a better climate, too!

One suspects that there is more wrong with the Swedish system than with the Swedes themselves. They are kind, intelligent, steadfast people who want to do well, although it will not be easy for them to eradicate their work-to-rule mentality when things get tougher. An overly regulated society, irrespective of its politics, can engender very boring members, with all spontaneity taxed out of them.

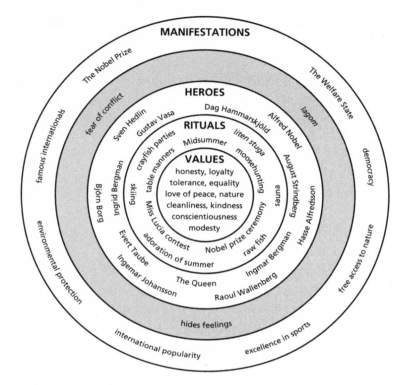

Figure 43.1 Swedish Ripple Graph

How to Empathize with Swedes

When dealing with Swedes, remember:

+ They believe that they are honest and always tell the truth.
+ They don't like to contradict their own colleagues.
+ They believe strongly in their group consensus, so don't ask them for quick, individual decisions.
+ They are not as profit-minded as you are, so don't focus too much on the bottom line.
+ In spite of their caring nature, they are more deal- than people-oriented, so you can always be pragmatic.
+ Their strong points when selling are quality, design, and prompt delivery, so you should try to match these.
+ They entertain well and generously when this is part of their program; do not hesitate to reciprocate.
+ Although they run out of small talk after 10–15 minutes, their jokes and anecdotes are first-class! Tell some of your own.
+ They are formal in toasting and expect speeches during and after dinner.

- ✦ They are extremely informal in address, so use first names.
- ✦ Silence in Sweden is not necessarily negative. Like Finns, they are reflective and rather introverted. Give them space.
- ✦ They are never overbearing and don't use brute force, even if they have the upper hand.
- ✦ Your best approach is to defer to their wish for long, all-round consultation; demonstrate clearly your own patience and understanding, allied to firmness and integrity.

MOTIVATION	
KEY	Consulting them, asking for their opinions
Cross-century mood	✦ Determined to preserve their welfare state, showing some nervousness about how it will be financed in the future (aging population).
	✦ Pushing to keep to the forefront in some areas of technology.
	✦ Following EU directives but often feeling the Swedish way was/is best.
	✦ Seeing traditional Swedish "feminine" values increasing and gaining recognition in the twenty-first century.

Motivating Factors

- ✦ Be diplomatic rather than frank.
- ✦ See business as beneficial to society rather than profit-oriented.
- ✦ Promote harmony over the cold truth.
- ✦ Delegate tasks downward as much as possible.
- ✦ Wait for them (patiently) to reach decisions by consensus.
- ✦ Discuss technical points at length and in detail.
- ✦ Remember that they will follow accepted procedures, even if you think you are close to them personally.
- ✦ Make humorous after-dinner speeches.
- ✦ Smile when they smile.
- ✦ Always try to compromise (Swedes don't understand that in some cultures compromise has the negative meaning of surrendering one's principles).

Avoid

- ✦ Confrontation.
- ✦ Rushing them.
- ✦ Talking tough; always be consultative and understanding.
- ✦ Being overly assertive or appearing overconfident.
- ✦ Attacking cherished Swedish institutions.

44

Norway

I was once discussing cultural relativity with a Norwegian friend and asked him how he would go about categorizing nationalities. "It's simple," he replied. "There are only two types of human beings—Norwegians and those who wish they were Norwegians."

This Norway centeredness, so often commented on by Danes and Swedes, is one of the three most striking characteristics of the Norwegian people. The other two are their stubbornness, which serves to reinforce their ethnocentricity, and their immense capacity for national soul-searching, which to some extent counterbalances it.

Norway is solvent, secure, well organized and poised for the twenty-first century. Its population of 5.2 million is well cared for in terms of housing, food, welfare and economic opportunity. The 28th economy in the world in size, it is an astounding eighth in GDP per capita and the world's twelfth biggest oil producer, enabling it to be the tenth largest exporter of energy.

Quality of life matches the economic foundation. Norway has the third oldest population in the world and ranks first in quality of life, according to the Human Development Index in 2018. It is the world's second largest donor of bilateral aid as a percentage of GDP (after Sweden). The educational system is remarkable in that Norwegians study longer than anyone else in Europe (12 years) and have the fourth highest tertiary enrollments, in spite of the difficult terrain and elongated country.

Geographically on the fringe of Europe, Norwegians are greatly admired by two other peoples on the European periphery—the Finns and the British. Opinion polls conducted by the Finnish Ministry of Labor consistently rank Norwegians as the most popular nationality, with the English second.

The warmth of feeling existing between the Norwegians and the British is no surprise. Viking blood flows through the veins of Britons in no small measure. Sea-going people like the English, Norwegians have left thousands of place names in their settlements in the British Isles. The city of Bergen always found the northeast of England more accessible in winter than the rest of Norway, and the history of Anglo-Norwegian trade stretches from the Hanseatic era to the present. Britain buys more Norwegian products than anybody else. Other factors binding the two countries are democracy with royalty, the parliamentary system, social justice, love of the outdoors, expeditions to the North and South Poles, Protestantism, seafaring, similarities in philosophic beliefs, calm attitudes and a shared sense of humor, especially in adversity. Norway also has good relations with the U.S. and feels in many ways part of the English-speaking world.

Norway's relations with European nations who are neither Anglo-Saxon nor Nordic are more enigmatic. Though viewed as clean dealers, Norwegians are seen by Southern Europeans as distant, excessively introverted, strong-willed and disinclined to mix. Germans see them as less susceptible to influence than the Danes, Swedes and Finns. The Slavic nations have had little contact due to the buffer position of Sweden and Finland.

Norwegians remain a proud, independent, reserved, essentially Nordic nation with their house clearly in good order. Their eventual adherence or non-adherence to the EU and other European structures would probably have less importance in the economic area than in the cultural sphere. If Finland is rapidly engaged in shedding her image as Europe's cultural lone wolf, it is hard to imagine Norway, with her close historical and cultural ties to her neighbors, continuing to isolate herself spiritually from the common European heritage.

Culture

Values

Norway's secure and comfortable standing, both economically and spiritually, during the first decade of the century is further cemented by a comprehensive array of deep-rooted and traditional values deriving not only from the resolutions of Protestant Christianity but also from the attitudes and culture of the Viking era culminating in the period A.D. 800–1000 Christianity had some difficulty in establishing its relevance to everyday lives in the far north and for this reason heathen philosophies lived on for centuries.

Others may not be able to make them change their minds, but Norwegians constantly do battle with their own feelings. Like the Dutch, they wish to be seen as a progressive, tolerant, modern people but are reluctant to demolish the traditional pillars of a rather straitlaced society. Thrift, caution, playing cards close to one's chest and strict word-and-deed correlation preclude the flexibility and communicative ease more readily observable in Denmark. Norwegian values can be summarized as follows:

honesty	pragmatism
cautious thrift	taciturnity
dislike of extravagance	obstinacy, introversion
belief in the individual	love of nature
self-reliance	prudence and foresight
controlling resources	Norway-centered
sense of humor	prefer action to words

Concepts

Leadership and Status

In democratic Norway, the boss is very much in the center of things, and staff enjoy access to him or her most of the time. Middle managers' opinions are heard and acted upon in egalitarian fashion, but top executives rarely abandon responsibility and accountability.

Norwegian managers addressing their staff have a strong and effective linguistic tool at their disposal. Spoken Norwegian is brisk, strident and cheerful—it has a fresh-air style about it. The distinctive, emphatic, rising tones of the language emphasize the Norway-centered nature of the medium, which serves to link managers more closely to their staff. It is not too low-key and hints at great energy. Essentially democratic, the recent standardization of the language (since the 1950s) enables managers to identify with all Norwegians.

The position of women in Norway is unrivaled anywhere in the world. Active in business, they are particularly powerful in politics. Gro Brundtland was one of Europe's first and best-known female prime ministers. Her cabinet had a male minority. Norwegian women often appear strong-willed and forthright, but retain feminine charm.

Space and Time

Norwegians have a low population density and like a lot of personal and working space. Norwegian offices and other public buildings are light, airy and often spacious. Their distance of comfort is 47 inches (1.2 meters). The nature of Norwegian terrain engenders a love of the wide open spaces, the mountains and the outdoor life. Fresh air and also the sea are very important for Norwegians' well-being. As many communities live in isolated valleys, a certain amount of parochialism results.

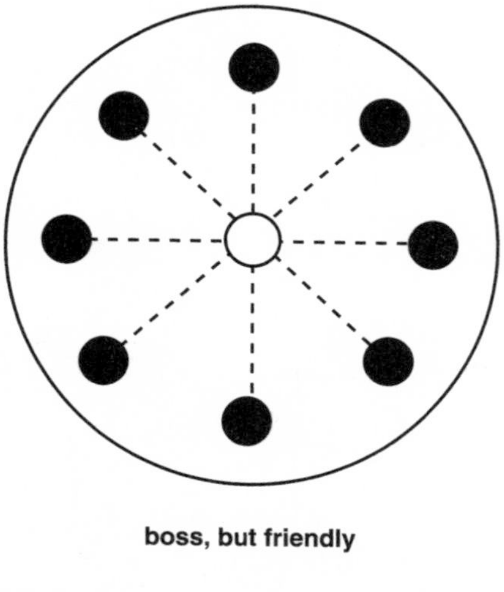
boss, but friendly

Figure 44.1 Norwegian Leadership Style

Norwegians are punctual, especially in the cities. In rural areas and among the sea-going population, attitudes to time are more relaxed. Norway is not an easy country to travel around in and allowances are often made for late arrivals over long distances, especially in the winter.

Cultural Factors in Communication

Communication Pattern

Norwegians' sterling qualities and warm feelings are not readily communicated in their speech style. Cold climates tend to produce introverts and the Norwegians, along with the Finns, are the shyest of Europeans. Meetings in Norway are frank, healthy occasions where people get quickly to the point and get feelings off their chests in a good-humored fashion. Deviousness is taboo and once everyone has obtained a clear view of the big picture, agreement is usually achieved. Once a decision has been reached, it is not likely to be changed.

Listening Habits

Norwegians listen in good humor, but quickly develop strong opinions that they soon expose. They are data-oriented and Norway-centered. They like speakers to introduce a personal touch, though one may not depart from the facts.

How to Empathize with Norwegians

Be frank, direct and strive to appear straightforward. They like clear-eyed, pragmatic dealing in a "fresh-air" atmosphere. They are looking for trust, energy and reliability. Always deliver what you have promised. Never appear in any way devious.

Do not praise the Swedes too much. Norwegians are "folksier" than Swedes and like a personal touch, although not overdone as in the Latin manner.

Talk about their mountains—they love them. Share outdoor pursuits with them if you can.

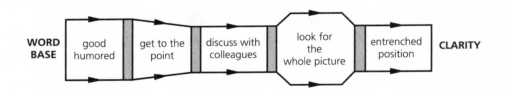

Figure 44.2 Norwegian Communication Pattern

MOTIVATION	
KEY	*Be straightforward*
Cross-century mood	✦ Oil is their trump card; their inclination is to keep some in the ground (under the sea) and invest wisely the profits they make from what they sell. ✦ Current mood is to keep out of the EU and maintain full national sovereignty. It is unlikely that this attitude will last more than a decade or two, given Norway's close historical and cultural ties to her neighbors. ✦ There is current national soul-searching—how to be seen as a progressive, tolerant, modern people and yet retain the traditional pillars of a rather straitlaced society.

Motivating Factors

✦ Be humorous whenever you can.
✦ Praise Norway, her scenery, people and achievements.
✦ Show modesty.
✦ Strive for mutual profit.
✦ Be robust and active; show that you are a "doer."
✦ Consult them on all important issues.
✦ Respect the power and pride of Norway's women.
✦ Know something about Norway's history.
✦ Eat *lapskaus* and codfish and be enthusiastic.
✦ Be generous without being extravagant.
✦ Keep your word.

Avoid

✦ Criticism of things Norwegian.
✦ Too much talk or charisma.
✦ Changing your mind frequently.
✦ Sarcasm.

45

Denmark

Denmark is a country that sells itself well and its customers, moreover, are generally well satisfied. For a land whose area is about 17,000 square miles (40,000 square kilometers)—smaller than both Latvia and Lithuania and dwarfed by its three Nordic neighbors—and whose population barely scrambles over 5.3 million, its ranking of 35th in the world's economies (well ahead of Finland, Pakistan, Venezuela and Chile, among others) is an economic miracle on a par with those witnessed in Korea, Singapore and Taiwan. Even more impressive than the total GDP figure is the fact that a large part of it consists of quality products, both in industry and agriculture. Danish goods do not come cheap, but there always seem to be takers. Visible exports usually exceed visible imports.

Trading successes mean that the Danes enjoy a high standard of living. GDP per capita, perhaps the most striking statistic, is just over $52,000, the highest in the EU except for Luxembourg, which enjoys special advantages. Denmark's population is the seventh oldest in the world and is one of the slowest growing.

Why are the Danes so successful? To begin with, they have been around for a long time and the country is only small in one sense. Not only is the Kingdom of Denmark the oldest monarchy in Europe, but it consists of Denmark proper, the Faeroe Islands and another not insignificant island landmass in the Western Hemisphere, namely Greenland. This last part of the kingdom is 415 miles (670 kilometers) from north to south and 650 miles (1,050 kilometers) from east to west. It is not all ice, either; 16 percent of the surface is ice free. Greenland was actually a Danish colony until 1953 and has had its own budget since 1979, but remains loyally in the kingdom and is administered by the Danish government. Danes, characteristically flexible, allow the Greenlanders considerable autonomy. They have their own flag, are exempt from military service and have not entered the EU. As in the case of Norway, fishing rights tend to complicate adherence. A similar arrangement exists in the case of the Faeroese, who have two representatives in the Danish parliament and are also represented on the Nordic Council.

Culture

Values

coziness (*hygge*)
flexibility
business acumen

tolerance
honesty
Protestant work ethic

cleanliness	social justice
egalitarianism	ironic
equality for women	frank
sarcastic	

Danes are mainly Lutheran and many of their values are Protestant ones, shared by their Nordic neighbors. But in some respects the Danes vary considerably from other Nordics. Often referred to as the Nordic Latins, they are more communicative, easy-going, uninhibited and smoothly international than Swedes, Norwegians or Finns. Consultation with colleagues before making decisions is mandatory, as in Sweden, but Danes get through it faster and then act quickly. After due discussion, they then want autonomy and independence. They believe that they are good at making decisions, more in the Finnish manner, pragmatically and with purpose.

Any form of bragging or aloofness is attacked without mercy, no less than it would be in Australia. Danes are fond of listing their "ten commandments":

+ You shall not think you are somebody.
+ You shall not put yourself on a par with us.
+ You shall not think you are cleverer than we are.
+ You shall not think you are better than we are.
+ You shall not think you know more than we do.
+ You shall not think you are more than we are.
+ You shall not think you are worth anything.
+ You shall not laugh at us.
+ You shall not think that anybody cares about you.
+ You shall not think that you can teach us anything.

However, if these admonitions and warnings seem formidable, remember that you will escape them if you are suitably modest and low-key in your dealings with Danes. Indeed, their good humor and apparently laid-back business style generally put other nationalities at ease.

Concepts

Leadership and Status

Basic Danish assumptions are generally in line with their essentially democratic stance and Protestant fine tuning. Leadership is by achievement and demonstration of technical competence. Leaders are expected to be low profile and benign and to consult colleagues for opinions.

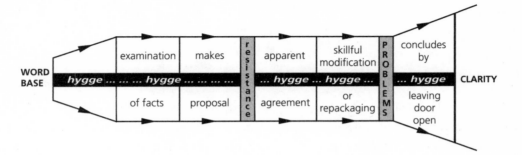

Figure 45.1 Danish Communication Pattern

The country has very few huge firms and has over 5,000 companies with fewer than 250 employees. Managers in Danish industry tend therefore to be owner-managers, just as there are many owner-captains. Personal involvement in the business results in a favorable view of inward investment and plowing back profits into companies to improve them further. Other by-products are dynamism and drive.

Status is based on qualifications, competence and results, yet materialism is downplayed. There is a focus on welfare.

Space and Time

The Danish concept of space is that they function best in an ample, airy, well-designed, hygienic environment. Offices are generally very tasteful and colorful.

As far as time-keeping is concerned, they are punctual without being obsessively so. Danes like early lunches and don't like long office hours. They spend their spare time creatively.

Cultural Factors in Communication

Communication Pattern

Danes are fluent speakers but calm and low voiced. They are the most loquacious of the Nordic countries, although not obtrusively so. Swedes, Finns and Norwegians consider them somewhat facile and clever. Serious discussions are frequently interspersed with humor. They have a sense of humor that is close to Anglo-Saxon. Linguistic ability is outstanding, particularly in English and German.

Listening Habits

The Danes are good listeners who rarely interrupt but are quite willing to ask questions afterward. Questions are good and pertinent, showing that absorption of facts was efficient. They are skillful at establishing a meaningful dialogue.

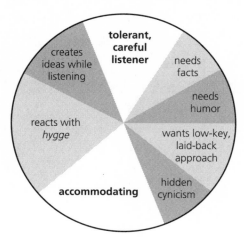

Figure 45.2 Danish Listening Habits

Behavior at Meetings and Negotiations

Danes are among the most congenial of nationalities, being neither too aggressive nor too passive. Like the British, they plot a reasonable line of argument as a basis for progress. They show flexibility in the face of obstacles and do not lack patience in seeking solutions. They show concerns regarding egalitarian procedures and processes—this is the only area in which they refuse to compromise. All members of a delegation will voice their opinions. They are good, level-headed negotiators with the knack of securing good deals without making enemies.

In their own companies and internal affairs Danes are blunt (like the Dutch) and believe that they can negate an opinion without negating the person who expresses it. They expect horizontal communication to be taken for granted and the few hierarchical influences that may come into play to be transparent. Heavy persuasion is taboo and too much lobbying is suspect. Agendas are generally adhered to and time is kept. If no decision has been reached by the end of the day it will be left until tomorrow, but there are no *mañana* tendencies. Working hours are short and overtime will not necessarily produce better results.

Manners and Taboos

Danes are generally very hospitable and congenial, quickly creating trust and confidence. *Hygge* (making things "cozy" for everyone) is an ever-present concern and objective. Danes are big eaters and underachieve when hungry. They drink willingly when socializing, but are not noted for overindulgence.

Handshakes are formal with heels together and a sharp snap down of the head (men), but easy-going informality ensues almost immediately afterward. Taboos include any attacks on egalitarianism, rights of women, social welfare and various minorities. Danes generally disparage rapid accumulation of personal wealth and are envious of outstanding individual achievement.

How to Empathize with Danes

Danes always appear reasonable, laid-back and well balanced. Focus on social progress rather than the benefits of capitalism. Avoid head-on arguments or unpleasant subjects. Danes generally want to hear the truth, but hate abrasiveness or brusqueness. They love anecdotes, particularly those that purport to provide wise analysis of a current situation.

Humor is key in Denmark. The trick is to introduce informality while at the same time maintaining correctness and properness. They are Anglophiles, and also firm believers in Nordic cooperation. Military matters and strict political alignments are not favorite subjects. Being a nation of preponderantly small- and middle-sized enterprises, they are less impressed by their own big companies than are the Swedes.

MOTIVATION	
KEY	*Be tolerant, utterly democratic*
Cross-century mood	✦ Human and individual rights question becoming more sensitive. ✦ Misgivings about surrendering Danish way of life to EU. ✦ Increasing distaste for interference from authorities. ✦ Resolved to maintain one of Europe's highest standards of living.

Motivating Factors

- ✦ Danes like to charm people (*hygge*). Enter into the spirit.
- ✦ Humor is an important factor.
- ✦ Pleasant follow-up is always advisable.
- ✦ They are very interested in profit but often pretend it is only secondary.
- ✦ They insist on tolerance of views and flexibility.
- ✦ Mild cynicism is acceptable—they will consider you less naïve and gullible.
- ✦ Remain generally low-key.
- ✦ Stick to facts and analyze them intelligently.
- ✦ Make all proposals seem reasonable.

(continued)

MOTIVATION (continued)

Avoid

+ Any form of boasting.
+ Showing you think you are cleverer than they are.
+ Laughing at them or at things Danish.
+ Patronizing them in any way.
+ Showing too much interest in materialism or bottom-line focus.
+ Infringing on *anybody's* rights.
+ Being overly serious; Danes think Swedes are so.

46

The Baltic States

The development of the Baltic region into a new growth area within Europe not only harks back to the golden era of Hanseatic cooperation but heralds the prospect—if we include parts of Poland and the St. Petersburg hinterland—of a vigorous, cold-climate market of 80 million people. The exploitation of this market, with its enticing mix of such ingredients as high GDP per capita, low labor costs and skilled workforces, could be more attractive and viable in the long term than many areas of Southern Europe and elsewhere. The historical opportunity beckons, as the Danes and Swedes link their countries with the Oresund Bridge and the eastern Baltic states, encouraged by Finland, seek to revive the old Hanseatic trade routes.

The three Baltic states (Estonia, Latvia and Lithuania) qualified for and were admitted to the European Union in 2004. In the past, the three nations have rarely cooperated effectively, divided as they have been by language, religion, foreign rulers and dreams of separation and independence. Lithuanians, an emotional and grandiloquent people, feel more at home with Slavic Poles and Russians than they do with Latvians and Estonians. The Polish–Lithuanian Commonwealth was the largest and most powerful state in Eastern Europe in the eighteenth century. Lutheran Latvians, blond and stocky, are more like northern Germans, who colonized them as early as the thirteenth century. Estonians, also Lutheran and even more reserved, strongly resemble their Finnish cousins and speak a Finno-Ugrian tongue.

If the Hanseatic highway and trade routes are to be resurrected—and this would bring enormous benefit and prolific growth to the region—the three small Baltic states will have to cooperate closely with one another, as well as with other nations on the Baltic shores. A subtle but important consideration in this regard is the common sprinkling among the Balts of a sizeable number of Russophones (speakers of Russian). Any exponential increase in the Balts' growth and prosperity can only take place if Russia's economy takes a turn for the better. The part of Russia showing most commercial promise is the northwest, particularly around St. Petersburg, with its huge potential pool of skilled workers, and to a lesser extent the hinterland extending to Minsk and Moscow.

Estonia

The smallest of the former states of the Soviet Union, with a population of just over 1.4 million, Estonia lies on the southern shore of the Baltic, her capital, Tallinn, only a few miles across the water from Helsinki. Closely related to the Finns, whom they resemble physically, Estonians speak a Finno-Ugrian language that sounds like Finnish when heard from a distance. In fact, Finns barely understand it when spoken at an average speed, but most Estonians understand Finnish, since under the period of Soviet domination *Suomen Televisio* was their "window to the West."

Estonians, a proud, organized and individualistic people, do not readily accept a close comparison with the Finns; they feel that they are more European than the Finns and that they have more cosmopolitan elements in their culture. Also, they complain that Finns patronize them, having gained international experience denied to Estonians during the Soviet years. Third parties visiting Estonia, however, cannot fail to be struck by the similarity that exists between Finnish and Estonian behavior.

Culture

Values

work ethic, good planners	home and family
individualism	independence and national identity
nature and its preservation	intellectual; skills and education
careful with money	good taste and well-mannered
creative and original	reserved and non-emotional
cynical about power	honest
introversion	order and cleanliness

Concepts

Leadership and Status

Estonians are very individualistic. Each person feels capable and prefers to lead rather than be led. Since the Soviet collapse, they have shown impatience toward those who have tried to tell them how to run their country. They have a deep sense of capability. Of the three Baltic states, the Estonians were the ones who seized independence most emphatically, with a show of some belligerence (in spite of their smallness and the large number of Russian minority citizens on their soil). They chose incredibly young leaders to guide them through the first delicate years after Soviet withdrawal. They were also the fastest to embrace (rather unpopular) market reforms and resolutely pegged their currency to the German mark.

Status is gained in Estonia by achievement, decisiveness and energy. Estonians have no former aristocracy to draw on, only foreign occupiers. Status is therefore demonstrated by educational qualifications, money and possessions.

Space and Time

Estonians are a particularly non-tactile people. They need body space and cannot bear close contact. A handshake is the maximum—there is no hugging or kissing in public. Family members are of course exceptions, but even among them physical contact is restrained. Young people are becoming more expressive; rural Estonians are the most reserved.

Estonians have a Northern European attitude toward punctuality, although the Russian minority has a more relaxed view. Estonians do not like to leave tasks unfinished and often work overtime at the end of the day without seeking extra remuneration.

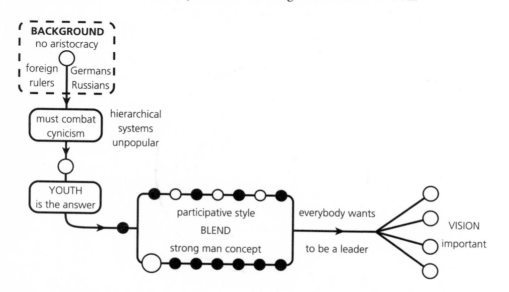

Figure 46.1 Estonian Leadership Style

Cultural Factors in Communication

Communication Pattern

The usual Estonian style is slow, drawn-out speech; there is no rush to express an opinion. When asked a question, Estonians allow a significant pause before embarking on the answer.

If asked to describe their own communication style, they use words such as *reserved, critical, closed, stubborn* and *wooden*. They believe that questions should be answered directly and summarily, without any extra information being volunteered. Their body language gives very few clues away—no gestures, no noticeable movement and the face also may not register any emotions. Self-praise is not considered polite—modesty is a virtue, which sometimes causes people to undervalue themselves. Businesspeople have to be skilled at making speeches that are concise and appropriate to the situation and the audience. Long speeches are considered boring.

Listening Habits

Estonians listen carefully and do not interrupt. Natural cynicism (reinforced in Soviet times) is concealed by good manners. After listening they give almost no feedback. Silence can be positive as well as negative. When satisfied with the information received, they feel no need to gush. Americans and multi-active Europeans are normally disappointed at the lack of responsiveness; Finns and Swedes understand perfectly.

Behavior at Meetings and Negotiations

Estonians are reputedly the most skillful businesspeople in the three Baltic states—they certainly speak the best English and face Finns and Scandinavians with confidence. They

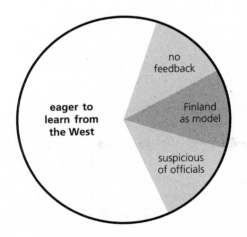

Figure 46.2 Estonian Listening Habits

are calm and level-headed, prizing their ability to show self-control, even when they are not happy with the turn of events. They are tenacious in their arguments, using facts and figures to combat emotive arguments. Although cautious and in no hurry to conclude deals, they have a strong desire to develop Western partners and trade and mop up any business they see lying around.

Once contracts are secured, they impress by their industriousness in production and fulfilling their commitments. For example, the Viisnurk ski factory in Pärnu, before independence, churned out cheap cross-country skis for sale throughout the Soviet Union. When the Soviet Union collapsed, so did that market. Undeterred, the factory improved the quality of the product and quickly secured markets in Finland and other Western countries for 250,000 pairs of skis per annum. It then went further and started producing Rossignol skis for the U.S. market. Unfortunately, this business has not proven viable in the long run.

The versatility of Estonian businesspeople is a quality born of necessity. Although Estonia has several advantages over neighboring Latvia and Lithuania—it has enormous oil-shale deposits and is a net exporter of electricity— its small economy makes it difficult for Estonians to compete in mass markets. Niche products are the solution. In this respect, high-quality Estonian handicrafts are among the most original in the world. At meetings Estonians present their products and policies confidently and with frankness. They are well aware that low labor costs give them useful leverage when dealing with Scandinavians.

Manners and Taboos

A visitor to Estonia cannot fail to be impressed by the importance of folklore and adherence to ancient customs. As a people they are very self-aware, keenly conscious of their uniqueness.

In social life, as in business dealings, Estonians impress by their orderliness (they don't cut in lines and are self-contained). Good manners, neatness and tidiness are mandatory. Young people are relatively well-behaved and disciplined. You see few gangs on street corners, and people rarely get drunk in public (although they do in private). Neighbors help each other build houses, and children generally support parents in housework and building activities. Estonians love the sauna, which for centuries has been pivotal in cultural life, often used for giving birth and during illness.

How to Empathize with Estonians

Estonians will respect a foreigner who shows respect for them and their flag. They expect no sentimental outpouring or show of affection, only calm admiration for their achievements and capability for survival. In business they expect no favors, just straightforward dealing on the basis that they can be trusted and will perform. Modesty and understatement will carry you a long way. The key to doing business is to establish reliable personal connections. It is a small country where most efficient businesspeople already know each other.

MOTIVATION	
KEY	*Acknowledgment of their efficiency and reliability*
Cross-century mood	✦ Currently determined to "make it" as an independent nation with its own future. ✦ They see EU membership as a guarantee for this. ✦ Proud of their rapid qualifications for EU entry by economic criteria.

Motivating Factors

✦ Respect the "new" nation and their flag.

✦ Admire their capacity for survival.

✦ Assume they can be trusted and will perform.

✦ Keep your commitments to them.

✦ Help them when they are under-resourced.

✦ Work through personal relationships as well as official channels.

✦ Share their passion for music, choirs and folklore festivals.

✦ Know something about Estonian heroes.

✦ Acknowledge their work ethic and individualism.

✦ Deal in a straightforward manner at all times.

Avoid

✦ Charisma, charm or sentiment.

✦ Trying to persuade or push.

✦ Lumping them together with the other Baltic states.

✦ Seeing them as pure Finns.

Latvia

Of the three Baltic republics, Latvia has suffered the most from Russian infiltration. In early 1994, Latvians made up only 54 percent of the population, with Russians totaling 33 percent. During the Soviet occupation, 750,000 foreigners (mainly Russians) arrived in Latvia. Of these, 99 percent applied for Latvian citizenship. Although present law stipulates 16 years' residence and knowledge of the Latvian language, Russians are not only anxious to secure a Latvian passport, but they are extremely supportive of Latvian independence.

This says something about the Latvians' attitude to foreigners. While resentful of Soviet influence, they show no evidence of systemic discrimination. They are, of course, used to foreigners in large numbers being on their soil; they had seven centuries of Germanic rule. The weight of Russian numbers remains, however, a practical problem. Russians actually outnumber Latvians in the cities and carry on most of the trade. Latvians, traditionally farmers and soldiers, have a problem in reasserting their influence in commercial life. This is a vital issue for the future, as Riga, by far the most important port in the area, holds the key to Latvia's prosperity and international involvement.

Culture

Values

honesty and loyalty	work ethic, discipline
arts (especially singing)	respect for nature, attachment to the land
entrepreneurship	family; clean, neat homes
conservatism	old-fashioned politeness
melancholy	physical strength
individualism	love of books

Following decades of foreign occupation and "Russification," Latvians are very conscious of their nationality and guard their cultural independence vigorously. Other ethnic groups on the fringes of Russia have been absorbed, losing much of their separate identity and all of their independence. Latvians wish to avoid this fate and have a strong sense of ethnic and linguistic separateness.

Concepts

Leadership and Status

Similar to Estonians, Latvians are individualistic. Everybody wants to be not so much a leader, but a manager in his or her own right. However, there is a tendency to respect firm, confident, knowledgeable leadership. Latvians also always want to be on the side that is winning. They are sometimes reluctant to show initiative.

Intellectuals and artists (literature, music, visual art) are acclaimed. However, image is also important (as in dress, evidence of financial security or well-being, or having a car, especially an imported one).

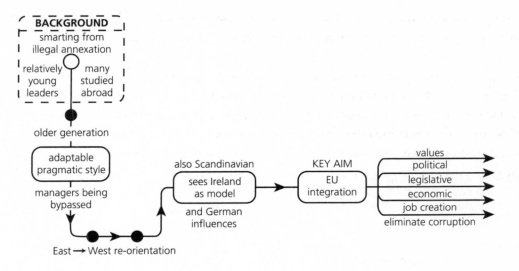

Figure 46.3 Latvian Leadership Style

Managers address staff in a cool, measured manner, reacting against the former rhetorical style of the Russians. They emphasize the use of Latvian as the language of local business and mix optimism with realism.

Space and Time

Latvians are not given to flamboyant, public displays of affection, although family and friends will kiss and/or hug on greeting. With strangers reserve is expected.

Latvians are usually punctual for actual appointments, but are sometimes slow to respond. Occasionally there is a feeling of "If not today, then tomorrow. Why rush?"

Cultural Factors in Communication

Communication Pattern

Speech is serious, almost Germanic in its precision and deliberate delivery. Rhetoric is taboo; even outward displays of emotion or lightheartedness are detrimental to the establishment of trust. Latvians do have a sense of humor, but they usually let the other side initiate joking. They are sometimes reluctant to volunteer information. A famous saying in Latvia goes like this: "We measure our cloth nine times, but we cut it only once."

Latvian speech is not only measured, but is basically very polite. There are hardly any swear words in Latvian, unlike Estonian, which resembles Finnish in its rich store of sonorous curses and oaths. Latvian uses subtleties of expression for effect. This occasionally comes out in their English or German, although such things are not easily translatable. They expect a speech to be well organized, with a cool approach.

Listening Habits

Latvians are unlikely to interrupt. They will listen closely, not revealing very much, and giving little feedback at the end.

Behavior at Meetings and Negotiations

Latvians are similar to Estonians, although less reserved and introverted. Although apparently compliant (they hesitate to disagree), they can be difficult to persuade or convince. They may be cool on the first meeting or among strangers; however, once acquainted with you, they become warm and more open-hearted. They are not likely to rush into things and some thought and consideration are necessary. They will at times exhibit signs of agreement when that may not be entirely the case.

During negotiations, certain rural attitudes are discernible among managers, such as a distrust of lawyers, bankers and marketing types and a feeling that excess profits are illegitimate. The large number of Russophones in business prolongs a tendency to follow the Soviet top-down system, especially with older individuals.

Younger managers are more amenable to change, but they often have a poor understanding of Western management processes in accounting, finance and marketing. Latvians in general have a desire to do things right legally and technically, which gives rise to an overemphasis on process as opposed to exploring imaginative ideas. Contracts and commitments are almost invariably respected and adhered to.

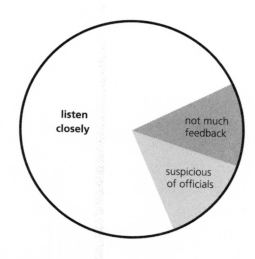

Figure 46.4 Latvian Listening Habits

Manners and Taboos

Many old-fashioned courtesies still exist: shaking hands on meeting, introductions, no first names unless mutually agreed upon. Latvians open doors for women and allow them to go through first, as well as helping them on with their coats. Women do not smoke in the street (although this is beginning to change), nor do they help themselves to a drink. Men expect to pay; this is a matter of pride.

The custom of holding dinner parties has not caught on yet. Generally the home is open only to family and close friends, except on name days. If you are invited to dinner, a bunch of flowers is obligatory and a bottle of something special may also be welcome.

Impolite, boastful, loud or condescending behavior is not acceptable, nor is prying or inquisitiveness about personal affairs.

How to Empathize with Latvians

Latvians are proud and usually quite bright; they appreciate being treated as intellectual equals. In fact, some tact is required to let them know when they may be wrong. Respect for a unique Latvian identity is important. While there is obviously some lack of what may be termed *commercial culture*, this is not due to any inability on their part but rather to the previously prevailing system (a command economy, with all decisions made in Moscow), which also resulted in isolation from the Western world. Those exploring Latvian culture will quickly gain respect. Language problems (e.g., not always speaking English) are also a vestige of the previous regime and should be evaluated in that light.

MOTIVATION	
KEY	*Showing solidity and good manners*
Cross-century mood	◆ Their biggest current problem is the presence of a resident Russian population of more than 40 percent. ◆ This is mitigated by the local Russians' liking for Latvia and support of Latvian independence. ◆ Riga, by far the most important port in the area, holds the key to Latvia's prosperity and international development.

Motivating Factors
- Show your own efficiency and competence—Latvians like to be on the winning side.
- Encourage them to show initiative—they are sometimes reluctant.

(continued)

MOTIVATION *(continued)*

- ✦ Admire their artistic and aesthetic achievements, especially their feeling for music.
- ✦ They are looking for honesty, loyalty and reliability, and seriousness.
- ✦ They like to see some Germanic qualities in you—competence, discipline, punctuality, predictable behavior.
- ✦ Respect them as intellectual equals.
- ✦ Respect their feeling for family and home.
- ✦ Share their enthusiasm and attachment to nature and the land (they are great gardeners).
- ✦ They do not reveal too much initially, so it is better not to pry.

Avoid

- ✦ Tactlessness when showing them they are wrong.
- ✦ Too much respect for officialdom.
- ✦ Hasty comments (on politics).
- ✦ Rhetoric.
- ✦ Outward displays of emotion.

Lithuania

Western Europeans may consider Lithuania to be a small, insignificant state situated in a remote, far-off corner of northeastern Europe. Lithuanians would say that they are wrong on all counts. Lithuania is bigger than not only Estonia and Latvia but also the Netherlands, Belgium, Denmark, Switzerland, Taiwan and other economic powerhouses such as Hong Kong, Singapore and Luxembourg. Secondly, there is nothing insignificant about her history—when she joined Poland through a dynastic union in 1386, the subsequent Polish–Lithuanian Commonwealth was the largest and most powerful state in Eastern Europe, stretching from the Baltic to the shores of the Black Sea. If you look more closely at the map and include European Russia and Ukraine as part of the continent, the geometric center of Europe is in fact just north of Vilnius.

Throughout its history, Lithuania has literally been a European crossroads, absorbing Russians, Poles, Germans, Jews, Belarusians and Ukrainians. In spite of its cosmopolitan nature, it was much more successful than Latvia and Estonia in protecting its national identity during the Soviet era—80 percent of its population remains ethnic Lithuanian.

Lithuania first gained independent statehood in the thirteenth century. The return to full independence in 1991 brought a wave of national sentiment and a rediscovery of Lithuania's language, culture and history. The new era has also brought a reorientation toward the West.

The desire to find a national path, a Lithuanian way of doing things, following a rejection of foreign domination, has to be reconciled with the need to catch up internationally by learning new techniques from abroad.

Culture

Values

preservation of national identity
generosity
Catholicism
strong historical consciousness
music (esp. choirs) and dancing
love of nature

hospitality
family
spontaneous attitude
sentiment
morality
romanticism

Concepts

Leadership and Status

Lithuania was the only Baltic state that previously had an aristocracy. However, political privilege still exists. Managers and other employees still often "toe the Communist Party line" despite a certain resistance to official policies. The older generation of Lithuanian managers has not completely freed themselves of bureaucratic habits from Soviet times, but young leadership is developing a more dynamic style, with Nordic encouragement. Lithuanian women are beginning to play vigorous roles in business and politics.

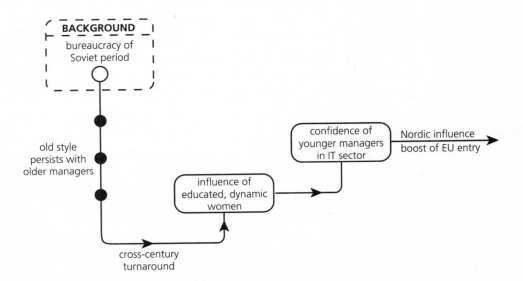

Figure 46.5 Lithuanian Leadership Style

Space and Time

Lithuanians stand somewhat closer to interlocutors than do Latvians and Estonians. They are occasionally tactile, though less so than Latins or Slavs. They are not as punctual as their northern neighbors. Hospitality can go on into the early hours.

Cultural Factors in Communication

Communication Pattern

Lithuanians are less reserved than Latvians and Estonians and are regarded by the former as talkative, even loquacious. Poles, however, consider them cold. The level of education is quite high and conversations are interesting, at times riveting. Their opinions are often laced with romantic idealism and nostalgia.

Lithuanian is a rich, expressive language, enabling managers to revel in its aesthetic, archaic constructions. The fact that Lithuanian is replacing Russian as the principal language of business is satisfying to employees.

Listening Habits

Lithuanians are good listeners, although somewhat impatient if they have opinions to offer. They are quick to perceive the feelings of others. Official-sounding statements and opinions are likely to turn off a Lithuanian listener.

Behavior at Meetings and Negotiations

Lithuanians do not follow agendas as strictly as Estonians, although in general they consider themselves organized and orderly. Good manners are of the essence. They tend to be more persuasive than other Balts, and when negotiating, emotion occasionally creeps in.

Lively, friendly small talk begins meetings and negotiations. A courteous introduction of proposals and a cautious reaction to counterproposals follow. Discussions may become heated (in comparison with Latvia or Estonia) if Lithuanian proposals are resisted strongly. Lithuanian counterproposals are expressed vigorously, without giving much away; this is often followed by a charming offensive, Baltic style (with some reasonable concessions, often with clever repackaging).

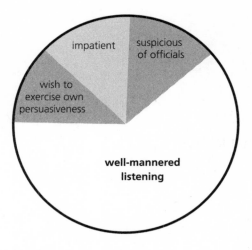

Figure 46.6 Lithuanian Listening Habits

Lithuanians are less pragmatic than their fellow Balts and will only compromise in Nordic style if they lose no face in the process. They can switch styles from Nordic reasonableness and factuality to Polish-style sensitivity and periodic opaqueness. Lithuanians generally honor contracts and commitments, especially when these are in written form. Hints at renegotiation may be given when circumstances change in favor of their partner, but they generally stick to the law.

Manners and Taboos

Lithuanians' sense of loyalty involves family, children and friends, although they have a strong sense of national identity and cultural traditions. Eating and drinking are considered important; unfortunately, alcoholism is a problem. A Lithuanian proverb says, "Each one drinks as much as he can—not less or more—until the glass is empty."

How to Empathize with Lithuanians

Treat Lithuanians as persons and as friends. Show a strong interest in their countryside, arts and aesthetic achievements. Play down your desire to make money as quickly as possible. Give personal opinions, rather than those of your company, officials or national policy. Develop a personal working relationship based on mutual affection. Show sentiment and be willing to indulge in soul-searching with them—it is a favorite pastime.

MOTIVATION	
KEY	*Good manners combined with liveliness*
Cross-century mood	✦ They share the Baltic states' hopes of reviving the old Hanseatic trade routes. ✦ They are happy to be in the EU—they point out that Vilnius is the geographic center of Europe!

Motivating Factors

✦ Share their strong sense of national identity.
✦ Show some interest in their language—it is the oldest and most archaic Indo-European language.
✦ Discussion can be livelier than in the other two Baltic states—you can express personal opinions strongly, but with good taste.
✦ Some sentiment is welcomed.
✦ They are proud of having "kept the Russians out" more effectively than the other Baltic states.
✦ They like good manners but accept persuasiveness.
✦ They are good listeners, but like to speak, so it is better not to address them at too great a length.
✦ Eating and drinking assume more importance than in Latvia or Estonia.

Avoid

✦ Sounding too official or boring them with cold facts and figures.
✦ Confusing them with Latvians.
✦ Lumping all Baltic states together.
✦ Roughness at any time.

47

Russia

The disintegration of the Soviet Union has eliminated the gigantic, multicultural phenomenon constituted by the bewildering assortment of countries, races, republics, territories, autonomous regions, philosophies, religions and credos that conglomerated to form the world's vastest political union. The cultural kaleidoscope had been so rich it boggled the mind. Its collapse, however, serves to make us focus on something simpler yet unquestionably fecund per se—the culture of Russia itself.

It is only too easy to lump Soviet ideology and the Russian character together, since during 70 years of strife and evolution, one lived with the other. Yet Soviet Communist Russian officials were no more than one regimented stream of Russian society—a frequently unpopular, vindictive and shortsighted breed at that, although their total grasp of power and utter ruthlessness enabled them to remain untoppled for seven decades.

Russian individuality was obliged in a sense to go underground, to mark time in order to survive, but the Russian soul is as immortal as anyone's. Its resurrection and development in the twenty-first century is of great importance to us all.

Some of the less attractive features of Russian behavior in the Soviet period— exaggerated collectivism, apathy, suspicion of foreigners, pessimism, petty corruption, lack of continued endeavor, inward withdrawal—were visible hundreds of years before Vladimir Lenin or Karl Marx were born. Both Czarist and Soviet rule took advantage of the collective, submissive, self-sacrificial, enduring tendencies of the romantic, essentially vulnerable subjects under their sway. Post-Soviet Russian society is undergoing cataclysmic evolution and change, and it remains to be seen how some eventual form of democracy and the freeing of entrepreneurial spirit will affect Russia's impact on the rest of the world.

The two chief factors in the formation of Russian values and core beliefs were over and above any governmental control. These prevailing determinants were the incalculable vastness of the Russian land and the unvarying harshness of its climate. The boundless, often indefensible steppes bred a deep sense of vulnerability and remoteness that caused groups to band together for survival and develop hostility to outsiders.

Climate (a potent factor in all cultures) was especially harsh on Russian peasants, who were traditionally forced, virtually, to hibernate for long periods, then struggle frantically to till, sow and harvest during the short summer. Anyone who has passed through Irkutsk or Novosibirsk in the depths of winter can appreciate the numbing effect of the temperature, with an annual average for January of -25 degrees celcius.

The long-suffering Russian peasants, ill-favored by cruel geography and denied (by immense distances and difficult terrain) chances to communicate among themselves, were easy prey for those with ambitions to rule. Small uneducated groups, lacking in resources and cut off from potential allies, are easy to manipulate. The Orthodox Church, the Czars, the Soviets, all exploited these hundreds of thousands of pathetic clusters of backward rustics. Open to various forms of indoctrination, the peasants were bullied, deceived, cruelly taxed and, whenever necessary, called to arms. Russians have lived with secret police not just in KGB times, but since the days of Ivan the Terrible, in the sixteenth century. Figure 47.1 shows how oppressive, cynical governance over many centuries developed further characteristics—pervasive suspicion, secrecy, apparent passivity, readiness to practice petty corruption, disrespect for edicts—as added ingredients to the traditional Russian pessimism and stoicism in adversity.

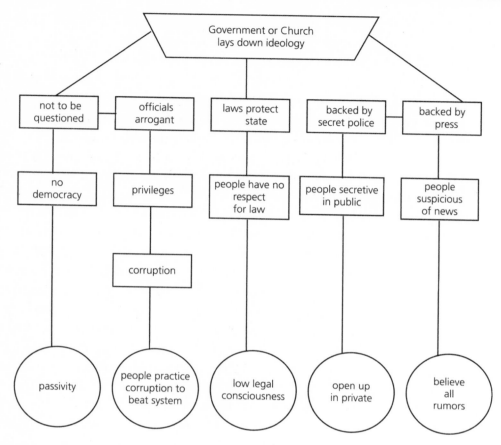

Figure 47.1 Governance of Russia

Values

If all this sounds rather negative, there is good news to come. Although resorting to expediency for survival, Russians are essentially warm, emotional, caring people, eagerly responding to kindness and love, once they perceive that they are not being "taken in" one more time. Finns—victims of Russian expansionism on more than one occasion—readily acknowledge the warmth and innate friendliness of the individual Russian. Even Americans, once they give themselves time to reflect, find a surprising amount of common ground. Both peoples distrust aristocrats and are uncomfortable, even today, with the smooth eloquence of some Europeans. Bluntness wins friends both in Wichita and Kazan. Both nations think big and consider they have an important role to play—a "mission" in world affairs.

Our familiar "horizon" comparison in Figure 47.2 shows that while Russians and Americans are destined by history and location to see the world in very different manners, there is sufficient commonality of thinking to provide a basis for fruitful cooperation. Their common dislikes are as important in this respect as some of their mutual ambitions.

Behavior at Meetings and Negotiations

As far as their attitudes to the world in general are concerned, how do Russians see the rest of us and—importantly—how do they do business? While it is clear that they are a society in transition, certain features of their business culture inevitably reflect the style of the command economy that organized their approach to meetings over a period of several decades. Russian negotiating characteristics, therefore, not only exhibit traditional peasant traits of caution, tenacity and reticence, but indicate a depth of experience born of thorough training and cunning organization. They may be as follows:

- ✦ They negotiate like they play chess: they plan several moves ahead. Opponents should think of the consequences of each move before making it.
- ✦ Russian negotiators often represent not themselves, but part of their government at some level.
- ✦ Russian negotiating teams are often composed of veterans or experts; consequently, they are very experienced.
- ✦ Sudden changes or new ideas cause discomfort, as they have to seek consensus from higher up.
- ✦ Negotiations often relate the subject under discussion to other issues outside the scope of the negotiations. This may not be clear to the other side.
- ✦ Russians often regard willingness to compromise as a sign of weakness.
- ✦ Their preferred tactic in case of deadlock is to display patience and "sit it out"; they will only abandon this tactic if the other side shows great firmness.
- ✦ The general tendency is to push forward vigorously if the other side seems to retreat, to pull back when meeting stiff resistance.
- ✦ Delivery style is often theatrical and emotional, intended to convey clearly their intent.

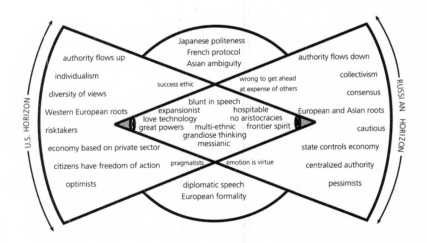

Figure 47.2 Russian/U.S. Horizons

+ Like Americans, they can use "tough talk" if they think they are in a stronger position.

+ They maintain discipline in the meeting and speak with one voice. When Americans or Italians speak with several voices, the Russians become confused about who has real authority.

+ Russians often present an initial draft outlining all their objectives. This is only their starting position and far from what they expect to achieve.

+ They often make minor concessions and ask for major ones in return.

+ They may build into their initial draft several "throwaways"—things of little importance which they can concede freely, without damaging their own position.

+ They usually ask the other side to speak first, so they may reflect on the position given.

+ They are sensitive and status conscious and must be treated as equals and not "talked down to."

+ Their approach to an agreement is conceptual and all-embracing, as opposed to American and German step-by-step settlement.

+ Acceptance of their conceptual approach often leads to difficulties in working out details later and eventual implementation.

+ They are suspicious of anything that is conceded easily. In the Soviet Union days, everything was complex.

+ Personal relationships between the negotiating teams can often achieve miracles in cases of apparent official deadlock.

+ Contracts are not as binding in the Russian mind as in Western minds. Like Asians, Russians see a contract as binding only if it continues to be mutually beneficial.

A study of this list may lead you to the conclusion that Russian negotiators are not easy people to deal with. There is no reason to believe that the development of entrepreneurism in Russia, giving added opportunities and greater breadth of vision to those who travel in the West, will make Russians any less effective around the negotiating table. Westerners may hold strong cards and may be able to dictate conditions for some length of time, but the ultimate mutual goal of win–win negotiations will only be achieved through adaptation to current Russian mentality and world attitudes.

How to Empathize with Russians

+ If you have strong cards, do not overplay them. Russians are proud people and must not be humiliated.

+ They are not as interested in money as you are; therefore, they are more prepared to walk away from a deal than you.

+ Russians are people-rather than deal-oriented. Try to make them like you.

- If you succeed, they will conspire with you to "beat the system." Indicate your own distrust of blind authority or excessive bureaucracy as often as you can.
- Do them a favor early on, but indicate it is not out of weakness. The favor should be personal, rather than relating to the business being discussed.
- Do not be unduly influenced by their theatrical and emotional displays, but do show sympathy with the human aspects involved.
- When you show your own firmness, let some glimmer of kindness shine through.
- Drink with them between meetings if you are able to; it is one of the easiest ways to build bridges.
- They like praise, especially related to Russian advances in technology, but also about their considerable artistic achievements.
- Do not talk about the Second World War. They are sensitive about war talk and consider most Russian wars as defensive ones against aggressive neighbors. They have not been given your version of history.
- They particularly love children, so exchanging photographs of your children is an excellent way to build relationships.
- They respect old people and scorn Americans' treatment of the elderly. Mention your own family closeness, if appropriate.
- Indicate your human side—emotions, hopes and aspirations. They are much more interested in your personal goals than in your commercial objectives.
- Bear in mind during your business discussions that their priorities will be personal relationships, form and appearance, and opportunity for financial gain—in that order.
- The Eastern and Western elements in their makeup often cause them to appear schizophrenic. Do not let this faze you—the other face will always reappear in due course.
- They have, in their history, never experienced democracy; therefore, do not expect them to be automatically egalitarian, fair, even-handed and open to straightforward debate. Explain to them clearly how you think about such matters and how you are basically motivated by these factors.
- Anything you introduce as an official directive or regulation they will distrust. What you indicate as a personal recommendation, though, they will embrace.
- Russians are basically conservative and do not accept change easily. Introduce new ideas slowly and keep them low key at first.
- They often push you and understand being pushed, but they rebel if they feel the pressure is intolerable. Try to gauge how far you can go with them.
- Dissidence in general is not popular with them, as security has historically been found in group, conformist behavior. Do not try to separate a Russian from his or her "group," whatever that may be.
- They love conversation. Do not hesitate to unburden yourself in front of them. Like Germans, they are fond of soul-searching.

- They achieve what they do largely through an intricate network of personal relationships. Favor is repaid by favor. They expect no help from officials.
- Like Germans, they enter meetings unsmiling. Like Germans, they can be quickly melted with a show of understanding and sincerity.
- When they touch another person during conversation, it is a sign of confidence.

MOTIVATION	
KEY	*Form personal alliances to "beat the system"*
Cross-century mood	<ul><li>Russians are in transition and need to be helped and encouraged.</li><li>They needed to be oriented toward eventual economic and political goals. There may be an outside chance that they will align with the EU.</li><li>Russians are still licking their political and economic wounds and trying to regain confidence.</li><li>Having lost most of the "Eastern Empire," there is an increasing tendency to face West.</li></ul>

Motivating Factors

- Emphasize the breadth of Russian horizons and viewpoints.
- Show that their many characteristics are mirrored in Western Europe: compassion in Italy, sentimentality in Germany, love of tradition in Britain, warmth and generosity in Spain, artistic achievements in France.
- Stress their "Europeanness."
- Envisage their eventual entry into the EU.
- Praise their volte-face after the demise of communism.
- Point out that traditional Russian traits have survived the vicissitudes of history.
- Focus on Russian positive characteristics: warmth, generosity, compassion, artistry and aesthetics, stamina, powers of improvisation, deep friendships.
- Offer help and advice where appropriate.
- Show camaraderie.
- Indicate trust.

Avoid

- Talking down to them.
- Discussing past failures.
- Causing loss of face.

(continued)

MOTIVATION *(continued)*
✦ Bad manners.
✦ Being too casual or flippant.
✦ Paying insufficient attention or respect to elderly people.
✦ Pushy behavior.

48

Central Asia

In the southern part of the former Soviet Union, sandwiched between Russia, Iran and Afghanistan from north to south and between the Caucasus Mountains and China from west to east, lie six Muslim republics that gained independence when the Soviet Union disintegrated. These countries—Kazakhstan, Uzbekistan, Kyrgyzstan, Tajikistan, Turkmenistan and Azerbaijan—have become a focus of international interest on account of the wealth of their natural resources.

The geographic location of these states gives them considerable strategic importance. They really do straddle Europe and Asia, and when the oil begins to flow fully (some routes are as yet uncertain), the politics of wealth and influence will intensify.

Only Tajikistan has an Indo-European language, akin to Persian. The other five republics speak Turkic tongues that are mutually intelligible. This has inspired Turkey, so far unsuccessful in her application to join the EU, to seek an alternative route by forming a Central Asian trading bloc of Turkic-speaking countries. This concept has met with cautious approval from the six Muslim republics, ever aware of Russian pressure from the north and the Chinese colossus to the east.

The Soviets had redrawn the map of Central Asia in the 1920s along rough linguistic lines. This divide-and-rule policy was their way of dealing with a large, scattered horde of nomadic and semi-nomadic tribes that roamed the deserts and steppes. These groups formed settlements and lived in dome-like tents made of felt called *yurts*. They migrated seasonally to find pastures for their herds of horses, sheep and goats. The Kazakhs, for instance, were rarely united as a simple nation under one leader, although they had chiefs. Today there are three levels of identity awareness: first, a person defines him- or herself by tribe; secondly, there is a strong national awareness; and third, a supra-national awareness, a sense of belonging to the pan-Turkestani movement. These levels are replicated in several of the republics. Whether the pan-Turkestani dream will ever be realized is highly doubtful, but the cultural backgrounds of the six nations have much in common.

Definitions are complicated. Between the Black Sea and the Chinese border 60 million people live in six countries that were part of the Soviet Union a short time ago. Russian immigration was massive, especially in Kazakhstan, where nearly 40 percent of the citizens are Russian. So are almost 20 percent of the inhabitants of Kyrgyzstan. One million Kazakhs live in China, a large number of Uzbeks are to be found in Afghanistan and more Azeris live in Iran than in Azerbaijan. One-fifth of the people of Tajikistan are Uzbeks. This situation is what you might expect where nomads are concerned, but immobilize them inside artifi- cially created boundaries and you have a recipe for friction and conflict. There have been no major explosions to date, but the Turkestani awareness is fading in the face of growing nationalism and divergence of aims with regard to the exploitation of unevenly distributed natural resources.

The Central Asian republics share many cultural characteristics on account of their com- mon history. To a greater or lesser extent, they are governed by Islamic tenets and profess rather a high level of morality, though pragmatism is creeping in more and more in states that are beginning to realize how rich they may become one day. In general, anti-Russian feeling runs high, not unsurprising in view of earlier Soviet purges.

Central Asians are loquacious, excitable and tough. They have long memories and can be vindictive if they feel wronged or exploited. Males dominate society, as in other Muslim states. Regional rivalries are fierce, as sentiments are often clannish or tribal rather than national. Turkey enjoys a certain popularity as a regional leader, though this may change if it gains entry into the EU. The abundance of oil and gas in the western half of the area sug- gests closer links to the main European nations in the future and a growing U.S. influence on commercial practices and even culture.

Owing to lack of space, I have analyzed only the two most populous Central Asian republics—Kazakhstan and Uzbekistan—in some detail. Many cultural characteristics are common to the region, though obviously each country has its own special traits and agenda. The Tajiks, particularly, have a different ethnic and linguistic background.

Kazakhstan

Kazakhstan is a vast, sparsely populated area (more than twice the size of Texas) with huge deposits of oil, natural gas, gold, copper, uranium and many other minerals. The Kazakhs were the first of all the Central Asian Muslims to acquire a national, purely Kazakh consciousness in the middle of the nineteenth century. Thus, they have a strong national consciousness, which is a result of several factors: pride and a feeling of superiority over the sedentary groups on the part of the nomads; a long tradition of power going back to the Mongol empire; and the existence of an authentic, purely Kazakh culture with a brilliant literature and numerous and highly intellectual and sophisticated Kazakh elite. Kazakhs were mostly nomads until the Russian Revolution. They were subjected to a very brutal settlement program in the 1930s, although tribal organization survived and is still perceived by the population as a reality.

The Kazakhs are currently rediscovering their national past and progressing toward a new sense of solidarity with other Central Asian Turks, especially the Uzbeks. They have no need to defend their cultural nationalism. Neither the Russians nor the Uzbeks have threatened Kazakh culture. Since 1970 the release of census data shows that despite the continued immigration of Europeans to Kazakhstan, the Kazakhs (because of their high fertility rate) are steadily regaining their position as the leading community in their republic. Kazakhstan is being wooed by oil companies from many nations, not least by the Americans.

Culture

Islam in its Sunni form dominates the culture of the Kazakhs. As in Turkmenistan, however, Islam does not have such deep roots as it has with the settled population of other Central Asian republics. Also, alongside their Muslim beliefs, they retain some earlier beliefs—superstition, witchcraft and even vestiges of shamanism.

Values

pride in their past	strong tribal affinities
nomadic traditions	adventuresome
love of horses	love of physical contests
daring and bravery	respect for age
suspicion of Uzbek chauvinism	warm and hospitable to strangers

Concepts

Leadership and Status

The Kazakh leadership model is autocratic and hierarchical and applies to the home and family, business circles and the political sphere. The influence of Islam is less pervasive than in neighboring Central Asian countries and is balanced by the pragmatism of the government, especially where the connections with foreigners (usually in the oil industry) are concerned. Kazakh leadership is characterized by national, as well as tribal, confidence and energy.

Kazakh managers address their staff in a vigorous, expressive style, using the richness of the Kazakh language, with its great literary and poetic tradition. Elements of paternalism are common in the managerial style, encouraging obedience and compliance.

Space and Time

With a sparse population inhabiting the ninth largest country in the world, the Kazakh sense of space is probably unique. Used to roaming the wide open spaces, usually on fast-galloping horses, the Kazakhs are a free and nomadic people, a breed apart.

Nomadic people are jealous of territory and resent encroachment by others. Kazakhs are, however, animated conversationalists and enjoy physical proximity when arguing. Older people are generally given more than a one meter "distance of comfort."

Kazakhs carry on social and business activities at a slow pace, and punctuality is not of the essence unless an older, senior person is involved. Meals are of considerable duration—feasting is typically Kazakh. Contact with Westerners is slowly imparting a sense of urgency among Kazakhs working for foreign companies. It is important to devote sufficient time to the many rituals in Kazakh society and safest to follow their tempo on ceremonial occasions and in formal business meetings.

Cultural Factors in Communication

Communication Pattern

Kazakhs have a rich literary tradition and they pride themselves on their eloquence when using their own language. Nearly all are fluent in Russian; fluent speakers of English are rare but increasing in number. Kazakhs argue tenaciously, but always with dignity. They protect not only their own face, but also that of others.

They are used to speaking with Russians and are interested in Westerners in general. Be sure to respect their nationalism and, when you aware of it, their tribal affinities. Address older people in an extremely courteous manner, looking directly at them. Kazakhs like energy in a conversationalist or interlocutor and like to get a feel for how sincere he or she is. They do not accept direct criticism, but are hungry for know-how and knowledge of others' experiences.

Listening Habits

Kazakhs listen carefully and courteously, not without a certain cynicism where Westerners, including Russians, are concerned. They rarely interrupt. Their Islamic defensiveness is of a moderate nature.

Behavior at Meetings and Negotiations

A business meeting in Kazakhstan can be a very satisfactory but complex experience. Kazakhs take their time in getting to know you before indulging in clear communication. They like proposals presented clearly, forcefully, in an energetic manner, but their own suggestions are initially tinged with caution. Conversations start in a formal manner, but as time goes by, Kazakhs try to form a strong personal relationship with their chief interlocutor. Talks will normally be interspersed with socializing and feasting and there may be a noticeable increase in joviality when they learn to trust you.

Because English is not widely spoken, interpreters are usually a must for visiting delegations. Business cards, written in both Russian and English, are widely used, and associates should be addressed by their first and patronymic names, as in Russia. Kazakhs are warm and hospitable people who enjoy getting to know their business counterparts socially. Typically, foreign delegates might be invited to drink tea (*chai*) at an associate's home, visit a communal sauna (*banya*) or attend a formal dinner in a restaurant. Kazakh society is intensely hierarchical and seating arrangements at business dinners will be dictated by rank, with the most senior people seated farthest from the door. Honored guests may be offered a lamb's head; be aware that refusing to sample this traditional dish would be considered rude. Vodka and cognac are drunk at social occasions and frequent toasts to fruitful business or personal relationships are customary. Here, the Russian influence is noticeable.

Kazakh negotiators are usually well prepared and are tenacious. Discussions are likely to become extremely animated. Be careful not to openly contradict senior members of the Kazakh team, as this could be interpreted as a lack of respect. Opposition to ideas should be indicated in an indirect manner. They may feign anger or display occasional intransigence, but these are generally tactics rather than deeply rooted emotions. They are not without humor but will only resort to it if you do.

They criticize in a roundabout way; you must listen carefully. Local business contacts may be able to help introduce you to the relevant decision-making officials. The pace of business can be slow. They are not in a hurry to conclude agreements and are usually happy to postpone discussion until the next day if some things are unclear. It may take more than one visit to conclude a deal successfully. Kazakhs bargain hard for the contract they want, but generally keep their word when it has been given.

How to Empathize with Kazakhs

- ✦ Talk about Kazakhstan rather than Central Asia in general.
- ✦ Be hearty, generous and jovial.
- ✦ Feast and drink with them as much as you are able.
- ✦ Attend local or regional ceremonies; learn about their customs and folklore.
- ✦ Know something about horses.

+ Display any physical prowess or skills you may have.
+ Praise their significant cultural heritage.
+ Develop friendships—Kazakhs are staunch, loyal friends once trust has been established.
+ Do what you have promised to do.
+ Let them see benefits are mutual.
+ Be modest about your abilities but let them see your expertise.

Uzbekistan

Uzbekistan has a relatively large population in comparison with the other Central Asian republics. Although independent since 1991, it remains in some ways the least changed of the former Soviet republics. The Communist Party was renamed and the country is still run largely as a command economy, with farmers obliged to sell their products to the state at well below world market prices. Central Asians regard Uzbeks as "businesspeople" who are enjoying increasing cultural autonomy, and there is a growing and aggressive Uzbek imperialism, especially felt in Tajikistan, where 20 percent of citizens are Uzbeks. Industry is relatively modern in Uzbekistan. Oil and gas are of major importance, and the country is the world's third largest producer of cotton.

Culture

Values

Islamic tenets
fierce independence and sense of history
admiration for physical strength and skill
love of horses
poetic talent
anti-Russian
Western orientation

respect for scholars
business sense
dynamism
opportunism
superiority over other Central Asians
respect for elders

Concepts

Leadership and Status

The current dictatorship is long-lived and hardly encourages freewheeling or innovative leadership at any level. A generation of younger managers is emerging with an increasing familiarity of U.S. management style due to the American presence on Uzbek soil. Democracy is probably a long way off, but Uzbeks learn quickly and are known for their opportunism.

Space and Time

"Distance of comfort" is closer than that of Americans and Northern Europeans, but greater than that of Latins. Uzbeks give more space to Westerners than to other Central Asians.

Like most Central Asians, Uzbeks have a relaxed attitude toward time, but increased contact with the West, particularly with the Americans during and after the war in Afghanistan, has made them more time-conscious. Among Central Asians, they are the most punctual.

Cultural Factors in Communication

Communication Pattern

Uzbeks are more outspoken than most other Central Asians and have a confidence born of business dealings over many centuries. Other Central Asians regard them as cunning, voluble and clever in the use of speech. They begin in a polite manner, with the usual courtesies, but show extreme caution in phrasing their proposals. Even in purely social situations they are noted for their circumspection. They are nobody's fools and can be cynical at times. They are very experienced commercially and must be addressed with a certain amount of sophistication. After several decades of Soviet preaching, they are very wary of empty "officialese." Normally suspicious of foreigners, they also exhibit some Muslim defensiveness. Other Central Asians, who respect their patience and persistence, feel that they must be constantly on guard against their savoir faire. Uzbeks are certainly eloquent, dynamic and very loquacious when dealing with each other.

Listening Habits

Uzbeks are less patient when listening than other Central Asians and may interrupt.

Behavior at Meetings and Negotiations

Uzbeks are used to lively, often noisy meetings, where everyone seems to talk at once. Their arguments are circular rather than linear, as they wish to examine all aspects of a proposal or project. They often wish to revisit issues that you may think have been settled. They like personal attention and wish to think that you are doing business on a personal basis, as opposed to formal discussion between companies. They will use praise and flattery and expect you to do the same.

Uzbeks may well be excited about modern developments in Uzbekistan and are ready to exploit any opportunities offered by Westerners. They are opportunists by nature and will try to extract know-how, technology and business secrets from partners/opponents at minimum cost to themselves. Care must be taken not to surrender leverage. It is wise to have an adequate entertainment budget, as meetings are normally interspersed with socializing and feasting. You need to be careful not to appear too naïve or gullible in relaxed interludes with Uzbeks. They are watchful and vigilant; they pounce on any contradictory remarks you may make. Do not let them take advantage of you at any time; if you do, they will press for more. Between their talkative (often noisy) sessions, they often lapse into noncommittal silences to disorient you. But in the end, remember that they are flexible, though they take great pains to disguise this.

Increasing contact with Westerners causes Uzbeks to adhere more closely to written contracts than previously. Formerly agreements were often made on an oral basis (a handshake) and generally respected in the main. That said, their innate opportunism also encourages them to seek renegotiation of any contract they feel is becoming less favorable to them because of changing circumstances.

How to Empathize with Uzbeks

+ Be dignified but canny at the same time.
+ Share your know-how generously but don't give away too much.
+ Praise Uzbeks over Kazakhs and other neighbors.
+ Avoid being too political.
+ Express enthusiasm about their rich cultural heritage.
+ Socialize energetically.
+ Establish good contacts and relations with older men.
+ Visit places of historical interest and learn their history.
+ Show sincerity at all times.
+ Be prepared to invest (for mutual benefit).
+ Be courteous and protect everyone's face.
+ Apply pressure only indirectly.
+ Use flattery when appropriate.
+ Never rush them.
+ Respect their spiritual values.

Azerbaijan

Azerbaijan is a small country the size of Austria, adjoining the Caspian Sea in a strategic position between Europe and Asia. Its neighbors are Russia, Georgia, Armenia and Iran. Across the Caspian, it faces Kazakhstan and Turkmenistan. One of its provinces—Nakhchivan—is separated from the main part by Armenia. The province of Nagorno-Karabakh (inhabited mostly by Armenians) is still disputed territory.

Two million people live in Baku, Azerbaijan's capital—an attractive modern city on the Caspian, though pollution is a problem. The Caspian Sea is rich in oil and gas. It also holds most of the world's sturgeon.

Like most of its neighbors in the Caucasus region, Azerbaijan was ruled periodically by many invaders, including Arabs, Turks, Persians, Mongols and Russians. As part of Russia since 1828, Azerbaijan became a Soviet republic in 1920. Just before the dissolution of the Soviet Union, Azerbaijan declared its independence in 1991. The Aliyev dynasty, father and son, have ruled the country ever since. Although the Arabs introduced the Arabic language in the seventh century A.D., and though Russian became prevalent in Soviet times, the Azeri language is currently the only official one, resembling modern Turkish in structure. This Turkic language enables Azeris to converse freely with Turks, Kazakhs and Uzbeks, as well as the inhabitants of Kyrgyzstan and Turkmenistan.

Apart from its ventures into oil exploration, Azerbaijan has featured in world news mainly on account of its war with Armenia over the sovereignty of Nagorno-Karabakh. The fate of this region is still undecided. The construction of an important oil pipeline from Baku to the southern coast of Turkey has enhanced the country's revenues since 2006.

The official language is Azeri, which can be written in Latin letters. Russian is widely used. The use of English is increasing among younger Azeris.

Culture

Religion

Over 95 percent of Azeris are Shiite Muslims, though a generally secular attitude toward religion enables Azeris to enjoy local vodka and other alcoholic drinks. Islamic tenets are observed in moderation. Eating pork and the use of the left hand are forbidden, but Islamic headscarves are rare and may not be worn by girls in secondary schools.

Kyrgyzstan

Kyrgyzstan occupies the western end of the Tian Shan mountain range and is one of the world's most rugged and mountainous areas. The Kyrgyz live mostly in rural communities, while Russians, Tartars and Uzbeks dominate the cities. The Kyrgyz are anti-Uzbek, due to past brutalities when the latter ruled the country in the nineteenth century, but they harbor no hostility toward the Kazakhs, who share a common history. There is a solid anti-Russian tradition, and the Kyrgyz have alienated many Russians (many of them have left) by their refusal to accept Russian as an official language. Kyrgyzstan has sought to establish strong relations with Turkey and wishes to establish democracy along the lines of the Turkish model.

Turkmenistan

Turkmenistan has a small population but vast reserves of gas. Created in 1924, it has a unique position among former Soviet Muslim republics. At present it is a tribal confederation rather than a modern nation. Turkmen Muslim society differs from others of Central Asia by the vitality of various social customs and traditions: sex discrimination, the persistence of polygamy and various traditional marital customs, such as the early marriage of girls, marriage by abduction, *karshylyk* marriages (a sister and a brother married to a brother and a sister), frequent religious marriages, and refusal to let Turkmen girls marry outside the tribe.

Turkmen nationalism is of the most pronounced anti-Russian character. The Turkmen consider themselves different from the other Central Asian Turks, but there are no anti-Uzbek or anti-Kazakh trends in Turkmen nationalism.

Tajikistan

Since the Second World War there is a growing sense among Tajik intelligentsia of their kinship with the Tajiks of Afghanistan and even with the Shia Iranians. Tajiks resent the pushy Uzbeks (fueled by their memory that some of the hallowed cities of Central Asian culture—Samarkand, Bukhara and Khiva—formerly belonged to them). The Tajiks are the most religious of the Central Asian nationalities.

49

Turkey

Turkey, an applicant for EU membership, would make quite an impact if it were to enter. To begin with, it would be by far the biggest country, being approximately three times the size of the U.K. and Italy and outsizing France, Spain and Germany by more than 50 percent. It would be second in population after Germany. It is the leader of a Turkic-speaking trading bloc of six former Russian-dominated Central Asian republics, and most of the country is not in Europe. Furthermore, Turkey has not fully satisfied European standards on human rights. It is no wonder that EU members want to take a deep breath before approving entry. Yet where else can Kemal Atatürk's modern, industrializing, secular NATO nation (which, remember, joined the West during the Korean and Gulf wars) go?

Anyone who has been to Turkey could hardly fail to notice how dissimilar it is from other Muslim states. The nation's modern character is largely the result of the influence of its founder, Kemal Atatürk. The first president of Turkey was born in 1881 in Salonika, then an Ottoman city. In 1905 Mustafa Kemal, as he was then known, graduated from the War Academy in Istanbul. In 1915, when the Dardanelles campaign was launched, he had reached the rank of colonel.

The War of Independence from the Ottomans began in 1919 when Kemal, then a general, rallied a liberation army in Anatolia and convened a congress. This was the forerunner of the Grand National Assembly, which was inaugurated in April 1920 with Mustafa Kemal elected president. He set about transforming his country with unabated zeal, creating a new political and legal system, abolishing the Caliphate and making both government and education secular. The Islamic calendar was replaced by the Western calendar, Western hats were worn instead of the fez and women stopped wearing the veil.

In 1934 the Turkish parliament gave Kemal the name Atatürk, which means "father of the Turks." His emphasis on secularism continues today. "Turkey is not a land of sheikhs, dervishes, disciples and lay brothers," he declared, having developed a lasting hatred for religious fundamentalism. He saw Westernization and return to Turkish roots as being entirely compatible, inasmuch as Islam was tolerated as a religion but banned as a lifestyle.

Culture

Values

belief in one's own honesty, reliability	hospitality, gallantry
Western-oriented	warmth, likeability
modified Islamic tenets	preservation of heritage
fierceness, tenacity	male dominance
national pride	adherence to Kemal Atatürk's reforms
macho traits	suspicion of Greeks

Concepts

Leadership and Status

In the Ottoman Empire and for most of Turkish history, power has been concentrated in a few hands. Sultans and Caliphs were all-powerful, and autocratic leadership was a fact of life. Kemal Atatürk changed all that and founded a democratic republic that, in spite of many troubled periods, has worked as well as many other theoretical democracies. It is true that the army has acted undemocratically on some occasions, seeing itself as "the guardian of the nation," but after each coup it has handed control back to civilians. Atatürk gave women the vote in 1934, and there has been one female prime minister. Still, women have a long way to go to achieve parity, and their position is often under threat from Islamic fundamentalists.

Space and Time

Turkey is a large country with a low population density. There is generally a "distance of respect" of more than one meter between speakers. Having said that, Mediterranean Turks are somewhat tactile among friends (this is usually confined to one's own sex). In many towns and villages, men dancing with men is a common spectacle. Foreigners are often invited to participate—don't be shy!

Things take time in Turkey and people turn up late for appointments. Istanbul—the largest urban sprawl in Europe—is not easy to move around in, and many delays originate from traffic problems.

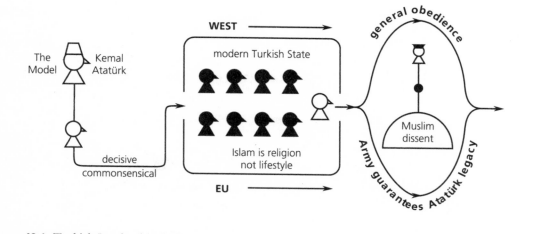

Figure 49.1 Turkish Leadership Style

Cultural Factors in Communication

Communication Pattern

The Turkish communication style derives from its three main roots: Islamic, Mediterranean and Eastern (Ottoman, Seljuk). The first two are sources of their liveliness—they are in the main both multi-active and dialogue-oriented. The third (Eastern) strand is, however, clearly visible—they are more reactive than any Europeans, except perhaps the Finns, and could also be classified as a listening culture, akin to several Central Asian republics as well as some Confucian societies. (reactive cultures let the other side speak first and slowly try to modify their reply or position to fit in with their interlocutor.)

In business circles their style is exploratory—they are very interested in all forms of change that lead to progress. They are polite and courteous (more than Westerners), but they wish to be seen as Western and modern. They show natural exasperation at being rejected by the West, but they are patient and persistent in trying to open and maintain acceptable communication channels.

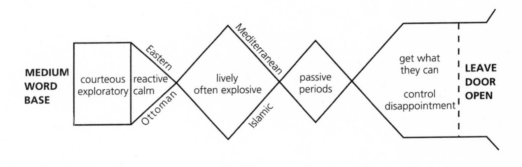

Figure 49.2 Turkish Communication Pattern

Listening Habits

As reactives, Turks are good listeners, wishing desperately to learn from Western colleagues. They control their Mediterranean ebullience and their Islamic righteousness to the extent that they normally refrain from interrupting their interlocutor. Nor do they try to speak over him or her in the French or Arab manner. They listen with some skepticism, but generally impute best motives and are rarely unreasonable unless they feel that they are being duped.

Behavior at Meetings and Negotiations

Meetings are usually conducted in a friendly, semiformal atmosphere. As hosts, Turks are extremely polite and solicitous. They are by no means inexperienced at negotiating, given their immense exposure to trading in the vast, enduring Ottoman Empire. Haggling is

Figure 49.3 Turkish Listening Habits

normal for them and they are disappointed if it does not ensue. Starting prices bear little relation to the intrinsic value of items. Turkish salespeople who are beaten down, or simply rejected, keep their cool, showing no signs of anger or annoyance. Doors are kept open for future deals.

Turks are willing to take risks in business, though they exercise a natural caution when investing in new and sizeable projects. Looking at markets, they know the value of their geographic location ("the bridge between East and West").

Manners and Taboos

Turks are very accommodating people, but they can easily be put off when encountering indelicate responses. They do not wish to discuss things Greek, but have few other national prejudices. The Kurdish question is, of course, delicate and best avoided by foreigners.

Islamic customs prevail in rural areas, but they are much more relaxed than in Arab countries and often invisible in the big cities. Turkish food and coffee are unique; enjoy them. Turks also produce and drink wine, as well as their own strong spirit, *raki*. Men wear ties less frequently than in European countries, though dress for both men and women is, in the main, typically Western.

How to Empathize with Turks

A golden rule would be to see them as they are, not as they are described in misleading accounts. They want respect and recognition. They want to play ball. If you refrain from attacking the current shortcomings of Turkish society, if you believe that Turks are doing their best to cooperate and put their house in order, if you place trust in them and exercise patience, you may end up with extremely reliable and (one day) very influential friends.

MOTIVATION

KEY	*Help to enter EU*
Cross-century mood	◆ Anxiety to gain entry to the EU is the number one concern. Where else should they go? ◆ They wish the West would realize that they are not Arabs or Iranians and do not wish to form an economic or political (or Islamic) bloc with them. They want to face west. ◆ There is a growing awareness that Europe links EU entry with the human rights question. The Kurdish problem is extremely thorny. ◆ If the cultural gap could be bridged, Turkey would strengthen Europe considerably.

Motivating Factors

◆ Show sympathy for Turkey's European aspirations.
◆ Exhibit solidarity as often as possible.
◆ Show early trust and warmth. Socialize with them.
◆ Respect their religion, even though the state is secular.
◆ Keep calm at all times.
◆ Try to show them the way to profit and other benefits.
◆ Praise Turkish hospitality and eat, drink and socialize with them.
◆ Speak a few words of Turkish.
◆ Respect older people.
◆ Allow for some ambiguity.
◆ Give them room to express their opinions.

Avoid

◆ Diminishing their dignity.
◆ Expressing strong opinions until you know theirs.
◆ Discussing the position of women.
◆ Discussing Greece or Cyprus.
◆ Referring to Turkish cruelty or aggressiveness in the Ottoman period.

50

Iran

This sizeable country (1,648,000 square kilometers/628,000 square miles) is largely a plateau averaging 1,200 meters (3,940 feet) in elevation. It attracted migrating Indo-Europeans, then occupying Europe, as early as 2000 B.C. Another Indo-European invasion took place (from the Caucasus Mountains) around 1000 B.C.; this introduced iron, copper and horses, thereby strengthening the area. These factors, as well as an extreme climate that has engendered a tough, vigorous populace, have enabled Persians to enjoy dominance of the region up to modern times.

The Pahlavi monarchy (the Shah) was overthrown in 1979, and the Islamic Republic of Iran was established and endorsed by a universal referendum a month later. Ayatollah Khomeini emerged as the undisputed leader. Rule by religious leaders has continued into the twenty-first century. In economic terms, it is important to understand that currently the Iranians are cautious about signing large new contracts with foreign firms. There are big differences in attitude between the private and the public sectors: whereas trade with the private sector can be fast, mobile and present-oriented, the state has put on the brakes and is more long-term and future-oriented in the types of businesses it will consider. Priorities for acceptance of projects are a willingness on the part of the Western company to invest now—with little financial help from Iran—and reap the rewards later; to create employment for Iranians; and to produce products in Iran that can also be exported to other countries in the region.

Culture

Values

Iranian, or Persian, culture goes back more than 3,000 years, and Iranians proudly adhere to their traditions and to their sense of leadership and power south of the Caspian. While Muslim, they identify little with the numerous Arab states in the Gulf, and they carried on an inconclusive but economically damaging war with Iraq that ended in 1987. Their cultural classification is multi-active and dialogue-oriented, although they are much less loquacious than Arabs. (See Chapter 3 for an explanation of these terms.)

Islamic faith and values, spirituality	hospitality
new technology, research, invention	family
neighborliness	design and pattern

traditional music and literature	seriousness, dignity
caution in decision making	academic achievement
respect for the wisdom of the old	respect for the Islamic role of women
politeness and clemency	their cultural achievements

Concepts

Leadership and Status

In general terms, spiritual leadership is dominant. When the spiritual leader Ayatollah Khomeini decided that it was time for the Shah to step down, support was massive and immediate (over 98 percent). In business, the leader may be identified as the last person to enter the room at a meeting, and he (and it will be a "he") will sit in the middle. Alternatively, he may show his hospitality by greeting the visitors at the entrance to the room.

Academic achievement is of high importance: in government the Iranian leader must be a "fully qualified theologian," selected by "experts." In business, education and specialized knowledge give managers status. Managers may have been educated in the West as well as in Iran.

Space and Time

Iranians keep their distance more than Arabs; they are used to this, as the population density is considerably lower than general in the region. They are perhaps somewhat more punctual than Arabs and would claim to have a greater respect for other people's time. Lack of punctuality in Tehran may be blamed, justifiably, on the traffic.

Cultural Factors in Communication

Communication Pattern

Iranians are talkative (although they appear taciturn to their more talkative neighbors) but respect dignity and seriousness of intent in speech. They can be loquacious but are not idle chatterers, particularly in business. They have a strong sense of what is appropriate and courteous according to context. They are keen to draw contrasts between what is proper in polite society and situations and what is suitable for the marketplace. They can be persuasive and admire persuasiveness in others. They can tolerate small talk, particularly mutual praise of the hospitality of others, but they soon wish to turn to the heart of the matter, to show that they have a sharp intellect and to demonstrate that they have something to say.

Listening Habits

Iranians like to talk, but they will listen attentively if they think that their interlocutor has something new to say. They are greedy for technical know-how and, because of their admiration for "experts," will listen eagerly to the latest technological ideas. However, care should be taken not to give the impression that the West is superior, as they will respond very negatively if they feel that you lack respect for them or undervalue them. After all, they have a powerful sense of the superiority of their own spiritual values and wish to build a better future for themselves, through technology, without espousing values that they view as decadent and doomed to eventual failure.

Behavior at Meetings and Negotiations

Some sort of introduction is required before getting down to business: a good topic is praise for their hospitality and the arrangements made for you. However, they are keen to enter into serious negotiation fairly early on, and will signpost this quite clearly by asking directly for your purpose and intentions. They may evince a certain amount of suspicion until they are absolutely certain what the "real aim" of the negotiation is.

It is important to show how the business you are discussing will benefit Iran. Concentrate on this rather than on appearing too greedy or showing you know best. Listen carefully to what they say, as they are prepared to talk at length, and be prepared to analyze the underlying message later as it may not be immediately apparent. Ensure that what you offer them is absolutely the latest technology; they will not appreciate being offered anything they consider outdated. They are won over by solid information and are likely to take copious notes—so be careful not to contradict yourself later. Once you have won their trust and respect, more business may follow. Emphasize your company name; the fame and reputation of names is of great importance.

The Iranians are very persuasive and will expect you to persuade them in return. If at first they seem to respond negatively to an idea, this does not mean that you should give up. Try again, about three more times. They have immensely strong faith in their ideas and will expect you to have faith in yours. Giving up immediately would arouse suspicions of weakness or lack of conviction. This applies also to invitations—they love inviting and being invited, but will often refuse before accepting.

Iranians are eager to demonstrate that they have sharp minds unclouded by decadent Western vices such as alcohol and recreational drugs, and they will not admire vagueness or uncertainty in others. Contracts and agreements should be short but complete; Iranians do not appreciate long-windedness. Be prepared for differences in approach from those managers who have been educated in the West and those whose education has been in Iran. It may be easier to strike a chord with the former.

Remember that meetings may be broken by long prayer sessions, and that it is pointless to arrange business trips to Iran during Ramadan.

Manners and Taboos

+ Body language is reserved and limited compared to that of Arabs.
+ No alcohol.
+ Dietary restrictions (especially pork).
+ Don't shake a woman's hand.
+ Use of the left hand is forbidden for "clean" tasks.

How to Empathize with Iranians

The key is to show Iranians respect. A good way to demonstrate this positively might be to praise their cultural heritage, of which they are justifiably proud. They feel that they have a much richer culture than that of the Arab world, so any praise of their art, craftsmanship, design or architecture (perhaps the easiest areas to appreciate readily) would be welcome. They particularly admire craftsmanship that has been laborious and painstaking, as in their carpets and the interior decoration of their mosques.

Avoid humor unless you are absolutely certain that the context permits it. It is particularly important to avoid humor at the expense of others, as this is viewed as unkind. Do not smile too much: they don't.

MOTIVATION	
KEY	*Show them respect*
Cross-century mood	✦ Would like to modernize and acquire technology without losing their spiritual poise. ✦ They accept investment on the basis that rewards must come later. ✦ They welcome help in producing products in Iran that also can be exported. ✦ Women's movements are restricted but growing in strength.

Motivating Factors

+ Respect dignity and seriousness in speech.
+ Be persuasive—they admire this.
+ Acknowledge academic achievement, especially in theology.
+ Offer them technology without "cultural strings."
+ Praise their hospitality before getting down to business.
+ Indicate your purpose and intentions early on.

(continued)

MOTIVATION *(continued)*

+ Show that what you are proposing will benefit Iran.
+ Listen carefully for their real message.
+ Show kindness, gentleness, courtesy.

Avoid

+ Giving strong opinions on political subjects.
+ Discussion of Islamic taboos (alcohol, pork, etc.).
+ Too much body language (they are not Arabs).
+ Idle chatter.
+ Giving any gifts with a representation of the human face (considered idolatrous).
+ Contradicting yourself (they take notes).
+ Discussing the situation in Iraq unless they bring it up.

51

The Arab Countries

Westerners and Arabs have very different views about what is right and wrong, good and evil, logical and illogical, acceptable and unacceptable. They live in two different worlds, each organized in its own manner. Unless one gains a deeper understanding of how these two mindsets differ, one group will end up with an unfavorable impression of the other. Before we go further, it is important to define what makes an Arab. The answer: the Arabic language.

It is worthwhile, therefore, to list the main cultural divergences, which go a long way toward explaining why each side sees certain events in a completely different light. The following is only a summary:

+ The West sees Arab society as one that is in decline, propped up temporarily by oil revenues. The Arabs, by contrast, are very conscious that their civilization once led the world and believe that they are capable of doing so again (in a moral sense).

- The West generally separates church and state. Most Islamic countries do not, and religion strongly influences social behavior, politics and even business.
- In the West, the individual is the basic social unit; with the Arabs it is the family.
- In the West, status is gained by achievement; in the Arab world, by class.
- Westerners like to deal in cold facts; Arabs will not let facts destroy their honor.
- Westerners want to be fair, but just; Arabs want to be just, but flexible.
- The West believes in organizations and institutions; Arabs believe in people (guided by God).
- Westerners in principle wish to modernize. Arabs strive to find a way of adopting modern modes of behavior without disrupting the traditions they value.
- Most Western countries have succeeded in creating equality for men and women. Arabs believe the two sexes have vastly different personalities and roles.
- Western societies differ greatly in their world views. Arabs, by contrast, largely subscribe to the same tenets of morality.
- Westerners must appear to behave rationally; for Arabs, it is important to impress others with their integrity.
- Westerners respect the strong. In Arab societies the weak must be respected and protected, and piety is one of the most admirable qualities. This characteristic has been implanted by the Arabs into Spanish cultural attitudes.
- In the West, friends are good company. In the Arab world a friend is a person who cannot refuse your request; neither can you refuse his or hers.
- When introducing themselves, Westerners usually restrict the amount of information they give. Arabs tend to talk a lot about their family and connections.
- Westerners like to use official channels to further their business interests; Arabs use personal relationships.
- Arabs expect regular praise when they have done good work, and are more hurt by criticism than Westerners, who are content to keep their job.
- When negotiating, Westerners try to find logical conclusions, whereas Arabs use personalized arguments, appeals and persistent persuasion. Arabs stand or sit much closer to their interlocutor than does a Westerner. It is normal for Arabs to breathe on each other and touch each other frequently.
- Arabs are less private than Westerners. Visiting and long conversations are frequent.
- Men and women mingle freely in Western societies; in most Arab countries they do not. Muslim sexuality is territorial; women trespassing in public places (male spaces) are expected to wear a veil to make themselves invisible. They are rarely seen by Westerners indoors.
- Hospitality is more effusive, even to strangers, in the Arab world than in the West. They have the tradition of "open house." A Bedouin will supposedly kill his last camel to feed his guest.

✦ Westerners, especially Swiss, Swedes and other Northern Europeans, arrive on time to dinner and other appointments. Arabs are much more relaxed in their timing. Social occasions or business meetings need not have fixed beginnings or endings.

✦ Unlike Westerners, Arabs prefer arranged marriages, which on the whole are very stable, involving mutual respect.

✦ Pork is taboo to Muslim Arabs, unlike in the West.

The British, Americans and Northern Europeans will realize that they and Arabs are at the two extremes of the monochronic–polychronic scale; therefore, communication will not take place in a natural manner. The exigencies of the Muslim religion complicate the interchange of ideas even further. Yet Arabs are used to dealing with foreigners and readily forgive them for not behaving like Arabs. You will even be forgiven for behaving like an infidel, as long as you make certain modifications. The most important thing is to avoid saying or doing anything they consider insulting or derogatory. This includes drinking alcohol, dressing improperly, being overly familiar with the few women they allow you to meet, and challenging the basic concepts of Islam. Foreign women are accepted without veils provided they dress conservatively. They may go shopping and travel alone but should avoid all-male cafés (which is most of them).

Arabs are looking for sincerity in your dealings with them and expect to be shown the same respect they show you. If you come across as sincere and true, you will have no problem. The natural tendency of Northern Europeans, Americans and Canadians to look down on multi-active behavior (talkativeness, invasion of privacy, poor time keeping, demonstrative body language) must be firmly suppressed, as the Arabs are not going to change their personality.

It is virtually impossible for multi-active people, especially Arabs, to act like Nordics or Americans. The only solution, therefore, is for the linear-active foreigner to make some concessions in the direction of extroversion. Many find this difficult, even painful, but the rewards for doing so can be considerable. To begin with, you must stand much closer to an Arab when talking to him than you would with a Briton or a German. If you keep your distance, the Arab will think you find his physical presence distasteful or that you are a particularly cold individual. Arabs speak volubly and earnestly to someone they like, so you must attempt to do the same. They are very dependent on eye contact, so take your sunglasses off when talking to them and look them right in the eye (normally not difficult). Northerners may be uncomfortable with flattery or professions of friendship, but Arabs love these utterances; therefore, you should not hesitate to praise their countries, their arts, their dress and their food (but not their women!).

When talking business with Arabs, remember that relationships are intensely personal. You want to do the business, but above all you want to do it with the person you are talking with, in whom you must always show close personal interest. If the Arab boasts about his connections and network, he is showing you the value of personal relationships, and if his uncle is influential in a government department (or is the minister), he will expect you to take delight in the possibility of that influence being helpful in the furthering of your business. Do not appear detached and reluctant to accept favors. Your Arab friend will ask favors of you in due course.

Because the family structure is of paramount importance in Arab life, you should pay close attention to all family members your Arab colleague introduces you to. You should inquire regularly about the health (and happiness) of his brothers, uncles, cousins and sons; it is a sure (and easy) way to gain your Arab friend's affection and loyalty. When visiting his country it is appropriate to take gifts for all these relatives, but do not expect Arabs to open the gifts in front of you.

At mealtimes, eat only with your right hand, take only the food that is offered to you and, while you must praise the food, do not pay too much attention to those who have cooked it. Do not ask to meet the cooks (wives, mothers or sisters) who have labored so long over the preparation of your meal. Your hosts will offer you the best morsels to eat, which you must accept. They will force too much on you; you will have to overeat a little in order not to upset them. You are not expected to talk much at mealtimes, so in that sense, a meal can be a welcome break.

Returning to the subject of words, not only do you have to speak *more* when you are with Arabs, but you have to step up the *volume* as well. Loudness of voice, rising pitch and tone, even shouting, all denote sincerity in Arab discourse. You may find this very hard to do, but try your best. Remember the Gulf War took place partly because President Bush (Senior) spoke softly and Saddam did not believe that he meant what he said (about declaring war, etc.). In Arab society it is quite normal to use speech in a rhetorical, almost aggressive manner to make a point clearly. Arabs are great admirers of eloquence, and if you can aspire to eloquence in their presence, they will take it as a sign of education, refinement and sincerity, no matter how verbose it may sound in your own ears.

Oaths are quite common in Arabic, so even if you slip in one of your less vehement ones when you get excited, it would not sound offensive to Arabs, who bring Allah into their arguments in almost every conversation. Arabs do not like discussing unpleasant matters such as illness, misfortune, accidents or death; do not introduce any. They are even reluctant to tell you bad news about business, so bear this in mind when everything looks rosy. Connected with this habit is the Arab tendency to use euphemisms. Someone who is sick is described as "tired," teachers magically become "professors" and slums are referred to as "low-cost dwellings."

Arabs have great respect for the written word, especially if it has a religious connotation. Do not wrap up anything in an Arabic-language newspaper—it might have Allah's name on it. If you handle a copy of the Koran, you should show it even more respect than a Japanese business card.

We have referred earlier to the Arab concept of the "open house," where visitors may gain access at all times. In the twentieth century the concept or tradition was extended to include "open office." This may sound friendly enough, but things can become chaotic if you have the first appointment. Northerners expect to be guaranteed some kind of privacy while they discuss business matters. In England and Germany, secretaries do not allow bosses to be disturbed by new arrivals during the course of a meeting. Even in Portugal, Spain, South

America and Sicily, newcomers are often asked to wait. In Arab countries they are shown straight into the office, according to the age-old tradition. Northern Europeans, Americans and Canadians, who normally expect the privilege of speaking without interruption, soon become nonplussed as anywhere up to half a dozen Arab visitors join your "private" meeting.

Not only will you be uncomfortable hearing several people speak at the same time, but you will also stand little chance of making your sober tones heard in the general hubbub. Arabs shout and speak loudly for dramatic effect or out of pure joy at seeing friends. They also seem to have the knack of absorbing three or four conversations at once. Even more problematic is how to proceed with the proposals you have traveled so far to present. Making an appointment for the next day is of no help, since the number of interruptions is unlikely to be fewer. Recently I asked the commercial counselor at one of the embassies in Abu Dhabi how to solve this dilemma. He answered as follows: You have to maneuver your chair so that you are sitting right next to the man you are doing business with. On the other side of his desk is not close enough—you have to be no more than a foot away and nearer to him than anybody else. When you have secured this position, you then shout into his right or left ear, depending on which side you are on. You continue to pound his ear with your propositions until he agrees with them. He is unlikely to give any trouble as he is suffering from numerous distractions from various angles, and acquiescence is usually the easiest way out. Enterprising multi-actives, such as Italians, often push documents to sign in front of the Arab in these circumstances. You may be unable to do this, but modesty will get you nowhere.

In conclusion, although the cultural gulf yawns wide, there is a fair chance you can make a favorable impression. Arabs admire education and expertise and welcome representatives of small countries who show less arrogance than the Americans, French and British. A Nordic or Dutch person will never be completely comfortable with Arab loquacity, subjectivity, lax sense of punctuality and fatalism, but they can make progress in their relations with Arabs by showing keen personal interest in them, praising and flattering rather than criticizing, memorizing the basic tenets of Islam, dressing smartly, receiving and extending favors without qualms, showing great respect for old people and traditions and being very flexible and relaxed at all times.

MOTIVATION	
KEY	*Showing compassion*
Cross-century mood	◆ Arabs are acutely conscious of their former historical glory and believe their moral leadership is still important in the future. ◆ Their new-found wealth (oil) may continue to aid them in this goal. ◆ They are content with the fast growth of Islam (e.g., in countries such as the U.S. and the U.K.) and foresee Islam as a great cultural force in the twenty-first century.

(continued)

MOTIVATION (continued)

Motivating Factors

+ Show interest in Islam.
+ Show Arabs as much respect as they show you.
+ Come across as sincere and true.
+ Make concessions in the direction of extroversion.
+ Be intensely personal.
+ Offer friendship as well as business opportunities.
+ Reciprocate favors.
+ Take gifts for your Arab colleague and his male relatives.
+ Always impute the best motives.
+ Bargain in a friendly manner—Arabs expect it.
+ Always appear just in their eyes.
+ Show kindness, compassion and moral integrity.
+ Speak confidently, without hesitation.
+ Minimize the importance of punctuality.

Avoid

+ Being reluctant to accept favors.
+ Saying anything that might be construed as insulting or derogatory.
+ Questioning Islamic taboos (alcohol, pork, use of left hand, discussion of related females).
+ Discussing Israel or Iraq.
+ Expressing a wish to be left alone in the evenings when in their country.

Differences among Arabs

Arabs behave in a strikingly similar manner everywhere in the huge swathe of territory stretching from Mauritania and Morocco in the west to Oman, Yemen and the Gulf States in the east. Although these countries lack political unity, Arab nationalism exists alongside, for instance, Egyptian or Iraqi nationalism. They are in a sense a cultural unit, bound by a common language, Arabic, and a major religion, Islam. Whereas a French person might say, "I am first a Frenchman and then a European," an Arab might say he is first and foremost an Arab and then a Syrian or an Algerian.

Various Arab countries have attempted some form of unification, most notably in 1958, when Egypt, Syria and Yemen formed the short-lived United Arab Republic. While political unity would strengthen the Arab cause, Arab leaders have rarely managed to speak with one voice; meetings of the Arab League are often scenes of dissension and even chaos. This is partly because peoples such as desert Bedouins, commercially minded Lebanese and Abu Dhabi oil executives differ wildly in their national and individual agendas. Significantly, even the common bond of Islam has contributed little toward unity in practical terms, not least because most Muslims are not Arabs (Turks living in Germany would have little sympathy with the aspirations of Algerian fundamentalists or Indonesian insurgents).

Consequently, when making comparisons of the cultures of the Arab lands, you encounter enduring similarities and familiar reactions, but also regional differences caused by variation in geography, economics, governmental structure and historical background. The following descriptions of the individual Arab countries will, hopefully, point out some of the distinctions.

Algeria

Algeria is the third most populous Arab country and the second biggest in area after the Sudan. Most of the population are Berbers and speak Berber as well as Arabic and, to a large degree, French. A strong nationalist spirit is evident, a result of the long struggle for independence from France. Unfortunately, the country has not enjoyed much political stability since its independence from France. Many years of one-party socialist rule was ended in 1989 by a new constitution, which allowed for multiparty rule. When the Islamic fundamentalists seemed sure to win, the army took power. There have been nearly two decades of violence and political unrest since. Two-thirds of Algeria is desert. Half the population works in agriculture in the northern coastal region. Unemployment is high (often 20 percent), and many thousands of males have immigrated to France. Industry is, however, significant inasmuch as Algeria is one of the world's largest producers of liquefied natural gas. Oil production has declined in recent years. GDP per capita is average for Arab countries. There is a growing managerial class, but women are not very active in the workforce. Veils are more common than in neighboring Tunisia or Morocco.

Although 99 percent of Algerians are Muslim, they are influenced by the French in certain aspects of social life. Wine is not taboo except among extreme fundamentalists, and the country actually had the fifth highest wine production in the world in the 1960s. Algerian athletes have consistently achieved success at the Olympic Games.

Bahrain

Bahrain is the smallest Arab state in terms of both population and area (only 1,000 square kilometers/300 square miles). It is actually an archipelago of 33 islands, all tiny, sandy and low-lying, with Manama, the capital, located on the largest island, Bahrain Island.

Prosperity came to Bahrain on account of the discovery of oil and natural gas. It was the first Gulf state to produce oil, which accounts for more than 50 percent of the country's revenues. Cheap gas supplies are also abundant and provide the basis for the country's promising aluminum smelting industry.

Bahrain has wisely used its oil revenues—its reserves are significantly smaller than those of neighboring states—to develop service industries that will probably provide the basis for the country's future prosperity. Tourism is important (most visitors are Arabs), and the construction of the King Fahad Causeway connecting Bahrain to Saudi Arabia greatly enhanced the hotel trade. Bahrain is an important trading center for the Gulf and one of the most influential banking and financial centers in the Middle East. The government has also introduced dry dock services and light engineering projects.

In spite of its affluence and current progress, Bahrain faces some internal and local problems. The even split between Sunni and Shia followers gives rise to the usual tensions in this area. Also, the state has an ongoing dispute with Qatar over the sovereignty of the oil-rich Hawar Island.

In Bahrain health and education programs are well-established, and women enjoy both university schooling and opportunities for a career. In contrast to Qatar and the United Arab Emirates (UAE), Bahrain's workforce is largely native. Fewer than half of its workers are immigrants. GDP per capita is the fourth highest in the Arab world, after Qatar, UAE and Kuwait.

Egypt

Egypt, with almost exactly 1,000,000 square kilometers (626,000 square miles), is only the twelfth largest African country, but it is the third most populous after Nigeria and Ethiopia. With over 90 million people, it has a population considerably bigger than the United Kingdom or France and is easily the most populous of the Arab lands (followed by Sudan with just over 40 million). One-third of all Arabs are Egyptian, and the capital of Egypt, Cairo, is crowded with over 32,000 people per square kilometer (75,000 people per square mile). Its 20 million inhabitants make it Africa's largest city. Most of Egypt is desert, and almost all the people live in the Nile Valley or in the delta, alongside the Suez Canal.

The Egyptian state was one of the very earliest urban and literate societies. Its culture had an important influence on both ancient Israel and ancient Greece, which subsequently helped to form the civilization of the modern West. Egypt also provided Africa with its first developed civilization and had considerable influence on many African cultures.

Perhaps the first and most important quality that has typified this civilization has been continuity. In every aspect of Egyptian life, in every manifestation of its culture, a deep conservatism can be observed. This clinging to the traditions and ways of earlier generations was the particular strength of the Egyptians. Life in the Nile Valley was determined to a great extent by the behavior of the river itself. The pattern of rising and falling water, of high Nile and low Nile, established the Egyptian year and controlled the lives of the Egyptian farmers—and most Egyptians were tied to a life on the land—from birth to death, from century to century. On the seasonal behavior of the Nile rested the prosperity, the very continuity, of the land.

In a sense Egypt was an island, cut off from other habitable lands—to the north by the sea and in all other directions by deserts. Being thus isolated, it was both protected from invasion and insulated from external influences. This isolation contributed in no small degree toward the conservative, inward-looking character of the Egyptians. For the Egyptians there could be no doubt that their country was quite distinct; it was a universe on its own, unrelated to other lands abroad. To be away from Egypt was to be divorced from reality; being an Egyptian meant living in Egypt, worshipping Egyptian gods (who had nothing to do with the world outside), dying and, above all, being buried in Egypt. Egyptian techniques in working materials were in many respects different from those practiced elsewhere in the ancient world; artistic methods and conventions, established at the very beginning of the Dynastic Period, were quite peculiar to Egypt; even Egyptian writing, the hieroglyphic script, was a medium of communication developed specifically for the use of the language spoken in Egypt, and it was incapable of adaptation to the requirements of other languages.

On the practical level, the Egyptians were outstanding among the peoples of antiquity. In the techniques of stone working they particularly excelled. The Nile Valley served as a vast quarry from north to south, providing the building stone that Egyptian architects employed so magnificently. Working with simple but efficient tools, the Egyptian craftsmen mastered all available materials, while Egyptian artists wrought masterpieces in many media.

Modern Egypt is intensely aware of the splendor of its unique and ancient civilization. It considers itself the leader of the Arab world culturally (there are more films made and publications printed in Egypt than in other Arab countries). English is common, and there exists a dominant elite and a growing middle class. The education system is good, and women are largely integrated; there have been no veils for 100 years. Tourism is a vital industry, though 50 percent of Egyptians are farmers. Coptic Christians enjoy freedom of worship.

Jordan

Jordan is one of the Arab countries where Westerners feel most comfortable, certainly those who speak English, because English is widely spoken as a second language, and the British connections of the Jordanian Royal Family have been influential in maintaining a pro-Western atmosphere in general. Visitors are welcomed to the magnificent tourist attractions of Petra, Wadi Rum, Aqaba, Jerash, the Dead Sea and the bustling cosmopolitan capital of Amman.

Most Jordanian citizens are of Palestinian or Bedouin origin. More than 90 percent of Jordanians are Sunni Muslims; 5 percent are Christians. There have been very few religious disputes, tolerance being traditional in the country.

Although Jordan has only the sixth highest GDP in the Arab world, it is in the top ten or eleven of the Arab world in GDP per capita, and the population of just over 7 million is relatively prosperous. The education and health systems are good, and the level of literacy is rising rapidly. Women are very visible in the tourist industries, in offices, schools and hospitals. They dress mainly in Western styles and even eat in public restaurants in Amman with their men. Amman is increasing in popularity as a center for international conferences and functions effectively as a modern metropolis.

In spite of the country's modernization, due not only to British influence but also to the huge influx of worldly Palestinians (more than a million), Jordan remains essentially a conservative Islamic state, maintaining its tribal affiliations with the part of Saudi Arabia that forms most of Jordan's eastern border. The traditional Bedouin values of this area, including hospitality and stability, have been beneficial to domestic policies and to the thriving tourist industries near the Red Sea.

Kuwait

Kuwait is a small, low-lying state on the Persian Gulf, bordered by Iraq on the north and west and by Saudi Arabia to the south. It consists mainly of desert plains. Eight percent of the land is meadows; there is no arable land.

Kuwait, an independent state, was founded in the early eighteenth century. In 1899 it became a protectorate of the British, who thereafter managed its foreign relations and defense until the country became independent in 1961. The present dynasty of rulers, the Al-Sabah family, was established as early as 1756. The country is a monarchy, the amir being chosen from family members. No political parties are permitted, though several informal associations exist. The most traumatic event in modern Kuwaiti history was its invasion by Iraq in 1990. In the Gulf War, which the invasion precipitated, the U.S.-led alliance defeated the Iraqis, with support from various countries including Saudi Arabia, which also felt threatened.

Disputes over Kuwait territory are not new, and actually the origins of the 1991 Gulf War can be traced back to 100 years earlier, a story too complex to tell in its entirety here.

On June 19, 1961, the British government announced its recognition of the full independence of the sheikhdom; six days later the Iraqi prime minister claimed Kuwait as an integral part of Iraq, his argument being that Kuwait had been a part of the Ottoman Empire and that ethnically, geographically and socially, Kuwait and Iraq were one country that had been arbitrarily divided by Britain. Threatened with invasion, the ruler of Kuwait appealed to Britain for military aid. In early July, British troops landed in Kuwait, and on July 20 the Arab League admitted the sheikhdom to its membership, thus recognizing its independence and refusing to admit the Iraqi claim. Almost two years later, on May 14, 1963, Kuwait was admitted to the United Nations. Relations with Iraq meanwhile improved, and in October 1963 Iraq recognized Kuwait's independence.

Today Kuwaitis drink distilled seawater and live and work in air-conditioned surroundings. In and around the city are schools, hospitals and tall office buildings. Education, health care and transportation are virtually free. As of now, there are no taxes, though taxation may be considered in the future in view of the substantial budget deficit. Power, water and electricity are cheap—heavily subsidized by the government.

There is planning for still further expansion of public and civic facilities. Engineers, doctors, contractors and merchants from every corner of the earth can be seen busily at work in Kuwait. In fact, 80 percent of the workforce is foreign. The city is booming.

Behind all this dynamism is oil, 90 percent of Kuwait's exports. Both working conditions and wages are superior in Kuwait compared with surrounding countries. Many of the foreign personnel and almost all of the Anglo-Americans are connected with either the oil companies or the government's industrial development projects.

Oil dominates the economy and accounts for the incredibly high standard of living in this barren, desert country. The oilfields have largely recovered from the devastation caused by the Iraqi invasion.

Kuwait is still tribal, religious and conservative. There are strong class distinctions among native Kuwaitis. Kuwaiti women are allowed to work in the same environment as men, but in the markets and on the streets they are veiled. Many of them nevertheless are well-educated and often wealthy. Foreigners can feel at ease with Kuwaitis, who cooperate readily on most issues. Deep personal friendships, however, are not easy to come by.

Lebanon

It is difficult to find a country with a society as diverse and divisive as that of Lebanon. Although it is the third smallest Arab country (only 10,000 square kilometers/4,000 square miles), more than two dozen major religious groups as well as substantial ethnic minority communities live there.

Lebanon cannot be described in simple terms as an Arab Islamic state. Although almost 60 percent of the people are Muslims, Christians (over 40 percent) possess a larger proportion of the wealth and power. There are 14 or 15 Christian denominations, the Maronite sect being the largest. Adherents of the Druze religion (deriving from Islam) are also numerous. Muslims are divided almost equally between Sunni and Shia. Kurds and Armenians are the largest ethnic minorities.

This rich diversity has led to Lebanon's development as a kind of cosmopolitan and international "clearinghouse" for the Middle East. Prior to the civil war in 1975, the country was a regional leader in banking, commerce and tourism. Despite continuing hostility and the destruction of buildings and infrastructure, a considerable amount of individual wealth remains, and the network of overseas Lebanese living all over the world may yet facilitate the resurrection of many Lebanese service industries. The population, whatever their affiliations, are generally well-educated and skillful in a variety of commercial activities. The

Lebanese rival Jews and Armenians in their reputation for doing business. Women are very active in commerce and the civil service and are openly Westernized. Foreign investment is likely to return to the country, especially to Beirut (which was once the most important Arab city after Cairo) once the Arab-Israeli question has been satisfactory resolved. In all, the diverse and sophisticated features of Lebanese society make it a unique semi-Western country in the Middle East.

Libya

Libya, the fourth largest country in Africa after Algeria, Congo-Kinshasa and Sudan, has a population of nearly 7 million people. 90 percent of the country consists of the vast Sahara Desert, which receives only 2.5cm of rain per year. The land has no permanent rivers.

The country, scene of important desert battles between the Allied and Axis powers in the Second World War, is unique among North African nations, inasmuch as it was colonized not by the French or the British, but by the Italians.

Libya is somewhat paradoxical in several ways. Formerly extremely poor, the discovery of oil has led to a prosperous society, even at lower levels. Although Arab nationalism is strong and the West (who imposed sanctions) is denigrated, Libya sends over 10,000 university students to the United States and other Western seats of learning. The land is mainly desert, but until recently most of the population was engaged in farming. Sanctions formerly imposed by the West, on account of Libya's alleged support to terrorists, did not apply to oil; an embargo on this would have had an adverse effect on the economies of Italy, Spain and Germany.

Owing to the size of the country and its relatively sparse population, immigrants have been imported on a large scale, but because most of the foreign workers have come from Arab neighbors, society, in spite of some Western and Asian presence, has remained in the main Islamic and Arabic-speaking. Owing to the government's strong support of Arab nationalism, Libyans mingle less with Europeans than do their neighbors in Tunisia and Egypt.

Libya's earliest inhabitants were Berber tribes, who often refer to themselves as Imazighen. According to the Columbia Encyclopedia the Berber culture "derives from earlier than 2400 B.C." By the eighth century BCE Phoenicians were trading there, and subsequent invaders included the Greeks, the Romans (146 BCE), Vandals, the Byzantine Empire and Arabs (A.D. 40). The Arabization of Libya continued until the Ottoman Empire took control from the mid-1500s to the early 1900s.

Modern Libyan history dates from the Italian colonization in 1911. When Italy was defeated in the Second World War, Libya gained independence in 1951 under King Idris, who was friendly to the Allies. Oil was discovered in 1959 and in 1969 Muammar Gaddafi led a coup that resulted in his despotic rule until October 2011, when large-scale rebellions and foreign intervention ended in Gaddafi's capture and killing as he tried to escape.

After forty years of Gaddafi's one-man rule, Libya has experienced a confused sequence of attempts at establishing a democratic system of government. At various intervals, bodies such as, the General National Congress, the Libya Dawn Militia, the House of Representatives and (in 2016) the Government of National Accord have tried to gain authority and restore security. The terrorist group ISIS is still active at the time of writing and the general situation is unsettled.

In 2017 representatives of the EU met to tackle the Mediterranean migration crisis. The Libyan coast is the main departure point for African migrants heading for Europe. Over 5,000 deaths by drowning were recorded by 2016.

Mauritania

Sparsely populated Mauritania is the fifth largest Arab country (slightly bigger than Egypt), but it is last in GDP, which stands at just under $5 billion. This is because almost the entire area of Mauritania is desert, much of it completely uninhabitable. Only in the extreme south, where the waters of the Senegal River are sufficient to allow irrigation, is there arable land for farming. Year after year the Sahara Desert, aided by relentless droughts, continues to bury grazing land.

It is little wonder that interaction between Mauritanians and Westerners is minimal. Large numbers of people are forced to migrate to the few cities, such as the capital, Nouakchott, where social problems and food shortages oblige the government to concentrate on internal issues. Not that foreign policy has been without complications. When Spain withdrew from Western Sahara in the 1960s, Mauritania agreed on a division of that country with Morocco. The activity of Polisario guerrillas, however, caused the government to renounce its claim in 1979.

A multiparty democracy of sorts has been in existence since 1992. The economy, dependent on and hampered by the severe climatic conditions, is aided to some extent by mineral reserves of iron ore and copper in the north of the country, though income from the latter is greatly reduced because of depressed world prices.

The sudden discovery of oil in the country has helped. Until recently, Mauritania was not thought of as a promising area in oil production. But since the discovery of huge reserves of black gold in early 2004, much has changed. In January 2004, the Australian firm Woodside announced that the Chinguetti Oilfield could yield as much as 75,000 barrels of oil per day. Another oilfield promises a total of 287 million barrels.

Most of Mauritania's people are Sunni Muslims. The population is one of the youngest in the Arab world, the median age currently at 20 years. Mauritania is a member of the Organization of African Unity (OAU) and the Arab League.

Morocco

Situated in the northwest corner of Africa and separated from Spain by only a narrow strait 16 kilometers (10 miles) wide, Morocco is the Arab nation closest to the West in more senses than one. All educated Moroccans are bilingual in French and Arabic, and many in the northern part of the country speak Spanish. It was, moreover, from Morocco that the "Moorish" conquest of southwestern Europe from A.D. 711 to 1492 was launched, providing Andalusia and the Moors themselves with the most shining cultural civilization that the area has ever experienced.

In the year A.D. 1000, Córdoba was the greatest city in the world, far larger than London, Paris or Rome and far more advanced in art, science and civic splendor. The Córdoba medina contained 80,000 shops and workshops; in the city were 600 mosques, 300 baths, 50 hospitals, nearly 100 public schools, 17 colleges and universities and 20 public libraries. A population of one million enjoyed a high standard of living equaled in other centers in Seville, Granada, Toledo and impressive cities all the way across Southern Europe from Lisbon to Palermo. Nor was this a civilization that existed just for a moment in history. It began with the Moorish incursions into Spain in A.D. 711 and ended *781 years later* with the fall of Islamic Granada.

The Moroccan connection with Europe has continued. Massive emigration of males to France has made the Moroccan population in that country a significant ethnic factor. In Morocco itself, men and women dress in Western styles. There are many Christians of European origin in the country, and Jews number over 15,000. The veil is worn in public only by older women, mainly in rural areas. Religious tolerance persists, as it did in the days of Al-Andalus. Many of the Moroccans in the southern part of the country are of black African origin.

Their closeness and general friendliness to the West notwithstanding, Morocco is still basically a Muslim country. The royal family traces its descent from the Prophet Muhammad, and campaigns of "Moroccanization" are not unpopular. Most Moroccans are of Berber descent and nearly 40 percent of the people speak Berber in the northern highlands.

The economy has been subject to considerable liberalization in recent years and foreign investment is encouraged. Tourism strengthens Morocco's links with the West, and the country has some aspirations to eventually join the EU, though early membership is unlikely, especially if the exportation of illegal drugs continues.

Oman

Oman, with a territory of 310,000 square kilometers (119,500 square miles), is roughly the same size as Italy or Poland but is thinly populated (4.5 million). Most of the country is composed of deserts and mountains, and what agriculture exists is hampered by severe water shortages.

The economy was rescued in the late 1960s by the exploitation of the nation's oil reserves. Currently oil accounts for over 80 percent of export revenue. In 1989 important discoveries of gas were made; it is possible that gas will eventually surpass oil as a major asset.

Oman is a Muslim country where religious adherence is split: 25 percent are Sunni and 75 percent belong to the moderate Ibadi sect of Islam. Oman enjoys a good relationship with the neighboring Emirates but has had friction with the Yemenis in the south.

Most Omanis are Arabs (about 80 percent), but the population inhabiting Oman's coastal strip is an ethnocultural mixture consisting of over a million Indians, Baluchi and black Africans. Omani Arabs, though relatively prosperous, are not sufficiently rich to avoid manual labor. They are helped by over a million foreign workers from the Indian subcontinent and the Far East. Omani women enjoy considerable freedom in most professions and many continue their education after marriage. Traditional Islamic social practices prevail throughout the country, but relations with Westerners and other non-Muslims are relaxed, often warm. The country is ruled by a sultan, an absolute ruler from a dynasty going back to the eighteenth century; no political parties are permitted.

Qatar

Qatar is a flat, barren peninsula jutting northward into the Gulf, its western side lining the Gulf of Bahrain; Bahrain is its tiny neighbor. Qatar is the only other country besides Saudi Arabia, its giant neighbor to the south, to adhere to the puritanical Wahhabi sect of Islam. Qatar is ruled by a conservative emir, whose family assumed power immediately after the state gained its independence from British protectorate status in 1972. In spite of its religious conservatism, the government is outward-looking and has sought partnerships that have not always been to the liking of its Gulf neighbors. Examples are the construction of a water pipeline from Qatar to Iran and economic ties with Israel. Territorial disputes have also occurred with Saudi Arabia and Bahrain.

The one factor that has enabled Qatar to pursue its independent policies was and is the huge deposits of oil and natural gas within its sandy territory. What had been a poor, sleepy fishing and pearling community in the 1950s was suddenly transformed into an affluent state with unlimited commercial opportunities for the country's young men, and in spite of continued adherence to traditional Islamic social practices, women enjoy an excellent education. Most of them, however, are "married off" between the ages of 15 and 20. Literacy is very high among Qataris, and the median age (31) is the highest in the Arab world. Living standards are also the highest, with a GDP per capita being the seventh highest in the world, ahead of the UAE, Saudi Arabia, Kuwait and Bahrain.

Qatar's profile as an energetic actor in the Gulf has been further raised by the establishment of the Al-Jazeera radio and TV station, giving all-around commentaries on the war the U.S. initiated in Iraq in 2003.

Saudi Arabia

Saudi Arabia is by far the largest country on the Arabian Peninsula; in fact, it is the 13th biggest nation in the world. Most of the territory is desert or semi-desert plateau (about 95 percent), where some nomadic livestock herders remain.

The two largest cities in Saudi Arabia are Riyadh, the capital, and Jeddah, the main port and commercial center. The most famous city, of course, is Mecca, the birthplace of the prophet Muhammad.

Muhammad, founder of Islam, was born in Mecca about A.D. 570; even then the city had long been a religious center for various Arabian clans and tribes. They came to Mecca to worship a black stone, probably a meteorite, that had been placed in the Kaaba, a pilgrimage shrine. After Muhammad spent several years in Medina gaining and organizing converts to his religion, he defeated the leading tribe that had opposed him and returned to Mecca. Today, all the world's Muslims face Mecca during their daily prayers, and they are encouraged to make a pilgrimage to Mecca at least once in their lifetime. Non-Muslims are not allowed in Mecca.

In the eighteenth century, the Wahhabi (a strict Islamic sect) gained the allegiance of the Saud family, who, with the support of the Bedouin, rapidly conquered most of the Arabian Peninsula. In 1810 the region was conquered by Turkey. Abdul Aziz ibn Saud later laid the foundations of the modern state of Saudi Arabia, and by 1925 he had conquered the entire area of what is now Saudi Arabia. In 1932 Ibn Saud formed the kingdom of Saudi Arabia and became its king, ruling in accordance with the sharia of Wahhabi Islam.

Oil was discovered in 1936 by the U.S. company Arabian Standard Oil, which later became the Arabian American Oil Company (Aramco). In 1945 Saudi Arabia joined the Arab League. When Ibn Saud died in 1953, he was succeeded by a number of kings from the royal Saud family. In the 1970s, King Khalid's rule was challenged by the growth of Islamic fundamentalism, especially in Iran. In 1979 Shia fundamentalists captured the Great Mosque in Mecca, but the rebellion was brutally suppressed. Saudi Arabia's support for Iraq in the Iran-Iraq War (1980–1988) led to Iranian attacks on Saudi shipping. In 1982 Khalid died and was succeeded by Prince Fahd. When Iraq invaded Kuwait in 1990, King Fahd requested coalition forces to protect it against possible Iraqi aggression. Saudi air and land forces played a significant role in the Allied victory in the 1991 Gulf War.

Oil dominates the Saudi Arabian economy. Saudi Arabia is the world's largest producer and exporter of crude oil, with around 25 percent of the world's known oil reserves. Saudi oil and oil products supply over 10 percent of the world demand and make up 90 percent of the nation's exports and 40 percent of its GDP. There are between one and two million foreigners in Saudi Arabia. Some Western experts are indispensable, but recently Saudis have preferred to hire Asian workers, who are less likely to pose a cultural threat. Oil revenue has been used to develop health, education, services, industry, farming and the nation's military hardware. The construction of desalination plants has played an important part in improving the supply of fresh water. Crops grown in Asir and at oases include dates and other fruits, vegetables and wheat. Pilgrimages to Mecca number more than 1.5 million pilgrims a year, making a vital addition to state revenue.

The popular image of Saudi Arabia as an extremely wealthy nation is not entirely true. It does have considerable oil wealth and can expect to extract at least eight million barrels a day for the next century and probably beyond. Despite this, a budget deficit of more than 10 years' duration is growing, prompting warnings from the International Monetary Fund. The situation could be remedied if the Saudi government were to withdraw some of its subsidies and start raising taxes, but so far such measures have been regarded as socially and politically unacceptable.

Arabic is spoken everywhere in Saudi Arabia; the language originated there. Society, though changing fast, remains under strict conservative control, especially as far as Islamic tenets are concerned. Foreigners must conform: alcohol is completely prohibited, socializing with Saudi females is taboo and certain formalities of dress must be observed. Saudi women are the most restricted of all: they must be fully veiled in public, cannot travel alone, and usually eat separately from the men. The ban on Saudi women driving cars was only lifted in June 2018.

Tens of thousands of young Saudis have studied in Britain and the United States and they, on account of their widened horizons, as well as the underprivileged lower classes, are likely to seek constitutional changes in the near future. Also, the turmoil created by the U.S.-led invasion of Iraq, with its effects on Saudi politics, may well hasten the reformation or revision of the country's structure and the role of the monarchy.

Sudan

Sudan, often referred to as *the Sudan*, is the third largest Arab country in area and the second largest in population, with just over 40 million people. Its GDP per person is one of the lowest in the Arab world, ahead of only Yemen and the West Bank and Gaza. Sudan is split into two, with basically an Arab north and an African south. Most northerners are bilingual in Arabic and the regional language. In the south, tribalism is dominant and over 10 percent of the people are Christians. A civil war was fought from 1955 to 1972, leading to the eventual creation of South Sudan in 2011. There are 100 local languages in the south, where animism mingles with Christianity. The Sudanese economy is agricultural and highly dependent on the river Nile to provide irrigation for cereals, groundnuts, sugarcane and cotton. Livestock rearing, on a nomadic basis, is the main occupation of the population, 70 percent of whom are villagers and herders. In spite of widespread poverty, the Sudanese people have an enduring reputation for honesty. Many of them are obliged to immigrate to the Arabian Peninsula to find work. Few women work outside the home.

Syria

Syria, with ancient Damascus as its capital, possesses cultural riches almost unrivaled in the Arab world. Its antiquity and well-preserved historical sights are a magnet for Europeans, and its well-educated French-oriented society and sophisticated middle and upper classes make it a rival to Lebanon and Morocco in terms of close links to the West. Unfortunately, the policy of the Syrian government since the Israeli-Arab War of 1967 has steered the Syrian people away from closer connections with Europe. The Israeli occupation of the Golan Heights is the sorest point, and the revolutionary socialist nature of the ruling Baath party has gained the nation few friends, apart from Iraq. Paradoxically, Syria, in an attempt to mend its fences with the West, joined the coalition of allied forces in the 1991 Gulf War.

Syrians identify strongly with their Muslim heritage. Damascus was adopted as the first capital of the Islamic world in A.D. 661, until Baghdad was built for this role in 762. Although Syrians are consequently conservative in their interpretation of Islam, the influence of the French and the sizeable minority groups in their society have led to the relaxation of certain Muslim rules, especially those regarding the position of women. Education for girls is a long-established right, and veils are worn by almost none of the younger women, who are readily visible in the workforce and in public life.

The richness of the Syrian cultural scene is enhanced by the considerable diversity of its population. Minority groups include Christians (10 percent), Kurds (10 percent), Druze, Armenians, Jews and Assyrians. Many languages are heard in public alongside Arabic—Kurdish, Turkish, French, Armenian, English and the ancient Syriac and Aramaic.

In 1970 an air force pilot named Hafez al-Assad seized power. He ruled the country as a despot for thirty years, declaring martial law from time to time. On his death in 2000, his son, Bashar al-Assad, was elected in a referendum. He started his tenure on good terms with the international community, but the deterioration in Syria's human-rights record led to the U.S. suspending diplomatic relations. In 2011 violence escalated into widespread civil conflict between government forces and a large number of rebel groups. Al-Assad's use of chemical weapons in 2013 and massacres carried out by ISIS led to hundreds of thousands of deaths and the displacement of millions of Syrians in a never-ending and complex conflict involving neighbors Turkey and Iran, and ultimately military forces from Russia and displaced persons inside Syria itself, many of them subjected to torture and poor humanitarian conditions in Syrian government prisons. It seems that this situation will not improve as long as Assad remains in power.

At the time of writing, the number of Syrian refugees has reached 5 million and there are additional displaced persons inside Syria itself.

Tunisia

The republic of Tunisia is the smallest country in North Africa. Tunis, the capital, and Bizerte are excellent ports. Carthage, the ancient capital, survives in magnificent ruins in the Gulf of Tunis. Kairouan is the fourth most holy city in Islam.

The Phoenician Queen, Dido, founded Carthage in 814 B.C. In 46 B.C. the Romans destroyed the city, and the region was subsumed into the Roman Empire. In A.D. 640 the Arabs invaded. The Berbers slowly converted to Islam and Arabic became the principal language. Spain's capture of much of Tunisia's coast in the seventeenth century led to the intervention of the Turks and later the French.

Tunisia was a major battleground of the North Africa campaigns in the Second World War. In 1956, the battle-torn nation gained independence and in 1957 Habib Bourguiba was elected as the country's first president. Tunisia has weathered the changes brought about by the "Arab Spring" better than most countries.

Tunisia is a middle-income developing country. Tunisia is the world's fourth largest producer of olives. Other major crops include barley, dates, grapes for wine-making and wheat. Several fine wines are produced in the country. Tourism is a vital source of foreign exchange. Most of Tunisia's trade is with EU countries, and it is seeking to negotiate an accord with the EU.

The Tunisian government is quite liberal and encourages private enterprise. Nearly 50 percent of the people belong to the middle and upper classes and are bilingual in Arabic and French. The budget for education is ample, but because there are more educated young men than available jobs, many seek employment in France and Libya. Women are westernized and work in most commercial and academic sectors. Ninety-eight percent of the population is Muslim; Jewish and Christian minorities are comfortably tolerated.

United Arab Emirates

The United Arab Emirates consists of seven emirates: Abu Dhabi, Dubai, Sharjah, Ajman, Fujairah, Ras al Khaimah and Umm-al-Qaiwain. Formerly known as the Trucial States, the UAE is a group of Arabic-speaking sheikhdoms bordered by Qatar on the northwest, Saudi Arabia on the west and south and Oman on the east and northeast. Most of the union's area of 83,650 square kilometers (32,300 square miles) is occupied by Abu Dhabi, which lies along the mainland coast. The total population is concentrated on the peninsula and along the coast. Upon formation of the UAE in 1971, the town of Abu Dhabi was chosen as the national capital.

Nearly the entire union is desert, containing broad patches of sand and numerous salt flats. Most of the union's native inhabitants are Arabs who adhere to the Sunni and Shia sects of Islam. Many of the Bedouins who once roamed the interior in search of pasturage for their flocks have migrated to the towns.

The United Arab Emirates came into being in 1971 when Britain relinquished responsibility for defense and foreign policy. There were originally six emirates; Ras al Khaimah became the seventh in 1972.

The seven hereditary rulers of the emirates make up the Supreme Council of Rulers, who elect a president from their members. There is a forty-member advisory council, but there are no political parties or parliamentary democracy.

The population of the UAE is overwhelmingly made up of immigrants, many of whom come from the Indian subcontinent. There are also large numbers of construction workers from Korea and the Philippines. Since the Gulf War, the emirates, like Kuwait, have also felt threatened, in view of their proximity to Kuwait and the existence of their own substantial oil reserves. Since 1991 the government has invested large sums of money in defense and currently maintains an all-volunteer military force of 70,000 to 80,000 men.

Exports are dominated by oil, more than 40 percent of which is sold to Western Europe and 20 percent to Japan. Other than oil products, there is little industry in the union. The five states without oil, especially Ajman, produce stamps, mainly for philatelists. Dubai has factories, assembly plants and a dry dock for oil tankers. Desalination and irrigation has led to many cultivated areas. Dubai also has an important entrepôt trade. There are no railways, but there are 5,000 kilometers (3,100 miles) of excellent paved roads. Tourism is becoming very important, especially in Dubai.

Education is free, and facilities are developed by the former Abu Dhabi Education Ministry. Medical services are concentrated in Dubai, which contains hospitals and child-welfare clinics. Hospital services are also free, and most people are treated in hospital outpatient clinics; there is little private medical practice.

Desert tribalism figured large in the days when the seven emirates were poor, divided and backward. Even with the impact of oil revenue, UAE society remains very traditional and conservative. Sexes are separated. Women do not eat with men, are veiled in public and do not mix with foreigners. The exception is in the ADNOC national oil company, which employs westernized female staff. Most young males speak good English.

The West Bank and Gaza

The political and economic situation in the West Bank and Gaza is currently very fluid because of the turmoil with Israeli and Palestine Liberation Organization relations, which have improved somewhat since Yasser Arafat's death. Their population of 3.2 million has an estimated GDP of $4.4 billion—second lowest among the Arab countries. Living standards are low, given the present political climate, as is the median age of the population (just under 17)—the second lowest in the Arab world.

Given political stability and time for reconstruction, (and an eventual Israeli withdrawal) the people of the West Bank and Gaza will hopefully find their niche in the service industries. Palestinians are good linguists and have traditionally pursued education. Many of them are valuable employees in clerical sectors in Jordan, the UAE and other Arab countries.

Yemen

North and South Yemen were unified in May 1990 and the first multiparty elections (judged reasonably fair) were held in 1993. The merger between the two states was a combination of an essentially private sector economy in the north and a centrally planned Marxist system of state ownership in the south.

Modern Yemen has the lowest GDP per person of any Arab country as well as the lowest median age (15 years). Yemen is strategically located at the entrance of the Red Sea.

There are considerable social and cultural differences between the northern and southern halves of the country. Women in the north are veiled in public and do not work outside the home. In the more commercially minded south, they are well-integrated in society. Cotton and coffee are major sources of national income. Yemenis are famous as craftsmen in construction, stone masonry and carpentry, and thousands of them work in Saudi Arabia in these trades. Fishing is an important industry in the south, and Indian Ocean commerce beckons. The country has a long way to go in terms of economic development, and violence and terrorist activity have hampered economic progress. Territorial disputes continue with Saudi Arabia, and relations with that country and Kuwait were strained during the 1991 Gulf War. At the time of writing the prolonged period of hostilities with Saudi Arabia makes it impossible to forecast with any certainty the outcome of the war or the future structure and type of government that will prevail in the region. If political stability and improved relations with its neighbors and the West can be maintained, Yemen's oil and gas reserves hold some promise of future prosperity. Most Yemenis are industrious and friendly toward foreigners.

52

Iraq

The Republic of Iraq is not just one more Arab, Islamic state. The Arab conquest in A.D. 637 introduced the Muslim religion and gave the country its Arabic name, *iraq*, meaning the "well-rooted country," but this event took place late in the day in terms of the area's history. For the previous 3,000 years, "the Land between the Two Rivers" (the Tigris and the Euphrates) was known as Mesopotamia and had hosted four great and sophisticated civilizations that were neither Arab nor Islamic. Mesopotamia, most of which is contained within the present Republic of Iraq, was "well-rooted" in the sense that it was the home of some of the earliest, if not *the* earliest, civilized (urban and literate) communities in the world. The Sumerians, the Akkadians, the Assyrians and the Babylonians—the "cuneiform cultures"—all made their successive contributions, laying the basis for the civilizations of Egypt, Crete and the West.

Babylon itself, only 89 kilometers (55 miles) south of Baghdad, was one of the most famous cities of antiquity. In 331 B.C., Babylon surrendered to Alexander the Great, who planned to make it his imperial capital. On his death in 323, the building of the city was continued by King Nebuchadnezzar II. Situated on the banks of the Euphrates, it was the largest city in the world at the time, covering 10,000 hectares, or almost 100 square kilometers (40 square miles). One of the central features was the great temple of Marduc, with its associated seven-story tower, known popularly as the Tower of Babel. Greek tradition refers to the Hanging Gardens of Babylon, a simulated hill of vegetation-clad terracing, deemed to be one of the Seven Wonders of the World.

What was so unique about the fertile alluvial basins of the Tigris and the Euphrates? It was in these lowland areas of the Near East that cereal cultivation began. As early as 7500 B.C., the stability engendered by the development of agriculture led to the emergence of mud-brick dwellings constituting, in effect, the world's first farming villages. These became in time the world's first city–states. Wood, stone and metal were all rare or entirely absent in Mesopotamia; the raw material that epitomizes Mesopotamian civilization is clay. It is visible in the almost exclusively mud-brick architecture, and in the number and variety of clay figurines and pottery artifacts, none more important than the clay tablets that led to the invention of writing.

Mesopotamia was inventive: the potter's wheel, architectural techniques, irrigation, elaborate drainage and, above all, writing gave the region superiority over neighbors in terms of power and advantageous trade. The Sumerians, the original owners of writing, set up large, compact social organizations. Cuneiform spread to influence the writing systems of Egypt, Crete and the Indus Valley.

Given this wealth of historical background, it is not surprising that the people of Iraq consider themselves special. Although the Arab conquest came late in the history of Mesopotamia, its advent has had great significance. Medina and Mecca—Muhammad's homes—were too remote geographically to be the administrative centers for the rapidly expanding Islamic empire, which burgeoned after the middle of the seventh century. Damascus was chosen as the empire's capital in A.D. 661, but in 762 the Abbasid Caliphate was established in Iraq and Baghdad became the first planned capital city to be built by Muslims. As such, it has enormous historical importance in the eyes of Arabs everywhere and explains pan-Arab sensitivity to the turmoil created there in the 2003 war. Other cities revered by Arabs in a similar symbolic manner are Alexandria, Cairo, Tunis, Córdoba and (on Iraqi soil) Basra, an important center of Muslim culture, religion and learning.

Although Mesopotamia was "Arabized" in 637 and is essentially an Arab country today (75 percent of the people are Arabs), it witnessed many centuries of non-Arab rule in between. The Mesopotamian land has always been vulnerable to attack. The Mongols captured Baghdad in 1258 and held sway for centuries before being displaced by the Ottoman Empire in 1534, then the British, in 1916. From 1920 to 1921 the British "created" (and renamed) modern Iraq by merging Mosul, Baghdad and Basra and setting up an Arab monarchy. The monarchy was overthrown in 1958 by an army-led coup d'état. Another coup brought the Baath party to power in 1963.

Iraq has succeeded in creating a nationally homogeneous society, but this has not been accompanied by political stability. Mesopotamian civilizations were characterized by a predilection for multiplicity and variety. It has had many languages, many cultures and no real geographical unity. Tolerance has been a continuing feature: Kurds, Turks, Turkmens, Jews, Christians, Arabs and Mongols have shared the land for centuries. A small ethnic group—the Yazidis—living near Mosul speak a special Kurdish dialect and are thought to be descendants of the ancient Iraqi population. In any eventual Iraqi state, the characteristics of minorities (especially the Kurds, who number over 20 percent) will have to be taken into account. (Cultural divergences between Arabs and the West are listed in Chapter 51, "The Arab Countries.")

The cultural heritage is one of immense prestige—aesthetic, moral, scientific, legal, and literary. The current centering of culture around religious schools, colleges and mosques is centuries old and is likely to continue, in spite of the secularization attempted by Saddam Hussein. Iraq is the only Arab state where Shias outnumber Sunni Muslims. The schism between the two sects and the country's eventual relations with Shia Iran hold the key to the future of the land.

The U.S.-led invasion of Iraq in 2003 has naturally had a profound impact on the country's economy. At the time of writing, both the economic as well as political situations are in transition. Iraq's first free elections were held in 2005. Future prosperity will largely depend on the rehabilitation of the oil industry as well as on the development of trade with the West and other areas.

Culture

Values

Iraqi values derive from two sources—traditional Islamic and Mesopotamian (multi-ethnic).

Islamic	Mesopotamian
Muslim tenets	pride in 5,000-year-old heritage
gender inequality	primacy of sacred sites
moralistic society	used to war, violence, occupation
sensitivity	Shia majority
hospitality	multi-ethnic familiarity (Kurds, Turkmen, Yazidis, Turks,
passion	Persians)
rhetoric	religious tolerance (of Christians, Jews, Chaldeans,
Allah is the only god	Nestorians, Orthodox, Catholics)

(continued)

Islamic	Mesopotamian *(continued)*
anti-Western	well-trained professional classes
sincerity	educated upper-class women
devoutness	conservatism

Concepts

Leadership and Status

In most Arab countries the ruler is at the pinnacle of power. This person may be a king (Jordan, Morocco), a leading sheikh (the Gulf States) or a dictator (Libya and Iraq prior to 2003). Age is important—great respect is shown to elders. Women have a much lower status.

In Iraq, leadership was in the hands of a despot (Saddam Hussein) and his Sunni clique. It seems likely that an important element of future leadership will be the Shia clergy, though they are not as powerful as their Iranian colleagues.

Space and Time

Iraqi sense of space is typically Arab. Interlocutors stand and sit close to each other and life is often in a crowd. Under the present circumstances, punctuality has little meaning.

Cultural Factors in Communication

Behavior at Meetings and Negotiations

Business life has not yet resumed its normal tempo in Iraq. Most meetings are of a political nature and are mainly adversarial and unruly.

How to Empathize with Iraqis

Under the present circumstances, one can only offer sympathy and, when possible, help and advice. The Arab majority will naturally respond well to warmth, generosity and any form of aid. Iraqi hospitality in times past was legendary, stemming from both Mesopotamian and Arab tradition. In view of the evident hostility between Iraqi Shias and Sunnis, it is clear that foreigners should stay out of their quarrels when possible. Kurds and other minority groups will have a tendency to claim special Western understanding and attention. The best you can do is to treat *all* Iraqis as fellow human beings who are undergoing a difficult period in their lives and who merit our deepest sympathy and help.

53

Israel

Following the United Nations partition of Palestine, Israel emerged as a nation on May 15, 1948. It was the first Jewish state to be established in nearly 2,000 years. Its creation represented a fulfillment of the historic national idea of the Jewish people, stemming from the traditional religious belief in God's promise of the land of Israel to the people of Israel. The ideal found practical expression in a desire to forge the national destiny without dependence on the goodwill of others. The establishment of Israel as an internationally recognized member of the family of nations signified a decisive step in modern Jewish history. It increased the possibility of normal social, cultural and economic conditions being created for the Jewish people in their ancient homeland.

Among the population are numbered hundreds of thousands of immigrants, many of them survivors of Nazi persecution in Europe or victims of anti-Semitism elsewhere. Israeli society is engaged in a variety of pioneering activities, including the rehabilitation of neglected agricultural lands. This led to the creation of a Jewish rural population, which, though it represented only about 10 percent of the total Jewish population, also represented something almost unknown in the diaspora (the historical scattering of the Jews in countries outside of Palestine). The revival of the Hebrew language made possible the cultural integration of the newcomers. Hostile relations between Israel and neighboring Arab states have prevailed from the outset and continue at the time of writing, though there is relative peace within Jordan and Egypt.

Culture

Values

obsession to survive	articulateness
courage	impatience
energy	morality
opinionated views	modernity

In origin, as well as in physical features, the Jewish population lacks uniformity. Immigrants differed in color and culture and brought with them languages and customs from a variety of countries. Consciousness of geographic origin and descent is, however, gradually being superseded by a national consciousness, especially among the young. This melting pot of cultures leads to a certain unpredictability in Israeli behavior, even among the Jews. The most significant divide is that between the religious Jews and the secularists. However, as in the United States, the mixing of nationalities and cultures produces an overlying *mainstream national* culture that is typified by the characteristics listed here.

Religion

The religious divide of Israel is as follows: 85 percent Judaism, 13 percent Muslim, 2 percent Christian.

Judaism, the oldest of the three monotheistic religions originating in the Middle East (the others are Christianity and Islam), is concentrated in Israel, but large Jewish populations exist in many European and American cities.

Judaism was developed by the ancient Hebrews in the Near East during the third millennium B.C. Tradition holds that Judaism was founded by Abraham, who was chosen by God to receive favorable treatment in return for obedience and worship. Having entered into this covenant with God, Abraham moved to Canaan from where, centuries later, his descendants migrated to Egypt and became enslaved. God accomplished the Hebrews' escape from Egypt and renewed the covenant with their leader, Moses. The religious hearth of Judaism is centered in Jerusalem. When the Romans drove out the Jews from this area in the first century A.D., others inhabited the land. For centuries, until the twentieth century, the region was called Palestine and was populated by Muslims. In the 1880s the Zionist movement started, whereby Jews began returning in steadily increasing numbers.

Religious Jewish groups immigrating to Israel generally continue to pray in the synagogues (Jewish houses of worship) of their respective communities. Religious Jewry in Israel constitutes a significant and articulate section of the population. There is, however, also a strong movement that seeks to prevent religious bodies and authorities from dominating national life or from interfering with individual freedom of conscience.

The largest religious minority group is formed by the Muslims, who constitute about two-thirds of the Arab population. Practically all of the Muslims are Sunni. The state helps to maintain their customs and religious institutions. Among the Muslims about 37,000 are Bedouin; about three-quarters of these live in the Negev, and the rest live in Galilee.

The Holocaust remains the major Jewish "cultural black hole," with repercussions in Israeli society. Nowadays a more immediate problem is the state of the Israeli-Palestinian relationship.

Concepts

Leadership and Status

Lacking an aristocracy, Israeli society attaches importance to achievement and dynamism when looking for leadership. The troubled time with Israel's Palestinian neighbors since

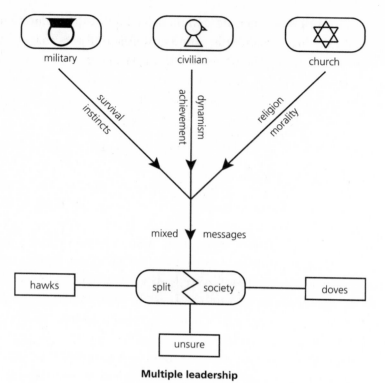

Multiple leadership

Figure 53.1 Israeli Leadership Style

1945 has led to an enhanced role for the military and hawkish politicians, though the Israeli center and left have not been without their charismatic figures. It is hard to judge how a period of prolonged peace would affect Israel's choice of leaders. The present hostile situation means that the choice cannot be divorced from political and security-bound realities. It is likely that in less troubled times cultural luminaries would be in the ascendancy, given the level of Israeli education. Religious leaders also exert considerable influence on Israeli life.

    Status is granted through achievement.

Space and Time

Israelis are fairly tactile; kissing, hugging and touching are fairly frequent at all levels of society. Population density is not particularly high at 295 people per square kilometer (755 people per square mile). The most significant Israeli issue of space is the government policy of taking possession of land through building settlements. This has naturally created intense hostility among Palestinians, who dispute the territory. The need and use of space is therefore crucial to the future political and cultural destiny of the Israeli people.

Israelis like to think that they are time-conscious and quick off the mark in the American manner, but in fact they are considerably more casual about punctuality than the Americans. Nevertheless, appointments must be made in advance, and people do not show up outrageously late. While generally efficient in keeping to business schedules, Israelis often fail to keep deadlines. Activity ceases on the Sabbath (sunset on Friday through sunset on Saturday).

Cultural Factors in Communication

Communication Pattern

Hebrew, like Arabic, is a Semitic language. Originally spoken in Palestine, it is the language of the Old Testament. Its use declined during the Babylonian Captivity (when Jews were deported to Babylon after the capture of Jerusalem by Nebuchadnezzar in 586 B.C.) and was overtaken by Aramaic, the language spoken by Jesus. Hebrew persisted as a literary language and was revived as a spoken language by the nineteenth century Zionist movement and became the official language of Israel in 1948.

Israelis are in general loquacious and opinionated. An American journalist who visited Jerusalem in 2004 remarked that people there never seemed to stop talking. Politics, religion and soul-searching were the exclusive topics of conversation.

Israelis are bold and direct—they see themselves as U.S.-style straight talkers in a devious Middle Eastern cultural environment. In fact, many Anglo-Saxons and Americans would find Israelis manipulative and transparently persuasive, though they stick to facts on the whole. Israelis are argumentative and do not concede their position easily. They back up their opinions with logic and erudition. The hard school of experience has engendered a considerable degree of irony and cynicism. They do have a sense of humor but are generally earnest and serious. Their critics would call them occasionally pushy and brash. Subtlety is not an Israeli strong point. They rival the French in their adherence to rationality but are more emotional on political issues.

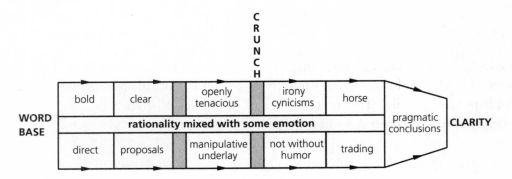

Figure 53.2 Israeli Communication Pattern

Listening Habits

Impatience and an urge to voice their opinions make Israelis poor listeners. They often feel that foreigners cannot put themselves in Israeli shoes. They are conscious of an innate intelligence, which causes them to discount many of the opinions of their interlocutors. They can, though, be swayed by good speakers who stick to facts and reason and who know something that they do not know.

Behavior at Meetings and Negotiations

Israelis are an informal people. There is little protocol and first names are used early. Dress is casual, and seating is only occasionally hierarchical. Everyone is allowed his or her say. The atmosphere is friendly, but businesslike. Israelis are keen to get to the point and though they are loquacious, digression is only permitted if it has some relevance to the business in hand. Time must not be wasted. Abstract theory is avoided—practical matters gain full attention. While being pragmatic, Israelis like to believe that they do not abandon principle. Religious beliefs play a small or greater part depending on who the participants are.

- ✦ Israelis negotiate tenaciously on price and other conditions, but avoid appearing unreasonable, as they are often in a weaker position.
- ✦ They make full use of high technology and are always seeking innovation and improvement.
- ✦ They make concessions in due course, but not easily, and when they do, they are quick to look for a quid pro quo.
- ✦ They are rarely delicate or subtle.

Manners and Taboos

Orthodox Jews have many rules and customs particular to their sect. These include special formal attire, prohibited foods (e.g., pork) and insistence that other foods be prepared in a special manner. Observance of the Sabbath is strict (Orthodox Jews are not even supposed to push buttons in elevators on Saturdays). In their eyes, modern Zionists brought the heresy of logic to Israel and a vision of a secular Jewish homeland. Various religious rites and ceremonies are visible at certain locations in the cities, especially Jerusalem.

How to Empathize with Israelis

As a young state (since 1948), Israel and Israelis want recognition first and foremost; this is a question of survival. As in Poland, survival is always at the forefront of the national consciousness, and Israelis will do almost anything for people who seem genuinely keen to help their country. Such empathy can, of course, be demonstrated in subtle ways. Israelis are grateful to people who improve their economic opportunities. Younger generations also like a good time, so regular socializing helps too. You must always appear democratic and put forward the best motives. Enthusiasm without too much charisma is a good recipe for success.

MOTIVATION	
KEY	*Support the existence of the state of Israel*
Cross-century mood	✦ Anxiety to protect the state. ✦ Developing tiredness of prolonged conflict. ✦ Pursuit of technology.

Motivating Factors

✦ Be sincere at all times.
✦ Appear confident, even forceful.
✦ Maintain a good tempo.
✦ Respect their religion or sect.
✦ Be straightforward.
✦ Understand their limitations and/or lack of resources.
✦ Speak to them as equals.
✦ Assume a high level of culture.

Avoid

✦ Too much idealism.
✦ Dwelling on political conflicts.
✦ Criticizing Israel.
✦ Lack of enthusiasm.
✦ Pulling rank.

54

India

By the middle of the twenty-first century, India will have passed China in terms of numbers of inhabitants, making it the most populated nation on earth. Its land area is also immense, with 3,287,000 square kilometers (126,900 square miles), making India the seventh largest nation in the world. India's GDP ranking was in seventh place in 2018, the country is developing rapidly in the technological and service sectors and its rapidly growing middle class numbers over 300 million. The origins of the Indus Valley civilization, with settled agriculture and trade with the Middle East, date from around 3000 B.C.

Now the heart of India beats in the densely populated plains of the Ganges, farmed for several millennia. To the north the mighty Himalayan range constitutes the world's most awesome frontier. To the south lies the peninsula, less fertile than the plains and often politically fragmented. Here the Tamils speak Dravidian languages, far removed structurally from the hundred or more Indo-European languages and dialects spoken in the rest of the country. Hindi, Urdu, Bengali and Gujarati are the most widely spoken tongues in this family, which also included Sanskrit in former times.

Pakistan and Bangladesh, after the partition, represent the two other major states on the Indian subcontinent. English serves as a lingua franca in the region, as many of the local languages are mutually unintelligible.

All three countries hope to benefit from extensive outsourcing of services from developed countries such as Britain and the United States. Outsourcing companies have experienced rapid growth in India, whose inhabitants speak English at a level of fluency adequate for performing the services involved. Bangladesh, Pakistan, Malaysia and several other Southeast Asian countries (possibly China, too) envisage enhancing their economies through outsourcing, though the Chinese and Indonesians currently lack the required language skills.

However, it is in the field of high technology where India has been surging ahead in the opening decade of the twenty-first century. Bangalore is now another "Silicon Valley," and there is every evidence that Indians will create a technological gap vis-à-vis other Asian countries and rival the Americans and Northern Europeans in the creation of software and other high-tech products.

Culture

Values

The British Raj left both a social and a cultural influence on many Indians. Commonalities with the British include cricket, tea, army traditions, Oxford and Cambridge elite, protection of accumulated wealth, titles of nobility, admiration for (English) literature, a democratic constitution, parliamentary rule, early industrialism, a class system, the English language as a vehicle of culture and administration, a large civil service, a legal system, and respect for property.

Indians have a special and unique culture that varies considerably from those of East Asia. Their communicative style is more loquacious than the Chinese, Japanese and Korean, and they are as dialogue-oriented as most Latins. Essentially multi-active, they have created a society where privacy is rarely indulged in and even more rarely sought. They make little attempt to conceal their feelings—joy, disappointment and grief are expressed without inhibition.

family orientation	loyalty to a group, often professional
honor of both family and group	arranged marriages
material success and creativity	do-it-yourself mentality
problem solving	fatalism
risk takers and experimenters	savvy at business

Concepts

Leadership and Status

Indians accept a hierarchical system with its obligations and duties. The boss must be humanistic and initiate promotion for his subordinates. In family businesses the elder son rarely decides what he wants to be—he is born to carry on the trade of the father; the father is expected to groom him for the job. First a good education will be provided. The son must study hard, then the next step will be indicated.

A strong work ethic is visible in Indian commerce, especially when people are working in their own or family business; however, Indians do not work by the clock. There is an easy acceptance of foreigners in business dealings; Indians do not fear foreigners—many invasions have brought familiarity. They are, however, suspicious of the iniquity that the foreigners may bring with them (perhaps a certain fear of division and subsequent loss of national identity). Nepotism is a way of life in traditional Indian companies. Family members hold key positions and work in close unison. Policy is also dictated by the trade group, for example, fruit merchants, jewelers and so forth. These groups work in concert and come to each other's aid in difficult times.

Space and Time

India is a crowded country, and people are used to living and working close together. Bus lines are real scrambles. Indians are fairly tactile, but a certain restraint is visible regarding closeness in public. Women are clearly subordinate to men. There is also the question of class consciousness, which lessens the tendency to embrace all and sundry.

There is great latitude regarding punctuality, according to class. The reincarnation factor also influences the Indian concept of time. Opportunities need not always be seized greedily. Time is cyclical, so such opportunities will inevitably reoccur (perhaps in another life!).

Cultural Factors in Communication

Communication Pattern

Indian English is old-fashioned, flowery and verbose. It is essentially a human, sympathetic language showing respect and often humility to the listener. It is generous in praise, yet reluctant to criticize, since failure in Indian business may quickly be attributed to bad karma. Indian English excels in ambiguity, and such things as truth and appearances are often subject to negotiation. Above all, the language of the Indian manager emphasizes the collective nature of the task and challenge. India is far from being a classless society, but the groups will often sink or swim together in the hard world of the subcontinent.

Listening Habits

The key to Indian attention is to be eloquent, humble and respectful. They admire a person with an extensive vocabulary. They are willing to listen at length, to enable a relationship to develop, and their aim, in the subsequent feedback, is to make a friend of the speaker. They do not make a difficult audience, but their sagacity must not be underestimated.

Behavior at Meetings and Negotiations

Indians remain polite while modifications are proposed, and repackage energetically to reach an agreement. They hate turning down any business. As far as negotiating style is

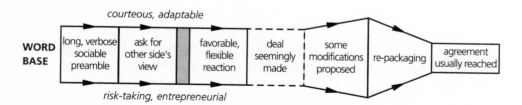

Figure 54.1 Indian Communication Pattern

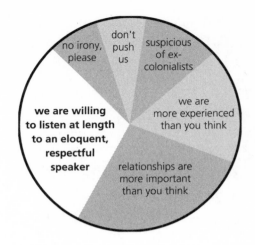

Figure 54.2 Indian Listening Habits

concerned, the Indians have few superiors. Although highly collectivist in their local group, they develop individuality and brilliance when dealing on their own with outsiders. They are clever at buying and selling. The following points indicate just one pattern of negotiation that an Indian employs with great skill when selling (each successive step may take place after days or weeks of negotiation).

1. I don't want to sell at all.
2. This business is the jewel in the crown of all the businesses that my family controls.
3. We don't need the money.
4. I am not intending to sell, but if I ever did sell, I would sell to you.
5. If I should sell, I have no idea whatsoever how we should evaluate such a successful business.
6. If one should try to estimate a price, it would be by analogy with similar deals that were done in the past.
7. When A sold X to B, that was such a deal.
8. A only sold X to B because he needed the money.
9. Perhaps I would like to sell to you, but I shall never be able to carry my family with me.
10. I have heard your proposed price and I have stormed out of the room.
11. I have to tell you in all honesty that we have received a very serious bid from a third party. It is higher than yours.
12. I do not expect you to pay more than they are willing to, but I expect you to match their offer.
13. I am willing to give the deal to you and not them, because I promised to sell to you.
14. I know that this price is not based on the usual multiple of profit, but how do you decide the worth of a business that has 70 percent of the market?

There are many other ploys that Indians use. Basically, they are disappointed if you do not engage in bargaining with them. Determination of price must come last, after all the benefits of the purchase or deal have been elaborated. Indians use all their communicative skills to get to the price indirectly. When negotiating, remember these points:

+ They are very skillful and can often fool you.
+ Understand their needs and objectives.
+ Be humble at all times.
+ Avoid sarcasm and irony.
+ Be patient—few Asians like to decide things quickly.
+ Focus on relationships; they see this as more important than any specific deal.
+ Indians will accept losses if they mean future gains.
+ Their negotiation concept is win–lose, but they are very flexible.

Manners and Taboos

Hinduism dominates Indians' social behavior, with the associated taboos. Women show great deference to men. Dress is opulent, often ostentatious. Brothers and sons generally live under one roof, which results in the fragmentation of land.

How to Empathize with Indians

Indians tend to complain openly about the injustices of the colonial period. If treated with respect, they quickly put the past behind them, especially where good business is in the offing. Play the Indians at their own game: be reasonable, solicitous and flexible. The country has a magnificent history, which should be referred to and admired. Learn all the basic facts about Mahatma Gandhi and avoid confusing him with Indira and Rajiv Gandhi's family, to which he was not related. A knowledge of Hinduism is also advisable, as is an awareness of the geography of India, Pakistan and Bangladesh.

Indians emanate and expect warmth, respect and properness. Do not risk joking with them—they tend to take things seriously. Be flexible at all times. Accept that there is a great deal of chaos, and remember that they manage it better than you do.

Learn to cope with the Indian bureaucracy, which can be slow and tedious; even more important, learn how to function within its constraints and restrictions. Maintain multiple channels of communication, both with government and commercial entities. Develop your own linkages, independent of your partner.

Try not to be judgmental about Indian failings or limitations. Remember that truth has many aspects—most Asians consider that there is no absolute truth: facts and appearances are often subject to negotiation.

Show sympathy and empathy whenever you see the other side in difficulties. Never use brute force or gain unfair advantage when dealing from strength.

Recognize and respect the unwritten word. In Asia oral agreements are weightier than documents. Operate within the context of a medium- to longer-term horizon.

MOTIVATION	
KEY	*Don't talk down to them; show sensitivity and understanding*
Cross-century mood	✦ India is overtaking China as the world's most populous nation. This motivates them to "think big." ✦ Creation of their own "Silicon Valley" is giving them unwonted confidence. Future progress in this area lies in cooperation with the U.S. ✦ Equality for women is rapidly becoming a major issue. ✦ Growing world acceptance of spiritual tenets and values is in India's favor.

Motivating Factors

✦ Show some knowledge of India's glorious past. The Indus Valley civilization dates from 3000 B.C.
✦ Show respect when dealing with Indians, who often have a complex over the injustices of the colonial period.
✦ Treat older people with great deference.
✦ Make yourself familiar with Indian family arrangements, e.g., brothers and sons usually living under one roof.
✦ Make yourself familiar with the respective positions of men and women and the system of arranged marriages.
✦ Develop a tolerance for ambiguity—it is common in Asia.
✦ Truth, facts and appearances are often subject to negotiation.
✦ Look at things from their point of view; you can learn a lot from them.
✦ Share gains and losses equitably, irrespective of contractual agreements.

Avoid

✦ Taking sides in the internal rivalry between Hindus and Muslims; many Indians are Muslims.
✦ Ideology once the discussion is clearly business.
✦ Humiliating them; always "give face."
✦ Discussing the caste question.
✦ Discussing Kashmir.

55

Pakistan

Pakistan, located in the northwest corner of the Indian subcontinent, is bordered by China and Afghanistan in the north, Iran in the west and India to the east and southeast.

The Indus Valley civilization developed 5,000 years ago. Waves of invaders later entered the area: Arabs, the Moguls and the British. The dominance of Hindus in British India led to the formation of the Muslim League in 1906. In the 1940s the League gained popular support for the idea of a separate state of Pakistan in Muslim-majority areas. When India achieved independence in 1947, it was partitioned into India and Pakistan. The resulting mass migration and communal violence claimed over 500,000 lives.

Muslim Pakistan was divided into two parts: East Bengal and West Pakistan, which were 1,600 kilometers (about 1,000 miles) apart. Pakistan was faced with enormous political and administrative problems, including East Pakistan's claim for greater autonomy. In 1971 East Pakistan declared independence as Bangladesh. West Pakistani troops invaded, and the ensuing civil war killed hundreds of thousands of people. Millions fled to India, and India sent troops to support Bangladesh.

In 1998 Pakistan became the world's seventh nuclear power. The war between India and Pakistan over Kashmir, which began in 1947, continues, but after September 11, 2001, the country's juxtaposition to Afghanistan caused it to be closely connected with the crisis. General Musharraf took complete power and edged Pakistan into an alliance with the United States, which has continued up to the writing of this edition. Strong Islamic beliefs give Pakistanis defensive attitudes toward peoples of other religions and philosophies. Antipathy to Indians, in spite of thousands of years of common heritage, is a major issue, which is further deepened by the ongoing bitter controversy over Kashmir.

Ninety percent of the Pakistanis are Muslim, and their cultural classification is multi-active, dialogue-oriented.

The languages of Pakistan—Urdu (the official language), Punjabi, Pashto, Sindhi and English—are written in modified forms of the Arabic-Persian script, which is written from right to left. Urdu is the first language taught in schools in Punjab, so every educated Punjabi can read and write it.

English is used for official purposes except in local administration, where the local vernacular is used. English is the de facto official language, even though it is spoken by only about 2 percent of the people of Pakistan.

Culture

It is difficult to speak of Pakistani culture in the singular. Family organization is strongly patriarchal, as in most agrarian societies, and most people live in large extended families. Women are, for the most part, restricted to the performance of domestic chores and to fulfilling the role of a dutiful wife and mother. Rich peasants, landowners and members of urban middle classes keep their women in seclusion (*pardah*); on the rare occasions they set foot outside their houses, they must be veiled. Poor peasant women have duties on the farm as well as in the house and do not observe pardah.

Pardah has been eliminated among the very rich, but, in general, even among this group attitudes toward women in society and the family are akin to those of Victorian England. Change is happening most rapidly among the urban lower-middle income group. These women, forced to seek employment under the pressure of economic necessity, are encouraged to be educated and thus are casting off pardah. Consequently, some women have gained distinction in the professions; significantly, some of the country's leading trade unionists are women.

While Pakistan claims a cultural heritage dating back more than 5,000 years, the emphasis on Islamic ideology has brought about a strong romantic identification with Islamic culture—not only that of India but of the whole Islamic world. Poetry is popular, and public poetry recitations are organized like musical concerts. Urdu, Sindhi, and Pashto poets are regional and national heroes. Literary tradition is the richest of all Pakistani art forms.

Values

For thousands of years the behavior of people living in the entire subcontinent was very similar. When the territory was split, millions of people had to leave one part of the subcontinent for another, taking their culture with them. Although religious tenets on both sides of the partition are diverse and opposed, many behavioral and social characteristics are common to Indians and Pakistanis. This is especially true in the areas of communication patterns, concepts of space and time, and comportment during meetings and negotiations. Where concepts differ is largely in terms of core beliefs (basically religious) that impart separate values, which are likely to diverge further as time goes by.

There is, however, an underlying behavioral pattern that exists throughout the subcontinent, and that differs sharply from the Confucian and Southeast Asian cultures of China, Japan, Korea, Malaysia, Thailand, Vietnam and so on.

Islam	devoutness
sincerity	energetic, assertive attitudes
loquacity, emotion, sensitivity, warmth	respect for education
suspicion of foreign influence	ambivalent attitude to neighbors
British influences—cricket, army	proclivity for coups and military
traditions	dominance

Concepts

Leadership and Status

Currently leadership is provided by the army. As in India, nepotism is common in traditional Pakistani companies. Family members hold key positions and work in close unison. Like Indians, Pakistanis accept a hierarchical system with its obligations and duties. The boss must be humanistic and initiate promotion for his subordinates. In family businesses the elder son rarely decides what he wants to be—he is born to carry on the trade of the father, and the father is expected to groom him for the job. Although women rise to the higher positions in politics and occasionally in business, they are invariably from the ranks of the well-born and wealthy. In general, wives in the lower classes are abused and degraded.

In recent years status has been entirely determined by the military.

Space and Time

The cities of Pakistan are horribly crowded; people are used to living and working close together. The situation in the mountainous areas is the opposite. Population density overall is much lower than in India. Pakistanis are less tactile than Indians.

Pakistanis are not punctual, though punctuality varies according to class. High-ranking persons generally make people wait.

Cultural Factors in Communication

Communication Pattern

Communication is usually courteous with lengthy small talk preceding getting down to business. When business is ultimately discussed, the reactive side of Pakistani nature is revealed in their request to hear the other side's view first. Their (multi-active) loquacity is held in check while the other speaks. Initial reaction usually seems favorable, but Pakistanis have the ability to modify and prepackage skillfully as they work their way toward a mutually acceptable agreement.

Pakistanis are extroverted but are still considered restrained in comparison with Latins and Arabs. Emotions are conveyed more through eye contact and facial expressions rather than by hand movements.

Listening Habits

The key to Pakistani attention is to be imaginative yet courteous. They like colorful speech. They are willing to listen at length, to enable a relationship to develop.

Behavior at Meetings and Negotiations

A meeting in Pakistan can be a kind of aesthetic experience: flowery, Victorian English can set the scene for exaggerated deference and flattering approaches. Pakistanis, like Danes, maintain the semi-euphoric atmosphere as long as possible until some holes are detected in the apparently agreed upon arrangement. They remain polite while modifications are proposed and then repackage their proposals energetically to reach an agreement. They hate turning down any business.

Basically Pakistanis, like most Asians, are disappointed if you do not engage in bargaining with them. Determination of price must come last, after all the benefits of the purchase or deal have been elaborated. Pakistanis use all their communicative skills to get to the price indirectly. In general, Pakistanis have the same attitude about contracts as their former British mentors, although they are more flexible.

How to Empathize with Pakistanis

Like Indians, Pakistanis have a complex over the injustices of the colonial period, and consequently tend to complain openly about these. If treated with respect, they, like Indians, quickly put the past behind them, especially where good business is in the offing. Be reasonable and flexible. A basic knowledge of Urdu is also advisable. Pakistanis emanate and expect warmth, zest and respect. British people can reach them by talking about cricket and army traditions.

MOTIVATION	
KEY	*Distinguish them from Indians*
Cross-century mood	✦ Exploration of potential alliances (U.S.? China?). ✦ Follow India's example in developing information technology.

Motivating Factors

✦ Show some knowledge of the glorious past of the subcontinent, including the advent of Islam.

✦ Learn something about the basic tenets of Islam.

✦ Make yourself familiar with family arrangements, the respective positions of men and women, and the system of arranged marriages.

✦ Be very clear about the geography of India, Pakistan and Bangladesh.

✦ Try to be nonjudgmental about Pakistani failings or shortcomings.

✦ Truth, facts and appearances are often subject to negotiation.

(continued)

MOTIVATION *(continued)*

- ◆ Show sympathy and empathy whenever you see the other side in difficulties.
- ◆ Never use brute force or gain unfair advantage when dealing from strength.
- ◆ Look at things from their point of view; you can learn a lot from them.
- ◆ Recognize the importance of the unwritten word. In Asia oral agreements are weightier than documents.
- ◆ Communicate clearly and often. Pakistanis like follow-up.

Avoid

- ◆ Sarcasm and other indelicate forms of humor.
- ◆ Impatience.
- ◆ Humiliating them (or using brute force).
- ◆ Any criticism of Islam.
- ◆ Talking about Kashmir.

56

Bangladesh

Although Bangladesh is dwarfed by India, Pakistan and neighboring Myanmar, it is one of the most densely populated countries on earth. It is also one of the poorest—but it was not always so. The Bengal region was probably the wealthiest part of the Indian subcontinent in the Middle Ages and up to the sixteenth century.

The incredible density of population as well as the low-lying nature of the territory are the principal ingredients of Bangladeshi geography. Rivers are naturally the dominant geographical feature in Bangladesh. Only the Amazon and Congo river systems are more prolific. Dhaka, the capital, and Chittagong are the major cities. Every three years Bangladesh is hit by a major cyclone; more people are killed by cyclones than anything else.

The dominant cultural group is Bengali, about 86 percent of whom are Muslim. The Muslims belong principally to the Sunni sect. Christian people in Bangladesh mostly have Portuguese names and are frequently English-speakers. More than 60 percent of people are engaged in agriculture; fishing is also important. The cultural classification of the Bangladeshis is multi-active, dialogue-oriented. Languages include Bengali (Bangla), Hindi, English and many local dialects.

Culture

Values

Bengali language and literature	Bengali Muslim tenets
"home village" roots	Islamic rule
respect for elders	abstinence
extended family	struggle for identity
secularism	passion
fatalism	imagination
hospitality	warmth
pride in ancestry	courtesy

Religion

In the last century significant changes occurred in the religious makeup of what is now Bangladesh. One hundred years ago, Hindus represented about 35 percent of the population; today this figure has dropped to around 10 percent. Bangladesh is now 85 percent Muslim and is the fourth biggest Muslim country in the world, after Indonesia, Pakistan and India. Part of the reason for the dramatic decline of Hindus in Bangladesh is due to the incursions of the Pakistani army in the 1960s, which caused many Bengali Hindus to flee to India, where they settled in the state of Tripura. Since 1971 relations between Hindus and Muslims have improved, partly on account of the sacrifices and suffering of Hindu Bangladeshis during the struggle for independence.

Bangladesh Muslims belong mainly to the Sunni sect, but there is also a small Shia community, mostly descended from Iranian traders who live mainly in the big cities. More important than the Sunni–Shia schism in Bangladesh is the fact that Islam was mainly spread in this area by Sufis, who are followers of a branch of Islam from Central Asia. Sufism emphasizes tolerance of other religions as well as abstinence and self-denial. This less aggressive version of Islam made it possible for Sufi missionaries in Bangladesh to convert Hindus in large numbers, as many of the beliefs of both Sufis and Hindus were similar. Sufis in Bangladesh organize a huge Muslim gathering annually just outside Dhaka. It is second in size only to the hajj in Mecca.

The Bangladeshi version of Hinduism differs from that in India. Being a minority creed it is less pompous than in India—its ceremonies, though colorful, are simpler than Indian ones.

Concepts

Leadership and Status

The Bangladeshi mode of government today is democracy, though in past years it was mostly despotic. Tradition still inclines Bangladeshis toward hierarchical leadership, as is apparent in government, home village systems and in the family itself. Religious leaders also rule autocratically.

In business circles, the patron or manager makes most decisions. The decision-making process often takes the form of wordy debate, but in the end the most powerful figure normally has his way. Educated women are also accepted as strong leaders.

Space and Time

Bangladeshis like to stand and sit close together, and there are points to be gained in accepting this proximity in terms of reciprocating warmth, even in business discussions.

As in many tropical areas, people have a flexible attitude toward time and punctuality. In Bangladesh, this is changing somewhat among the younger generation, partly due to their increasing involvement with information technology, where success often depends on fast-moving development. Bangladesh seems destined to emulate certain parts of India in becoming an outsourcing location for Western companies. Due to more contact with foreign companies and aid organizations, Bangladeshis are in general receptive to suggestions that punctuality be improved.

Cultural Factors in Communication

Communication Pattern

Foreign visitors to Bangladesh often find the people somewhat abrupt and unsophisticated in their opening conversational exchanges. This feature probably derives from the rural traditions and character of many people. They quickly warm to you, though, if you show them some empathy. Bangladeshis can then become extremely helpful and hospitable, almost to the point of embarrassment. Their traditional interest in poetry and literature makes them eloquent and at times oratorical. They are not averse to flattery; their discourse is essentially courteous. They tend to avoid strongly worded statements or affirmations, preferring to indicate their opinions in an indirect and rather pleasant manner. They are inclined to find solutions through compromise on most matters. They are uncomfortable with silence, filling in gaps in the conversation with pleasantries. Beware, though, that their courteous dialogue often disguises their skill at pursuing arguments.

Bangladeshi body language is similar to that used in most of the subcontinent, but you must to watch the "head-waggle" carefully. Waggling the head from side to side in response to a question may mean "no" or "I'm not sure." A single tilt to one side means agreement or consent.

Listening Habits

Bangladeshis listen carefully, as they have a thirst for knowledge. Their natural courtesy prevents them from interrupting frequently, though they may do so if they fail to understand what the speaker is driving at. As they listen, they are seeking areas of common interest and opportunities to create empathy. Sometimes they are reluctant to admit something is above their head, out of respect for a foreigner or senior figure.

Behavior at Meetings and Negotiations

Business meetings in Bangladesh are quite formal; various niceties of dress, protocol and manners should be observed. Meetings usually begin with small talk, which can be extensive if it proves interesting. During this time, the Bangladeshi participants are beginning to feel relaxed and are increasingly receptive to fruitful business discussion. This small-talk session should also be enjoyed at subsequent meetings with the same people. It is considered un-sophisticated to launch into business discussion right from the outset.

When you get down to the business itself, the process must not be rushed ("only a fool tries to hustle the East"). Exchanges must remain unhurried, pleasant and non-confrontational. As long as this type of harmony is maintained, Bangladeshis will continue to endeavor to advance goals and seek acceptable solutions. Even if you should fail to reach an immediate agreement, the door should be left open for future discussion. Whatever the result of a meeting, it should end on a pleasant note.

As Bangladeshis, owing to their weak economy, are often the weaker party, it behooves you to show generosity and refrain from extracting maximum advantage from the situation.

Bangladeshis are not famous for adhering strictly to agendas. They may often wish to digress and may talk among themselves in Bengali. Don't take offense; accept this as part and parcel of Bangladeshi behavior.

Manners and Taboos

Manners are molded by Islamic and Hindu traditions and rules. Dress is generally conservative, especially for women. Western women are advised not to leave too much flesh exposed, especially when entering mosques. Men wear shirts without jackets at informal dinners and functions, while women wear casual evening dresses or long skirts.

In business circles a handshake is very common, though men should not shake hands with a woman unless she offers her hand first.

Exchanging gifts is frequent in social circumstances, but less common between business colleagues. Corporate gifts, however, are widely used.

As in Arab countries, it is impolite to use the left hand or to point your feet at any person. Muslims of course do not eat pork; Hindus do not eat beef. Alcohol is not normally available, except in four- or five-star hotels and restaurants.

How to Empathize with Bangladeshis

+ Be sensitive to local customs, which vary from region to region.
+ Women and men cannot form friendships except at the most formal level.
+ Respect this situation. It is one area where Hindu and Islamic views coincide.
+ It is normal for men and boys to hold hands in public. Foreign men can participate if circumstances are appropriate.
+ You may offer advice when it seems appropriate or wanted, but do not preach, though you may talk at length on your particular speciality or technical skill.
+ Don't judge things in absolute terms, for example, right and wrong, true and untrue, good and bad. Truth in Bangladesh is situational and contextual.

MOTIVATION	
KEY	*Acknowledge their national identity*
Cross-century mood	+ Tendency to follow India's lead in modernization (e.g., outsourcing and IT). + Reconciling Bengali and Muslim beliefs.

Motivating Factors

+ Know Bangladeshi history accurately—it has many twists and turns.
+ Knowledge and expertise strongly motivate Bangladeshis to follow you.
+ Be modest rather than opinionated.
+ Show you see things from their point of view.
+ Know and respect the basic tenets of Islam and Hinduism.
+ When affording Bangladeshis benefits, allow them to reciprocate (however humbly) to maintain their "face."
+ Always protect their face.
+ Accept ambiguous remarks and leave your options open.
+ Learn some Bengali and use it humbly.

(continued)

MOTIVATION *(continued)*
Avoid
✦ Indelicate use of humor.
✦ Talking down to them.
✦ Calling them Indians.

57

Southeast Asia

Although Japan, China and Korea constitute the three great powerhouses of East Asia, the seven major countries of Southeast Asia (Indonesia, Vietnam, Thailand, Singapore, Philippines, Malaysia and Taiwan) count a combined population of 500 million and have a rapidly increasing significance in terms of future markets, resources of labor and industrial and technological development. Indonesia is the world's fourth most populated state, the Philippines is twelfth, Vietnam is fourteenth and Thailand is twentieth. Malaysia and Singapore are already high tech and actually manufacture a great deal of the technology. Western firms face fewer problems with trading and investment opportunities in most of these countries, which are less inclined to set up protectionist barriers than, for instance, Japan and Korea.

In order for Westerners to do business successfully in this area, they have to acquire certain insights into the Southeast Asian mindset. National traits vary considerably within this group—Vietnam is the odd one out—but Indonesians, Malaysians, Thais and Filipinos subscribe to a remarkable number of shared characteristics that have little in common with the more austere work-and-duty ethics of the Japanese, Koreans and Chinese. The Southeast Asian worldview is relatively relaxed, time is seen as a limitless commodity, the value of efficiency is often ambiguous and gentleness and virtue are prized above all.

One good way of discovering the Southeast Asian mentality is to examine the Western businessperson's model and to put it in perspective in relation to theirs.

The differences are striking. Westerners are of course generally self-determined and dynamic; Southeast Asians have deep cultural dynamics embedded in deeply rooted practices and customs. They wish to please their Western partners but must remain true to their cultural traditions.

Western	Southeast Asian
Love of individualism	Fondness for the collective
Personal ego	Personal interests subordinated to the group
Life is a challenge	Security and harmony
Achievement and self-actualization goals	Achievements must contribute to group goals
Competitiveness, aggression, direct confrontation	Cooperation, restraint, adaptation to the other
Overt action	Subtle, sometimes ambiguous action
Persuasion, argument, competition	Persuasion is presumptuous, Asians seek common ground, sharing
Technological change is rapid	Social and cultural change is evolutionary
External rewards	Internal rewards
Profit-sensitive	Sensitive to social pressures
Law, contractual obligations define behavior	Face saving, face giving define behavior
Western banter, familiarity, nicknames	Politeness, gentleness, low voice, social rank, mutual respect
Delegate to professionals	Delegate to kinship
Meritocracy	Patronage system
Planning top down	Policies and guidelines top down, tactical plans bottom up

Management goals:	Management goals:
✦ profit maximization	✦ social responsibility
✦ organizational efficiency	✦ harmonious work atmosphere
✦ high productivity	✦ high performance seen as ruthless

Westerners are really quite unaware of the rough ride that many Asians have when beginning to deal with the West. Let us take the case of an Indonesian gentleman arriving in the United States for a business negotiation. The first evening, while he is still suffering from jet lag, he is taken out for dinner by his American partner. After experiencing a crushing handshake, he is made to drink a couple of martinis, then red wine with a huge steak which he manages to get down with difficulty.

The next morning he is hung over but attends his meeting at the ridiculous time of 9:00 A.M. After more excruciating handshakes from other enormous Americans, he is subjected to the indignity of being addressed by his first name. Where are their manners? Small talk and friendly socializing at the beginning of the meeting were restricted to two minutes, unappetizing coffee is served in plastic (!) containers, and before he has gathered his wits, they are straight into the negotiation, giving him no chance to deliver his ten-minute background speech with a view to creating initial harmony between the parties. The negotiating style is confrontational, and he is being asked yes and no questions and badgered for quick decisions before he has even got his pens and pencils in a row.

The Americans, already physically overpowering, don't seem to be able to sit correctly—they are slumped and slouched and showed the soles of their shoes at him in ankle-on-knee crosses. When he indicates polite rejection of some of their proposals by the traditional reluctant-assent method, the Americans take it as yes and throw in more proposals. At times they become very tough, then friendly, then tough again—what a strange custom! They seem to think that attack is the best method of defense, bluff shamelessly, then concede quickly when their bluff is called. Obviously, face saving doesn't count! They blurt out many slangy expressions, which he doesn't understand and which they don't bother to explain. They use a lot of tough expressions like "That will blow it out of the water" (what water?) and "I tell you, I can walk away from this deal," when it is quite clear that they want to do the deal and make the profit. He wonders what kind of a company he is getting involved with…

The Muslim Cultures of Southeast Asia

Malaysia and Indonesia share many of the basic characteristics prevalent among East Asian people. However, the fact that Islam is the dominant religion in these two countries gives rise to certain important differences in behavior and attitudes.

In the following respects the Malaysians and Indonesians are *similar* to the Chinese, Koreans and Japanese:

+ The family is the basic unit of life. A great deal of time is spent developing interpersonal relationships with family members and close friends.
+ Harmony is important in social and business life. Head-on confrontation is to be avoided if at all possible.
+ Loss of face is very serious.
+ Conversations, including business discussions, are roundabout and indirect in the interest of politeness and avoiding offense.
+ Society is organized hierarchically, based on age and seniority.
+ Etiquette, good manners, protocol and gentleness are mandatory.
+ Collectivism prevails over individualism.

The Muslim cultures *diverge* from their Buddhist-Confucian-Taoist neighbors in the following respects:

+ Islam affects their social and business life on a daily basis.
+ Islamic taboos, such as pork and alcohol and the use of the left hand, are observed.
+ In Malaysia, the status and partial segregation of women are in accordance with Islamic practice.

- The work ethic shared by the Chinese, Japanese and Koreans is noticeably absent in Malaysia and Indonesia.
- Indonesians and Malaysians do not adhere to the same standards of punctuality as their neighbors.
- Compared with the Chinese, Japanese and Koreans, the Southeast Asian Muslims seem to lack drive and ambition and are less interested in profit and material success.

58

Indonesia

The world's largest Islamic country, with a population approaching 260 million, Indonesia is the world's largest archipelago, consisting of over 13,000 islands. It stretches over 5,000 kilometers (3,000 miles) from east to west and over 2,000 kilometers (1,200 miles) from north to south.

Fierce independence movements have flared in many of the islands, and Indonesia is described by many as the world's largest colonial power. It obtained independence from the Dutch in 1945, when the Japanese ceased to occupy the country. Guerrilla warfare delayed total independence until 1949. Achmad Sukarno was the country's first president, then Mohamed Suharto from 1966 until 1998. On Sukarno's overthrow, aversion to the influence of communist China led to the slaughter of many Chinese living in Indonesia, where, as in Malaysia, they controlled many aspects of commerce. The Chinese today keep a low profile, but they are still active in business. Indonesia is very poor, the per capita income not reaching $4,000 per annum. About 50 percent of national income comes from oil. Bahasa Indonesia, the national language, is closely related to Malay. Dialects of Bahasa Indonesia are numerous and are, unfortunately, often mutually incomprehensible.

The position of women is quite different from other Muslim countries: they can vote and have full civil rights; on many islands they hold leadership positions; they have never been veiled or secluded; and in Jakarta they often shake hands like men, though sometimes they bow with hands folded.

Indonesians are dialogue-oriented and a mix of reactive and multi-active in their cultural orientation. (See Chapter 3 for an explanation of these terms.)

Culture

Values

loquacity	face saving
hierarchy	courtesy
desire to please	gentleness
family	friendly hospitality
no work ethic in the Protestant sense	unity and conformity
age is respected	avoidance of confrontation
polygamy is permitted but rare	*adat* customary law usually prevails over Islam

Concepts

Leadership and Status

Leaders are expected to be paternalistic and are usually from chosen families or emanate from the higher ranks in the army. Leaders often seek consensus, which is the mode followed by all persons. In colonial times, leadership came from the Dutch. Under Sukarno and Suharto, leadership was exercised principally by the military and therefore was autocratic. The indifferent nature of many Indonesians to the business process has, however, resulted in a lot of business management being entrusted to resident Chinese. The Chinese professional class has the commercial know-how and international connections. Overseas Chinese shareholding in many Indonesian companies encourages this situation.

Space and Time

Indonesians are used to being crowded. They are comfortable in a group and need relatively little personal space.

Time in Indonesia is a "limitless pool." It is often referred to as "rubber time." Punctuality is not observed. Public and municipal meetings can begin one hour late or more. Indonesians do not like to be hurried, and there is little sense of urgency about anything.

Cultural Factors in Communication

Communication Pattern

Indonesians are loquacious, but they conduct their conversations in a quiet voice and without displaying intensity of emotion. Confrontation is avoided and problems or areas of difference are alluded to in an indirect manner. Indonesians excel in respectful language and, in the reactive manner, modify their own proposals out of deference. They are clever at saying what you want to hear; they can be tantalizingly ambiguous. They can engage in prolonged questioning to clarify intent, but even so, meetings often end with a few loose ends floating around. They also are reluctant to admit that they do not know the answer to a question. They often give wrong directions!

Listening Habits

Indonesians listen deferentially and do not interrupt. Speeches at public meetings are long and boring, but people show no dissension. In business meetings they listen carefully to foreigners but do not always fully understand the content; unfortunately, they do not indicate this, and misunderstandings may arise as a result. The general level of English is quite low. Indonesians rarely say anything that might be offensive; consequently, it is often difficult to judge the relative success of your presentation.

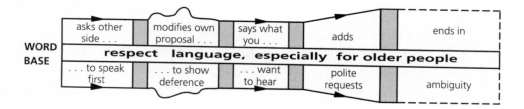

Figure 58.1 Indonesian Communication Pattern

Behavior at Meetings and Negotiations

Deferential listening and quiet speaking are aimed at maintaining harmony. No one must be made to feel *malu* (ashamed or embarrassed). Everything is negotiable, and everything takes time. Bargaining is expected, and hard bargainers are respected. There are, in reality, no fixed prices, and starting positions may be way out of line. Indonesians act in a collectivist manner and, like the Japanese, prefer to negotiate in numbers. They are almost never aggressive, but you will need a lot of patience and must forget about time pressures.

Indonesians have a strong multi-active streak that sometimes overlies their basic (Asian) reactive nature. The result of this is that meetings, although generally conducted in a restrained, courteous manner, can be extremely long and verbose. This can test a Westerner's patience, especially if translation and interpreting are involved. Delegations (also when traveling abroad) can be large. Many delegates do not seem to take a very active part in the discussion but attend in order to "get to know the other side." Older people are expected to do most of the speaking and be responsible for the progression of the meeting. Repetition is frequent, and it is often hard for a Westerner to discern the direction of the Indonesian side.

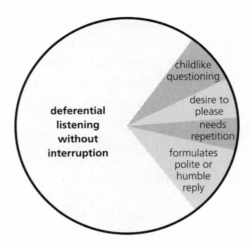

Figure 58.2 Indonesian Listening Habits

Indonesians, for their part, seem comfortable with ambiguity and often appear to promote it. They shy away from too much Western directness or bluntness. As in many Asian countries, confrontation is anathema.

Manners and Taboos

Respectability in dress is important; women can wear shorts, but they should reach the knees and be baggy rather than tight.

Greetings are always courteous, and shaking hands with women is acceptable. Men often hold hands.

Indonesians touch each other more than most East Asians, but the head remains sacred. One's head may not be held higher than that of a superior or older person, which means that Indonesians often bend or lower their head, even duck (or drop shoulders) when passing "superiors" in the street!

Things are handed over with the right hand or with both hands for added respect. A hands-on-hip stance is seen as aggressive.

Taboos include the Muslim prohibition on alcohol and pork as well as the use of the left hand. It is bad manners to point, ask personal questions or completely finish the food on your plate. Unfortunately bribery is common at most levels of society and is called "speed money."

How to Empathize with Indonesians

Indonesians are very friendly and you should reciprocate this. Courtesy and gentleness are mandatory. Indonesians will buy from people who treat them with deference and who show they like them; generally, they crave recognition and affection. References to corruption, military influence or other problems or shortcomings evident in the country will only serve to embarrass them. Women are not secluded as in many Muslim countries, so you may converse with them. Ask Indonesians about their families a lot—they appreciate concern for relations. Sympathize with them over the tsunami disaster in December 2004.

MOTIVATION	
KEY	*Show gentleness and respect*
Cross-century mood	✦ Satisfaction at toppling a military regime is tempered by uneasiness about possible revolutions and chaos. ✦ Growing awareness of their size and future market potential. ✦ Not yet oriented as to which politics or regional goals they will pursue. ✦ Tendency to soften Islamic discipline (in contrast to Iran and Afghanistan, for example).

Motivating Factors

✦ Although they show great humility, Indonesians are well aware that they are the fourth largest country in the world. Show respect for the size of their market!

✦ Corruption is endemic. As you cannot avoid it, learn to make the best of the system, dealing with it pragmatically and with grace.

✦ Most Indonesians are Muslims, though *adat* (customary law) usually prevails over Islam. Become familiar with the basic tenets of both creeds—and respect them.

✦ Conformity is valued above individuality, so always take into account the interest of groups. The same applies to rewards and incentives.

✦ Bear in mind that Indonesians are less aggressive in business than many other nationalities. They are motivated not so much by prospects of profits and material success as by a smooth relationship with their associates.

✦ A lot of business in Indonesia is carried on by resident Chinese. You may profitably use these channels, but always keep Indonesians in the picture.

✦ Indonesians have a positive orientation toward work only if it is fun. Try to maintain a pleasant atmosphere in the workplace or during discussions.

✦ If you are in a position of leadership, you are expected to be paternalistic.

✦ They often will turn to you when they are in difficulty; give advice and personal help readily.

✦ You should always speak in a quiet voice and show little emotion (except compassion).

✦ Indonesians respect Westerners and expect you to be clean, neat and well-dressed. Women must dress in a respectable and somewhat conservative manner.

(continued)

MOTIVATION *(continued)*

+ Small talk before commencing business is expected.
+ The level of English throughout Indonesia is not high. You should speak slowly and clearly and in a kind manner. Repeat your remarks whenever you suspect there might be a misunderstanding.

Avoid

+ Pressuring them or insisting on Western punctuality.
+ Being confrontational. Refer to problems in an indirect manner.
+ Getting involved in political issues.
+ Referring to possible dismemberment of the Indonesian state.

59

Malaysia

Malaysia has a population of around 30 million, of whom 50 percent are Malay, 36 percent Chinese, and 14 percent Indian and other groups. The political structure is a federation of 13 states, 11 on the Malay peninsula and 2 (Sabah and Sarawak) on the island of Borneo. Chief exports are rubber, palm oil, tropical timber, tin, petroleum, cocoa beans and pepper.

Racial tension between the Malays and Chinese exists. As Malay people have traditionally been only minimally involved in the economic sector of the community, an occupational void was largely filled by the Chinese. When the Malays eventually gained control over the economy, riots occurred. In 1969 a twenty-year plan was introduced to increase the Malay labor force at all levels of business and to reduce the foreign share of the Malay market from 60 to 30 percent by 1990. Due to a continuing lack of interest in business by the Malays, these percentages have been difficult to achieve. Work and idleness are not clearly delineated in Malay culture and language. Work is only one of many activities pursued by the Malays. Deepening of relationships and time spent with the elderly may be seen as idle pursuits by Westerners, but not by Malays.

The near balance of power between Malays and Chinese requires close cooperation between the two cultures, but because of cultural differences in customs, religions and values, an atmosphere of distrust still exists.

Culture

Values

gentleness (*budi*)	family and friends
respect, courtesy	formality giving way to informality
love of children	wealth not pursued for its own sake
trust	lack of motivation for worldly success
compromise	fatalism—God's will
goodness of humanity	preference to study arts instead of science
strong Islamic beliefs	

Concepts

Leadership and Status

People born in high positions are expected to demonstrate leadership capabilities. A good leader is religiously devout, sincere, humble and tactful.

Status is inherited, not earned, and is confirmed by demonstrating leadership and a caring attitude. Malays feel comfortable in a hierarchical structure in which they have a definite role.

Malays are modest and rarely request promotion. They expect it to be accorded by a caring senior when the time is ripe.

Space and Time

An adequate distance of comfort is respected. Malays are environmentally conscious.

There is little attention to the past, and the future is regarded as vague and unpredictable (God's will), so the present must be spent virtuously.

Cultural Factors in Communication

Communication Pattern

Conversations are roundabout, avoiding giving offense. Malays are skilled at indirect references. Communication is formal at first, with gradual informality being introduced over time. A certain elegance of expression is maintained, both when speaking Malay and English. Some British influence is evident in debating.

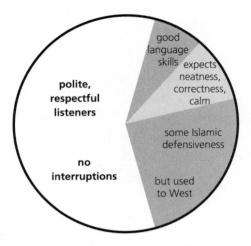

Figure 59.1 Malay Listening Habits

Listening Habits

Malays are respectful, especially to seniors and elderly people; they will not interrupt. They listen for virtue and caring comments. Most can understand English spoken at normal speed.

Behavior at Meetings and Negotiations

Harmony and balanced discussion are sought. Malays' relative indifference to business reduces ambition and competition. There is little attempt to alter the environment (in direct contrast to Singapore, Hong Kong, Korea and Japan). People who compromise most in business negotiations are the ones who are respected most. The Malays are not given to great shows of determination.

Manners and Taboos

Most taboos are Muslim. Malays are comfortable in a hierarchical structure, showing deference to seniors and authority.

Greetings are important. It is customary for men and women to shake hands with each other. In the Malay handshake the man offers both hands, but without the grip. He lightly touches his friend's hands, then brings his hands to his breast. This means "I greet you from my heart." Women often salaam, bowing very low.

The index finger is not used for pointing. It is more polite to use the right thumb, with fingers closed. As in Indonesia, the head is sacred and should not be touched (no patting children on the head!).

How to Empathize with Malays

Malays are more group-oriented than many other people. Try to apply synergistic skills to the relationship. This is a good approach with people who think in terms of divisions between Malay/Chinese/Western or Muslim/Buddhist/Christian.

Familiarize yourself with the basic concepts of Islam. Show respect for seniors and religious beliefs. Younger Malays are very proud of the modern Malay orientation toward industrialization and high tech; share this enthusiasm with them.

MOTIVATION	
KEY	*Man is basically good*
Cross-century mood	✦ Malays wish to be at the forefront of technology and modernization without sacrificing Islamic or Asian values. ✦ Currently see their own spiritual and moral standards as high. ✦ Would like to settle the cultural differences between Malays and the numerous local Chinese.

Motivating Factors

✦ Impute best motives (man is good).
✦ Be courteous and gentle at all times; speak in a low, kindly voice.
✦ Look always to the collective good.
✦ Seek harmony and balanced discussion at meetings.
✦ Make indirect references to problems and save face for all.
✦ Show you possess dignity and are (possibly) devout.
✦ Show affection for children.
✦ Remember that Malays see time spent deepening relationships as work, not idleness.
✦ Compromise wisely.
✦ Remember that correct greetings are important.

Avoid

✦ Roughness or loudness.
✦ Direct criticism of people.
✦ Pointing at people or patting children on the head.
✦ Focusing on the bottom line.

60

Singapore

Perhaps Singapore never intended to become a tiger. Its name, *Singapura,* is Sanskrit meaning "Lion City," but even that description was euphemistic for a port that was notorious as a pirate haunt. It remained a jungle backwater from 1400 to 1800, but better times were soon to come. Singapore is not a tale of two cities but rather a tale of two men, both remarkable individuals and visionaries to whom the city owes its present prosperity.

If you have stayed at the Raffles Hotel, you may be aware that it was named after Thomas Raffles, son of an undistinguished sea captain. He joined the East India Company at the age of 14 and in his mid-twenties was posted to Penang, where he took the trouble to learn Malay, an initiative that contrasted strongly with the linguistic lethargy of better-educated colonial officials. His common sense and ability to communicate with all manner of people stood him in good stead. He held many important posts as an administrator, but his most significant achievement was the founding of Singapore. By 1822 Singapore had developed into a booming port with 10,000 inhabitants.

Raffles, who is still greatly honored in Singapore, was the right man in the right place at the right time. Besides Singapore, he also founded the London Zoo and the Raffles Institution. It was at this college that the second of the two great men of Singapore was educated, the first prime minister, Lee Kuan Yew.

While Thomas Raffles fathered the original colony, Lee Kuan Yew can truly be described as the father of modern Singapore. His parents were Straits-born Chinese of Hakka origin. After studying at the Raffles Institution, he went to Cambridge University, where he got a First (degree) in law, with distinction. He set up a law firm in Singapore but became increasingly involved in politics and became prime minister in 1959. His tenure lasted 31 years. It was characterized by benevolent dictatorship based on efficiency, honesty, intolerance and an unswerving sense of mission. At the time of its breakaway from the Malaysian Federation, Singapore was considered by many critics to be a nonviable economy on account of its bulging population and complete lack of natural resources. Lee proved them all wrong. He perceived that the teeming inhabitants of Singapore, like those of the Japanese islands, were the country's greatest asset. Unlike the homogeneous Japanese, however, Singaporeans had to be welded into a team. Although imbued with a desire to create wealth (here they resemble the people of Hong Kong), Singaporeans were of extremely diverse origin—Chinese, Malay, Indian, European and Eurasian. Lee took it on himself to create a sense of national identity, to build a nation, to run it as it should be run. As the *Economist* said, "Lee ran Singapore like a well-run nursery." He felt he knew what was best for the country and, showing great political adroitness, he allowed no one to defy him. In his three decades in power he created a powerful economy: Singaporeans who might have wished to oppose or obstruct him were crushed by the sheer weight of the city–state's achievements. In one of his speeches he exclaimed, "The greatest satisfaction in life comes from achievement. To achieve is to be happy . . . Achievement generates inner or spiritual strength, a strength which grows out of an inner discipline."

Discipline there certainly was. Chewing gum, littering and (for some time) long hair were taboo. Fines were heavy, including ones for failing to flush the toilet. Singaporeans were imbued with Lee's Confucian values—filial respect, duty, moderation and the work ethic were mandatory. (See Chapter 65 for a description of the basic tenets of Confucianism.) Censorship of the media, including television, was strict. Welfare, job stability, good education, cheap housing and affluence were thrust on Lee's citizens. The people of Singapore were going to be happy, whether they liked it or not.

Concepts

Leadership and Status

The current leadership model is very similar to Lee Kuan Yew's. Singaporean Asians are comfortable in hierarchical structures. Value is, however, also placed on good teamwork, especially among the younger generations.

Space and Time

Singapore and Hong Kong have the world's highest density of population. Consequently, Singaporeans are used to crowds and crowding. However, during conversation they maintain a respectful 1 to 1.2 meters (39 to 47 inches) from interlocutors. Space is valuable and Singaporeans like to own some. They have the highest rate of home ownership in the world.

Singaporeans also value time. They do not waste any and are in general extremely punctual.

Cultural Factors in Communication

Communication Pattern

Singaporeans are largely fluent in English and are characterized by articulateness and verbal clarity. Speech is courteous. They are by no means long-winded.

Listening Habits

Singaporeans are courteous, careful listeners in the Asian manner. They do not interrupt, but give good feedback at the end. They often reply with, "My modest opinion is . . ."

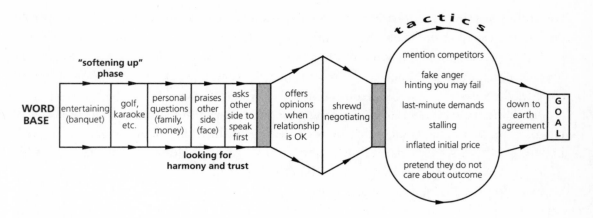

Figure 60.1 Singaporean Communication Pattern

Figure 60.2 Singaporean Listening Habits

How to Empathize with Singaporeans

+ Bear in mind the racial mix and react accordingly:
+ The Chinese dominate and play a big part in running the state; they are efficient, frugal and have an impeccable social and business network that you should respect and try to join.
+ Westerners tend to be very experienced (old hands) and are also well connected.
+ Eurasians can be sensitive about their origins.
+ Indians are mainly Tamils and speak that language.
+ Malays tend to be less ambitious in business than the other groups.

◆ Try to acquire a smattering of the languages spoken in Singapore (other than English): Mandarin Chinese, Malay and Tamil.

◆ Remember and be sensitive to the varying religious beliefs: Christian, Buddhist, Muslim, Hindu and Taoist.

◆ Conform to the republic's disciplined, law-abiding, somewhat sober way of life; eccentricity will win you few medals and will erode your credibility.

MOTIVATION	
KEY	*Showing efficiency and leanness*
Cross-century mood	◆ Determined to maintain their prosperity and stability. ◆ Somewhat nervous about Indonesian instability. ◆ See possibilities of continued good relations with China in spite of different political systems.

Motivating Factors

◆ Show personal efficiency.

◆ Demonstrate frugality.

◆ Try to think multiculturally.

◆ Praise Singapore's fantastic economic achievements.

◆ Respect elders.

◆ Show you know Singapore is an independent country.

◆ Respect academic achievement.

◆ Stay clean and well-dressed.

Avoid

◆ Looking or sounding like an ex-colonialist.

◆ Querying Eurasians about their origins.

◆ Discussing religion.

◆ Criticizing China too much.

61

Thailand

The nineteenth century saw extensive colonization in Southeast Asia, but one nation–state in the area remained independent: Thailand, formerly known to the West as Siam. *Thai* means "free," so Thailand is the "Land of the Free," also known as the "Land of Smiles" and the "Land of the Yellow Robes." The last title vividly describes the Buddhist religion embraced by the Thai people.

The odds against Thailand remaining free from either the British or the French sphere of interest were considerable, but various factors combined to enable the country to preserve its sovereignty. Thailand was in fact not an easy nut to crack. A nation of successful fighters, it had enjoyed unbroken control over its own territory since 1238, when the Thais revolted against the Khmers, whose tradition they share, and established the Kingdom of Sukhothai in the north central part of the country.

Relatively populous throughout the following 600 years, the Thais were no pushover for any power and in fact dominated their neighbors for the period. They also had the territorial advantage of not being adjacent to a nearby colossus—India or China—where British influence was strong. Geographically, they were cushioned by weaker states: Laos, Cambodia, Burma and former Malaya. The fact that they had the colonialist British to the west and their French rivals to the east gave the Thais opportunities to play one off against the other, and they eventually concluded treaties with both European powers. Neither did they neglect the Americans: the first American ship arrived in Thailand in 1821; in 1833 the Thai-American Treaty of Amity and Commerce was signed in Bangkok. The good relations with the United States have been maintained into the twenty-first century, and the U.S. is Thailand's biggest export market.

The astuteness of Thai diplomacy, their fiercely independent spirit and the paramount importance of their religion—Buddhism—are the main factors in Thailand's cultural differentiation from the other Southeast Asian states.

Thailand is the world's biggest exporter of rubber. Textiles are now a major export item and the nation is also an important exporter of more sophisticated products such as hard-disk drives for computers, precision micro-ball bearings and integrated circuits.

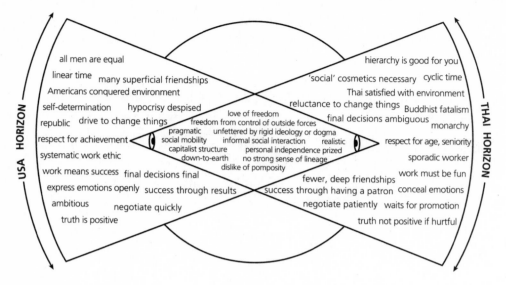

Figure 61.1 USA/Thai Horizon

Culture

Values

pragmatism	simplicity
fatalism, karma	love of freedom
dislike of pomposity	form and proper behavior
family, filial piety	compassion, kindness
respect, face, deference	dignity, honor
belief in moderation	reluctance to initiate change
satisfaction with nature's tempo	interest in Western education
rejection of Western work ethic	desire for inward comfort

Religion

Of the total population of over 65 million, 95 percent have declared themselves Buddhists, mostly of the Theravada school. About 4 percent of the people are Muslims.

In Thailand, Laos, Cambodia and Vietnam, Theravada Buddhism is the most important form of Buddhism. This is distinct from Mahayana Buddhism, as practiced in China, Korea, Japan and the Hanoi area of Vietnam, which has a long history of Chinese influence. Theravada Buddhism is more influential, meaningful and especially visible in the lives of the common people than the Mahayana variant, which is often interlaced with rigid Confucian doctrines. (A description of the basic tenets of Confucianism is given in Chapter 65.)

During many centuries of Thai history, education, which has long been considered a key to national security and development, was almost exclusively in the hands of Buddhist monks. The Thai alphabet was invented by King Ramkhamhaeng in the thirteenth century. Buddhist monasteries (called *wats*) established schools within their grounds and the monks, in addition to their religious duties, taught reading, writing and arithmetic, as well as other subjects, to local youngsters. Today there are over 30,000 temples scattered throughout Thailand's 73 provinces. In modern Thailand, schools are now run by the government, but many of them are still located within the compounds of monasteries.

To understand the importance of the wat and of popular Buddhism in controlling Thai thought, it is necessary to appreciate the multifunctional nature of these monasteries and how much they are used by the common people. Families in rural areas often feel insecure about keeping their valuables in their homes, so they ask the abbot to store them in the monastery. The wat is not only the villager's "safe deposit box," it is also a storehouse for documents and artifacts of historical significance. Thousands of Buddha images are also kept there and used for public veneration and objects of meditation.

Travelers may stay overnight in wats, especially when traveling to festivals; children sent to schools in Bangkok can use them as hostels, their parents making donations. The young schoolboys live with the monks and assist them with their daily chores, such as washing, cleaning and carrying food containers. They also receive instruction in the Buddhist tenets. Government functions take place in wats (elections, conscription), and some are even used as clinics.

Concepts

Leadership and Status

In 1257 the Kingdom of Sukhothai adopted the paternalistic system of government. The king, while enjoying absolute sovereign power, looked after his subjects like a father and personally paid close attention to their well-being. The Khmer system had been based on the concept of Divine Right (not unlike England's). The bloodless coup of 1932 that led to Thailand changing from absolute to constitutional monarchy did little to alter this structure. Today the king's power emanates from the people; he is head of state and of the armed forces and is upholder of Buddhism and all other religions.

In Thailand authority and power are considered natural to the human condition. The holder of power has accumulated merit in a previous life. The best leader is one who empathizes most with his subordinates.

There is a clear hierarchy of status: king, aristocracy, government officials, priests, doctors, professors, businesspeople, others. The military, while influential, is always in the background. Hierarchy is good for you, subordinates are happy with their station in life. There is a certain amount of social mobility, but one doesn't challenge the system.

Space and Time

Thais are friendly and stand close, but are basically non-tactile.

Buddhists have a cyclical concept of time. Days and seasons succeed each other, as do kings and governments. Opportunities and options recur and multiply irrespective of one's anxiety to seize them. The use of time does not equate with earning a living. Success depends more on luck than on timing. Thais dislike deadlines.

Cultural Factors in Communication

Communication Pattern

People who keep cool are respected, so conversation is conducted with Buddhist moderation. When angered, Thais use a subtle method of revenge.

In general, they avoid unpleasant truths and describe only a small percentage of personal problems. Saving face for others is vital. Hypocrisy is not always negative.

Humor is used (largely puns). Smiles may cover tragic situations.

Listening Habits

Thais are docile, obedient listeners. They never interrupt a speaker, and unless requested, they give no feedback. Sensitive discussions must be initiated from the top.

Behavior at Meetings and Negotiations

Buddhism discourages competition; therefore, Thais are not overly ambitious and are reluctant to initiate change. Easy work with sufficient pay is better than hard work with high pay. Authority is respected when present but often ignored when absent. Work tempo increases or decreases according to the presence of the boss. Discussion of issues is welcomed, but decisions (and blame) are passed upward.

Social affairs are discussed during work hours, but business is pursued after hours in social situations, thus blending the two. There is a patronage system for getting ahead. Decisions are often ambiguous, so that nobody loses face. Negotiations should not be hurried: three or four days of building relationships are advisable first. The central part of business is approached slowly and concentrically. Giggles mean that a favor is to be asked for (or withheld).

Manners and Taboos

Direct confrontations must be avoided at all costs; everyone's face must be maintained. Socializing includes meals, theater and music, kickboxing, going to the beach and badminton. Care should be taken to observe the pecking order in social and business situations. Superiors are not to be challenged, but they generally strive to get on well with subordinates.

How to Empathize with Thais

- ✦ Know Thai history.
- ✦ Emphasize their independence.
- ✦ Be easy-going socially.
- ✦ Don't rush them.
- ✦ Learn the basics of Theravada Buddhism.
- ✦ Think of time as cyclical.
- ✦ Respect the monarchy.
- ✦ Dress neatly.

MOTIVATION	
KEY	*Make work pleasant*
Cross-century mood	✦ Thais have little objection to maintaining friendly relations with the United States; this is growing through student grants. ✦ Thais are happy to continue to pursue their traditional independent path in the twenty-first century; it has stood the test of time. ✦ Thais seem content to let overseas Chinese run a lot of their business, and this feature may well gain importance as China becomes more powerful economically. ✦ Thais are happy to be increasingly involved in the manufacturing of technological products.

Motivating Factors

- ✦ Show sincerity and kindness when addressing Thais.
- ✦ Clarify your position in the hierarchy and exercise your powers according to your rank.
- ✦ Develop a client–patron relationship with your subordinates.
- ✦ Moderate your expressions of emotion.
- ✦ Distribute responsibility gradually, simultaneously encouraging staff.
- ✦ Adopt a relaxed attitude toward the work tempo, avoiding too many deadlines.
- ✦ Encourage enthusiasm for launching new projects.
- ✦ Maintain form and properness at all times.

(continued)

MOTIVATION *(continued)*

+ Protect everyone's face at all times. White lies are permissible.
+ Introduce as much "fun" as possible into your directives.
+ Introduce changes gradually and with full explanation.
+ Accord promotion regularly. Thais expect it to be initiated by superiors.
+ Emphasize security rather than risk-taking in the work context.
+ Keep in mind that blame in a Thai company is passed upward.
+ Remember that there is no clear division between life and work. Thais discuss personal matters during business hours.
+ Allow time off for employees who have urgent family problems.
+ Discuss problems with contextual sensitivity.

Avoid

+ Being pompous.
+ Being blunt or overly frank.
+ Getting heated.
+ Overlooking people in your presence.
+ Seeming to be overly materialistic.

62

Myanmar (Burma)

Burma, or Myanmar as it is now called, is no tiny appendage to the Asian mega-powers of China, India, or Japan. It is a huge variegated landmass of 673,000 square kilometers, bigger than Britain and France combined, comfortably peopled by over 60 million sturdy inhabitants. It features a bustling capital of 6 million citizens—Yangon (formerly Rangoon in the days of the British Empire)—and boasts an impressive array of national assets such as oil, natural gas, minerals (jade, sapphires, rubies, emeralds), gold, timber (especially teak), as well as agricultural products like rice, maize, beans, tea, jute, tobacco, betel nuts, cotton and sugar cane.

In spite of its atmosphere of poverty, backwardness and lack of urgency, it is a rich country of untapped wealth, blessed geographically by a horseshoe formation of mountain ranges guarding the vast interior plains around the River Irrawaddy from invasion, whether from India, China or Thailand. Her northern border with China is flanked by the Tibetan range of mountains, where passes are rarely lower than 3,000 meters above sea level and which contains Southeast Asia's highest peak—Hkakabo Razi (5,881 meters or 19,295 feet).

In spite of its size, natural wealth and advantageous geographical location, Myanmar has never been a totally homogeneous nation. In fact, one has to stretch one's imagination to call it a state. The land is made up of seven regions (or divisions), plus seven separate states (Kachin, Shan, Chin, Kayin, Kayah, Mon and Rakhine). Each state has different histories and traditions, costumes, philosophies, agendas and aspirations. The biggest state (Shan) has nearly 5 million inhabitants, its area of 60,000 square miles forming Burma's eastern border with China, Laos and Thailand.

At the time of writing, there are some signs of change (it has been described as 'a fragile opening'). Aung San Suu Kyi's long struggle and repeated periods of house arrest have borne some fruit. The junta of generals resigned in March 2011. Parliamentary rule was established and the multi-party elections held in October 2010 had resulted in the government party winning a rigged contest. The Prime Minister of the former military government, Thein Sein, became the new civilian President in March 2011 and began to initiate courageous reforms in August. His first meeting with Aung San Suu Kyi took place the same month and her party, the NLD, was allowed to stand in the elections the following April. She and her party won 43 of the 45 seats up for election. Thein Sein left office on 30 March 2016, and Aung San Suu Kyi became State Counselor.

This modest opening of the political system may have a much greater significance. Over the next few years, Asia's geography will see a fundamental reorientation, bringing China and India together in an unprecedented manner. For millennia these two countries have been separated by near-impenetrable barriers: jungle, deadly malaria, the Himalayas, the high wastelands of the Tibetan plateau, the difficult terrain of North Myanmar. For the last decade India and China have united many of their commercial aims and aspirations for greater power by creating, along with Russia and Brazil, the significant union BRICS, an alliance that embraces five states with nearly 50 percent of the world's population and soon to surpass more than half of the planet's GDP. What they currently lack is smooth coordination, hampered by incomplete geographical proximity and differences in cultural make-up. Dr. Thant Myint-U has written about the proposed new configuration of the East, where Asia's last great frontier may disappear, and Asia be woven together as never before. At the heart of this change lies Myanmar. China refers to the "Malacca Dilemma," because 80 percent of her vital oil imports have to pass through Strait of Malacca near Singapore. She is now building a pipeline across Myanmar, which will significantly shorten oil routes. Along new Myanmar highways, China will be able to export her own goods directly to European markets, bypassing the Indian Ocean route. Both China and India can help develop Myanmar's raw-materials riches, particularly useful for the industrial development of China's southwest. Some experts predict the making of a new Silk Road like the one that in ancient times coupled China to Central Asia and Europe. The new Silk Road lately proposed does not go through Burma, but there seems to be a linked project that does.

However things turn out, it seems likely that Myanmar's key location will cause her to be increasingly involved in the movements of her giant neighbors. Tourism is already exploding, but the prospect of bilateral treaties and industrial development may rapidly transform this conservative land into something quite different during the course of the twenty-first century. The four Asian Tigers—Korea, Hong Kong, Taiwan and Singapore—have undergone their transformation and prospered. Myanmar's territory is more than five times as big as all the Tigers combined. Her area is almost as extensive as the whole of Indo-China (Vietnam, Laos and Cambodia). Will Myanmar figure, along with Vietnam, as one of the next bunch of Asian Tigers? Sandwiched between two ambitious BRICS, will she be carried to prosperity in tandem with them?

Culture

Values

religiosity	humility
serenity	quietness
sense of duty	sacrifice
respect	fatalism
neatness	anti-Muslim

Religion

One is amazed at the intensity of the people's preoccupation with religion. Burmese regard themselves as one of the champions of Theravada Buddhism, influencing Buddhist followers in neighboring countries. Burmese of all ages seem to devote one or two hours daily to religious pursuits—prayers, worshipping, maintaining their Buddhist structures. On the Sagaing hill cluster, overlooking Mandalay, there are no fewer than 554 monasteries and nunneries; there are over 4,000 pagodas in Bagan alone, while near Monywa, where the world's tallest Buddha (424 feet) is visible from a distance of 16 km, there are 500,000 almost identical images and life-size statues of Buddha lined up in a cemetery-like array over several acres.

It is clear that the scrupulous maintenance of these structures and the support of the huge monastic population imposes heavy demands on the national economy, yet society seems to expect nothing in return save the merit gained through their religious devoutness and the guardianship of the monks. Building pagodas guarantees better reincarnation in the next world, while imposing considerable financial hardship in this one! This search for merit is observable in practically every aspect of Burmese daily life. With the advent of globalization (and Burma has, until recently, been one of the last strongholds of its exclusion), one asks oneself: what is the future of this long-hidden land? Continued preoccupation with religious pursuits or a switch to concerns of economic progress? Comforting spiritual seclusion or international integration?

Concepts

Leadership and Status

On the whole, public obedience is typical, particularly vis-à-vis the military authorities. The decades-long support of Aung San Suu Kyi indicates, however, a refusal to abandon certain aspects of dissent. At the time of writing, public opinion is deeply split with regard to the Rohingya question resulting in political turmoil and over 700,000 refugees forced into exile. People are also led by the religious tenets of Theravada Buddhism.

Space and Time

The distance of comfort during conversation is a respectful minimum of 1.5 meters. Burmese are non-tactile in general. An inordinate amount of space is afforded to religious structures and rituals.

The concept of time is typically Buddhist, i.e. cyclical. The time devoted to religious duties in Myanmar is unparalleled elsewhere. No great attachment to punctuality. As in Japan, timeliness is more important.

Cultural Factors in Communication

Communication Pattern

Burmese tend to be slow and cautious in self-expression. They strive for articulacy when addressing foreigners. They are reluctant to reveal strong views or opinions, preferring a certain vagueness when pushed to be explicit. Humility is a general characteristic, though they are gently persistent.

Listening Habits

Again, humility precludes interruptions. Largely passive when listening, they conceal their real feelings. The speaker gets the impression of overall compliance. Buddhist tenets govern their attitude.

Behavior at Meetings and Negotiations

Face protection is vital during all meetings, which may often appear protracted, with no little measure of ambiguity. Toleration is preached in general, though the persecution of the Rohingya in recent years has blighted this reputation. The military are often involved in business discussions and tend to deny their own shortcomings in the area of tolerance and consent.

Manners and Taboos

In spite of striking regional differences, anomalies and conflicts, the biggest tribe—the Burmese themselves—form a visible national core. Burmese count 70 percent of the country's population. They would not be described as ardent nationalists, but speak of their country with some pride, though in humble terms. Certain features are common to all the area's inhabitants, even the outlying states. These are the wearing of the *longyi* by both men and women, the use of *thanaka* yellow cosmetics on cheeks, betel and *lapet* (pickled tea), peasants' carts drawn by twin oxen, weaving and lacquer ware, ubiquitous monks in the countryside and in the streets of the cities, groups of nuns, novice monks (children) carrying rice-bowls, millions of Buddhist structures—pagodas, shrines, statues, images of Buddha, frequent festivals and processions, numerous monasteries and nunneries dotting the landscape.

How to Empathize with the Burmese

Any form of political discussion, in either business or social encounters, is difficult for outsiders. There are ample opportunities for foreigners to enjoy exchanges with Burmese in terms of appreciating the restful and scenic landscape, the comforts and intricacies of their faith and the general friendliness of the populace. It remains to be seen how the variegated influences of the military, the reformists, the turmoil on the Bangladeshi frontier and the ultimate impact of China and India will settle the Burmese and the empathies they seek.

MOTIVATION	
KEY	*Express opinions in a non-assertive manner*
Cross-century mood	◆ Positioning themselves between China and India. ◆ Contemplating part in "Silk Road." ◆ Rohingya Turmoil.
	(continued)

MOTIVATION *(continued)*

Motivating Factors

- ✦ Be courteous at all times.
- ✦ Show interest in their religious activities.
- ✦ Enjoy touring their temples etc.
- ✦ Always be patient with them.
- ✦ Impute best motives.

Avoid

- ✦ Taking sides in political disputes.
- ✦ Talking too loud.
- ✦ Criticizing any Burmese regional group.

63

The Philippines

Among East and Southeast Asians, Filipinos are an anomaly. They are talkative in the Latin manner; they demonstrate warmth and emotion openly; they are cosmopolitan and travel the world; they are comfortable with Americans and with Westerners in general; they are committed to democratic institutions, including freedom of speech; and they distrust and reject authoritarianism whenever possible.

The repressive and corrupt Marcos era was hard on the easygoing Filipinos, not least because the dictator was propped up by the Americans, from whom Filipinos had learned much better attributes. Their enthusiasm for liberty, their will to debate, their commitment to free enterprise and their open borders were all part of the U.S. legacy. With the overthrow of Ferdinand Marcos in 1986, Corazon Aquino introduced political reforms. Her successor, President Fidel Ramos, proved more adept and, though formerly an autocratic figure, he kept the country firmly on the path of reform. He perceived clearly the effect of Western countries on Filipino thought and pointed out that his people could not be governed in the

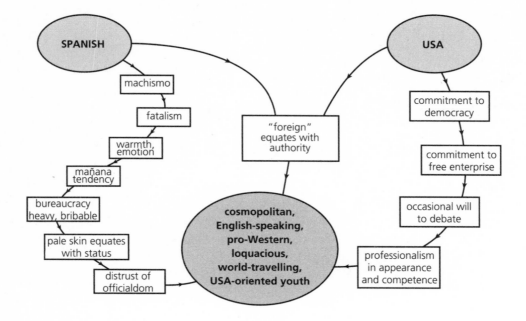

Figure 63.1 The Philippines—Colonial Influences

same authoritarian manner as the Japanese, Chinese, Koreans and Singaporeans. For example, over 100,000 Americans live in the Philippines, and almost 2 million Filipinos reside in the U.S., where they are the fastest growing Asian minority. A Filipino governor was elected in Hawaii.

The "non-Asianness" of Filipinos derives not only from their 100-year contact with the Americans, but also to a great degree from the 350-year period of Spanish colonialism. Indeed, the islands were named after Philip II of Spain!

Culture

Values

family most important   hospitality
education highly valued   authority highly valued
respect for old people   sensitivity to overly aggressive behavior
no criticism in public   (American)
hiya (avoidance of shame at all costs)   fatalism
love of gambling and games of chance   machismo
Roman Catholicism   flexibility
loyalty sought and reciprocated   personalization of business essential

Concepts

Leadership and Status

Leadership is based on family name, age and connections. Subordinates are generally obedient and avoid dissension. Managers often strive to do well, as the subordinates' expectations inspire them. Paternalism is common. Employees may ask superiors to help them in various matters. Older people are expected to give advice to younger ones, who listen to them attentively. Managers must give clear instructions to achieve progress. The military may sometimes be involved in political leadership.

Status is established by family name, connections and education. In spite of the Filipino love of democracy, senior- and even middle-ranking Filipinos can be hypersensitive in matters of status and quickly take offense if there is an imagined slight.

Space and Time

The distance of comfort is closer than that of most Europeans but similar to that of Spaniards. The everyday greeting for acquaintances and friends is a handshake for both men and women. A pat on the back has been inherited from the Spanish.

A *mañana* tendency has also been inherited from the Spanish. When making appointments, it is advisable to ask if they are "American time" or "Filipino time." In the case of the latter, being one or two hours late is not unusual.

Cultural Factors in Communication

Communication Pattern

Filipinos' multi-active, dialogue-oriented communication somewhat resembles the Spanish, but is less forceful and exuberant. (See Chapter 3 for an explanation of these terms.) Oratory is valued and speeches can be lengthy. Although Tagalog is used throughout the country, the Philippines is, at a functional level, the second largest English-speaking nation in the world. Some politicians even make speeches half in Tagalog and half in English.

Listening Habits

Although somewhat excitable and scattered in thought, Filipinos' Asian side makes them good, polite listeners. They like warm but modest speakers and can understand English speakers at normal speed. They rarely interrupt, but give ready feedback.

Behavior at Meetings and Negotiations

Politeness, especially to older people and persons of senior rank, is absolutely essential. The tone of discussion is generally conciliatory, and avoidance of heated discussion or opinionated expression is advisable. Filipinos like to be conformist and rarely say no openly. They conceal their feelings well, so you should try to read the hidden signals they give at meetings. The fatalistic phrase *bahala na* (God wills it) is often heard—you can even use it on them if you wish!

Raising the eyebrows or jerking the head upward are both affirmative. A jerk of the head downward means no. If someone says yes while putting their head downward, you can be reasonably sure that they really feel negatively about the matter. Filipino body language is generally more overt than that of other Asians, but it is more restrained than that of Latin people.

There is a general commitment to free enterprise and friendly relations with the West. Filipino managers pay lip service to the democratic ideal but are rather autocratic in their management style. They maintain a considerable power distance vis-à-vis subordinates. Business efficiency, however, is affected negatively by having to seek contacts in high places to cut through bureaucratic red tape. Bribery is not unknown.

Manners and Taboos

In restaurants men still hiss to attract waiters; women often signal with their fans. Filipinos are extremely hospitable and love parties, singing, dancing and good food. Flowers are a suitable gift when visiting their homes.

Men usually wear the *barong tagalog*, a loose, frilly, white- or cream-colored shirt with tails out, no jacket or tie. Most foreign men do the same after a while.

Taboos include confrontation and topics such as corruption, foreign aid, religion and poverty. Public criticism of any person must be avoided. Gift giving is fairly common, but do not accept a gift (or any other service) without first refusing it *twice*.

How to Empathize with Filipinos

As Asians, Filipinos expect modesty, gentleness and courtesy. Because of their Spanish influence, they expect warmth, respect and close personal relations. Try to make them like you—if they do, then price, although still important, becomes secondary.

Adapt to their time concept—they will not change it. Show respect for their education, English ability and qualifications, connections and personality. Be very polite to all senior people. Above all, ask continually about their family and their well-being.

Speak calmly, sensitively and in a low voice. Shake hands briefly and without too much firmness or energy. When criticizing, praise other things at the same time. Leaving something unsaid can also be a subtle way of indicating mild disapproval. Take an interest in Filipino culture and language. Always be professional in look, manner and competence: they expect it.

MOTIVATION	
KEY	*Flexibility and courtesy*
Cross-century mood	✦ Ties with the United States may well strengthen in the twenty- first century. ✦ Their commitment to democracy and free speech and their antipathy to authoritarianism distinguish them from other Asians. ✦ The Philippines is the second largest English-speaking country in the world—this is unlikely to change!

Motivating Factors

✦ Learn to read between the lines.

✦ Satisfy their Asian and Spanish requirements.

✦ As they are also American-influenced, show your commitment to democracy and free trade.

✦ Do business at their tempo and in the relaxed Filipino manner.

✦ Dress neatly, as they do, and always maintain a professional appearance.

✦ Show great sympathy for any difficulties they may face and help them as much as you can.

✦ Take an interest in Filipino culture and language.

✦ Distinguish between Christians and Muslims and adapt accordingly.

✦ Make appropriate gifts to business colleagues.

✦ Be flexible, as they are.

✦ Know Filipino geography and history.

Avoid

✦ Being brusque.

✦ Causing anyone to lose face in public.

✦ Tucking in the barong tagalog—the frilly shirts.

✦ Making comments that might be construed as too direct.

64

Vietnam

Even though it has been devastated by warfare and economic chaos, Vietnam must ultimately emerge as a major player in the Southeast Asian region. Its substantial land area of
330,000 square kilometers (127,000 square miles)—considerably bigger than Italy and the
U.K.—is occupied by 95 million hard-working, frugal, relatively well-educated people. It is
the 14th most populous country in the world and is also arguably the most schizophrenic.
The densely inhabited areas of the Red River Delta in the north and the Mekong Delta in
the south are not only 1,500 kilometers (930 miles) apart but are separated by a slender
bottleneck of mountainous terrain, where it is difficult to obtain anything beyond life's basic
necessities, mobility is minimal and English is rarely spoken.

Two very different Vietnams have existed for centuries. Chinese colonization of the country from 208 B.C. to A.D. 939 left behind it a neo-Confucian *yang* sub-system that has persisted
in the north up to the present. (A description of the basic tenets of Confucianism is given
in Chapter 65.) The more freewheeling, commercially minded south was always the bastion
of *yin* reaction—more open villages, more tolerance of individual initiatives and cultural
diversity. The yang concept was embedded in age-old Vietnamese traditions and expounded
Confucianism, order and discipline, male dominance, common welfare and replication of
uniformity. The yin concept was directly opposed: Taoism, Buddhism and Catholicism; liberalism; supportive of freedom rather than of excessive discipline; individual rights rather
than collectivism; diversity as opposed to uniformity; and promotion of women as influential
members of society.

From 1932 Vietnam consciously and vigorously strove to create a viable modern identity.
The first part of the twentieth century witnessed an extreme case of social conflict over the
yin–yang polarization; it is easy to forget that the Vietnam War was fought mainly by Vietnamese against other Vietnamese.

Vietnam lost ground, economically and politically, due to 30 years of war and its struggles
with the French. Its neighbors progressed greatly during this time. Former premier Van Linh
is seen as the "Vietnamese Gorbachev," but democracy has never fared well in Vietnam.
Today Christians and the Buddhist monks seek human rights and freedom of expression;
a growing middle class seeks political freedoms; an entrepreneurial class (especially in the
South) seeks accelerated economic reforms.

Currently the Vietnamese are trying to solve their problems by following the Chinese
model rather than the Russian, that is, to liberalize the economy as quickly as possible and
encourage investment, while at the same time maintaining strict political control (socialism
with a market economy).

Culture

Values

Confucian: work ethic, duty, morality
filial piety (pre-Chinese)
resistance to foreigners
nationalism
forbearance
collectivism (society over individual)
pride, self-respect (especially the north)

respect for learning
theme of sacrifice
resilience, tenacity
restraint
sense of proportion
pro-Western
entrepreneurism (especially the south)

Concepts

Leadership and Status

Collective leadership according to Confucian tenets has been the traditional model. Until recently, leaders had to possess a good war record and adhere to socialist thinking. Old Vietnamese society was organized along hierarchical feudal lines. Tribal chiefs—civil, religious and military—often owned large plots of land and controlled serfs. Power was hereditary. A shogun-like figure was usually king. Today, the Communist Party still leads most activities.

Space and Time

The Vietnamese, as a group-oriented society, are used to living and working in close proximity to each other. The Red River Delta, with over 10 million inhabitants, is one of the most densely populated areas on earth. Nevertheless, the Vietnamese are not tactile.

Their sense of time, basically Asian and cyclic, has been influenced by French colonialists and the Americans, so that *mañana* tendencies observable in the Philippines and Indonesia are less visible in Vietnam.

Cultural Factors in Communication

Communication Pattern

French influence is readily observable. Facial expression is much more evident than in, for instance, Japan, Korea or China, and you will observe some body language reminiscent of the French. Emotional factors can be used in argument. Good education and a high rate of literacy lend people confidence in communication. Vietnamese literary tradition is strong, particularly in poetry. People in the South tend to be more open and frank than many Asians (no doubt due to prolonged contact with Americans).

Listening Habits

The Vietnamese are good listeners and expect speakers to be clear and logical. They are well versed in French-style debate.

Behavior at Meetings and Negotiations

In essence, Vietnamese style is a combination of French rationality and Vietnamese tenacity. Although basically courteous, they are often willing to use counter-arguments, are cautious and give little away. Because of their history, the Vietnamese do not trust the Chinese, Japanese or Westerners, being suspicious of all. The current easing of hostility toward Americans is because they see the U.S. as a political counterweight to China, as well as an economic counter weight to Japan. Vietnam is opening up to the Association of Southeast Asian Nations (ASEAN) countries for the same reasons.

Decision making is by consensus. Political (socialist) considerations have up to now dominated business, but the *doi moi* (renovation) process has done a great deal to liberalize the economy and to soften attitudes. Ideals of equality have been abandoned. Salary differentials have been vastly widened. Bureaucracy is, however, still tortuous and corrupt, according to most standards.

Manners and Taboos

The age-old tradition of respect for the elderly is reflected in the leadership. Traditions, especially in the countryside and mountains, still include totemism, animism, tattooing, chewing betel nuts and blackening of teeth. Even though such practices have little application to modern city life, they do indicate the cultural affinities of the Vietnamese to the Khmer and Melano-Indonesian peoples and stress the non-Chinese side of their culture. Political dissension is, of course, currently taboo.

How to Empathize with the Vietnamese

Consider everything from the Vietnamese viewpoint—their long struggles against the Chinese, French and American "invaders"; their fierce independent streak, duty and morality in resistance; the provocations they suffered at the hands of the Khmer Rouge; and their current economic difficulties. Also remember that the Vietnamese have some Western characteristics, including French rationality and emotive behavior as well as occasional American freewheeling traits.

Self-respect and loss of face are very much on their mind. Although they are not dealing from strength, the Vietnamese have a great sense of pride and will not be humiliated. Always defer to their "old men"; in any case, they are currently in control. They are tenacious and surrender anything only with reluctance.

MOTIVATION	
KEY	*Always appear just in their eyes*
Cross-century mood	✦ The major aim is currently that of consolidating the unification of North and South. ✦ They like the idea of capitalism, but government bureaucracy currently stifles progress. ✦ They would like to get closer to the United States to counterbalance their traditional enemy, China.

Motivating Factors

✦ Bear in mind and respect their Confucianism.
✦ Know Vietnamese history accurately.
✦ Sympathize with their difficulties and the years lost to wars and struggle.
✦ Utilize their Western traits—French rationality and U.S.-style entrepreneurism (in the south).
✦ Protect their face.
✦ Respect their high level of education and their literary tradition.
✦ Read some of their poetry (in translation).
✦ Be logical.
✦ Admire their bravery and tenacity.
✦ Negotiate with them firmly, cautiously and fairly.
✦ Remember that women play an important role in the workplace.

Avoid

✦ Talking down to them or humiliating them in any way.
✦ Assuming they have a natural alignment with China (they don't).
✦ Talking about two Vietnams.
✦ Discussing the "domino theory."
✦ Expecting things to be done quickly.

65

China and Hong Kong

China

China is not only the world's most populated country, it also boasts the planet's oldest civilization—an agricultural-based society formed on the Yellow River 5,000 years ago. During this long period—practically all of recorded human history—China was essentially an isolated country, cut off from other peoples by a vast ocean to the east, jungles to the south, towering mountain ranges to the west and freezing steppes to the north. It has never formed a lasting, friendly relationship with a distant country. For two millennia the Chinese empire was its own universe, sucking in Korea, Vietnam and other neighbors, while exacting tributes from others, including Japan. Its unbroken culture spread itself over many centuries throughout East Asia, where its influence is manifest in music, dance, paintings, religion, philosophy, architecture, theater, societal structure, administration and, above all, language and literature.

Westerners who, in the second half of the twentieth century, may have seen China as a Third-World, relatively backward nation in terms of crude technology, sparse infrastructure, appalling hygiene, rampant pollution, outdated politics and inadequate communication fell into the trap of misjudging, underestimating and misunderstanding the power and impact of the Chinese people on their neighbors and now, the world at large.

China sees herself as *Chung-Kuo*—the middle kingdom, the center of the universe and the world's oldest culture and society. A visitor from the Tang Dynasty (China's golden age) would still see its legacy intact in the streets and fields of China today. The Chinese, 1.4 billion strong, see no diminishment of their moral authority, exercised with such power for thousands of years. Their sense of cultural superiority is greater than even that of the Japanese, to whom they brought a rich civilization. Foreigners in the eyes of Chinese are inferior, corrupt, decadent, disloyal and volatile, frequently hegemonic, barbaric and, in essence, "devils."

Once you are fully aware of how the Chinese view foreigners, you will find it easier to deal with them. They did not make these assumptions lightly. In the "Opium Wars" between 1839 and 1860, Britain forced Bengal opium on the Chinese, annexed Hong Kong and claimed enclaves in several Chinese ports, including Shanghai. France, Germany and Russia soon followed the British, while the Japanese, imitating the West, smashed China in the war of 1894–1895 and annexed Taiwan. This proved merely a prelude to a full-scale invasion of the mainland, followed by civil war after the Japanese withdrawal, culminating in victory for

Mao Tsetung's forces in 1949. The foreign devils had to abandon their profitable ghettos in Shanghai and other cities, leaving only Hong Kong in alien hands (until 1997).

That xenophobia might be an understandable reaction to these events can be readily perceived. Whether the Chinese actually possess cultural superiority over the rest of us is another matter. They believe they do. However, the numerous and magnificent spiritual and artistic achievements of the Chinese civilization do not go unrivaled in other parts of the world, and the Chinese would not deny this. They are capable of expressing admiration for European artistic creation, *dans son genre,* just as they appreciate the efficiency of the British, French and Nordic political systems, as well as American technological progress. Where they feel superior is in the area of moral and spiritual values. Inasmuch as most nations feel that their norms are the correct ones—that their behavior alone is truly exemplary—this is not surprising in itself.

The Chinese, however, like the Russians and Muslims, combine their sense of moral right-eousness with fierce criticism of Western societies. They see the European nations of former imperial glory—Britain, France, Spain and Portugal—in decline, decay and spiritual disin-tegration. They see the American culture as having begun to decline before it reached its peak, and they perceive the Japanese, once earnest students of Chinese philosophies and pre-cepts, as having succumbed to materialism and consumerism. They never admired Russia.

What are these superior Chinese values? They are not slow to tell you:

modesty

tolerance

filial piety • courtesy • thrift

patience • respect for elderly

sincerity • loyalty • family closeness • tradition

trustworthiness • stoicism • tenacity • self-sacrifice • kindness

moderation • patriotism • asceticism • diligence • harmony

resistance to corruption • learning • respect for hierarchy

generosity • adaptability • conscientiousness

sense of duty • pride (no losing face)

undemanding nature • friendships

gratitude for favors

impartiality • purity

gentleness

wisdom

A Westerner, plowing through this list of self-ascribed values, might wonder about mod-esty and impartiality, but, in the main, the Chinese *do* go about their daily lives, especially at the individual level, exhibiting many of these characteristics. Whatever they might think of us, we can hardly fail to see them as hardworking, conscientious, patient, undemanding and thrifty. They seem generally to be in harmony with each other (good team members), and toward us they are usually courteous and compliant.

To understand why the Chinese go about their affairs in an orderly, respectful fashion, we would do well to examine some of the basic tenets of their beliefs and philosophies. The most important influence is that of Confucianism.

Stability of society in China, according to Confucian views, is based on unequal relationships between people. This is almost diametrically opposed to British, American and Scandinavian ideas, but it is hardly questioned in China. The five relationships basic to ethical behavior are ruler-subject, father-son, older brother-younger brother, husband-wife and senior friend-junior friend.

The Chinese believe that the disorder, crime and lack of societal responsibility in many Western countries is the result of not observing these relationships.

Unequal relationships do not, however, simply imply unlimited advantages for the superiors. While their authority must not be questioned, their obligations are also mandatory. They must protect and exhibit kindness to those who show them obedience and allegiance. The basic teaching of Confucius can be summarized as follows:

- We should observe and respect unequal relationships.
- The family is the prototype of all social organization. We are members of a group, not individuals.
- We must behave in a virtuous manner toward others. Everybody's "face" must be maintained.
- Education and hard work must be prized.
- We should be moderate in all things. Save, stay calm, avoid extremes and shun indulgence.

Confucianism exercises a strong influence on the daily lives and business cultures in China, Hong Kong, Japan, Korea, Taiwan, Singapore and, to a lesser extent, other East Asian countries. Westerners wishing to deal with these Asians should take Confucianism into account and adapt accordingly.

The Chinese are also influenced by several other factors that are usually not part of the Western mindset, although feng shui and acupuncture have been catching on in the past decade or so. These factors are, among others:

- Taoism: insistence on a healthy lifestyle, adequate vegetarianism, generosity of spirit
- Buddhism: harmony through meditation
- Ancestor worship: past figures strongly influencing present action
- Feng shui: "wind and water" superstition, affecting decisions on building and arrangement of furniture, mirrors and doors
- Herbal medicine and acupuncture: frequently used and believed in
- Animal years: giving an individual the qualities of his or her birth animal

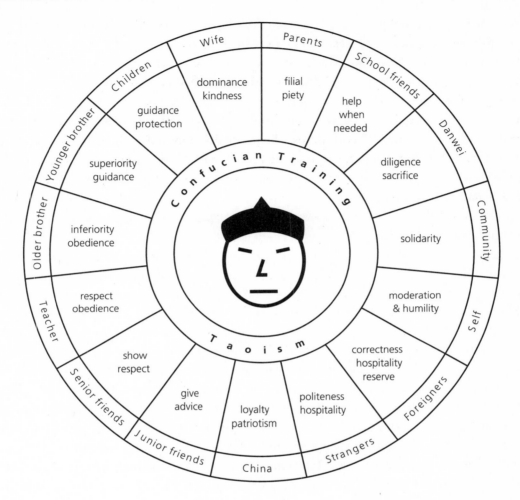

Figure 65.1 Confucian Training

What might seem old-fashioned superstition to Europeans is present-day reality to the Chinese. If, for example, you were born in the Year of the Horse, the Chinese will conclude that you have stamina and they will not try to outlast you. If you are a Rat, they will exercise great care in dealing with you, as you are smart, brave and clever. Similarly, the Chinese may consider that you will be unlucky if your office has two doors in a straight line (not in accordance with feng shui), but their natural courtesy will make them refrain from telling you. They will agree in a compliant manner to most of your business proposals, especially if you show great keenness in making them, because they wish to avoid a discordant note. They may let you wait half an hour at the bus stop rather than disappoint you with the news that the bus had left just before you arrived.

Collectivism is very strong in China. It originated in the early agrarian economies and is enhanced in the teachings of Confucius; it is not a product of communism, although the

Communist Party and regime found it useful. A Chinese person belongs to four basic groups and is, to some degree, a prisoner: the work unit (*danwei*), family, school and community. Obligations to each group, from which the Chinese may not distance themselves, mean that they have virtually no social or geographic mobility. Because no Westerners labor under such constraints, they find it hard to understand to what extent Chinese hands may be tied when it comes to making a decision requiring sudden change or independence of action. Lack of mobility also gives the Chinese an added problem as to the question of losing face. An American who disgraces him- or herself in New York can begin again next week in California. The Chinese who loses face may well have to guts it out for the next 40 years in the same community, workplace or academic environment. Neither do individuals have just one face to maintain. Their different social obligations (laid down by Confucius) force them to be many things to many people.

Traditionally the Chinese have been locked into the "extended" family system, where links between children and parents, uncles and aunts, cousins, grandchildren, husband's and wife's families and a host of distant relations both in China and overseas are much closer than anything we experience in the West. The "networking" advantages of such a system are obvious, although the acute interdependence involved can cause considerable stress. Additional responsibilities toward school friends, teachers and neighbors increase the strain. Under the communist regime, however, the *danwei,* or work unit, pinned the Chinese down to the greatest degree. One's relationship with the work unit went much deeper than simply collecting wages for a job done. The danwei solves disputes; administers government regulations; sees to housing, medical care, day care and kindergarten; arranges recreation, picnics and vacation homes; makes funeral arrangements; and sometimes even helps to arrange marriages.

Americans, Britons and northern Europeans, unused to paternalistic companies or "work units" and jealous of individual rights and privacy, abhor this type of group interference. Yet the Chinese blame Western insistence on individualism at all costs for their problems of crime, addiction and family breakdown. China is not alone among Asian nations in adhering to an alternative philosophy—that of group rights, where the extended family is seen as more important than the individual. According to Confucius, the individual owes as much to society as the other way around and, if the duties involved are scrupulously carried out, the resulting social cohesion, mutual protection of face and continuing harmony will lead to economic success.

This leads us to the question of human rights. Virtually all European countries see these as a prerequisite to other areas of development, while in the United States they are the bedrock of the Constitution itself; there is nothing Americans hold more dear. China, in company with some other Asians, has a different set of priorities. "Starving people are not in a position to exercise human rights" is the argument.

The West may well argue that after 5,000 years of civilization China should already be further along the road toward individual prosperity than she is today. The Chinese will answer that their late development is partly due to nineteenth century Western colonialism (look how Japan has prospered) and that with 1.3 billion people speaking umpteen different dialects of Chinese, group prosperity and cohesion are safer goals. Each nation shies away from the problems of its past history and takes steps to avoid their repetition.

The Chinese cannot adhere to their strong Confucian beliefs and other age-old traditions without their business culture being affected. Some of the consequences include the following:

+ Power distance is large; inequalities are expected and desired.
+ Less powerful people depend on the powerful to protect them and take care of their careers and welfare.
+ Parents, teachers and bosses must all be obeyed.
+ Age brings seniority.
+ There is a wide salary range between the top and bottom of the organization.
+ The ideal boss is a benevolent autocrat.
+ Privileges for managers are expected and popular.
+ Subordinates expect to be told what to do.
+ Individualism is taboo.
+ Relationships are more important than tasks.
+ Confrontation is avoided; harmony and consensus are ultimate goals.
+ The search for virtue is more important than the search for truth. A and B can both be right if both are virtuous.
+ Long-term orientation and goals are advisable.

Another aspect of Chinese culture that has clear ties to business is *guanxi*, the linking of two people in a relationship of mutual dependence. Guanxi involves reciprocal gifts and favors. While this is a charming custom, it can also be fraught with danger, as the recipient of an unusually expensive gift will almost certainly be asked shortly for a huge personal favor. It may well compromise a business situation and cause embarrassment to those who are closely restricted by their companies in the area of discounts, arbitrary pricing, and so on.

Concepts

Leadership and State

Consensus is generally highly valued in China. In companies controlled by the state, a leadership group (often invisible) will decide policy. In the developing expansion of capitalist-style companies, leaders are emerging with reputations of competence; also, locally elected officials (e.g., mayors) are becoming influential in the business sphere and may have only loose ties with Beijing. In Chinese family businesses (and there are many), the senior male is the patriarch and generally follows the usual nepotistic structure.

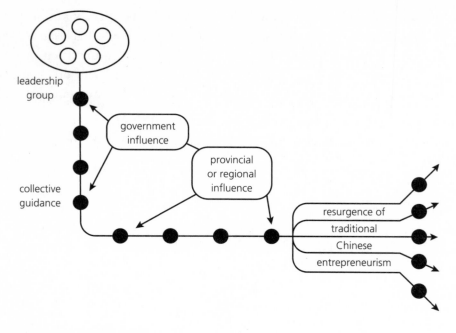

Figure 65.2 Chinese Leadership Style

Space and Time

China has relatively low population density, but the big cities are incredibly crowded. Although used to "rubbing shoulders" at home, on public transportation, on the street and in the factory or office, Chinese have respect for privacy when possible and maintain a distance of more than one meter in conversation.

As mentioned later in this chapter, the Chinese are extremely punctual and abhor wasting anyone's time.

Cultural Factors in Communication

Communication Pattern

The Chinese are courteous and considerate interlocutors in the Asian manner, but they are more direct than the Japanese and some other East Asians. They do not depart from their polite behavior but often ask you bluntly how you feel about certain important matters. This enables them not to contradict or devalue your opinions. Although they will express any criticism of their partner indirectly, a general pleasant openness helps Westerners feel they know where the conversation is going. Mild flattery is appropriate from both sides.

Listening Habits

Traditional Chinese suspicion of Westerners (the result of exploitation in the nineteenth and twentieth centuries) is gradually giving way to a more open-minded acceptance of some Western views. Younger Chinese, particularly, wish to gain access to American and European "modernity" and respond well to interlocutors who display no arrogance. Finns and Swedes, with their modest and caring speech styles, are especially well-received in China. Other Nordics, as well as Britons, Canadians, New Zealanders and South Africans do not find it hard to get along with the Chinese. Latins and Americans, however, often talk too much for Chinese tastes, though the flexible Italians have had great success in establishing their brand names in Beijing and Shanghai.

Behavior at Meetings and Negotiations

+ The Chinese prefer meetings to be formal, although dress is usually comfortable.
+ Seating will be according to hierarchy. Business cards are exchanged.
+ The senior man must be shown great respect and attention at all times, even though he takes little part; the deputy or vice chairman is often the decision maker.
+ The meeting is principally for information gathering; the real decisions will be made elsewhere.
+ The pace of negotiations will be slow and repetitious. The time frame is too long for Westerners, who may see the slow-down techniques as bargaining ploys.
+ Politeness is observed at all times. Confrontation and loss of face (for both sides) must be avoided.
+ The Chinese rarely say no—they only hint at difficulties.
+ A collective spirit prevails; nobody says "I," only "we."
+ In a collectivist culture, accountability for decisions is avoided in many meetings. Authority is not passed downward from the leaders.
+ Decisions have a long-term orientation. Negotiations in China are important social occasions during which one fosters relationships and decides if the people on the other side of the table are suitable partners for the long run. The Chinese, who have been doing business for 4,000 years, certainly are.
+ They consider you technically competent but otherwise inexperienced in business relations.
+ They negotiate step by step in an unhurried manner. They prefer to open proceedings with a discussion of general principles of mutual interest. That is probably enough for the first day.
+ They dislike U.S. eagerness to sign a contract.
+ Deal-oriented Americans and many Europeans agree to perform specific tasks over an agreed period of time. The Chinese, looking beyond the deal, prioritize mutual trust in the long term.

+ They are thrifty, cautious and patient. You will have to match their patience and stamina; otherwise, deals and opportunities will be lost.
+ They combine flexibility with firmness and expect both these qualities in you.
+ Once they have decided who, what, when and how is best, they are very trustworthy.
+ They know the size of their market and use this in their pricing strategy.

Manners and Taboos

The Chinese are basically very welcoming people who extend generous hospitality and courtesy both to Asians and "barbarians." Sit-down dinners are the norm, usually lasting about two hours and ending when the host stands up. On these occasions you should try all the delicacies put in front of you by your host, without actually leaving any dish empty. Protocol is easy-going. The Chinese slurp and make all sorts of noises when eating; they may also smoke at the table. You are unlikely to disgrace yourself unless you are particularly inept with chopsticks, handle food with your fingers or insist on paying the bill before your host has had the chance to do so.

As far as meetings are concerned, it is often necessary to make appointments one or two weeks in advance with officials, only a day or so with entrepreneurs and acquaintances. You should turn up on time. Individual Chinese often arrive 15 minutes early and say they can finish the business before the meeting is scheduled to begin, so as not to waste your time. You need not take punctuality to these lengths but you should not be late.

When saying farewell, the Chinese mention their imminent departure early on in the meeting, as opposed to Westerners who delay it until just before leaving. A Chinese prolongs the farewell on the street, perhaps accompanying you part of your way.

It is good manners in China to show courtesy as often as possible. This involves excessive humility and self-disparagement. All good Asians are self-effacing, but the Chinese take it to ridiculous lengths. You may try to fit into the picture by being a good listener, by using deference and understatement in your replies, by never mentioning your impressive business or academic qualifications and by trying to get in the back row when someone takes a photograph.

Chinese taboos include egotism, loudness, arrogance, lack of consideration for others and, of course, any form of boasting.

The Twenty-First Century, China and You

Asians are destined to be world leaders in industrial, economic and trade growth in this century. China, with her mammoth population and land area, will be the dominant force in the region. Japan will also be a major player, but China has 10 times Japan's population and 25 times its land area. Breathtaking development and growth in China are already well underway. The West would be wise to start establishing meaningful and durable links and relationships now.

The return on investment, provided it is long-term, may well be staggering. China is embarking on the biggest economic development in world history. What happened in Japan between 1954 and 1990 is starting to happen in China, but on an unimaginably greater scale. Forecasts indicate that the average GDP per capita in China will rise exponentially between 2005 and 2050. A country with a GDP of US$20 trillion a year will be the world's biggest producer, manufacturer and possibly leading exporter. Along with the Indian subcontinent, it will also be the world's biggest consumer (market). Americans, Europeans and other Asians will compete ferociously to sell into that market.

How can you go about establishing your position and image in Chinese eyes? Policy and planning must be long-term, otherwise you will be wasting your time on relatively unimportant ventures.

How to Empathize with the Chinese

You are dealing with people who place values and principles above money and expediency. Bear this in mind. The Chinese will not stray from their reverence of Confucian views on order, family and consensus. Show unqualified respect for these as well as Buddhist tenets.

The Chinese see their language not only as a cultural tool that has historically influenced Japan, Korea, Southeast Asia and other areas, but as a repository for transmitting cultural values. The undisputed link between language and culture gives them a strong motive to increase the currency of the Chinese language, at least on a regional basis. You would do well to have one or two individuals in your company or organization develop reasonable fluency in Chinese.

Britain in particular has had long experience in China and many connections in East Asia. Chinese also react favorably to Nordic calmness, German technology and French savoir faire. Americans and Europeans should study Buddhist and Confucian behavior and show compassion for Chinese difficulties. It will pay off.

Final golden rules: be extremely deferential at all times, combine courtesy with firmness, show humility and respect for age and rank, don't overdo the logic, prepare your meetings in detail, don't speak in a loud voice or rush them, know your Chinese history, always keep your calm and remember that patience and allowing adequate time for reflection are the keys to making progress, however slow it may seem.

MOTIVATION

KEY	*Humility, giving face*

Cross-century mood	◆ Regaining Taiwan is foremost in their minds. It will be difficult to motivate them at all if you oppose them on this issue.
	◆ They make progress on human rights at their own pace; accusation is counterproductive.
	◆ The Chinese expect to regain Asian and hemispheric hegemony during this century; they see the eighteenth and nineteenth centuries as an aberration.
	◆ Deng said "to make money is glorious," and this is quickly becoming a goal.

Motivating Factors

◆ Show compassion for Chinese difficulties. It will pay off.

◆ Learn all you can about guanxi.

◆ Prepare well—the Chinese will appreciate it.

◆ Know Chinese history, and praise their inventiveness and artistic achievements.

◆ Remember that power distance is large and that inequalities are expected and desired. Find your "rank" and behave accordingly.

◆ When a big deal is cooking, visit, visit and visit again. Chinese desire follow-up! Your rank must be as high as possible.

◆ Tell subordinates what to do (kindly).

◆ When entertaining, do not hesitate to be lavish. The Chinese are frugal people, but not when feasting.

◆ Preserve harmony by saving face for everybody on all occasions. This is guiding principle number one.

◆ Be careful how you look at the concept of truth. The Chinese do not believe in absolute, scientific truth.

◆ They consider themselves extremely experienced, knowledgeable and shrewd. You may think you are more au fait (competent) with international business methods, but don't let this show through.

◆ They won't do business with you if they don't trust you. Show your reliability through your deeds.

◆ Imitate their skill in combining affability with arm's-length politeness.

(continued)

MOTIVATION *(continued)*

- ✦ Learn to read between the lines. Chinese arguments often go around in circles. Try to triangulate to get a fix on the real point.
- ✦ Don't hesitate to do business through go-betweens. It often speeds up progress strikingly.
- ✦ Remember that gift-giving is an important feature in business and social relationships. Choose appropriate rather than lavish gifts.
- ✦ Remember that in China the buyer comes first and expects added respect.
- ✦ Dress neatly and conservatively. Beards and other excessive hair cause the Chinese to feel uncomfortable.
- ✦ Close all meetings you control by thanking everyone for attending.

Avoid

- ✦ Showing anger or appearing upset.
- ✦ Rushing Chinese business partners.
- ✦ Rejecting a Chinese proposal out of hand. When you negate someone's idea, you negate the person.
- ✦ Boasting.
- ✦ Ignoring anyone brought into your presence.
- ✦ Discussing Taiwan or Tibet.
- ✦ The topic of human rights (for Chinese).

Hong Kong

Hong Kong was acquired by the British government from China by way of a 99-year lease that expired in 1997. The seventh biggest port in the world, Hong Kong's historic function was to serve as an entrepôt for trade between China and Western countries. In this role it developed successfully up to the Second World War, but when the United Nations placed an embargo on trade with China and North Korea during the Korean War, Hong Kong could no longer survive on trade alone. The colony was forced to change from a trading to an industrial economy. Rapid development ensued—in garment and textile industries, electronics, shipbuilding, steel rolling, cement manufacture, aluminum extrusion, and a variety of light products from toys and wigs to plastic flowers.

From the very beginning Hong Kong had a clear raison d'être—to make money. It certainly succeeded. In the absence of any significant natural resources, Hong Kong's wealth, like that of Singapore, Japan and Korea, is created by its one asset—industrious people. In this case 99 percent of them are Chinese, about half of whom immigrated from the neighboring Chinese provinces of Guangdong and Fujian. The other half are native Hong Kongers. The dominant Chinese dialect in Hong Kong is Cantonese, which is quite different from Mandarin.

The major non-Chinese population groups are from Britain and the Commonwealth, the United States, Portugal and Japan. As in the case of Singapore, the combination of Western commercial know-how and Eastern diligence has produced several decades of impressive productivity and prosperity.

The seemingly unending boom has been facilitated by several factors. Although China coveted its "South Gate," the colony functioned as an excellent point of contact with the West, even at the most critical periods of the Cold War. Trade between Hong Kong and China flourished. In 1994 China exported $72 billion worth of goods. Of these 45 percent went to or through Hong Kong, which, in turn, sent 30 percent of its exports to China.

Hong Kong is valuable to China as a conduit for trade, investment and technology transfer. Its existence enables China to trade extensively with two other "Tigers"—Taiwan and South Korea—without having to compromise her political stance. Western confidence in the ability to continue trading strongly in the area after 1997 is reflected in the rising value of real estate, the frenetic construction in both Hong Kong and Shenzhen (Guangdong Province of China) and the increasing number of foreign companies actually entering Hong Kong. There are more than 500 American trading companies doing business with China from Hong Kong and Kowloon.

Hong Kong is many things that Singapore is not, and vice versa. Both Tigers take gold medals for industriousness, tenacity, risk taking and efficiency. Both have made their fortunes by shrewdly combining strengths from East and West. Both populations are predominantly Chinese, who have demonstrated their infinite potential and talent, given the right conditions for development. After that the comparison becomes more of a striking contrast.

Hong Kong has expensive housing, high salaries and job mobility, little red tape, no inhibitions and people who live from deal to deal. Singapore, in contrast, has cheap housing, moderate salaries and job stability, strict regulations, decorum and long-term planning. Opinions vary, among both Westerners and Asians, about which is the better place to live and work. Singapore impresses with its discipline, racial tolerance and successful multiculturalism. Westerners frown on the direct control of business exercised by parliament but admire the overall efficiency and honesty of conduct. Hong Kong dazzles you with sheer, unbridled energy, single-mindedness and pluralism. It is interesting to note that, although Hong Kong is 99 percent Chinese, Singapore generally enjoyed better relations with China than the former colony did. China finds pluralism hard to understand; Singapore speaks with one voice—a more traditional Asian practice. Moreover, the voice is in Mandarin, which is better accepted in Beijing than singsong Cantonese!

There is naturally a question mark about Hong Kong's future. The reincorporation of a ninety-nine-year-old British colony into a motherland possessing 5,000 years of unbroken heritage is truly a collision of cultures, in spite of racial commonalities. Communication styles and listening patterns are far apart.

Hong Kong, with entrepreneurism in its blood, its sense of urgency, driving always in the fast lane, stands in close comparison in its business activities to the bustling United States. It remains to be seen what the cultural collision with the bureaucratic motherland will eventually produce, although China has done little to interfere with the East-West flow of business since devolution.

Communication Pattern

Hong Kongers negotiate briskly and factually to achieve quick results. They often show impatience. The tempo is American. Figure 65.3 compares the communication patterns of Hong Kong and China.

Listening Habits

Hong Kongers want only facts, hardly any preamble and no "padding." They may interrupt if the interlocutor is too slow. They show perspicacity and clear-sightedness when asking questions. Figure 57.4 shows the significant differences between the listening habits of the Chinese and Hong Kongers.

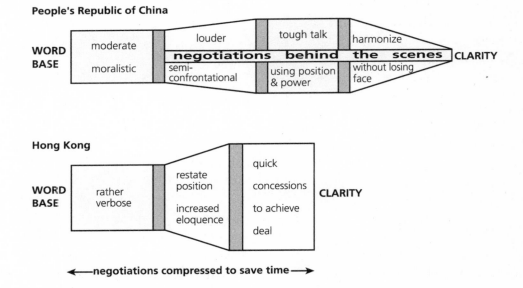

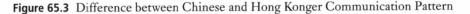

Figure 65.3 Difference between Chinese and Hong Konger Communication Pattern

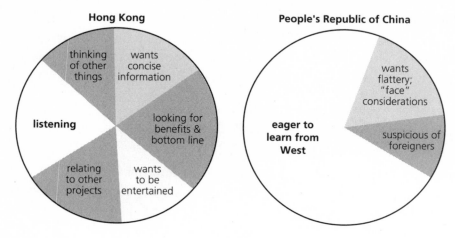

Figure 65.4 Difference between Chinese and Hong Konger Listening Habits

MOTIVATION	
KEY	*Do things fast*
Cross-century mood	✦ The reincorporation of the colony into China is naturally the dominant cross-century event. ✦ Hong Kongers show current determination to maintain the Basic Law agreed upon between the British and Chinese. ✦ Hong Kong will face increased competition in the twenty-first century as a major entrepôt. Shanghai is the main rival.

Motivating Factors

✦ Take risks and show them how to make money.
✦ Show efficiency and industriousness.
✦ Do things quickly, and cut red tape to a minimum.
✦ Shed most inhibitions.
✦ Pragmatism must rule.
✦ Be prepared to trade (work) with anybody.
✦ Be single-minded.
✦ Demonstrate tenacity and stamina.
✦ Impatience is not taboo.
✦ Use strengths from East and West.
✦ Respect Chinese family businesses.

(continued)

MOTIVATION *(continued)*

Avoid

✦ Unnecessary delay or procrastination.

✦ Criticism of China (Hong Kongers are quite capable of doing this).

✦ Colonialist attitudes.

✦ Underestimating middle-class Hong Kongers.

✦ Ignoring old men.

66

Korea

Korea is the only (officially) still-divided country in the world. Both Koreas are armed, dangerous and technically at war. This chapter focuses principally on South Korea (often referred to as the Republic of Korea, or ROK), but in terms of deeply rooted culture, all Koreans are the same. Differences in the political structure between the communist North and capitalist South have, since 1945, obliged North and South Koreans to lead very different lives, but the Korean core beliefs of *kibun, hahn,* Confucianism, tenacity and obsession with survival dominate thinking on both sides of the border and distinguish Koreans strongly from their Chinese and Japanese neighbors.

Korea will eventually be reunified, and when that happens the combined population of more than 75 million will put it on a par with Vietnam and increase its clout in East Asia. South Korea's influence is already remarkable. On a limited land area less than half the size of the United Kingdom, South Koreans have built the fourth largest economy in Asia, based on low-cost, high-quality export production. Its GDP of nearly US$1400 billion dwarfs those of the three other Asian Tigers—Taiwan (US$525 billion), Hong Kong (US$309 billion) and Singapore (US$297 billion). South Korea is the eighth largest trading economy in the world and actually grew at an average rate of more than 15 percent between 1960 and 1995!

The South Korean miracle is beginning to show signs of both maturity and age and is changing the focus of its economy from low-cost, low-technology production to high-tech, high-value-added, capital-intensive products. The strength of ROK's large conglomerates (*chaebols*) and the industriousness of its businesspeople and workers suggest that it will successfully make the transition to a new economy appropriate to current twenty-first century conditions.

On account of its proximity to China, Korea has been, and still is, strongly influenced by the teaching of Confucius. (A description of the basic tenets of Confucianism is given in Chapter 65.) *Hahn* is something different and more peculiarly Korean. This is the word used to describe the pent-up energies and frustrations that developed in the Korean psyche under conditions of extreme hardship and oppression. We must remember that Japan occupied Korea from 1895 to 1945, and the Korean War of 1950–1953 caused unimaginable suffering throughout the peninsula. *Hahn*, which stems not only from foreign occupation but also from social immobility, sexual discrimination, family vendettas and abject poverty, has translated into extreme nationalism, a release of energy and in the end to Korean prosperity.

Kibun, roughly translated as "face" or "reputation," is a more sensitive issue in Korea than perhaps anywhere else in the world. For a Korean, *kibun* is an intuitive sensitivity to social balance and correct behavior. Koreans are able to deal even with people they dislike under a veneer of courtesy. Foreign people dealing with them can easily be fooled into thinking that Koreans are easy-going and good-natured.

The Korean *chaebol* is the rough equivalent of the *keiretsu* or former *zaibatsu* in Japan. It is a conglomerate of a dozen or more companies owned by or closely linked to a prominent family. Personal and family connections are extremely important in Korea, where clans are seen as bastions against the outside world. The very size of the chaebol in modern Korea has necessitated the employment of a large class of well-educated professional managers. Even they, however, generally have close personal ties with the owning family.

Foreigners working with Koreans do well if they can cultivate good relationships within Korean power structures. This is difficult to do, and third-party introductions are both advisable and necessary.

Culture

Values

Confucian ethic	protection of *kibun* (inner feelings)
vertical society	respect for elders
observance of protocol	competitive spirit
toughness	obsession with survival
creativity	adaptability
tendency toward violence	suspicion of neighbors (China, Japan)
tenacity	dislike of foreigners in general (*hahn*)
nationalism	willingness to suffer hardship for the good of the country

Concepts

Leadership and Status

Leadership is Confucian in essence, but the importance, influence and power of certain families are more in evidence than in Japan and China. Power, once acquired, is not easily conceded, and the history of violence between the authorities and the people is top down in Korea, as opposed to frequently being bottom up in Japan.

Family name, wealth and the power of the chaebols decide status.

Space and Time

Korea is a crowded country, and space, especially in the big cities, is at a premium. Koreans are used to working close to each other, but require clearly defined personal space in formal situations. They are non-tactile. Koreans are very hard working (they try to outperform the Japanese) and rarely waste time. They are relatively punctual and have an American-like attitude of packing as much action as they can into a given time period.

Cultural Factors in Communication

Communication Pattern

Koreans are energetic conversationalists, very intense when serious, believe they can handle Westerners better than other Asians can and often try their hand at humor. They have a very elastic concept of truth and it is advisable to double-check anything that is promised. They are often looking for quick profits and one should be careful about granting exclusivity. It is better to judge their statements against past performance rather than future forecasts.

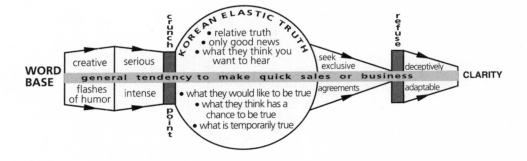

Figure 66.1 Korean Communication Pattern

Listening Habits

Koreans are courteous listeners in true Asian style, but they often give the impression that they know in advance what you are going to tell them. They often give lively feedback and may ask original questions. Giving them face is important both during and after a presentation.

Behavior at Meetings and Negotiations

It can be more difficult to create a lasting agreement with quick-moving Koreans than with the highly structured Japanese or bureaucratic Chinese officials. Historically, their collective experience is that compromise leads to defeat, second place spells disaster. This makes them extremely competitive and continually on the lookout for further advantage. This is annoying to the Westerner who is trying to negotiate a win–win situation.

Negative aspects of doing business with Koreans include the following:

+ Deception: they will tell you this or that has been done, while not actually doing anything.
+ When they wish you to withdraw from a deal (to leave them in sole charge), they often create difficulties for your staying with it. These difficulties can sometimes be arranged with official or government compliance.
+ They may show you a good time and send you home happy, but fail to implement the agreement signed in the cordial atmosphere that they create.
+ They often seek long-term, exclusive agreements; it is better to sign agreements for the short term based on Korean performance!
+ Koreans often break a relationship suddenly if they find a better deal elsewhere.
+ Knowledge is power; Koreans tend to keep it to themselves.

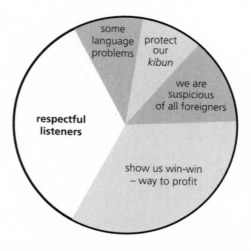

Figure 66.2 Korean Listening Habits

+ If selling to you, they may let quality fall if they get bigger orders elsewhere.
+ When buying, they tend to look at price rather than the useful life of your product.
+ They prefer quick sales to the development of solid business relations. (This is due to Korea's chronic instability, historically.)

Positive aspects of dealing with Koreans include the following:

+ They are willing to experiment and take risks.
+ They hustle and bustle.
+ They are creative and show initiative.
+ They are accessible.
+ They are adaptable and amenable to last-minute changes.
+ They have a strong sense of honor, which they display once you have won their trust.

Manners and Taboos

Protocol is extremely important. If you fail to give a Korean the respect due to his rank, status or age, he will withdraw and avoid you in the future. If you fail to observe the basic rules of social exchange and proper respect in Korea, you become an "unperson" and Koreans will henceforth have no concern for your welfare, even while continuing to be polite. They can actually be violent to unpersons.

Touching another person is an affront. Businessmen now shake hands to show that they are modernized but will often bow at the same time. They sometimes become more affectionate after a few drinks but will usually apologize for being drunk (the same evening and again the next day).

Punctuality is reasonable but less important than in China or Japan. When in their office or in contemplation, Koreans build imaginary walls round themselves, then disappear for a time. You can break through this wall by coughing discreetly at a distance of 3 to 5 meters (10 to 16 feet).

Koreans do not introduce others formally but say to a stranger, "I am seeing you for the first time." The elder then suggests an introduction, whereupon both parties mumble names unclearly and exchange cards. Koreans avoid calling each other by name, preferring titles.

Table manners include serving the guest, slurping soup, smacking lips and belching heartily to show appreciation of the meal.

How to Empathize with Koreans

Koreans consider themselves very different from the Chinese and Japanese, and due respect must be paid to their long history, artistic riches and national uniqueness. They believe that they can handle Westerners better than other Asians. Your reaction should be to express willingness to go along with their ideas, sharing humor with them whenever possible, but maintaining a firm, pragmatic stance at all times.

Pay great attention to protecting their *kibun*—loss of face in Korea is more serious than anything else. Do not overemphasize your Japanese connections and do not refer to the Korean language as an offshoot of Japanese.

MOTIVATION	
KEY	*Praise Korean achievement*
Cross-century mood	✦ As usual, they are thinking about beating the Japanese. ✦ Korean survival is always their first concern. In this respect reunification is on their mind. ✦ There is no lessening of their ambition or energy in the first decade of the twenty-first century. ✦ There is a tendency to follow in Japanese footsteps in exploiting cheap labor and resources in Southeast Asia.

Motivating Factors

✦ When negotiating with Koreans, show toughness allied with respect. Never appear gullible.
✦ Although they often appear idealistic and somewhat touchy, they usually end up being very pragmatic. Work toward practical solutions in a cool manner.
✦ Remember that they have an obsession with survival. They have had a hard history in the course of which they usually came off second best in conflicts. Always let them see that you want a win–win situation and allow them room for profit and advancement.
✦ They are suspicious of all foreigners and their motives. Work hard at demonstrating and building up trust.
✦ They have a vertical society; be careful how you move within the hierarchy.
✦ Encourage their creativity—they are proud of it. Don't be afraid to introduce new and innovative ideas. They are more amenable to quick change than are the Japanese or Chinese.
✦ They like thoughtful gifts. No Japanese products, please.
✦ Try to match their work ethic, punctuality and tenacity.
✦ Remember that Koreans wield several varieties of truth. Take everything with a pinch of salt and avoid taking offense when you discern that facts do not correspond exactly to appearances.
✦ Admire their risk taking and use it to your advantage. Show your willingness to share risks and problems.
✦ It is important to socialize and drink with them in the evening. A certain degree of inebriation on both sides is permissible and expected.

(continued)

MOTIVATION *(continued)*

Avoid

✦ Ignoring or showing a lack of respect for Confucian values.

✦ Being put off by sudden Korean volte-faces. They may occur frequently.

✦ Dwelling on past misdemeanors.

✦ Expectations of smooth or problem-free business with them. Make allowances.

67

Japan

The Japanese are culturally very different from anyone else, their uniqueness probably deriving in the main from three principal factors: their history of isolation, the crowded conditions imposed by their geography, and the Japanese language itself.

Although Japan for many centuries had a close cultural connection with China, the period of autocratic Tokugawa rule beginning in 1603 led to almost complete isolation from the rest of the world until the arrival of Commodore Matthew Perry of the United States in 1853. During the 250 years of isolation, Japan developed a distinct society and culture that still has no equal in terms of group cooperation in spite of the evident changes that occurred in the twentieth century.

Packed together in large numbers in big cities, the Japanese developed complex social skills, which led to the phenomenon known as the *web society*—that is, great interdependence between all members of a group and an abundance of moral and social obligations, both vertically and horizontally. It all begins at birth. Whereas Western babies are soon separated from their mothers and put in a room of their own, Japanese children are kept close to their parents' side day and night, for two or three years. Western children quickly develop initiative on their own and gain early experience in problem solving. Japanese children, by contrast, are encouraged to be completely dependent on those close to them and to develop a sense of interdependence that will stay with them throughout life. They can demand favors from people in their group, and these have to be granted. Their first group is their family, but later it becomes high school, then university, then the company.

Age and seniority have their priorities but also their obligations. The Japanese language has separate words for *elder brother, younger brother* and so forth because the duties of one to the other are different and must be sharply defined. Protection can be demanded from those who have "gone before." Section leaders will unashamedly demand promotion for mediocre employees in their section, simply because they are under their wing and have remained loyal. It is almost impossible for a general manager to resist these demands.

The web society structure is advantageous to the Japanese businessperson in terms of what many Westerners today call networking. The Japanese, although great respecters of privacy, are very gregarious in business situations. Consequently, the spider's web of which they are part provides them with an unrivaled high-context information network.

Culture

Values

ultra-honesty	protection of everyone's face
modesty	sense of honor
shyness	ultra-politeness
distrust of verbosity	belief in Japanese uniqueness
sense of duty	punctuality
hospitality	avoidance of debt
uneasiness with foreigners	mutual obligations

Concepts

Leadership and Status

Although Japanese top executives have great power in conformity with Confucian hierarchy, they actually have little involvement in the everyday affairs of the company. (For a description of the basic tenets of Confucianism, see Chapter 57.) On appropriate occasions they initiate policies that are conveyed to middle managers and to the rank and file. Ideas often originate on the factory floor or with other lower-level sources. Suggestions, ideas and inventions make their way up the company hierarchy by a process of collecting signatures among workers and middle managers. Many people are involved. Top executives take the final step in ratifying items that have won sufficient approval.

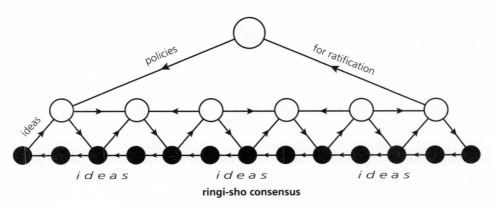

Figure 67.1 Japanese Leadership Style

Space and Time

Although living and working in crowded conditions (home, office and factory), the Japanese are essentially non-tactile and apologize immediately to anyone they bump into or inadvertently touch or brush against.

Japanese are very punctual and often turn up 15 to 20 minutes early for appointments. Tokyo traffic jams can, however, foil these good intentions! The Japanese use of time has been described in full in Chapter 4.

Cultural Factors in Communication

Communication Pattern

Japanese behavior is strongly affected by the nature of their language. According to the Benjamin Whorf theory, the language we speak determines to a significant degree our way of thinking. The Japanese themselves use language in a completely different way from the rest of us. Japanese is often described as a vague or ambiguous language. For instance, the verbs are impersonal, so often you do not know who is being referred to. This vagueness is frequently used on purpose by Japanese conversationalists who wish to absolve anyone of possible blame and demonstrate politeness. The well-known honorific terms in Japanese enhance this politeness, while often adding to the vagueness. Long indirect clauses usually precede the main statement. Everything must be placed in context in Japan; therefore, blunt language is too brief and out of place. No Japanese boss would say "Tidy up the office." They are obliged to say to their subordinates, "As we have some important visitors coming at twelve o'clock and since we wish them to get the best impression of our company, perhaps we could improve the orderliness around here." Another way in which the language reflects the society is the lack of a reported speech mechanism in Japanese. Japanese people do not like to report other people's statements; failure to be accurate could result in embarrass-ment or injustice. My secretary in Japan always refused to describe the contents of incoming telephone calls when I was absent and invariably asked me to ring back the caller to get the message.

Listening Habits

Japanese audiences are disciplined and attentive but may understand almost nothing in any foreign language spoken at normal speed. They do not come to understand; they are there to be courteous and to create personal harmony. *How* you address them is what matters. *What* you say is irrelevant; they will get the information they need from your printed material. (See Chapter 5 for a diagram of Japanese listening habits.)

Behavior at Meetings and Negotiations

The Japanese are conditioned by exceptional historical and geographical constraints as well as by their thought processes in a language very different from any other. How does this affect foreign businesspeople dealing with them?

At the beginning there is the first meeting. The Japanese, unlike Westerners, worry about meeting newcomers. In their own web society Japanese executives know exactly the man-ner they should use to address someone, depending on a superior, inferior or equal status. Americans who stride across the room and pump their hands are a source of great embar-rassment. First, unless they have been properly introduced, the Japanese are unable to define the stranger's rank. Secondly, it is likely that Westerners will initiate a person-to-person exchange of views in the first meeting, which poses an even greater danger to the Japanese. They represent their group; therefore, they cannot pronounce on any matters there and then without consultation. The exchange of visiting cards is a familiar ceremony in Japan, although the information gained from these will be insufficient without prior knowledge.

Westerners are individuals, but the Japanese represent their company, which is part of their group, which in turn represents Japan. In these circumstances, how can they deal face-to-face, alone?

Westerners often complain that on 6 visits to a company they will be met by 18 different people in groups of 3 and will have to say the same thing six times. This is time-consuming but necessary for the Japanese, as all the members of the group have to become acquainted with the visitors.

After this ordeal, Westerners often press for a quick decision. They will not get one. If they impose a time limit, the Japanese will back out quietly.

As we all know, Asians do not like to lose face. I had a striking example of this during my first week in Japan when a colleague and I were negotiating for the lease of a building. With some difficulty we had secured an appointment with the president of the company that owned the building. He was a seventy-year-old man, and he spoke for half an hour (through an interpreter), explaining the merits and high reputation of the building, terminating his remarks with the price for the rental. It seemed a little on the high side to me. My colleague, who had been brought up in an Arab country, promptly offered him half. The elderly president and the interpreter immediately rose to their feet, smiled and bowed simultaneously and left the room. We never saw them again.

The Japanese do in fact negotiate, but not in the Arab manner. Face must not be lost and politeness must be maintained at all times. The Japanese go to incredible lengths to be polite. Their reluctance to say no is well known. If the Japanese do not wish to enter into a deal with a foreign partner, they will not come out with a negative reply. However, you will not be able to get in touch with your contact in that company thereafter. He or she will always be ill, on vacation or attending a funeral.

The following list includes those points most important to remember when negotiating with the Japanese.

+ The first person you contact in a Japanese company (or who contacted you) will be present throughout the negotiating period.
+ The Japanese normally negotiate in teams, each member of which has a different specialty.
+ The members of the team may change or increase, as the Japanese wish as many members of their company as possible to get to know you.
+ There will be a senior staff member present who will dictate tactics, but he is rarely the one who does the talking. Each member will ask questions within the field of his or her competence, using the best linguist as the interpreter.
+ Their questions constitute an information-gathering process only. They are not about to make a decision based on your answers.
+ However strong the team, they will have to refer back to the head office. Therefore, no decision will be made at the first meeting and probably not at the second.
+ Their decisions will eventually be made by consensus; therefore, no person will stick out as an individual.
+ The second meeting tends to go over the same ground as the first, but the questions will be in more depth—and will come from a different team.
+ The Japanese negotiators bring their company's position to the table with little authority to change it, so there is little flexibility in their position.
+ Flexibility is more evident *between* meetings, when they have checked with their head office.
+ The Japanese are willing to go over the same information many times to avoid later misunderstandings and achieve clarity, although the ambiguities of their own speech style often leave Westerners far from clear on their intentions.
+ They are cautious, skilled in stalling tactics and won't be rushed.

- ✦ Their decisions are long-term, for example: Do we want these people as partners in the future? Do we trust them? Is this the right direction for the company to be heading? Big decisions take time.

- ✦ Once the Japanese company has made its decision, the negotiating team then expects quick action and will criticize the partner if there is a delay.

- ✦ The Japanese will break off negotiations if the other side is too blunt, impatient or fails to observe protocol.

- ✦ If great respect is shown and very reasonable demands are made, they are capable of modifying their own demands greatly.

- ✦ They go to great lengths to preserve harmony throughout the negotiations and will strive to bring the two "respectable" companies closer together. They are happy to socialize in between meetings.

- ✦ They never say no, never refute entirely another's argument and never break off negotiations as long as harmony prevails. This leaves them room for renegotiation some time in the future if circumstances change.

- ✦ They will cancel a meeting if they think the conditions on which it was set up have changed.

- ✦ They will show exaggerated respect to your senior negotiator and expect you to do the same to theirs.

- ✦ They will sometimes bring to the meeting a very senior person (e.g., former minister) who is only a consultant to the company, but commands (your) respect and deference.

- ✦ They will use a middleman or go-between if they can find one. After all, if both sides trust him, then there must be harmony.

- ✦ Negotiating style will be non-individualistic, impersonal and unemotional, but emotion is important (it is just under the surface). Logic and intellectual argument alone cannot sway the Japanese. They must like you and trust you wholeheartedly, otherwise no deal!

Why are Japanese companies so successful? If there is one key to Japanese success it is their ability to conduct a company's internal affairs in a spirit of harmony and cooperation. Americans and Europeans seem to have more energy as individuals, but they are often pulling in different directions within a company. There is certainly submarine infighting below the surface in Japanese companies, but once unanimity of agreement has been reached (and the president insists on it), then everyone pulls together. The Japanese will discuss and discuss until everybody agrees. Such endless discussion often results in slow decisions, but the Japanese think the gain in solidarity is worth it. Results seem to show that they are right. All this is not without its tension, however, since Japanese executives frequently have to give in, even if their ideas are good ones.

The Japanese attitude toward foreigners, even educated people and high-ranking businesspeople, is clear: you are always an outsider. Your efforts to speak Japanese will be smiled on, but seldom taken seriously. As many senior Japanese do not speak English, Japanese interpreters are often used. They can be unbelievably bad and seldom give real translations when Americans or Europeans wish to be blunt. Often the message, lost in an endless labyrinth of polite vagueness, will not get across at all. Translators and interpreters in Japan have an unhappy time. Usually they will be abused by Westerners for not translating properly and criticized by their own superiors for being unclear. They are not really trusted anyway; after all, they speak two languages.

THE JAPANESE AS SEEN BY OTHERS

Appearance	Reality
They are aloof.	Extreme shyness makes it difficult for them to initiate conversation.
They are short on words.	True. The Japanese distrust words. Also, they may have poor command of the language you speak.
They deafen you with silence.	Silence shows respect for the speaker.
They often look glum.	In Japan, happiness hides behind a straight face.
When they smile, they don't look sincere.	Japanese often smile to make you feel comfortable. You should be thankful.
They say yes when they mean no.	They don't like to offend you by showing open disagreement or refusal.
We can never tell what they really think.	By generally keeping a straight face, they are rather impassive, but they are not trying to deceive you.
They never look you right in the eye.	The Japanese are taught that it is rude to stare.
They sit up straight all the time and don't seem to relax in meetings.	The Japanese don't like to slouch. Maintaining correct posture is polite.
They go to sleep during meetings.	Not often. When they close their eyes, it means they are concentrating on what you are saying.
They delay in making decisions, don't answer letters and faxes when we press them.	They don't like to be rushed. They must complete their consensus.
They lack individualism and all behave the same way.	They prefer teamwork and group decisions to individualism. Homogeneity makes them act alike.
They talk Japanese during meetings so we can't understand them.	It is their language! Also, they may find it difficult to concentrate for long periods in a foreign language.
They are often ambiguous. We are never quite sure what they mean.	Japanese is an ambiguous, vague language which carries over into the English translation. Also, their language level may be low.

(continued)

THE JAPANESE AS SEEN BY OTHERS *(continued)*

Appearance	Reality
They delay making an order for six months, then they expect you to deliver tomorrow!	Japanese companies tend to proceed with implementation while they await an order. That way they are never caught flat-footed.
Sometimes they don't seem interested in immediate profit. This is annoying to Westerners.	Japanese shareholders do not press for dividends. They believe more in increasing market share, improving share price and eventually making capital gains. They think long term.
They are tough negotiators, often refusing to change their position.	Tough negotiators are good negotiators! The Japanese meet force with intransigence. But when treated with respect, they are often willing to modify their position considerably.
They don't like foreigners, believing they are a superior race.	It is true that the Japanese people consider themselves unique, but they have often been willing to learn from others. In Japan they treat foreigners very well. Their hospitality is unsurpassed.
They don't mix easily with other nationalities.	Those Japanese who have had little contact with foreigners are often afraid to mix with them, as they feel they won't know how to behave.
They are noisy in groups and behave badly when abroad.	In Japan there are very strict rules on social behavior. When abroad the relaxation of these rules tends to make them let their hair down and be boisterous. Also, they tolerate alcohol badly.
They try to bribe Westerners with gifts.	Not true. Gift giving is a tradition in Japan and applies also to foreign guests. You can reciprocate.
They do not always respect contracts, often asking for renegotiation after several months.	They respect oral contracts and the spirit in which they were made. They wish to renegotiate if market or other conditions have changed.

How to Empathize with the Japanese

What should a foreign businessperson who goes to Japan do? First, restrict your body language. Do not wave your arms about, do not touch people unnecessarily and above all do not put your arm around their shoulders as you pass through doorways. Do not report conversations you have had with a Japanese to third parties unless it is clear that you may do so. Do not mention business for the first 15 minutes of any conversation. Never address any Japanese businessman by his first name and never, ever talk about the Second World War.

If you are dealing with a group of Japanese (and they usually come to see you in groups), address your remarks to the senior man and bow to him as low as he bows to you, but watch carefully; he may put out his hand Western-style when you attempt to bow Japanese-style. You may talk about golf or ski jumping as much as you like, but do not tell jokes unless they are at your own expense and can easily be understood.

Manners and Taboos

It is not a good idea to ask to see a Japanese home; even important businesspeople often live in tiny apartments, a fact that causes them some embarrassment. They are quite happy to go to your home, however, since you are likely to have more space. Do not shake hands with them more than necessary as they regard this practice as unhygienic. However, you should always present your visiting card immediately at the first meeting.

When dealing with a Japanese company that may superficially resemble your own, do not assume similarities that are not there. Japan has *modernized, not westernized,* and true similarities are mainly only technical. Don't assume that they mean the same as you do when they use words like *leadership* or *motivation.* They have something quite different in mind.

If there seem to be a lot of *don'ts* with regard to your behavior when dealing with the Japanese, there is also a list of *dos.* Above all you should be modest and reserved. Bow if you can manage it and begin your conversation by asking about their families. It is quite correct to enthuse over the Japanese economic miracle, as well as their reputation for honesty and lavish hospitality. Another positive subject is the long unbroken history of Japan and its achievements in the arts.

It is also quite correct for you to apologize for your rudeness when you last met. The Japanese always do this whether they were rude or not. What it means is that you speak in a disparaging manner about your unpunctuality or poor hospitality or any other personal defect you can think of. For instance, the Japanese apologize regularly for having had a cold, having taken you to see a poor film, having given you a ride in their noisy car or having beaten your country at karate.

Finally, if you want to do business with the Japanese you must also try to look the part. Remember that normally all Japanese executives dress conservatively in dark blue or gray with a white shirt and dark tie. A Japanese businessman looks at you in a manner not unlike that of the Spaniard. He must like you and he must trust you, otherwise no deal. He likes people who are clean, well-dressed, not too hairy, not too young, modest, of quiet voice and above all, polite. You must also convince him that you are respectable. For a Japanese, respectability comprises a certain age and several of the qualities just mentioned, and also a proven record in business, an absence of any doubtful partners or deals and evidence of unquestioned solvency. Many Japanese businesspeople will ask you openly at the first meeting for a list of your board of directors, the financial state of your company, your chief customers and a chairman's report.

MOTIVATION

KEY	*Courtesy, giving face*
Cross-century mood	◆ Want more leisure, foreign travel and less regimentation. ◆ Wish to share trend setting with the West in regard to fashion, music, art, and food. ◆ Inclination to put an end to (or modify) "salaryman" drudgery. ◆ Increasing dissatisfaction with banks and political parties.

Motivating Factors

◆ Be very polite at all times. This involves often standing up when you would normally sit down, perhaps bowing when you would shake hands and apologizing several times a day for rudeness you have not committed.

◆ Entertain generously with splendid meals—which you apologize for afterwards.

◆ Flatter them a lot. They like it.

◆ Show great respect for their company.

◆ Emphasize the size, age, wealth and reputation of your own company.

◆ Remember that anything you say they take literally. Flippant remarks such as "This is killing me" or "You must be kidding" will be misconstrued.

◆ Be less direct in your utterances than you would be with others.

◆ You must never hurt their feelings.

◆ Learn some Japanese and use it to show you have an interest in their culture. Don't overdo it—they don't like foreigners who speak fast Japanese.

◆ When speaking English (if this is your common language), speak slowly and distinctly. They smile and nod constantly but may not understand much.

◆ Be prepared to say everything 5 times at a succession of meetings and anything vital at least 10 times.

◆ If they make an oral agreement, they will stick to it, but they do not necessarily want to shake hands on it. A nod or slight bow is much better.

◆ Find common ground when you can. They love sharing.

◆ Things are often agreed upon between meetings, so be prepared to talk business while socializing.

Avoid

◆ Saying "No," or "It's impossible" or "We can't." If you disagree, just be silent.

◆ Cornering them or making them lose face.

(continued)

MOTIVATION *(continued)*

◆ Pushing documents at them until they are ready; they prefer oral agreements to written ones anyway.

◆ Trying to extract decisions from them at meetings. Remember, they have to check with the head office.

68

Latin America

The term New World is a great and somewhat impertinent misnomer used by Europeans to describe the Americas. It is in fact a very old world, which witnessed a kaleidoscopic array of diverse cultures, civilizations and stupendous feats of human endeavor over many millennia before Europe emerged from the Dark Ages.

You have to scrutinize a map of the North/South American continent to appreciate the enormity and magnificence of the subsequent migrations through Alaska, North, Central and South America around 40 to 60 thousand years ago.

Only 500 years have passed since the beginning of the Iberian conquest of Latin America—a mere blip in relation to the history of human activity there. It is clear, however, that the Hispanic-Portuguese advent, devastating the indigenous cultures that preceded them and imposing their own civilization, had a decisive impact on the molding of Latin American life.

But Latin Americans are not Spaniards or Portuguese. They are a distinctly separate breed, and we would be remiss in our assessment of them if we were to ignore not only the bloodlines of some of their ancestors as well as their unique cultural achievements but also the vast, inaccessible stretches of wild and savage terrain, which for tens of millennia challenged the pioneering, migrating "Indians" as they pressed inexorably southward. Although originating in error, the name *Indian* was not so misplaced as it once seemed. These hunters were perhaps not from the Indian subcontinent, but they were certainly Asians, and not only did they bring with them the physical characteristics of their homelands (Andean Indians resemble many Asians), but they also possessed Asiatic psychologies and enduring traits that left their mark on the conquistadors who subjugated them, "civilized" them and intermarried with them.

Such a blending of races and ancestry, such an exciting mixing of pioneers, adventurers and warriors, such a vast, wild and exhilarating geographical environment, in a southern ocean setting of relative isolation (even in the twenty-first century), produces a special type of person with whom their northern neighbors and the Europeans are not yet fully familiar. Although the inhabitants of Latin America vary to a considerable degree in their world views and lifestyles, there is a common quality that distinguishes the Latin American from the rest of humankind. Latin America has, and increasingly will have, its own special impact on the world in the twenty-first century, just as their North American neighbors had in the twentieth century.

Latin American Characteristics

When we attempt to define or evaluate a distinctive Latin American culture, it is inevitable that we take Hispanic traits as our starting point. The conquistadors, at least in the early years of conquest, ruthlessly imposed their own type of civilization upon the indigenous peoples. If the driving force of conquest was greed, it came disguised as a crusading faith—Catholicism—with the backing not only of the Pope and two Iberian monarchies, but with all the trappings of southwest Europe—merciless soldiering, bureaucratic impositions, taxes and levies, zealous missionaries, churches, schools, courts, even the Spanish Inquisition itself. The indigenous cultures were occasionally exploited (to seek allies) but in the main were crushed, destroyed or, in the case of inaccessible terrains, ignored.

But from the Indians' point of view all was not lost. History teaches us that when one civilization conquers another, very often vestiges of the original way of life remain. In some cases the victors are influenced by the local culture and even absorb many of its characteristics. In Latin America, the only-too-evident Iberian theatricality, machismo and individualism are subtly tempered by ephemeral, more ambiguous undertones emanating from indigenous and (in the case of Brazil) African lifestyles.

What are basic Hispanic traits? The Iberian Peninsula was part of the Roman Empire, and just as the Spanish language is clearly a legitimate daughter of Latin, Spaniards inherited most of the characteristics of the European Mediterranean people—extroverted behavior, loquacity, volatility, love of argument and rhetoric, openly expressed emotions, a quick temper balanced by ready compassion, capacity for intrigue and conspiracy, love of gossip, overt body language, quickness of perception and slow to trust. In these respects Spanish people differ little from their Italian, French and Portuguese cousins.

But Spain was occupied by many legions of many races, including the Moors, who remained in the southern part of the country for 700 years. Crossing the straits from nearby Morocco in A.D. 711, they dominated Spanish intellectual life until the late fifteenth century. Their last stronghold—Granada—fell in 1492, coincidentally the year in which Columbus "discovered" America.

The diverse influence of the Muslims, Vizigoths, Vandals and other tribes on the Roman Spaniards gave rise to distinctive Hispanic traits that are not shared with the French or Italians. Some of these are, for example, the exaggerated sense of personal honor that a Spaniard cherishes; the subsequent desire for revenge if this is slighted; the persistent machismo allied to gallantry toward women; the perception of a "double truth," which distinguishes between present immediacy and ultimate reality; and the fierce loyalty engendered by a crusading spirit on behalf of religious convictions or a revered leader. These qualities, which the Spaniards inherited from their non-Roman conquerors, were also imported into Central and South America in the cultural baggage of the conquistadores—many of whom came from Moor-influenced Andalusia and Extremadura. Machismo, double truth, mañana tendencies and chauvinism are prominent among them.

The influence of the American Indian cultures in its turn causes Latin Americans to differ from their Spanish cousins. The invaders rapidly acquired the ability to adapt themselves to the "strange" and "exotic" environment of the Indians. They slept in hammocks, paddled canoes, smoked tobacco, ate maize and potatoes and married local women. They shared the Indians' attachment to the land; they were equally exhilarated by the vast expanses of the wild continent. Mingling with the natives, they acquired a deep and new understanding of human suffering, which widened their worldview and made them see exploitation from another angle. They learned to resent European authority and felt the incongruity of the norms of an old society imposed on new lands and situations. The beckoning pampas grasslands and mountains made them impatient with European caution. Like the Indians, they cooperated feebly and tardily with the Spanish court and sometimes not at all. Like the Moors and Indians, they developed the habit of rejecting rational criteria. Optimism, engendered by the limitless spaces and opportunities, joined hands with native fatalism. If one trusted in bountiful nature, all would end well. When Europe's kings and queens pressed too hard, the subsequent sense of powerlessness led to native-style passivity and inactivity. Like Aztec, Incan and Mayan subjects, the Hispanic settlers developed traits of indecisiveness leading to a lack of accountability and reliance on paternalism. The seeds of eventual rebellion were thus being sown.

Latin American Characteristics

Trait	Origin
◆ love of space	geographic
◆ optimism bordering on arrogance	and
◆ impatience with European caution	environmental
◆ isolationism	
◆ lack of international experience	
◆ rural habits	Indian
◆ attachment to the land	
◆ resentment against exploitation	
◆ poor cooperation with authorities	*(continued)*

(continued from previous page)

- ✦ sense of fatalism
- ✦ periods of inactivity
- ✦ understanding of human suffering
- ✦ compassion
- ✦ fear of the unknown
- ✦ indecisiveness
- ✦ imitation

✦ fatalism ✦ machismo ✦ *mañana* ✦ view of women	Moorish (via conquistadores)
✦ importance of status ✦ idealism over materialism ✦ art of conversation ✦ feeling of cultural superiority to North Americans ✦ good grasp of human values ✦ theatricality ✦ Catholicism and crusading spirit	Hispanic
✦ human beings as more important than rules ✦ little correlation between law and actual life ✦ little aptitude for parliamentary rule ✦ lack of internal discipline	conquistadores

69

Argentina

Of the 18 independent Spanish-speaking republics in Central and South America, Argentina is the largest, the richest, the most influential, arguably the most scenic and colorful and certainly the most enigmatic. With over 2.8 million square kilometers (over 1 million square miles) of territory (the eighth largest nation in the world), Argentina is gifted with enormous resources in the form of oil, minerals, gas, cotton, sugar, timber and tobacco, with pampas covering a topsoil reputedly 3 to 6 meters (10 to 20 feet) deep, capable of supporting 55 million head of cattle and 30 million sheep, with a 95 percent literacy rate and an extremely sophisticated, well-educated middle class concentrated in a strikingly beautiful and smoothly functioning capital of over 15 million people. Why then is Argentina in the first decade of the twenty-first century struggling to achieve a GDP half that of Spain and a GDP per capita of less than a third of that of little Denmark? Why have the Argentineans, so intellectually brilliant and analytical, failed to realize their beckoning potential? Why did this heady brew of nationalities—Spaniards, Anglos, Welsh, Italians, Indians as well as liberal sprinklings of Poles, Ukrainians, Germans and Bolivians—fail to match the economic achievements of the parallel multicultural giants, the United States and Canada?

The factors are many and complex, though 40 years of political squabbling and glaring economic errors would seem to point the finger of blame at atrociously inefficient and corrupt government. A major problem is the fact that the riches of the country lie in the interior, but political, commercial and financial control have been rigidly centered in Buenos Aires. This conflict of interests between the top-heavy capital and the widespread rural areas has been a major obstacle to the development of the country.

Buenos Aires in fact got off to a bad start, the first settlers being killed or driven out by hostile Indians. Even when a beachhead was established, it remained very much a swampy backwater, for the Spaniards were much more interested in Peruvian gold, so neighboring northwest Argentina was the center of trade. The Spanish king actually forbade direct trade between Spain and Rio de la Plata, as he felt he could not protect the Atlantic trade routes. Goods came and went first via the Caribbean and Panama, then overland to the Pacific, then by boat to Lima and finally by oxcart to Buenos Aires! The shortsightedness of the Spanish Crown led to the development of illegal trading along the Rio de la Plata, and the wily *porteños* (inhabitants of Buenos Aires) indulged in big-time smuggling, slave traffic and other nefarious activities in direct defiance of Spanish laws. Fortunes were made out of leather and cattle hides, and when technical advancement enabled refrigerated beef to be exported to Europe, it was clear that Buenos Aires would acquire a stranglehold on the economy of the interior—a grip which has never been loosened or relinquished.

Since, as they say, every country gets the government it deserves, any analysis of Argentina must inevitably focus on the paradoxical nature of the country's inhabitants.

The Many Faces of Argentina

Who are the Argentineans? What are they really like? This is a popular subject of discussion in South America, as Chileans, Brazilians, Venezuelans and others are forthright in their opinions about Argentine conceit. The Argentineans themselves, in soul-searching fashion, are quick to scrutinize their own defects—even to make fun of themselves. In Buenos Aires you often hear the definition, "An Argentinean is an Italian who speaks Spanish, lives in a French house and thinks he is British." In fact, this description pertains more to *porteños* than to people in rural districts.

Buenos Aires has the appearance of (and to all intents and purposes is) a European city, reminiscent of Paris and Madrid and bearing no resemblance to other South American cities. Eighty-five percent of the 15 million inhabitants of the Buenos Aires metropolitan area are of European descent; Indians and even mestizos (a mixture of Europeans and Indians) are hardly visible. Indeed the *porteños* find themselves frequently asking the question, "Am I a European or an American?" Millions of Argentineans in less sophisticated rural regions would say "European" while feeling themselves distinctively "American." But the demographic patchwork of Argentina is far more complex than a straight rural-urban divide. As you travel around the vast country, you encounter groups possessing a striking variety of psychologies and world views.

Tierra del Fuego

On a recent visit to Ushuaia in Tierra del Fuego, one month after being in Reykjavik, Iceland, I had a distinct sense of déjà vu. The steeply roofed, wooden houses of Ushuaia were Scandinavian in appearance; the staggering wild beauty of the Beagle Channel reminded me of the Lofoten Islands off the northwest coast of Norway; the fish-and-sheep economy mirrored that of Iceland; the pioneering, rough-and-ready attitudes of the settlers in the far south were a world apart from the practiced cosmopolitan nature of the *porteños*.

In Ushuaia, 3,000 kilometers (1,900 miles) from Buenos Aires, the youngish, hardy and distinctly self-reliant islanders face south rather than north and are concerned with snowfall and skiing, the development of "adventure" tourism, the nearby Falkland Islands and the 1,200,000 square kilometer (463,000 square mile) slice of not-so-distant Antarctica.

Tierra del Fuegans are acutely conscious of the epic peculiarities of their history and geography. Ushuaia is located at the very end of the trek that faced Asian migrants crossing the Bering Straits around 50,000 years ago. It took a long time to walk (and to settle on the land) from the Bering Straits to Tierra del Fuego. The Yamana and Ona Indians completed the entirety of the journey perhaps 20,000 years ago. Almost entirely eradicated by the colonists, the last ones died a few decades ago; the city's museums exhibit numerous black-and-white pictures of these primitive people. Although pure Indians no longer exist, mestizos abound. Another characteristic of the "wild south" atmosphere is the consciousness of the town having been a penal colony from 1902 to 1947 (shades of Australia).

The Northwest

The diversity of Argentinean demographics can be highlighted by a quick trip from Tierra del Fuego to Salta in the republic's northwest corner near the borders with Chile, Bolivia and Paraguay. This colorful, wind-sculpted desert is the epicenter of Argentina's colonial and pre-Columbian cultures. Salta was founded in the second half of the sixteenth century, but the region had been inhabited for over 10,000 years before that and was culturally the most developed area in Argentina when the Spaniards arrived. The northwest provinces, nearest gold-rich Peru, were the focus of Spanish activity in the country until far-off Buenos Aires achieved preeminence. If Tierra del Fuego is the least Latin part of Argentina, the northwest is certainly the most Indian. This is evident not only in the physiology of the inhabitants, but also in the relaxed, slow-paced tempo of village and town life, in the exotic local dishes and in the traditional music, arts and crafts. As you approach the Chilean border, you increasingly see deep-chested (because of lack of oxygen) native Indians. The staggering Andean altitudes remind you how natural barriers are major factors in the delineation of frontiers between the South American republics.

The Gaucho

Unlike the *porteño*, the inhabitants of Buenos Aires and its environs, there is nothing enigmatic about the gaucho. Far removed from the psychiatric clinics and complicated goings-on of the capital, he (the gaucho is unequivocally male) pursues a purposeful and steadfast, quintessentially Argentinean existence. Unlike many of his countrymen, he knows who he is and is proud of it. The gaucho has been known as "the man who was born on horseback." Lest you think that he is an obsolete species, note that over 150,000 gauchos work every day, caring for a livestock population of 55 million cattle, 30 million sheep and 2 million horses.

It is no wonder that the annual per capita meat consumption is between 80–85 kilograms (174–187 pounds)! The gaucho, who has the blood of many ethnic groups in his veins, has evolved in tandem with the country's turbulent history. Acquiring unrivaled skills in horsemanship during the period of 1580–1750, he received his baptism of fire before the country gained its independence and distinguished himself by feats of valor in the ferocious battles of the Desert War.

Often spurned, downtrodden and cheated by Argentine society, the gaucho has held fast to solid principles throughout the centuries. He learned hardiness, the power of resistance and a code of nobility from the Indians with whom he mingled and occasionally fought. He trusts the word of another and believes in true friendship. He has a defined concept of superior and subordinate and practices a code of honor that respects both authority and freedom. He cultivates patriotism without making a show of it, and contributes to aesthetics through his artisanship as applied to silver working, textiles and braided leather. He is close to the land, his animals and his family. He is a poet, musician, dancer and a great storyteller. He respects women, children and strangers. Perhaps more than any other of his countrymen, he represents the true spirit of Argentina.

The Porteños

The continuing dominant position of Buenos Aires in Argentinean commerce means that international business partners will normally have to deal with *porteños* in their activities in or related to Argentina. Consequently, you will have to learn the *porteño* mindset to deal successfully. What are the *porteños* like? How do they think? What makes them tick?

To begin with, you will need to examine the Argentinean national malaise, which is particularly evident in Buenos Aires. This somewhat melancholy phenomenon,which parallels national soul-searching in Holland and Norway, pervades *porteño* thought, leading to an indecisiveness and over-analysis that is often mocked by other South Americans. Foreigners have barely stepped onto Argentinean soil before they are asked, "What do you think of Argentina?" The beauty of the country and the courtesy and hospitality of the *porteños* will enable you to reply positively, but the question goes much deeper than that. It is as if they are asking, "Do you think we are doing things right?" Or "What is Argentina's reputation abroad?" Buenos Aires reputedly has more psychiatrists per capita than anywhere else in the world. Most likely, the acute slippage in the standard of living has undermined people's confidence.

To foreigners, *porteños* are the kindest people on earth, but they admit that they are more testy among themselves, that they look down on their rural cousins and that they feel intellectually superior to all other Latin Americans, who in turn call them arrogant. *Porteños* like Uruguayans ("they are similar to us"), dislike Chileans ("territorially aggressive"), think Bolivians, Paraguayans and Ecuadorians are Indians, but have some respect for Peruvians. Colombia and Venezuela are too far off to matter much. They admit that the exuberant Brazilians are a lot of fun, but they have a complex about the enormous size of Brazil and fear that a flood of cheap Brazilian imports would threaten Argentine industry if markets were fully freed.

The *porteños* are compassionate souls, with impeccable manners indoors and out. In restaurants they are quiet (compared to Mediterranean people), and on the street they are considerate pedestrians and citizens. Waiters, taxi drivers, hotel staff and most people in public offices do their jobs efficiently, and you won't see the "chip on the shoulder" that is so common among poorly paid people in Southern Europe. They are extremely sentimental, emotion often creeping into business dealings.

Porteños are certainly overly politicized, and you may have to listen to their woes more than you want to. About 80 percent of their national and local newspapers are devoted to politics; this hardly makes fascinating reading for those foreigners who have taken the trouble to learn Spanish. Corruption at high levels is endemic, and one tires of wondering how long it will take Argentineans to rid themselves of bad government—when did they have a good one? The power of the military establishment over the political process does seem to have been restrained, but scandals among elected administrators continue. Opinion polls show that Argentineans want a strong executive restrained by the judiciary and the media, but the absence of any tradition of representative government is a serious impediment to achieving these goals.

Porteños are good Catholics and resemble the Italians in their attitude toward extended, close families. They feel European but know relatively little about Europe, which seems very distant and expensive to reach. In reality their waking hours are filled with animated discussions of the exciting life of the bustling capital—politics, scandals, crime, business, soccer and other sports, theater and cinema and the tango (an obsession). They also keep themselves busy cultivating a lively social circle where wining and dining attain a standard unrivalled in most countries. Many will tell you that they eat meat 13 times a week, pasta once a week and fish once a month.

Porteños show some British influence (blue blazers, rugby, golf, tennis, polo and tea are popular), and Britain was Argentina's chief trading partner until the Second World War. Like Western Europeans, *porteños* are highly literate, spend money rather than save it, are extremely brand-oriented and sustain low population growth.

Others

There are other Argentineans. Around Tilcara you can see Bolivian-influenced cultures; in Humahuaca and Purmamarca the brown faces, colorful garments and adobe dwellings emphasize the resilience of the indigenous peoples. Four thousand eight hundred kilometers (three thousand miles) further south, a different kind of resilience is evident in Trelew and Gaiman—Welsh Patagonia— where stone cottages, chapels and meticulously cultivated fields bear witness to the determined Celtic settlers who created an agricultural and social paradise in the Chubut Valley. The Welsh arrived in the area in 1865, and some of the descendants of the settlers still speak Welsh, thereby contributing to the richness of pan-Argentine culture.

Culture

Values

eloquence	courtesy
conceit	distrust of authorities
Europeanness	suspicion of Anglo-Saxons
emotion	feeling of superiority over other South
family closeness	Americans

Concepts

Leadership and Status

Leadership in most Hispanic American countries has traditionally been centered around a strong dictator or military figure or, in the case of Argentina, dominant political parties. Nepotism is common and staff are manipulated by a variety of persuasive methods ranging from (benign) paternalism to outright exploitation and coercion.

Space and Time

Argentineans sit close to interlocutors and often pat their arm or grip their elbow to show trust. Out of doors they love the exhilarating space that their country offers.

Their sense of time is typically South American. They can be quite unconcerned about punctuality, though they are not the worst offenders on the continent.

Cultural Factors in Communication

Communication Pattern

Meetings with Latin Americans are more complicated than with, say, Nordics or Australians. To begin with, a lot of small talk is expected, and Americans and Northern Europeans need to give clear signs of respecting the national honor of their counterparts. Initial proposals are often far removed from realistic conclusions, and protracted haggling is part of the process. Argentineans can be very persuasive. Agreements reached are often somewhat inconclusive and strict adherence to contracts is questionable.

Listening Habits

Traditionally, Argentineans are poor at cooperating with authorities and with carrying out any external plans that do not correspond to their immediate needs. Consequently they are not among the best of audiences. Only charismatic speakers can get them to listen for any length of time, and even they must be very respectful and present the listeners with an intrinsic learning opportunity.

Behavior at Meetings and Negotiations

Argentineans conduct meetings and negotiations in a courteous and sophisticated style. They tend to overanalyze in the Latin manner and can be quite opinionated if they are given the chance. It is best to stick to your guns with them.

How to Empathize with Argentineans

Reciprocate their obvious courtesy and appreciate their level of sophistication. Argentineans can be won over by a combination of intellectual argument and openly friendly stance. It is advisable not to dwell on the country's numerous political problems and financial disasters.

70

Mexico

Argentina and Mexico, the two Spanish-speaking giants of Latin America, both have to contend with a culturally different "colossus" to the north (Brazil and the United States, respectively). Argentina, relatively isolated in the southern ocean and at the bottom end of the continent's cone, has surprisingly little contact with Brazil and is visited by fewer than four million people per year. The U.S. is far distant in another hemisphere; consequently, Argentineans have had the legroom to fashion their present-day culture along preferred European lines.

Mexico, by contrast (so far from God, so near the United States), has a 2,500 kilometer (1,553 mile) northern border with the U.S., which is crossed 20 million times each year, mainly by Americans, who account for 85 percent of Mexico's exports and 70 percent of her imports. Mexico's involvement with the U.S., and particularly the loss in 1845–1846 of her territories that are now California, New Mexico, Arizona, Nevada, Utah and part of Colorado, has had a decisive influence on the history of the nation and the shaping of Mexican mentality. The Mexican psyche, even before the U.S. ascended to dominance, was already profoundly different from that of other European- or Asian-influenced Latin American cultures, on account of the dramatic and irreversible fusion of indigenous and Muslim-affected Hispanic civilizations in the years following Hernan Cortés' victory in 1521. For all living Mexicans, the Aztec legacy and the *Yanqui* trauma are ever-present realities, shaping their thoughts, attitudes, actions, values, plans and unique mindset.

Culture

Values

personal dignity	uniqueness of the individual
hypersensitivity	national honor
exaggerated emotion, passion, rhetoric	mysticism, fatalism
apathy, passivity	obedience to authority
group loyalty	family closeness
deference to age	saving face at all costs
resentment of exploitation	acceptance of stratification of society
demoralization, inferiority complex	idealism as reaction to defeat
dual truth and reality	concern for status and appearances
machismo	historical perspectives
mañana, cyclical time	disdain for menial labor per se
human relations orientation	

Mexicans, like other Latin Americans, derive many of their characteristics from Spain, whose language, religion, values and lifestyle were rapidly imported by the conquistadores. The subsequent fusion of cultures was, however, quite different in Mexico from what it was in the United States, Brazil or Argentina, where the indigenous people were decimated, marginalized or ignored culturally. When Cortés arrived in Mexico, a magnificent civilization was already in place. It is true that the Aztec armies were defeated and the population subjugated, but the indigenous influence remained to pervade every aspect of Mexican life—food, involvement with nature, beliefs, concepts of time and space, attitudes toward authority, the eventual world view itself. The readiness of the Spaniards to intermarry with the indigenous people (absent in Argentina and the U.S.) soon produced a rapidly expanding mestizo population and culture that gave Mexico the most Indian-oriented mindset among the major American countries.

Which are the Indian-influenced characteristics of the Mexican? If passion, rhetoric, exuberance, extroversion and imagination are Hispanic traits, the subtler, deeper, more inscrutable side of the Mexican reveals his affinity to indigenous life. Though normally bouncy and gregarious, Mexicans frequently slip into melancholy and despairing modes, where fatalism, apathy and a sense of powerlessness combine to produce an inferiority complex far removed from Argentinean conceit or Brazilian gay abandon. At such times Mexicans "put on a mask," concealing feelings behind an impassive countenance that denotes stoicism in adversity and a quiet understanding of human suffering. From the indigenous people, Mexicans also inherit the passive acceptance of the stratification of society—just as it was in the Aztec caste system, a readiness to assume a preordained role in the hierarchy, an exaggerated deference for age and its assumed wisdom, and an ability to face poverty, hardship and death itself without undue fuss or complaint. This is a product of the Indian concept of cyclical time: compensation is achieved when the wheel turns full circle, and no human endeavor, however strenuous, can really affect the immediate sequence of events. Like the indigenous people, the Mexican believes in the solidity and comforting support of the group, where oral agreements are kept, commitments honored, and trustworthiness is paramount.

These time-honored values dominate Mexican business and social life today. The modern Mexican is preoccupied with face and credibility, far more than most Latin Americans, who are often more pragmatic. *La dignidad del hombre*—certainly a Spanish concept—is a more sensitive issue in Mexico than anywhere in Europe, with the possible exception of Sicily. Mexican face saving and obsession with respect and status resembles the Asian (Japanese) variety in its finickiness and intensity. This Asian characteristic was carried over the Bering Straits and has lost no significance in Indian-affected cultures all the way from Alaska to Tierra del Fuego. Indian influence is also seen in the slow Mexican tempo in building relationships, unwillingness to commit oneself to involvement with others if trust has not been established, suspicion of the *gringo* (how often the indigenous people have been betrayed!) and a tendency to look for a go-between if agreement cannot be reached in discussion. Above all, the Mexican mestizo is united with his Indian forebears by a sense of historical perspective gained from ongoing contemplation of and research into a history of 3,000 years and a conviction that anything that happens now in the present is an inevitable result of past actions and destinies.

Mexicans are extremely warm-hearted and hospitable people who are not slow to invite you into their homes, where you will encounter strong family ties and an unequivocally moralistic ambience based on Catholic principles. The father is the head of the family, his wife and children are normally happily obedient; he is also devoted to his mother. Mexican women take great pains to enhance and preserve their considerable beauty, normally use heavier makeup than European women and are fond of gold and silver jewelry (following Aztec tradition!). Like their husbands, they are animated and charming conversationalists; Mexican eye contact is very strong, and the distance of comfort is close. Men in particular hug other men (even you when they get to know you), slap backs affectionately and grip elbows to show trust.

No account of Mexican customs would be complete without reference to *la mordida*. While the Mexican gives freely to his guest, conducting business and obtaining many social services incur a cost which is normally obviated in U.S. and Northern European societies. Mexican civil servants, officials and police are paid very little and usually seek to augment their meager salaries by accepting what Americans call *bribes* to facilitate the granting of permits and other services. Mexicans consider this to be rather normal and not unreasonable. The custom sits well both with the traditional Spanish willingness to help the underdog ("There but for the grace of God go I") and the historical precedent of the Aztec system of exacting tributes. The dilemma for the foreigner lies not in knowing whether you should pay or not, but in how much you should pay. There is a going rate for everything, whether it is securing a government contract, an import permit or quick access to the head of a line in a post office. Mexicans are familiar with expected rates and it is often wise to consult them.

Concepts

Leadership and Status

Leadership in Mexico is very autocratic, particularly in business circles. Insight into leaders' mentality can be gained from the following paragraphs on status and the section "Behavior at Meetings and Negotiations."

In many Western societies status is achieved through hard work, accomplishment, and sometimes wealth. In Mexico it is less a matter of achievement than of "completeness." The Mexican leader may have acquired his position initially by birthright or nepotism, but he will not be successful unless he takes great pains to develop a huge network of friends, business partners and officials who will help him to consolidate his power base. As in the Aztec *cacique* system, these relationships are built on complex personal ties that allow favors to be sought, usually granted and ultimately reciprocated.

In business, a senior manager will command unquestioned obedience and respect from his subordinates, but as in Confucian systems, he is obliged to reward them with loyalty, courtesy and protection. The *patrón* wields his power openly and with machismo, but he will show immediate compassion for a worker's misfortunes and come readily to the aid of his family in the case of undue hardship or bereavement.

The *patrón* is himself a family man, a good Catholic and moralist, as well as a shrewd tactician and negotiator. When the chips are down, he has the connections and levers of power to attain the goals of the group he leads. This is what the Mexicans mean by *completeness*. He does not have to work hard at establishing his authority over staff—it is *assumed* from the very beginning.

Space and Time

Mexicans are exhilarated by the open spaces readily available in Mexico. When conversing, however, the distance of comfort is very close. They are a tactile culture.

Punctuality is not high on the list of Mexican priorities. In most hierarchical societies it is accepted that the powerful make others wait. Easy access to the presence of superiors casts doubt on their status. In Mexico life is not organized around a clock—a mere machine—but around a succession of encounters and relationships which are qualified and quantified not in linear fashion but in terms of depth of personal involvement, excitement, opportunity or caprice. Human transactions must be satisfactorily completed—not interrupted by the ringing of a bell or a knock on the door.

A second crucial aspect of time concerns late deliveries or tardy payments and is often accompanied by a paucity of communication. This is an unending source of irritation to linear Americans, Germans and others who accuse Mexicans of laziness. But Mexicans are not lazy—they cannot afford to be! Delays may be caused by the necessity to juggle options or assets due to a lack of resources, or simply because one is not ready to make a move yet. Cheated so often in the past, the Mexican has good reason to move slowly! Mexicans recognize that fate has many things in store for us that we cannot foresee, that the sequence of events in God's calendar may not correspond to man-made schedules and deadlines. Sometimes one has to make changes to accommodate changes elsewhere. One has to choose one's priorities.

Cultural Factors in Communication

Communication Pattern

Scandinavians, Japanese and some other reticent peoples often convey their thoughts and values through quiet, reliable actions. Mexicans prefer words. Of all the varieties of Spanish, Mexican Spanish, with its abundant use of diminutives and colorful imagery, is perhaps the most flowery. Like Italians, they leave little unsaid, are generous in their praise and flattery when talking to foreigners and rarely say anything that you do not want to hear.

In Mexico people are expected to discuss issues at length, seeking the agreement or conversion of the other and leaving no stone unturned to make oneself clear. As with most Latins, conversation is regarded as an art, and Mexicans fully expect you as their partner to give as good as you get. This is not always easy for Asians, Finns, Swedes and many Anglo-Saxons, who prefer to deal with facts and figures without the embroidery. Such calculating discourse does not, however, sit well with Mexicans, since it represents for them less than half of the whole picture. Feelings are more important than facts, and any statistical description of a business activity fails to take into account the complex web of human entanglements that surround a project. Lateral clearances, concerns of superiors and subordinates, current hopes and aspirations all have to be taken into account and thoroughly debated. There is also the question of real truth, which is not as readily available in charted or graphed form as the Anglo-Saxon may think. Mexicans in full fling of rhetoric may seem to many foreigners to barely have their emotions under control. Yet passion and eloquence are central to Mexicans' style of delivery, and their oratory is designed to show their extensive understanding of complex issues.

The Mexican manager, though macho in appearance and resilient in approach, still regards language as a beautiful tool and may quote well-known writers, even poets, as he constructs his arguments. Humor, also, is a frequently used tool, though in contrast to the dry Anglo-Saxon or Scandinavian varieties, it usually involves a play on words that non-Spanish speakers cannot always appreciate!

Listening Habits

Mexicans are courteous and polite listeners, always ready to learn from people of other nationalities. They are, however, very suspicious of Americans.

Behavior at Meetings and Negotiations

Meetings are always preceded with friendly small talk and only begin when the time feels right. The Mexican leader of the delegation will be highly visible, will claim priority seating and will probably be the chief spokesman. Initially, great politeness will be displayed by all and surnames with formal titles will be used. Any relaxing of formality, as the meeting progresses, will be initiated by the senior Mexican.

Dress is important—usually neat, conservative and of good quality.

The Mexican delegation will expect their leader to call the shots, will always concur with him and protect his status through attention and deference. Mexican specialists or experts will make contributions, but this will be coordinated by the leader. The other side should address all remarks to the senior Mexican, not to an interpreter, and only briefly to specialists.

Mexicans rarely discuss details at plenary sessions. The senior Mexican is expected to outline the background of the project in clear, broad terms and to convey his approval of general principles without taking any fixed position. The delegation leader will be skilled in exhibiting a detached approach to any issues that appear thorny, so as to avoid unpleasantness.

Foreigners must be sensitive to the Mexican "national honor" at all times. Mexicans are descendants of the Aztecs and know all about power, superiority and inferiority issues. They may accept the superior firepower of the other side, but they must never be humiliated. Opponents should be firm, but always respectful, even delicate. Because of the need for saving face, clear escape routes should always be signposted during negotiations.

Abstract principles count little for Mexicans if they contradict or clash with the views of one of their leaders. Credibility is the most powerful factor in persuading Mexicans to do something. It is unlikely you can outtalk them or win by wheeling and dealing.

Mexicans do not follow agendas rigidly and feel they can discuss any point when it seems opportune. They are less concerned about the completion or profitability of the deal under current discussion, thinking much more long-term. For them, successful business is all about creating a large number of long-lasting and reliable alliances. Insistence on deadlines and overly meticulous details in a contract signify (for the Mexicans) lack of trust.

You may gain advantage, when the strengths of each party are roughly equal, by according to the Mexican leader the status of *patrón*. As such he will be obliged to grant you courtesies and some privilege.

How to Empathize with Mexicans

Mexicans are not difficult people to get along with as long as you bear in mind their preoccupation with personal and national honor and take great pains to protect their face at all times. People used to interacting with the Japanese will have few problems with Mexicans. However, it is even better to be proactive in terms of improving relations.

Indeed, any foreigner will do well by displaying quiet respect and distinct moral values to contradict squarely the Mexican-held stereotype of the "ugly American." The Mexican sees a *Yanqui* as a money-minded materialist, therefore an incomplete human being, lacking in religious principles and family values and leading a way of life that produces undisciplined children who leave home early and disrespectful wives who sue for divorce. Men die early of heart attacks caused by the stress of American working life, long hours in the office and short vacations. Widows are quickly ushered into old folks' rest homes by uncaring sons who proceed to repeat the ghastly cycle.

Many Americans and Northern Europeans do not fit this stereotype, often being good family members and possessing a set of principles (though perhaps Protestant, not Catholic) that are just as solid as those of Latin Americans. The Anglo-Saxon, German or Scandinavian, given a modicum of sensitivity and willingness to adapt, can quickly distance himself from this damaging image and gain the confidence of his Mexican partner. If you display patience, go for a win–win situation in business, nurture a solicitous relationship with the Mexican's family members as well as sharing with them the details of your own private life, you will quickly convince the Mexican that there are good gringos and bad ones. Once this has been established and the question of relative status has been sorted out, many doors will open.

MOTIVATION

KEY	*Discuss ideals and honor*
Cross-century mood	✦ Inclination to achieve eventual economic and spiritual integration with the U.S. and Canada. ✦ Tendency to be seen as "North American" rather than Central or Latin American. ✦ Continued Mexican immigration to California currently causes problems, but is seen as eventually strengthening ties with Mexico and the western U.S.

Motivating Factors

✦ Show affection for Mexico and show warmth.
✦ Be compassionate.
✦ Give advice and help, but in a humble manner.
✦ Accept social invitations.
✦ Accept physical closeness.
✦ Use strong eye contact.
✦ Be relaxed about time.
✦ Use charisma if you can.
✦ Accept lengthy discussions when they want to express their point of view.
✦ Respect older people and ask about relatives.
✦ Accept interruptions.
✦ Allow for a certain amount of euphoria and exaggeration.
✦ Learn about Mexico's fascinating and colorful history, its literature and art.
✦ Admire their wonderful painting and architecture.

Avoid

✦ U.S. exploitive methods.
✦ Causing Mexicans to lose face.
✦ Pouring cold water on their occasional grandiosity.
✦ Stuffiness; merely sustain your dignity.
✦ Asking about how much Indian blood they have; it's a matter of status.
✦ Criticizing Mexican politics.
✦ Discussing corruption or political unrest in Chiapas.

71

Brazil

Just as children inherit and imitate the behavioral characteristics of their parents, new-born states (usually colonies) inherit and adopt the cultural traits of the mother country. Brazilians—the only Portuguese-speaking people of Latin America—act quite differently from other South Americans because their mother country is Portugal, not Spain.

The turbulent history of Spain since the days of the Roman Empire produced a headstrong race of impetuous individualists who readily exploded into violence in interregional disputes and internecine struggles. This combination of factionalism and violence was reflected in the arduous and protracted struggles of the South American wars of independence and echoed once more, centuries later, in the bloody Spanish Civil War. The Portuguese, by contrast, have a much gentler touch, tending to resolve their disputes by protracted discussion rather than by physical means. Portuguese rule in Brazil was nowhere near as harsh or autocratic as the Spanish. The people never felt the need to launch a war of independence. Brazil's emancipation took the form of a gentle transition and occurred virtually without bloodshed. Another striking example of history repeating itself was seen in 1974, when the Portuguese Revolution took place with no loss of life (the soldiers had carnations peeping out of their gun barrels!).

The Portuguese "conquest" of Brazil is almost laughable in its casualness. In the first place, Pedro Alvares Cabral discovered it by accident when he seems to have strayed off course on his way to India in 1500. At least he took the trouble to raise the Portuguese flag while he was there, but the Portuguese court was much more interested in extracting spices from the East. Spain consequently completed the conquest of most of South America by 1550, the Portuguese barely hanging on to their huge colony. However, Jesuit missionaries lent the occupation more seriousness. Black slaves were imported from Angola, and Indians were enslaved to help work the sugar plantations. The Portuguese settlers cohabited with the blacks and Indians, producing mulattos and mestizos. Thus the bloodlines of the new nation were rapidly being established.

The Portuguese mixed easily with other races (as they do today). Observers of life in early Brazil noted the patriarchal and expansive atmosphere on the plantations, "where children of all colors played together and were treated with equal tenderness by all." The mingling of races in a tropical climate produced a people of easy-going disposition. The diverse, illiterate populations of early Brazil, scattered along huge coastal plains, plateaus, rivers and jungles, rendered orthodox parliamentary government impossible. Monarchs and dictators were always necessary; fortunately, many of them were benevolent.

The Portuguese-Brazilian genius for compromise has continually enabled the nation to make tolerance and exploitation compatible. Autocratic rule is accepted along with an attachment to constitutionalism. The Brazilians are happy to be Brazilian, believing implicitly in the prolific potential of their country. "Our country grows at night when the politicians are asleep."

Brazilians are predominantly Roman Catholic, with some influence from African religions. Its cultural classification is multi-active, dialogue-oriented (see Chapter 3 for an explanation of these terms).

The Brazilians tend to be, like the Americans, very futuristic in their outlook, tearing down the old and constantly building anew, although they are traditional with respect to family and social customs.

Culture

Values

loquacious, exuberant	optimistic
emotional, theatrical	flexible
future-oriented	hospitable
group-oriented	avoid unpleasantness
impatient	cheerful
enjoy being Brazilian	relaxed time
compassionate	break rules
friendly, tolerant	easy racial relations
love music, dancing	imaginative
grandiose, exaggerating	unruly
patriotic	

The Brazilians enjoy a sense of national self-confidence: they have the fifth largest country in the world; it is extremely rich in resources, many of them as of yet undeveloped; and they have a growing population, soon approaching 220 million. They are happy to believe that God is Brazilian. To quote one Brazilian ambassador to England, "We are extrovert, impetuous, tropical. We like to march towards the unknown, without considering latitudes."

Concepts

Leadership and Status

Brazil is still essentially led by the upper and upper-middle classes. The country has been struggling toward democracy since 1986, before which it was a military dictatorship.

Nepotism is still widespread. Meritocracy is slowly creeping in, but will still take some time to be fully accepted.

Although on the surface Brazil seems to be free from racial intolerance, it is still very much a class society—one need only look at the composition of governing bodies. It is still important to "come from a good family," although status is slowly beginning to derive from entrepreneurial success and political influence.

Space and Time

Brazilians have a very close distance of comfort and are quite happy working close to each other. They are a tactile, hugging and very extroverted people. Women almost always greet each other with a kiss on each cheek, while men shake hands *and* give each other a warm pat on the back.

Brazilians actually believe it is impolite to arrive at someone's house for dinner on time. Business appointments rarely begin as scheduled and often run much longer than anticipated, thus delaying all further appointments.

They are generous with their time (often too generous), and they have a tendency to focus on the process rather than the product, which often causes them to lose sight of objectives. They favor interdependence in business and expect help in times of tragedy or failure. Brazilian companies are generally paternalistic and forgiving.

Cultural Factors in Communication

Communication Pattern

Loquacious and verbose to the extreme, the Brazilians use gestures and facial expressions to emphasize their point of view. Although appearing overly emotional at times, they only want you to understand that what they are saying "comes from the heart."

Their heart-felt emotions are accompanied by strong eye contact. Brazilians are very expressive, particularly when it comes to showing emotions such as disbelief, joy, sympathy or disappointment.

The lengthier their discourse, the more they feel they will have cemented your loyalty as a basis on which they can build further transactions and create long-term goodwill.

Listening Habits

Owing to their exuberance of expression, Brazilian listening habits tend to be somewhat erratic; they interrupt each other with ideas of their own, each individual wanting to make his or her personal contribution. You will have to learn to do the same. Their aim will be to form an in-depth impression of you from watching your movements, gestures and eye contact, rather than from listening intently to what you are saying. It makes sense, then, that Brazilian attention span is relatively short.

Behavior at Meetings and Negotiations

The Brazilian manager will use the *tu* (informal) form to subordinates, but do not let this fool you. His oratorical delivery makes what he says a fait accompli. Brazilian Portuguese, with its many diminutive endings, is highly suitable for expressing emotions and nuances, and for making a harsh statement appear less so.

Meetings tend to be erratic, even chaotic, with constant interruption of the agenda under discussion, as participants all come up with their own very creative ideas. Because Brazilians like to please, they will often tell people what they want to hear, stretching the truth to some extent. In this respect they always claim to have a solution to problems, though in reality this is often not the case. Excessive concern about job security leads to a reluctance to express their own opinions if they fear their view will run contrary to those of their superiors. Brazilians like to grab at easy, immediate solutions, the result often being a lack of long-term planning.

While demonstrating exuberance and energy at the outset of a new project, Brazilians tend to run out of steam and frequently leave projects unfinished, seemingly without qualms of conscience. Their enthusiasm for initiating exciting schemes is not matched by commitment to results. You will find that constant tracking and monitoring becomes a necessity.

This Brazilian inclination to look for a new bonanza rather than to persevere with a current project is a direct result of the pattern of the country's development. Since the early days of the dye-wood monopoly, the economic cycle has been one of boom-bust-boom. One bonanza succeeded another—sugar, cotton, gold, diamonds, coffee, rubber, iron ore. Quick fortunes were made in each commodity. When world prices declined, Brazilians showed little aptitude for cost cutting, finding it easier to move on to new pastures in a country of seemingly limitless resources.

Manners and Taboos

Brazilians excel as "space invaders." *Do not* change places if a Brazilian sits down as the fourth person on a three-seater sofa! As they are tactile in the extreme, accept with grace their arm-patting and warm embrace.

Do not become annoyed at their lack of concern about punctuality. Remember, 15 minutes to a half hour is not considered late in Brazil. Because they have a very open and informal society, there is very little you can do to upset them anyway—but don't try.

How to Empathize with Brazilians

Try not to react suspiciously to the warmth emanating from the Brazilians; they strive to be liked and to please others. If you are stiff and formal, they will not know how to react. Similarly, do not hesitate to accept their invitations to social activities—it is a wonderful way to get to know your counterparts and will prove to be a very worthwhile experience for you personally.

Brazilians often find it difficult to compete with their peers for a promotion, and even talented individuals need frequent encouragement and ongoing training to further their careers. They are hesitant to accept responsibility; you may find that you constantly need to build up their confidence. Always show that you have a big heart and that you care about their personal problems as well as their competence on the job. It also helps to show them that you have your own personal problems, too, and ask them for advice.

MOTIVATION	
KEY	*Always be cheerful and show affection for Brazil*
Cross-century mood	✦ Growing feeling that this will be the South American (Brazilian) century. ✦ Awareness that Brazilian compassion and human understanding may soon be gaining ground. ✦ Encouraged by NAFTA, MERCOSUR and similar organizations. ✦ Awareness of the enormity of their country and size of their market in years to come.

Motivating Factors

✦ Show great compassion for people's problems and give advice and help.
✦ Be friendly, informal, happy.
✦ Talk about soccer.
✦ Be cool about Argentina.
✦ Accept social invitations enthusiastically.
✦ Be forward-looking and futuristic.
✦ Put relationships before product and procedure.
✦ Be relaxed about time.
✦ Inquire about elderly relatives.
✦ Accept physical closeness, kissing and hugging.

(continued)

MOTIVATION *(continued)*

+ Accept lengthy discussions as Brazilians put forward their point of view.
+ Remember that Brazilians often interrupt without intending to be rude.
+ Accept the fact that the truth appears in many guises.
+ Be charismatic in outlining plans and projects.

Avoid

+ Stuffiness and formality.
+ Focusing too much on profits.
+ Turning down appeals for help or support.
+ The appearance of exploiting them.
+ Flaunting wealth or power.

72

Chile

Chile is a curious shape, being either the longest narrow country in the world or the narrowest long one. A glance at the map of South America shows Chile apparently being pushed into the Pacific Ocean by a beefier Argentina much in the same way that Norway seems edged into the North Sea by land-rich Sweden. Both Norway and southern Chile have sunken coastlines to the west, with a succession of fjords giving the land a drowning appearance. Both countries are nonetheless rich in resources, Chile possessing one-third of the world's copper reserves and Norway being the biggest oil producer in Western Europe.

Mountain ranges often decide where frontiers are located. In the north of Italy, the mighty Alps separate the peninsula from neighbors France, Switzerland and Austria. The frontier between China and India is demarcated by the Himalayas. Chile's border with Argentina is hardly less formidable, with its 7,800-meter (26,000-foot) Aconcagua in the Andes—the highest peak in the Western Hemisphere—presenting a spectacular barrier to west-looking Argentineans. Only at the southernmost tip of Tierra del Fuego do the Argentines get the merest glimpse of the Pacific Ocean.

Land-hungry nations often show vigor in making the best of what they have. The Chileans, handicapped by difficult terrain—uninhabitable mountains, deserts and rain-soaked forests—have maximized their options by exploiting a variety of land resources and exporting them vigorously in three different directions: Asia, North America and Europe.

The "Andes barrier" has effectively diminished Chile's interaction with her own continent. Although she gets substantial imports from Argentina, Brazil and Mexico, her chief export destinations are China, Japan, United States, Britain, Brazil, South Korea, Germany and Taiwan. Chile has been referred to as a South American "Tiger" or "like Taiwan but with better wine." Although her exports are puny compared with those of the four Asian Tigers, Chile provides her customers with vital supplies of copper, aluminum, nitrates, lithium, iodine, borax and selenium. She is the world's eighth producer of silver and twelfth of gold.

So much for the deserts of the north. Chile has also assumed an important position in the export of timber, fresh fruit, fish meal, farmed salmon (to Japan), several other foodstuffs and agricultural products, and is carving out a reputation for the production of high-quality, low-cost wine. The United States and Britain are the chief buyers, but Chilean wine is making substantial inroads in the wine markets of Scandinavia, Germany, the Netherlands and even Japan. Only Chile and Argentina on the South American continent have the right conditions for producing wines of high quality, and reasonable prices are giving Chilean wine producers an advantage over other "new world" wines such as those the U.S. and Australia produce.

Chile's energetic role as a world trader is facilitated to some extent by her reputation for stability, relative to most other Latin American countries. This stability is by no means restricted to recent times. Pedro de Valdivia, the Spanish explorer who founded the city of Santiago de Chile in 1541, had a lot of trouble with the Araucanian Indians (they captured and killed him in 1554), but by clever distribution of land before his death, he laid the basis for the Chilean oligarchy, which, after independence, dominated Chilean history until the twentieth century. Spaniards and Indians began to mingle peaceably (Araucanians worked on the estates), and by 1850 Chile had become the leading power on the Pacific coast. A large number of Germans immigrated to work the forests and British mercantile pioneers settled in the port of Valparaiso.

Chile's fight for independence from Spain caused less dislocation than in most Spanish American countries, and the land-owning class maintained autocratic rule until a brief civil war in 1891. British capital helped to develop the northern deserts, and a war with Peru in 1880–1881 granted Chile land as far north as Arica.

As an urban class appeared, they pressed for parliamentary government and a centralized educational system. Immigration became more selective, allowing many people with specialized skills to enter the country. The Allende-Pinochet period caused great social unrest, but Chile approached the end of the century with an open market, democratic rule and the highest credit rating on the continent.

Tension with Argentina (Chile helped Britain during the Falklands dispute) has lessened, and the country seems set to play the role of Latin America's most industrious trader (and perhaps safest bet) in the first decades of the twenty-first century.

Culture

Values

emotional and personal stability	European orientation
internationalism	fast payers
education	insecure, hesitant
loyalty	short-termers
eloquence	respectful
loquacious, extroverted	dignified
perceptive	

Visitors to Chile are struck by the European nature of the country, matched on the continent only by the ambience in Buenos Aires. Although the German and British connections remain strong, the Spanish heritage is evident (85 percent of the people are Catholic), and the cultural values are mainly Hispanic.

It is difficult to estimate the cultural influence of the Araucanian Indians, but Chileans do display some South American characteristics that differ from the Spanish: reluctance to accept responsibility, difficulty seeing objectives at work, little long-term planning, lack of commitment to results, tendency to imitate rather than innovate, failure to recognize mistakes, expectation of help when things go wrong, lack of initiative and invention and an exaggerated concern over job security.

On the other hand, Chileans have many positive features, not the least of which is that they are the fastest payers in South America. They are well-educated, very loyal once they are won over and have an intelligently pragmatic view of doing business. Although they are at first indirect and conceal their opinions, they open up splendidly once friendship and trust have been established. They are eloquent conversationalists and good listeners. Their national pride is everpresent, but they respect the histories and achievements of other nations, particularly European ones. Their "triangular target" for trade—Asia, Europe and the United States—shows the Chileans' burgeoning internationalism and feel for the future. While NAFTA and MERCOSUR are important connections, they wish to maintain strong European ties, and they realize that their geographic position (as that of Australia) offers lucrative opportunities in an Asian-Pacific context.

Concepts

Leadership and Status

Chilean leadership is traditionally autocratic in the South American manner, but the nation has gone further down the road toward democracy than many others in the area. Reaction to the Pinochet era encourages Chileans to speak up, both in politics and business. Consequently the modern Chilean executive is not easy to lead, and differences of attitude toward authority abound.

Space and Time

Chileans are basically a tactile and affectionate people, but they display some restraint, particularly with foreigners. The Chilean distance of comfort is around one meter.

Chileans are the most punctual of Latin Americans (up to 15 minutes delay for appointments is normal).

Cultural Factors in Communication

Communication Pattern

Chileans are eloquent and persuasive conversationalists, but they are somewhat more restrained and pragmatic than most other Latin Americans. Although they are long-winded, they are able to structure their remarks in a way that Anglo-Saxons and even Asians can follow them. They are also capable of giving patient explanations.

Listening Habits

Chileans are somewhat nervous listeners inasmuch as they wish to break in, but are often too polite to do so. Because they often believe they know best, they can barely tolerate long monologues from others.

Behavior at Meetings and Negotiations

Meetings are conducted Latin-style with lengthy preambles, wordy monologues and frequent digressions from the agenda. An underlying pragmatism does, however, keep the business on track. Chileans are not particularly aggressive when negotiating, often showing some insecurity and fear of loss of business (or jobs). Their negotiating style resembles the Italian, encompassing lots of flexibility and accommodation. After meetings, they tend to have second thoughts, so it is necessary to monitor follow-up activities. The business atmosphere in general is pleasant and "civilized." Options are left open when business cannot be concluded during the first round of discussion.

How to Empathize with Chileans

Chileans are warm-hearted Latins who wish nothing more than to mingle with Europeans (even Anglo-Saxons) and to trade energetically with them. If you maintain a positive attitude, treat them as equals, do business in a friendly manner and enjoy their magnificent countryside (and wine), you will find that you can easily build good relations with Chileans.

MOTIVATION	
KEY	*Showing concern for their welfare*
Cross-century mood	✦ Determination to maintain their triangular target in trade—the U.S., Europe and Asia. ✦ Historical friction with Argentina—mainly over territory—is diminishing. ✦ A major aim is consolidation of a democratic framework accepted by the major powers.

Motivating Factors

- ✦ Learn Chilean history and geography.
- ✦ Allow for flexibility of the truth; Chileans often say what they think you want to hear.
- ✦ Respect their culture.
- ✦ Compliment them on being the fastest payers in South America.
- ✦ Protect their dignity.
- ✦ Be kind as much and as often as you can.

Avoid

- ✦ Taking sides in the Pinochet issue (Chileans are divided in their views).
- ✦ Talking down to them.
- ✦ Discussing Indian heritage (indigenous groups are the lowest in status).
- ✦ Praising Argentina too much.

73

Venezuela

Venezuela is indeed a land of paradoxes. This is not only immediately apparent in its scenic contrasts—snow-capped Andes to the west, 3,000 kilometers (1,900 miles) of golden Caribbean beaches to the north and a dense Amazon rain forest to the south—but also in its erratic historical development.

First settled around 13,000 B.C. by the Yanomami Indians (whose descendants still live in remote isolated pockets without direct contact with the outside world), Venezuela has another face, which is the most "Yankeefied" in South America, with a modern road network and developed infrastructure paid for by the immense oil wealth generated after 1910.

Oil, too, is a Venezuelan paradox, inasmuch as it has proven both a boon and a disaster for the Venezuelan people. The oil boom enabled a high standard of living unheard of in South America, but agriculture and ranching went into decline, sinking the peasants into ever-increasing poverty. The oil wealth was systematically squandered by corrupt leaders (the oil price quadrupled following the outbreak of the Arab-Israeli war (1967), but the subsequent glut in the 1970s cut the country's revenue in half.

Venezuela boasts the continent's superhero—Simón Bolívar. His bravery and foresight brought independence to Venezuela, Colombia, Panama, Peru, Ecuador and Bolivia, but he died in poverty, proclaiming, "There have been three great fools in history: Jesus, Don Quixote and I."

Bolívar once called Quito a monastery, Bogotá a university and Caracas a barracks. Venezuelans in fact suffered more than any other country from the wars of independence, fighting in all the armies that Bolívar led. One-quarter of the country's population died in these conflicts. After that, Venezuela alternated between despotism and anarchy. Therein lies another Venezuelan paradox: its enduring yoke of *caudillos* and its recurring experiments with democratic rule.

Venezuela means "Little Venice" in Spanish. When the conquistadores sailed into Lake Maracaibo in 1499, they saw local Indians living in rustic thatched houses on stilts above the water. The Spaniards were, of course, making a sarcastic comparison with Venetian opulence.

Venezuela is a country of mixed blood. About 70 percent of the population is a blend of European, Indian and African ancestry, or any two of the three. The rest are whites (about 21 percent), blacks (8 percent) and pure-blood Indians (1 percent). Venezuela experienced significant post–the Second World War immigration from Europe (estimated at about a million), mostly from Spain, Italy and Portugal until the 1960s, when many of them returned home. From the 1950s on, there has been a stream of immigrants from other South American countries, particularly from Colombia. Caracas is the country's most cosmopolitan city.

There is some friction between Venezuelans and Colombians, and some ambivalence toward the not-so-distant United States. However, the Venezuelans, in view of their wild extravagance in the 1980s, have proven to be their own worst enemies.

Because of their proximity to the U.S., Venezuelans think they understand North Americans better than other South Americans. In fact, many of them buy retirement or vacation homes in Florida.

Culture

Values

patriotic	optimistic
loyal	adaptable
critical of others	emotional, warm
compassionate	education
bound by rules and regulations	respect family, property, elderly

By and large Venezuelans are friendly, lively and hospitable. However, the oil crises have brought difficult times, with somewhat diminished hospitality, especially in the big cities.

Concepts

Leadership and Status

Wealth counts most. Venezuelans also accord status to people whom they consider very civilized, such as artists, writers, teachers, doctors and engineers. Leadership in Venezuela has traditionally been centered around a strong dictator or president. Nepotism is common, and staff are manipulated by a variety of persuasive methods ranging from (benign) paternalism to outright exploitation and coercion.

Space and Time

Venezuelans, like most other South Americans, sit or stand close to their interlocutor and are fairly tactile. In terms of their sense of national space, they are conscious of being dwarfed by their huge neighbor Brazil.

Venezuelans have a South American concept of time inasmuch as punctuality has only relative importance; people arriving late for appointments are not regarded as rude. Venezuelans tend to lose all sense of time when they are engaged in animated conversations.

Cultural Factors in Communication

Communication Pattern

Lengthy in discourse, Venezuelans rarely get directly to the point but rather tend to talk around the subject matter and will rarely tell you what they think. Expressing strong or personal opinions is not considered polite.

Body language is overt, with great use of hands and facial expression. Venezuelans are very expressive except in areas where Indians predominate. Gripping one's upper arm signifies confidence in the other.

The common language is, of course, Spanish, but there are also 25 Indian languages spoken in the country.

Listening Habits

Most Venezuelans are loquacious Latins. Traditionally they are poor at cooperating with authorities or on any external plans that do not correspond to their immediate needs. Consequently, they are not among the best of audiences. Only charismatic speakers can get them to listen for very long, and even they must show them they know more than Venezuelans do.

Behavior at Meetings and Negotiations

Business meetings in Venezuela are usually conducted in a pleasant, sociable atmosphere with foreigners and begin with a lot of small talk. Protocol is generally observed to a considerable degree, including the order of seating, particularly with regard to the senior Venezuelan delegate. He or she will expect a lot of respect, but in turn must appear affable and generous. Maintaining a high level of politeness is essential. Initial proposals are often far removed from realistic conclusions, and protracted haggling is part of the process. Agreements reached are often somewhat inconclusive. Meetings are often preceded or followed by socializing and entertaining. Dress is usually smart and tasteful.

When running the meeting, Venezuelans are jealous of their reputation of being affable hosts. The leader is always obvious as he or she will be dutifully supported at all times by other delegates. You can gain points by showing great respect and by addressing most of your remarks to the senior person.

Venezuelans are somewhat unpredictable in the way they conduct meetings and behave in them. One thing is sure: they will talk a lot and often several at the same time. The following features can be disconcerting to North Americans, Northern Europeans and some Asians:

+ the gap between concept and implementation
+ low productivity (more hours, same results)
+ social envy

+ reluctance to accept responsibility
+ exaggerated sensitivity to insults
+ expectation to be helped when things aren't going well
+ lacking in punctuality
+ not committed to results
+ excessive concern about job security
+ little long-term planning
+ poor sense of time, schedules and agendas
+ imitators rather than innovators
+ often live in advance of themselves (as if dreams were already reality)

On the other hand, there are many positive aspects of dealing with the Venezuelans:

+ loyalty (if properly motivated)
+ teamwork (if properly motivated)
+ warmth
+ desire to please others
+ optimism
+ adaptability

During negotiations, the leader of a team will probably be a well-educated, personable male with a power base locally or back home. It is unlikely his team will ever contradict him.

Manners and Taboos

Venezuelans are colorful people, both the Indians and those descended from the conquistadores. Idealism is rampant, and most people think they have a good grasp of human values. Taboos include cruelty (though it does exist), lack of consideration for the dignity of others, too close an identification with U.S. values and any form of rough treatment.

How to Empathize with Venezuelans

Show an interest in Venezuelan history and know something about Simón Bolívar. You should offer your help frequently when they have business or personal problems and be willing to share their conspiracies and avoid strict adherence to rules and regulations. Try to strike the golden mean between dignified distance and informal approach. Accept certain ambiguities; the truth appears in many guises. Ascribe many of your good ideas to them and their inspiration. Avoid dampening their enthusiasm, even when inexperience shows through and be compassionate and solicitous in your dealings, especially with those less fortunate than you.

MOTIVATION	
KEY	*Be optimistic about Venezuela's future*
Cross-century mood	✦ Venezuelans are determined to make better use of their oil revenues in the twenty-first century. ✦ Recent leadership has aligned itself with Cuba. ✦ Attitude to the U.S. will be critical.

Motivating Factors

✦ Treat Venezuelans with respect and as equals.

✦ Remember national honor is very important for them.

✦ Develop strong personal relationships.

✦ Ask often about their close family members.

✦ Entertain lavishly.

✦ Make allowances when contracting with them.

✦ When you deal from strength, do not wield your power openly.

✦ Always impute the best motives, even if you think they might be planning to cheat you.

✦ Show trust in them, but take precautions.

✦ Be generous in your praise, even for small achievements.

Avoid

✦ Referring to Venezuela's profligacy and economic fragility.

✦ Questioning people about their Indian heritage. Indigenous people occupy the bottom rung of the social ladder.

✦ Praising or identifying too much with the United States.

✦ Emphasizing the bottom line; results are only part of the picture.

✦ Rushing them or giving them deadlines—they won't observe them anyway.

74

Colombia

Colombia is the only South American country to have coastlines on both the Pacific Ocean and the Caribbean Sea. It is also the only country named after Christopher Columbus. Twice the size of France, it is the fourth largest country in South America and borders on Panama, Venezuela, Brazil, Peru and Ecuador.

In 2018 the population of Colombia was over 48 million. Ninety percent of the people live in the western half of the country, with its densely settled valleys and tablelands.

Colombians are of Spanish, Indian and, to a lesser degree, African ancestry. About 60 percent of the people are mestizo, a mixture of Europeans and Indians.

Mulattos and blacks represent approximately 20 percent and whites about the same. Pure or nearly pure indigenous groups make up less than 2 percent.

Throughout the 1970s Colombia's illegal trade in cocaine grew steadily, creating wealthy drug barons. In the 1980s, armed cartels (such as the Cali) became a destabilizing force, and political and media assassinations were frequent.

Recent years have been dominated by endemic violence in Colombia, with threats to government control coming from both left-wing guerrillas and drug-trafficking cartels. Revenue from other crops offers a poor substitute to growers in place of their illegal coca.

The guerrilla problem, which was adversely affecting the economy, was to a large extent settled in 2016.

The most ancient inhabitants of the land which is now Colombia were the Chibcha, who occupied the fertile plateaus and valleys of the "cordillera oriental" (eastern Andes). They had migrated southward from North America and presumably were descended from the groups that crossed the Bering Straits around 12,000 B.C.

In 1499, the Spanish conquistadores arrived on present-day Colombian territory looking for gold and emeralds. Colombia had plenty of both. In 1525 the Spanish established their Colombian settlement at Santa Marta. By 1538 the conquistador Gonzalo Jimenez de Quesada had conquered the Chibcha and established Bogotá. Colombia became part of the New Kingdom of Granada, whose territory also included Ecuador, Panama and Venezuela. The Venezuelan general Simón Bolívar led the fight against Spain and won a decisive victory on August 7, 1819, at Boyacá.

Colombia has experienced more than ten civil wars. These internal conflicts have had a very strong impact on the mentality and behavior of Colombians. Colombians are not by nature an aggressive people, but so many internal confrontations have made them rather defensive and more intolerant. They now react rather quickly.

Culture

Values

Colombia strongly reflects its history as a colony of Spain. It is often referred to as the most Roman Catholic of the South American countries, and its people are proud of the relative purity of their Spanish language. Although its population is largely mestizo, Spanish culture has predominated over indigenous Indian forms. Two centuries of intensive colonization eliminated most (but not all) Indian traits. Colombians now share the following characteristics:

reasonable punctuality	elaborate greeting ritual
honesty	good conversation
loyalty and allegiance to family	poor correlation between law and actual life
extreme politeness	traditional habits
dignity of the individual, pride	friendship
generosity	need to feel useful in one's work
perception about others	

Concepts

Leadership and Status

Wealth is still an important factor and is becoming increasingly so. Unfortunately, the acquisition of wealth in Colombia frequently has doubtful origins. University professors, doctors and leading church figures are respected. Of course, Colombia has a great literary tradition. Her novelists and poets enjoy a great reputation and the most famous writer, Gabriel García Márquez, was the Nobel Prize winner for literature in 1982. Painters and sculptors such as Obregón, Botero and Negret are widely known throughout South America.

Because the country has been through so many difficult years with civil wars, it is hard for Colombians to know what kinds of leaders are best. Many feel that the only type of person who could sort out the country would be a dictator, but others feel that a flexible leader who is able to negotiate is needed. In a business context, most Colombians would like a leader who is midway between being very strong and weak—someone strong enough to make decisions and carry them through but not so strong as to impose his or her will without consultation, someone with analytical skills and vision, but the ability to see another's point of view when making decisions.

Space and Time

In general terms, Colombians feel comfortable closer to people than Northern Europeans and Americans, but it also depends on the relationship. With strangers or business acquaintances they maintain distance, whereas with friends and family they are more physically intimate in terms of touching someone's arm when speaking or patting someone on the back (between men).

Punctuality in official environments is very important for Colombians. It is a matter of culture and respect for the other person. On social occasions, however, guests are expected to arrive 30 minutes late. In terms of preparation, Colombians tend to be spontaneous rather than planners, except for a big business meeting.

Cultural Factors in Communication

Communication Pattern

Colombians are verbose by nature and express their ideas in an eloquent manner. Although respecting logic, they will often become emotional during discussions, where feelings take precedence. Their conversation is often versatile. For instance, they can maintain dignity of expression while at the same time introducing an element of humor. Humor is used relatively frequently in business discussions, anecdotes being extremely popular. Communication style varies to some extent according to the area of origin. In the highlands of Bogotá and Medellín, a more European style exists, with its balanced seriousness and moderate results orientation. Cali and the coastal strip are much more relaxed, indicative of people from the Caribbean. Politeness is mandatory in all regions, and people are reluctant to criticize openly. As the level of education is high in the cities, people are able to hold discussions on many subjects, and they do this even in business settings.

Listening Habits

Colombian mandatory politeness and courtesy carries over into their listening habits. People rarely interrupt a speaker, and the listening posture is uniformly deferential. Foreign interlocutors, especially European, are accorded extra respect. There is a certain defensiveness with Americans, but Colombians are eager to acquire know-how from U.S. partners. Feedback is slow and measured but generally quite perceptive. At presentations, Colombians watch the presenter carefully; they are absorbing the speaker's body language as well as content. You should listen attentively and pay attention to body language as well.

Behavior at Meetings and Negotiations

Colombian businesspeople take meetings seriously, observing rules of hierarchy and protocol and generally following an agenda in a disciplined manner. They are usually successful in striking the right balance between formality and friendliness, especially when dealing with foreigners.

Meetings begin with protracted small talk in order for people to get to know each other and to formulate a mutually appropriate approach to the objectives in question. You should enjoy the conversation and leave the initiation of the serious business talk in Colombian hands. They have an innate sense of timing in this respect. It is not unusual for preparatory discussions to be accompanied by some refreshment—even lunch or dinner. Colombian businesspeople regard hospitality as an integral part of the business process. Remember that personal relationships dominate business deals.

Once issues are tackled, the senior Colombian may outline the general approach to the project, painting with a broad brush, avoiding details at this stage. Accord this senior figure great respect (reciprocating the deference he or she will accord you). The accompanying (subordinate) Colombians will at all times respect the hierarchical position of their leader, but specialists are allowed to voice their opinions without inhibition. Colombians like to make decisions by consensus; this also includes consensual attitudes with the other side. Discussions are usually conducted in a dignified and mild manner; disagreement is expressed indirectly, and pressure should be gentle.

Americans and Northern Europeans should be wary of depending only on facts and figures to advance their cause; human feelings are important too. Colombians are results-oriented, but the route to profitability should take into consideration the aspirations and reputation of all people involved.

Emotion is not far from the surface with Colombians, especially when the going gets tough, but they are skillful in controlling their feelings and rarely take refuge in intransigence. Unlike some Latin businesspeople, Colombians control meetings in a calm manner and generally avoid situations where several people speak at once. Apart from a certain impatience, turn-taking during discussion is fairly similar to that common among Anglo-Saxons.

Meetings are begun with handshakes all around, also repeated on departure. Handshakes and polite greetings are exchanged again at subsequent meetings. Business cards, printed in English and Spanish, are a necessary courtesy.

Colombians are late payers, but payment ethics are generally good and therefore Colombia has a favorable credit status. Remember—nothing is certain until it is in writing, but once a contract has been signed, it will be observed to the letter. Colombians are serious businesspeople with an eye for good quality, a reasonable price and favorable terms of delivery.

Manners and Taboos

Manners and customs vary enormously in different regions of Colombia. Because of the country's geographic composition, isolation is an important factor in Colombian life. People are often known by the region in which they live, each recognizable by their dress, diet and speech. The most important social group is that of the *Antiqueños*.

Colombian businesspeople dress smartly with a somewhat conservative taste. Dark gray and dark blue are most popular for suits. In rural areas and in the coastal tropical zones, dress is more casual, certainly more colorful, but generally in good taste. Women usually wear sleeveless dresses. You may even wear neat shorts on the coast on social occasions. People are judged by the quality of their clothes and their degree of cleanliness.

Colombians drink in an elegant manner, not dissimilar to the French and Italians. They rarely drink to get drunk. Colombians used to be heavy smokers, but this habit is declining rapidly. In restaurants, the person who issues the invitation normally pays the bill, but it is not uncommon for Colombian guests to try to pay when a foreigner has invited them.

How to Empathize with Colombians

Colombians generally embarrass foreigners through their profuse hospitality and attention to their needs. Try to reciprocate as much as possible, as they may be spending beyond their means. Colombians appreciate closeness and even compassion from foreign colleagues or partners; don't hesitate to show warmth whenever possible. It is the best way to gain their loyalty. The optimal way to empathize with them is to combine consistent respect for their dignity with sympathy and understanding of their hopes and aspirations.

MOTIVATION	
KEY	*Maintenance of courtesy and dignity*
Cross-century mood	✦ Preoccupation with the long-drawn-out drug problem. ✦ Eagerness to maintain a good credit rating. ✦ Hope for better inter-American trade.

Motivating Factors

✦ Colombians are educated; you cannot pull wool over their eyes.
✦ Compassion: the Colombian people are used to hardship and adversity.
✦ Try to help them with their problems.
✦ Clearly state your objectives—Colombians are pragmatic as well as idealistic.

(continued)

MOTIVATION *(continued)*

✦ Remember Colombian national honor.

✦ Accept that truth may be situational or ambiguous—not always literal.

✦ Let them speak at length (they are long-winded, but can get upset if not given a full hearing).

✦ Respect Catholic values.

✦ Praise frequently; criticize only indirectly.

✦ Help Colombians move up in their careers; they are often nervous about career stagnation.

✦ Share their South American sense of opportunism.

Avoid

✦ Loss of face for anyone.

✦ Patronizing them.

✦ Focusing too much on drug problems, the cartels and so on.

✦ Discussing bribery.

✦ Politics in general.

75

Sub-Saharan Africa

Africa is staggering in its size and complexity. With 48 different countries in a land area three times the size of the United States, it qualifies as the world's most culturally diverse continent. Even Europe has fewer countries and languages. The Americas, also vast in area, have only twenty-odd Spanish-speaking republics plus Brazil, Canada and the U.S. Asia, the world's biggest continent, hosts fewer cultures than Africa does.

Though regional variations are numerous, there is a firm, enduring underlay of African culture stretching all the way from the Sahara desert to the Cape of Good Hope. (Francophone Morocco, Algeria and Tunisia form a separate cultural unit and, along with Libya, Egypt and part of Sudan, are classified as Arab rather than African.)

All of Africa was colonized in an earlier era, with the exception of Ethiopia and Liberia. British and French influence is noticeable in most countries, and Spanish, German, Dutch and Portuguese echoes remain where they once ruled. There are approximately 1,000 languages and dialects spoken in Africa, most of them in the sub-Saharan region. The most well known are Hausa, Shona, Xhosa and Swahili. Swahili, a Creole mix, acts as a lingua franca in large parts of East Africa. Nigeria, Africa's most populous country, has more Muslims than any Arab country does. Nigeria alone is home to 280 different languages and many more dialects.

Africa's major problem is an explosive population growth that swamps most efforts at progressive development. Sub-Saharan Africa is currently home to about 12 percent of the world's population. In 1950 the population was less than 200 million; at the end of the twentieth century it approximated 650 million. Projections suggest that it will expand to around 900 million by the year 2020. This is in spite of reduced population growth due to AIDS and having lost a staggering 15 million people from the sixteenth to the nineteenth centuries in the slave trade. It is hoped that advanced nations will turn a more sympathetic eye in the future in terms of facilitating entry of African products into Western markets.

Life is hard in Africa, and many of its inhabitants live on the edge of survival. Procreation is seen as a means of guaranteeing immortality through lineage continuation. Release from the vicissitudes of life is obtained through song and dance, feasting and festivals—short-term enjoyment of what life offers. The concept of the extended family guarantees that children will look after people in their old age— the African equivalent to Medicare. Africans, often seen as fatalistic by Americans and Europeans, adapt to their environment rather than fight or try to change it.

Sub-Saharan Africa is divided into more than 600 culture groups: Zulu, Yoruba, Hausa, Hottentot, Masai and Igbo are among the major ones. Indians and Europeans form significant minorities, especially in South Africa. Because of its great size (the world's second largest continent after Asia), Africa is still relatively thinly populated. More than 70 percent of the population is rural. Agriculture, however, is greatly restricted in many areas by counterproductive natural phenomena. These include the Sahara desert—supporting only a sparse, nomadic herding community—and a huge tropical rain forest stretching across Central Africa. East and South Africa are the most fertile areas.

The continent is, nevertheless, rich in minerals: gold, diamonds and coal in South Africa; some of the world's largest deposits of copper ore in Zambia; oil and bauxite in abundant quantities in West Africa. Apart from South Africa, the entire sub-Saharan continent is industrially underdeveloped on account of geography and political unrest.

The Sahara is by far the world's largest desert; the Nile (6,600 kilometers/4,100 miles), is the world's longest river. The enormous sunken valley in East Africa—the Great Rift Valley—is reputed to be the home of the first hominids. Most of the continent is hot and humid (outside the desert areas) and forms a huge plateau between the Indian and Atlantic Oceans. Most likely Africa was originally joined to South America and formed the supercontinent of Pangaea.

The first known African pottery was produced in the Sahara region about 7500 B.C. Around 6000 B.C., agriculture and the domestication of sheep and goats were introduced from Egypt, but the incipient desertification of the Sahara around the same time impeded further development south until horses entered the sub-Sahara region around 1000 B.C.

The Portuguese reached the West African coast in 1416 and established supremacy there between 1478 and 1500. In 1498 Vasco da Gama called at Mombasa en route for India, but it was not until 1574 that the Portuguese founded the city of Luanda in Angola. Dutch settlers founded the colony of Cape Town in South Africa in 1652.

The slave trade flourished between the sixteenth and nineteenth centuries, as mentioned earlier in this chapter, largely from a West African base. In the late nineteenth century the discovery of mineral wealth on the continent led to the "scramble for Africa," and the whole of the continent (except for Liberia and Ethiopia) was under foreign domination by 1900. The European powers met in Berlin in 1884 and agreed on boundaries and spheres of influence. The British claimed West African colonies such as Ghana and Nigeria, East African ones such as Kenya, and Botswana in the south, as well as South Africa itself. The French took central African regions such as Chad, Gabon and Brazzaville Congo, and the Belgians acquired the Congo River Basin. The Portuguese retained their colonies in Angola and Mozambique; they were the first to arrive and the last to leave (in 1975). Italy briefly claimed Ethiopia and Somalia; Germany, Togo, Namibia and Tanzania.

Such arbitrary divisions were disastrous for African culture, as the political map bore very little resemblance to the cultural, traditional one. This means that the term *nation* has little meaning for most Africans. Tribes were split up, and even though most countries achieved independence in the 1960s, not all ethnic units have been successfully reunited. Disastrous civil wars have ensued in Nigeria, Sudan, Rwanda and Burundi. Thus, the greed of the European powers in the nineteenth and twentieth centuries has been the political root of African poverty and backwardness. South Africa is so far the only bright spot, its GDP equaling approximately that of the rest of sub-Saharan Africa altogether and ranking 33rd in the world. The total African GDP (including the countries in the north) is only roughly the same as South Korea or the Netherlands.

Resentment over centuries of political and economic exploitation (especially the slavery question) has left all Africans with a sense of deep distrust of whites. This also extends to descendants of Africans in the United States, Caribbean and Central America. A by-product of white domination is an inferiority complex, although this has been offset to some extent in the second half of the twentieth century by increasing black supremacy in athletics, including boxing, basketball, baseball, cricket and even tennis, as well as the rise to prominence of descendants of Africans in the U.S. (Colin Powell, Condoleezza Rice, Louis Armstrong, Toni Morrison, Martin Luther King, Duke Ellington, Mohammed Ali, among many others). Nelson Mandela, at one time, was considered the most universally respected human on earth.

Culture

Africans see themselves in a close pattern of kinship, to which they make sincere contributions and are consequently protected and secure. Only tribalism has rescued many Africans from the sense of loss created by the artificially created political states in the 1880s (e.g., I may be Kenyan, but really I am Kikuyu, or South African perhaps, but Zulu for sure).

Values

African values, strong and enduring, find many parallels in multi-active and reactive cultures (see Chapter 3 for an explanation of these terms). Their collectivism is greatly reminiscent of China and many other East Asian countries; their overriding sense of family and kinship reminds one of Japan, China and the islands of the Pacific. Hierarchy in Africa differs little from that in Japan, China, India and the Pacific. Sub-Saharan Africans are warm, joyous, tolerant, often laid-back and have a great sense of humor. A hard life engenders patience and fortitude. No people are more colorful or exuberant.

specific rights of kinship	ancestral mediators and a remote god
duty (social obligations)	tribal ethics/morals (weakens state concept)
cooperation before competition	respect for elderly
hospitality and generosity	tendency toward consumption
love of dance and music	respect for magic
fatalistic	fondness for the exotic
theatrical	hope for trust

Women's participation in labor varies from country to country. There are generally fewer women in paid employment than men, though a large proportion of women in sub-Saharan countries are engaged in subsistence agriculture—if only part of the time. Women are also employed in the civil service, in trade (especially in West Africa), in domestic service and to an increasing extent in light industry. The high birth rate in most countries places a heavy burden on the African woman in terms of frequent pregnancies and time-consuming childcare, so few African females occupy high positions in large companies or political institutions.

However, women generally run the markets in West Africa and are widely seen as better money managers than men. As many of the men have to leave home for long periods (working in mines, etc.), women also act as heads of families for many months of the year. Especially in rural areas they greatly outnumber men. They work hard, hauling, sowing and harvesting, and they produce the lion's share of food for local markets, where they are almost exclusively the vendors. In general their influence is increasing. It is as well to remember that in precolonial times there were many female chiefs.

In the battle of the sexes, many African women are still at a disadvantage. Most marry very young to much older men. Spousal abuse is not unknown and female subservience is often expected. Women are expected to eat after men and may be addressed only indirectly in some cases. Female circumcision (excision) persists in most countries, often supported by traditionalists and the parents of wives. Many marriages are arranged; the husband's family must pay "brideswealth" to compensate for the loss of a daughter.

Polygamy, which predated Islam in Africa, is common. Unhappy brides may elope, seeking parents' permission retrospectively.

In spite of these disadvantages, as well as less schooling than the men, the African woman is charismatic, reliable and possesses great integrity. Her ultimate advancement will be a great boon to the welfare of the continent.

Religion

Many Africans adopted the religion of their conquerors or colonizers; consequently, they adhere to Islamic and nearly all Christian sects. Their spirituality, necessary and cherished because of the difficulties they face in this life, is mirrored in many poor countries where Catholicism (e.g., South America) and Islam prevail.

Sub-Saharan peoples have a rich and varied collection of traditional beliefs. Almost all recognize a supreme being who created the universe. Many Africans also believe in the power of the spirit world: spirits are thought to be capable of exerting a friendly or malignant influence. Many of the spirits are associated with agriculture and receive special offerings at harvest time.

Other beliefs (also found in many parts of Asia) are those of reincarnation and ancestor worship. Important social rituals are held in connection with the ancestors, who are feared, as the dead are believed to have greater power than the living. Reincarnation may occur in the form of living animals and even inanimate objects. Magic is important and plays a significant part in the everyday life of many people. All over sub-Saharan Africa medicine men fashion all kinds of charms (necklaces, bracelets, etc.) that, when worn, will ward off evil. They also make other objects to protect crops or to bring rain. Westerners should not underestimate Africans' belief in magic. It has proven more enduring than the traditional mythologies, many of which were dismantled by the advance of Islam and Christianity.

It must be remembered that the traditional African religions are much older than either Islam or Christianity, and that ancestor worship and animism were practiced in Europe and the Americas long before Christianity. When the Western missionaries came to Africa, they showed no reluctance to incorporate traditional African practices (dances around the altar, food offerings, use of village drums) into their own church rituals and doctrines. There is a great overlapping of religious beliefs in Africa, where in general religious tolerance is high, except for clashes along the Islamic-Christian divide in the Sahel fringe of the Sahara desert. It is also noteworthy that religion is not a decisive factor in politics: Christian leaders can usually be elected in predominantly Muslim countries, and vice versa.

Whatever their sect or religion, Africans are monotheists. Atheism is alien to the continent. Even the animists, who are probably the majority in sub-Saharan Africa, think of one God, albeit visible in the form of inanimate objects such as trees, rocks, stones and so forth. Such objects are intermediaries for God. There are Western parallels in good luck charms.

Animism in Africa entails festivals, sacred objects and various exotic practices under the guidance of priests, medicine men and rainmakers. Africans fear spirits and go to great lengths to appease them. They are extremely conscious of the vulnerability of weaker members of the community, such as ailing people, pregnant women and small children. Children are regarded not just as the descendants of ancestors; they *are* the ancestors in reincarnation. Such beliefs are not unknown in other cultures such as Japan, Russia and Hispanic America. Ancestors are considered as nearby and are often consulted. In Madagascar houses are built for them, usually of a higher standard of construction than the home dwelling!

These traditional beliefs exert the major influence in defining the morals and ethics of the community. If Christianity or Islam happen to support these, so much the better!

Concepts

Leadership and Status

Traditionally, many societies were based on clans and lineages, with most authority being held by elders. Clans might consist of a single kinship unit, but would be linked with neighboring bands by ties of intermarriage and consciousness of common cultural identity. This type of leadership still exists, but economic change has weakened clan and tribal influence. The traditional equality of living standards has been affected, especially in the cities, by the growth of new elites and the appearance of a poor and typically exploited urban proletariat.

As military dictatorships are common in modern Africa, status is frequently achieved through power and coercion, but traditionally status belonged to tribal chiefs and leaders who promoted and protected the beliefs and tenets of the tribe. This cultural status still exists in most areas, though it often has to take a back seat to a prevalent political campaign or situation. Nelson Mandela, of course, is an all-African hero.

Medicine men are both respected and feared and have traditional status. Tribal artists, using mainly wood and, after the twelfth century, also bronze as their medium, are usually professionals and receive great respect and cultural status.

Space and Time

In spite of burgeoning populations, Africa as a whole has a relatively low population density. The sense of space in such countries as Kenya and South Africa is exhilarating, and rural communities all over sub-Saharan Africa cling passionately to the wide open spaces of their land and their herds. Cities, by contrast, are overcrowded and cramp the traditional African lifestyle.

With regard to personal space, African behavior is exceptional. Not only are they a very tactile people in terms of hugging and squeezing, but it is common for Africans to maintain a handshake while conversing—even on the street. More use is made of the eyes and facial expressions than would be the norm for even Southern Europeans. The African love of dance and rhythm is visible in their body language, which accompanies speech. They often sway in rhythm with their verbal utterances, almost enacting a dance in moments of excitement. All this body language occasionally causes Europeans some embarrassment (especially when speaking to relative strangers), but in reality it is a positive characteristic, emanating warmth, closeness and trust.

Multi-active sub-Saharan Africans are not renowned for punctuality or any sense of urgency. Hot climates inhibit rushing around to keep appointments, and you will have to adjust to African time. Africans themselves wait patiently for delayed transportation or meetings with important persons. VIPs usually make both Africans and Westerners wait for an hour or more. But when they do see you, they will give you plenty of time. Meetings often begin when enough people (or the VIPs) show up. The causes of this *mañana* behavior are similar to those in Spain and Mexico: insufficient resources, lack of adequate planning, not ready to make a commitment yet.

Cultural Factors in Communication

Communication Pattern

African communication is at the outset warm and friendly, and in many cases it is couched in poetic and symbolic terms. Color, charisma and rhetoric come naturally to Africans, and of course are enhanced by improved education. When conducting a business meeting, warmth is tempered by tenacity in defending tribal interests.

For the African, communication is a vital process, since Africans—like the Japanese, Chinese and Mexicans, among others—believe that *a person is not a person* unless he or she has someone to communicate with.

Communication in Africa is at its best face-to-face, not by phone or other means. Ideally messages are given in a soft voice and are not confrontational. A mutually satisfactory agreement is sought through full discussion. In negotiation, a win–win result is sought.

Africans have considerable oratorical skills and call on various forms of expression, such as poetry, proverbs, stories, parables, riddles, conundrums and even songs. You should try to respond in a similar manner (with Western proverbs, etc.). Parables are expected to provide indirect answers to problems or issues.

Storytelling is an age-old African tradition. Business discussions retain some of this folksiness, inasmuch as they are conducted in an unhurried, relaxed manner, with many human and personal references. You will have everything to gain by reciprocating this friendly, consultative style. Silence may indicate disagreement. Africans may talk around an issue in a circular fashion, that is, similar to Asian discourse, in order to find a mutually satisfactory solution.

Humor is an important part of communication. It is normally gentle but can turn to light slapstick. Jokes are common, usually situational, often touching on ethnic differences. You should also indulge in gentle humor, using first names when possible, to soften procedures.

In Francophone Africa, spoken French is formal and flowery and concentrates on theory. In Anglophone regions there is a more pragmatic approach to applying theory to practice. Anglophones like to look at issues one at a time and find solutions as they go along, while Francophones tend to open up a "menu" or list of items to be discussed in order to eventually find an all-embracing solution. Here we see African exploratory warmth combined with elegant French discourse. In schools in Francophone Africa, students tend to be attentive but passive, respecting the teacher's mastery of language. In Anglophone countries there is much more interaction and querying of concepts.

Listening Habits

Africans are courteous listeners who drink in information, though some repetition is advisable. They do not like being rushed verbally—their own elders have innate patience putting forward concepts and discussing problems from all angles. Though suspicious of "ex-colonialists," Africans are quickly gratified by reasonable establishment of trust between parties.

Behavior at Meetings and Negotiations

When holding meetings with Africans, try to observe certain important points of African protocol. Africans come to meetings dressed in a neat, clean, often smart manner (more formal in East and Southern Africa than West Africa); you should follow suit. Respect the traditions of the continent; these include initial use of surnames (and titles, where applicable), formal hierarchical seating, respect for older members present and initiating procedures in a reasonable, conciliatory manner. The business of the day is not broached at the outset. African tradition decrees that first one "sits under a tree" and enjoys an unhurried preamble of friendly small talk, including inquiring after the health and comfort of participants and their relatives or associates.

Let the African members decide when to shift from socializing to business. An elderly African will indicate when this point has been reached.

At first meetings, do not push yourself forward too quickly. Instead, concentrate on evincing sincerity and giving evidence of trustworthiness. Business cards are essential (as in Japan) and should indicate all of your qualifications and rank. This early stage of getting to know your African partners is not only a trust-building process, but also one of creating reciprocal obligations that will serve as a basis for a smooth development of relations and a modus operandi in meetings to follow.

If there are language or other communication problems, intermediaries should be used. As in Asia, go-betweens can be very valuable in Africa for facilitating, apologizing and (when needed) complaining.

Africans do not adhere strictly to agendas. Points are discussed in order of importance (not necessarily according to logical chronology). When certain items are seen as vital, they may be revisited many times, irrespective of the agenda. Points are not abandoned until some measure of mutual satisfaction has been achieved. Older men will decide when this has happened.

Decisions are almost invariably made by consensus and must reflect *all* opinions voiced by the group. If you have difficulty obtaining agreement from a senior African, it is a wise policy to sound him out in private (perhaps using an intermediary) to see if he can develop support for your proposal. As in Asia, vigorous airing of differences of opinion in public is frowned upon. No one must lose face.

A pleasing feature of attending meetings with Africans is that they are quick to protect Westerners they have befriended. They may make concessions out of sheer generosity, and you should reciprocate without delay. Three important points to remember are (1) fairness, (2) soft sell and (3) no hurry. Africans will often strive to please, though there are one or two areas where they may be hampered in meeting your requirements or standards. It is difficult for them to discipline members of their own tribe, and they will be expected to show favoritism to their own tribe members in matters of promotion. Promotion in Africa is often on the basis of age (as in Japan) or ethnic consideration.

The African custom of expecting *dash* (some gift or payment for facilitating a request) is also common. Although Americans and some Europeans find this tradition unseemly, it should be viewed against an African background of poverty and disparity of income and may in fact be the smoothest way of getting things done. This custom is by no means confined to the African continent, as anyone who has been in business in Italy, Indonesia or Brazil well knows.

The necessity for Africans to share their gains with their extended family means that they are rarely able to achieve substantial savings or amass capital in the Western or Asian manner. A tendency toward consumption rather than saving derives from this obligation to share. Westerners should see occasional lavish consumption as being a result of African societal conditions rather than personal weakness.

Finally, when Africans seem poor at long-term planning, you must remember that survival is the first consideration, and it is essentially a short-term proposition. Bear in mind that the memories of ancestors—their words and deeds—will not only influence African behavior at meetings, but Africans mentally consider them *present* at business discussions, straddling the past and the immediate future. You will be greatly helped in this respect if you are cognizant of the past history of the tribe concerned. Culture changes slowly, so reference to past traditions will help guide you to forecast likely behavior now and tomorrow.

Negotiating Characteristics

- ✦ African initial proposals or demands bear little resemblance to final outcomes.
- ✦ The tribal or clan interest usually serves as a background to other commercial considerations.
- ✦ Conviviality and affability are usually maintained (but not always).
- ✦ Theatrical demands and explosive outbursts are not uncommon, usually followed by conciliatory periods.
- ✦ Older men are usually calm and make most of the decisions.
- ✦ In the modern economy, Africans continue to show traditional wisdom, but inexperience of new economic factors is often a handicap.
- ✦ The goal of negotiation is normally "win–win."
- ✦ Bargaining and haggling is part of the negotiation process. Skillful hagglers are admired.
- ✦ Offers must come from the *buyer*, so that the seller does not lose face.
- ✦ Negotiations are often conducted in a folksy or chatty manner.
- ✦ Meetings can often be noisy, but not necessarily aggressive.
- ✦ Westerners are expected to lead meetings at which they are present or at least to make significant contributions.
- ✦ Witnesses are often called in to meetings to see and hear agreements reached.
- ✦ Customary law (which existed in Africa long before Islamic or Western law) is often applied.

Manners and Taboos

More than one thousand tribal traditions entail many different customs, beliefs, rituals and taboos. Beliefs in a supreme being and other supernatural elements affect behavior continent-wide. Islamic core beliefs and taboos are in conformity with those of other Muslim communities. Various Christian sects exert their own influences. The Western appreciation of traditional jazz music gives white people a certain feel for African cultural sensitivity, poetry and drive. Music is one of the fruitful meeting grounds for black and white people and gives clues as to how common desires and feelings could, in better eras to come, be developed, coordinated and enjoyed.

Society manners include formal greetings (with enthusiasm)—shaking hands, touching arms and so on. Shoes are normally removed before entering a home. Africans eat their big meal in the evening; men are usually fed first. Africans who are invited to dinner often bring friends along. Eating and drinking take place usually seated, when relationship-building is extensive. Servants are treated as servants. Privacy has little meaning in Africa; you are not left alone very much, as you might get lonely!

Gifts might include alcohol (not for Muslims), flowers, candy and items such as T-shirts with logos, baseball caps or food in rural locations. One must take gifts for children and certainly to the chief or headman!

Beer is a popular drink in all parts of Africa except in the stricter Muslim communities. Africans get tipsy, as do Americans and Europeans, but excess of inebriation is frowned upon. Tipping is expected in upscale restaurants and, of course, in taxis.

Manners differ considerably in Anglophone and Francophone countries, though African traditions dominate. Anglophones tend to be well-dressed in the Western fashion; Francophones go more for traditional, colorful attire.

How to Empathize with Sub-Saharan Africans

Africans in general need warmth, kindness, sympathy and practical help. They are also proud, so that aid and advice must be offered discreetly. Recognize African strengths, which are numerous in many artistic, aesthetic and humanitarian fields. These should be seen as compensating for shortcomings (e.g., organizational and economic), which derive from situations often created by whites. From any point of view, Africans have an uphill struggle in the next few decades. Empathy will be detected if you help them by giving plentiful recognition where it is due; by paying in full for good African products, labor and services; and by sacrificing short-term profit for long-term policies to develop trade, exchange and viable commercial prospects. Look at African efforts positively and keep an open mind as to their eventual potential.

MOTIVATION	
KEY	*Compassion and understanding*
Cross-century mood	✦ Widespread recognition of Nelson Mandela's achievements. ✦ Hope for increased Western acceptance of African products at fair prices. ✦ Consideration in some areas of increased contact (or trade) with non-European countries (e.g., China).

Motivating Factors

- ✦ Greet everyone fully (shaking hands).
- ✦ Shed any hint of ex-colonial style.
- ✦ Accept physical closeness and tactile behavior.
- ✦ Communicate face-to-face whenever possible.
- ✦ Maintain steady eye contact.
- ✦ Talk loudly, clearly and slowly.

(continued)

MOTIVATION *(continued)*

- ✦ Evince sincerity; be cheerful and enthusiastic.
- ✦ Respect elders.
- ✦ Give repeated evidence of being trustworthy.
- ✦ Deliver what you promise.
- ✦ Repeat assurances many times, especially to influential and elderly people.
- ✦ Socialize to the extent they permit you to.
- ✦ Remember that they are thinking collectively (and possibly tribally!).
- ✦ Praise group performance.
- ✦ Be generally protective.
- ✦ Evince sympathy.
- ✦ Permit absences.
- ✦ Allow friends to "drop in" at work.
- ✦ Allow private use of office phones.
- ✦ Attend weddings and funerals.
- ✦ Criticize only indirectly, through the use of parables or fictitious stories.
- ✦ Wait six months before making final decisions.
- ✦ Respect African knowledge of local conditions.
- ✦ Utilize African innovative skills.

Avoid

- ✦ Criticizing Africans, especially in front of others.
- ✦ Dwelling on African shortcomings and failures.
- ✦ Being patronizing in any way.
- ✦ Undue exploitation of their economic condition.
- ✦ Firing anyone (it's better to promote someone to another job).

Epilogue
Achieving Empathy

Changing Perspectives in International Management Strategy

The political changes in Europe and other parts of the world in recent years have been quite startling in their suddenness and dimensions. The rapid volte-face in what was Czechoslovakia, Romania and the former East Germany, the increasing self-confidence visible in Hungary and Poland, the break-up of Yugoslavia, the rapprochement between the United States and Russia, and the regaining of independence in the Baltic republics are all signs of a global transformation in ideological alignments and longstanding alliances.

The new century was quickly plunged into crises, both man-made and natural. The attacks of September 11, 2001, engendered swift American retaliation: the war in Afghanistan, the removal from power of the Taliban, the establishment of a U.S. base in Uzbekistan and the deepening of relations with Pakistan and Georgia augmented substantially American influence in Central Asia. The American administration's impatience with the slowness of the UN's handling of Saddam Hussein led to the invasion of Iraq, the subsequent capture of the Iraqi leader and an unsatisfactory occupation with the aim of establishing a "democracy" in a country that has never known one.

The greenhouse effect, global warming and the restive nature of the earth's crust has led to earthquakes, disastrous flooding in many areas and the super catastrophe of the Asian tsunami on Boxing Day (December 26), 2004.

But these political, military and natural crises are only symptoms of much more deeply rooted changes, over which politicians, governments and international organizations have little or no control. Forces are at work beyond anything we have previously had to deal with. The Industrial Revolution had a tremendous impact on society, but it never quite ran away with us. One invention led to another, and the capitalist system organized the finance, labor and production techniques to deal with it. The Information Technology Revolution, on the other hand, has left us all floundering. Too much information is available, at too great a speed, from too many sources.

Modern business has faster access to more information than ever before, but by the time it has been sifted, analyzed, codified and processed, by the time managers and board members have decided on its impact and implementation, it is often already obsolete.

Furthermore, information management systems are frequently wrong. Information coming from news broadcasts, TV, the press and even news agencies are more often than not biased or at least flavored by the source. People at the top of management don't really know where they are going, don't get the information on time, face contradictions such as simultaneous centralization versus decentralization, teamwork versus initiative, consensus versus speed of decision, and so on.

The ubiquitous use of e-mail and mobile phone text messaging worldwide, usually in English and often wielded by non-English speakers, is resulting in a rapid deterioration of the English language.

Besides the irreversible changes being brought about by the information explosion and computer dictatorship, other tides that sweep us helplessly along are the incredible advances in medicine, the greenhouse effect and the changes in climate, the unstoppable march of science, the killing of hundreds of species, the drive for ecological awareness, the collapse of communism and the rising strength of Islam. Add to these factors the reunification and burgeoning power of Germany; the prospect of a Pacific Basin economic club for the twenty-first century; the elimination of most small, middle and even big companies by the multinational giants; a few jokers in the pack like the export powerhouses of Taiwan and Singapore—and it is no wonder that planning a global strategy is beyond the abilities of the great majority of managers and business leaders today.

Moreover, leading management consultants tell us that the bigger the company, the more difficult the internal and external communication, the more cumbersome the decision making, the more chaotic the organization. Nevertheless, the vaster the conglomerate, the bigger its domestic market, the greater seems its need to expand, export and establish itself abroad. The latter part of the twentieth century witnessed takeovers, mergers and acquisitions on a hitherto unimaginable scale, and the trend is for even large national companies to merge or become insignificant. Large banks have begun to group themselves in twos and threes. Citigroup became the biggest bank in the world through amalgamation with others. Ford bought Jaguar; Toyota and Nissan manufacture heavily in Britain; Deutsche Bank has a large stake in Mercedes; IVECO is a merger of the Fiat, Magirus-Deutz and Unic truck companies; AT&T tried to work with Olivetti; and even Finland's Kone, Nokia and Huhtumäki have become international conglomerates.

How well are companies prepared for global integration? If the solution is cultural synergy, do we know how to achieve it? What is the route to take?

The interdependence of nations also becomes clearer every day. Leaders are at the center of an ongoing dialogue to achieve mutual security, lessening of tension and confrontation, control of nuclear threat and all-around raising of living standards.

At the business level, global interdependence is emerging fast. The European Union is trying to create a market equal in size to that of the United States. Japan depends on the Middle East for oil and on the U.S. to buy its products. Russia needs American and Argentinean grain. China shops around the world for everything from oil to soy crops. Countries such as Italy, Britain and Korea, with few natural resources, depend on manufacturing and exports for survival. Small nations such as Finland, Denmark and Singapore develop niche industries with high-quality products to assure they maintain the standard of living they have already achieved. Countries not belonging to one of the large economic blocs hunt desperately around to find one. Geographically isolated countries such as New Zealand and Australia have an ever-increasing problem.

In terms of regional cooperation, there can be no better example than the collaboration and goodwill evident in the Nordic area, where Scandinavian Swedes, Danes, Norwegians and Icelanders enjoy relatively untroubled relations and mutual benefits with Altaic Finns. These peoples often look askance at each other, but there is little doubt that the overriding factor in arrangements between Scandinavians and Finns is common sense. The rest of Europe would do well to study its merits!

Europeans form a large, fascinating, talented, original family. Unfortunately, like real families, they have their ups and downs, moods, disputes, loves and hates. Yet although impetuous and quarrelsome, this family can be quite brilliant. The calm, disciplined Nordics have demonstrated what regional cohesion can do. British, Dutch and Germans are equally tranquil and organized, though less capable of cooperation. The French have vision, the Italians and Spaniards flair and, once harnessed, great energy. Romania, Poland and the Ukraine have huge agricultural potential. Czechs and Hungarians are knowledgeable, inventive and strikingly capable.

There can be no accurate assessment of the ultimate size, composition or political nature of the European Union. Its realization in terms of economic, monetary, political, military and cultural integration will, of necessity, be slow, frustrating and painful. One tends to forget that the United States, powerful as it is now, took nearly 150 years to emerge as a unified, purposeful power—and they speak the same language!

But cohesive or not, Europe has several cards to play. First, it is big. Second, it also has a sizeable workforce. Third, Europeans are educated. The United States and China have the world's two biggest economies, but Europe claims 4 out of the top 10. As far as GDP per capita and purchasing power are concerned, European countries have 10 places in the top 20. National debt is also very low.

The United States and Japan, currently undisputed leaders in production and finance, take Europe very seriously. Both countries have invested heavily in the continent and created strong bases inside the EU.

It remains to be seen how Britain's proposed exit from the EU (referred to as Brexit) will affect the above intentions.

However, if we are considering a management model for the twenty-first century, we cannot ignore Japanese systems. The Japanese people do not cast themselves in the role of teachers or mentors, but in an age when our own analysts advocate teamwork before individualism, collaboration and amalgamation before competition, we are seeing a shift from Western to Eastern culture. It could just be that the Asian model fits the era. The current success of Japan, Korea, Taiwan, Singapore and Hong Kong would suggest this. Indonesians, Malaysians and Thais follow in their wake.

The Chinese model, of course, promises to be preeminent. On my lecture tour of Peking and Shanghai universities in December 2004, I encountered progressive executives and academics who matched their Western counterparts in everything save international experience. They are open to new styles of management, and they are eager to internationalize.

The physical aspects of twenty-first century Beijing and Shanghai are stunning. Both cities are so huge that New York looks modest by comparison. Beijing stretches for miles both in length and breadth, and the number of skyscrapers is such that one finds it hard to define where downtown is. Shanghai, which is even bigger, has admirably preserved the noble curves of the former colonial bund while juxtaposing, across the river in Putong, the world's most impressive super-high-tech skyline. In Shanghai, particularly, one is assured that the twenty-first century has really arrived. The streets of both Beijing and Shanghai sport gleaming show windows for Gucci, Versace, Ferragamo, Armani, Prada, Nokia, Starbucks and other Western glitterati. Pedestrians are elegantly dressed and friendly. Well-polished cars—Mercedes, Volkswagen, Toyota and Peugeot (among many others)—patrol the wide boulevards, ostensibly expensive imports from the West, but, in fact, are *made in China*. While I was there, incidentally, Chinese Lenovo casually bought the computer division of IBM. A changing world! Soon (if it is not already), China will become the factory of our planet.

In the first decade of the twenty-first century, the world labors under warfare and threats of warfare, political dissension, inequality of wealth, uncertainty of the future, lack of morality, complexity of change. But on the plus side we have increasing opportunities for social justice, world peace and growth for all. Many new technologies are widely available, mobilization of labor is easier and some elements of the new generation show moral strength, a desire for peace and ecological awareness.

Sixty nations met in 2002 and contributed US$4 billion for the rebuilding of a destroyed Afghanistan. Médecins sans Frontières is a positive concept. Worldwide sympathy regarding the Asian tsunami unified a large number of nations as they mobilized their efforts to donate massive financial and logistical aid to the unfortunate victims of the disaster. If one could marshal the best outcomes of Western vibrancy, Chinese wisdom, Russian humanity, the sincere morality of Islamic moderates and aid the strivings of millions of Africans and Indians, this century might end on a less discordant note than the last one.

How do we translate good ideas into action? Study of good models shows us that teamwork and training make an enormous difference. Managers must have multinational skills. They will have to work shoulder to shoulder with people from many nationalities in the global village of the twenty-first century. They must understand them, speak to them, cooperate with them, manage them effectively, not lose out to them, yet like and praise them. These are our cultural challenges.

The Multicultural Executive

In this book we have discussed the phenomenon of *cultural myopia*—how ethnocentrism blinds us to the salient features of our own cultural makeup, while making us see other cultures as deviations from our correct system. For some powerful societies, confident of their historical success or brilliance (United States, France), it is a short leap from cultural myopia to *cultural imperialism.*

At the height of their power, American, British, French and Spanish conquerors did not hesitate to set up policies and regulations that were congruent with their own cultural values and not with those of their "subjects." Economic imperialism in our present era has hardly lessened this tendency and is in fact further complicated by the desire of multinational companies to impose strong (global) corporate cultures.

I have stated earlier that we shall never fully understand the "others," particularly if the separating factors of language, geography and ideology have been distant. The best we can hope for is to acquire an orientation that enables us to lessen the communication gap between ourselves and our partners. All of us are wrapped up in prejudice, subject to a *natural dynamic of bias.* We cannot proceed to an evaluation or judgment of another without starting with an acute sharpening of our own self-awareness.

A Behavioral Spectrum

All of us have our place on a complicated spectrum of comportment, with dizzying extremes of rudeness and courtesy, violence and gentleness, humility and conceit, and dozens of other behavioral dimensions. We perceive and judge others from the point in the spectrum where we stand rooted. We have a relative, not complete, view. If Swedes look at others through blue-and-yellow spectacles, they will fail to see them or their manners as they really are. They will suspect that all Italians are neurotic poseurs and see the individualistic Americans as lacking in respect for the beloved Swedish consensus. Americans will perceive the Japanese as having "shifty" eyes, while the same Japanese consider Spaniards rude because they constantly "stare." The route to self-understanding is to question many of those values that were pumped into us when we were young. Is it always wise for a Finn or a Brit to keep a stiff upper lip? What is wrong with a little Italian feeling? Can't the French, obsessed with logic, appreciate the power of Japanese intuition? What is special about Spanish honor? If you can't ask a friend (or relative) to do a business favor for you, what are friends and relatives for?

Once you realize that many of your cherished values or core beliefs were drummed into you by a biased community that possibly represents only a very small percentage of international opinion, presenting a very limited or blinkered world view, you are more likely to accept the opinions and manners of others as being at least equally valid, if not occasionally superior.

Eliminating Your Own Barriers

If you are able to see yourself or your culture from the outside and think more objectively as a consequence, you will have a good chance of clearing away certain cultural barriers that would have impeded access to others' thoughts or personalities. Finns must shed their excessive shyness, their bumbling modesty and their distrust of fast talkers. The French must rid themselves of their sense of intellectual superiority, and the Germans must realize that their cult of efficiency may indeed have counterproductive overtones. Americans must occasionally see themselves as insensitive, materialistic pragmatists who erect barriers of misunderstanding, often through well-meant bluntness or excessive informality.

Empathy

Better self-evaluation and elimination of your principal cultural idiosyncrasies will lead you to the final step toward achieving harmony, that of developing empathy with the other side. Empathy is based on accepting differences and building on these in a positive manner. The Japanese may come to accept that American directness is, after all, honest. The American may perceive that exaggerated Japanese courtesy is, after all, better than hostility. If the Italian wants to talk 90 percent of the time with a Finn, who is content to be silent (in Finland, silence is fun), then are they not both happy and doing what they do best?

The characteristics that best describe empathy are as follows:

+ tact
+ humor
+ sensitivity
+ flexibility
+ compromise
+ politeness
+ calm
+ warmth
+ patience
+ willingness to clarify objectives
+ observation of the other side's protocol
+ care to avoid irritants
+ careful listening
+ respect of confidentiality
+ inspiration of trust, and, above all,
+ constantly trying to see things from the other's (cultural) point of view

This is the profile of the *international negotiator*. Small side-effects such as eye-contact, posture, personal space and etiquette are all important, but the overriding factor is the ability to decipher what is basic human nature (which can be trusted by all) and which learned cultural habits will cause variation in human behavior and therefore must be recognized, accepted and adapted to.

The very act of adaptation, however, is fraught with difficulties. Culture is designed for success and survival; if we are alive, healthy and solvent, we have compelling reasons to believe in our particular formula. Temporary setbacks or, in certain cases, shocking failures, can undermine this confidence. The humiliating defeat of Japan in 1945 led to many Japanese, especially the youth, imitating various aspects of American culture. But certain features of Japanese behavior could not be subject to adaptation. In Japan, men do not report to women, whatever system of administration the Americans installed.

How much should we try to change others if we truly believe that our culture is superior? A safe answer is that we should *not,* thereby escaping the charge of cultural imperialism. But moral conflicts can arise. If we live in a culture where wife-beating is the norm, do we advise, accept or adapt?

It is important that we examine closely the nature of conflicts. Besides the clearly moral type mentioned here, other real conflicts arise from deeply rooted philosophical, religious or even political convictions. Thus Islamic beliefs with regard to alcohol, pork and the status of women, or Chinese attitudes toward basic inequalities in humans, will continue to clash with what we perceive as more tolerant and humanitarian Western attitudes. But such core beliefs are so well buttressed in their respective societies that we are well advised not to persist in challenging them, as changes can only come from within. In fact, it is not often that we try.

Another type of clash is pseudo-conflict, that is to say, that we feel irritated, bemused or even offended by some aspect of another's behavior and proceed to condemn it (strongly or mildly) without really attempting to see it in perspective. We see *mañana* mentality, Swiss pedantry and the assumed Asian smile as essentially negative, instead of trying to put these qualities into an understandable framework of cultural behavior. Pseudo-conflict equates with misunderstanding, or overfondness for the stereotype.

We cannot exist without stereotyping—it gives us points of reference in determining our behavior toward strangers. The mind tends to simplify complex feelings and attitudes, including our own. For intercultural understanding we must learn to *manage* stereotypes, that is, to maximize and appreciate the positive values we perceive, and minimize and laugh off (if we can) what we see as conflicting or negative.

We tend toward excessive stereotyping when we are under stress. Stress also reinforces our own cultural characteristics, so a vicious circle develops. Stressful conflict during meetings causes Americans to speak louder, South Americans to gesticulate, Japanese to clam up, Germans to bridle in righteousness and French to restate their position with icy logic. Without stress, Americans are friendly and generous, South Americans affectionate, Japanese courteous, Germans fair and French charming.

Self-criticism, avoidance of irritants and stress, more accurate assessment of the individual, tact, tolerance, adaptation without sacrificing one's integrity, substantial study of our partner's culture, history and language—all these are resources to be drawn on when cultures collide.

We may enrich our own existence by absorbing certain features of other cultures—change them by our own efforts we will not. History has so far allowed cultures that have not been militarily overrun to prosper, survive, languish or atrophy at their own rate of persistence or decline. It remains to be seen if the new forces represented by galloping information technology, rapid globalization of business and ferociously competing giant countries and economies will result in the devastation of weakened cultures that lack the ability to adapt to the truly dynamic changes of the twenty-first century.

Bibliography

Axtell, Roger E. ed. (1985) *Do's and Taboos Around the World,* compiled by the Parker Pen Company.

Barzini, Luigi (1964) *The Italians,* London: Hamish Hamilton.

Berry, Michael (1992) *Know Thyself and the Other Fellow Too: Strategies for Effective Cross-Cultural Communication,* Institute for European Studies.

Bradnock, Robert and Roma eds. (1995) *India Handbook,* with Sri Lanka, Bhutan and The Maldives, Bath: Trade & Travel Publications.

Condon, John C. (1985) *Communicating with the Mexicans,* Yarmouth, ME: Intercultural Press.

Dahl, Øyvind, *Malagasy and Other Time Concepts and Some Consequences for Communication,* Centre for Intercultural Communication.

Fieg, John Paul (1989) *A Common Core: Thais and Americans,* Yarmouth, ME: Intercultural Press.

Fisher, Glen (1980) *International Negotiation: A Cross-Cultural Perspective,* Yarmouth, ME: Intercultural Press.

Furnham, Adrian and Bochner, Stephen (1986) *Culture Shock: Psychological Reactions to Unfamiliar Environments,* Methuen.

Gochenour, Theodore (1990) *Considering Filipinos,* Yarmouth, ME: Intercultural Press. Hall, Edward T. and Reed Hall, Mildred (1983) *Hidden Differences, Studies in International Communication: How to Communicate with the Germans,* Hamburg, Stern Magazine/ Gruner & Jahr.

Hall, Edward T., and Reed Hall, Mildred (1983) *Understanding Cultural Differences: Germans, French, and Americans,* Yarmouth, ME: Intercultural Press.

Hampden-Turner, Charles and Trompenaars, Fons (1993) *The Seven Cultures of Capitalism: Value Systems for Creating Wealth in the United States, Britain, Japan, Germany, France, Sweden and The Netherlands,* New York: Doubleday.

Harris, Philip R. and Moran, Robert T. (1979) *Managing Cultural Differences: High-Performance Strategies for Today's Global Manager,* Houston: Gulf.

Hendry, Joy (1993) *Wrapping Culture: Politeness, Presentation, and Power in Japan and Other Societies,* Oxford: Clarendon Press.

Hofstede, Geert (1980) *Culture's Consequences: International Differences in Work-Related Values,* Newbury Park, CA: Sage.

Hofstede, Geert (1991) *Cultures and Organizations: Software of the Mind, Intercultural Cooperation and Its Importance for Survival,* Maidenhead: McGraw-Hill.

Holden, Nigel J. (1992) *Management, Language and Eurocommunication, 1992 and Beyond,* Institute for European Studies.

Hu, Wenzhong and Grove, Cornelius, L. (1991) *Encountering the Chinese: A Guide for Americans,* Yarmouth, ME: Intercultural Press.

James, Clive (1991) *Brrm! Brrm! or The Man from Japan or Perfume at Anchorage,* London: Pan.

Kawaskai, Ichiro (1969) *Japan Unmasked,* Rutland, Vermont/Tokyo: Charles E. Tuttle. Kulke, Hermann and Rothermund, Dietmar (1986) *A History of India,* Croom Helm Australia.

Kusy, Frank (1987) *Cadogan Guides—India: Kathmandu Valley—Nepal,* Old Saybrook, CT: Globe Pequot Press.

Lanier, Alison R. (1990) *The Rising Sun on Main Street: Working with the Japanese,* Morrisville, PA: International Information Associates.

Lehtonen, Jaakko (1990) *Kultur, Språk och Kommunikation,* University of Jyväskylä Press.
Lewis, Richard D. (1993) *Finland, Cultural Lone Wolf,* Otava.

Mole, John (1995) *Mind Your Manners: Managing Business Cultures in Europe,* London: Nicholas Brealey.

Morris, Desmond (1985) *Bodywatching, A Field Guide on the Human Species,* London: Jonathan Cape.

Nurmi, Raimo (1986) *A Cross Cultural Note on Australian and Finnish Values,* Deakin University.

Nurmi, Raimo (1989) *Management in Finland,* Turku Commercial High School.

Nydell, Margaret K. (1987) *Understanding Arabs: A Guide for Westerners,* Yarmouth, ME: Intercultural Press.

Peers, Allison E. (1992) *Spain: A Companion to Spanish Studies,* London: Methuen.

Phillips-Martinsson, Jean (1991) *Swedes as Others See Them: Facts, Myths or a Communication Complex?* Lund: Studentlitteratur.

Rearwin, David (1991) *The Asia Business Book,* Yarmouth, ME: Intercultural Press.
Reischauer, Edwin O. (1977) *The Japanese,* Cambridge, MA: Belknap.

Richmond, Yale (1992) *From Nyet to Da: Understanding the Russians,* Yarmouth, ME: Intercultural Press.

Sapir, Edward (1966) *Culture, Language and Personality, Selected Essays,* Berkeley and Los Angeles: University of California Press.

Sinclair, Kevin with Wong Po-yee, Iris (1991) *Culture Shock! China,* London: Kuperard.
Steward, Edwards C. and Bennett, Milton J. (1991) *American Cultural Patterns: A Cross-Cultural Perspective,* Yarmouth, ME: Intercultural Press.

Storti, Craig (1989) *The Art of Crossing Cultures,* Yarmouth, ME: Intercultural Press.
Tan, Terry (1992) *Culture Shock! Britain,* London: Ernest Benn.

Trompenaars, Fons and Hampden-Turner, Charles (1997) *Riding the Waves of Culture: Understanding Cultural Diversity in Business,* 2nd edn., London: Nicholas Brealey.

Wanning, Esther (1991) *Culture Shock! USA,* London: Kuperard.

Whorf, Benjamin Lee (1956) *Language, Thought and Reality,* Cambridge, MA: Massachusetts Institute of Technology Press.

Glossary

◆

Albania	from Albanian word for "speak" (or "eagle")
atavistic (atavism)	reappearance in a person of a characteristic which has not been seen for generations
Azerbaijan	a small country adjoining the Caspian Sea
Azeri	language of Azerbaijan
Belarus	formerly known as "White Russia"
besa	to keep one's promises (Albanian)
borscht	beetroot soup
BRICS	economic union of Russia, China, India, Brazil and South Africa
Buddhism	a religion of east and central Asia growing out of the teachings of Buddha, that one must become free of human desires in order to escape from suffering
Burma	former name of Myanmar
cadres	an inner group of highly trained and active people in a particular group (company, army, etc.) (French)
Cartesian	relating to René Descartes, French philosopher and mathematician
Caucasus	mountainous area in South Eastern Europe
chauvinism	very great and often unthinking admiration for one's country; proud and unreasonable belief that one's country is better than all others
collective programming	the way a particular group of people or nationalities is trained from a very early age to internalize the behavior and attitudes of the group
communication gap	lack of understanding of people of other cultures, because of differences in language, cultural attitudes, etc.
compartmentalize projects	concentrate single-mindedly on a project, not allowing it to projects be influenced by other goals or activities
complete action chains	finish one task completely before commencing another one
complete human transactions	finish all one's business with a particular individual before going on to another task
Confucianism	a Chinese way of thought which teaches that one should be loyal to one's family, friends and rulers, and treat others as one would like to be treated, developed from the ideas of Confucius
context centered	depending on a situation
core beliefs	basic concepts of a national group which have been learned and internalized from an early age
cross-culture	comparison of beliefs, attitudes, etc. of different cultural groups of nationalities
cultural display event	something we do or say which reveals our core beliefs (cultural attitudes) to people of other cultures

cultural imperialism	attempt to impose the tenets of one's culture on others
cultural myopia	inability to see another culture's points of view
"cultural spectacles"	the way our own core beliefs influence how we view other cultures
culture	the customs, beliefs, art and all the other products of human thought made by a particular group of a people at a particular time
culture shock	the feeling of shock or of being disoriented which someone has when they experience a different and unfamiliar culture
cyclic time	recurring events
Cyprus	derives from Greek word for Cypress tree
danwei	work unit (Chinese)
data-oriented (culture)	a culture whose people gather information mainly through print and database sources
deviants	people who are different in moral or social standards from what is considered normal
dialogue-oriented (culture)	a culture whose people gather information through direct contact with other people
diaspora	external or overseas community of a given nationality
double truth	two ways of looking at things: the immediate reality and the poetic whole
dusha	the Russian soul (Russian)
école normale supériéure	prestigious tertiary level institute of learning in France specializing in various ares of pedagogy, leading to a career in higher education of research (French)
empathy	the ability to imagine oneself in the position of another person and so to share and understand that person's feelings
Enosis	union of Cyprus and Greece
extrovert	a person who likes to spend time in activities with other people rather than being quiet and alone
faux pas	social mistake in words or behavior (French)
feng shui	wind-and-water superstition (Chinese)
force majeure	an event beyond one's control (French)
gaffe	an unintentional social mistake (French)
GDP	gross domestic product
genocide	killing of an entire people
Georgia	originates from Greek "geo" meaning "earth"
giri	duty (Japanese)
guanxi	the linking of two people in a relationship of mutual dependence (Chinese)
hara kiri	ritual suicide using a sword to cut open one's stomach, formerly practised by Japanese Samurai to avoid dishonor
hautes écoles	tertiary level in education in France in specialized areas, such as commerce, engineering etc. (French)
high context (culture)	networking, dialogue-oriented culture
honorific expression	indicating respect for the person being addressed, especially in Oriental languages
horizon (cultural)	one's world view (limited)

human mental programming	the practice of instilling one's beliefs in the young programming under one's responsibility (or any "captive" audience)
Indo-European	major language group
inscrutable	describes people whose meaning or way of thinking is not at all clear, mysterious
introvert	concerning oneself with one's own thoughts rather than sharing activities with others
Islam	the Muslim religion started by Mohammand
itadakimasu	literally: I am receiving (Japanese)—similiar to *bon appétit*
kaisha	company, firm (Japanese)
kanun	customary law (Albanian)
karma	the force produced by a person's actions in life which will influence him or her later or in future lives
kibun	saving face (Korean)
lagom	spirit of moderation in all things (Swedish)
language mold	the way our language channels or molds our thoughts
language of mangement	how certain management styles are facilitated by the nature of the language of the manager and the group being managed
linear time	a concept of time as a "line" of sequential events with the past behind us and the future in front
linear-active (culture)	a culture whose people are task-oriented, highly organized planners, perferring to do one thing at a time in the sequence shown in their diary
listening (culture)	a culture whose people listen well, never interrupt and show great deference to others' opinions; they do not precipitate improvident action, allowing ideas to mature
longyi	garment worn by men or women
low context (culture)	data-oriented culture, few oral contacts
Malta	from Greek "meli" (honey)
meritocracy	a social system which gives the highest positions to those with the most ability
messianic	belief that one has an important mission
monochronic (culture)	a culture dominated by precision and propriety, preferring to concentrate on doing one thing at a time
mores	the moral customs of a particular group
"muddling through"	achieving one's goals without proper planning
multi-active (culture)	a culture whose people tend to do many things at once, often in an unplanned order, usually people oriented, extrovert
networking	the establishing of professional connections with the aim of sharing information, advice or support
NGO	non-government organization
notions	the perception by a cultural group of certain basic concepts
on	obligation (Japanese)
Ordnung	order (German)
patronymic	name, based on name of a father
polychronic	someone who likes to do many things at once, often without precise planning

power distance	a measure of the interpersonal power of influence between superior and subordinate as perceived by the latter, often determined by the national culture
pundonor	honor, dignity (Spanish)
pysanky	Easter egg tradition
reactive (culture)	a culture whose people rarely initiate action or discussion, preferring first to listen to and establish the other's position, then react to it and formulate their own
ringi-sho	decision making through consensus (Japanese)
Romantic nationalism	type of patriotism
sardechna zaprashayem	greeting when welcoming guests (Belarusian)
saudades	nostalgia, sentimentality (Portuguese)
sisu	perseverance, stamina (Finnish)
skål	cheers! to your health! (Swedish)
space bubble	the personal space which an individual dislikes being encroached on
stereotyping	fixing a set of ideas about what a particular type of person or nationality is like, which is (wrongly) believed to be true in all cases
sturgeon	fish from which caviar is obtained
task orientation	giving instructions or directions to colleagues or subordinates
tatami	straw floor mat, the number of which is often used to denote the size of a room in Japan
tenets	principles, beliefs
Theravada Buddhism	Buddhist sect
Ukraine	borderland
USP	unique selling point
values	standards or principles, ideas about the importance of certain qualities, especially those accepted by a particular group
Volkswirtschaftshochschule	tertiary level education in Germany in the area of economics and commerce (German)
web society	an interdependent society excelling in networking
Weltanschauung	world view (German)
Weltschmerz	"world pain," i.e., depressed state (German)

Index